SOFTWARE TESTING TECHNIQUES

Second Edition

Boris Beizer

VNR **VAN NOSTRAND REINHOLD** New York

Library of Congress Catalog Card Number 89-27639
ISBN 0-442-20672-0

I⊤P Van Nostrand Reinhold is an International Thomson Publishing company.
     ITP logo is a trademark under license.

Printed in the United States of America

Van Nostrand Reinhold   ITP Germany
115 Fifth Avenue   Königswinterer Str. 418
New York, NY 10003   53227 Bonn
                                         Germany

International Thomson Publishing   International Thomson Publishing Asia
Berkshire House,168-173   38 Kim Tian Rd., #0105
High Holborn, London WC1V 7AA   Kim Tian Plaza
England   Singapore 0316

Thomas Nelson Australia   International Thomson Publishing Japan
102 Dodds Street   Kyowa Building, 3F
South Melbourne 3205   2-2-1 Hirakawacho
Victoria, Australia   Chiyada-Ku, Tokyo 102
                                          Japan

Nelson Canada
1120 Birchmount Road
Scarborough, Ontario
M1K 5G4, Canada

16 15 14 13 12 11 10 9 8 7 6 5 4

Library of Congress Cataloging-in-Publication Data

Beizer, Boris, 1934-
     Software testing techniques / Boris Beizer.—2nd ed.
          p.   cm.
     Includes bibliographical references.
     ISBN 0-442-20672-0
     1. Computer software—Testing. I. Title.
QA76.76.T48B45   1990
005.1'4—dc20]   89-27639
                                                         CIP

Dedicated to several unfortunate, very bad software projects for which I was privileged to act as a consultant (albeit briefly). They provided lessons on the difficulties this book is intended to circumvent and led to the realization that this book is needed. Their failure could have been averted—requiescat in pace.

THE RUNNING OF THREE-OH-THREE

(With apologies to Robert W. Service)

There are bugs adrift on the midnight shift
  That cannot be foretold.
The audit trails have their secret tales
  That would make your blood run cold.
Debugging nights have seen queer sights,
  But the queerest they ever did see
Was that time on the way to cutover day
  I ran test three-oh-three.

Now three-oh-three in its infancy
  Was simple and sublime;
A bit set here or a patch put there;
  All done in record time.
"A trivial test is always best,"
  Consultants love to state;
But a test gone sour at the midnight hour,
  Is a test you'll learn to hate.

All through that day we slugged away
  At data errors in memory
Talk about dumps! They lay in lumps
  Between and on the machinery.
The printer's hammer beat like a hammer
  In sonic tyranny.
It wasn't much fun and we hadn't yet run
  The infamous three-oh-three.

That very night by the dismal light
  Of an empty Coke machine,
The problems solved, we all resolved
  To start the next day clean.
"Another test," the boss suggests,
  "Before we end this session.
You're doing well, I'm proud to tell,
  But humor this last obsession."

We really were beat; we'd been on our feet
    For eighteen hours or more.
Our eyes were glazed and through the haze,
    We couldn't tell "NEITHER" from "NOR."
But he smiled and said, "Before you bed—
    Just one little test to run;
And if you do, I tell you true,
    Next payday you'll have fun."

Now talk about pay was an eloquent way
    To make our adrenalin rise;
And one little pest of a simple test
    Was trivial enterprise.
We fell for this tact and swore to a pact
    That before the hour was done
Our victory over three-oh-three
    Would be absolutely won.

We said "What the heck," and loaded the deck,
    Then toggled the bootstrap switch;
But the ROM was burned and a bit had turned—
    'Twas the ever present hitch.
We keyed in the code as in days of old.
    With nary an audible murmur;
But 'neath our breath, we snarled of death,
    Misery, mayhem, and murder.

I loaded the patch; the floppy was scratched,
    Its backup locked in a drawer.
I cursed the slob who did that job,
    A damnable disc destroyer.
We reversed ten yards, picked up the shards
    Of a version he'd discarded.
It rankled like hell—it was sad to tell,
    Of the bugs he'd disregarded.

I shouted "Nix! I refuse to fix
    Bugs that have been glossed over!"
I flung my pencil, listing, stencil
    In disgust and went for the door.
But the boss asked to chat, gave me a pat
    And said it's a night he'd remember.
He promised booze and great reviews,
    And a bonus in December.

Another hour, with tempers sour,
    'Til we could try again.
That code was mangled, tortured, tangled,
    Unstructured, dumb, inane.
But after a while we began to smile;
    We'd corrected every blunder.
Just one little test and we could rest
    In sweet repose and slumber.

I hit the key for three-oh-three,
    But the system wouldn't have it.
I tried once more from the monitor,
    On the verge of throwing a fit.
The more I tried, the more I cried
    As the output mocked by silence.
It wasn't fair—I tore my hair;
    The time had come for violence.

I kicked the frame and kicked again:
    The printer burped the beginning.
Ignoring the risk, I stomped the disc,
    Sure now that I was winning.
I relished my hate as I beat the tape,
    Enjoying its rewinding.
That proc knew fear! The fact was clear
    From its internal grinding.

With every hit, I advanced one bit;
    Approaching the conclusion.
My fists were sore, replete with gore,
    Abrasions, and contusions.
The tapes were rocking, no more mocking:
    I drove that system, beaming!
And by morning's light, the end in sight;
    I knew I'd soon be dreaming.

But then its bowels began to howl—
    My guts turned into jelly.
The metal shrieked, disc platters streaked
    Across the room pell-melly.
About the hall, from wall to wall,
    They dove at us; we cowered.
One did a flip, and in a nip,
    The boss was disemboweled.

It didn't wait, but threw a tape
    Which bounded and entangled.
The loops unwound, around and round;
    My partner died—enstrangled.
The printer dumped, gallumped and thumped,
    The platen leapt and zoomed.
As in a dream, there was a scream;
    The analyst was doomed.

There wasn't much fuss for the rest of us—
    Just fracture and concussion,
An eye gouged out, a busted snout,
    From which the red was gushin'
As for the fire, you shouldn't inquire;
    Nor of the flood that followed.
Those with skin called next of kin;
    Their memory forever hallowed.

There are bugs adrift on the midnight shift
    That cannot be foretold.
The audit trails have their secret tales
    That would make your blood run cold.
Debugging nights have seen queer sights,
    But the queerest they ever did see
Was that time on the way to cutover day
    I ran test three-oh-three.

PREFACE TO THE SECOND EDITION

I started to write the first edition of *Software Testing Techniques* in 1978. It was published in 1983, but most of the references predated 1980: the first edition was a book for the 80s that reported on the state of software testing as of the late 70s. This edition will be published at the beginning of a new decade. The years between have been a decade of intensive research and development in software testing as an art and science; a decade in which the vocabulary of testing evolved from idiosyncratic usages into an accepted set of concepts and terms for those concepts; a decade that saw intensive research on the relative strength of different testing techniques; a decade in which testing emerged as a discipline in its own right; a decade that began with evangelism for proper testing and ended with widely accepted testing norms; a decade that saw testing change from a mostly manual process to an intensely automated process; the decade in which PCs and workstations became ubiquitous personal data management, programming, and test tools.

A new edition was needed to update the technical material, but also for other reasons: software testing and quality assurance evangelism is no longer needed; there's less about which to be iconoclastic; some of the "hot" ideas of the 70s have passed into obscurity while formerly obscure concepts have come to the fore; testers have emerged as skilled professionals along with "programmers" and "system analysts." Most important of all, many professional testers who began the decade as the whipping boys of software developers are ending it with the roles reversed. The final reasons for a new edition is the shift in audience. Although I wrote the first edition for all programmers (because testers as such hardly existed), *Software Testing Techniques* became one of the standard reference books on the professional tester's shelf. A new edition was needed to shift the focus from a book for programmers (and testers) to a balanced book for testers and programmers.

The most obvious change was the removal of Chapter 8—Data-Base-Driven Test Design. Its remnants are now in Chapter 6—Domain Testing, Chapter 13—Implementation, and scattered elsewhere. I removed material that the reader can find, better said, in *Software System Testing and Quality Assurance* (BEIZ84). The material based on a manual test development process, unaided by workstations and PCs, had a quaint ring to it—so that went. I also removed other process material that I've subsequently learned must be taken for granted if there's to be testing worth the doing—data dictionaries, to name one. Finally, I wanted to sharpen the focus of this book even more toward techniques and farther away from process because process is too big and too important to treat superficially. It is covered more thoroughly in BEIZ84, and there are many other sources for process information, which was not the case when I wrote the first edition.

As for additions, the biggest changes reflect the rapid development of automated aids to programming and testing. Advanced testing techniques are processing-intensive and can't be applied without tools. The first edition did not meet the needs of test tool builders or users. The final major addition is the section on testability tips in most chapters. We've gone full circle, back to putting the primary responsibility for software quality on the programmer. This approach requires that all test techniques be interpreted in the light of design for testability.

Software testing and quality assurance can be looked at from three points of view: (1) our tools and techniques, (2) what we are testing, (3) and the process by which testing is done and quality is assured. *This* book concerns test techniques and tools. What we test can likewise be divided into three domains: components (units), integration, and systems. Component testing is also covered in this book because most techniques are most easily applied to components. The rest of the subject is fully covered in *Software System Testing and Quality Assurance* (BEIZ84). The two books are inseparable. As befits their contents, I expect that individual testers and programmers will have the greatest use out of this book, and system engineers, testers, managers and QA/QC workers out of the other.

This book is intended for four kinds of readers, as follows:

Programmers (including designers, system analysts, system architects, database managers, be it for new systems or for the maintenance of old systems). A solid foundation in test techniques will make your own testing and debugging easier and more predictable at the cost of being less exciting. The techniques in this book, though usually applied to units or components, are also fundamental to integration and system testing. The most important thing you can get out of this book is *testability:* to use testing technique knowledge to change your design so that it can be verified and integrated with much less testing than you might think is necessary—that is, to design testable software.

Testers (including independent testers, system testers, beta testers, functional testers, software buyers, quality assurance specialists, test tool buyers). Testing is your stock in trade and, directly or indirectly, comprises half of your tool kit. The test tools you may buy are often based on deep properties of specific testing techniques—and it is difficult to understand how such tools work, or what their limitations and strengths might be, without understanding the underlying technique. Your task has always been to do a good job of testing with inadequate resources: your resources will always be inadequate when compared to a virtual infinity of justifiable tests but if you understand the techniques and where they are best applied, you'll have an easier time of effectively allocating your scant resources.

Teachers (including university professors and testing trainers). This book is intended to be a cohesive structure around which testing training can be organized. That means a consistent mainstream terminology, a structure, a portal to the more advanced literature, and many hooks on which you can hang your personal perspective and needs, be it theory on the one hand or practice on the other.

Researchers and Developers (including testing theorists and test tool builders). The literature is vast, the terminology conflicting and confused, the time is short and the need is urgent. If this book helps you get on board, then it has done for you what I intended it to do.

I hope all readers will find this book to be what I want it to be: a clear presentation of the state of the art that bridges the often awesome gap between theory and practice: a recapitulation and synthesis of the important concepts with guidance on their practical application. Also, I hope that you will benefit from the combined glossary/index, which has proved a time saver in other books. Readers of the first edition will see a clarification of concepts that were sometimes muddy, new material and a consistent vocabulary with more formal definitions mostly based on ANSI/ IEEE 729, Glossary for Software Engineering (ANSI83A). The single biggest change was to replace "element" in the first edition with "component" in the second. I have also stuck to the use of "bug" and "symptom" rather than "fault" and "failure," respectively, because I find that people in the field tend to confuse the two terms, perhaps because they both start with an "f" and also because "bug" is one of the most frequently used word in this book, coming just after "the," "a," and "test."

If you've read this far, I don't have to sell you on the importance of testing. But I recognize that *you* may have a selling job to do to your management or peers. I hope that within these pages you find arguments that can help you to make the sale.

Boris Beizer
Abington, Pennsylvania

PREFACE TO THE FIRST EDITION

This book concerns testing techniques that are applied to individual routines. The companion volume, *Software System Testing and Quality Assurance* [BEIZ84], is concerned with integration testing, development of system test plans, software quality management, test teams, and software reliability. Most software is produced by the cooperative effort of many designers and programmers working over a period of years. The resulting product cannot be fully understood by any one person. Consequently, quality standards can only be achieved by emplacing effective management and control methods. However, no matter how elegant the methods used to test a system, how complete the documentation, how structured the architecture, the development plans, the project reviews, the walkthroughs, the data-base management, the configuration control—no matter how advanced the entire panoply of techniques—all will come to nothing, and the project will fail, if the unit-level software, the individual routines, have not been properly tested. Quality assurance that ignores unit-level testing issues is a construct built on a foundation of sand.

Although I set out to write a book on software quality assurance, it became clear to me as I progressed that I was assuming that programmers know how to do unit testing. Good programmers *do* know how to do unit testing—it is one of the things that makes them good programmers—but their knowledge and their techniques are hard won; and if they communicate those lessons to others, it is as master to apprentice. The literature of programming is dominated by design issues. Some otherwise excellent textbooks have nothing to say about testing other than "try everything" or "be sure to test thoroughly." And those texts that do address testing do not give testing an emphasis that even remotely reflects the 50% or more of labor that is expended in testing. The same can be said for programming courses. Typically, although testing will consume more than half of a programmer's professional life, less than 5% of the programmer's education will be devoted to testing.

xiii

Yet there has evolved a large body of techniques and an abundant technical literature on testing. The purpose of this book is to extract from that literature those techniques that are most useful to the individual programmers, to merge and modify them by the lessons of practice—the lessons of the art of testing as it is actually done—and to present a tool kit that the programmer can use to design and execute comprehensive unit tests. I have stressed unit-level testing, but the reader will realize that most of the techniques can be applied at all system levels and should be.

Although this is a text, it does not include problems to solve. Programmers have enough real problems, and I don't think it is appropriate to add contrived ones to those they already have. Testing should be taught in a testing laboratory course. In the ideal course, as I see it, the student does not write one line of code. Small modules of 50 to 100 statements are provided as exercises. These modules are bad pieces of code—ugly, convoluted horrors with hidden own-data, self-modification, inadvertent recursion, and bugs—lots and lots of bugs. Each exercise is given a fixed computer-time budget. The student's progress is measured by the number of known bugs discovered in that time. The student who carefully structures the test cases, who does proper desk checking, and who thinks about test objectives, is more likely to find the bugs in the budgeted time than the student who relies on intuition as a sole tool. The language used and the nature of the exercises should be tailored to the environment—in terms of factors that include computer availability, terminals, and built-in test tools. The language is not important, although assembly language and older languages, such as FORTRAN and COBOL, have the distinct advantage of permitting entire categories of bugs that are impossible in modern languages such as Pascal.

ACKNOWLEDGMENTS

My first thanks go to the buyers of the first edition: without their generous support, a second edition would not have been possible. Next, I thank those readers who took the trouble to write to me with their suggestions, criticism, and ideas. Third, I thank the respondents of my several questionnaires on testing and quality assurance. The many students who attended my testing and quality assurance seminars were a valuable source of insights into testing, but more important, their continual and creative feedback exerted a powerful influence on how best to present this material. Also, the following persons graced me with their incisive and constructive criticism and/or data: Victor Basili, Walter Ellis, Mike Fagan, Dave Gelperin, Bill Hetzel, Elaine Weyuker, and Lee White. Finally, to my consulting clients from whom I continue to learn the real problems of testing and how to solve them. To all of you, my thanks. This is your book; I've been a mere recorder.

CONTENTS

10. LOGIC-BASED TESTING   320

11. STATES, STATE GRAPHS, AND TRANSITION TESTING   363

1
INTRODUCTION

1. THE PURPOSE OF TESTING

1.1. What We Do

Testing consumes at least half of the labor expended to produce a working program (BOEH75C, BROW73, GOOD79, RADA81, WOLV75).* Few programmers like testing and even fewer like test design—especially if test design and testing take longer than program design and coding. This attitude is understandable. Software is ephemeral: you can't point to something physical. I think, deep down, most of us don't believe in software—at least not the way we believe in hardware. If software is insubstantial, then how much more insubstantial does software testing seem? There isn't even some debugged code to point to when we're through with test design. The effort put into testing seems wasted if the tests don't reveal bugs.

There's another, deeper, problem with testing that's related to the reason we do it (MILL78B, MYER79). It's done to catch bugs. There's a myth that if we were really good at programming, there would be no bugs to catch. If only we could really concentrate, if everyone used structured programming, top-down design, decision tables, if programs were written in SQUISH, if we had the right silver bullets, then there would be no bugs. So goes the myth. There are bugs, the myth says, because we are bad at what we do; and if we are bad at it, we should feel guilty about it. Therefore, testing and test design amount to an admission of failure, which instills a goodly dose of guilt. And the tedium of testing is just punishment for our errors. Punishment for what? For being human? Guilt

---

* The numbers vary, but most of the apparent variability results from creative accounting. A debugger spends much time testing hypothesized causes of symptoms; so does a maintenance programmer. If we include all testing activities, of whatever they are a part, the total time spent testing by all parties ranges from 30% to 90%. If we only count formal tests conducted by an independent test group, the range is 10%–25%.

1

for what? For not achieving inhuman perfection? For not distinguishing between what another programmer thinks and what he says? For not being telepathic? For not solving human communication problems that have been kicked around by philosophers and theologians for 40 centuries?

The statistics show that programming, done well, will still have one to three bugs per hundred statements (AKIY71, ALBE76, BOEH75B, ENDR75, RADA81, SHOO75, THAY76, WEIS85B).* Certainly, if you have a 10% error rate, then you either need more programming education or you deserve reprimand *and* guilt.** There are some persons who claim that they can write bug-free programs. There's a saying among sailors on the Chesapeake Bay, whose sandy, shifting bottom outdates charts before they're printed, "If you haven't run aground on the Chesapeake, you haven't sailed the Chesapeake much." So it is with programming and bugs: I have them, you have them, we all have them—and the point is to do what we can to prevent them and to discover them as early as possible, but not to feel guilty about them. Programmers! Cast out your guilt! Spend half your time in joyous testing and debugging! Thrill to the excitement of the chase! Stalk bugs with care, methodology, and reason. Build traps for them. Be more artful than those devious bugs and taste the joys of guiltless programming! Testers! Break that software (as you must) and drive it to the ultimate—but don't enjoy the programmer's pain.

1.2. Productivity and Quality in Software

Consider the manufacture of a mass-produced widget. Whatever the design cost, it is a small part of the total cost when amortized over a large production run. Once in production, every manufacturing stage is subjected to quality control and testing from component source inspection to final testing before shipping. If flaws are discovered at any stage, the widget or part of it will either be discarded or cycled back for rework and correction. The assembly line's productivity is measured by the sum of the costs of the materials, the rework, and the discarded components, and the cost of quality assurance and testing. There is a trade-off between quality-assurance costs and manufacturing costs. If insufficient effort is

---

* Please don't use that 1% rate as a standard against which to measure programmer effectiveness. There are big variations (from 0.01 to 10) which can be explained by complexity and circumstances alone. Also, lines-of-code (usually, *k*-lines-of-code) is one of the worst complexity measures there is. See Chapter 7.
** The worst I ever saw was a 500-instruction assembly language routine with an average of 2.2 bugs per instruction after syntax checking by the assembler. That person didn't belong in programming.

spent in quality assurance, the reject rate will be high and so will the net cost. Conversely, if inspection is so good that all faults are caught as they occur, inspection costs will dominate, and again net cost will suffer. The manufacturing process designers attempt to establish a level of testing and quality assurance that minimizes net cost for a given quality objective. Testing and quality-assurance costs for manufactured items can be as low as 2% in consumer products or as high as 80% in products such as spaceships, nuclear reactors, and aircraft, where failures threaten life.

The relation between productivity and quality for software is very different from that for manufactured goods. The "manufacturing" cost of a software copy is trivial: the cost of the tape or disc and a few minutes of computer time. Furthermore, software "manufacturing" quality assurance is automated through the use of check sums and other error-detecting methods. Software costs are dominated by development. Software maintenance is unlike hardware maintenance. It is not really "maintenance" but an extended development in which enhancements are designed and installed and deficiencies corrected. The biggest part of software cost is the cost of bugs: the cost of detecting them, the cost of correcting them, the cost of designing tests that discover them, and the cost of running those tests. The main difference then between widget productivity and software productivity is that for hardware quality is only one of several productivity determinants, whereas for software, quality and productivity are almost indistinguishable.

1.3. Goals for Testing

Testing and test design, as parts of quality assurance, should also focus on bug prevention. To the extent that testing and test design do not prevent bugs, they should be able to discover symptoms caused by bugs. Finally, tests should provide clear diagnoses so that bugs can be easily corrected. Bug prevention is testing's first goal. A prevented bug is better than a detected and corrected bug because if the bug is prevented, there's no code to correct. Moreover, no retesting is needed to confirm that the correction was valid, no one is embarrassed, no memory is consumed, and prevented bugs can't wreck a schedule. More than the act of testing, the act of *designing* tests is one of the best bug preventers known. The thinking that must be done to create a useful test can discover and eliminate bugs before they are coded—indeed, test-design thinking can discover and eliminate bugs at every stage in the creation of software, from conception to specification, to design, coding, and the rest. For this reason, Dave Gelperin and Bill Hetzel (GELP87) advocate "Test, then code." The ideal test activity would be so successful at bug prevention that actual testing would be unnecessary because all bugs would have been found and fixed during test design.*

Unfortunately, we can't achieve this ideal. Despite our effort, there will be bugs because we are human. To the extent that testing fails to reach its primary goal, *bug prevention,* it must reach its secondary goal, *bug discovery.* Bugs are not always obvious. A bug is manifested in deviations from expected behavior. A test design must document expectations, the test procedure in detail, and the results of the actual test—all of which are subject to error. But knowing that a program is incorrect does not imply knowing the bug. Different bugs can have the same manifestations, and one bug can have many symptoms. The symptoms and the causes can be disentangled only by using many small detailed tests.

1.4. Phases in a Tester's Mental Life

1.4.1. Why Testing?

What's the purpose of testing? There's an attitudinal progression characterized by the following five phases:

PHASE 0—There's no difference between testing and debugging. Other than in support of debugging, testing has no purpose.

PHASE 1—The purpose of testing is to show that the software works.

PHASE 2—The purpose of testing is to show that the software doesn't work.

PHASE 3—The purpose of testing is not to prove anything, but to reduce the perceived risk of not working to an acceptable value.

PHASE 4—Testing is not an act. It is a mental discipline that results in low-risk software without much testing effort.

1.4.2. Phase 0 Thinking

I called the inability to distinguish between testing and debugging "phase 0" because it denies that testing matters, which is why I denied it the grace of a number. See Section 2.1 in this chapter for the difference between testing and debugging. If phase 0 thinking dominates an organi-

---

* I think that's what good programmers do—they test at every opportunity. "Test early and often" is their motto. It's not that they have fewer bugs, but that the habit of continual testing keeps their bugs private, and therefore cheaper.

zation, then there can be no effective testing, no quality assurance, and no quality. Phase 0 thinking was the norm in the early days of software development and dominated the scene until the early 1970s, when testing emerged as a discipline.

Phase 0 thinking was appropriate to an environment characterized by expensive and scarce computing resources, low-cost (relative to hardware) software, lone programmers, small projects, and throwaway software. Today, this kind of thinking is the greatest cultural barrier to good testing and quality software. But phase 0 thinking is a problem for testers and developers today because many software managers learned and practiced programming when this mode was the norm—and it's hard to change how you think.

1.4.3. Phase 1 Thinking—The Software Works

Phase 1 thinking represented progress because it recognized the distinction between testing and debugging. This thinking dominated the leading edge of testing until the late 1970s when its fallacy was discovered. This recognition is attributed to Myers (MYER79) who observed that it is self-corrupting. It only takes one failed test to show that software doesn't work, but even an infinite number of tests won't prove that it does. The objective of phase 1 thinking is unachievable. The process is corrupted because the probability of showing that the software works *decreases* as testing increases; that is, the more you test, the likelier you are to find a bug. Therefore, if your objective is to demonstrate a high probability of working, that objective is best achieved by not testing at all! Although this conclusion may seem silly to the conscious, rational mind, it is the kind of syllogism that our unconscious mind loves to implement.

1.4.4. Phase 2 Thinking—The Software Doesn't Work

When, as testers, we shift our goal to phase 2 thinking we are no longer working in cahoots with the designers, but against them. The difference between phase 1 and 2 thinking is illustrated by analogy to the difference between bookkeepers and auditors. The bookkeeper's goal is to show that the books balance, but the auditor's goal is to show that despite the appearance of balance, the bookkeeper has embezzled. Phase 2 thinking leads to strong, revealing tests.

While one failed test satisfies the phase 2 goal, phase 2 thinking also has limits. The test reveals a bug, the programmer corrects it, the test designer designs and executes another test intended to demonstrate another bug. Phase 2 thinking leads to a never-ending sequence of ever more diabolical tests. Taken to extremes, it too never ends, and the result is reliable software that never gets shipped. The trouble with phase 2 thinking is that we don't know when to stop.

1.4.5. Phase 3 Thinking—Test for Risk Reduction

Phase 3 thinking is nothing more than accepting the principles of statistical quality control. I say "accepting" rather than "implementing" because it's not obvious how statistical quality control should be applied to software. To the extent that testing catches bugs and to the extent that those bugs are fixed, testing does improve the product. If a test is passed, then the product's quality does not change, but our perception of that quality does. Testing, pass or fail, reduces our perception of risk about a software product. The more we test, the more we test with harsh tests, the more confidence we have in the product. We'll risk release when that confidence is high enough.*

1.4.6. Phase 4 Thinking—A State of Mind

The phase 4 thinker's knowledge of what testing can and can't do, combined with knowing what makes software testable, results in software that doesn't need much testing to achieve the lower-phase goals. Testability is the goal for two reasons. The first and obvious reason is that we want to reduce the labor of testing. The second and more important reason is that testable code has fewer bugs than code that's hard to test. The impact on productivity of these two factors working together is multiplicative. What makes code testable? One of the main reasons to learn test techniques is to answer that question.

1.4.7. Cumulative Goals

The above goals are cumulative. Debugging depends on testing as a tool for probing hypothesized causes of symptoms. There are many ways to break software that have nothing to do with the software's functional requirements: phase 2 tests alone might never show that the software does what it's supposed to do. It's impractical to break software until the easy demonstrations of workability are behind you. Use of statistical

---

* It would be nice if such statistical methods could be applied as easily to software as they are to widgets. Today, statistical quality control can only be applied to large software products with long histories such as 20 million lines of code and 10 years of use. Application to small products or components as a means to determine when the component can be released is dangerous.

methods as a guide to test design, as a means to achieve good testing at acceptable risks, is a way of fine-tuning the process. It should be applied only to large, robust products with few bugs. Finally, a state of mind isn't enough: even the most testable software must be debugged, must work, and must be hard to break.

1.5. Test Design

Although programmers, testers, and programming managers know that code must be designed and tested, many appear to be unaware that tests themselves must be designed and tested—designed by a process no less rigorous and no less controlled than that used for code. Too often, test cases are attempted without prior analysis of the program's requirements or structure. Such test design, if you can call it that, is just a haphazard series of ad-lib cases that are not documented either before or after the tests are executed. Because they were not formally designed, they cannot be precisely repeated, and no one is sure whether there was a bug or not. After the bug has been ostensibly corrected, no one is sure that the retest was identical to the test that found the bug. Ad-lib tests are useful during debugging, where their primary purpose is to help locate the bug, but ad-lib tests done in support of debugging, no matter how exhausting, are not substitutes for *designed* tests.

The test-design phase of programming should be explicitly identified. Instead of "design, code, desk check, test, and debug," the programming process should be described as: "design, test design, code, test code, program inspection, test inspection, test debugging, test execution, program debugging, testing." Giving test design an explicit place in the scheme of things provides more visibility to that amorphous half of the labor that often goes under the name "test and debug." It makes it less likely that test design will be given short shrift when the budget's small and the schedule's tight and there's a vague hope that maybe this time, just this once, the system will come together without bugs.

1.6. Testing Isn't Everything

This is a book on testing techniques, which are only *part* of our weaponry against bugs. Research and practice (BASI87, FAGA76, MYER78, WEIN65, WHIT87) show that other approaches to the creation of good software are possible and essential. Testing, I believe, is still our most potent weapon, but there's evidence (FAGA76) that other methods may be as effective: but you can't implement inspections, say, *instead* of testing because testing and inspections catch or prevent different kinds of bugs. Today, if we want to prevent all the bugs that we can and catch those that we don't prevent, we must review, inspect, read, do walkthroughs, *and then test*. We don't know today the mix of approaches to use under what circumstances. Experience shows that the "best mix" *very much* depends on things such as development environment, application, size of project, language, history, and culture. The other major methods in decreasing order of effectiveness are as follows:

Inspection Methods—In this category I include walkthroughs, desk checking, formal inspections (FAGA76), and code reading. These methods appear to be as effective as testing, but the bugs caught do not completely overlap.

Design Style—By this term I mean the stylistic criteria used by programmers to define what they mean by a "good" program. Sticking to outmoded style, such as "tight" code or "optimizing" for performance destroys quality. Conversely, adopting stylistic objectives such as testability, openness, and clarity can do much to prevent bugs.

Static Analysis Methods—These methods include anything that can be done by formal analysis of source code during or in conjunction with compilation. Syntax checking in early compilers was rudimentary and was part of the programmer's "testing." Compilers have taken that job over (thank the Lord). **Strong typing** and **type checking** eliminate an entire category of bugs. There's a lot more that can be done to detect errors by static analysis. It's an area of intensive research and development. For example, much of **data-flow anomaly** detection (see Chapters 5 and 8), which today is part of testing, will eventually be incorporated into the compiler's static analysis.

Languages—The source language can help reduce certain kinds of bugs. Languages continue to evolve, and preventing bugs is a driving force in that evolution. Curiously, though, programmers find new kinds of bugs in new languages, so the bug rate seems to be independent of the language used.

Design Methodologies and Development Environment—The design methodology (that is, the development process used and the environment in which that methodology is embedded), can prevent many kinds of bugs. For example, configuration control and automatic distribution of change information prevents bugs which result from a programmer's unawareness that there were changes.

1.7. The Pesticide Paradox and the Complexity Barrier

You're a poor farmer growing cotton in Alabama and the boll weevils are destroying your crop. You mortgage the farm to buy DDT, which you spray on your field, killing 98% of the pest, saving the crop. The next year, you spray the DDT early in the season, but the boll weevils still eat your crop because the 2% you didn't kill last year were resistant to DDT. You now have to mortgage the farm to buy DDT *and* Malathion; then next year's boll weevils will resist both pesticides and you'll have to mortgage the farm yet again. That's the pesticide paradox* for boll weevils and also for software testing.

> *First Law: The Pesticide Paradox*—Every method you use to prevent or find bugs leaves a residue of subtler bugs against which those methods are ineffectual.

That's not too bad, you say, because at least the software gets better and better. Not quite!

> *Second Law: The Complexity Barrier*—Software complexity (and therefore that of bugs) grows to the limits of our ability to manage that complexity.

By eliminating the (previous) easy bugs you allowed another escalation of features and complexity, but this time you have subtler bugs to face, just to retain the reliability you had before. Society seems to be unwilling to limit complexity because we all want that extra bell, whistle, and feature interaction. Thus, our users always push us to the complexity barrier and how close we can approach that barrier is largely determined by the strength of the techniques we can wield against ever more complex and subtle bugs.

2. SOME DICHOTOMIES

2.1. Testing Versus Debugging

Testing and debugging are often lumped under the same heading, and it's no wonder that their roles are often confused: for some, the two words are

---

* The pesticide paradox for boll weevils is resolved by surrounding the cotton field with a sacrificial crop that the boll weevils prefer to cotton. Would that we could create a sacrificial subroutine in all software systems that would attract all the bugs.

synonymous; for others, the phrase "test and debug" is treated as a single word. The **purpose of testing** is to show that a program has bugs. The **purpose of debugging** is find the error or misconception that led to the program's failure and to design and implement the program changes that correct the error. Debugging usually follows testing, but they differ as to goals, methods, and most important, psychology:

1. Testing starts with known conditions, uses predefined procedures, and has predictable outcomes; only whether or not the program passes the test is unpredictable. Debugging starts from possibly unknown initial conditions, and the end cannot be predicted, except statistically.
2. Testing can and should be planned, designed, and scheduled. The procedures for, and duration of, debugging cannot be so constrained.
3. Testing is a demonstration of error or apparent correctness. Debugging is a deductive process.
4. Testing proves a programmer's failure. Debugging is the programmer's vindication.
5. Testing, as executed, should strive to be predictable, dull, constrained, rigid, and inhuman. Debugging demands intuitive leaps, conjectures, experimentation, and freedom.
6. Much of testing can be done without design knowledge. Debugging is impossible without detailed design knowledge.
7. Testing can often be done by an outsider. Debugging must be done by an insider.
8. Although there is a robust theory of testing that establishes theoretical limits to what testing can and can't do, debugging has only recently been attacked by theorists—and so far there are only rudimentary results.
9. Much of test execution and design can be automated. Automated debugging is still a dream.

2.2. Function Versus Structure

Tests can be designed from a functional or a structural point of view. In **functional testing** the program or system is treated as a black box. It is subjected to inputs, and its outputs are verified for conformance to specified behavior. The software's user should be concerned only with functionality and features, and the program's implementation details should not matter. Functional testing takes the user's point of view.

Structural testing does look at the implementation details. Such things as programming style, control method, source language, database design, and coding details dominate structural testing; but the boundary between function and structure is fuzzy. Good systems are built in layers—from the outside to the inside. The user sees only the outermost layer, the layer of pure function. Each layer inward is less related to the system's functions and more constrained by its structure: so what is structure to one layer is function to the next. For example, the user of an online system doesn't know that the system has a memory-allocation routine. For the user, such things are structural details. The memory-management routine's designer works from a specification for that routine. The specification is a definition of "function" at that layer. The memory-management routine uses a link-block subroutine. The memory-management routine's designer writes a "functional" specification for a link-block subroutine, thereby defining a further layer of structural detail and function. At deeper levels, the programmer views the operating system as a structural detail, but the operating system's designer treats the computer's hardware logic as the structural detail.

Most of this book is devoted to models of programs and the tests that can be designed by using those models. A given model, and the associated tests may be first introduced in a structural context but later used again in a functional context, or vice versa. The initial choice of how to present a model was based on the context that seemed most natural for that model and in which it was likeliest that the model would be used for test design. Just as you can't clearly distinguish function from structure, you can't fix the utility of a model to structural tests or functional tests. If it helps you design effective tests, then use the model in whatever context it seems to work.

There's no controversy between the use of structural versus functional tests: both are useful, both have limitations, both target different kinds of bugs. Functional tests can, in principle, detect all bugs but would take infinite time to do so. Structural tests are inherently finite but cannot detect all errors, even if completely executed. The art of testing, in part, is in how you choose between structural and functional tests.

2.3. The Designer Versus the Tester

If testing were wholly based on functional specifications and independent of implementation details, then the designer and the tester could be completely separated. Conversely, to design a test plan based only on a system's structural details would require the software designer's knowledge, and hence only she could design the tests. The more you know about the design, the likelier you are to eliminate useless tests, which, despite functional differences, are actually handled by the same routines over the same paths; but the more you know about the design, the likelier you are to have the same misconceptions as the designer. Ignorance of structure is the independent tester's best friend and worst enemy. The naive tester has no preconceptions about what is or is not possible and will, therefore, design tests that the program's designer would never think of—and many tests that never should be thought of. Knowledge, which is the designer's strength, brings efficiency to testing but also blindness to missing functions and strange cases. Tests designed and executed by the software's designers are by nature biased toward structural considerations and therefore suffer the limitations of structural testing. Tests designed and executed by an independent tester are bias-free and can't be finished. Part of the artistry of testing is to balance knowledge and its biases against ignorance and its inefficiencies.

In this book I discuss the "tester," "test-team member," or "test designer" in contrast to the "programmer" and "program designer," as if they were distinct persons. As one goes from **unit testing** to **unit integration,** to **component testing** and integration, to **system testing,** and finally to formal **system feature testing,** it is increasingly more effective if the "tester" and "programmer" are different persons. The techniques presented in this book can be used for all testing—from unit to system. When the technique is used in system testing, the designer and tester are probably different persons; but when the technique is used in unit testing, the tester and programmer merge into one person, who sometimes acts as a programmer and sometimes as a tester.

You must be a constructive schizophrenic. Be clear about the difference between your role as a programmer and as a tester. The tester in you must be suspicious, uncompromising, hostile, and compulsively obsessed with destroying, utterly destroying, the programmer's software. The tester in you is your Mister Hyde—your Incredible Hulk. He must exercise what Gruenberger calls "low cunning." (HETZ73) The programmer in you is trying to do a job in the simplest and cleanest way possible, on time, and within budget. Sometimes you achieve this by having great insights into the programming problem that reduce complexity and labor and are almost correct. And with that tester/Hulk lurking in the background of your mind, it pays to have a healthy paranoia about bugs. Remember, then, that when I refer to the "test designer" and "programmer" as separate persons, the extent to which they are separated depends on the testing level and the context in which the technique is applied. This saves me the effort of writing about the same technique twice and you the tedium of reading it twice.

2.4. Modularity Versus Efficiency

Both tests and systems can be modular. A **module** is a discrete, well-defined, small component of a system. The smaller the component, the easier it is to understand; but every component has interfaces with other components, and *all* interfaces are sources of confusion. The smaller the component, the likelier are interface bugs. Large components reduce external interfaces but have complicated internal logic that may be difficult or impossible to understand. Part of the artistry of software design is setting component size and boundaries at points that balance internal complexity against interface complexity to achieve an overall complexity minimization.

Testing can and should likewise be organized into modular components. Small, independent test cases have the virtue of easy repeatability. If an error is found by testing, only the small test, not a large component that consists of a sequence of hundreds of interdependent tests, need be rerun to confirm that a test design bug has been fixed. Similarly, if the test has a bug, only that test need be changed and not a whole test plan. But microscopic test cases require individual setups and each such setup (e.g., data, inputs) can have bugs. As with system design, artistry comes into test design in setting the scope of each test and groups of tests so that test design, test debugging, and test execution labor are minimized without compromising effectiveness.

2.5. Small Versus Large

I often write small analytical programs of a few hundred lines that, once used, are discarded. Do I use formal test techniques, quality assurance, and all the rest I so passionately advocate? Of course not, and I'm not a hypocrite. I do what everyone does in similar circumstances: I design, I code, I test a few cases, debug, redesign, recode, and so on, much as I did 30 years ago. I can get away with such (slovenly) practices because I'm programming for a very small, intelligent, forgiving, user population— me. It's the ultimate of small programs and it is most efficiently done by intuitive means and complete lack of formality.

Let's up the scale to a larger package. I'm still the only programmer and user, but now, the package has thirty components averaging 750 statements each, developed over a period of 5 years. Now I *must* create and maintain a data dictionary and do thorough unit testing. But I'll take my own word for it and not bother to retain all those test cases or to exercise formal configuration control.

You can extrapolate from there or draw on your experiences. **Programming in the large** (DERE76) means constructing programs that consist of many components written by many different persons. **Programming in the small** is what we do for ourselves in the privacy of our own offices or as homework exercises in an undergraduate programming course. Size brings with it nonlinear scale effects, which are imperfectly understood today. Qualitative changes occur with size and so must testing methods and quality criteria. A primary example is the notion of **coverage**—a measure of test completeness. Without worrying about exactly what these terms mean, 100% coverage is essential for unit testing, but we back off this requirement as we deal with ever larger software aggregates, accept 75%–85% for most systems, and possibly as low as 50% for huge systems of 10 million lines of code or so.

2.6. The Builder Versus the Buyer

Most software is written and used by the same organization. Unfortunately, this situation is dishonest because it clouds accountability. Many organizations today recognize the virtue of independent software development and operation because it leads to better software, better security, and better testing. Independent software development does not mean that all software should be bought from software houses or consultants but that the software developing entity and the entity that pays for the software be separated enough to make accountability clear. I've heard of cases where the software development group and the operational group within the same company negotiate and sign formal contracts with one another—with lawyers present. If there is no separation between builder and buyer, there can be no accountability. If there is no accountability, the motivation for software quality disappears and with it any serious attempt to do proper testing.

Just as programmers and testers can merge and become one, so can builder and buyer. There are several other persons in the software development cast of characters who, like the above, can also be separated or merged:

1. The **builder,** who designs for and is accountable to
2. The **buyer,** who pays for the system in the hope of profits from providing services to

3. The **user,** the ultimate beneficiary or victim of the system. The user's interests are guarded by

4. The **tester,** who is dedicated to the builder's destruction and

5. The **operator,** who has to live with the builder's mistakes, the buyer's murky specifications, the tester's oversights, and the user's complaints.

3. A MODEL FOR TESTING

3.1. The Project

Testing is applied to anything from subroutines to systems that consist of millions of statements. The archetypical system is one that allows the exploration of all aspects of testing without the complications that have nothing to do with testing but affect any very large project. It's medium-scale programming. Testing the interfaces between different parts of your own mind is very different from testing the interface between you and other programmers separated from you by geography, language, time, and disposition. Testing a one-shot routine that will be run only a few times is very different from testing one that must run for decades and may be modified by some unknown future programmer. Although all the problems of the solitary routine occur for the routine that is embedded in a system, the converse is not true: many kinds of bugs just can't exist in solitary routines. There is an implied context for the test methods discussed in this book—a real-world context characterized by the following model project:

Application—The specifics of the application are unimportant. It is a real-time system that must provide timely responses to user requests for services. It is an online system connected to remote terminals.

Staff—The programming staff consists of twenty to thirty programmers— big enough to warrant formality, but not too big to manage—big enough to use specialists for some parts of the system's design.

Schedule—The project will take 24 months from the start of design to formal acceptance by the customer. Acceptance will be followed by a 6-month cutover period. Computer resources for development and testing will be almost adequate.

Specification—The specification is good. It is functionally detailed without constraining the design, but there are undocumented "understandings" concerning the requirements.

Acceptance Test—The system will be accepted only after a formal acceptance test. The application is not new, so part of the formal test already exists. At first the customer will intend to design the acceptance test, but later it will become the software design team's responsibility.

Personnel—The staff is professional and experienced in programming and in the application. Half the staff has programmed that computer before and most know the source language. One-third, mostly junior programmers, have no experience with the application. The typical programmer has been employed by the programming department for 3 years. The climate is open and frank. Management's attitude is positive and knowledgeable about the realities of such projects.

Standards—Programming and test standards exist and are usually followed. They understand the role of interfaces and the need for interface standards. Documentation is good. There is an internal, semiformal, quality-assurance function. The database is centrally developed and administered.

Objectives—The system is the first of many similar systems that will be implemented in the future. No two will be identical, but they will have 75% of the code in common. Once installed, the system is expected to operate profitably for more than 10 years.

Source—One-third of the code is new, one-third extracted from a previous, reliable, but poorly documented system, and one-third is being rehosted (from another language, computer, operating system—take your pick).

History—One programmer will quit before his components are tested. Another programmer will be fired before testing begins: excellent work, but poorly documented. One component will have to be redone after unit testing: a superb piece of work that defies integration. The customer will insist on five big changes and twenty small ones. There will be at least one nasty problem that nobody—not the customer, not the programmer, not the managers, nor the hardware vendor—suspected. A facility and/or hardware delivery problem will delay testing for several weeks and force second- and third-shift work. Several important milestones will slip but the delivery date will be met.

Our model project is a typical well-run, successful project with a share of glory and catastrophe—neither a utopian project nor a slice of hell.

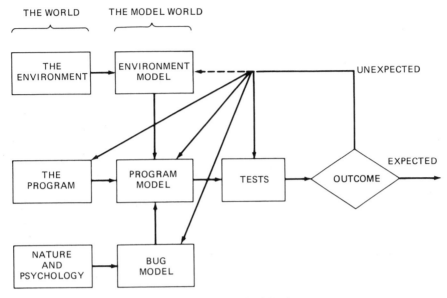

Figure 1.1. A Model of Testing.

3.2. Overview

Figure 1.1 is a model of the testing process. The process starts with a program embedded in an environment, such as a computer, an operating system, or a calling program. We understand human nature and its suceptibility to error. This understanding leads us to create three models: a model of the environment, a model of the program, and a model of the expected bugs. From these models we create a set of tests, which are then executed. The result of each test is either expected or unexpected. If unexpected, it may lead us to revise the test, our model or concept of how the program behaves, our concept of what bugs are possible, or the program itself. Only rarely would we attempt to modify the environment.

3.3. The Environment

A **program's environment** is the hardware and software required to make it run. For online systems the environment may include communications lines, other systems, terminals, and operators. The environment also includes all programs that interact with—and are used to create—the program under test, such as operating system, loader, linkage editor, compiler, utility routines.

Programmers should learn early in their careers that it's not smart to blame the environment (that is, hardware and firmware) for bugs. Hardware bugs are rare. So are bugs in manufacturer-supplied software. This isn't because logic designers and operating system programmers are better than application programmers, but because such hardware and software is stable, tends to be in operation for a long time, and most bugs will have been found and fixed by the time programmers use that hardware or software.* Because hardware and firmware are stable, we don't have to consider all of the environment's complexity. Instead, we work with a simplification of it, in which only the features most important to the program at hand are considered. Our model of the environment includes our *beliefs* regarding such things as the workings of the computer's instruction set, operating system macros and commands, and what a higher-order language statement will do. If testing reveals an unexpected result, we may have to change our beliefs (our model of the environment) to find out what went wrong. But sometimes the environment could be wrong: the bug could be in the hardware or firmware after all.

3.4. The Program

Most programs are too complicated to understand in detail. We must simplify our concept of the program in order to test it. So although a real program is exercised on the test bed, in our brains we deal with a simplified version of it—a version in which most details are ignored. If the program calls a subroutine, we tend not to think about the subroutine's details unless its operation is suspect. Similarly, we may ignore processing details to focus on the program's control structure or ignore control structure to focus on processing. As with the environment, if the simple model of the program does not explain the unexpected behavior, we may have to modify that model to include more facts and details. And if that fails, we may have to modify the program.

3.5. Bugs

Bugs are more insidious than ever we expect them to be. Yet it is convenient to categorize them: initialization, call sequence, wrong variable, and so on. Our notion of what is or isn't a bug varies. A bad specification may lead us to mistake good behavior for bugs, and vice versa. An unexpected

---

* But new operating systems and firmware are as buggy as new application software.

test result may lead us to change our notion of what a bug is—that is to say, our model of bugs.

While we're on the subject of bugs, I'd like to dispel some optimistic notions that many programmers and testers have about bugs. Most programmers and testers have beliefs about bugs that express a naivete that ranks with belief in the tooth fairy. If you hold any of the following beliefs, then disabuse yourself of them because as long as you believe in such things you will be unable to test effectively and unable to justify the dirty tests most programs need.

Benign Bug Hypothesis—The belief that bugs are nice, tame, and logical. Only weak bugs have a logic to them and are amenable to exposure by strictly logical means. Subtle bugs have no definable pattern—they are wild cards.

Bug Locality Hypothesis—The belief that a bug discovered within a component affects only that component's behavior; that because of structure, language syntax, and data organization, the symptoms of a bug are localized to the component's designed domain. Only weak bugs are so localized. Subtle bugs have consequences that are arbitrarily far removed from the cause in time and/or space from the component in which they exist.

Control Bug Dominance—The belief that errors in the control structure of programs dominate the bugs. While many easy bugs, especially in components, can be traced to **control-flow** errors, **data-flow** and data-structure errors are as common. Subtle bugs that violate data-structure boundaries and data/code separation can't be found by looking only at control structures.

Code/Data Separation—The belief, especially in HOL programming, that bugs respect the separation of code and data.* Furthermore, in real systems the distinction between code and data can be hard to make, and it is exactly that blurred distinction that permit such bugs to exist.

Lingua Salvator Est—The hopeful belief that language syntax and semantics (e.g., structured coding, strong typing, complexity hiding) eliminates most bugs. True, good language features do help prevent the simpler component bugs but there's no statistical evidence to support the notion that such features help with subtle bugs in big systems.

---

* Think about it. How do most programs crash? Either by executing data or by inadvertent modifications of code—in either case, a supposedly impossible violation of code/data separation.

Corrections Abide—The mistaken belief that a corrected bug remains corrected. Here's a generic counterexample. A bug is believed to have symptoms caused by the interaction of components A and B but the real problem is a bug in C, which left a residue in a data structure used by both A and B. The bug is "corrected" by changing A and B. Later, C is modified or removed and the symptoms of A and B recur. Subtle bugs are like that.

Silver Bullets—The mistaken belief that X (language, design method, representation, environment—name your own) grants immunity from bugs. Easy-to-moderate bugs may be reduced, but remember the pesticide paradox.

Sadism Suffices—The common belief, especially by independent testers, that a sadistic streak, low cunning, and intuition are sufficient to extirpate most bugs. You only catch easy bugs that way. Tough bugs need methodology and techniques, so read on.

Angelic Testers—The ludicrous belief that testers are better at test design than programmers are at code design.*

3.6. Tests

Tests are formal procedures. Inputs must be prepared, outcomes predicted, tests documented, commands executed, and results observed; all these steps are subject to error. There is nothing magical about testing and test design that immunizes testers against bugs. An unexpected test result is as often cause by a test bug as it is by a real bug.* Bugs can creep into the documentation, the inputs, and the commands and becloud our observation of results. An unexpected test result, therefore, may lead us to revise the tests. Because the tests are themselves in an environment, we also have a mental model of the tests, and instead of revising the tests, we may have to revise that mental model.

3.7. Testing and Levels

We do three distinct kinds of testing on a typical software system: **unit/ component testing, integration testing,** and **system testing.** The objectives

---

* Not universal. For mature organizations with an established, sophisticated design and independent testing process in place, bug rates are approximately equal, where we can (roughly) equate one line of source code to one subtest. An immature process, characterized by inadequate component tests, appears to show programmer bug rates that are about 10 times higher than independent testers' bug rates (in tests). As programmers get better at component testing and inspections, their bug rates go down and eventually approximates the testers' bug rates. Tester bug rates also drop, but not as fast. Actually, we should expect programmer bug rates to be slightly lower than tester bug rates because there are more aspects of test design that cannot be automated than for comparable programming activities. Supporting evidence for comparisons of tester and programmer bug rates is sparse and mostly anecdotal.

of each class is different and therefore, we can expect the mix of test methods used to differ. They are:

Unit, Unit Testing—A **unit** is the smallest testable piece of software, by which I mean that it can be compiled or assembled, linked, loaded, and put under the control of a **test harness** or **driver**. A **unit** is usually the work of one programmer and it consists of several hundred or fewer, lines of source code. **Unit testing** is the testing we do to show that the unit does not satisfy its functional specification and/or that its implemented structure does not match the intended design structure. When our tests reveal such faults, we say that there is a **unit bug.**

Component, Component Testing—A **component** is an **integrated aggregate** of one or more units. A unit is a component, a component with subroutines it calls is a component, etc. By this (recursive) definition, a component can be anything from a unit to an entire system. **Component testing** is the testing we do to show that the component does not satisfy its functional specification and/or that its implemented structure does not match the intended design structure. When our tests reveal such problems, we say that there is a **component bug.**

Integration, Integration Testing—**Integration** is a *process* by which components are aggregated to create larger components. **Integration testing** is testing done to show that even though the components were individually satisfactory, as demonstrated by successful passage of component tests, the combination of components are incorrect or inconsistent. For example, components A and B have both passed their component tests. Integration testing is aimed as showing inconsistencies between A and B. Examples of such inconsistencies are improper call or return sequences, inconsistent data validation criteria, and inconsistent handling of data objects. Integration testing should not be confused with testing integrated objects, which is just higher level component testing. Integration testing is specifically aimed at exposing the problems that arise from the combination of components. The sequence, then, consists of component testing for components A and B, integration testing for the combination of A and B, and finally, component testing for the "new" component (A,B).*

---

* I'm indebted to one of my seminar students for the following elegant illustration of component and integration testing issues. Consider a subroutine A, which calls itself recursively. Initial component testing does not include the called subcomponents; therefore the recursive call of A by A is not tested. Integration testing is the test of the A call and return. The new, integrated component is clearly a different kind of component because it invokes the recursive call support mechanisms (e.g., the stack), which were not tested before; therefore, as a "new" component, it needs additional testing.

System, System Testing—A **system** is a big component. **System testing** is aimed at revealing bugs that cannot be attributed to components as such, to the inconsistencies between components, or to the planned interactions of components and other objects. System testing concerns issues and behaviors that can only be exposed by testing the entire integrated system or a major part of it. System testing includes testing for performance, security, accountability, configuration sensitivity, start-up, and recovery.

This book concerns component testing, but the techniques discussed here also apply to integration and system testing. There aren't any special integration and system testing techniques but the mix of effective techniques changes as our concern shifts from components to integration, to system. How and where integration and system testing will be covered is discussed in the preface to this book. You'll find comments on techniques concerning their relative effectiveness as applied to component, integration, and system testing throughout the book. Such comments are intended to guide your selection of a mix of techniques that best matches your testing concerns, be it component, integration, or system, or some mixture of the three.

3.8. The Role of Models

Testing is a process in which we create mental models of the environment, the program, human nature, and the tests themselves. Each model is used either until we accept the behavior as correct or until the model is no longer sufficient for the purpose. Unexpected test results always force a revision of some mental model, and in turn may lead to a revision of whatever is being modeled. The revised model may be more detailed, which is to say more complicated, or more abstract, which is to say simpler. The art of testing consists of creating, selecting, exploring, and revising models. Our ability to go through this process depends on the number of different models we have at hand and their ability to express a program's behavior.

4. PLAYING POOL AND CONSULTING ORACLES

4.1. Playing Pool

Testing is like playing pool. There's real pool and there's kiddie pool. In kiddie pool you hit the balls, and whatever pocket they fall into you claim as the intended pocket. It's not much of a game and, though suitable for 10-year-olds, it's no challenge for an adult. The objective of real pool is to specify the pocket in advance: similarly for testing. There's real testing and there's kiddie testing. In kiddie testing the tester says, after the fact, that the observed outcome of the test was the expected outcome. In real testing *the outcome is predicted and documented before the test is run.* If a programmer can't reliably predict the outcome of a test before it is run, then that programmer doesn't understand how the program works or what it's supposed to be doing. The tester who can't make that kind of prediction doesn't understand the program's functional objectives. Such misunderstandings lead to bugs, either in the program or in its tests, or both.

4.2. Oracles

An **oracle** (HOWD78B) is any program, process, or body of data that specifies the expected outcome of a set of tests as applied to a tested object. There are as many different kinds of oracles as there are testing concerns. The most common oracle is an **input/outcome oracle**—an oracle that specifies the expected outcome for a specified input. When used without qualification, the term means input/outcome oracle. Other types of oracles are defined in the glossary and will be introduced as required.

4.3. Sources of Oracles

If every test designer had to analyze and predict the expected behavior for every test case for every component, then test design would be very expensive. The hardest part of test design is predicting the expected outcome, but we often have oracles that reduce the work. Here are some sources of oracles:

Kiddie Testing—Run the test and see what comes out. No, I didn't lie and I'm not contradicting myself. It's a question of discipline. If you have the outcome in front of you, and especially if you have intermediate values of internal variables, then it's much easier to validate that outcome by analysis and show it to be correct than it is to predict what the outcome should be and validate your prediction. The problem with kiddie testing as an oracle is that it is very hard to distinguish between its use as an adjunct to prediction and as pure kiddie testing. If the personal discipline and the controls are there, and if there is a documented analysis that justifies the predicted outcomes, then does it matter if that analysis was aided by kiddie testing?

Regression Test Suites—Today, software development and testing are dominated not by the design of new software but by rework and maintenance of existing software. In such instances, most of the tests you need will have been run on a previous version. Most of those tests should have the same outcome for the new version. Outcome prediction is therefore needed only for changed parts of components.

Purchased Suites and Oracles—Highly standardized software that (should) differ only as to implementation often has commercially available test suites and oracles. The most common examples are compilers for standard languages, communications protocols, and mathematical routines. As more software becomes standardized, more oracles will emerge as products and services.

Existing Program—A working, trusted program is an excellent oracle. The typical use is when the program is being rehosted to a new language, operating system, environment, configuration, or to some combination of these, with the intention that the behavior should not change as a result of the rehosting.

5.   IS COMPLETE TESTING POSSIBLE?

If the objective of testing were to *prove* that a program is free of bugs, then testing not only would be practically impossible, but also would be theoretically impossible. Three different approaches can be used to demonstrate that a program is correct: tests based on structure, tests based on function, and formal proofs of correctness. Each approach leads to the conclusion that complete testing, in the sense of a *proof* is neither theoretically nor practically possible (MANN78).

Functional Testing—Every program operates on a finite number of inputs. Whatever pragmatic meaning those inputs might have, they can always be interpreted as a binary bit stream. A complete functional test would consist of subjecting the program to all possible input streams. For each input the routine either accepts the stream and produces a correct outcome, accepts the stream and produces an incorrect outcome, or rejects the stream and tells us that it did so. Because the rejection message is itself an outcome, the problem is reduced to verifying that the correct outcome is produced for every input. But a 10-character input string has 2^{80} possible input streams and corresponding outcomes. So complete functional testing in this sense is impractical.*

But even theoretically, we can't execute a purely functional test this way because we don't know the length of the string to which the system is responding. Let's say that the routine should respond to a 10-charac-

---

* At one test per microsecond, twice the current estimated age of the universe.

ter string. It should be reset after the tenth character, and the next 10 characters should constitute a new test. Unknown to us, the routine has a huge buffer and is actually responding to 10,000-character strings. The bug is such that the program will appear to provide a proper outcome for every 10-character sequence the first thousand times and fail on the 1001st attempt. Without a limit to the routine's memory capacity, which is a structural concept, it is impossible even in principle to prove that the routine is correct.

There are two more problems: the input sequence generator and the outcome verifier. Should we assume that the hardware and software used to generate the inputs, to compare the real outcome to the expected outcome, and to document the expected outcome are bug-free? Pure functional testing is at best conditional on an unverifiable assumption that all test tools and test preparation tools are correct and that only the tested routine is at fault; in the real world of testing, that assumption is silly.

Structural Testing—One should design enough tests to ensure that every path through the routine is exercised at least once. Right off that's impossible, because some loops might never terminate. Brush that problem aside by observing that the universe—including all that's in it—is finite. Even so, the number of paths through a small routine can be awesome because each loop multiplies the path count by the number of times through the loop. A small routine can have millions or billions of paths, so total **path testing** is usually impractical, although it can be done for some routines. By doing it we solve the problems of unknown size that we ran into for purely functional testing; however, it doesn't solve the problem of preparing a bug-free input, a bug-free response list, and a bug-free test observation. We still need those things, because pure structural testing can never assure us that the routine is doing the right thing.

Correctness Proofs—Formal proofs of correctness rely on a combination of functional and structural concepts. Requirements are stated in a formal language (e.g., mathematics), and each program statement is examined and used in a step of an inductive proof that the routine will produce the correct outcome for all possible input sequences. The practical issue here is that such proofs are very expensive and have been applied only to numerical routines or to formal proofs for crucial software such as a system's security kernel or portions of compilers. But there are theoretical objections to formal proofs of correctness that go beyond the practical issues. How do we know that the specification is achievable? Its consistency and completeness must be proved, and in general, that is a provably unsolvable problem. Assuming that the specification has been proved correct, then the mechanism used to prove the program, the steps in the proof, the logic used, and so on, must be proved (GOOD75). Mathematicians and logicians have no more immunity to bugs than programmers or testers have. This also leads to never-ending sequences of unverifiable assumptions.

Manna and Waldinger (MANN78) have clearly summarized the theoretical barriers to complete testing:

"We can never be sure that the specifications are correct."

"No verification system can verify every correct program."

"We can never be certain that a verification system is correct."

Not only are all known approaches to absolute demonstrations of correctness impractical, but they are impossible. Therefore, our objective must shift from an absolute proof to a suitably convincing demonstration—from a deduction to a seduction. That word "suitable," if it is to have the same meaning to everyone, implies a quantitative measure, which in turn implies a statistical measure of software reliability. Our goal, then, should be to provide enough testing to ensure that the probability of failure due to hibernating bugs is low enough to accept. "Enough" implies judgment. What is enough to a video game is insufficient to a nuclear reactor. We can expect that each application will eventually evolve its own software reliability standards. Concurrently, test techniques and reliability models will evolve so that it will be possible, based on test results, to make a quantitative prediction of the routine's reliability.

2

THE TAXONOMY OF BUGS

1. SYNOPSIS

What are the possible consequences of bugs? Bugs are categorized. Statistics and occurrence frequency of various bugs are given.

2. THE CONSEQUENCES OF BUGS

2.1. The Importance of Bugs

The importance of a bug depends on frequency, correction cost, installation cost, and consequences.

Frequency—How often does that kind of bug occur? See Table 2.1 on page 57 for bug frequency statistics. Pay more attention to the more frequent bug types.

Correction Cost—What does it cost to correct the bug after it's been found? That cost is the sum of two factors: (1) the cost of discovery and (2) the cost of correction. These costs go up dramatically the later in the development cycle the bug is discovered. Correction cost also depends on system size. The larger the system the more it costs to correct the same bug.

Installation Cost—Installation cost depends on the number of installations: small for a single-user program, but how about a PC operating system bug? Installation cost can dominate all other costs—fixing one simple bug and distributing the fix could exceed the entire system's development cost.

Consequences—What are the consequences of the bug? You might measure this by the mean size of the awards made by juries to the victims of your bug.

A reasonable metric for bug importance is:

$$\text{importance (\$)} = \text{frequency} * (\text{correction\_cost} + \text{installation\_cost} + \text{consequential\_cost})$$

Frequency tends not to depend on application or environment, but correction, installation, and consequential costs do. As designers, testers, and QA workers, you must be interested in bug importance, not raw frequency. Therefore you must create your own importance model. This chapter will help you do that.

2.2. How Bugs Affect Us—Consequences

Bug consequences range from mild to catastrophic. Consequences should be measured in human rather than machine terms because it is ultimately for humans that we write programs. If you answer the question, "What are the consequences of this bug?" in machine terms by saying, for example, "Bit so-and-so will be set instead of reset," you're avoiding responsibility for the bug. Although it may be difficult to do in the scope of a subroutine, programmers should try to measure the consequences of their bugs in human terms. Here are some consequences on a scale of one to ten:

1. *Mild*—The symptoms of the bug offend us aesthetically; a misspelled output or a misaligned printout.
2. *Moderate*—Outputs are misleading or redundant. The bug impacts the system's performance.
3. *Annoying*—The system's behavior, because of the bug, is dehumanizing. Names are truncated or arbitrarily modified. Bills for $0.00 are sent. Operators must use unnatural command sequences and must trick the system into a proper response for unusual bug-related cases.
4. *Disturbing*—It refuses to handle legitimate transactions. The automatic teller machine won't give you money. My credit card is declared invalid.
5. *Serious*—It loses track of transactions: not just the transaction itself (your paycheck), but the fact that the transaction occurred. Accountability is lost.
6. *Very Serious*—Instead of losing your paycheck, the system credits it to another account or converts deposits into withdrawals. The bug causes the system to do the wrong transaction.
7. *Extreme*—The problems aren't limited to a few users or to a few

transaction types. They are frequent and arbitrary instead of sporadic or for unusual cases.

8. *Intolerable*—Long-term, unrecoverable corruption of the data base occurs and the corruption is not easily discovered. Serious consideration is given to shutting the system down.

9. *Catastrophic*—The decision to shut down is taken out of our hands because the system fails.

10. *Infectious*—What can be worse than a failed system? One that corrupts other systems even though it does not fail in itself; that erodes the social or physical environment; that melts nuclear reactors or starts wars; whose influence, because of malfunction, is far greater than expected; a system that kills.

Any of these consequences could follow from that wrong bit. Programming is a serious business, and testing is more serious still. It pays to have nightmares about undiscovered bugs once in a while (SHED80). When was the last time one of your bugs violated someone's human rights?

2.3. Flexible Severity Rather Than Absolutes

Many programmers, testers, and quality assurance workers have an absolutist attitude toward bugs. "Everybody *knows* that a program must be *perfect* if it's to work: if there's a bug, it *must* be fixed." That's untrue, of course, even though the myth continues to be foisted onto an unwary public. Ask the person in the street and chances are that they'll parrot that myth of ours. That's trouble for us because we can't do it now and never could. It's *our* myth because we, the computer types, created it and continue to perpetuate it. Software never was perfect and won't get perfect. But is that a license to create garbage? The missing ingredient is our reluctance to quantify quality. If instead of saying that software has either 0 quality (there is at least one bug) or 100% (perfect quality and no bugs), we recognize that quality can be measured on some scale, say from 0 to 10. Quality can be measured as a combination of factors, of which the number of bugs and their severity is only one component. The details of how this is done is the subject of another book; but it's enough to say that many organizations have designed and use satisfactory, quantitative, quality metrics. Because bugs and their symptoms play a significant role in such metrics, as testing progresses you can see the quality rise from next to zero to some value at which it is deemed safe to ship the product.

Examining these metrics closer, we see that how the parts are weighted depends on environment, application, culture, and many other factors.

Let's look at a few of these:

Correction Cost—The cost of correcting a bug has almost nothing to do with symptom severity. Catastrophic, life-threatening bugs could be trivial to fix, whereas minor annoyances could require major rewrites to correct.

Context and Application Dependency—The severity of a bug, for the same bug with the same symptoms, depends on context. For example, a roundoff error in an orbit calculation doesn't mean much in a space-ship video game but it matters to real astronauts.

Creating Culture Dependency—What's important depends on the creators of the software and their cultural aspirations. Test tool vendors are more sensitive about bugs in their products than, say, games software vendors.

User Culture Dependency—What's important depends on the user culture. An R&D shop might accept a bug for which there's a workaround; a banker would go to jail for that same bug; and naive users of PC software go crazy over bugs that pros ignore.

The Software Development Phase—Severity depends on development phase. Any bug gets more severe as it gets closer to field use and more severe the longer it's been around—more severe because of the dramatic rise in correction cost with time. Also, what's a trivial or subtle bug to the designer means little to the maintenance programmer for whom all bugs are equally mysterious.

2.4. The Nightmare List and When to Stop Testing

In George Orwell's novel, *1984,* there's a torture chamber called "room 101"—a room that contains your own special nightmare. For me, sailing through 4-foot waves, the boat heeled over, is exhilarating; for my seasick passengers, that's room 101. For me, rounding Cape Horn in winter, with 20-foot waves in a gale is a room 101 but I've heard round-the-world sailboat racers call such conditions "bracing."

The point about bugs is that you or your organization must define your own nightmares. I can't tell you what they are, and therefore I can't ascribe a severity to bugs. Which is why I treat all bugs as equally as I can in this book. And when I slip and express a value judgment about bugs, recognize it for what it is because I can't completely rid myself of my own values.

How should you go about quantifying the nightmare? Here's a workable procedure:

1. List your worst software nightmares. State them in terms of the symptoms they produce and how your user will react to those symptoms. For end users and the population at large, the categories of Section 2.2 above are a starting point. For programmers the nightmare may be closer to home, such as: "I might get a bad personal performance rating."
2. Convert the consequences of each nightmare into a cost. Usually, this is a labor cost for correcting the nightmare, but if your scope extends to the public, it could be the cost of lawsuits, lost business, or nuclear reactor meltdowns.
3. Order the list from the costliest to the cheapest and then discard the low-concern nightmares with which you can live.
4. Based on your experience, measured data (the best source to use), intuition, and published statistics postulate the kinds of bugs that are likely to create the symptoms expressed by each nightmare. Don't go too deep because most bugs are easy. This is a bug design process. If you can "design" the bug by a one-character or one-statement change, then it's a good target. If it takes hours of sneaky thinking to characterize the bug, then either it's an unlikely bug or you're worried about a saboteur in your organization, which could be appropriate in some cases. Most bugs are simple goofs once you find and understand them.
5. For each nightmare, then, you've developed a list of possible causative bugs. Order that list by decreasing probability. Judge the probability based on your own bug statistics, intuition, experience, etc. The same bug type will appear in different nightmares. The importance of a bug type is calculated by multiplying the expected cost of the nightmare by the probability of the bug and summing across all nightmares:

$$\text{importance of bug type } i = \sum_{\text{all nightmares}} C_{ij} P_{(\text{bug type } i \text{ in nightmare } j)}$$

6. Rank the bug types in order of decreasing importance to you.
7. Design tests (based on your knowledge of test techniques) and design your quality assurance inspection process by using the methods that are most effective against the most important bugs.
8. If a test is passed, then some nightmares or parts of them go away. If a test is failed, then a nightmare is possible, but upon correcting the

bug, it too goes away. Testing, then, gives you information you can use to revise your estimated nightmare probabilities. As you test, revise the probabilities and reorder the nightmare list. Taking whatever information you get from testing and working it back through the exercise leads you to revise your subsequent test strategy, either on this project if it's big enough or long enough, or on subsequent projects.

9. Stop testing when the probability of all nightmares has been shown to be inconsequential as a result of hard evidence produced by testing.

The above prescription can be implemented as a formal part of the software development process, or it can be adopted as a guideline or philosophical point of view. The idea is not that you implement elaborate metrics (unless that's appropriate) but that you recognize the importance of the feedback that testing provides to the testing process itself and, more important, to the kinds of tests you will design.

The mature tester's problem has never been how to design tests. If you understand testing techniques, you will know how to design several different infinities of justifiable tests. The tester's central problem is how to best cull a reasonable, finite, number of tests from that multifold infinity—a test suite that, as experience and logic leads us to predict, will have a high probability of putting the nightmares to rest—that is to say, an effective, revealing, set of tests. Look at the pesticide paradox again and observe the following consequence:

Corollary to the First Law—Test suites wear out.

Yesterday's elegant, revealing, effective, test suite will wear out because programmers and designers, given feedback on their bugs, do modify their programming habits and style in an attempt to reduce the incidence of bugs they know about. Furthermore, the better the feedback, the better the QA, the more responsive the programmers are, the faster those suites wear out. Yes, the software is getting better, but that only allows you to approach closer to, or to leap over, the previous complexity barrier. True, bug statistics tell you nothing about the coming release, only the bugs of the previous release—but that's better than basing your test technique strategy on general industry statistics or on myths. If you don't gather bug statistics, organized into some rational taxonomy, you don't know how effective your testing has been, and worse, you don't know how worn out your test suite is. The consequences of that ignorance is a brutal shock. How many horror stories do you want to hear about the sophisticated outfit that tested long, hard, and diligently—sent release 3.4 to the field, confident that it was the best tested product they had ever shipped—only to have it bomb more miserably than any prior release?

3. A TAXONOMY FOR BUGS*

3.1. General

There is no universally correct way to categorize bugs. This taxonomy is not rigid. Bugs are difficult to categorize. A given bug can be put into one or another category depending on its history and the programmer's state of mind. For example, a one-character error in a source statement changes the statement, but unfortunately it passes syntax checking. As a result, data are corrupted in an area far removed from the actual bug. That in turn leads to an improperly executed function. Is this a typewriting error, a coding error, a data error, or a functional error? If the bug is in our own program, we're tempted to blame it on typewriting;** if in another programmer's code, on carelessness. And if our job is to critique the system, we might say that the fault is an inadequate internal data-validation mechanism. A detailed taxonomy is presented in the appendix. The major categories are: requirements, features and functionality, structure, data, implementation and coding, integration, system and software architecture, and testing. A first breakdown is provided in Table 2.1, whereas in the appendix the breakdown is as fine as makes sense. Bug taxonomy, as testing, is potentially infinite. More important than adopting the "right" taxonomy is that you adopt *some* taxonomy and that you use it as a statistical framework on which to base your testing strategy. Because there's so much effort required to develop a taxonomy, don't redo my work—you're invited to adopt the taxonomy of the appendix (or any part thereof) and are hereby authorized to copy it (with appropriate attribu-

---

* I'm sticking with "bug" rather than adopt another word such as "fault," which is the current fad in publications because: (1) everybody knows what "bug" means; (2) the standards are inconsistent with one another and with themselves in the definition of "fault," "error," and "failure"; (3) according to the Oxford English Dictionary, the usage of "bug" the way we use it, contrary to popular belief, *predates* its entomological use by centuries—the first written reference to "bug" = "goblin" is from 1388, but its first use to mean a small, six-legged creature with a hard carapace dates from 1642; (4) I prefer short, strong, Anglo-Saxon words to effete Norman words. The genesis of "bug" as a computer problem being derived from a moth fried on the power bus of an early computer, thus bringing the system down, is apocryphal. "Bug" is an ancient and honorable word (Welsh *bwg*) and not newly coined jargon peculiar to the computer industry.
** Ah, for the good old days when programs were keypunched onto cards by a keypunch operator; then we could blame the operator for the bugs. Today, with code entered directly by the programmer at a terminal or PC, we can try blaming the communication interface or the local area network, which isn't as convincing.

tion) without guilt or fear of being sued by me for plagiarism. If my taxonomy doesn't turn you on, adopt the IEEE taxonomy (IEEE87B).

3.2. Requirements, Features, and Functionality Bugs

3.2.1. Requirements and Specifications

Requirements and the specifications developed from them can be incomplete, ambiguous, or self-contradictory. They can be misunderstood or impossible to understand. The specification may assume, but not mention, other specifications and prerequisites that are known to the specifier but not to the designer. And specifications that don't have these flaws may change while the design is in progress. Features are modified, added, and deleted. The designer has to hit a moving target and occasionally misses.

Requirements, especially as expressed in a specification (or often, as *not* expressed because there is no specification) are a major source of expensive bugs. The range is from a few percent to more than 50%, depending on application and environment. What hurts most about these bugs is that they're the earliest to invade the system and the last to leave. It's not unusual for a faulty requirement to get through all development testing, beta testing, and initial field use, only to be caught after hundreds of sites have been installed.

3.2.2. Feature Bugs

Specification problems usually create corresponding feature problems. A feature can be wrong, missing, or superfluous. A missing feature or case is the easiest to detect and correct. A wrong feature could have deep design implications. Extra features were once considered desirable. We now recognize that "free" features are rarely free. Any increase in generality that does not contribute to reliability, modularity, maintainability, and robustness should be suspected. Gratuitous enhancements can, if they increase complexity, accumulate into a fertile compost heap that breeds future bugs, and they can create holes that can be converted into security breaches. Conversely, one cannot rigidly forbid additional features that might be a consequence of good design. Removing the features might complicate the software, consume more resources, and foster more bugs.

3.2.3. Feature Interaction

Providing clear, correct, implementable, and testable feature specifications is not enough. Features usually come in groups of related features.

The features of each group and the interaction of features within each group are usually well tested. The problem is unpredictable interactions between feature groups or even between individual features. For example, your telephone is provided with call holding and call forwarding. Call holding allows you to put a new incoming call on hold while you continue talking to the first caller. Call forwarding allows you to redirect incoming calls to some other telephone number. Here are some simple feature interaction questions: How about holding a third call when there is already a call on hold? Forwarding forwarded calls (i.e., the number forwarded to is also forwarding calls)? Forwarding calls in a loop? Holding while forwarding is active? Initiating forwarding when there is a call on hold? Holding for forwarded calls when the telephone forwarded to does (doesn't) have forwarding? . . . If you think these variations are brain twisters, how about feature interactions for your income tax return, say between federal, state, and local tax laws? Every application has its peculiar set of features and a much bigger set of unspecified feature interaction potentials and therefore feature interaction bugs. We have very little statistics on these bugs, but the trend seems to be that as the earlier, simpler, bugs are removed, feature interaction bugs emerge as a major category. Other than deliberately preventing some interactions and testing the important combinations, we have no magic remedy for these problems.

3.2.4. Specification and Feature Bug Remedies

Most feature bugs are rooted in human-to-human communication problems. One solution is the use of high-level, formal specification languages or systems (BELF76, BERZ85, DAVI88A, DAVI88B, FISC79, HAYE85, PROG88, SOFT88, YEHR80). Such languages and systems provide short-term support but, in the long run, do not solve the problem.

Short-Term Support—Specification languages (we'll call them all "languages" hereafter, even though some may be interactive dialogue systems) facilitate formalization of requirements and (partial)* inconsistency and ambiguity analysis. With formal specifications, partially to fully automatic test case generation is possible. Generally, users and developers of such products have found them to be cost-effective.

Long-Term Support—Assume that we have a great specification language and that it can be used to create unambiguous, complete specifications with unambiguous, complete tests and consistent test criteria. A specification written in that language could theoretically be compiled

---

* "Partial" rather than "complete" because total consistency and completeness analysis is a known unsolvable problem.

into object code (ignoring efficiency and practicality issues). But this is just programming in HOL squared. The specification problem has been shifted to a higher level but not eliminated. Theoretical considerations aside, given a system which can generate functional tests from specifications, the likeliest impact is a further complexity escalation facilitated by the reduction of another class of bugs (the complexity barrier law).

The long-term impact of formal specification languages and systems will probably be that they will influence the design of ordinary programming languages so that more of *current* specification can be formalized. This approach will reduce, but not eliminate, specification bugs. The pesticide paradox will work again to eliminate the kinds of specification bugs we now have (simple ambiguities and contradictions), leaving us a residue of tougher specification bugs that will need an even higher order specification system to expose.

3.2.5. Testing Techniques

Most **functional test techniques**—that is, those techniques which are based on a behavioral description of software, such as **transaction flow testing** (Chapter 4), **syntax testing** (Chapter 9), **domain testing** (Chapter 6), **logic testing** (Chapter 10), and **state testing** (Chapter 11) are useful in testing functional bugs. They are also useful in testing for requirements and specification bugs to the extent that the requirements can be expressed in terms of the model on which the technique is based.

3.3. Structural Bugs

3.3.1. Control and Sequence Bugs

Control and sequence bugs include paths left out, unreachable code, improper nesting of loops, loop-back or loop-termination criteria incorrect, missing process steps, duplicated processing, unnecessary processing, rampaging GOTO's, ill-conceived switches, **spaghetti code,** and worst of all, **pachinko code.**

Although much of testing and software design literature focuses on control flow bugs, they are not as common in new software as the literature might lead one to believe. One reason for the popularity of control-flow problems in the literature is that this area is amenable to theoretical treatment. Fortunately, most control-flow bugs (in new code) are easily tested and caught in unit testing.

Another source of confusion and therefore research concern is that novice programmers working on toy problems do tend to have more control-flow bugs than experienced programmers. A third reason for concern with control-flow problems is that dirty old code, especially assembly language and COBOL code, can be dominated by control-flow bugs. In fact, a good reason to rewrite an application from scratch is that the old control structure has become so complicated and so arbitrary after decades of rework that no one dare modify it further and, further, it defies testing.

Control and sequence bugs at all levels are caught by testing, especially structural testing, more specifically, path testing (Chapter 3), combined with a bottom-line functional test based on a specification. These bugs are partially prevented by language choice (e.g., languages that restrict control-flow options) and style, and most important, lots of memory. Experience shows that many control-flow problems result directly from trying to "squeeze" 8 pounds of software into a 4-pound bag (i.e., 8K object into 4K). Squeezing for short execution time is as bad.

3.3.2. Logic Bugs

Bugs in logic, especially those related to misunderstanding how case statements and logic operators behave singly and in combinations, include nonexistent cases, improper layout of cases, "impossible" cases that are not impossible, a "don't-care" case that matters, improper negation of a boolean expression (for example, using "greater than" as the negation of "less than"), improper simplification and combination of cases, overlap of exclusive cases, confusing "exclusive OR" with "inclusive OR."

Another problematic area concerns misunderstanding the semantics of the order in which a boolean expression is evaluated for specific compilers, especially in the context of deeply nested IF-THEN-ELSE constructs. For example, the truth or falsity of a logical expression is determined after evaluating a few terms, so evaluation of further terms (usually) stops, but the programmer expects that further terms will be evaluated. In other words, although the boolean expression appears as a single statement, the programmer does not understand that its components will be evaluated sequentially. See index entries on **predicate coverage** for more information.

If these bugs are part of logical (i.e., boolean) processing not related to control flow, then they are categorized as processing bugs. If they are part of a logical expression (i.e., **control-flow predicate**) which is used to direct the control flow, then they are categorized as control-flow bugs.

Logic bugs are not really different in kind from arithmetic bugs. They are likelier than arithmetic bugs because programmers, like most people, have less formal training in logic at an early age than they do in arithmetic. The best defense against this kind of bug is a systematic analysis of cases. Logic-based testing (Chapter 10) is helpful.

3.3.3.   Processing Bugs

Processing bugs include arithmetic bugs, algebraic, mathematical function evaluation, algorithm selection, and general processing. Many problems in this area are related to incorrect conversion from one data representation to another. This is especially true in assembly language programming. Other problems include ignoring overflow, ignoring the difference between positive and negative zero, improper use of greater-than, greater-than-or-equal, less-than, less-than-or-equal, assumption of equality to zero in floating point, and improper comparison between different formats as in ASCII to binary or integer to floating point.

Although these bugs are frequent (12%), they tend to be caught in good unit testing and also tend to have localized effects. Selection of covering test cases, especially domain-testing methods (Chapter 6) are the testing remedies for this kind of bug.

3.3.4.   Initialization Bugs

Initialization bugs are common, and experienced programmers and testers know they must look for them. Both improper and superfluous initialization occur. The latter tends to be less harmful but can affect performance. Typical bugs are as follows: forgetting to initialize working space, registers, or data areas before first use or assuming that they are initialized elsewhere; a bug in the first value of a loop-control parameter; accepting an initial value without a validation check; and initializing to the wrong format, data representation, or type.

The remedies here are in the kinds of tools the programmer has. The source language also helps. Explicit declaration of all variables, as in Pascal, helps to reduce some initialization problems. Preprocessors, either built into the language or run separately, can detect some, but not all, initialization problems. The test methods of Chapter 5 are helpful for test design and for debugging initialization problems.

3.3.5.   Data-Flow Bugs and Anomalies

Most initialization bugs are a special case of data-flow anomalies. A **data-flow anomaly** occurs when there is a path along which we expect to do something unreasonable with data, such as using an uninitialized variable, attempting to use a variable before it exists, modifying data and then not storing or using the result, or initializing twice without an intermediate use. Although part of data-flow anomaly detection can be done by the compiler based on information known at compile time, much can be detected only by execution and therefore is a subject for testing. It is generally recognized today that data-flow anomalies are as important as control-flow anomalies. The methods of Chapters 5 and 12 will help you design tests aimed at data-flow problems.

3.4. Data Bugs

3.4.1. General

Data bugs include all bugs that arise from the specification of data objects, their formats, the number of such objects, and their initial values. Data bugs are at least as common as bugs in code, but they are often treated as if they did not exist at all. Underestimating the frequency of data bugs is caused by poor bug accounting. In some projects, bugs in data declarations are just not counted, and for that matter, data declaration statements are not counted as part of the code. The separation of code and data is, of course, artificial because their roles can be interchanged at will. At the extreme, one can write a twenty-instruction program that can simulate any computer (a Turing machine) and have all "programs" recorded as data and manipulated as such. Furthermore, this can be done in any language on any computer—but who would want to?

Software is evolving toward programs in which more and more of the control and processing functions are stored in tables. I call this the third law:

Third Law—Code migrates to data.

Because of this law there is an increasing awareness that bugs in code are only half the battle and that data problems should be given equal attention. The bug statistics of Table 2.1 support this concept; that is, structural bugs and data bugs each have frequencies of about 25%. If you examine a piece of contemporary source code, you may find that half of the statements are data declarations. Although these statements do not result in executable code, because they are specified by humans, they are as subject to error as operative statements. If a program is designed under the assumption that a certain data object will be set to zero and it isn't, the operative statements of the program are not at fault. Even so, there is still an initialization bug, which, because it is in a data statement, could be harder to find than if it had been a bug in executable code.

This increase in the proportion of the source statements devoted to data definition is a direct consequence of two factors: (1) the dramatic reduction in the cost of main memory and disc storage, and (2) the high cost of creating and testing software. Generalized software controlled by tables is not efficient. Computer costs, especially memory costs, have decreased to the point where the inefficiencies of generalized table-driven code are not usually significant. The increasing cost of software as a percentage of system cost has shifted the emphasis in the software industry away from single-purpose, unique software to an increased reliance on prepackaged, generalized programs. This trend is evident in the computer manufacturers' software, in the existence of a healthy proprietary software industry, and in the emergence of languages and programming environments that support code reusability (e.g., object-oriented languages). Generalized packages must satisfy a wide range of options, host configurations, operating systems, and computers. The designer of a generalized package achieves generality, in part, by making many things parametric, such as array sizes, memory partition, and file structure. It is not unusual for a big application package to have several hundred parameters. Setting the parameter values particularizes the program to the specific installation. The parameters are interrelated, and errors in those relations can cause illogical conditions and, therefore, bugs.

Another source of database complexity increase is the use of control tables in lieu of code. The simplest example is the use of tables that turn processing options on and off. A more complicated form of control table is used when a system must execute a set of closely related processes that have the same control structure but are different in details. An early example is found in telephony, where the details of controlling a telephone call are table-driven. A generalized call-control processor handles calls from and to different kinds of lines. The system is loaded with a set of tables that corresponds to the protocols required for that telephone exchange. Another example is the use of generalized device-control software which is particularized by data stored in device tables. The operating system can be used with new, undefined devices, if those devices' parameters can fit into a set of very broad values. The culmination of this trend is the use of complete, internal, transaction-control languages designed for the application. Instead of being coded as computer instructions or language statements, the steps required to process a transaction are stored as a sequence of constants in a transaction-processing table. The state of the transaction, that is, the current processing step, is stored in a transaction-control block. The generalized transaction-control processor uses the combination of transaction state and the control tables to direct the transaction to the next step. The transaction-control table is actually a program which is processed interpretively by the transaction-control processor. That program may contain the equivalent of addressing, conditional branch instructions, looping statements, case statements, and so on. In other words, a **hidden programming language** has been created. It is an effective design technique because it enables fixed software to handle many different transaction types, individually and simultaneously. Furthermore, modifying the control tables to install new transaction types is usually easier than making the same modifications in code.

In summary, current programming trends are leading to the increasing use of undeclared, internal, specialized programming languages. These are languages—make no mistake about that—even if they are simple compared to normal programming languages; but the syntax of these languages is rarely debugged. There's no compiler for them and therefore no source syntax checking. The programs in these languages are inserted as octal or hexadecimal codes—as if we were programming back in the early days of UNIVAC-I. Large, low-cost memory will continue to strengthen this trend and, consequently, there will be an increased incidence of code masquerading as data. Bugs in this kind of hidden code are at least as difficult to find as bugs in normal code. The first step in the avoidance of data bugs—whether the data are used as pure data, as parameters, or as hidden code—is the realization that *all* source statements, including data declarations, must be counted, and that all source statements, whether or not they result in object code, are bug-prone.

The categories used for data bugs are different from those used for code bugs. Each way of looking at data provides a different perspective. These categories for data bugs overlap and are no stricter than the categories used for bugs in code.

3.4.2. Dynamic Versus Static

Dynamic data are transitory. Whatever their purpose, they have a relatively short lifetime, typically the processing time of one transaction. A storage object may be used to hold dynamic data of different types, with different formats, attributes, and residues. Failure to initialize a shared object properly can lead to data-dependent bugs caused by residues from a previous use of that object by another transaction. Note that the culprit transaction is long gone when the bug's symptoms are discovered. Because the effect of corruption of dynamic data can be arbitrarily far removed from the cause, such bugs are among the most difficult to catch. The design remedy is complete documentation of all shared-memory structures, defensive code that does thorough data-validation checks, and centralized-resource managers.

The basic problem is leftover garbage in a shared resource. This can be handled in one of three ways: (1) cleanup after use by the user, (2) common cleanup by the resource manager, and (3) no cleanup. The latter is the method usually used. Therefore, resource users must program under the assumption that the resource manager gives them garbage-filled resources. Common cleanup is used in very secure systems where subsequent users of a resource must never be able to read data left by a previous user in another security or privacy category.

Static data are fixed in form and content. Whatever their purpose, they appear in the source code or data base, directly or indirectly, as, for example, a number, a string of characters, or a bit pattern. Static data need not be explicit in the source code. Some languages provide **compile-time processing,** which is especially useful in general-purpose routines that are particularized by interrelated parameters. Compile-time processing is an effective measure against parameter-value conflicts. Instead of relying on the programmer to calculate the correct values of interrelated parameters, a program executed at compile time (or assembly time) calculates the parameters' values. If compile-time processing is not a language feature, then a specialized preprocessor can be built that will check the parameter values and calculate those values that are derived from others. As an example, a large commercial telecommunications system has several hundred parameters that dictate the number of lines, the layout of all storage media, the hardware configuration, the characteristics of the lines, the allowable user options for those lines, and so on. These are processed by a site-adapter program that not only sets the parameter values but builds data declarations, sizes arrays, creates constants, and inserts processing routines from a library. A bug in the site adapter, or in the data given to the site adapter, can result in bugs in the static data used by the object programs for that site.

Another example is the postprocessor used to install many personal computer software packages. Here the configuration peculiarities are handled by generalized table-driven software, which is particularized at run (actually, installation) time.

Any preprocessing (or postprocessing) code, any code executed at compile or assembly time or before, at load time, at installation time, or some other time can lead to faulty static data and therefore bugs—even though such code (and the execution thereof) does not represent object code at run time. We tend to take compilers, assemblers, utilities, loaders, and configurators for granted and do not suspect them to be bug sources. This is not a bad assumption for standard utilities or translators.

But if a highly parameterized system uses site-adapter software or prepro- cessors or compile-time/assembly-time processing, and if such proces- sors and code are developed concurrently with the working software of the application—watch out!

Software used to produce object code is suspect until validated. All new software must be rigorously tested even if it isn't part of the applica- tion's mainstream. Static data can be just as wrong as any other kind and can have just as many bugs. Do not treat a routine that creates static data as "simple" because it "just stuffs a bunch of numbers into a table." Subject such code to the same testing rigor that you apply to running code.*

The design remedy for the preprocessing situation is in the source language. If the language permits compile-time processing that can be used to particularize parameter values and data structures, and if the syntax of the compile-time statements is identical to the syntax of the rest of the language, then the code will be subjected to the same validation and syntax checking as ordinary code. Such language facilities eliminate the need for most specialized preprocessors, table generators, and site adapters. For postprocessors, there is no magic, other than to recognize that users judge developers by the entire picture, installation software included.

3.4.3. Information, Parameter, and Control

Static or dynamic data can serve in one of three roles, or in a combination of roles: as a parameter, for control, or for information. What constitutes control or information is a matter of perspective and can shift from one processing level to another. A scheduler receives a request to start a process. To the scheduler the identity of the process is information to be processed, but at another level it is control. My name is used to generate a hash code that will be used to access a disc record. My name is informa- tion, but to the disc hardware its translation into an address is control (e.g., move to track so-and-so).

Information is usually dynamic and tends to be local to a single transac- tion or task. As such, errors in information (when data are treated as information, that is) may not be serious bugs. The bug, if any, is in the lack of protective data-validation code or in the failure to protect the routine's logic from out-of-range data or data in the wrong format. The

---

* And the winner for consistently bad software of this ilk is PC installation software. Clean, robust, "friendly," operational software (e.g., word processing) is saddled with a hostile but overly tender installation package whose operation is closer to clearing mine fields than to processing.

only way we can be sure that there is data-validation code in a routine is to put it there. Assuming that the other routine will validate data invites latent bugs and maintenance problems. The program evolves and changes, and it is forgotten that the modified routine did the data validation for several other routines. *If* a routine is vulnerable to bad data, the only sane thing to do is to block such data within the routine; but it's even better to redesign it so that it is no longer vulnerable.

Inadequate data validation often leads to finger pointing. The calling routine's author is blamed, the called routine's author blames back, they both blame the operators. This scenario leads to a lot of ego confrontation and guilt. "If only the other programmers did their job correctly," you say, "we wouldn't need all this redundant data validation and defensive code. I have to put in this extra junk because I'm surrounded by slobs!" This attitude is understandable, but not productive. Furthermore, if you really feel that way, you're likely to feel guilty about it. Don't blame your fellow programmer and don't feel guilt. Nature has conspired against us but given us a scapegoat. One of the unfortunate side effects of large-scale integrated circuitry stems from the use of microscopic logic elements that work at very low energy levels. Modern circuitry is vulnerable to electronic noise, electromagnetic radiation, cosmic rays, neutron hits, stray alpha particles, and other noxious disturbances. No kidding—alpha-particle hits that can change the value of a bit are a serious problem, and the semiconductor manufacturers are spending a lot of money and effort to reduce the random modification of data by alpha particles. Therefore, even if your fellow programmers did thorough, correct data validation, dynamic data, static data, parameters, and code can be corrupted. Program without rancor and guilt! Put in the data-validation checks and blame the necessity on sun spots and alpha particles!*

3.4.4. Contents, Structure, and Attributes

Data specifications consist of three parts:

Contents—The actual bit pattern, character string, or number put into a data structure. Content is a pure bit pattern and has no meaning unless

---

* There are always two sides to the coin. The best routine accepts any kind of input garbage and returns with an "invalid input data" code, whereas the worst routine just crashes. How, when, and where data validation should be done, and how defensive low-level routines should be, are architecture and integration issues. Locally defensive code—that is, code that is defensive in accordance with local notions of correctness—may block or reject good transactions and therefore create integration problems. What it comes down to is that defensiveness should be (but isn't usually) a part of the routine's functional specification and should be attributed to routines in accordance with a global plan.

it is interpreted by a hardware or software processor. All data bugs result in the corruption or misinterpretation of content.

Structure—The size and shape and numbers that describe the data object, that is, the memory locations used to store the content (e.g., 16 characters aligned on a word boundary, 122 blocks of 83 characters each, bits 4 through 14 of word 17). Structures can have substructures and can be arranged into superstructures. A hunk of memory may have several different structures defined over it—e.g., a two-dimensional array treated elsewhere as N one-dimensional arrays.

Attributes—The specification of meaning, that is, the semantics associated with the contents of a data object (e.g., an integer, an alphanumeric string, a subroutine).

The severity and subtlety of bugs increases as we go from content to attributes because things get less formal in that direction. Content has been dealt with earlier in this section. Structural bugs can take the form of declaration bugs, but these are not the worst kind of structural bugs. A serious potential for bugs occurs when data are used with different structures. Here is a piece of clever design. The programmer has subdivided the problem into eight cases and uses a 3-bit field to designate the case. Another programmer has four different cases to consider and uses a 2-bit field for the purpose. A third programmer is interested in the combination of the other two sets of cases and treats the whole as a 5-bit field that leads to thirty-two combined cases. We cannot judge, out of context, whether this is a good design or an abomination, but we can note that there is a different structure in the minds of the three programmers and therefore a potential for bugs. The practice of interpreting a given memory location under several different structures is not intrinsically bad. Often, the only alternative would be increased memory and many more data transfers.

Attributes of data are the meanings we associate with data. Although some bugs are related to misinterpretation of integers for floating point and other basic representation problems, the more subtle attribute-related bugs are embedded in the application. Consider a 16-bit field. It could represent, among other things, a number, a loop-iteration count, a control code, a pointer, or a link field. Each interpretation is a different attribute. There is no way for the computer to know that it is proper or improper to add a control code to a link field to yield a loop count. We have used the same data with different meanings. In modern parlance, we have changed the **data type.** It is generally incorrect to logically or arithmetically combine objects whose types are different. Conversely, it is almost impossible to create an efficient system without doing so. Shifts in interpretation usually occur at interfaces, especially the human interface that is behind every software interface. See GANN76 for a summary of **type bugs.**

The preventive measures for data-type bugs are in the source language, documentation, and coding style. Explicit documentation of the contents, structure, and attributes of all data objects is essential. The database documentation should be centralized. All alternate interpretation of a given data object should be listed along with the identity of all routines that have access to that object. A proper **data dictionary** (which is what the database documentation is called) can be as large as the narrative description of the code. The data dictionary and the database it represents must also be designed. This design is done by a high-level design process, which is as important as the design of the software architecture. My point of view here *is* dogmatic. Routines should not be administratively treated as if they have their "own" data declarations.* All data structures should be globally defined and centrally administered. Exceptions, such as a private work area, should be individually justified. Such private data structures must never be used by any other routine but the structure must still be documented in the data dictionary.

It's impossible to properly test software of any size (say 10,000+ statements) without central database management and a configuration-controlled data dictionary. I was once faced with such a herculean challenge. My first step was to try to create the missing data dictionary preparatory to any attempt to define tests. The act of dragging the murky bottoms of a hundred minds for hidden data declarations and semiprivate space in an attempt to create a data dictionary revealed so many data bugs that it was obvious that the system would defy integration. I never did get to design

---

* I've had more flack and misinterpretations of this position than almost anything else I've written. It seems to fly in the face of contemporary programming trends and language advances. To support the reasoning, I'll cite what I call the Fourth Law:

Fourth Law—Local migrates to global.

There is a tendency, over a period of time (years), for previously local data objects to become global because there are intermediate (local) results that some other programmer can use to "fix" a maintenance problem or to add new functionality. Although the originating programmer may have intended object X to be local, own data, 20 years later enough of these have been migrated to a more global scope to cause serious problems. For this reason all data objects should be administratively treated as if they were global from the very start. The issue is centralized administration of data structures and data. Where the language requires data declarations within the body of the routine the desired effect can be achieved by use of macros, by preprocessors, etc. The point is that even if the language permits or requires private data objects, administratively they should be treated as if they are global—i.e., in the data dictionary. An alternate, and possibly concurrent position, is to enforce locality rigidly and permanently. That means making the global use of local data as heinous a crime as say, modifying the computer's backplane wiring. This is part of what's behind object-oriented programming. We'll have to wait for a decade, preferably two, to see if locality is retained over time and if the Fourth Law does or does not hold (in practice, rather than in theory) for object-oriented software.

tests for that project—it collapsed; and a new design was started surreptitiously from scratch.

The second remedy is in the source language. **Strongly typed languages** prevent the inadvertent mixed manipulation of data that are declared as different types. A conversion in usage from pointer type to counter type, say, requires an explicit statement that will do the conversion. Such statements may or may not result in object code. Conversion from floating point to integer, would, of course, require object code, but conversion from pointer to counter might not. Strong typing forces the explicit declaration of attributes and provides compiler facilities to check for mixed-type operations. The ability of the user to specify types, as in Pascal, is mandatory. These data-typing facilities force the specification of data attributes into the source code, which makes them more amenable to automatic verification by the compiler and to test design than when the attributes are described in a separate data dictionary. In assembly language programming, or in source languages that do not have user-defined types, the remedy is the use of **field-access macros.** No programmer is allowed to directly access a field in the database. Access can be obtained only through the use of a field-access macro. The macro code does all the extraction, stripping, justification, and type conversion necessary. If the database structure has to be changed, the affected field-access macros are changed, but the source code that uses the macros does not (usually) have to be changed. The attributes of the data are documented with the field-access macro documentation. Another advantage of this approach is that the data dictionary can be automatically produced from the specifications of the field-access macro library.

3.5. Coding Bugs

Coding errors of all kinds can create any of the other kinds of bugs. Syntax errors are generally not important in the scheme of things if the source language translator has adequate syntax checking. Failure to catch a syntax error is a bug in the translator. A good translator will also catch undeclared data, undeclared routines, dangling code, and many initialization problems. Any programming error caught by the translator (assembler, compiler, or interpreter) does not substantially affect test design and execution because testing cannot start until such errors are corrected. Whether it takes a programmer one, ten, or a hundred passes before a routine can be tested should concern software management (because it is a programming productivity issue) but not test design (which is a quality-assurance issue). But if a program has many source-syntax errors, we should expect many logic and coding bugs—because a slob is a slob is a slob.

Given good source-syntax checking, the most common pure coding errors are typographical, followed by errors caused by not understanding the operation of an instruction or statement or the by-products of an instruction or statement. Coding bugs are the wild cards of programming. Unlike logic or process bugs, which have their own perverse rationality, wild cards are arbitrary.

The most common kind of coding bug, and often considered the least harmful, are documentation bugs (i.e., erroneous comments). Although many documentation bugs are simple spelling errors or the result of poor writing, many are actual errors—that is, misleading or erroneous comments. We can no longer afford to discount such bugs because their consequences are as great as "true" coding errors. Today, programming labor is dominated by maintenance. This will increase as software becomes even longer-lived. Documentation bugs lead to incorrect maintenance actions and therefore cause the insertion of other bugs. Testing techniques have nothing to offer for these bugs. The solution lies in inspections, QA, automated data dictionaries, and specification systems.

3.6. Interface, Integration, and System Bugs

3.6.1.   External Interfaces

The external interfaces are the means used to communicate with the world. These include devices, actuators, sensors, input terminals, printers, and communication lines. Often there is a person on the other side of the interface. That person may be ingenious or ingenuous, but is frequently malevolent. The primary design criterion for an interface with the outside world should be **robustness.** All external interfaces, human or machine, employ a protocol. Protocols are complicated and hard to understand. The protocol itself may be wrong, especially if it's new, or it may be incorrectly implemented. Other external interface bugs include: invalid timing or sequence assumptions related to external signals; misunderstanding external input and output formats; and insufficient tolerance to bad input data. The test design methods of Chapters 6, 9, and 11 are suited to testing external interfaces.

3.6.2.   Internal Interfaces

Internal interfaces are in principle not different from external interfaces, but there are differences in practice because the internal environment is more controlled. The external environment is fixed and the system must adapt to it but the internal environment, which consists of interfaces with other components, can be negotiated. Internal interfaces have the same problems external interfaces have, as well as a few more that are more closely related to implementation details: protocol-design bugs, input and output format bugs, inadequate protection against corrupted data, wrong subroutine call sequence, call-parameter bugs, misunderstood entry or exit parameter values.

To the extent that internal interfaces, protocols, and formats are formalized, the test methods of Chapters 6, 9, and 11 will be helpful. The real remedy is in the design and in standards. Internal interfaces should be standardized and not just allowed to grow. They should be formal, and there should be as few as possible. There's a trade-off between the number of different internal interfaces and the complexity of the interfaces. One universal interface would have so many parameters that it would be inefficient and subject to abuse, misuse, and misunderstanding. Unique interfaces for every pair of communicating routines would be efficient, but N programmers could lead to N^2 interfaces, most of which wouldn't be documented and all of which would have to be tested (but wouldn't be). The main objective of integration testing is to test all internal interfaces (BEIZ84).

3.6.3. Hardware Architecture

It's easy to forget that hardware exists. You can have a programming career and never see a mainframe or minicomputer. When you are working through successive layers of application executive, operating system, compiler, and other intervening software, it's understandable that the hardware architecture appears abstract and remote. It is neither practical nor economical for every programmer in a large project to know all aspects of the hardware architecture. Software bugs related to hardware architecture originate mostly from misunderstanding how the hardware works. Here are examples: paging mechanism ignored or misunderstood, address-generation error, I/O-device operation or instruction error, I/O-device address error, misunderstood device-status code, improper hardware simultaneity assumption, hardware race condition ignored, data format wrong for device, wrong format expected, device protocol error, device instruction-sequence limitation ignored, expecting the device to respond too quickly, waiting too long for a response, ignoring channel throughput limits, assuming that the device is initialized, assuming that the device is not initialized, incorrect interrupt handling, ignoring hardware fault or error conditions, ignoring operator malice.

The remedy for hardware architecture and interface problems is two-fold: (1) good programming and testing and (2) centralization of hardware interface software in programs written by hardware interface specialists. Hardware interface testing is complicated by the fact that modern hardware has very few buttons, switches, and lights. Old computers had lots of them, and you could abuse those buttons and switches to create wonderful anomalous interface conditions that could not be simulated any other way. Today's highly integrated black boxes rarely have such controls and, consequently, considerable ingenuity may be needed to simulate and test hardware interface status conditions. Modern hardware is better and cheaper without the buttons and lights, but also harder to test. This paradox can be resolved by hardware that has special test modes and test instructions that do what the buttons and switches used to do. The hardware manufacturers, as a group, have yet to provide adequate features of this kind. Often the only alternative is to use an elaborate hardware simulator instead of the real hardware. Then you're faced with the problem of distinguishing between real bugs and hardware simulator implementation bugs.

3.6.4. Operating System

Program bugs related to the operating system are a combination of hardware architecture and interface bugs, mostly caused by a misunderstanding of what it is the operating system does. And, of course, the operating system could have bugs of its own. Operating systems can lull the programmer into believing that all hardware interface issues are handled by it. Furthermore, as the operating system matures, bugs in it are found and corrected, but some of these corrections may leave quirks. Sometimes the bug is not fixed at all, but a notice of the problem is buried somewhere in the documentation—if only you knew where to look for it.

The remedy for operating system interface bugs is the same as for hardware bugs: use operating system interface specialists, and use explicit interface modules or macros for all operating system calls. This approach may not eliminate the bugs, but at least it will localize them and make testing easier.

3.6.5.   Software Architecture

Software architecture bugs are often the kind that are called "interactive." Routines can pass unit and integration testing without revealing such bugs. Many of them depend on load, and their symptoms emerge only when the system is stressed. They tend to be the most difficult kind of bug to find and exhume. Here is a sample of the causes of such bugs: assumption that there will be no interrupts, failure to block or unblock interrupts, assumption that code is reentrant or not reentrant, bypassing data interlocks, failure to close or open an interlock, assumption that a called routine is resident or not resident, assumption that a calling program is resident or not resident, assumption that registers or memory were initialized or not initialized, assumption that register or memory location content did not change, local setting of global parameters, and global setting of local parameters.

The first line of defense against these bugs is the design. The first bastion of that defense is that there *be* a design for the software architecture. Not designing a software architecture is an unfortunate but common disease. The most elegant test techniques will be helpless in a complicated system whose architecture "just growed" without plan or structure. All test techniques are applicable to the discovery of software architecture bugs, but experience has shown that careful integration of modules and subjecting the final system to a brutal stress test are especially effective (BEIZ84).*

3.6.6. Control and Sequence Bugs

System-level control and sequence bugs include: ignored timing; assuming that events occur in a specified sequence; starting a process before its prerequisites are met (e.g., working on data before all the data have arrived from disc); waiting for an impossible combination of prerequisites; not recognizing when prerequisites have been met; specifying wrong priority, program state, or processing level; missing, wrong, redundant, or superfluous process steps.

The remedy for these bugs is in the design. Highly structured sequence control is helpful. Specialized, internal, sequence-control mechanisms, such as an internal job control language, are useful. Sequence steps and prerequisites stored in tables and processed interpretively by a sequence-control processor or dispatcher make process sequences easier to test and to modify if bugs are discovered. **Path testing** as applied to **transaction flowgraphs,** as discussed in Chapter 4, is especially effective at detecting system-level control and sequence bugs.

---

* Until the stress test wears out, that is.

3.6.7. Resource Management Problems

Memory is subdivided into dynamically allocated resources such as buffer blocks, queue blocks, task control blocks, and overlay buffers. Similarly, external mass storage units such as discs, are subdivided into memory-resource pools. Here are some resource usage and management bugs: required resource not obtained (rare); wrong resource used (common, if there are several resources with the same structure or different kinds of resources in the same pool); resource already in use; race condition in getting a resource; resource not returned to the right pool; fractionated resources not properly recombined (some resource managers take big resources and subdivide them into smaller resources, and Humpty Dumpty isn't always put together again); failure to return a resource (common); **resource deadlock** (a type A resource is needed to get a type B, a type B is needed to get a type C, and a type C is needed to get a type A); resource use forbidden to the caller; used resource not returned; resource linked to the wrong kind of queue; forgetting to return a resource.

A design remedy that prevents bugs is always preferable to a test method that discovers them. The design remedy in resource management is to keep the resource structure simple: the fewest different kinds of resources, the fewest pools, and no private resource management.

Complicated resource structures are often designed in a misguided attempt to save memory and not because they're essential. The software has to handle, say, large-, small-, and medium-length transactions, and it is reasoned that memory will be saved if three different-sized resources are implemented. This reasoning is often faulty because:

1. Memory is cheap and getting cheaper.
2. Complicated resource structures and multiple pools need management software; that software needs memory, and the increase in program space could be bigger than the expected data space saved.
3. The complicated scheme takes additional processing time, and therefore all resources are held in use a little longer. The size of the pools will have to be increased to compensate for this additional holding time.
4. The basis for sizing the resource is often wrong. A typical choice is to make the buffer block's length equal to the length required by an average transaction—usually a poor choice. A correct analysis (see BEIZ78, pp. 301–302) shows that the optimum resource size is usually proportional to the square root of the transaction's length. However, square-root laws are relatively insensitive to parameter changes and consequently the waste of using many short blocks for

long transactions or large blocks to store short transactions isn't as bad as naive intuition suggests.

The second design remedy is to centralize the management of all pools, either through centralized resource managers, common resource-management subroutines, resource-management macros, or a combination of these.

I mentioned resource loss three times—it was not a writing bug. Resource loss is the most frequent resource-related bug. Common sense tells you why programmers lose resources. You need the resource to process—so it's unlikely that you'll forget to get it; but when the job is done, the successful conclusion of the task will not be affected if the resource is not returned. A good routine attempts to get resources as soon as possible at a common point and also attempts to return them at a common point; but strange paths may require more resources, and you could forget that you're using several resource units instead of one. Furthermore, an exception-condition handler that responds to system-threatening illogical conditions may bypass the normal exit and jump directly to an executive level—and there goes the resource. The design remedies are to centralize resource fetch-and-return within each routine and to provide macros that return all resources rather than just one. Resource-loss problems are exhumed by path testing (Chapter 3), by transaction-flow testing (Chapter 4), data-flow testing (Chapter 5), and by stress testing (BEIZ84).

3.6.8. Integration Bugs

Integration bugs are bugs having to do with the integration of, and with the interfaces between, presumably working and tested components. Most of these bugs result from inconsistencies or incompatibilities between components. All methods used to transfer data directly or indirectly between components and all methods by which components share data can host integration bugs and are therefore proper targets for integration testing. The communication methods include data structures, call sequences, registers, semaphores, communication links, protocols, and so on. Integration strategies and special testing considerations are discussed in more detail in BEIZ84. While integration bugs do not constitute a big bug category (9%) they are an expensive category because they are usually caught late in the game and because they force changes in several components and/or data structures, often during the height of system debugging. Test methods aimed at interfaces, especially domain testing (Chapter 6), syntax testing (Chapter 9), and data-flow testing when applied across components (Chapter 5), are effective contributors to the discovery and elimination of integration bugs.

3.6.9. System Bugs

System bugs is a catch-all phrase covering all kinds of bugs that cannot be ascribed to components or to their simple interactions, but result from the totality of interactions between many components such as programs, data, hardware, and the operating system. System testing as a discipline is discussed in BEIZ84. The only test technique that applies obviously and directly to system testing is transaction-flow testing (Chapter 4); but the reader should keep in mind two important facts: (1) all test techniques can be useful at all levels, from unit to system, and (2) there can be no meaningful system testing until there has been thorough component and integration testing. System bugs are infrequent (1.7%) but very important (expensive) because they are often found only after the system has been fielded and because the fix is rarely simple.

3.7. Test and Test Design Bugs

3.7.1. Testing

Testers have no immunity to bugs (see the footnote on page 20). Tests, especially system tests, require complicated scenarios and databases. They require code or the equivalent to execute, and consequently they can have bugs. The virtue of independent functional testing is that it provides an unbiased point of view; but that lack of bias is an opportunity for different, and possibly incorrect, interpretations of the specification. Although test bugs are not software bugs, it's hard to tell them apart, and much labor can be spent making the distinction. Also, consider the maintenance programmer—does it matter whether she's worked 3 days to chase and fix a real bug or wasted 3 days chasing a chimerical bug that was really a faulty test specification?

3.7.2. Test Criteria

The specification is correct, it is correctly interpreted and implemented, and a seemingly proper test has been designed; but the criterion by which the software's behavior is judged is incorrect or impossible. How would you, for example, "prove that the entire system is free of bugs?" If a criterion is quantitative, such as a throughput or processing delay, the act of measuring the performance can perturb the performance measured. The more complicated the criteria, the likelier they are to have bugs.

3.7.3. Remedies

The remedies for test bugs are: test debugging, test quality assurance, test execution automation, and test design automation.

Test Debugging—The first remedy for test bugs is testing and debugging the tests. The differences between test debugging and program debugging are not fundamental. Test debugging is usually easier because tests, when properly designed, are simpler than programs and do not have to make concessions to efficiency. Also, tests tend to have a localized impact relative to other tests, and therefore the complicated interactions that usually plague software designers are less frequent. We have no magic prescriptions for test debugging—no more than we have for software debugging.

Test Quality Assurance—Programmers have the right to ask how quality in independent testing and test design is monitored. Should we implement test testers and test-tester tests? This sequence does not converge. Methods for test quality assurance are discussed in *Software System Testing and Quality Assurance* (BEIZ84).

Test Execution Automation—The history of software bug removal and prevention is indistinguishable from the history of programming automation aids. Assemblers, loaders, compilers, and the like were all developed to reduce the incidence of programmer and/or operator errors. Test execution bugs are virtually eliminated by various test execution automation tools, many of which are discussed throughout this book. The point is that "manual testing" is self-contradictory. If you want to get rid of test execution bugs, get rid of manual execution.

Test Design Automation—Just as much of software development has been automated (what is a compiler, after all?) much test design can be and has been automated. For a given productivity rate, automation reduces bug count—be it for software or be it for tests.

3.8. Testing and Design Style

This is a book on test design, yet this chapter has said a lot about programming style and design. You might wonder why the productivity of one programming group is as much as 10 times higher than that of another group working on the same application, the same computer, in the same language, and under similar constraints. It should be obvious—bad designs lead to bugs, and bad designs are difficult to test; therefore, the bugs remain. Good designs inhibit bugs before they occur and are easy to test. The two factors are multiplicative, which explains the large productivity differences. The best test techniques are useless when applied to abominable code: it is sometimes easier to redesign a bad routine than to attempt to create tests for it. The labor required to produce new code plus the test design and execution labor for the new code can be much less than the labor required to design thorough tests for an undisciplined, unstructured monstrosity. Good testing works best on good code and good designs. And no test technique can ever convert garbage into gold.

4. SOME BUG STATISTICS

The frequency of bugs taken from many different sources (see the appendix) shows approximately 2.4 bugs per thousand source statements.* But because some of the sample did not include unexecutable statements, the real value is probably lower. These data (usually) describe bugs caught in independent testing, integration testing, and system testing. The number of bugs discovered by the programmer in self-testing at the component level is unknown. The importance of Table 2.1 is not the absolute frequency of bugs (e.g., how many bugs per thousand lines of code) but the relative frequency of the bugs by category. You should examine the sources for these statistics yourself so that you can rearrange the categories to match your own taxonomy. Other references with useful statistics are: AKIY71, BELF79, BOEH75A, BOIE72, DNIE78, ELSH76B, ENDR75, GANN76, GILB77, GOEL78B, HAUG64, HOFF77, ITOH73, LITE76, REIF79A, RUBE75, SCHI78, SCHN75, SCHN79A, SCHW71, SHOO75, and WAGO73.

---

* This is not a contradiction to the 1%–3% rate stated on page 2 in Chapter 1. The 1%–3% rate applies to all bugs, from unit testing out to the field, and typically includes all the bugs discovered by the programmer during self-testing and inspections. The 0.24% rate is dominated by our data source, which included mostly independent testing, integration testing, and system testing—after thorough component testing by the programmers. But even that shouldn't be taken seriously because there's a lot of variation in the source on that score also. What counts in Table 2.1 is the relative frequency of various bug types as a guide to selecting effective testing strategies, and not the absolute bug rate to be used as club on the programmer's head.

SIZE OF SAMPLE—6,877,000 STATEMENTS (COMMENTS INCLUDED)
TOTAL REPORTED BUGS—16,209—BUGS PER 1000 STATEMENTS—2.36

1xxx REQUIREMENTS	1317	8.1%
11xx Requirements Incorrect	649	4.0%
12xx Requirements Logic	153	0.9%
13xx Requirements, Completeness	224	1.4%
15xx Presentation, Documentation	13	0.1%
16xx Requirements Changes	278	1.7%
2xxx FEATURES AND FUNCTIONALITY	2624	16.2%
21xx Feature/Function Correctness	456	2.8%
22xx Feature Completeness	231	1.4%
23xx Functional Case Completeness	193	1.2%
24xx Domain Bugs	778	4.8%
25xx User Messages and Diagnostics	857	5.3%
26xx Exception Condition Mishandled	79	0.5%
29xx Other Functional Bugs	30	0.2%
3xxx STRUCTURAL BUGS	4082	25.2%
31xx Control Flow and Sequencing	2078	12.8%
32xx Processing	2004	12.4%
4xxx DATA	3638	22.4%
41xx Data Definition and Structure	1805	11.1%
42xx Data Access and Handling	1831	11.3%
49xx Other Data Problems	2	0.0%
5xxx IMPLEMENTATION AND CODING	1601	9.9%
51xx Coding and Typographical	322	2.0%
52xx Style and Standards Violations	318	2.0%
53xx Documentation	960	5.9%
59xx Other Implementation	1	0.0%
6xxx INTEGRATION	1455	9.0%
61xx Internal Interfaces	859	5.3%
62xx External Interfaces, Timing, Throughput	518	3.2%
69xx Other Integration	78	0.5%
7xxx SYSTEM, SOFTWARE ARCHITECTURE	282	1.7%
71xx O/S Call and Use	47	0.3%
72xx Software Architecture	139	0.9%
73xx Recovery and Accountability	4	0.0%
74xx Performance	64	0.4%
75xx Incorrect Diagnostics, Exceptions	16	0.1%
76xx Partitions, Overlays	3	0.0%
77xx Sysgen, Environment	9	0.1%
8xxx TEST DEFINITION AND EXECUTION	447	2.8%
81xx Test Design Bugs	11	0.1%
82xx Test Execution Bugs	355	2.2%
83xx Test Documentation	11	0.1%
84xx Test Case Completeness	64	0.4%
89xx Other Testing Bugs	6	0.0%
9xxx OTHER, UNSPECIFIED	763	4.7%

Table 2.1. Sample Bug Statistics.

5. SUMMARY

1. The importance of a bug depends on its frequency, the correction cost, the consequential cost, and the application. Allocate your limited testing resources in proportion to the bug's importance.
2. Use the nightmare list as a guide to how much testing is required.
3. Test techniques are like antibiotics—their effectiveness depends on the target—what works against a virus may not work against bacteria or fungi. The test techniques you use must be matched to the kind of bugs you have.
4. Because programmers learn from their mistakes, the effectiveness of test techniques, just as antibiotics, erodes with time. *TEST SUITES WEAR OUT.*
5. A comprehensive bug taxonomy is a prerequisite to gathering useful bug statistics. Adopt a taxonomy, simple or elaborate, but adopt one and classify all bugs within it.
6. Continually gather bug statistics (in accordance to your taxonomy) to determine the kind of bugs you have and the effectiveness of your current test techniques against them.

3

FLOWGRAPHS AND PATH TESTING

1. SYNOPSIS

Path testing based on the use of the program's control flow as a structural model is the cornerstone of testing. Methods for generating tests from the program's control flow, criteria for selecting paths, and how to determine path-forcing input values are discussed.

2. PATH-TESTING BASICS

2.1. Motivation and Assumptions

2.1.1. What Is It?

Path testing is the name given to a family of test techniques based on judiciously selecting a set of test paths through the program. If the set of paths is properly chosen, then we have achieved some measure of test thoroughness. For example, pick enough paths to assure that every source statement has been executed at least once.

2.1.2. Motivation

Path-testing techniques are the oldest of all structural test techniques. They are recorded as being in use at IBM for more than two decades (HIRS67, SCHI69, WARN64). The commonsense idea of executing every statement and branch at least once under some test comes to almost every person who examines software testing in depth. Path-testing techniques were also the first techniques to come under theoretical scrutiny. There is considerable (anecdotal) evidence that path testing was independently discovered and used many many times in many different places.

Path testing is most applicable to new software for unit testing. It is a structural technique. It requires complete knowledge of the program's structure (i.e., source code). It is most often used by programmers to unit-test their own code. The effectiveness of path testing rapidly deteriorates as the size of the software aggregate under test increases. Path testing is rarely, if ever, used for system testing. For the programmer, it is *the* basic test technique.

I'm often asked by independent testers and system testers why they should bother learning path testing because they're not likely to ever use it directly: the reason to learn path testing is that it's fundamental to all testing techniques. That's also the reason this chapter is the longest in the book. It is almost impossible to discuss any testing strategy without relying on the conceptual vocabulary established in path testing. And when we discuss functional testing techniques such as transaction-flow testing (Chapter 4) or domain testing (Chapter 6), which are very useful to system testers even though we don't deal with paths directly, understanding the strategy depends on understanding that there are paths that can be distinguished from one another.

2.1.3. The Bug Assumption

The bug assumption for the path-testing strategies is that something has gone wrong with the software that makes it take a different path than intended. As an example, "GOTO X" where "GOTO Y" had been intended. As another example, "IF A is *true* THEN DO X ELSE DO Y", instead of "IF A is *false* THEN . . .". We also assume, in path testing, that specifications are correct and achievable, that there are no processing bugs other than those that affect the control flow, and that data are properly defined and accessed. Structured programming languages prevent many of the bugs targeted by path testing: as a consequence, the effectiveness of path testing for these languages is reduced. Conversely, old code, especially in assembly languages, COBOL, FORTRAN, and Basic, has a higher proportion of control-flow bugs than contemporary code, and for such software path testing is indispensable.

2.2. Control Flowgraphs

2.2.1. General

The **control flowgraph** (or **flowgraph** alone when the context is clear) is a graphical representation of a program's control structure. It uses the elements shown in Figure 3.1: **process blocks, decisions,** and **junctions.** The control flowgraph is similar to the earlier **flowchart,** with which it is not to be confused. The differences between control flowgraphs and flowcharts are discussed in Section 2.2.5 below.

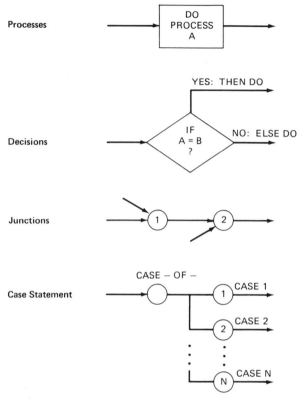

Figure 3.1. Flowgraph Elements.

2.2.2.   Process Block

A **process block*** is a sequence of program statements uninterrupted by either decisions or junctions. Formally, it is a sequence of statements such that if any one statement of the block is executed, then all statements thereof are executed. Less formally, a process block is a piece of straight-line code. A process block can be one source statement or hundreds. The point is that, bugs aside, once a process block is initiated, every statement within it will be executed. Similarly, there is no point within the process block that is the target of a GOTO. The term "process" will be used interchangeably with "process block."

A process has one entry and one exit. It can consist of a single statement or instruction, a sequence of statements or instructions, a single-

---

* Also called "process," "block," "basic block," and "program block."

entry/single-exit subroutine, a macro or function call, or a sequence of these. The program does not (rather, is not intended to) jump into or out of processes. From the point of view of test cases designed from control flowgraphs, the details of the operation within the process are unimportant if those details do not affect the control flow. If the processing does affect the flow of control, the effect will be manifested at a subsequent decision or case statement.

2.2.3. Decisions and Case Statements

A **decision** is a program point at which the control flow can diverge. Machine language conditional branch and conditional skip instructions are examples of decisions. The FORTRAN IF and the Pascal IF-THEN-ELSE constructs are decisions, although they also contain processing components. While most decisions are two-way or **binary,** some (such as the FORTRAN IF) are three-way branches in control flow. The design of test cases is generally easier with two-way branches than with three-way branches, and there are also more powerful test-design tools that can be used. A **case statement** is a multiway branch or decision. Examples of case statements include a jump table in assembly language, the FORTRAN-computed GOTO and assigned GOTO, and the Pascal CASE statement. From the point of view of test design, there are no fundamental differences between decisions and case statements.

2.2.4. Junctions

A **junction** is a point in the program where the control flow can merge. Examples of junctions are: the target of a jump or skip instruction in assembly language, a label that is the target of a GOTO, the END-IF and CONTINUE statements in FORTRAN, and the Pascal statement labels, END and UNTIL.

Unconditional branches such as FORTRAN's GOTO or unconditional jump instructions are not fundamental to programming. Although it can be proven (BOHM66) that unconditional branches are not essential to programming, their use is ubiquitous and often practically unavoidable. Testing and testing theory are easier if there are no GOTOs, but in the real world we must often test dirty old software. The methods discussed in this book apply to any kind of software—assembly languages, FOR-TRAN, COBOL, C, Pascal, Ada, etc. Some of the differences between the old and new languages is that the newer languages are generally nicer from the point of view of control flow and test design. Whatever language you program, if you can apply test techniques to assembly language spaghetti code, you'll have no trouble with the newer, gentler languages.

2.2.5. Control Flowgraphs Versus Flowcharts

A program's **flowchart** resembles a control flowgraph, but differs in one important way. In control flowgraphs, we don't show the details of what is in a process block; indeed, the entire block, no matter how many statements in it, is shown as a single process. In flowcharts, conversely, every part of the process block is drawn: if a process block consists of 100 steps, the flowchart may have 100 boxes. Although some flowcharting conventions permit grouping adjacent processing statements into "higher-level" steps, there are no fixed rules about how this should be done.* The flowchart focuses on process steps, whereas the control flowgraph all but ignores them. The flowchart forces an expansion of visual complexity by adding many off-page connectors, which confuse the control flow, but the flowgraph compacts the representation and makes it easier to follow.

Flowcharts have been falling out of favor for over a decade, and before another decade passes they'll be regarded as curious, archaic relics of a bygone programming era. Indeed, flowcharts are rarely used today; they're created mainly to satisfy obsolete documentation specifications. But before we throw flowcharts forever into the dustbin of programming practices past, we should ask why they had been so popular and why otherwise rational thinkers about the programming process (myself included) should have so fervently promoted their use. I can't speak for others, but I think that the flowchart was a first step toward the control flowgraph: when we used flowcharts for design we were actually using cluttered-up control flowgraphs. The trouble with them is that there's too much information—especially if the flowcharting standard requires one flowchart box per source statement.

So while the exercise of drawing detailed flowcharts may not be an effective step in the design process, the act of drawing a control flowgraph (and also data flowgraph—Chapter 5) is a useful tool that can help us clarify the control flow and data flow issues. Accordingly, because we are all good programmers, I'll assume that there is a design control–flowgraph

---

* Flowcharts as usually drawn do combine program steps so that there may be only a few boxes for many statements but the rules by which program steps are combined into flowchart boxes are arbitrary and peculiar to the flowcharting convention used. This makes it difficult, if not impossible, to create theoretical constructs for flowcharts. Control flowgraphs, conversely, use mathematically precise formation rules.

that has been created and checked prior to coding. There may also be specification control–flowgraphs prior to design.

2.2.6. *Notational Evolution*

The control flowgraph is a simplified (i.e., more abstract) representation of the program's structure. To understand its creation and use, we'll go through an example, starting with Figure 3.2—a little horror written in a FORTRAN-like **program design language** (PDL). The first step in translating this to a control flowgraph is shown in Figure 3.3, where we have the typical one-for-one classical flowchart. Note that complexity has increased, clarity has decreased, and that we had to add auxiliary labels (LOOP, XX, and YY), which have no actual program counterpart. In Figure 3.4 we merged the process steps and replaced them with the single process box. We now have a control flowgraph. But this representation is still too busy. We simplify the notation further to achieve Figure 3.5, where for the first time we can really see what the control flow looks like. To do that we had to make several more notational changes.

1. The process boxes weren't really needed. There is an implied process on every line joining junctions and decisions, especially if we allow do-nothing or dummy processes.
2. We don't need to know (at this time) the specifics of the decisions, just the fact that there is a branch—so we can do away with things such as "U > V?", "yes", "no", and so on.

CODE* (PDL)

```
        INPUT X, Y                    V(U−1):=V(U+1) + U(V−1)
        Z := X + Y               ELL:V(U+U(V)) := U + V
        V := X − Y                    IF U = V GOTO JOE
        IF Z >=Ø GOTO SAM             IF U > V THEN U := Z
  JOE:  Z := Z − 1                    Z := U
  SAM:  Z := Z + V                    END
        FOR U = Ø TO Z
        V(U),U(V) := (Z + V)*U
        IF V(U)= Ø GOTO JOE
        Z := Z − 1
        IF Z = Ø GOTO ELL
        U := U + 1
        NEXT U
```

* A contrived horror

Figure 3.2. Program Example (PDL).

3. The specific target label names aren't important—just the fact that they exist. So we can replace them by simple numbers.

Figure 3-5 is the way we usually represent the program's control flow-graph. There are two kinds of components: circles and arrows that join circles. A circle with more than one arrow leaving it is a **decision;** a circle with more than one arrow entering is a **junction.** We call the circles **nodes** and the arrows **links.** Note also that the entry and exit are also denoted by circles and are thereby also considered to be nodes. Nodes are usually numbered or labeled by using the original program labels. The link name can be formed from the names of the nodes it spans. Thus a link from

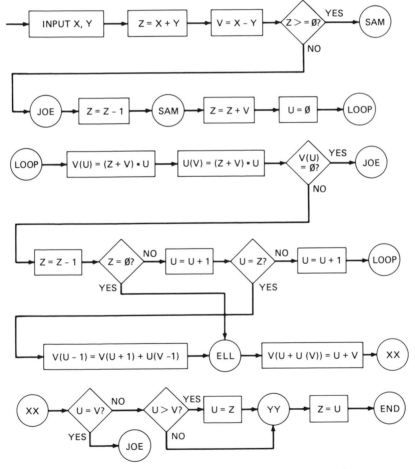

Figure 3.3. One-to-one Flowchart for Figure 3.2 Example.

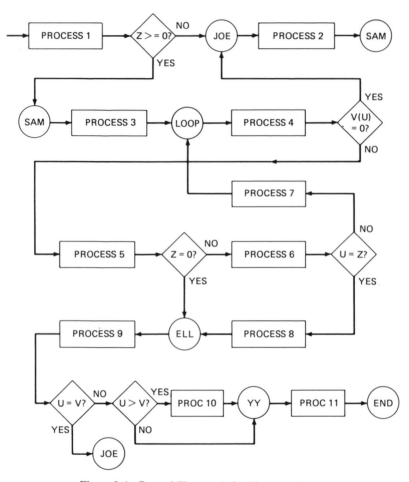

Figure 3.4. Control Flowgraph for Figure 3.2 Example.

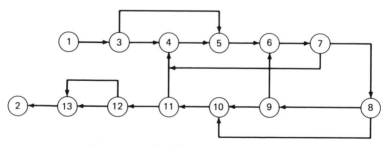

Figure 3.5. Simplified Flowgraph Notation.

node 7 to node 4 is called link (7,4), whereas one from node 4 to node 7 is called link (4,7). For parallel links between a pair of nodes, (nodes 12 and 13 in Figure 3.5) we can use subscripts to denote each one or some unambiguous notation such as ''(12,13 upper)'' and ''(12,13 lower)''. An alternate way to name links that avoids this problem is to use a unique lowercase letter for each link in the flowgraph.

The final transformation is shown in Figure 3.6, where we've dropped the node numbers to achieve an even simpler representation. The way to work with control flowgraphs is to use the simplest possible representation—that is, no more information than you need to correlate back to the source program or PDL.

Although graphical representations are revealing, they are often inconvenient—especially if we have to work with them. The alternative is to use a **linked-list** representation, shown in Figure 3.7. Each node has a name and there is an entry on the list for each link in the flowgraph. Only the information pertinent to the control flow is shown—that is, the labels and the decisions. The linked list is the representation of choice for programs that manipulate or create flowgraphs.

2.2.7. Flowgraph-Program Correspondence

A flowgraph is a pictorial representation of a program and not the program itself, just as a topographic map, no matter how detailed, is not the terrain it represents. This distinction is important: failure to make it can lead to bugs. You can't always associate the parts of a program in a unique way with flowgraph parts because many program structures, such as IF-THEN-ELSE constructs, consist of a combination of decisions, junctions, and processes. Furthermore, the translation from a flowgraph element to a statement and vice versa is not always unique. Myers (MYER77) cites an anomaly based on different representations of the

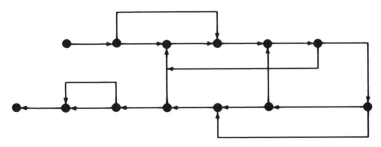

Figure 3.6. Even Simpler Flowgraph Notation.

```
 1 (BEGIN)    : 3
 2 (END)      :                    Exit, no outlink
 3 (Z>∅?)     : 4 (FALSE)
              : 5 (TRUE)
 4 (JOE)      : 5
 5 (SAM)      : 6
 6 (LOOP)     : 7
 7 (V(U)=∅?)  : 4 (TRUE)
              : 8 (FALSE)
 8 (Z=∅?)     : 9 (FALSE)
              :10 (TRUE)
 9 (U=Z?)     : 6 (FALSE) = LOOP
              :10 (TRUE) = ELL
10 (ELL)      :11
11 (U=V?)     : 4 (TRUE) = JOE
              :12 (FALSE)
12 (U>V?)     :13 (TRUE)
              :13 (FALSE)
13            : 2 (END)
```

Figure 3.7. Linked-List Control-Flowgraph Notation.

FORTRAN statement "IF (A=0) .AND. (B=1) THEN . . .". It has the alternate representations shown in Figure 3.8.

A FORTRAN DO has three parts: a decision, an end-point junction, and a process that iterates the DO variable. The FORTRAN IF-THEN-ELSE has a decision, a junction, and three processes (including the processing associated with the decision itself). Therefore, neither of these statements can be translated into a single flowgraph element. Some computers have looping, iterating, and EXECUTE instructions or other instruction options and modes that prevent the direct correspondence between instructions and flowgraph elements. Such differences are so familiar to us that we often code without conscious awareness of their existence. It is, however, important that the distinction between a program and its flowgraph representation be kept in mind during test design. An improper translation from flowgraph to code during coding can lead to bugs, and an improper translation (in either direction) during test design can lead to missing test cases and consequently, to undiscovered bugs. When faced with a possibly ambiguous translation from code to flowgraph or from flowgraph to code, as in the above example, it is better to pick the more complicated representation rather than the simpler one. At worst, you will design a few extra test cases.

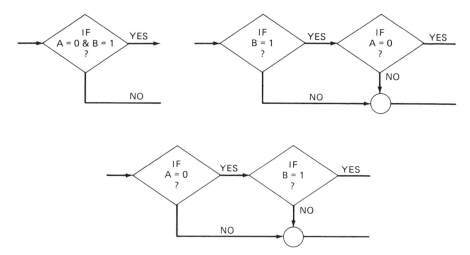

Figure 3.8. Alternative Flowgraphs for the Same Logic.

2.2.8. Flowgraph and Flowchart Generation

The control flowgraph is a simplified version of the earlier flowchart. Although there are many commercially available flowcharting packages, there are relatively few control flowgraph generators as of the time of writing. This situation is especially irksome because the information needed to generate the control flowgraph is a by-product of most compilers. Therefore, we will have to discuss the earlier flowchart generators and hope that, sooner or later, you'll be able to substitute "control flowgraph" for "flowchart" throughout the sequel.

Flowcharts can be (1) hand-drawn by the programmer, (2) automatically produced by a flowcharting program based on a mechanical analysis of the source code, or (3) semiautomatically produced by a flowcharting program based in part on structural analysis of the source code and in part on directions given by the programmer. The semiautomatic flowchart is most common with assembly language source code. A flowcharting package that provides controls over how statements are mapped into process boxes can be used to produce a flowchart that is reasonably close to the control flowgraph. You do this by starting process boxes just after any decision or GOTO target and ending them just before branches or GOTOs.

The designer's original flowchart and the automatically produced flowchart would be identical in a perfect world, but often they are not. The programmer's design control–flowgraph or flowchart is a statement of intentions and not a program. Those intentions become corrupted through the action of malevolent forces such as keyboards, compilers, and other programmers. A typographical error in a case statement can cause a different path to be implemented or can make a path unachievable. In assembly language, the possibility of manipulating addresses, registers, page boundaries, or even instructions (inadvertently, it is to be hoped) makes the potential differences between the specification control–flowgraph and the actual control flow wilder yet. If you have automatically produced flowcharts, then it is effective to check the correspondence between the specification control–flowgraph and the flowchart produced from code. Better yet, have someone else, someone who has not seen the specification flowgraph, translate the code back into a flowgraph, or compare the automatically produced flowchart with the specification flowgraph. Do it as part of an inspection or review. Many bugs can be caught this way. It may seem like a lot of extra work, but consider which you would rather do:

1. A calm, manual retranslation of the code back into a flowgraph with an unbiased comparison, or
2. A frenzied plea to a colleague in the heat of the test floor late at night: "Look this over for me, will you? I just can't find the bug."

2.3. Path Testing

2.3.1. Paths, Nodes, and Links

A **path** through a program is a sequence of instructions or statements that starts at an entry, junction, or decision and ends at another, or possibly the same, junction, decision, or exit. A path may go through several junctions, processes, or decisions, one or more times. Paths consist of **segments.** The smallest segment is a link—that is, a single process that lies between two nodes (e.g., junction-process-junction, junction-process-decision, decision-process-junction, decision-process-decision). A direct connection between two nodes, as in an unconditional GOTO, is also called a "process" by convention, even though no actual processing takes place. A **path segment** is a succession of consecutive links that belongs to some path. The **length** of a path is measured by the number of links in it and not by the number of instructions or statements executed along the path. An alternative way to measure the length of a path is by the number of nodes traversed—this method has some analytical and theoretical benefits. If programs (by convention) are assumed to have an entry and an exit node, then the number of links traversed is just one less than the number of nodes traversed. Because links are named by the pair of nodes they join, the **name of a path** is the name of the nodes along the path. For example, the shortest path from entry to exit in Figure 3.5 is called "(1,3,5,6,7,8,10,11,12,13,2)". Alternatively, if we choose to label the links, the name of the path is the succession of link names along the path. A path has a **loop** in it if any node (link) name is repeated. For example, path (1,3,4,5,6,7,4,5,6,7,8,9,10,11,12,13,2) in Figure 3.5 loops about nodes 4,5,6, and 7.

The word "path" is also used in the more restricted sense of a path that starts at the routine's entrance and ends at its exit. In practice, test paths are usually entry-to-exit paths. Where we have to make a distinction between arbitrary paths and entry-to-exit paths, we'll use the term "entry/exit path" as needed. The terms **entry/exit path** and **complete path** are also used in the literature to denote a path that starts at an entry and goes to an exit. Our interest in entry/exit paths in testing is pragmatic because: (1) it's difficult to set up and execute paths that start at an arbitrary statement; (2) it's hard to stop at an arbitrary statement without setting traps or using patches and (3) entry/exit paths are what we want to test because we use routines that way.

2.3.2.   Multi-Entry/Multi-Exit Routines

Throughout this book I implicitly assume that all routines and programs have a single entry and a single exit. Although there are circumstances in which it is proper to jump out of a routine and bypass the normal control structure and exit method, I cannot conceive of any rational reason why one would want to jump into the middle of a routine or program.* You might want to jump out of a routine when an illogical condition has been detected for which it is clear that any further processing along that path could damage the system's operation or data. Under such circumstances, the normal return path must be bypassed. In such cases, though, there is only one place to go—to the system's recovery-processing software. Jumping into a routine is almost always done in a misguided attempt to save some code or coding labor (to be paid for by a manifold increase in test design and debugging labor). If the routine performs several variations on the same processing and it is effective to bypass part of the processing, the correct way to design the routine is to provide an entry parameter that within the routine (say, by a case statement), directs the

---

* Not to be confused with instances in which a collection of independent routines are accessed by a common name. For example, the set of routines is called "SET" and it is loaded as a set in order to have efficient overlays; but within "SET" there are independent, single-entry subroutines. It might superficially seem that "SET" is a multi-entry/multi-exit routine.

control flow to the proper point. Similarly, if a routine can have several different kinds of outcomes, then an exit parameter should be used. Another alternative is to encapsulate the common parts into subroutines. Instead of using direct linkages between multiple exits and entrances, we handle the control flow by examining the values of the exit parameter that can serve as an entry parameter for the next routine or a return parameter for the calling routine. Note that the parameter does not have to be passed explicitly between the routines—it can be a value in a register or in a common memory location.

The trouble with multi-entry and multi-exit routines is that it can be very difficult to determine what the interprocess control flow is, and consequently it is easy to miss important test cases. Furthermore, the use of multi-entry and multi-exit routines increases the number of entries and exits and therefore the number of interfaces. This practice leads to more test cases than would otherwise be needed. Multi-entry/multi-exit routine testing is discussed in further detail in Section 2.5 below.

2.3.3. Fundamental Path Selection Criteria

There are many paths between the entry and exit of a typical routine. Every decision doubles the number of potential paths, and every loop multiplies the number of potential paths by the number of different iteration values possible for the loop. If a routine has one loop, each pass through that loop (once, twice, three times, and so on) constitutes a different path through the routine, even though the same code is traversed each time. Even small routines can have an incredible number of potential paths (see Chapter 8 for path-counting methods). A lavish test approach might consist of testing all paths, but that would not be a complete test, because a bug could create unwanted paths or make mandatory paths unexecutable. And just because all paths are right doesn't mean that the routine is doing the required processing along those paths. Such possibilities aside for the moment, how might we define "complete testing"?

1. Exercise every path from entry to exit.
2. Exercise every statement or instruction at least once.
3. Exercise every branch and case statement, in each direction, at least once.

If prescription 1 is followed, then prescriptions 2 and 3 are automatically followed; but prescription 1 is impractical for most routines. It can be done only for routines that have no loops, in which case it includes all the cases included in prescriptions 2 and 3. Prescriptions 2 and 3 might appear to be equivalent, but they are not. Here is a correct version of a routine:

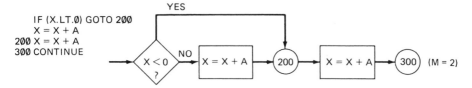

For X negative, the output is X + A, while for X greater than or equal to zero, the output is X + 2A. Following prescription 2 and executing every statement, but not every branch, would not reveal the bug in the following incorrect version:

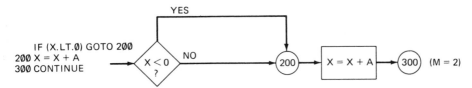

A negative value produces the correct answer. Every statement can be executed, but if the test cases do not force each branch to be taken, the bug can remain hidden. The next example uses a test based on executing each branch but does not force the execution of all statements:

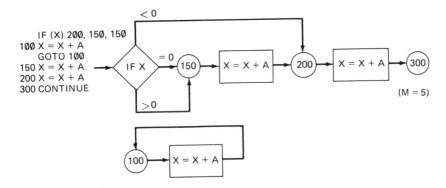

The hidden loop around label 100 is not revealed by tests based on prescription 3 alone because no test forces the execution of statement 100 and the following GOTO statement. Furthermore, label 100 is not flagged by the compiler as an unreferenced label and the subsequent GOTO does not refer to an undefined label.

A **static analysis** (that is, an analysis based on examining the source code or structure) cannot determine whether a piece of code is or is not reachable. There could be subroutine calls with parameters that are subroutine labels, or in the above example there could be a GOTO that targeted label 100 but could never achieve a value that would send the program to that label. Only a **dynamic analysis** (that is, an analysis based on the code's behavior while running—which is to say, to all intents and purposes, testing) can determine whether code is reachable or not and therefore distinguish between the ideal structure we think we have and the actual, buggy structure.

2.3.4.   Path-Testing Criteria

Although real bugs are rarely as blatant as the above examples, the examples demonstrate that prescriptions 2 and 3 alone are insufficient: but note that for software written in a structured programming language, satisfying prescription 3 *does* imply that prescription 2 is also satisfied.

Any testing strategy based on paths must at least both exercise every instruction and take branches in all directions. A set of tests that does this is not complete in an absolute sense, but it is complete in the sense that anything less must leave something untested. We have, therefore, explored three different **testing criteria** or **strategies** out of a potentially infinite family of strategies. They are:

1. *Path Testing (P_∞)*—Execute all possible control flow paths through the program: typically, this is restricted to all possible entry/exit paths through the program. If we achieve this prescription, we are said to have achieved **100% path coverage.*** This is the strongest criterion in the path-testing strategy family: it is generally impossible to achieve.

2. *Statement Testing (P_1)*—Execute all statements in the program at least once under some test. If we do enough tests to achieve this, we are said to have achieved **100% statement coverage.*** An alternate, equivalent characterization is to say that we have achieved **100%**

---

* We usually drop the ''100%,'' so when we say that we have ''achieved branch coverage'' it means we have achieved 100% branch coverage. Similarly for statement coverage, path coverage, and other notions of coverage that will be introduced in the sequel. The use of the word ''coverage'' in the literature is bound to be confusing to the newcomer. The term ''complete coverage'' or ''coverage'' alone is often used in the literature to mean 100% statement and branch coverage (i.e., C1 + C2). Because C2 usually implies C1, the term ''branch coverage'' usually means ''branch and statement coverage.'' The term ''coverage'' alone is also used to mean coverage with respect to the specific criterion being discussed, (e.g., predicate coverage), and also for C1 + C2. I will endeavor to make the specific coverage notion intended clear.

node coverage (of the nodes in the program's control flowgraph). We denote this by C1. This is the weakest criterion in the family: testing less than this for new software is unconscionable and should be criminalized.

3. *Branch Testing (P₂)*—Execute enough tests to assure that every branch alternative has been exercised at least once under some test. If we do enough tests to achieve this prescription, then we have achieved **100% branch coverage** (see page 74 footnote). An alternative characterization is to say that we have achieved **100% link coverage** (of the links in the control flowgraph of the program). For structured software, branch testing and therefore branch coverage strictly includes statement coverage. We denote branch coverage by C2.

What about strategies that are stronger than branch testing but weaker than path testing? The notation P_1, P_2, . . . P_∞ should alert you to the fact that there is an infinite number of such strategies, but even that's insufficient to exhaust testing.

2.3.5.   Common Sense and Strategies

Branch and statement coverage are accepted today as the minimum mandatory testing requirement. Statement coverage is established as a minimum testing requirement in the IEEE unit test standard (ANSI87B). Statement and branch coverage have also been used for more than two decades as minimum mandatory unit test requirements for new code at IBM (HIRS67, SCHI69, WARN64) and other major computer and software companies. The justification for insisting on statement and branch coverage isn't based on theory but on common sense. One can argue that 100% statement coverage (C1) is a lot of work, to which I reply that debugging is a lot more work. Why not use a judicious sampling of paths?** What's wrong with leaving some code, especially code that has a low probability of execution, untested? Common sense and experience show why such proposals are ineffectual:

1. Not testing a piece of code leaves a residue of bugs in the program in proportion to the size of the untested code and the probability of bugs.

** One reason that programmers and programming managers (especially) who are unfamiliar with testing may object to statement and branch coverage is that they confuse it with executing all possible paths. I recall several instances in which hours of argument ended when the recalcitrant programmer was finally made to realize that testing all paths was not at all the same as branch and statement coverage—whereupon she said, "Oh! Is *that* all you wanted?"

2. The high-probability paths are always thoroughly tested if only to demonstrate that the system works properly. If you have to leave some code untested at the unit level, it is more rational to leave the normal, high-probability paths untested, because someone else is sure to exercise them during integration testing or system testing.
3. Logic errors and fuzzy thinking are inversely proportional to the probability of the path's execution.
4. The subjective probability of executing a path as seen by the routine's designer and its objective execution probability are far apart. Only analysis can reveal the probability of a path, and most programmers' intuition with regard to path probabilities is miserable (see BEIZ78).
5. The subjective evaluation of the importance of a code segment as judged by its programmer is biased by aesthetic sense, ego, and familiarity. Elegant code might be heavily tested to demonstrate its elegance or to defend the concept, whereas straightforward code might be given cursory testing because "How could anything go wrong with that?"

Unit testing of new code based on less than C1 forces us to decide what code should be left untested. Ask yourself, "What immunity from bugs has been granted to the untested code?" If such code has no special immunity from bugs, then what criterion will you use to decide which code shall and which shall not be tested? Such criteria are inevitably biased, rarely rational, and always grievous. Realistically, the practice of putting untested code into systems is common, and so are system failures. The excuse I've most often heard for putting in untested code is that there wasn't enough time or money left to do the testing. If there wasn't enough time and money to test the routine, then there wasn't enough time and money to create it in the first place. What you think is code, before it has been properly tested, is not code, but the mere promise of code—not a program, but a perverse parody of a program. If you put such junk into a system, its bugs will show, and because there hasn't been a rigorous unit test, you'll have a difficult time finding the bugs. As Hannah Cowley said, "Vanity, like murder, will out." For it's vanity to think that untested code has no bugs, and murder to put such code in. It is better to leave out untested code altogether than to put it in. Code that doesn't exist can't corrupt good code. A function that hasn't been implemented is known not to work. An untested function may or may not work itself (probably not), but it can make other things fail that would otherwise work. In case I haven't made myself clear, leaving untested code in a system is stupid, shortsighted, and irresponsible.

How about branch coverage (C2)? Why does common sense lead us to this requirement? Control flow is at the heart of programming. Typical software has a high density of conditional branches, loops, and other control-flow statements—approximately 25% in most languages. If we stop at C1, then one of the alternatives in the IF-THEN-ELSE statements might never be tested. It's obviously worse with case statements and loops. Let's apply common sense to our testing. We should expect that if we apply a testing criterion to source code, say C1, then applying our test cases to the object code produced should achieve comparable coverage. For example, if we achieved C1 for Pascal source, then is it not reasonable to expect that we achieved C1 for the object code into which that source was translated? Statement coverage (C1) does not guarantee this result, nor does it even come close. A good piece of logic-intensive modern code might actually be only 75% or less C1 covered at the object level when C1 is the criterion used for source. One can easily design a routine in an HOL such that its machine language translation is at best covered at 50%, or for that matter, at an arbitrarily low percentage under C1. Therefore, the commonsense argument we used for statement coverage also forces us into branch coverage. That is, if we are to achieve object level C1, then we need at least source level C2 for most source languages.

Commonsense considerations will force us to even more thorough notions of testing, because for example, even C2 applied to source does not guarantee C1 for object. Every testing technique leads us to define more justifiable tests and leads us to a further recognition of just how weak statement and branch coverage are as criteria for "complete testing." Have we tested all reasonable data-usage patterns? Have we checked all the interesting extreme input combinations? Have we tested all interesting loop conditions? Have all features been verified? The more we learn about testing, the more we realize that statement and branch coverage are minimum *floors* below which we dare not fall, rather than ceilings to which we should aspire.

2.3.6.   Which Paths

You must pick enough paths to achieve C1 + C2. The question of what is the fewest number of such paths is interesting to the designer of test tools that help automate path testing, but it is not crucial to the pragmatic design of tests. It's better to take many simple paths than a few complicated paths. Furthermore, there's no harm in taking paths that will exercise the same code more than once. As an example of how to go about selecting paths, consider the unstructured monstrosity of Figure 3.9.

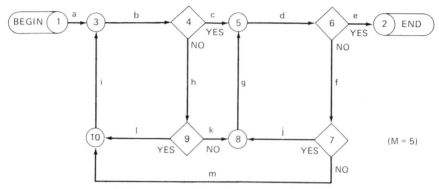

Figure 3.9. An Example of Path Selection.

Start at the beginning and take the most obvious path to the exit—it typically corresponds to the normal path. The most obvious path in Figure 3.9 is (1,3,4,5,6,2), if we name it by nodes, or *abcde* if we name it by links. Then take the next most obvious path, *abhkgde*. All other paths in this example lead to loops. Take a simple loop first—building, if possible, on a previous path, such as *abhlibcde*. Then take another loop, *abcdfjgde*. And finally, *abcdfmibcde*. Here are some practical suggestions:

1. Draw the control flowgraph on a single sheet of paper.
2. Make several copies—as many as you'll need for coverage (C1 + C2) and several more.
3. Use a yellow highlighting marker to trace paths. Copy the paths onto a master sheet.
4. Continue tracing paths until all lines on the master sheet are covered, indicating that you appear to have achieved C1 + C2.

I say "appear" because some of the paths you've selected might not be achievable. This is discussed in Section 3 below.

As you trace the paths, create a table that shows the paths, the coverage status of each process, and each decision. The above paths lead to the following table:

PATHS	DECISIONS				PROCESS–LINK												
	4	6	7	9	a	b	c	d	e	f	g	h	i	j	k	l	m
abcde	YES	YES			√	√	√	√	√								
abhkgde	NO	YES		NO	√	√			√	√	√	√			√		
abhlibcde	NO, YES	YES		YES	√	√	√	√	√			√	√			√	
abcdfjgde	YES	NO, YES	YES		√	√	√	√	√	√	√			√			
abcdfmibcde	YES	NO, YES	NO		√	√	√	√	√	√			√				√

After you have traced a covering path set on the master sheet and filled in the table for every path, check the following:

1. Does every decision have a YES and a NO in its column? (C2)
2. Has every case of all case statements been marked? (C2)
3. Is every three-way branch (less, equal, greater) covered? (C2)
4. Is every link (process) covered at least once? (C1)*

Select successive paths as small variations of previous paths. Try to change only one thing at a time—only one decision's outcome if possible. It's better to have several paths, each differing by only one thing, than one path that covers more but along which several things change.** The *abcd* segment in the above example is common to many paths. If this common segment has been debugged, and a bug appears in a new path that uses this segment, it's more likely that the bug is in the new part of the path (say *fjgde*) rather than in the part that's already been debugged. Using small changes from one test to the next may seem like more work; however,

1. Small changes from path to path mean small, easily documented, and gradual changes in the test setup. Setting up long, complicated paths that share nothing with other test cases is also a lot of extra work.
2. Testing is experimenting. Good experiments rely on changing only one thing at a time. The more you change from test to test, the likelier you are to get confused.
3. The costs of extra paths are a few more microseconds of computer time, the time to run another case, and the cost of additional documentation. Many more and different kinds of tests are required beyond path testing. A few extra paths represent only a small increment in the total test labor.

You could select paths with the idea of achieving coverage without knowing anything about what the routine is supposed to do. Path selection based on pure structure without regard to function has the advantage of being free of bias. Conversely, such paths are likely to be confusing, counterintuitive, and hard to understand. I favor paths that have some

---

* *Note:* For structured languages and well-formed programs this check is redundant.
** Not only does this strategy make sense, but it has been formally explored (PRAT87) to create the path prefix strategy, which is stronger than branch testing, but nevertheless efficient from the point of view of the number of test cases needed. It appears to be a satisfactory basis for building structural test generation tools.

sensible functional meaning.* With this in mind, the path selection rules can be revised as follows:

1. Pick the simplest, functionally sensible entry/exit path.
2. Pick additional paths as small variations from previous paths. Pick paths that do not have loops rather than paths that do. Favor short paths over long paths, simple paths over complicated paths, and paths that make sense over paths that don't.
3. Pick additional paths that have no obvious functional meaning only if it's necessary to provide coverage. But ask yourself first why such paths exist at all. Why wasn't coverage achieved with functionally sensible paths?
4. Be comfortable with your chosen paths. Play your hunches and give your intuition free reign as long as you achieve C1 + C2.
5. Don't follow rules slavishly—except for coverage.

2.4. Loops

2.4.1. The Kinds of Loops

I had a physics professor who said that there were only two kinds of mensuration systems: the metric and the barbaric. I say that there are only three kinds of loops: **nested, concatenated,** and **horrible.** Figure 3.10 shows examples of each kind.

2.4.2. Cases for a Single Loop

A single loop can be covered with two cases: looping and not looping. But experience shows that many loop-related bugs are not discovered by C1 + C2. Bugs lurk in corners and congregate at boundaries—in the case of loops, at or around the minimum and maximum number of times the loop can be iterated. The minimum number of iterations is often zero, but it need not be.

Case 1—Single Loop, Zero Minimum, N Maximum,
No Excluded Values

1. Try bypassing the loop (zero iterations). If you can't, you either have a bug, or zero is not the minimum and you have the wrong case.

---

* The term "function" is here understood to mean function in the context of the routine's specification and not necessarily in the sense of overall function as viewed by the user.

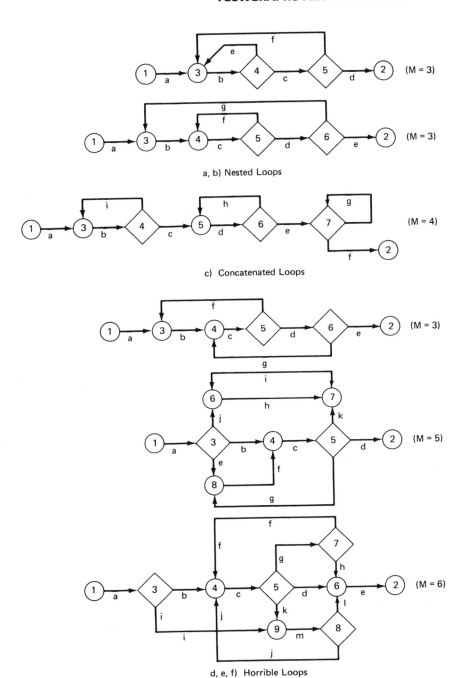

a, b) Nested Loops

c) Concatenated Loops

d, e, f) Horrible Loops

Figure 3.10. Examples of Loop Types.

2. Could the loop-control variable be negative? Could it appear to specify a negative number of iterations? What happens to such a value?
3. One pass through the loop.
4. Two passes through the loop for reasons discussed below.
5. A typical number of iterations, unless covered by a previous test.
6. One less than the maximum number of iterations.
7. The maximum number of iterations.
8. Attempt one more than the maximum number of iterations. What prevents the loop-control variable from having this value? What will happen with this value if it is forced?

The reason for two passes through the loop is based on a theorem by Huang (HUAN79) that states that some data-flow anomalies, such as some initialization problems, can be detected only by two passes through the loop. The problem occurs when data are initialized within the loop and referenced after leaving the loop. If, because of bugs, a variable is defined within the loop but is not referenced or used in the loop, only two traversals of the loop would show the double initialization. Similar problems are discussed in further detail in Chapter 5.

Case 2—Single Loop, Nonzero Minimum, No Excluded Values

1. Try one less than the expected minimum. What happens if the loop control variable's value is less than the minimum? What prevents the value from being less than the minimum?
2. The minimum number of iterations.
3. One more than the minimum number of iterations.
4. Once, unless covered by a previous test.
5. Twice, unless covered by a previous test.
6. A typical value.
7. One less than the maximum value.
8. The maximum number of iterations.
9. Attempt one more than the maximum number of iterations.

Case 3—Single Loops with Excluded Values

Treat single loops with excluded values as two sets of tests consisting of loops without excluded values, such as Cases 1 and 2 above. Say that the total range of the loop-control variable was 1 to 20, but that values 7, 8, 9, and 10 were excluded. The two sets of tests are 1–6 and 11–20. The test cases to attempt would be 0,1,2,4,6,7, for the first range and 10,11,15,19,20,21, for the second range. The underlined cases are not supposed to work, but they should be attempted. Similarly, you might want to try a value within the excluded range, such as 8. If you had two sets of excluded values, you would have three sets of tests, one for each allowed range. If the excluded values are very systematic and easily typified, this approach would entail too many tests. Say that all odd values were excluded. I would test the extreme points of the range as if there were no excluded values, for the extreme points, for the excluded values, and also for typical excluded values. For example, if the range is 0 to 20 and odd values are excluded, try $-1,0,1,2,3,10,11,18,19,20,21,22$.

2.4.3. Nested Loops

If you had five tests (assuming that one less than the minimum and one more than the maximum were not achievable) for one loop, a pair of nested loops would require 25 tests, and three nested loops would require 125. This is heavy even by my standards. You can't always afford to test all combinations of nested loops' iteration values. Here's a tactic to use to discard some of these values:

1. Start at the innermost loop. Set all the outer loops to their minimum values.
2. Test the minimum, minimum + 1, typical, maximum − 1, and maximum for the innermost loop, while holding the outer loops at their minimum-iteration-parameter values. Expand the tests as required for out-of-range and excluded values.
3. If you've done the outermost loop, GOTO step 5, ELSE move out one loop and set it up as in step 2—with all other loops set to typical values.
4. Continue outward in this manner until all loops have been covered.
5. Do the five cases for all loops in the nest simultaneously.

This procedure works out to twelve tests for a pair of nested loops, sixteen for three nested loops, and nineteen for four nested loops. Practicality may prevent testing in which all loops achieve their maximum values simultaneously. You may have to compromise. Estimate the processing time for the loop and multiply by the product of loop-iteration variables to estimate the time spent in the loop (for details in the general case and precise methods, see Chapter 8 or BEIZ78). If the expected execution time is several years or centuries, ask yourself whether this is reasonable. Why isn't there a check on the combination of values? Unbounded processing time could indicate a bug.

These cases can be expanded by taking into account potential problems associated with initialization of variables and with excluded combinations and ranges. In general, Huang's twice-through theorem should also be applied to the combination of loops to assure catching data-initialization problems. Hold the outer loops at the minimum values and run the inner loop through its cases. Then hold the outer loop at one and run the inner loop through its cases. Finally, hold the outer loop at two and run through the inner-loop cases. Next, reverse the role of the inner and outer loop and do it over again, excluding cases that have been tried earlier. A similar strategy can be used with combinations of allowed values in one loop and excluded values in another.

2.4.4. Concatenated Loops

Concatenated loops fall between single and nested loops with respect to test cases. Two loops are **concatenated** if it's possible to reach one after exiting the other while still on a path from entrance to exit. If the loops cannot be on the same path, then they are not concatenated and can be treated as individual loops. Even if the loops are on the same path and you can be sure that they are independent of each other, you can still treat them as individual loops; but if the iteration values in one loop are directly or indirectly related to the iteration values of another loop, *and* they can occur on the same path, then treat them as you would nested loops. The problem of excessive processing time for combinations of loop-iteration values should not occur because the loop-iteration values are additive rather than multiplicative as they are for nested loops.

2.4.5. Horrible Loops

Although the methods of Chapter 8 may give you some insight into the design of test cases for horrible loops, the resulting cases are not definitive and are usually too many to execute. The thinking required to check the end points and looping values for intertwined loops appears to be unique for each program. It's also difficult at times to see how deeply nested the loops are, or indeed whether there are any nested loops. The use of code that jumps into and out of loops, intersecting loops, hidden loops, and cross-connected loops, makes iteration-value selection for test cases an awesome and ugly task, which is another reason such structures should be avoided.

2.4.6. Loop-Testing Time

Any kind of loop can lead to long testing time, especially if all the extreme value cases are to be attempted (MAX − 1, MAX, MAX + 1). This situation is obviously worse for nested and dependent concatenated loops. In the context of real testing, most tests take a fraction of a second to execute, and even deeply nested loops can be tested in seconds or minutes. I said earlier that unreasonably long test execution times (i.e., hours or centuries) could indicate bugs in the software or the specification. Consider nested loops in which testing the combination of extreme values leads to long test times. You have several options:

1. Show that the combined execution time results from an unreasonable or incorrect specification. Fix the specification.
2. Prove that although the combined extreme cases are hypothetically possible, they are not possible in the real world. That is, the combined extreme cases cannot occur. Don't test the cases and accept the risk. The risk is high because hardware glitches or human input errors could drive you into the case.
3. Put in limits or checks that prevent the combined extreme cases. Then you have to test the software that implements such safety measures.
4. Test with the extreme-value combinations, but use different numbers.

What goes wrong at loop limits, especially at simultaneous limits on several nested or dependent loops? It's rarely the specific numbers; it's the fact that several limits are hit simultaneously. For example, three nested loops have limits at 10,000, 200, and 8,000 for a total of 16,000,000,000 iterations for one extreme-value check. The bug, if any, is not likely to be associated with the specific values 10,000, 200, and 8,000. Almost any other three limiting values would show the bug—for example, 100, 20, and 80. The new limiting values may not make operational sense, nor need they, because you're not trying to simulate reality, you're trying to break the software. The test time problem is solved by rescaling the test limit values to a set of numbers that lead to reasonable execution times. This can be done by a separate compile, by patching, by setting parameter values, etc. The only numbers that may be special are binary powers such as 2, 4, 8, and especially 256, and 65,536. These values should be avoided in rescaling a problem lest a peculiarity of the number mask a bug.

2.5. More on Testing Multi-Entry/Multi-Exit Routines

2.5.1. A Weak Approach

Suppose we have to test a program that has multi-entry and/or multi-exit routines. An approach to testing such junk, assuming that we cannot get the routines changed, is to create fictitious single-entry segments with fictitious case statements and fictitious processes that set fictitious exit parameters and go to a fictitious common junction. This fictitious code (provided you don't get trapped into confusing it with real code) will help you organize the test case design and keep the control flow relatively clean from an analytical point of view (see Figure 3.11).

This technique involves a lot of extra work because you must examine the cross-reference listings to find all references to the labels that correspond to the multiple entries. But it can be rewarding. Present the fictitious input case statement and the list of entrances to the designer of the

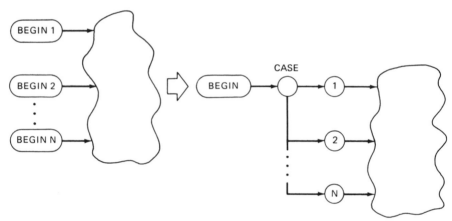

A MULTI-ENTRY ROUTINE IS CONVERTED TO AN EQUIVALENT SINGLE-ENTRY ROUTINE WITH AN ENTRY PARAMETER AND A CONTROLLING CASE STATEMENT.

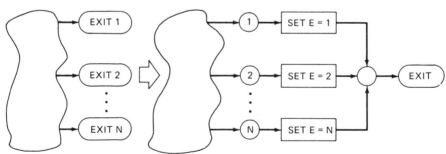

A MULTI-EXIT ROUTINE IS CONVERTED TO AN EQUIVALENT SINGLE-EXIT ROUTINE WITH AN EXIT PARAMETER.

Figure 3.11. Conversion of Multi-Exit or Multi-Entry Routines.

multi-entry routine, and you may be rewarded with a statement like, "That's not right! So-and-so isn't supposed to come in via that entry point." Similarly, every exit destination corresponding to your pseudoexit parameter should be discussed with the designer of the multi-exit routine, and again you may find that some targets are not correct, although this is less likely to happen because multiple entries are more likely to be misused than multiple exits. After all, the designers of routines should know how they want to exit, but it's difficult to control an entry that can be initiated by many other programmers.

In assembly language it's possible to calculate the address of the entry point either in absolute terms or relative to the routine's origin. Such multiple entries are truly abominable, because absolute address calculations make the routine's operation dependent upon location, and relative address calculations change the control flow when the routine is modified. Furthermore, there is no way to tell, without effectively simulating the machine's operation, just what is going on. Absolute addressing for control purposes should be forbidden in almost all instances, although there are mitigating circumstances in which it is not only desirable, but mandatory. In some computers, it is not possible to write an interrupt-handling routine or a device-control routine without resorting to absolute addresses. Where this is essential, all such code should be centralized, tightly controlled, and approved in writing, one such address at a time.

2.5.2. The Integration Testing Issue

Treating the multi-entry/multi-exit routine as if it were reasonably structured by using a fictional entry case statement and a fictional exit parameter is a weak approach because it does not solve the essential testing problem. The essential problem is an integration testing issue and has to do with paths within called components.

In Figure 3.12a we have a multi-entry routine with three entrances and three different callers. The first entrance is valid for callers A and B, the second is valid only for caller A, and the third is valid for callers B and C. Just testing the entrances (as we would in unit testing) doesn't do the job because in integration testing it's the interface, the validity of the call, that must be established. In integration testing, we would have to do at least two tests for the A and B callers—one for each of their entrances. Note also that, in general, during unit testing we have no idea who the callers are to be.

Figure 3.12b shows the situation for a multi-exit routine. It has three exits, labeled 1, 2, and 3. It can be called by components X or Y. Exits 1

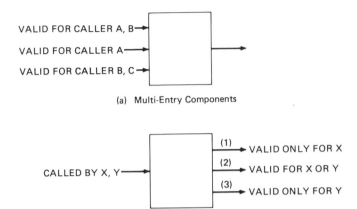

(a) Multi-Entry Components

Figure 3.12. Invalid Paths in a Multi-Exit Routine.

and 2 are valid for the X calls and 2 and 3 are valid for the Y calls. Component testing must not only confirm that exits 1 and 2 are taken for the X calls, but that there are no paths for the X calls that lead to exit 3— and similarly for exit 1 and the Y calls. But when we are doing unit tests, we do not know who will call this routine with what restrictions. As for the multi-entry routine, we must establish the validity of the exit for every caller. Note that we must confirm that not only does the caller take the expected exit, but also that there is no way for the caller to return via the wrong exit.

When we combine the multi-entry routine with the multi-exit routine, we see that in integration testing we must examine every combination of entry and exit for every caller. Since we don't know, during unit design, which combinations will or will not be valid, unit testing must at least treat each such combination as if it were a separate routine. Thus, a routine with three entrances and four exits results in twelve routines' worth of unit testing. Integration testing is made more complicated in proportion to the number of exits, or fourfold.

In an attempt to save 2% of the coding labor, the programmer has increased unit testing cost twelve-fold and integration testing cost by a factor of 4. If only the routine's designers would actually go through all the testing required, it would not be so bad. Unfortunately, most designers of multi-entry/multi-exit routines do not understand the testing ramifications and, as a consequence, quit at simple C1 or C2 (and we're lucky to get that). It's not that such routines can't be tested, but that they're hardly ever tested adequately.

2.5.3.   The Theory and Tools Issue

Another objection to multi-entry/multi-exit routines is that much of testing theory depends on the fact that such routines do not or cannot exist. Most of testing theory assumes that all routines have a single entry and exit. Software which has this property is called **well-formed.** Software which does not have this property is called **ill-formed.**

There are other characterizations of well-formed software: the most common variant is to insist on strict structuring in addition to single-entry/single-exit. In applying any result from theory, it is wise to check the notion of well-formed used and to see whether the software to which the result is to be applied does or does not conform—because the theoretical results may or may not be true in your case. The most common trap occurs in comparing testing strategies. Theory may show that strategy X includes strategy Y, but only for certain notions of well-formed. In other cases, they may be incomparable and thus, running tests based on X would not guarantee tests based on Y and you would have to do both sets of tests. Because multi-entry/multi-exit routines are ill-formed for most theories, the proofs of how strategies relate to one another may be invalid.

The theory issue extends to tools. Test tools, especially test generators based on structure, embody combinations of formal strategies and heuristics. Some of the strategies may be proprietary and may be based on theoretical results—which may or may not hold for ill-formed software. Consequently, the tool may fail to generate important test cases.

2.5.4.   Strategy Summary

The proper way to test multi-entry or multi-exit routines is:

1. Get rid of them.
2. Completely control those you can't get rid of.
3. Augment the flowgraph with fictitious, equivalent, input case statements and exit parameters to help you organize the tests for those that remain and accept the weakness of the approach.
4. Do stronger unit testing by treating each entry/exit combination as if it were a completely different routine.
5. Recognize that you are dealing with a much more complicated beast than you thought, and pay for it in much heavier integration testing.
6. Be sure you understand the strategies and assumptions built into your automatic test generators and confirm that they do (don't) necessarily work for multi-entry/multi-exit routines.

2.6. Effectiveness of Path Testing

2.6.1. *Effectiveness and Limitations*

Approximately 65% of all bugs can be caught in unit testing, which is dominated by path-testing methods, of which statement and branch testing dominates. Precise statistics based on controlled experiments on the effectiveness of path testing are sparse (but see BASI87). What statistics there are show that path testing catches approximately half of all bugs caught during unit testing or approximately 35% of all bugs (BASI87, BOEH75B, ENDR75, GANN79, GIRG86, HENN84, HOWD76, HOWD78D, KERN76, MILL77C, THAY76). When path testing is combined with other methods, such as limit checks on loops, the percentage of bugs caught rises to 50% to 60% in unit testing. Path testing is more effective for unstructured than for structured software. The statistics also indicate that path testing as a sole technique is limited. Here are some of the reasons:

1. Planning to cover does not mean you will cover. Path testing may not cover if you have bugs.
2. Path testing may not reveal totally wrong or missing functions.
3. Interface errors, particularly at the interface with other routines, may not be caught by unit-level path testing.
4. Database and data-flow errors may not be caught.
5. The routine can pass all of its tests at the unit level, but the possibility that it interferes with or perturbs other routines cannot be determined by unit-level path tests.
6. Not all initialization errors are caught by path testing.
7. Specification errors can't be caught.

2.6.2. *A Lot of Work?*

Creating the flowgraph, selecting a set of covering paths, finding input data values to force those paths, setting up the loop cases and combinations—it's a lot of work. Perhaps as much work as it took to design the routine and certainly more work than it took to code it. The statistics indicate that you will spend half of your time testing and debugging— presumably that time includes the time required to design and document test cases. I would rather spend a few quiet hours in my office doing test design than twice those hours on the test floor debugging, going half-deaf from the clatter of a high-speed printer that's producing massive dumps, the reading of which will make me half-blind. Furthermore, *the act of careful, complete, systematic, test design will catch as many bugs as the act of testing.* It's worth repeating here and several times more in this book: *The test design process, at all levels, is at least as effective at catching bugs as is running the test designed by that process.* Personally, I believe that it's far more effective, but I don't have statistics to back that claim. And when you consider the fact that bugs caught during test design cost less to fix than bugs caught during testing, it makes test design bug catching even more attractive.

2.6.3. More on How to Do It

Although fancy tools are nice, the only tools you need is the source code listing (or PDL), a yellow marking pen, and a copying machine. At first you may want to create the control flowgraph and use that as a basis for test design, but as you gain experience with practice (and I mean a few days, not months or years), you'll find that you can select the paths directly on the source code without bothering to draw the control flowgraph. If you can path trace through code for debugging purposes then you can just as easily trace through code for test design purposes. And if you can't trace a path through code, are you a programmer?

You do it with code almost the same way as you would with a pictorial control flowgraph. Make several copies of the source. Select your path, marking the statements on the path with the marking pen—but be sure to mark only the executed parts of IF. . .THEN. . .ELSE statements lest you achieve only C1 instead of C2. Transcribe your markings to a master sheet. When it's all yellow, you have a covering path set. Note the difference between C1 and C2. For C1, you only need to check the statement off; for C2, you must also mark out every part of the statement, especially for IF. . .THEN. . .ELSE and case statement parts.

2.7. Variations

Branch and statement coverage as basic testing criteria are well established as effective, reasonable, and easy to implement. How about the more complicated test criteria in the path-testing family? We know that there are an infinite number of such criteria and we seemed, for a while, destined to an infinite number of Ph.D. dissertations that explored them. There are two main classes of variations:

1. Strategies between P_2 and total path testing.
2. Strategies weaker than P_1 or P_2.

The stronger strategies, typically require more complicated path selection criteria, most of which are impractical for human test design. Typically, the strategy has been embedded in a tool that either selects a covering set of paths based on the strategy or helps the programmer to do so. While research can show that strategy A is stronger than B in the sense that all tests generated by B are included in those generated by A, it is much more difficult to ascertain cost-effectiveness. For example, if strategy A takes 100 times as many cases to satisfy as B, the effectiveness of A would depend on the probability that there are bugs of the type caught by A and not by B. We have almost no such statistics and therefore we know very little about the pragmatic effectiveness of this class of variations (but see WEYU88A). A survey of the main strategies can be found in NTAF88.

As an example of how we can build a family of path-testing strategies, consider a family in which we construct paths out of segments that traverse one, two, or three nodes or more. If we build all paths out single-node segments P_1 (hardly to be called a "path," then we have achieved C1. If we use two-node segments (e.g., links = P_2) to construct paths, we achieve C2.

The weaker strategies—that is, those based on doing less than C2 or C1—may seem to directly contradict our position that C2 is a minimum requirement. This observation is true for wholly new software, but not necessarily true for modified software in a maintenance situation. It does not appear to be reasonable to insist that complete C2 testing, say, be redone when only a small part of the software has been modified. Recent research (LEUN88, LINJ89) shows that the incremental testing (i.e., regression testing) situation is not the same as the new software situation and therefore, weaker path-testing strategies may be effective.

3.   PREDICATES, PATH PREDICATES, AND ACHIEVABLE PATHS

3.1.   General

Selecting a path does not mean that it is achievable. If all decisions are based on variables whose values are independent of the processing and of one another, then all combinations of decision outcomes are possible (2^n outcomes for n binary decisions) and all paths are achievable: in general, this is not so. Every selected path leads to an associated boolean expression, called the **path predicate expression,** which characterizes the input values (if any) that will cause that path to be traversed.

3.2. Predicates

3.2.1. Definition and Examples

The direction taken at a decision depends on the value of decision variables. For binary decisions, decision processing ultimately results in the evaluation of a logical (i.e., boolean) function whose outcome is either TRUE or FALSE. Although the function evaluated at the decision can be numeric or alphanumeric, when the decision is made it is based on a logical function's truth value. The logical function evaluated at a decision is called a **predicate** (GOOD75, HUAN75). Some examples: "A is greater than zero," "the fifth character has a numerical value of 31," "X is either negative or equal to 10," "$X + Y = 3Z^2 - 44$," "Flag 21 is set." Every path corresponds to a succession of TRUE/FALSE values for the predicates traversed on that path. As an example:

> "'X is greater than zero' is TRUE."

AND

> "'$X + Y = 3Z^2 - 44$' is FALSE."

AND

> "'W is either negative or equal to 10' is TRUE."

is a sequence of predicates whose truth values will cause the routine to take a specific path. A predicate associated with a path is called a **path predicate.**

3.2.2. Multiway Branches

The path taken through a multiway branch such as computed GOTO's (FORTRAN), case statements (Pascal), or jump tables (assembly language) cannot be directly expressed in TRUE/FALSE terms. Although it is possible to describe such alternatives by using multivalued logic, an easier expedient is to express multiway branches as an equivalent set of IF. . .THEN. . .ELSE statements. For example, a three-way case statement can be written as:

```
IF case=1 DO A1 ELSE
        (IF case=2 DO A2 ELSE DO A3 ENDIF) ENDIF
```

The translation is not unique because there are many ways to create a tree of IF. . .THEN. . .ELSE statements that simulates the multiway

branch. We treat multiway branches this way as an analytical convenience in order to talk about testing—we don't replace multiway branches
with nested IF's just to test them. Here is another possible variance
between our model (the flowgraph) and the real program. Although multiway branches are effective programming construct, we'll talk about predicates as if they are all binary. That means that we'll have to take special
care (such as the artificial construct above) to handle multiway predicates.

3.2.3. Inputs

In testing, the word **input** is not restricted to direct inputs, such as variables in a subroutine call, but includes all data objects referenced by the
routine whose values are fixed prior to entering it—for example, inputs in
a calling sequence, objects in a data structure, values left in a register.
Although inputs may be numerical, set members, boolean, integers,
strings, or virtually any combination of object types, we can talk about
data as if they are numbers. No generality is lost by this practice. Because
any array can be mapped onto a one-dimensional array, we can treat the
set of inputs to the routine as if it is a one-dimensional array, which we
call the **input vector.**

3.3. Predicate Expressions

3.3.1. Predicate Interpretation

The simplest predicate depends only on input variables. For example, if
X_1 and X_2 are inputs, the predicate might be "$X_1 + X_2 >= 0$". Given the
values of X_1 and X_2 the direction taken through the decision based on the
predicate is determined at input time and doesn't depend on processing.
Assume that the predicate is "$X_1 + Y >= 0$", that along a path prior to
reaching this predicate we had the assignment statement "$Y := X_2 + 7$",
and that nothing else on that path affected the value of Y. Although our
predicate depends on the processing, we can substitute the symbolic expression for Y to obtain an equivalent predicate "$X_1 + X_2 + 7 >= 0$".
The act of symbolic substitution of operations along the path in order
to express the predicate solely in terms of the input vector is called **predicate interpretation.** The interpretation may depend on the path; for
example,

```
          INPUT X
          ON X GOTO A, B, C, ...
       A: Z := 7 @ GOTO HEM
       B: Z := −7 @ GOTO HEM
       C: Z := 0 @ GOTO HEM
          .........


   HEM: DO SOMETHING
          .........


   HEN: IF Y + Z > 0 GOTO ELL ELSE GOTO EMM
```

The predicate interpretation at HEN (the IF statement) depends on the path we took through the first multiway branch (the assigned GOTO). It yields for the three cases respectively, "IF $Y + 7 > 0$ GOTO. . . .", "IF $Y − 7 > 0$ GOTO . . .", and "IF $Y > 0$ GOTO . . .". It is also possible that the predicate interpretation does not depend on the path and for that matter, appearances aside, when all is said and done (especially if there are bugs) that after interpretation the predicate does not depend on anything (for example, "$7 >= 3$"). Because every path can lead to a different interpretation of predicates along that path, a predicate that after interpretation does not depend on input values does not necessarily constitute a bug. Only if all possible interpretations of a predicate are independent of the input could we suspect a bug.

The **path predicates** are the specific form of the predicates of the decisions along the selected path after interpretation. In our discussion of path testing we assume, unless stated otherwise, that all predicates have been interpreted—ignoring for the moment the difficulty that such interpretation could entail.

3.3.2. Independence and Correlation of Variables and Predicates

The path predicates take on truth values (TRUE/FALSE) based on the values of input variables, either directly (interpretation is not required) or indirectly (interpretation is required). If a variable's value does not change as a result of processing, that variable is **independent** of the processing. Conversely, if the variable's value can change as a result of the processing the *variable* is **process dependent.** Similarly, a *predicate* whose truth value can change as a result of the processing is said to be **process dependent** and one whose truth value does not change as a result of the processing is **process independent.** Process dependence of a predicate does not always follow from dependence of the input variables on which that predicate is based. For example, the input variables are X and Y and the predicate is "X + Y = 10". The processing increments X and decrements Y. Although the numerical values of X and Y are process dependent, the predicate "X + Y = 10" is process independent. As another example, the predicate is "X is odd" and the process increments X by an even number. Again, X's value is process dependent but the predicate is process independent. However, if all the variables on which a predicate is based are process independent, it follows that the predicate must be process independent and therefore its truth value is determined by the inputs directly. Also keep in mind that we are looking only at those variables whose values can affect the control flow of the routine and not at all variables whose values may change as a result of processing.

Variables, whether process dependent or independent, may be **correlated** to one another. Two variables are **correlated** if every combination of their values cannot be independently specified. For example, two 8-bit variables should lead to 2^{16} combinations. If there is a restriction on their sum, say the sum must be less than or equal to 2^8, then only 2^9 combinations are possible. Variables whose values can be specified independently without restriction are **uncorrelated.** By analogy, a pair of predicates whose outcomes depend on one or more variables in common (whether or not those variables are correlated) are said to be **correlated predicates.** As an example, let X and Y be two input variables that are independent of the processing and are not correlated with one another. Let decision 10 be based on the predicate "X = Y" and decision 12 on the predicate "X + Y = 8". If we select values for X and Y to satisfy decision 10, we may have forced the predicate's truth value for decision 12 and may not be able to make that decision branch the way we wish. Every path through a routine is achievable only if all predicates in that routine are uncorrelated. If a routine has a loop, then at least one decision's predicate must depend on the processing or there is an input value that will cause the routine to loop indefinitely.

3.3.3. *Path Predicate Expressions*

The following is a conceptual exercise—an aid to understanding testing issues, but not the way you design test cases. Select an (entry/exit) path through a routine. Write down the uninterpreted predicates for the decisions you meet along the path, being sure if there are loops, to distinguish each passage through the predicates in the loop (or the loop-control predicate) by noting the value of the loop-control variable that applies to that pass. Interpret the predicates to convert them into predicates that contain only input variables. The result of this mental exercise is a set of boolean expressions, all of which must be satisfied to achieve the selected path. This set is called the **path predicate expression.** Assuming (for the sake of our example) that the input variables are numerical, the expression is equivalent to a set of inequalities such as

$$X_1 + 3X_2 + 17 >= 0$$
$$X_3 = 17$$
$$X_4 - X_1 >= 14X_2$$

Any set of input values that satisfy *all* of the conditions of the path predicate expression will force the routine to the path. If there is no such set of inputs, the path is not achievable. The situation can be more complicated because a predicate could have an .OR. in it. For example:

$$\text{IF } X_5 > 0 \text{ .OR. } X_6 < 0 \text{ THEN. . .}$$

A single .OR., such as the above, gives us two sets of expressions, either of which, if solved, forces the path. If we added the above expression to the original three we would have the following two sets of inequalities:

A: $X_5 > 0$	E: $X_6 < 0$
B: $X_1 + 3X_2 + 17 >= 0$	B: $X_1 + 3X_2 + 17 >= 0$
C: $X_3 = 17$	C: $X_3 = 17$
D: $X_4 - X_1 >= 14X_2$	D: $X_4 - X_1 >= 14X_2$

We can simplify our notation by using an uppercase letter to denote each predicate's truth value and then use boolean algebra notation to denote the predicate expression: concatenation means "AND", a plus sign means "OR", and negation is denoted by an overscore. The above example, using the boolean variable names shown above then becomes

$$ABCD + EBCD = (A+E)BCD$$

If we had taken the opposite branch at the fourth predicate, the inequality would be $X_4 - X_1 < 14X_2$ and the resulting predicate expression for that path would be

$$(A+E)BC\overline{D}$$

3.4. Predicate Coverage

3.4.1. Compound Predicates

Most programming languages permit **compound predicates** at decisions—that is, predicates of the form A .OR. B or A .AND. B. and more complicated boolean expressions. The branch taken at such decisions is determined by the truth value of the entire boolean expression. Even if a given decision's predicate is not compound, it may become compound after interpretation because interpretation may require us to carry forward a compound term. Also, a simple negation can introduce a compound predicate. For example, say the predicate at some decision is

$$X = 17 \quad \text{(that is, IF X=17 THEN. . .)}$$

The opposite branch is X .NE. 17, which is equivalent to $X > 17$ .OR. $X < 17$. Therefore, whether or not the language permits compound predicates, we can at any decision have an arbitrarily complicated compound predicate after interpretation.

3.4.2. Predicate Coverage

Assume for the sake of discussion that a predicate on a selected path is a compound predicate which depends directly on the input vector—i.e., interpretation is not required. Consider a compound predicate such as A+B+C+D. It consists of four subsidiary predicates, any of which must be true for the branch to be taken. We don't know, offhand, the order in which the subsidiary predicates will be evaluated: that depends on how the compiler implements things. It could be A,B,C,D, or more likely, D,C,B,A. It's difficult to predict the sequence in which the predicates are evaluated because the compiler can rearrange that sequence to optimize the code. Let's say it evaluates the terms in the order A,B,C,D. Typically (but not necessarily) the compiler will create code which will stop predicate evaluation as soon as the truth value of the compound predicate is determined. For example, if the first term (A) is true, evaluation stops because the direction of the branch is determined. Therefore, the desired path could be taken, but there could still be a bug in predicate B that would not be discovered by this test. The same situation holds for a form such as ABCD for the FALSE branch, because the negation of ABCD is $\overline{A} + \overline{B} + \overline{C} + \overline{D}$.

Returning to the general case in which we allow arbitrarily complicated compound predicates at any decision and in which compound predicates arise as a result of interpretation, it is clear that achieving the desired

direction at a given decision could still hide bugs in the associated predicates. The desired path is achieved for the test case you chose, but for
some other case, in which the truth value of the controlling predicate is
determined in some other order, the branch goes the wrong way. For
example, the predicate is A + B and A is correct, but B is buggy. The first
test makes A true, and consequently B is not exercised. The next test case
(the one we didn't try) has A false and B should be true, which would
make the path go the same way as the first case. The bug in B makes B
false and consequently we have the wrong path. An even nastier case is
A + B + C because the intended path will be taken despite the bug in B
because B's failure is masked by the fact that C is true.

We'll have a lot more to say about predicates and boolean algebra in
Chapter 10. For now, it's enough to realize that achieving C2 could still
hide control flow bugs. A stronger notion of coverage is indicated: **predicate coverage.** We say that **predicate coverage** has been achieved if all
possible combinations of truth values corresponding to the selected path
have been explored under some test. Predicate coverage is clearly
stronger than branch coverage. If all possible combinations of all predicates under all interpretations are covered, we have the equivalent of total
path testing. Just as there are hierarchies of path testing based on path-
segment link lengths, we can construct hierarchies based on different
notions of predicate coverage.

3.5. Testing Blindness

3.5.1. The Problem

Let's leave compound predicates for now and return to simple predicates.
Is it enough to run one path through a predicate to test its validity?
Consider the following example:

```
        IF A GOTO BOB ELSE GOTO COB
BOB:DO SOMETHING
        · · ·


        GOTO SAM
COB:DO SOMETHING ELSE
        · · ·


        GOTO SAM
        · · ·


    SAM:IF X DO ALPHA ELSE DO BETA
```

Our question concerns the X predicate in SAM. We can reach it either via the BOB sequence or via the COB sequence. Whichever we do, there are two alternatives at SAM and presumably, two different cases would be sufficient to test the SAM statement. Is it possible that we might have to actually do four cases, corresponding to two cases for reaching SAM via BOB and two more cases for reaching SAM via COB? The answer, unfortunately, is yes, because of **testing blindness** (ZEIL81).

Testing blindness is a pathological situation in which the desired path is achieved for the wrong reason. It can occur because of the interaction of two or more statements that makes the buggy predicate "work" despite its bug and because of an unfortunate selection of input values that does not reveal the situation. Zeil (ZEIL81, WHIT87) discusses three kinds of predicate blindness: **assignment blindness, equality blindness,** and **self-blindness.** There are probably many more kinds of blindness yet to be discovered. We don't know whether instances of different kinds of blindness bugs are significant to the point where it pays to design special test methods to discover them. The point of discussing blindness is to expose further limitations of path testing and to justify the need for other strategies.

3.5.2. Assignment Blindness

Assignment blindness occurs when the buggy predicate appears to work correctly because the specific value chosen for an assignment statement works with both the correct and incorrect predicate. Here's an example:

Correct	Buggy
X := 7	X := 7
.....	.....
IF Y > 0 THEN	IF X + Y > 0 THEN

If the test case sets Y:= 1 the desired path is taken in either case, but there is still a bug. Some other path that leads to the same predicate could have a different assignment value for X, so the wrong path would be taken because of the error in the predicate.

3.5.3. Equality Blindness

Equality blindness occurs when the path selected by a prior predicate results in a value that works both for the correct and buggy predicate. For example,

Correct	*Buggy*
IF Y = 2 THEN. . .	IF Y = 2 THEN. . .
.....	.....
IF X + Y > 3 THEN. . .	IF X > 1 THEN. . .

The first predicate (IF Y = 2) forces the rest of the path, so that for any positive value of X, the path taken at the second predicate will be the same for the correct and buggy versions.

3.5.4. Self-Blindness

Self-blindness occurs when the buggy predicate is a multiple of the correct predicate and as a result is indistinguishable along that path. For example,

Correct	*Buggy*
X := A	X := A
.....	.....
IF X − 1 > 0 THEN...	IF X + A −2 > 0 THEN

The assignment (X:= A) makes the predicates multiples of each other (for example, A − 1 > 0 and 2A − 2 > 0), so the direction taken is the same for the correct and buggy version. A path with another assignment could behave differently and would reveal the bug.

4. PATH SENSITIZING

4.1. Review; Achievable and Unachievable Paths

Let's review the progression of thinking to this point.

1. We want to select and test enough paths to achieve a satisfactory notion of test completeness such as C1 and/or C2.
2. Extract the program's control flowgraph and select a set of tentative covering paths.
3. For any path in that set, interpret the predicates along the path as needed to express them in terms of the input vector. In general, individual predicates are compound or may become compound as a result of interpretation.
4. Trace the path through, multiplying (boolean) the individual compound predicates to achieve a boolean expression such as

$$(A + BC)(D + E)(FGH)(IJ)(K)(L),$$

where the terms in the parentheses are the compound predicates met at each decision along the path and each letter (A, B, . . .) stands for simple predicates.

5. Multiply out the expression to achieve a **sum-of-products form:**

ADFGHIJKL + AEFGHIJKL + BCDFGHIJKL + BCEFGHIJKL

6. Each product term denotes a set of inequalities that, if solved, will yield an input vector that will drive the routine along the designated path. Remember that equalities are a special case of inequalities and that these need not be numerical; for example, A could mean "STRING ALPHA = 'Help Me'" and B could mean "BIT 17 IS SET".

7. Solve any one of the inequality sets for the chosen path and you have found a set of input values for the path.

If you can find a solution, then the path is **achievable.** If you can't find a solution to any of the sets of inequalities, the path is **unachievable.** The act of finding a set of solutions to the path predicate expression is called **path sensitization.**

Is there a general algorithm that will solve the inequalities in order to sensitize the path and failing that, tell us that there is no solution? The answer is a resounding no! The question is known to lead to unsolvable problems from several different points of view. In the pragmatic world of testing we never let trivial things such as provable unsolvability get in our way—especially if there are effective heuristics around.

4.2. Pragmatic Observations

The purpose of the above discussion has been to explore the sensitization issues and to provide insight into tools that help us sensitize paths. If in practice you really had to do the above in the manner indicated then test design would be a difficult procedure suitable only to the mathematically inclined. It doesn't go that way in practice: it's much easier. You select a path and with little fuss or bother you determine the required input vector. Furthermore, if there is any difficulty, it's likelier that there are bugs rather than a truly difficult sensitization problem.

4.3. Heuristic Procedures for Sensitizing Paths

Here is a workable approach. Instead of selecting the paths without considering how to sensitize, attempt to choose a covering path set that is easy to sensitize and pick hard to sensitize paths only as you must to achieve coverage.

1. Identify all variables that affect the decisions. Classify them as to whether they are process dependent or independent. Identify correlated input variables. For dependent variables, express the nature of the process dependency as an equation, function, or whatever is convenient and clear. For correlated variables, express the logical, arithmetic, or functional relation that defines the correlation.
2. Classify the predicates as dependent or independent. A predicate based only on independent input variables must be independent. Identify correlated predicates and document the nature of the correlation as for variables. If the same predicate appears at more than one decision, the decisions are obviously correlated.
3. Start path selection with uncorrelated, independent predicates. Cover as much as you can. If you achieve coverage and you had identified supposedly dependent predicates, something is wrong. Here are some of the possibilities:
   a. The predicates are correlated and/or dependent in such a way as to nullify the dependency. The routine's logic can probably be simplified. See the methods of Chapter 10.
   b. The predicates are incorrectly classified. Check your work.
   c. Your path tracing is faulty. Look for a missing path or incomplete coverage.
   d. There is a bug.
4. If coverage hasn't been achieved using independent uncorrelated predicates, extend the path set by using correlated predicates; preferably those whose resolution is independent of the processing— i.e., those that don't need interpretation.
5. If coverage hasn't been achieved, extend the cases to those that involve dependent predicates (typically required to cover loops), preferably those that are not correlated.
6. Last, use correlated, dependent predicates.
7. For each path selected above, list the input variables corresponding to the predicates required to force the path. If the variable is independent, list its value. If the variable is dependent, list the relation that will make the predicate go the right way (i.e., interpret the predi-

cate). If the variable is correlated, state the nature of the correlation to other variables. Examine forbidden combinations (if any) in detail. Determine the mechanism by which forbidden combinations of values are prohibited. If nothing prevents such combinations, what will happen if they are supplied as inputs?
8. Each path will yield a set of inequalities, which must be simultaneously satisfied to force the path.

4.4. Examples

4.4.1. Simple, Independent, Uncorrelated Predicates

The uppercase letters in the decision boxes of Figure 3.13 represent the predicates. The capital letters on the links following the decisions indicate whether the predicate is true (unbarred) or false (barred) for that link. There are four decisions in this example and, consequently, four predicates. Because they are uncorrelated and independent by assumption, each can take on TRUE or FALSE independently, leading to $2^4 = 16$ possible values; but the number of possible paths is far less (8) and the number of covering paths is smaller still. A set of covering paths and their associated predicate truth values can be trivially obtained from the flowgraph:

Path	Predicate Values
abcdef	A $\overline{\text{C}}$
aghcimkf	$\overline{\text{A}}$ B C D
aglmjef	$\overline{\text{A}}$ B $\overline{\text{D}}$

A glance at the path column shows that all links are represented at least once. The predicate value column shows all predicates appearing both

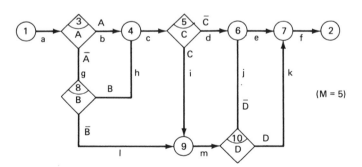

Figure 3.13. Predicate Notation.

barred and unbarred. Therefore, every link has been covered and every decision has been taken both ways. I violated my own rules here because two things changed on the second path. Using a few more but simpler paths with fewer changes to cover the same flowgraph, I get:

Path	Predicate Values
abcdef	A $\overline{C}$
abcimjef	A C $\overline{D}$
abcimkf	A C D
aghcdef	$\overline{A}$ B $\overline{C}$
aglmkf	$\overline{A}$ B $\overline{D}$

Because you know what each predicate means (for example, A means "X = 0?"), you can now determine the set of input values corresponding to each path.

4.4.2. Correlated, Independent Predicates

The two decisions in Figure 3.14 are correlated because they used the identical predicate (A). If you picked paths *abdeg* and *acdfg*, which seem to provide coverage, you would find that neither of these paths is achievable. If the A branch (c) is taken at the first decision, then the A branch (e) must also be taken at the second decision. There are two decisions and therefore a potential for four paths, but only two of them, *abdfg* and *acdeg*, are achievable. The flowgraph can be replaced with Figure 3.15, in which we have reproduced the common code, or alternatively, we can embed the common link *d* code into a subroutine.

Predicates correlation will not often be so blatant as when both decisions have exactly the same tests on the same variables. Suppose you didn't know or didn't realize that some predicates were correlated. You would find that setting one decision's variables would force another's and that you did not have the freedom to choose the rest of the path. In general, correlated predicates mean that some paths are not achievable,

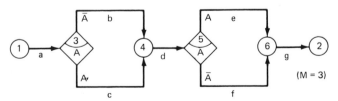

Figure 3.14. Correlated Decisions.

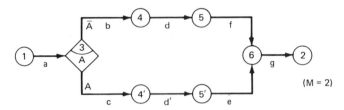

Figure 3.15. Correlated Decision of Figure 3.14 Removed.

although this does not mean that coverage is unachievable. If you select paths from the design flowgraph or the PDL specification without considering the details of path sensitization and subsequently you find that a path is not achievable, even though it was selected on the basis of seemingly meaningful cases, it is an occasion for joy rather than frustration. One of the following must be true:

1. You found a bug.
2. The design can be simplified by removing some decisions, possibly at the cost of a new subroutine or repeated code.
3. You have a better understanding of how the decisions are interrelated.

The question to ask is: "How did the decisions come to be correlated?" Correlated decisions are redundant. If you have n decisions in a routine and less than 2^n paths, there is redundancy in the design, even though you might not be able to take advantage of it. If n decisions give you only 2^{n-1} paths, then one decision is targeted for removal. If n decisions give 2^{n-2} paths, then two decisions should be targeted. Generally, $\log_2$(number of paths) tells you how many effective decisions you have. Comparing this with the actual number of decisions tells you whether any can be targeted for removal. Because getting rid of code is the best possible kind of test,* removing potentially redundant code is good testing at its best.

One common and troublesome source of correlated decisions is the reprehensible practice of "saving code." Link d in the above example is typical. The designer had thought to save common code by doing the initial processing that followed the first decision, merging to execute the

---

* The highest goal of testing is bug prevention. If bugs occur at 1% per source statement, then credit yourself with a bug "found" and "corrected" for every hundred lines of code you eliminate. Adjust this to the local bug rate. Bad routines tend to have a lot of superfluous code and a high bug rate—say, 3% to 4%; you can earn your pay on such routines.

common code, and then splitting again to do the different code based on the second decision. It's relatively harmless in this example. Most often, the second decision will be based on a flag that was set on the link appropriate to the predicate's value at the first decision. The second decision is based on the flag's value, but it is obviously correlated to the first. Think of these two pieces as being widely separated and embedded within a larger, more complicated routine. Now the nature of the correlation is subtle and obscure. The way it's usually done, though, is not even this sensible. The programmer sees a sequence of code that seems to correspond to part of a case that's yet to be programmed. He jumps into the middle of the old code to take advantage of the supposedly common code and puts in a subsequent test to avoid doing the wrong processing and to get him back onto the correct path. Maintaining such code is a nightmare because such "code-saving" tricks are rarely documented. This can lead to future bugs even though there are no bugs at first. The potential for future bugs exists because the correlation is essential. If maintenance removes the correlation, then the previously unachievable (and undesirable) paths become possible.

Correlated decisions on a path, especially those that prevent functionally sensible paths, are suspect. At best they provide an opportunity for simplifying the routine's control structure and therefore for saving testing labor, or they may reveal a bug. It's rare that correlated decisions that prevent functionally sensible paths are due to subtleties in the requirements.

4.4.3. Dependent Predicates

Finding sensitizing values for dependent predicates may force you to "play computer." Usually, and thankfully, most of the routine's processing does not affect the control flow and consequently can be ignored. Simulate the computer only to the extent necessary to force paths. Loops are the most common kind of dependent predicates; the number of times a typical routine will iterate in the loop is usually determinable in a straightforward manner from the input variables' values. Consequently it is usually easy to work backward to determine the input value that will force the loop a specified number of times.

4.4.4. The General Case

There is no simple procedure for the general case. It is easy to state the steps involved but much harder to accomplish them.

1. Select cases to provide coverage on the basis of functionally sensible paths. If the routine is well structured, you should be able to force most of the paths without deep analysis. Intractable paths should be examined for potential bugs before investing time solving equations or whatever you might have to do to find path-forcing input values.
2. Tackle the path with the fewest decisions first. Give preference to nonlooping paths over looping paths.
3. Start at the end of the path and not the beginning. Trace the path in reverse and list the predicates in the order in which they appear. The first predicate (the last on the path in the normal direction) imposes restrictions on subsequent predicates (previous when reckoned in the normal path direction). Determine the broadest possible range of values for the predicate that will satisfy the desired path direction.
4. Continue working backward along the path to the next decision. The next decision may be restricted by the range of values you determined for the previous decision (in the backward direction). Pick a range of values for the affected variables as broad as possible for the desired direction and consistent with the set of values thus far determined.
5. Continue until you reach the entrance and therefore have established a set of input conditions for the entire path.

Whatever manipulations you do can always be reduced to equivalent numerical operations. What you're doing in tracing the path backward is building a set of numerical inequalities or a combination of numerical inequalities, equations, and logical statements. You're trying to find input values that satisfy all of them—the values that force the path. If you can't find such a solution, the path is unachievable. Alternatively, it means that you couldn't solve the set of inequalities. Most likely it means that you've found a bug.

An alternate approach to use when you are truly faced with functionally sensible paths that require equation solving to sensitize is a little easier. Instead of working backward along the path, work forward from the first decision to the last. To do this, though, you may have to drop your preconceived paths. Let's say that you have already sensitized some paths and all the rest seem to be dependent and/or correlated.

1. List the decisions that have yet to be covered in the order in which you expect to traverse them. For each decision, write down the broadest possible range of input values that affect that decision.
2. Pick a direction at the first decision on the path that appears to go in the direction you want to go. Adjust all input values—that is, the

range of input values—that are affected by your choice. For example, X was restricted to positive integers at input and Y was any letter between "D" and "G". The first decision restricted X to less than 10 and Y to "E" or "F". This restricted set of input values is now used for the next decision.

3. Continue, decision by decision, always picking a direction that gets you closer to the exit. Because the predicates are dependent and/or correlated, your earlier choices may force subsequent directions.

4. Assuming that the procedure does not lead to impossible or contradictory input values (which means that the attempted path is not achievable), start a new path using the last decision at which you had a choice, assuming that such a path will provide additional coverage.

The advantage of the forward method over the backward method is that it's usually less work to get the input values because you are solving the simultaneous inequalities as you go. The disadvantage is that you don't quite know where you're going. The routine is the master and not you.

5. PATH INSTRUMENTATION

5.1. The Problem

We haven't said much about the outcome of the test—for example, the outputs produced as a result of the processing along the selected path. Note that we use the word "**outcome**" rather than "output." The **outcome** of a test is what we expect to happen as a result of the test. That includes outputs, of course, but what if the desired outcome is that there be no output? As with inputs, test outcomes include anything we can observe in the computer's memory, mass storage, I/O, registers, that should have changed as a result of the test, or *not* changed as a result of the test—that bears repetition: *the expected outcome includes any expected changes or the lack of change (if that's what's expected).* We're not doing kiddie testing, so we predict the outcome of the test as part of the test design process. We then run the test, observe the actual outcome, and compare that outcome to the expected outcome. If the predicted and actual outcomes match, can we say that the test has been passed? We cannot. We can only say that some of the necessary conditions for passing are satisfied, but the conditions are not sufficient because the desired outcome could have been achieved for the wrong reason. This situation is called **coincidental correctness.** Continuing in this (paranoid) vein, assume that we ran a covering set of tests and achieved the desired outcomes for each

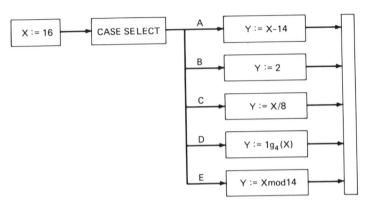

Figure 3.16. Coincidental Correctness.

case. Can we say that we've covered? Again no because the desired outcome could have been achieved by the wrong path.

Figure 3.16 is an example of a routine that, for the (unfortunately) chosen input value ($X = 16$), yields the same outcome ($Y = 2$) no matter which case we select. Therefore, the tests chosen this way will not tell us whether we have achieved coverage. For example, the five cases could be totally jumbled and still the outcome would be the same. **Path instrumentation** is what we have to do to confirm that the outcome was achieved by the intended path.

5.2. General Strategy

All instrumentation methods are a variation on a theme of an interpretive trace. An **interpretive trace program,** you'll recall, is one that executes every statement in order and records the intermediate values of all calculations, the statement labels traversed, etc. It's often part of a symbolic debugging package. If we run the tested routine under a trace, then we have all the information we need to confirm the outcome and, furthermore, to confirm that it was achieved by the intended path. The trouble with traces is that they give us far more information than we need. In fact, the typical trace program provides so much information that confirming the path from its massive output dump is more work than simulating the computer by hand to confirm the path. Even trace programs that provide some control over what is to be dumped usually do not give us the specific information we need for testing. Recognizing the limitations of the classical trace packages or symbolic debuggers, a variety of instrumentation methods more suitable to the testing process have emerged.

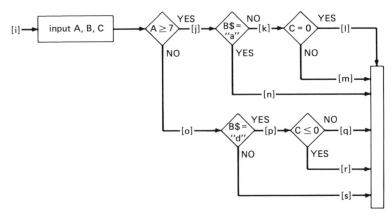

Figure 3.17. Single Link Marker Instrumentation.

5.3. Link Markers

A simple and effective form of instrumentation (RAMA75B) is called a **traversal marker** or **link marker.** Name every link by a lowercase letter. Instrument the links so that the link's name is recorded when the link is executed. The succession of letters produced in going from the routine's entry to its exit should, if there are no bugs, exactly correspond to the path name (i.e., the "name" you get when you concatenate the link names traversed on the path—e.g., *abcde*); see Figure 3.17.

Unfortunately, a single link marker may not do the trick because links can be chewed open by bugs. The situation is illustrated in Figure 3.18. We intended to traverse the *ikm* path, but because of a rampaging GOTO in the middle of the *m* link, we go to process B. If coincidental correctness is against us, the outcomes will be the same and we won't know about the bug. The solution is to implement two markers per link: one at the beginning of each link and one at the end; see Figure 3.19. The two link markers

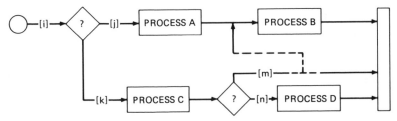

Figure 3.18. Why Single Link Markers Aren't Enough.

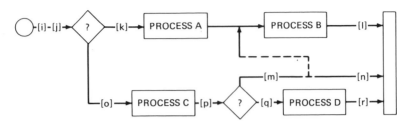

Figure 3.19. Double Link Markers.

now specify the path name and confirm both the beginning and end of the link.

5.4. Link Counters

A less disruptive (and less informative) instrumentation method is based on counters. Instead of a unique link name to be pushed into a string when the link is traversed, we simply increment a link counter. We now confirm that the path length is as expected. The same problem that led us to double link markers also leads us to double link counters. With these in place, we expect an even count that is exactly double the expected path length. This is probably paring instrumentation down to the point where it's almost useless, so we'll get a little more complicated and put a counter on every link. Then we can easily predict what the link counts should be for any test. If there are no loops, they will all equal 1. Similarly, we can accumulate counts over a series of tests, say a covering set, and confirm that the total link counts equals the sums we would expect from the series. The same reasoning as before leads us to double link counters— one at the start of the link and one at the end. The checkout procedure then consists of answering the following questions:

1. Do the begin-link counter values equal the end-link counter values for all links?
2. Do the input-link count of every decision equal the sum of the link counts of the output links from that decision?
3. Do the sum of the input-link counts for a junction equal the output-link count for that junction?
4. Do the counts match the values you predicted when you designed the test?

5.5. Other Instrumentation Methods

The methods you can use to instrument paths are limited only by your imagination. Here's a sample:

1. Mark each link by a unique prime number and multiply the link name into a central register. The path name is a unique number and you can recapture the links traversed by factoring. The order in which the links were traversed is lost, but it's unlikely that a bug would cause a reversal of link execution order—but reversals of statements within a link are possible.
2. Use a bit map with a single bit per link and set that bit when the link is traversed (or two bits per link if you want to be more elaborate and protect yourself against link busters).
3. Use a hash coding scheme over the link names, or calculate an error-detecting code over the link names, such as a check sum.
4. Use your symbolic debugger or trace to give you a trace only of subroutine calls and return. Instrument the links that don't have a real subroutine call on them by putting a call to a dummy subroutine, whose only interesting property is its name.
5. Set a variable value at the beginning of the link to a unique number for that link and use an assertion statement at the end of the link to confirm that you're still on it. The sequence of satisfied assertions is the path name.

Every instrumentation probe (marker, counter) you insert gives you more information, but with each probe the information is further removed from reality. The ultimate instrumentation, a full interpretive trace, gives you the most information possible but so distorts timing relations that timing and race-condition bugs will hide under your probes. Location-dependent bugs also hide under probes. If, for example, someone made an absolute assumption about the location of something in the data base, the presence or absence of probes could modify things so that the bug could be seen only when the probe was inactive and not with the probe in place. In other words, the very probe designed to reveal bugs may hide them. Such **peek-a-boo bugs** are really tough.

5.6. Implementation

For unit testing, path instrumentation and verification can be provided by a comprehensive test tool that supports your source language. Unfortunately for you, you may be working with an unsupported language, or may be doing higher-level testing, in which case, you'll have to consider how to install instrumentation the hard way.

The introduction of probes, especially if you have to put them in by hand, provides new opportunities for bugs. Automatically inserted probes are less bug-prone, but can only be inserted in terms of the real rather than the intended structure. This discrepancy can be great, especially if control is affected by what goes on in lower-level routines that are called by the routine under test. Instrumentation is relatively more important when path testing is used at the higher levels of program structure, such as with transaction flows (see Chapter 4), than when it is used at the unit level. Furthermore, at the higher levels the possibility of discrepancies between actual and intended structure is greater; but instrumentation overhead is relatively smaller.

It is easiest to install probes when programming in languages that support **conditional assembly** or **conditional compilation.** The probes are written in the source code and tagged into categories. Both counters and traversal markers can be implemented, and one need not be parsimonious with the number and placement of probes because only those that are activated for that test will be compiled or assembled. For any test or small set of tests, only some of the probes will be active. Rarely would you compile with all probes activated and then only when all else failed.

Conditional assembly and compilation must be used with caution, especially at higher program levels. A unit may take just a few seconds to compile or assemble. But (and this is language and language processor dependent), the same routine, if compiled or assembled in the context of a full system, could take many hours—thereby canceling many of the advantages of conditional assembly and compilation.

If conditional assembly or compilation are not available, use macros or function calls for each category of probe to be implemented. The probe can be turned on or off by modifying the macro or function definition or by setting ON/OFF parameters within the functions or macros. Use of macros or functions will also reduce bugs in the probes themselves. A general-purpose routine can be written to store the outputs of traversal markers. Because efficiency is not really an issue, you can afford the overhead and can use a piece of standard code to record things.

Plan your instrumentation in levels of ever-increasing detail so that when all probes are active at the most detailed level, they will serve as a diagnostic tool. Remember that path testing based on structure should comprise at most half of all the tests that are to be done, and although the instrumentation may be installed to verify path testing, it will also be useful in other tests.

6. IMPLEMENTATION AND APPLICATION OF PATH TESTING

6.1. Integration, Coverage, and Paths in Called Components

Path-testing methods are mainly used in unit testing, especially for new software. Let's consider an idealistic process by which components are integrated. The new component is first tested as an independent unit with all called components and corequisite components replaced by **stubs**—a simulator of lower-level components that is presumably more reliable than the actual component. This is classical unit testing. Path-testing methods at this stage are used to explore potential control-flow problems without the distraction of possible bugs in called or corequisite components. We then integrate the component with its called subroutines and corequisite components, one at a time, carefully probing the interface issues. Once the interfaces have been tested, we retest the integrated component, this time with the stubs replaced by the real subroutines and corequisite component. The component is now ready for the next level of integration. This bottom-up integration process continues until the entire system has been integrated. The idea behind integrating in this manner is that it avoids the confusion between problems in lower-level components and the component under test.

I said that the above procedure was idealistic—it's good pedagogy because it clarifies the integration issues, but that's hardly ever the way integration is done. Reality is more complicated, less rigid, far more dynamic, and more efficient. While a bottom-up integration strategy may be used in part, integration proceeds in associated blocks of components, some of which have been fully tested and are fully trusted and others of which have had little prior testing. Stubs may be correctly avoided because it is recognized that the bug potential for some stubs may be higher than that of the real routine. And there are always old, well-tested routines to be integrated.

As soon as we deal with partially tested lower-level subroutines to be integrated with the component on which we are momentarily focusing our attention, we have to think about paths within the subroutine—similarly for coroutines. The same situation, albeit less obviously, is true for corequisite component whose interface with our component is via a data object. What does it mean to achieve C1 or C2 coverage at this level when lower-level or corequisite components could affect our control flow? There are several consequences. First, predicate interpretation could require us to treat the subroutine as if it were in-line code, adding its complexity and processing to the problem. Sensitization obviously becomes more difficult because there's a lot more code to think about. Third, a selected path may be unachievable because the called component's processing blocks that path. In assembly language programming, all of these interactions and more must be considered, which is one of the reasons why, function-for-function, assembly language is much harder to program. One of the main services provided by higher-order languages is that they allow us to hide lower-level complexity. Although it is always possible to circumvent complexity hiding, the extent that the designer takes advantage of it is also the extent to which higher-level testing can ignore lower-level actions and paths within called components.

Path testing, and for that matter, most structural testing methods, rely on the assumption that we can do effective testing one level at a time without being overly concerned with what happens at the lower levels. It is a fundamental weakness, but no worse than the other weaknesses of path testing we've exposed, such as predicate coverage problems and blindness.

Although there are few hard statistics, we typically lose about 15% coverage (for most coverage metrics) with each level. Thus, while we may achieve C2 at the current level, path tests will achieve 85% one level down, 70% two levels down, 60% three levels down, and so on. When all testing, by all methods, is considered, C1 coverage at the system level ranges from a low of 50% to a high of 85%. We have no statistics for C2 coverage in system testing because it is impossible to monitor C2 coverage (in current hardware) without disrupting the system's operation to the point where testing is impossible. System-level coverage is generally restricted to C1, which can be done by tools that minimally disturb the system. There are unsupported claims of achieving 95% C1 coverage in system testing, but this result was for software that was designed with coverage and integration issues in mind.

6.2. New Code

Wholly new or substantially modified code should always be subjected to enough path testing to achieve C2 (with additional C1 monitoring if it's an unstructured language). Stubs are used where it is clear that the bug potential for the stub is significantly lower than that of the called component. That means that old, trusted components will not be replaced by stubs. Some consideration is given to paths within called components, but only to the extent that we have to do so to assure that the paths we select at the higher level is achievable. Typically, we'll try to use the shortest entry/exit path that will do the job; avoid loops; avoid lower-level subroutine calls; avoid as much lower-level complexity as possible. The unit test suite should be mechanized so that it can be repeated as integration progresses. As a mechanized suite, it will be possible to redo most of the tests with very little effort as we achieve larger and larger aggregates of integrated components. The fact that a previously selected path is no longer achievable often means that we've found a bug arising from an unsuspected interaction. The path may also be blocked because of error conditions or other exceptional situations that can't easily be tested in context. We should expect to drop some percentage of the tests because they can't be run in an integrated component: typical values are 10%–20%.

6.3. Maintenance

The maintenance situation is distinctly different. Path testing is first used on the modified component, as for new software, but called and corequisite components will invariably be real rather than simulated. If we have a configuration-controlled, automated, unit test suite, then path testing will be repeated entirely with such modifications as required to accommodate the changes. Otherwise, selected paths will be chosen in an attempt to achieve C2 over the changed code. As we learn more about the differences between maintenance testing and new code testing, new, more effective strategies will emerge that will change the current, intuition-driven, maintenance test methods into efficient methodologies that provide the kind of coverage we should achieve in maintenance.

6.4. Rehosting

Path testing with C1 + C2 coverage is a powerful tool for rehosting old software. When used in conjunction with automatic or semiautomatic structural test generators, we get a very powerful, effective, rehosting process. Software is rehosted because it is no longer cost-effective to support the environment in which it runs (hardware, language, operating system). Because it's old software, we may have no specification to speak of, much of its operation may be poorly understood, and it is probably as unstructured as software can be. Such software, though, has one great virtue—it works. Whatever it is the software does, it does so correctly, and it is as bug-free as any software can be. The objective of rehosting is to change the operating environment and not the rehosted software. If you attempt to do both simultaneously, all is lost.

Here's how it's done. First, a translator from the old to the new environment is created and tested as any piece of software would be. The bugs in the rehosting process, if any, will be in the translation algorithm and the translator, and the rehosting process is intended to catch those bugs. Second, a complete (C1 + C2) path test suite is created for the old software in the old environment. Components may be grouped to reduce total testing labor and to avoid a total buildup and reintegration, but C1 + C2 is not compromised. The suite is run on the old software in the old environment and all outcomes are recorded. *That test suite and the associated outcomes become the specification for the rehosted software.* Another translator may be needed to convert or adapt the tests and outcomes to the new environment: such translation, if needed, is kept to a minimum, even if it may result in an inefficient rehosted program. The translator is run on all units. The translated units and higher-level component aggregates are then retested using the specification test suite. Coverage is monitored. Test failures or failure to achieve coverage leads to changes in the translator(s) that could necessitate translation reruns and retesting. When the entire system has passed all of the above tests, it is subjected to system-level functional verification testing.

The cost of the process is comparable to the cost of rewriting the software from scratch; it may even be more expensive, but that's not the point. The point is that this method avoids the risks associated with rewriting and achieves a stable, correctly working, though possibly inefficient, software base in the new environment without operational or security compromises. Once confidence in the rehosted software has been established, it can then be modified to improve efficiency and/or to implement new functionality, which had been difficult in the old environment.

This process, designed by the author, was successfully used to rehost the DOD security-accredited Overseas AUTODIN software, operated by the Defense Communications Agency. Assembly language software was translated from an obsolete Philco-Ford 102 computer into VAX assembly language: this entailed substantially different hardware architectures and instruction repertoires. Rehosting from one COBOL environment to another is easy by comparison.

7. TESTABILITY TIPS

Testable software has fewer bugs, is easier to test, and is easier to debug. What has path testing taught us about testability and—more important—which design goals should we adopt to create more testable software? Here are some tips.

1. Keep in mind three numbers: the total number of paths, the total number of achievable paths, and the number of paths required to achieve C2 coverage. The closer these numbers are to each other, the more testable the routine is because:

a. Few unachievable paths means less sensitizing problems and fewer sensitizing dead ends (unsolvable equations).

b. Fewer total paths means reduced opportunities for blindness and coincidental correctness.

c. Testing is based on samples. The smaller the achievable path set is compared to the covering path set, the greater the relative size of the sample, and therefore the greater the confidence warranted in the test set we did execute.

2. Make your decisions once, only once, and stick to them—no correlated decisions. Design goal: n decisions means 2^n paths—all achievable, all needed for C2.

3. Don't squeeze the code.

4. If you can't test it, don't build it.

5. If you don't test it, rip it out.

6. Introduce no "extras," "freebies," unwanted generalizations, additional functionality, hooks, or anything else that will require more cases to cover if you won't or can't test them.

7. If you can't sensitize a path you need for coverage, you probably don't know what you're doing.

8. Easy cover beats elegance every time.

9. Covering paths make functional sense.

10. Deeply nested and/or horrible loops aren't a mark of genius but of a murky mind.

11. Flags, switches, and instruction modification, playing around with the program status word, and other violations of sane programming are evil. "The Devil made me do it!" is no excuse.

12. Don't squeeze the code. *Don't squeeze the code!* **DON'T SQUEEZE THE CODE!**

8. SUMMARY

1. Path testing based on structure is a powerful unit-testing tool. With suitable interpretation, it can be used for system functional tests (see Chapter 4).

2. The objective of path testing is to execute enough tests to assure that, as a minimum, C1 + C2 have been achieved.

3. Select paths as deviations from the normal paths, starting with the simplest, most familiar, most direct paths from the entry to the exit. Add paths as needed to achieve coverage.

4. Add paths to cover extreme cases for loops and combinations of loops: no looping, once, twice, one less than the maximum, the maximum. Attempt forbidden cases.

5. Find path-sensitizing input-data sets for each selected path. If a path is unachievable, choose another path that will also achieve coverage. But first ask yourself why seemingly sensible cases lead to unachievable paths.

6. Use instrumentation and tools to verify the path and to monitor coverage.

7. Incorporate the notion of coverage (especially C2) into all reviews and inspections. Make the ability to achieve C2 a major review agenda item.

8. Design test cases and path from the design flowgraph or PDL specification but sensitize paths from the code as part of desk checking. Do covering test case designs either prior to coding or concurrently with coding.

9. Document all tests and expected test results as copiously as you would document code. Put test suites under the same degree of configuration control used for the software it tests. Treat each path like a subroutine. Predict and document the outcome for the stated inputs and the path trace (or name by links). Also document any significant environmental factors and preconditions. Your tests must be reproducible so that they can serve a diagnostic purpose if they reveal a bug. An undocumented test cannot be reproduced. Automate test execution.

10. Be creatively stupid when conducting tests. Every deviation from the predicted outcome or path must be explained. Every deviation must lead to either a test change, a code change, or a conceptual change.

11. A test that reveals a bug has succeeded, not failed (MYER79).

4
TRANSACTION-FLOW TESTING

1. SYNOPSIS

Transaction flows are introduced as a representation of a system's processing. The methods that were applied to control flowgraphs are then used for functional testing. Transaction flows and transaction-flow testing are to the independent system tester what control flows and path testing are to the programmer.

2. GENERALIZATIONS

The control flowgraph discussed in Chapter 3 is the most often used model in test design. It is but one of an infinite number of possible models based on the same components—links and nodes. The control flowgraph was introduced as a structural model. We now use the same conceptual components and methods over a different kind of flowgraph, the **transaction flowgraph**—this time, though, to create a behavioral model of the program that leads to functional testing. The transaction flowgraph is, if you will, a model of the structure of the system's behavior (i.e., functionality).

We can either focus on how software is built (i.e., structure) or on how it behaves (i.e., function). A structural focus leads us to structural test techniques, whereas a functional (behavioral) focus leads us to functional test methods. In either case, for either point of view, the **graph**—that is, a representation based on circles (nodes) and arrows (links)—is a powerful conceptual tool. There are many different ways to represent software. Peters (PETE76) summarizes the most useful ones. Most of these representations can be converted to some kind of flowgraph.

Path testing (Chapter 3) is fundamental because we'll now see how the entire elaborate mechanism of path testing can be used in an analogous form as a basis for system testing. The point of all this is to demonstrate that testing consists of defining useful graph models and covering them.

Question—What do you do when you see a graph?

Answer—COVER IT!

3. TRANSACTION FLOWS

3.1. Definitions

A **transaction** is a unit of work seen from a system user's point of view. A transaction consists of a sequence of operations, some of which are performed by a system, persons, or devices that are outside of the system. Transactions begin with **birth**—that is, they are created as a result of some external act. At the conclusion of the transaction's processing, the transaction is no longer in the system, except perhaps in the form of historical records. A transaction for an online information retrieval system might consist of the following steps or **tasks**:

1. Accept input (tentative birth).
2. Validate input (birth).
3. Transmit acknowledgment to requester.
4. Do input processing.
5. Search file.
6. Request directions from user.
7. Accept input.
8. Validate input.
9. Process request.
10. Update file.
11. Transmit output.
12. Record transaction in log and cleanup (death).

The user sees this scenario as a single transaction. From the system's point of view, the transaction consists of twelve steps and ten different kinds of subsidiary tasks.

Most online systems process many kinds of transactions. For example, an automatic bank teller machine can be used for withdrawals, deposits, bill payments, and money transfers. Furthermore, these operations can be done for a checking account, savings account, vacation account, Christmas club, and so on. Although the sequence of operations may differ from transaction to transaction, most transactions have common operations. For example, the automatic teller machine begins every transaction by validating the user's card and password number. Tasks in a transaction flowgraph correspond to processing steps in a control flowgraph. As with control flows, there can be conditional and unconditional branches, and junctions.

3.2. Example

Figure 4.1 shows part of a transaction flow. A PC is used as a terminal controller for several dumb terminals. The terminals are used to process orders for parts, say. The order forms are complicated. The user specifies the wanted action, and the terminal controller requests the appropriate form from a remotely located central computer. The forms may be several pages long and may have many fields on each page. A compressed version of the form is transmitted by the central computer to minimize communication line usage. The form is then translated by the terminal control PC for display by the dumb terminal. The terminal controller only transmits the answers (i.e., the contents of the blanks) back to the central computer. As each page of the form is filled out, the terminal controller transmits the answers to the central computer, which either accepts or rejects them. If the answers are invalid, a diagnostic code is transmitted by the central computer to the terminal controller, which in turn translates the code and informs the user at the terminal. Finally, the system allows the user to review the filled-out form.

Decision D1 in Figure 4.1 is not part of the process as such; it is really a characteristic of the kinds of transactions that the terminal controller handles. However, there is a decision like this somewhere in the program. Process P1 probably consists of several subsidiary processes that are completed by the transmission of the request for an order from the central computer. The next step is "process P2," which involves no real processing. What the terminal controller does here depends on the software's structure. Typically, transactions for some other terminal will be processed. Process P3 is a real processing step, as is P4. Process P6 is another wait for input. This has no direct correspondence to a program step. Decisions D2 and D4 depend on the structure of the form. Which branch is taken at decision D3 is determined by the user's behavior. The system does not necessarily have actual decisions corresponding to D1, D2, D3, D4, or D5; D1 and D5 for example, might be implemented by interrupts caused by special keys on the terminal or, if the terminal was itself a PC, by function keys.

The most general case of a transaction flow, then, represents by a flowgraph a scenario between people and computers. In a more restricted example, the transaction flow can represent an internal sequence of events that may occur in processing a transaction.

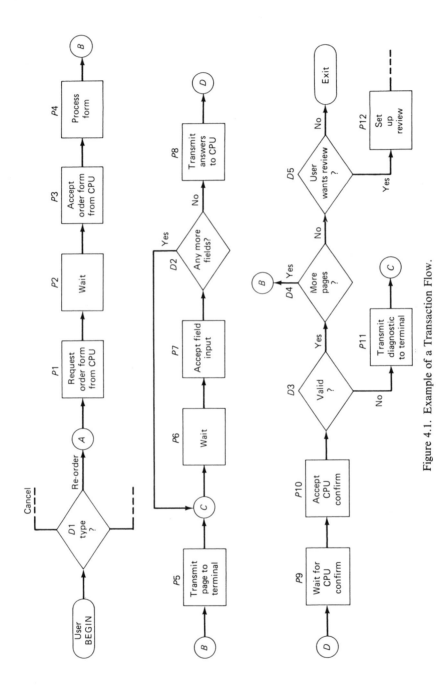

Figure 4.1. Example of a Transaction Flow.

3.3. Usage

Transaction flows are indispensable for specifying requirements of complicated systems, especially online systems. A big system such as an air traffic control or airline reservation system, has not hundreds, but thousands of different transaction flows. The flows are represented by relatively simple flowgraphs, many of which have a single straight-through path. Loops are infrequent compared to control flowgraphs. The most common loop is used to request a retry after user input errors. An ATM system, for example, allows the user to try, say three times, and will take the card away the fourth time.

3.4. Implementation

The implementation of a transaction flow is usually implicit in the design of the system's control structure and associated data base. That is, there is no direct, one-to-one correspondence between the "processes" and "decisions" of the transaction flows and corresponding program component. A transaction flow is a representation of a path taken by a transaction through a succession of processing modules. Think of each transaction as represented by a **token**—such as a transaction-control block that is passed from routine to routine as it progresses through its flow. The transaction flowgraph is a pictorial representation of what happens to the tokens; it is *not* the control structure of the program that manipulates those tokens.

Figure 4.2 shows another transaction flow and the corresponding implementation of a program that creates that flow. This transaction goes through input processing, which classifies it as to type, and then passes through process A, followed by B. The result of process B may force the transaction to pass back to process A. The transaction then goes to process C, then to either D or E, and finally to output processing.

Figure 4.2b is a diagrammatic representation of a software architecture that might implement this and many other transactions. The system is controlled by an executive/scheduler/dispatcher/operating system—call it what you will. In this diagram the boxes represent processes and the links represent processing queues. The transaction enters (that is, it is created by) an input processing module in response to inputs received, for example, at a terminal. The transaction is "created" by the act of filling out a transaction-control block and placing that token on an input queue. The scheduler then examines the transaction and places it on the work queue for process A, but process A will not necessarily be activated immediately. When a process has finished working on the transaction, it

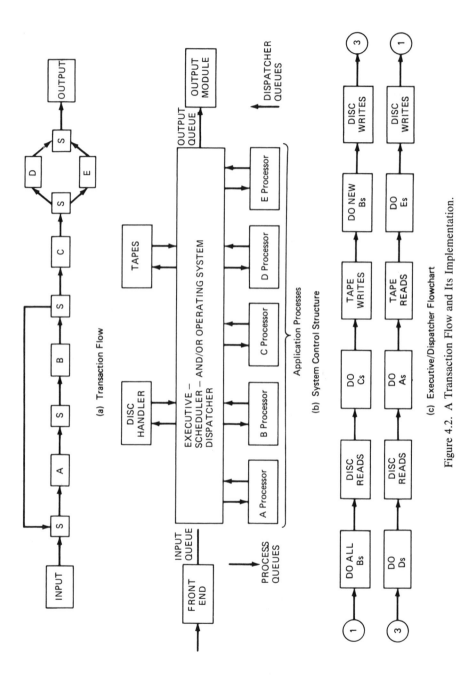

(a) Transaction Flow

(b) System Control Structure

(c) Executive/Dispatcher Flowchart

Figure 4.2. A Transaction Flow and Its Implementation.

places the transaction-control block back on a scheduler queue. The scheduler then examines the transaction control block and routes it to the next process based on information stored in the block. The scheduler contains tables or code that routes the transaction to its next process. In systems that handle hundreds of transaction types, this information is usually stored in tables rather than as explicit code. Alternatively, the dispatcher may contain no transaction control data or code; the information could be implemented as code in each transaction processing module.

Figure 4.2c shows a possible implementation of this transaction processing system (simplified). Let's say that while there could be many different transaction flows in the system, they all used only processes A, B, C, D, E, and disc and tape reads and writes, in various combinations. Just because the transaction flow order is A,B,C,D,E is no reason to invoke the processes in that order. For other transactions, not shown, the processing order might be B,C,A,E,D. A fixed processing order based on one transaction flow might not be optimum for another. Furthermore, different transactions have different priorities that may require some to wait for higher-priority transactions to be processed. Similarly, one would not delay processing for all transactions while waiting for a specific transaction to complete a necessary disc read operation.

In general, in multiprocessing systems there is no direct correspondence between the order in which processes are invoked and transaction flows. A given transaction will, of course, receive processing attention from the appropriate processing modules in the strict order required, but there could be many other things going on between the instances in which that transaction was being processed.

I left out the scheduler calls in Figure 4.2c to simplify things. Assume that there's a return of control to the scheduler after each process box. The whole program is organized as a simple loop. First, the scheduler invokes processing module B, which cleans up all transactions waiting for B processing at that moment. Then the disc reads are initiated and the scheduler turns control over to module C, which clears up all of its tasks. After the tape writes are initiated, module B is invoked again to take care of any additional work that may have accumulated for it. The process continues, and finally the entire loop starts over again. A cyclic structure like this is common in process control and communications systems, among many others. Alternatively, a more complex control structure can be used in which the processing modules are not invoked in fixed order but in an order determined by the length of the queues for those modules, the priority of the tasks, the priority of the active modules, and the state of the system with respect to I/O operations. A queue-driven approach is more common in commercial operating systems. The reasons for choosing one control architecture over another is not germane to testing. It is a performance and resource-optimization question. For more information, see BEIZ78.

3.5. Perspective

We didn't say how many computers there are: it could be one, it could be dozens, uniprocessor or parallel, single-instruction multiple data **(SIMD)** or multi-instruction multiple data **(MIMD).** We didn't restrict the communication methods between processing components: it could be via data structures, over communication lines, processing queues, or direct transfers in a call. We assumed nothing about the system's executive structure or operating system(s): interrupt driven, cyclic, multiprocessing, polled, free-running. There were no restrictions on how a transaction's identity is maintained: implicit, explicit, in transaction control blocks, or in task tables. How is the transaction's state recorded? Any way you want (but typically in the transaction's control block, assuming that such a thing exists). Transaction-flow testing is the ultimate black-box technique because all we ask is that there be something identifiable as a transaction and that the system will do predictable things to transactions.

Transaction flowgraphs are a kind of **data flowgraph** (KAVI87, KODR77, RUGG79). That is, we look at the history of operations applied to data objects. You'll note some stylistic differences in how we constructed data flowgraphs compared to the rules for constructing control flowgraphs. The most important of these is the definition of link or basic block. In control flowgraphs we defined a link or block as a set of instructions such that if any one of them was executed, all (barring bugs) would be executed. For data flowgraphs in general, and transaction flowgraphs in particular, we change the definition to identify all processes of interest. For example, in Figure 4.1 the link between nodes A and C had five distinct processes, whereas in a control flowgraph there would be only one. We do this to get a more useful, revealing, model. Nothing is lost by this practice; that is, all theory and all characteristics of graphs hold. We have broken a single link into several. We'll do the same with data flowgraphs in Chapter 5.

Another difference to which we must be sensitive is that the decision nodes of a transaction flowgraph can be complicated processes in their own rights. Our transaction-flow model is almost always a simplified version of those decisions. Many decisions have exception exits that go to central recovery processes. Similarly, links may actually contain decisions, such as a recovery process invoked when a queue integrity routine determines that the link (queue) has been compromised (for example, it was linked back to itself in a loop). The third difference we tend to ignore in our transaction-flow models is the effect of interrupts. Interrupts can do the equivalent of converting every process box into a many-splendored thing with more exit links than a porcupine has spines. We just can't put all that into our transaction-flow model—if we did, we'd gain "accuracy" at the expense of intelligibility. The model would no longer be fit for test design.

3.6. Complications

3.6.1. General

Although in simple cases transactions have a unique identity from the time they're created to the time they're completed, in many systems a transaction can give birth to others, and transactions can also merge. The simple flowgraph is inadequate to represent transaction flows that split and merge.

3.6.2. Births

Figure 4.3 shows three different possible interpretations of the decision symbol, or nodes with two or more outlinks.

Figure 4.3a shows a decision node, as in a control flowgraph. Interpreted in terms of transaction flowgraphs, this symbol means that the transaction will either take one alternative or the other, but not both. In other words, this is a decision point of a transaction flow. Figure 4.3b shows a different situation. The incoming transaction (the parent) gives birth to a new transaction (the daughter), whence both transactions continue on their separate paths, the parent retaining its identity as a transaction. I call this situation **biosis.** Figure 4.3c is similar to Figure 4.3b, except that the parent transaction is destroyed and two new transactions (daughters) are created. I call this situation **mitosis** because of its similarity to biological mitotic division.

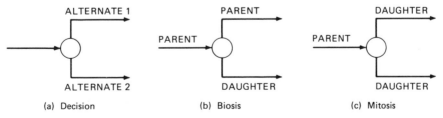

Figure 4.3. Nodes with Multiple Outlinks.

3.6.3. Mergers

Transaction-flow junction points (i.e., nodes with two or more inlinks) are potentially as troublesome as transaction-flow splits. Figure 4.4a shows the ordinary junction, which is similar to the junction in a control flowgraph. It is understood that a transaction can arrive either on one link (path 1) or the other (path 2). In Figure 4.4b (**absorption**) a predator transaction absorbs a prey. The prey is gone but the predator retains its identity. Figure 4.4c shows a slightly different situation in which two parent transactions merge to form a new daughter. In keeping with the biological flavor of this section, I call this act **conjugation.**

3.6.4. Theoretical Status and Pragmatic Solutions

The above examples do not exhaust the possible variations of interpretation of the decision and junction symbols in the context of real transaction flows. If we further consider multiprocessor systems and associated transaction coordination situations, our simple transaction-flow model no longer suffices. The most mature generic model for this kind of thing is a **Petri net** (KAVI87, MURA89, PETE76, PETE81, RAMA85, RUGG79). Petri nets use operations that can include and distinguish between all the above variations and more and also include mechanisms for explicitly representing tokens that traverse stages in the process. There is a mature theory of Petri nets (MURA89, PETE81), but it is beyond the scope of this book. Petri nets have been applied to hardware testing problems, protocol testing, network testing, and other areas, but their application to general software testing is still in its infancy. Nor do we yet have enough experience with the application of Petri nets to software testing to determine whether it is or is not a productive model for general software testing.

Recognizing that the transaction-flow model is imperfect but that a "correct" model is untried, what shall we, as testing practitioners, do? As

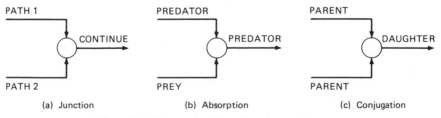

Figure 4.4. Transaction-Flow Junctions and Mergers.

with all models, we ignore the complexities that can invalidate the model and use what we can apply with ease. After all, models for testing are intended to give us insights into effective test case design—they're intuition joggers—so it doesn't matter that they're imperfect as long as the resulting tests are good. We have no problem with ordinary decisions and junctions. Here's a prescription for the troublesome cases:

1. *Biosis*—Follow the parent flow from beginning to end. Treat each daughter birth as a new flow, either to the end or to the point where the daughter is absorbed.
2. *Mitosis*—This situation involves three or more transaction flows: from the beginning of the parent's flow to the mitosis point and one additional flow for each daughter, from the mitosis point to each's respective end.
3. *Absorption*—Follow the predator as the primary flow. The prey is modeled from its beginning to the point at which it's eaten.
4. *Conjugation*—Three or more separate flows—the opposite of mitosis. From the birth of each parent proceed to the conjugation point and follow the resulting daughter from the conjugation point to her end.

Births, absorptions, and conjugations are as problematic for the software designer as they are for the software modeler and the test designer; as a consequence, such points have more than their share of bugs. The common problems are: lost daughters, wrongful deaths, and illegitimate births. So although you model transaction flows by simple flowgraphs, recognize that the likeliest place for bugs are where transactions are created, absorbed, or merged; keep track of such points and be sure to design specific tests to validate biosis, mitosis, absorption, and conjugations.

3.7. Transaction-Flow Structure

I've written harsh words about programmers who jump into the middle of loops to save a few lines of coding. The harsh words are warranted because more often than not (but not always), violations of so-called "rules" of structured design, have a deleterious impact on testability. How "well-structured" should transaction flows be? How well-structured should we expect them to be?

Just because transaction flows look like control flows, it does not follow that what constitutes good structure for code constitutes good structure for transaction flows—that's voodoo thinking based on the thaumaturgic principle of similarity.* As it turns out, transaction flows are often ill-structured and there's nothing you can do about it. Here are some of the reasons:

1. It's a *model* of a process, not just code. Humans may be involved in loops, decisions, and so on. We can't bind human behavior to software structure rules, no matter how fervently we might wish it.
2. Parts of the flows may incorporate the behavior of other systems over which we have no control. Why should we expect their behavior to be structured?
3. No small part of the totality of transaction flows exists to model error conditions, failures, malfunctions, and subsequent recovery actions. These are inherently unstructured—jumping out of loops, rampant GOTOs, and so on.
4. The number of transactions and the complexity of individual transaction flows grow over time as features are added and enhanced. Often, the world imposes the structure of the flows on us. Such structure may be the result of a congressional debate, a bilateral trade agreement, a contract, a salesman's boast after a four-martini "power lunch"—you name it. Should we expect good structure from politicians, salesmen, lawyers, and other drafters of social contracts? Try a transaction flowgraph for your income tax return if you still have doubts.
5. Systems are built out of modules and the transaction flows result from the interaction of those modules. Good system design dictates that we avoid changing modules in order to implement new transactions or to modify existing transactions. The result is that we build new paths between modules, new queues, add modules, and so on, and tie the whole together with ad hoc flags and switches to make it work. We may have to fool existing modules into doing the new job for us—that's usually preferable to changing many different modules. It's not unusual to deliberately block some paths in order to use a common part for several different kinds of transactions.
6. Our models are just that—approximations to reality. Interrupts, priorities, multitasking, multicomputers, synchronization, parallel processing, queue disciplines, polling—all of these make mincemeat out of structuring concepts that apply to units. The consequence of attempting to "structure" the transaction flows could be inefficient

---

* A fundamental law of magic. Objects and persons are manipulated through the principle of similarity by acting on an analog or facsimile of the object—for example, by sticking pins into the likeness of a hated person.

processing, poor response times, dangerous processing, security compromises, lost transaction integrity, and so on.

4. TRANSACTION-FLOW TESTING TECHNIQUES

4.1. Get the Transaction Flows

Complicated systems that process a lot of different, complicated transactions should have explicit representations of the transaction flows, or the equivalent, documented. If transaction flows are part of the system's specifications, half the battle is won. Don't expect to get pure transaction flows and don't insist on only that form of representing the system's processing requirements. There are other, equivalent representations, such as HIPO charts and Petri nets, that can serve the same purpose (MURA89, PETE76, PETE80). Also, because transaction flows can be mapped into programs, they can be described in a PDL. If such representations are used and if they are done correctly, it will be easy to create the transaction flows from them. The objective is to have a trace of what happens to transactions—a trace of the progression of actions, which, as we have seen, may not correspond to the design of the system executive or to the relation between the processing modules that work on the transaction. Transaction flows are like control flowgraphs, and consequently we should expect to have them in increasing levels of detail. It is correct and effective to have subflows analogous to subroutines in control flowgraphs, although there may not be any processing module that corresponds to such subflows.

Designers ought to understand what they're doing. And it's obvious that if they don't, they're not likely to do it right. I've made it a practice to ask for transaction flows—say, for the ten most important transactions that a system is to process—preparatory to designing the system's functional test. I hope that that information is in the specification. If it isn't, it's likely that there will be some disagreement as to what the system is supposed to be doing. More important, the system's design documentation should contain an overview section that details the main transaction flows (all of them, it is hoped). If I can't find that or the equivalent, then I don't need a lot of complicated tests to know that the system will have a lot of complicated bugs. Detailed transaction flows are a mandatory prerequisite to the rational design of a system's functional test.

Like so much in testing, the act of getting the information on which to base tests can be more effective at catching and exterminating bugs than the tests that result from that information. Insisting on getting transaction flows or the equivalent is sometimes a gentle way of convincing inept design groups that they don't know what they're doing. These are harsh words, but let's face it: superb code and unit testing will be useless if the overall design is poor. And how can there be a rational, effective design if no one on the design team can walk you through the more important transactions, step by step and alternative by alternative. I'm sure that mine is a biased sample, but every system I've ever seen that was in serious trouble had no transaction flows documented, nor had the designers provided anything that approximated that kind of functional representation; however, it's certainly possible to have a bad design even with transaction flows.*

To reiterate: the first step in using transaction flows as a basis for system testing is to get the transaction flows. Often, that's the hardest step. Occasionally, it's the only step before the project's canceled.

4.2. Inspections, Reviews, Walkthroughs

Transaction flows are a natural agenda for system reviews or inspections. It's more important over the long haul that the designers know what it is the system is supposed to be doing than how they implement that functionality. I'd start transaction-flow walkthroughs at the preliminary design review and continue them in ever greater detail as the project progresses.

1. In conducting the walkthroughs, you should:
   a. Discuss enough transaction types (i.e., paths through the transaction flows) to account for 98%–99% of the transactions the system is expected to process. Adjust the time spent and the intensity of the review in proportion to the perceived risk of failing to process each transaction properly. Let the nightmare list be your guide. The designers should name the transaction, provide its flowgraph, identify all processes, branches, loops, splits, mergers, and so on.
   b. Discuss paths through flows in functional rather than technical terms. If a nontechnical buyer's representative who understands the application is present, so much the better. The discussion should be almost completely design independent. If the designers keep coming back to the design, its a sign of trouble because they

---

* I needed transaction flows to do a throughput model of a big system. It was another one of those bad projects on which I was consulted. Timing flows only represent high-probability paths, and the detailed order in which processing occurs within a link does not usually affect the timing analysis. I was having such poor luck getting the designers to create the transaction flows that, in desperation, I sent them simplified versions suitable only to timing analysis and asked for a confirmation or a correction—hoping thereby to stir them into action. You guessed it—my model flows appeared in the next monthly design release as *the* design flows. Thankfully, my name wasn't on them.

may be implementing what they want to implement rather than what the user needs.

   c. Ask the designers to relate every flow to the specification and to show how that transaction, directly or indirectly, follows from the requirements. Don't insist on a slavish one-to-one correspondence because that could lead to a poor implementation.

2. Make transaction-flow testing the cornerstone of system functional testing just as path testing is the cornerstone of unit testing. For this you need enough tests to achieve C1 and C2 coverage of the complete set of transaction flowgraphs.

3. Select additional transaction-flow paths (beyond C1 + C2) for loops, extreme values, and domain boundaries (see Chapter 6).

4. Select additional paths for weird cases and very long, potentially troublesome transactions with high risks and potential consequential damage.

5. Design more test cases to validate all births and deaths and to search for lost daughters, illegitimate births, and wrongful deaths.

6. Publish and distribute the selected test paths through the transaction flows as early as possible so that they will exert the maximum beneficial effect on the project.

7. Have the buyer concur that the selected set of test paths through the transaction flows constitute an adequate system functional test. Negotiate a subset of these paths to be used as the basis for a formal acceptance test.

8. Tell the designers which paths will be used for testing but not (yet) the details of the test cases that force those paths. Give them enough information to design their own test cases but not so much information that they can develop a "Mickey Mouse" fix that covers a specific test case but is otherwise useless.

4.3. Path Selection

Path selection for system testing based on transaction flows should have a distinctly different flavor from that of path selection done for unit tests based on control flowgraphs. Start with a covering set of tests (C1 + C2) using the analogous criteria you used for structural path testing, but don't expect to find too many bugs on such paths.

   Select a covering set of paths based on functionally sensible transactions as you would for control flowgraphs. Confirm these with the designers. Having designed those (easy) tests, now do exactly the opposite of what you would have done for unit tests. Try to find the most tortuous, longest, strangest path from the entry to the exit of the transaction flow.

Create a catalog of these weird paths. Go over them not just with the high-level designer who laid out the transaction flows, but with the next-level designers who are implementing the modules that will process the transaction. It can be a gratifying experience, even in a good system. The act of discussing the weird paths will expose missing interlocks, duplicated interlocks, interface problems, programs working at cross-purposes, duplicated processing—a lot of stuff that would otherwise have shown up only during the final acceptance tests, or worse, after the system was operating. The entire cost of independent testing can be paid for by a few such paths for a few well-chosen transactions. This procedure is best done early in the game, while the system design is still in progress, before processing modules have been coded. I try to do it just after the internal design specifications for the processing modules are completed and just before those modules are coded. Any earlier than that, you'll get a lot of "I don't know yet" answers to your questions, which is a waste of both your time and the designer's. Any later, it's already cast into code and correction has become expensive.

This process has diminishing returns. Most competent designers won't be caught twice. You have only to show them one nasty case and they'll review all their interfaces and interlocks and you're not likely to find any new bugs from that module—but you can catch most modules and their designers once. Eventually the blatant bugs have been removed, and those that remain are due to implementation errors and wild cards. Bringing up a weird path after a few rounds of this will just make the designer smirk as she shows you just how neatly your weird cases, and several more that you hadn't thought of, are handled.

The covering set of paths belong in the system feature tests. I still try to augment cover with weird paths in addition to normal paths, if I possibly can. It gives everybody more confidence in the system and its test. I also keep weird paths in proportion to what I perceive to be the designer's lack of confidence. I suppose it's sadistic hitting a person who's down, but it's effective. Conversely, you do get fooled by supremely confident idiots and insecure geniuses.

4.4. Sensitization

I have some good news and bad news about sensitization. Most of the normal paths are very easy to sensitize—80%–95% *transaction flow* coverage (C1 + C2) is usually easy to achieve.* The bad news is that the remaining small percentage is often very difficult, if not impossible, to

---

* Remember, don't confuse *transaction-flow coverage* with *code coverage*.

achieve by fair means. While the simple paths are easy to sensitize there are many of them, so that there's a lot of tedium in test design. Usually, just identifying the normal path is enough to sensitizing it. In fact, many test designers who do mainly transaction flow testing (perhaps not by that name) are not even conscious of a sensitization issue. To them, sensitization *is* the act of defining the transaction. If there are sensitization problems on the easy paths, then bet on either a bug in transaction flows or a design bug.

How about the off-paths, the exception conditions, the path segments on which we expect to find most of the bugs? The reason these paths are often difficult to sensitize is that they correspond to error conditions, synchronization problems, overload responses, and other anomalous situations. A constant headache along this line is testing a protocol across an external interface. In order to test our abnormal paths we may have to ask the other system to simulate bad transactions or failures—it's usually a live system and getting that kind of cooperation is harder than catching Santa Claus coming down the chimney. I said that it was tough to sensitize such path segments if we were going to be fair about it. It's not as bad if we allow ourselves to play dirty. Here's a short list:

1. *Use Patches*—The dirty system tester's best, but dangerous, friend.* It's a lot easier to fake an error return from another system by a judicious patch than it is to negotiate a joint test session—besides, whom are we kidding? If we don't put the patch into *our* system, they (the ones on the other side of the interface) will have to put the patch into *their* system. In either case, somebody put in an ''unrealistic'' patch.

2. *Mistune*—Test in a system sized with grossly inadequate resources. By ''grossly'' I mean about 5%–10% of what one might expect to need. This helps to force most of the resource-related exception conditions.

3. *Break the Rules*—Transactions almost always require associated, correctly specified, data structures to support them. Often a system database generator is used to create such objects and to assure that all required objects have been correctly specified. Bypass the database generator and/or use patches to break any and all rules embodied in the database and system configuration that will help you to go down the desired path.

---

* And then there was the time I inadvertently cut off a major part of U.S. communications with Europe several times in one night by a badly installed patch during live testing.

4. *Use Breakpoints*—Put breakpoints at the branch points where the hard-to-sensitize path segment begins and then patch the transaction control block to force that path.

You can use one or all of the above methods, and many I haven't thought of, to sensitize the strange paths. These techniques are especially suitable for those long tortuous paths that avoid the exit. When you use them, you become vulnerable to the designer's cry of "foul." And there's some justification for that accusation. Here's the point, once you allow such shenanigans, you allow arbitrary patches. Who *can't* crash a system if she's allowed to patch anything anywhere, anytime? It's unreasonable to expect a system to stand up to that kind of abuse. Yet, you must do such things if you're to do a good job of testing. The solution to this dilemma is to be meticulous about such tests; to be absolutely sure that there's no other reasonable way to go down that path; to be absolutely sure that there's no error in the patch; and to be ready for a fight with the designers every time you employ such methods.

4.5. Instrumentation

Instrumentation plays a bigger role in transaction-flow testing than in unit path testing. Counters are not useful because the same module could appear in many different flows and the system could be simultaneously processing different transactions. The information of the path taken for a given transaction must be kept with that transaction. It can be recorded either by a central transaction dispatcher (if there is one) or by the individual processing modules. You need a trace of all the processing steps for the transaction, the queues on which it resided, and the entries and exits to and from the dispatcher. In some systems such traces are provided by the operating system. In other systems, such as communications systems or most secure systems, a running log that contains exactly this information is maintained as part of normal processing. You can afford heavy instrumentation compared to unit-testing instrumentation because the overhead of such instrumentation is typically small compared to the processing. Another, better alternative is to make the instrumentation part of the system design. Augment the design as needed to provide complete transaction-flow tracing for all transactions. The payoff in system debugging and performance testing alone is worth the effort for most systems. And it's a lot easier and better to design the instrumentation in than it is to retrofit it.

4.6.   Test Databases

About 30%–40% of the effort of transaction-flow test design is the design
and maintenance of the test database(s). It may be a third of the labor,
but it carries a disproportionately high part of the headaches. I've seen
two major, generic errors in the design of such databases—and they often
follow in sequence on the same project. The first error is to be unaware
that there's a test database to be designed. The result is that every programmer and tester designs his own, unique database, which is incompatible with all other programmers' and testers' needs. The consequence is
that every tester (independent or programmer) needs exclusive use of the
entire system. Furthermore, many of the tests are configuration-sensitive,
so there's no way to port one set of tests over from another suite. At
about the time that testing has ground to a halt because of this tower of
babble—when the test bed floor has expanded to several acres of gear
running around the clock—it's decided that test data bases must be configuration-controlled and centrally administered under a comprehensive
design plan. Often, because the independent testers need more elaborate
test setups than do the programmers, the responsibility is given to the test
group. That's when the second error occurs. In order to avoid a repetition
of the previous chaos, it is decided that there will be one comprehensive
database that will satisfy all testing needs. The design and debugging of
such a monster becomes a mighty project in its own right. A typical
system of a half-million lines of source code will probably need four or
five different, incompatible databases to support testing. The design of
these databases is no less important than the design of the system data
structures. It requires talented, mature, diplomatic, experienced designers—experienced both in the system design and in test design.

4.7.   Execution

If you're going to do transaction-flow testing for a system of any size, be
committed to test execution automation from the start. If more than a few
hundred test cases are required to achieve C1 + C2 transaction-flow
coverage, don't bother with transaction-flow testing if you don't have the
time and resources to almost completely automate all test execution.
You'll be running and rerunning those transactions not once, but hundreds of times over the project's life. Transaction-flow testing with the
intention of achieving C1 + C2 usually leads to a big (four- to fivefold)
increase in the number of test cases. Without execution automation you

can't expect to do it right. Capture/replay tools and other test drivers are essential. See Chapter 13 for more details.

5. IMPLEMENTATION COMMENTS

5.1. Transaction Based Systems

Let's go back to Figure 4.2b. There's a lot we can imply in this design that makes transaction-flow testing easy.

1. *Transaction Control Block*—There's an explicit transaction control block associated with every live transaction. The block contains, among other things, the transaction's type, identity, and processing state. Whether the block itself contains the information or just pointers to the information is immaterial. What matters is that there's a unique data object through which anything we want to know about a transaction is easily found. The control block is created when the transaction is born and is returned to the pool when the transaction leaves the system for archival storage.

2. *Centralized, Common, Processing Queues*—Transactions (actually, transaction control blocks) are not passed directly from one process to another but are transferred from process to process by means of centralized explicit processing queues. The dispatcher links control blocks to processes. Processes link control blocks back to the dispatcher when they are done. Instead of $O(n^2)$ ad hoc queues between n processors, the number of explicit queues is proportional to the number of processors.

3. *Transaction Dispatcher*—There is a centralized transaction dispatcher. Based on the transaction's current state and transaction type, the next process is determined from stored dispatch tables or a similar mechanism. For example, use a finite-state machine implementation (see Chapter 11).

4. *Recovery and Other Logs*—Key points in the transaction's life are recorded for several different purposes—the two most important being transaction recovery support and transaction accounting. At the very least, there are birth and death entries. Other entries may be provided on request as part of development support (e.g., debugging) or for tuning. The most complete instrumentation provides coverage certification (C1 + C2) over the transaction flows. These facilities obviate the need for special instrumentation.

5. *Self-Test Support*—The transaction control tables have privileged modes that can be used for test and diagnostic purposes. There are

special transaction types and states for normal transactions whose sole purpose is to facilitate testing. With these features in place, it is never necessary to use patches to force paths.

It's not my intention to tantalize you with a tester's paradise, but it's obvious that transaction-flow testing for a system with the above features is as easy as system testing gets. The designer has recognized that transactions are entities worth reckoning with, has probably done an explicit analysis of all transaction flows, and has implemented a design that is relatively invulnerable to even radical changes in the required flows—and, incidentally, has made the system tester's job much easier. The designer has also made it relatively unlikely that transaction-flow testing will reveal any bugs at all—the pesticide paradox.

A good system functional test achieves C1 + C2 over the transaction flows, no matter how hard that task may be or how easy the designer has made the job for us. If the design is an ad hoc mess of interprocess queues with decisions made here and there and everywhere, transaction routing determined locally in low-level routines, with most of the transaction state information implicit, then transaction-flow testing will yield rich rewards—personally, it's as much fun as taking candy away from sick babies. It's so easy to break such systems that I've sometimes been ashamed of it. But how about the testable design outlined above? Transaction-flow testing will reveal an occasional goof here and there, but rarely anything over which to panic. And whatever bugs are found are easily fixed. Our testing resources are limited and must be spent on the potentially most revealing tests. If you're testing a system with an explicit transaction-control mechanism, then don't do any more transaction-flow testing than you need to satisfy risk and contractual issues. Conversely, if it's a piece of ad hoc garbage, transaction-flow system testing is where it's at.

5.2. Hidden Languages

Don't expect to find neat decision boxes and junctions as in a control flowgraph. The actual decision may be made (and usually is) in a processing module, and the central dispatcher (if there is one) is usually indifferent to the transaction flows. Alternatively, the dispatcher may direct the flows based on control codes contained in the transaction's control block or stored elsewhere in the database. Such codes actually constitute an internal language. If an explicit mechanism of this kind does exist, the transaction flows are indeed implemented as "programs" in this internal language. A commercial operating system's job control language or the set of task control codes combined with execution files are examples of such "languages."

The trouble is that these languages are often undeclared, undefined, undocumented, and unrecognized. Furthermore, unlike formal higher-order languages and their associated compilers or interpreters, neither the language's syntax, semantics, nor processor has been debugged. The flow-control language evolves as a series of ad hoc agreements between module designers. Here are some of the things that can go wrong:

1. The language is rarely checked for self-consistency (assuming that its existence has been recognized).
2. The language must be processed, usually one step at a time, by an interpreter that may be centralized in a single routine but is more often distributed in bits and pieces among all the processing modules. That interpreter, centralized or distributed, may have bugs.
3. The "program"—i.e., the steps stored in a transaction-control table—may have bugs or may become corrupted by bugs far removed from the transaction under consideration. This is a nasty kind of bug to find. Just as a routine may pass its tests but foul the database for another routine, a transaction may pass all of its tests but, in so doing, foul the transaction-control tables for subsequent transactions.
4. Finally, any transaction processing module can have bugs.

If transaction-control tables are used to direct the flow, it is effective to treat that mechanism as if an actual language has been implemented. Look for the basic components of any language—processing steps, conditional-branch instructions, unconditional branches, program labels, subroutines (i.e., the tables can direct processing to subtables which can be used in common for several different flows), loop control, and so on. Assuming you can identify all of these elements, document a "syntax" for this primitive, undeclared language and discuss this syntax with whoever is responsible for implementing the transaction-control structure and software. The pseudolanguage approach was used to provide flexibility in implementing many different, complicated transaction flows. Therefore, it is reasonable to expect that any syntactically valid "statement" in this language should make processing sense. A syntactically valid, arbitrary statement might not provide a useful transaction, but at the very least, the system should not blow up if such a transaction were to be defined. Test the syntax and generate test cases as you would for any syntax-directed test, as discussed in Chapter 9.

6. TESTABILITY TIPS

1. Implement transaction flows along with supporting data structures as a primary specification and design tool.
2. Use explicit transaction-control blocks as a primary control mechanism.
3. Build all instrumentation in as part of the system design.
4. Use a centralized, table-driven, transaction dispatcher to control transaction flows.
5. Implement transaction control as table-driven finite-state machines (see Chapter 11) for which transaction state information is stored in the transaction-control block.
6. Be willing to add fields to transaction-control blocks and states to transaction flows if by doing so you can avoid biosis, mitosis, absorption, and conjugation.
7. Make sure there is one-to-one correspondence between transaction-flow paths and functional requirements, if possible.
8. To the extent that you can control it, apply the same structure rules to transaction flows that you apply to code—i.e., avoid jumping into or out of loops, unessential GOTOs, deeply nested loops, and so on.
9. Emulate the testability criteria for code; that is, keep the number of covering paths, number of feasible paths, and total path number as close as possible to one another.
10. Don't be afraid to design transaction-control languages. But if you do, validate the correctness and sanity of the syntax and semantics. Treat the design of the language and its translator or interpreter as you would the design of a new programming language. Test the language and its processor thoroughly before you test transactions.

7. SUMMARY

1. The methods discussed for path testing of units and programs can be applied with suitable interpretation to functional testing based on transaction flows.
2. The biggest problem and the biggest payoff may be getting the transaction flows in the first place.
3. Full coverage (C1 + C2) is required for all flows, but most bugs will be found on the strange, meaningless, weird paths.

4. Transaction-flow control may be implemented by means of an undeclared and unrecognized internal language. Get it recognized, get it declared, and then test its syntax using the methods of Chapter 9.
5. The practice of attempting to design tests based on transaction-flow representation of requirements and discussing those attempts with the designer can unearth more bugs than any tests you run.

5

DATA-FLOW TESTING

1. SYNOPSIS

Data-flow testing uses the control flowgraph to explore the unreasonable things that can happen to data **(data-flow anomalies).** Consideration of data-flow anomalies leads to test path selection strategies that fill the gaps between complete path testing and branch and statement testing. Comparisons of strategies, generalization, tools, and effectiveness.

2. DATA-FLOW TESTING BASICS

2.1. Motivation and Assumptions

2.1.1. What Is It?

Data-flow testing is the name given to a family of test strategies based on selecting paths through the program's control flow in order to explore sequences of events related to the status of data objects. For example, pick enough paths to assure that every data object has been initialized prior to use or that all defined objects have been used for something.

2.1.2. Motivation

I can't improve on Rapps and Weyuker's (RAPP82) eloquent motivation for data-flow testing:

> "It is our belief that, just as one would not feel confident about a program without executing every statement in it as part of some test, one should not feel confident about a program without having seen the effect of using the value produced by each and every computation."

For more motivation, reread Section 3.4, Chapter 2. *At least half of contemporary source code consists of data declaration statements—that is, statements that define data structures, individual objects, initial or default values, and attributes.* To the extent that we achieve the widely sought goal of reusable code, we can expect the balance of source code statements to shift ever more toward data statement domination.

In all known hardware technologies, memory components have been, are, and are expected to be cheaper than processing components. A flip-flop (basic storage element) requires two transistors, but 1 bit of an adder takes six transistors.* Another advantage to memory is geometrical regularity. Memory chips are regular—they look as if they were woven—conversely, logic elements are more haphazard.** The memory units' geometric regularity permits tighter packing and therefore more elements per chip. This fact will, as it has in the past, continue to push software into data-dominated designs.

2.1.3. New Paradigms—Data-Flow Machines

Low-cost computational and memory elements have made possible massively parallel machines that can break the time logjam of current architectures. Most computers today are **Von Neumann machines.** This architecture features interchangeable storage of instructions and data in the same memory units. The Von Neumann architecture executes one instruction at a time in the following, typical, microinstruction sequence:

1. Fetch instruction from memory.
2. Interpret instruction.
3. Fetch operand(s).
4. Process (execute).
5. Store result (perhaps in registers).
6. Increment program counter (pointer to next instruction).
7. GOTO 1.

The pure Von Neumann machine has only one set of control circuitry to interpret the instruction, only one set of registers in which to process the data, and only one execution unit (e.g., arithmetic/logic unit). This design leads to a sequential, instruction- by-instruction execution, which in turn

---

* Memory elements can be built with one transistor (or none) and adders can do with less than six, but for all known technologies, whatever design wizardry is applied, memory is cheaper than processing.
** Programmed logic arrays (PLAs) are geometrically regular, but they pay for that by effectively discarding many of their components, and therefore they can't achieve as high an effective density as memory.

leads to control-flow dominance in our thinking. The Von Neumann machine forces sequence onto problems that may not inherently be sequential.

Massively parallel **(multi-instruction, multidata—MIMD)** machines, by contrast, have multiple mechanisms for executing steps 1–7 above and can therefore fetch several instructions and/or objects in parallel. They can also do arithmetic or logical operations simultaneously on different data objects. While such machines are still in the R&D phase, it is clear that they are dominated by data-flow thinking to which control flow takes a back seat (OXLE84). Even though you may not now be programming a real MIMD machine, current language and compiler development trends are toward abstract MIMD machines in which the decision of how to sequence parallel computation steps are left to the compiler (SHIY87). Just as we found that compilers do a better job (on average) than humans at assigning registers, we can expect such compilers to do a better job of sequencing. If the implementation is for an MIMD machine, then the compiler will produce parallel (data-flow) instructions while for a conventional machine it will produce sequential instructions. In other words, the sequential (Von Neumann) machine is the special case of a parallel machine with only one processor. It is reasonable to expect languages to evolve toward the support of the more general case. Whether compiled to

Given L, t, and d, solve for Z and H_c.

$$\cos C = \cos L \sin t$$
$$\tan M = \cot L \cos t$$
$$\tan (Z + F) = -\sin L \tan t$$
$$\tan F = \cos C \tan (M + d)$$
$$\sin H_c = \sin C \sin (M + d)$$
$$Z = (Z + F) - F$$

$t_1 := \cot L$		$t_3 := t_3 * t_4$	*/ $\cos C$ /*
$t_2 := \cos t$		$t_4 := \tan t_1$	*/ $\tan (M + d)$ /*
$t_3 := t_1 * t_2$	*/ $\tan M$ /*	$t_4 := t_3 * t_4$	*/ $\tan F$ /*
$t_1 := \tan^{-1} t_3$	*/ M /*	$t_4 := \tan^{-1} t_4$	*/ F /*.
$t_1 := t_1 + d$	*/ $M + d$ /*	$Z := t_2 - t_4$	
$t_2 := -\sin L$		$t_3 := \cos^{-1} t_3$	*/ C /*
$t_3 := \tan t$		$t_3 := \sin t_3$	*/ $\sin C$ /*
$t_2 := t_2 * t_3$	*/ $\tan (Z + F)$ /*	$t_1 := \sin t_1$	*/ $\sin (M + d)$ /*
$t_2 := \tan^{-1} t_2$	*/ $Z + F$ /*	$H_c := t_1 * t_3$	*/ $\sin H_c$ /*
$t_3 := \cos L$		$H_c := \sin^{-1} H_c$	
$t_4 := \sin t$			

Figure 5.1. Von Neumann Navigation Calculation PDL.

one or many processing units, from the programmer's point of view, it will be data-flow software that has to be tested.

Figure 5.1 shows the PDL for solving some navigation equations (BOWD77) on a Von Neumann machine that has a coprocessor to calculate trigonometric functions. The control flowgraph corresponding to Figure 5.1 is trivial: it has exactly one link. The implementation shown requires twenty-one steps and four temporary memory locations. Figure 5.2

Given L, t, and d, solve for Z and H_c.

$$\cos C = \cos L \sin t$$
$$\tan M = \cot L \cos t$$
$$\tan (Z + F) = -\sin L \tan t$$
$$\tan F = \cos C \tan (M + d)$$
$$\sin H_c = \sin C \sin (M + d)$$
$$Z = (Z + F) - F$$

```
PAR DO: CSL  := cos L    SNT := sin t
        CTL  := cot L    CST := cos t
        SNL  := sin L    TNT := tan t
END PAR:
PAR DO: CSC  := CSL*SNT       */ cos C /*
        TNM  := CTL*CST       */ tan M /*
        TZF  := -SNL*TNT      */ tan (Z+F) /*
END PAR:
PAR DO:  C   := cos⁻¹ CSC    */ C /*
         M   := tan⁻¹ TNM    */ M /*
         ZPF := tan⁻¹ TZF    */ Z + F /*
END PAR
PAR DO: MPD := M + d        */ M + d /*
        SNC := sin C        */ sin C /*
END PAR:
PAR DO: TMD := tan MPD      */ tan (M + d) /*
        SMD := sin MPD      */ sin (M + d) /*
END PAR:
PAR DO: TNF := CSC*TMD      */ tan F /*
        SHC := SNC*SMD      */ sin Hc /*
END PAR:
PAR DO:  Hc := sin⁻¹ SHC
         F  := tan⁻¹ TNF    */ F /*
END PAR:
        Z   := ZPF − F
```

Figure 5.2. Data-flow Machine Navigation Calculation PDL.

shows a data-flow PDL for solving the same set of equations. A corresponding data flowgraph is shown in Figure 5.3. The "PAR DO" notation means that the calculations within its scope (PAR DO/END PAR) can be done in parallel. The nodes, which I've shown as expressions, denote operations (for example, tan(x), *, sin(x)) and the links denote that the result of the operation at the arrow's tail is needed for the operation at the arrow's head. This flowgraph is simplified because we're really doing two things at each node: an assignment and an arithmetic or trigonometric operation. As always when we have a graph, we should think about ways to cover it.

One of the advantages of the data flowgraph (as we saw for transaction flows) is that there's no restriction to uniprocessing as there is for the control flowgraph. There is a control flow here—actually, there are several independent, parallel streams. When we go back to the Von

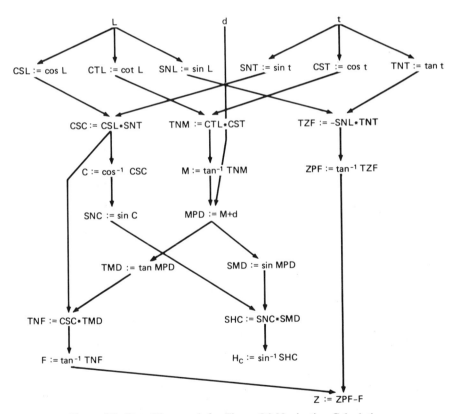

Figure 5.3. Data Flowgraph for Figure 5.2 Navigation Calculations.

Neumann machine for the rest of this book, we'll be forcing these control streams into one sequential control flow as usual. The Von Neumann machine implementation shown in Figure 5.1 is not unique. There are thousands of different orders, all correct, in which the operations could have been done. There might be a different control flowgraph for each such variant, but the underlying relation between the data objects shown in Figure 5.3 would not change. From our (Von Neumann) perspective, the kind of data flowgraph shown in Figure 5.3 is a specification of relations between objects. When we say that we want to cover this graph, we mean that we want to be sure that all such relations have been explored under test.

2.1.4. The Bug Assumptions

The bug assumption for data-flow testing strategies is that control flow is generally correct and that something has gone wrong with the software so that data objects are not available when they should be, or silly things are being done to data objects. Also, if there is a control-flow problem, we expect it to have symptoms that can be detected by data-flow analysis.

2.2. Data Flowgraphs

2.2.1. General

The **data flowgraph** is a graph consisting of nodes and **directed links** (i.e., links with arrows on them). Although we'll be doing data-flow testing, we won't be using data flowgraphs as such. Rather, we'll use an ordinary control flowgraph annotated to show what happens to the data objects of interest at the moment. If we were using a data-flow machine or language, the graph of Figure 5.3 would be the graph we would work with directly. With a Von Neumann machine, our objective is to expose deviations between the data flows we have (however they be implemented) and the data flows we want—such as that which might be specified by Figure 5.3.

2.2.2. Data Object State and Usage

Data objects can be created, killed and/or used. They can be used in two distinct ways: in a calculation or as part of a control flow predicate. The following symbols* denote these possibilities:

---

* I don't like these particular symbols because the literature is contradictory. Some authors use u to mean "undefined," c for "control use," p for "processing use," and r for "reference"; some use other conventions. Like it or not, the above notation is dominant.

d—defined, created, initialized, etc.

k—killed, undefined, released.

u—used for something.

   c—used in a calculation.

   p—used in a predicate.

1. *Defined*—An object is **defined** explicitly when it appears in a data declaration or implicitly (as in FORTRAN) when it appears on the left-hand side of an assignment statement. "Defined" can also be used to mean that a file has been opened, a dynamically allocated object has been allocated, something is pushed onto the stack, a record written, and so on. Be broad in your interpretation of "defined" or "create" and you'll find more applications to data-flow testing than you might think of at first.

2. *Killed or Undefined*—An object is **killed** or **undefined** when it is released or otherwise made unavailable, or when its contents are no longer known with certitude. For example, the loop control variable in FORTRAN is undefined when the loop is exited; release of dynamically allocated objects back to the availability pool is "killing" or "undefining"; return of records; the old top of the stack after it is popped; a file is closed. Note that an assignment statement can simultaneously kill and (re)define. For example, if A had been previously defined and we do a new assignment such as A := 17, we have killed A's previous value and redefined A. A very precise model would denote a typical assignment statement by *kd*. In practice, however, because killing the old value is usually implicit in an assignment statement and because a use between the (implicit) *k* and the *d* is impossible, we can drop the *k* and use a simple *d* to model assignment statements.

   Define and kill are complementary operations. That is, they generally come in pairs and one does the opposite of the other. When you see complementary operations on data objects it should be a signal to you that a data-flow model, and therefore data-flow testing methods, might be effective.

3. *Usage*—A variable is used for **computation** (*c*) when it appears on the right-hand side of an assignment statement, as a pointer, as part of a pointer calculation, a file record is read or written, and so on. It is **used** in a **predicate** (*p*) when it appears directly in a predicate (for example, IF A>B. . .), but also implicitly as the control variable of a loop, in an expression used to evaluate the control flow of a case

statement, as a pointer to an object that will be used to direct control flow. Predicate usage does not preclude computational use, or vice versa; in some languages, usage can be for both predicate and computation simultaneously—for example, a test-and-clear machine language instruction.

2.2.3. Data-Flow Anomalies

There are as many notions of data-flow anomalies as there are modelers. The notions presented here are by consensus those considered to be most useful. An anomaly is denoted by a two-character sequence of actions. For example, *ku* means that the object is killed and then used (possible in some languages), whereas *dd* means that the object is defined twice without an intervening usage. What is an anomaly may depend on the application. For example, the sequence

$$A := C + D$$
$$IF\ A > 0\ THEN\ X := 1\ ELSE\ X := -1$$
$$A := B + C$$

seems reasonable because it corresponds to *dpd* for variable A, but in the context of some secure systems it might be objectionable because the system doctrine might require several assignments of A to zero prior to reuse. For example,

$$A := C + D$$
$$IF\ A > 0\ THEN\ X := 1\ ELSE\ X := -1$$
$$A := 0$$
$$A := 0$$
$$A := 0$$
$$A := B + C$$

There are nine possible two-letter combinations for *d, k* and *u*. Some are bugs, some are suspicious, and some are okay.

dd—probably harmless but suspicious. Why define the object twice without an intervening usage?

dk—probably a bug. Why define the object without using it?

du—the normal case. The object is defined, then used.

kd—normal situation. An object is killed, then redefined.

kk—harmless but probably buggy. Did you want to be sure it was really killed?

ku—a bug. The object doesn't exist in the sense that its value is undefined or indeterminate. For example, the loop-control value in a FORTRAN program after exit from the loop.

ud—usually not a bug because the language permits reassignment at almost any time.

uk—normal situation.
uu—normal situation.

In addition to the above two-letter situations there are six single-letter situations. We'll use a leading dash to mean that nothing of interest (*d,k,u*) occurs prior to the action noted along the entry-exit path of interest and a trailing dash to mean that nothing happens after the point of interest to the exit.

−*k*: possibly anomalous because from the entrance to this point on the path, the variable had not been defined. We're killing a variable that does not exist; but note that the variable might have been created by a called routine or might be global.

−*d*: okay. This is just the first definition along this path.

−*u*: possibly anomalous. Not anomalous if the variable is global and has been previously defined.

k−: not anomalous. The last thing done on this path was to kill the variable.

d−: possibly anomalous. The variable was defined and not used on this path; but this could be a global definition or within a routine that defines the variables for other routines.

u−: not anomalous. The variable was used but not killed on this path. Although this sequence is not anomalous, it signals a frequent kind of bug. If *d* and *k* mean dynamic storage allocation and return respectively, this could be an instance in which a dynamically allocated object was not returned to the pool after use—not a bug if we expect some other routine to return it.

The single-letter situations do not lead to clear data-flow anomalies but only the possibility thereof. Also, whether or not a single-letter situation is anomalous is an integration testing issue rather than a component testing issue because the interaction of two or more components is involved. Although the easier data-flow anomalies can be exhibited by testing a single component, the more difficult (and more frequent) anomalies are those that involve several components—i.e., integration data-flow bugs.

2.2.4. Data-Flow Anomaly State Graph

Our data-flow anomaly model prescribes that an object can be in one of four distinct states:

K—undefined, previously killed, does not exist.

D—defined but not yet used for anything.

U—has been used for computation or in predicate.

A—anomalous.

Don't confuse these capital letters (K,D,U,A), which denote the state of the variable, with the program action, denoted by lowercase letters (k,d,u). Figure 5.4 (after HUAN79) shows what I call the "unforgiving model," because it holds that once a variable becomes anomalous it can never return to a state of grace.*

My data-flow anomaly state graph differs from Huang's because I call the kk sequence anomalous, whereas he does not. Assume that the variable starts in the K state—that is, it has not been defined or does not exist. If an attempt is made to use it or to kill it (e.g., say that we're talking about opening, closing, and using files and that "killing" means closing), the object's state becomes anomalous (state A) and, once it is anomalous, no action can return the variable to a working state. If it is defined (d), it goes into the D, or defined but not yet used, state. If it has been defined (D) and redefined (d) or killed without use (k), it becomes anomalous, while usage (u) brings it to the U state. If in U, redefinition (d) brings it to D, u keeps it in U, and k kills it.

Huang (HUAN79) has a more forgiving alternate model (Figure 5.5). This graph has three normal and three anomalous states and he considers the kk sequence not to be anomalous. The difference between this state graph and Figure 5.4 is that redemption is possible. A proper action from any of the three anomalous states returns the variable to a useful working state. The point of showing you this alternative anomaly state graph is to

---

* This state graph doesn't support the single-letter anomalies. We'd have to add more states to do that.

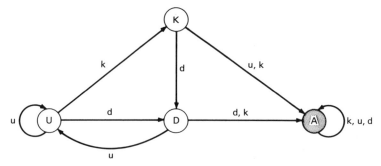

Figure 5.4. Unforgiving Data Flow Anomaly State Graph.

demonstrate that the specifics of an anomaly depends on such things as language, application, context, or even your frame of mind. In principle, you must create a new definition of data flow anomaly (e.g., a new state graph) in each situation. You must at least verify that the anomaly definition behind the theory or imbedded in a data flow anomaly test tool is appropriate to your situation.

2.2.5.   Static Versus Dynamic Anomaly Detection

Static analysis is analysis done on source code without actually executing it (GHEZ81). **Dynamic analysis** is done on the fly as the program is being executed and is based on intermediate values that result from the program's execution. Source-code syntax error detection is the archetypal static analysis result, whereas a division by zero warning is the archetypal

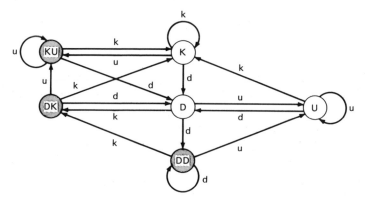

Figure 5.5. Forgiving Data Flow Anomaly State Graph.

dynamic analysis result. If a problem, such as a data-flow anomaly, can be detected by static analysis methods, then it does not belong in testing—it belongs in the language processor.

There's actually a lot more static analysis for data flow anomalies going on in current language processors than you might realize at first. Languages which force variable declarations (e.g., Pascal) can detect $-u$ and ku anomalies and optimizing compilers can detect some (but not all) instances of dead variables. The run-time resident portion of the compiler and/or the operating system also does dynamic analysis for us and therefore helps in testing by detecting anomalous situations. Most anomalies are detected by such means; that is, we don't have to put in special software or instrumentation to detect an attempt, say, to read a closed file, but we do have to assure that we design tests that will traverse paths on which such things happen.

Why isn't static analysis enough? Why is testing required? Could not a vastly expanded language processor detect all anomalies? No. The problem is provably unsolvable. Barring unsolvability problems, though, there are many things for which current notions of static analysis are inadequate.

1. *Dead Variables*—Although it is often possible to prove that a variable is dead or alive at a given point in the program (in fact, optimizing compilers depend on being able to do just that), the general problem is unsolvable.
2. *Arrays*—Arrays are problematic in that the array is defined or killed as a single object, but reference is to specific locations within the array. Array pointers are usually dynamically calculated, so there's no way to do a static analysis to validate the pointer value. And even if the pointer is within bounds, how do we know that the specific array element accessed has been initialized? In many languages, dynamically allocated arrays contain garbage unless explicitly initialized and therefore, $-u$ anomalies are possible. In Rocky Mountain Basic for example, arrays can be dynamically redimensioned without losing their contents. This feature is very handy, but think of what that does to static validation of array pointer values.
3. *Records and Pointers*—The array problem and the difficulty with pointers is a special case of multipart data structures. We have the same problem with records and the pointers to them. Also, in many applications we create files and their names dynamically and there's no way to determine, without execution, whether such objects are in the proper state on a given path or, for that matter, whether they exist at all.

4. *Dynamic Subroutine or Function Names in a Call*—A subroutine or function name is a dynamic variable in a call. What is passed, or a combination of subroutine names and data objects, is constructed on a specific path. There's no way, without executing the path, to determine whether the call is correct or not.

5. *False Anomalies*—Anomalies are specific to paths. Even a "clear bug" such as *ku* may not be a bug if the path along which the anomaly exist is unachievable. Such "anomalies" are **false anomalies.** Unfortunately, the problem of determining whether a path is or is not achievable is unsolvable.

6. *Recoverable Anomalies and Alternate State Graphs*—What constitutes an anomaly depends on context, application, and semantics. Huang provided two anomaly state graphs (Figures 5.4 and 5.5), but I didn't agree with his first one so I changed it. The second graph is also a good model, one based on the idea that anomaly recovery is possible. How does the compiler know which model I have in mind? It can't because the definition of "anomaly" is not fundamental. The language processor must have a built-in anomaly definition with which you may or may not (with good reason) agree.

7. *Concurrency, Interrupts, System Issues*—As soon as we get away from the simple single-task uniprocessor environment and start thinking in terms of systems, most anomaly issues become vastly more complicated. How often do we define or create data objects at an interrupt level so that they can be processed by a lower-priority routine? Interrupts can make the "correct" anomalous and the "anomalous" correct. True concurrency (as in an MIMD machine) and pseudoconcurrency (as in multiprocessing) systems can do the same to us. Much of integration and system testing is aimed at detecting data-flow anomalies that cannot be detected in the context of a single routine.

Although static analysis methods have limits, they are worth using and a continuing trend in language processor design has been better static analysis methods, especially for data flow anomaly detection. That's good because it means there's less for us to do as testers and we have far too much to do as it is.

2.3. The Data-Flow Model

2.3.1. *General*

Our data-flow model is based on the program's control flowgraph—don't confuse that with the program's data flowgraph. We annotate each link with symbols (for example, d, k, u, c, p) or sequences of symbols (for example, dd, du, ddd) that denote the sequence of data operations on that link with respect to the variable of interest. Such annotations are called **link weights.** There is a (possibly) different set of link weights for every variable and for every element of an array. The control flowgraph's structure (that is, the nodes and the links that connect them) is the same for every variable: it is the weights that change.*

2.3.2. Components of the Model

Here are the modeling rules:

1. To every statement there is a node, whose name (number) is unique. Every node has at least one outlink and at least one inlink except exit nodes, which do not have outlinks, and entry nodes, which do not have inlinks.
2. **Exit nodes** are dummy nodes placed at the outgoing arrowheads of exit statements (e.g., END, RETURN), to complete the graph. Similarly, **entry nodes** are dummy nodes placed at entry statements (e.g., BEGIN) for the same reason.
3. The outlink of **simple statements** (statements with only one outlink) are weighted by the proper sequence of data-flow actions for that statement. Note that the sequence can consist of more than one letter. For example, the assignment statement A:= A + B in most languages is weighted by cd or possibly ckd for variable A. Languages that permit multiple simultaneous assignments and/or compound statements can have anomalies within the statement. The sequence must correspond to the order in which the object code will be executed for that variable.
4. **Predicate nodes** (e.g., IF-THEN-ELSE, DO WHILE, CASE) are weighted with the p-use(s) on *every* outlink, appropriate to that outlink.
5. Every sequence of simple statements (e.g., a sequence of nodes with one inlink and one outlink) can be replaced by a pair of nodes that has, as weights on the link between them, the concatenation of link weights.

---

* Readers familiar with the data-flow testing literature may note (and object) that I assign the weights to the links rather than to the nodes, contrary to the usual practice, which assigns weights to nodes, except predicate uses, which are assigned to outlinks. The model described in Section 2.3.2 results in equivalent graphs because it is always possible to convert a node-weighted model to a link-weighted model, or vice versa. My use of link weights rather than node weights is not capricious—it is to provide consistency with the general node reduction algorithm of Chapters 8 and 12. I'd rather, especially in Chapter 12, use only relation matrices. Node weights would have forced me to introduce incidence matrices in addition to relation matrices in a text already overloaded with abstractions.

6. If there are several data-flow actions on a given link for a given variable, then the weight of the link is denoted by the sequence of actions on that link for that variable.

7. Conversely, a link with several data-flow actions on it can be replaced by a succession of equivalent links, each of which has at most one data-flow action for any variable. In all that follows, from the point of view of discussing the strategies, we'll assume that such a transformation has been done.*

2.3.3. Putting It Together

Figure 5.6a shows the control flowgraph that we first saw as Figures 3.2 to 3.6 in Chapter 3. I've kept the node labels and marked the decision nodes with the variables in the control-flow predicate. We don't need the actual predicate here—it's enough to know the names of the predicate variables. Also, the nodes are numbered so that we can more easily refer to them and to the intervening links.

Figure 5.6b shows this control flowgraph annotated for variables X and Y data flows (they're identical). There's a *dcc* on the first link (1,3) and nothing else because nothing else is done with these variables. I've assumed that killing is implicit in assignment and that explicit killing is not necessary.

Figure 5.6c shows the same control flowgraph annotated for variable Z. Z is first defined by an assignment statement on the first link. Z is used in a predicate ($Z >= 0$?) at node 3, and therefore both outlinks of that node—(3,4) and (3,5)—are marked with a *p*. Link (4,5) has $Z := Z-1$, which is a computational use followed by a definition and hence the *cd* annotation. There are two more instances of predicate use—at nodes 8 and 9.

The data-flow annotation for variable V is shown in Figure 5.6d. Don't confuse array V() with variable V; similarly for U() versus U. The assignment statement $V(U),U(V) := (Z+V)*U$ (see Figure 3.2) is compound. I've modeled it as two separate statements with the result that there are a total of three *c*-uses of this variable at link (6,7): two on the right-hand side of the assignment and once for the array pointer.

If there aren't too many variables of interest, you can annotate the control flowgraph by using the standard data-flow actions with subscripts to denote the variables. For example: d_x, k_x, u_x, c_x, and p_x denote the

---

* The strategies, as defined by Weyuker et al. (FRAN88, RAPP82, RAPP85) are defined over a model programming language that avoids complexities met in many real languages. For example, anomalies within a statement are effectively forbidden, as is isolated code. Although the strategies are developed, and theorems proved over a simplified language, it does not obviate the utility of the strategies when applied to real languages.

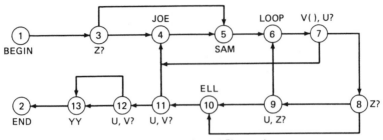

(a) Unannotated Control Flowgraph

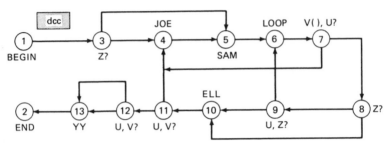

(b) Control Flowgraph Annotated for X and Y Data Flows

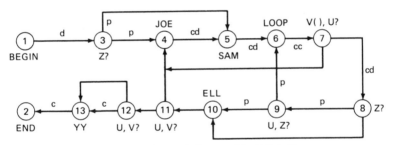

(c) Control Flowgraph Annotated for Z Data Flow

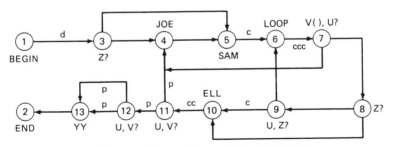

(d) Control Flowgraph Annotated for V Data Flow

Figure 5.6. Control Flowgraphs.

actions for variable x, whereas d_y, k_y, u_y, c_y, and p_y denote the actions for variable y.

3. DATA-FLOW TESTING STRATEGIES

3.1. General

Data-flow testing strategies are structural strategies. We saw in Chapter 3, Section 2.7, how to construct a family of structural testing strategies based on the length (in links or traversed nodes) of path segments to be used to construct test paths. This is only one family of an infinite number of families of possible test strategies. Ntafos (NTAF84B) generalizes the idea by defining **required element testing** as a way of generating a family of test strategies based on a structural characterization of the way test cases are to be defined (i.e., how we pick nodes, links, and/or sequences of nodes or links to be included in a test case) and a functional characterization that test cases must satisfy. Pure structural and functional testing as well as hybrid strategies can be defined within his conceptual framework.

Restricting ourselves to structural strategies, any algorithm for selecting links and/or nodes defines a corresponding (possibly useless) test strategy. In path-testing strategies, the only structural characteristic used was the raw program-control flowgraph without consideration of what happened on those links. In other words, nodes and links are considered to have no property other than the fact that they exist. Higher-level path-testing strategies based, say, on adjacent link pairs or triplets take more of the control-flow structure into account, but still no other information than is implicit in the control flowgraph.

In contrast to the path-testing strategies, data-flow strategies take into account what happens to data objects on the links in addition to the raw connectivity of the graph. In other words, data flow strategies require data-flow link weights (d,k,u,c,p).* Data-flow testing strategies are based on selecting test path segments (also called **subpaths**) that satisfy some characteristic of data flows for all data objects. For example, all subpaths that contain a d (or u, k, du, dk). Given a rule for selecting test path segments, a major objective of testing research has been to determine the relative strength of the strategy corresponding to that rule—that is, to find out whether it is stronger or weaker than some other strategy, or incomparable. A strategy X is **stronger** than another strategy Y if all test cases

---

* Other structural testing strategies could require some other property that can be expressed by link weights. For example, suppose our testing concern is the mean execution time of the routine and that passing or failing is determined by whether or not timing objectives are met. In that case, the link weights would be link execution time and branch probabilities (see Chapter 8, Section 5.5.3).

produced under Y are included in those produced under X—conversely for **weaker.** All structural strategies are weaker than total path testing. Data-flow testing strategies provide one set of families that fill the gap.

3.2. Terminology

We'll assume for the moment that all paths are achievable. Some terminology:

1. A **definition-clear path segment*** (with respect to variable X) is a connected sequence of links such that X is (possibly) defined on the first link and not redefined or killed on any subsequent link of that path segment. All paths in Figure 5.6b are definition clear because variables X and Y are defined only on the first link (1,3) and not thereafter. Similarly for variable V in Figure 5.6d. In Figure 5.6c, we have a more complicated situation. The following path segments are definition-clear: (1,3,4), (1,3,5), (5,6,7,4), (7,8,9,6,7), (7,8,9,10), (7,8,10), (7,8,10,11). Subpath (1,3,4,5) is not definition-clear because the variable is defined on (1,3) and again on (4,5). For practice, try finding all the definition-clear subpaths for this routine (i.e., for all variables).

   The fact that there is a definition-clear subpath between two nodes does not imply that all subpaths between those nodes are definition-clear; in general, there are many subpaths between nodes, and some could have definitions on them and some not. Note that a definition-clear path segment does not preclude loops. For example, a loop consisting of links (i,j) and (j,i) could have a definition on (i,j) and a use on (j,i). Observe that if we have included such loop segments in a test, by the definition of definition-clear path segment, there is no need to go around again. Thus, although these strategies allow

---

* The definitions of this section are informal variants of those presented in the literature, which do not usually take into account the possibility that a sequence of data-flow actions can take place on a given link for a given variable. The theory, as developed (e.g., FRAN88, RAPP82, RAPP85) is over a language that does not permit such complications. The strategies are based on models for which one and only one data-flow action occurs on each link (actually, at each node) for any variable. Associating the data-flow action with the links rather than with the nodes (as we do) and allowing multiple data-flow actions per link complicates the model considerably but does not change the fundamental results of the theory. The more realistic model, with multiple data-flow actions on links, can be converted to the simpler model of the theory by just breaking up a link on which multiple actions take place into a sequence of equivalent links. For example, a *dcc* link becomes three successive links with a *d*, a *c* and a *c* action on them, respectively. Then the definitions, as given, apply. Predicate uses in the literature are always associated with links and, in this respect, the models coincide.

loops, the loops need be traversed at most once; therefore, the number of test paths is always finite. As a consequence, all of these strategies must be weaker than all paths because we can always "create" a bug that is manifested only after a loop has been iterated an arbitrarily high number of times.

We consider one variable (X) at a time and look at all the links on which X is defined. We want to examine interactions between a variable's definition and the subsequent uses of that definition. If there are several definitions without intervening uses along a given path, then there can be no interaction between the first definition and its uses on that path. The test criteria are based on the uses of a variable which can be reached from a given definition of that variable (if any).

2. A **loop-free path segment** is a path segment for which every node is visited at most once. Path (4,5,6,7,8,10) in Figure 5.6c is loop free, but path (10,11,4,5,6,7,8,10,11,12) is not because nodes 10 and 11 are each visited twice.

3. A **simple path segment** is a path segment in which at most one node is visited twice. For example, in Figure 5.6c, (7,4,5,6,7) is a simple path segment. A simple path segment is either loop-free or if there is a loop, only one node is involved.

4. A **du path** from node i to k is a path segment such that if the last link has a computational use of X, then the path is simple and definition-clear; if the penultimate node is j—that is, the path is $(i,p,q,...,r,s,t,j,k)$ and link (j,k) has a predicate use—then the path from i to j is both loop-free and definition-clear.

3.3.   The Strategies

3.3.1.   Overview

The structural test strategies discussed below (FRAN88, RAPP82, RAPP85) are based on the program's control flowgraph. They differ in the extent to which predicate uses and/or computational uses of variables are included in the test set. The strategies also differ as to whether or not all paths of a given type are required or only one path of that type—that is, all predicate uses versus at least one predicate use; all computational uses versus at least one computational use; both computational and predicate uses versus either one or the other. Not all variations are interesting, nor have all been investigated.

3.3.2. All-du Paths

The **all-*du*-paths (ADUP) strategy** is the strongest data-flow testing strategy discussed here. It requires that *every du* path from *every* definition of *every* variable to *every* use of that definition be exercised under some test. In Figure 5.6b, because variables X and Y are used only on link (1,3), any test that starts at the entry satisfies this criterion (for variables X and Y, but not for all variables as required by the strategy). The situation for variable Z (Figure 5.6c) is more complicated because the variable is redefined in many places. For the definition on link (1,3) we must exercise paths that include subpaths (1,3,4) and (1,3,5). The definition on link (4,5) is covered by any path that includes (5,6), such as subpath (1,3,4,5,6, ...). The (5,6) definition requires paths that include subpaths (5,6,7,4) and (5,6,7,8). Variable V (Figure 5.6d) is defined only once on link (1,3). Because V has a predicate use at node 12 and the subsequent path to the end must be forced for both directions at node 12, the all-*du*-paths strategy for this variable requires that we exercise all loop-free entry/exit paths and at least one path that includes the loop caused by (11,4). Note that we must test paths that include both subpaths (3,4,5) and (3,5) even though neither of these has V definitions. They must be included because they provide alternate *du* paths to the V use on link (5,6). Although (7,4) is not used in the test set for variable V, it will be included in the test set that covers the predicate uses of array variable V() and U.

The all-*du*-paths strategy *is* a strong criterion, but it does not take as many tests as it might seem at first because any one test simultaneously satisfies the criterion for several definitions and uses of several different variables.

3.3.3. All-Uses Strategy

Just as we reduced our ambitions by stepping down from all paths (P_∞) to branch coverage (P_2), say, we can reduce the number of test cases by asking that the test set include *at least one* path segment from every definition to every use that can be reached by that definition—this is called the **all-uses (AU) strategy.** The strategy is that *at least one* definition-clear path from *every* definition of *every* variable to *every* use of that definition be exercised under some test. In Figure 5.6d, ADUP requires that we include subpaths (3,4,5) and (3,5) in some test because subsequent uses of V, such as on link (5,6), can be reached by either alternative. In AU either (3,4,5) or (3,5) can be used to start paths, but we don't have to use both. Similarly, we can skip the (8,10) link if we've included the

(8,9,10) subpath. Note the hole. We must include (8,9,10) in some test cases because that's the only way to reach the *c* use at link (9,10)—but suppose our bug for variable V is on link (8,10) after all? Find a covering set of paths under AU for Figure 5.6d.

3.3.4.   All-p-Uses/Some-c-Uses and All-c-Uses/Some-p-Uses Strategies

Weaker criteria require fewer test cases to satisfy. We would like a criterion that is stronger than P_2 but weaker than AU. Therefore, select cases as for AU (Section 3.3.3) except that if we have a predicate use, then (presumably) there's no need to select an additional computational use (if any). More formally, the **all-*p*-uses/some-*c*-uses (APU+C)** strategy is defined as follows: for every variable and every definition of that variable, include at least one definition-free path from the definition to every predicate use; if there are definitions of the variable that are not covered by the above prescription, then add computational-use test cases as required to cover every definition. The **all-*c*-uses/some-*p*-uses (ACU+P)** strategy reverses the bias: first ensure coverage by computational-use cases and if any definition is not covered by the previously selected paths, add such predicate-use cases as are needed to assure that every definition is included in some test.

In Figure 5.6b, for variables X and Y, any test case satisfies both criteria because definition and uses occur on link (1,3). In Figure 5.6c, for APU+C we can select paths that all take the upper link (12,13) and therefore we do not cover the *c*-use of Z: but that's okay according to the strategy's definition because every definition is covered. Links (1,3), (4,5), (5,6), and (7,8) must be included because they contain definitions for variable Z. Links (3,4), (3,5), (8,9), (8,10), (9,6), and (9,10) must be included because they contain predicate uses of Z. Find a covering set of test cases under APU+C for all variables in this example—it only takes two tests. In Figure 5.6d, APU+C is achieved for V by (1,3,5,6,7,8,10,11,4,5,6,7,8,10,11,12[upper],13,2) and (1,3,5,6,7,8,10,11,12[lower],13,2). Note that the *c*-use at (9,10) need not be included under the APU+C criterion.

Figure 5.6d shows a single definition for variable V. C-use coverage is achieved by (1,3,4,5,6,7,8,9,10,11,12,13,2). In Figure 5.6c, ACU+P coverage is achieved for Z by path (1,3,4,5,6,7,8,10, 11,12,13[lower],2), but the predicate uses of several definitions are not covered. Specifically, the (1,3) definition is not covered for the (3,5) *p*-use, the (7,8) definition is not covered for the (8,9), (9,6) and (9,10) *p*-uses.

The above examples imply that APU+C is stronger than branch coverage but ACU+P may be weaker than, or incomparable to, branch coverage.

3.3.5. All-Definitions Strategy

The **all-definitions (AD) strategy** asks only that every definition of every variable be covered by at least one use of that variable, be that use a computational use or a predicate use. Path (1,3,4,5,6,7,8, . . .) satisfies this criterion for variable Z, whereas any entry/exit path satisfies it for variable V. From the definition of this strategy we would expect it to be weaker than both ACU+P and APU+C.

3.3.6. All-Predicate-Uses, All-Computational Uses Strategies

The **all-predicate-uses (APU) strategy** is derived from the APU+C strategy by dropping the requirement that we include a *c*-use for the variable if there are no *p*-uses for the variable following each definition. Similarly, the **all-computational-uses (ACU) strategy** is derived from ACU+P by dropping the requirement that we include a *p*-use if there are no *c*-use instances following a definition. It is intuitively obvious that ACU should be weaker than ACU+P and that APU should be weaker than APU+C.

3.3.7. Ordering the Strategies

Figure 5.7 compares path-flow and data-flow testing strategies. The arrows denote that the strategy at the arrow's tail is stronger than the strategy at the arrow's head. Formal proofs of these relations are found in RAPP85 and FRAN88. The right-hand side of this graph, along the path from "all paths" to "all statements" is the more interesting hierarchy for practical applications. Note that although ACU+P is stronger than ACU, both are incomparable to the predicate-biased strategies. Note also that "all definitions" is not comparable to ACU or APU.

The discussion of data-flow testing strategies in this chapter is introductory and only minimally covers the research done in this area. Variations of data-flow strategies exist, including different ways of characterizing the paths to be included and whether or not the selected paths are achievable. The strength relation graph of Figure 5.7 can be substantially expanded to fit almost all such strategies into it. Indeed, one objective of testing research has been to place newly proposed strategies into the hierarchy. For additional information see CLAR86, FRAN86, FRAN88, KORE85, LASK83, NTAF84B, NTAF88, RAPP82, RAPP85, and ZEIL88.

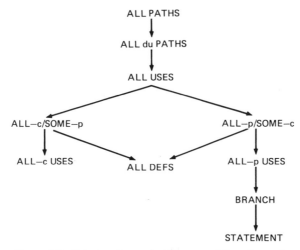

Figure 5.7. Relative Strength of Structural Test Strategies

3.4. Slicing, Dicing, Data Flow, and Debugging

3.4.1. General

Although an impressive theory of testing has emerged over the past 2 decades, debugging theory has lagged. Even those of us who eschew (unstructured) debugging because it is (in a sense) a failure of testing, recognize that debugging will always be with us. Testing in a maintenance context is not the same as testing new code—for which most testing theory and testing strategies have been developed. Maintenance testing is in many ways similar to debugging. I view debugging and testing as two ends of a spectrum of techniques in which maintenance testing falls some-place in the middle. It is interesting to note that the three concerns (test-ing, maintenance and debugging) come together in the context of data-flow testing techniques (KORE85, LASK83, LYLE88, OSTR88B).

3.4.2. Slices and Dices

A (static) program **slice** (WEIS82) is a part of a program (e.g., a selected set of statements) defined with respect to a given variable X (where X is a simple variable or a data vector) and a statement i: it is the set of all statements that could (potentially, under static analysis) affect the value of X at statement i—where the influence of a faulty statement could result from an improper computational use or predicate use of some other variables at prior statements. If X is incorrect at statement *i*, it follows that the bug must be in the program slice for X with respect to *i*. A program **dice** (LYLE87) is a part of a slice in which all statements which are known to be correct have been removed. In other words, a dice is obtained from a slice by incorporating information obtained through testing or experiment (e.g., debugging). The idea behind slicing and dicing is based on Weiser's observation (WEIS82) that these constructs are at the heart of the procedure followed by good debuggers. This position is intuitively sensible. The debugger first limits her scope to those prior statements that could have caused the faulty value at statement *i* (the slice) and then eliminates from further consideration those statements that testing has shown to be correct. Debugging can be modeled as an iterative procedure in which slices are further refined by dicing, where the dicing information is obtained from ad hoc tests aimed primarily at eliminating possibilities. Debugging ends when the dice has been reduced to the one faulty statement.

Dynamic slicing (KORE88C) is a refinement of static slicing in which only statements on achievable paths to the statement in question are included. Korel and Laski further extend the notion of slices to arrays and data vectors and also compare and contrast data flow relations such as *dc* and *dp* within dynamic slices to analogous relations in static data flows (for example, *dc* and *dp*).

Slicing methods have been supported by tools and tried experimentally on a small scale. Current models of slicing and dicing incorporate assumptions about bugs and programs that weaken their applicability to real programs and bugs. It is too early to tell whether some form of slicing will lead to commercial testing and/or debugging tools. It is encouraging, though, to find that data-flow concepts appear to be central to closing the gap between debugging and testing.

4. APPLICATION, TOOLS, EFFECTIVENESS

Ntafos (NTAF84B) compared random testing, P_2, and AU strategies on fourteen of the Kernighan and Plauger (KERN76) programs (a set of mathematical programs with known bugs, often used to evaluate test strategies). The experiment had the following outcome:

Strategy	Mean No. Test Cases	Bugs Found (%)
Random testing	35	93.7
Branch testing	3.8	91.6
All uses	11.3	96.3

A second experiment (NTAF84A) on seven similar programs showed the following:

Strategy	Mean No. Test Cases	Bugs Found (%)
Random testing	100	79.5
Branch testing	34	85.5
All uses	84	90.0

Sneed (SNEE86) reports experience with real programs and compares branch coverage effectiveness at catching bugs to data-flow testing criteria. Sneed's data-flow coverage definition is pragmatic rather than mathematically precise: it corresponds most closely to AD. He reports that the number of bugs detected by requiring 90% "data coverage" was twice as high as those detected by requiring 90% branch coverage.

Weyuker (WEYU88A, WEYU90) has published the most thorough comparison of data-flow testing strategies to date. Her study is based on twenty-nine programs from the Kernighan and Plauger set. Tests were designed using the ASSET testing system (FRAN88). Although the study is based on a small sample, the results are encouraging. The study examined the number of test cases needed to satisfy ACU, APU, AU, and ADUP. The number of test cases are normalized to the number of binary decisions in the program. A linear regression line of the form $t = a + bd$ was done for the four strategies; where a and b are constants obtained from the regression and d is the number of binary decisions in the program. The number of binary decisions in a program is an established program complexity metric (see Chapter 7). A loop-free program with d binary decisions requires at most $d + 1$ test cases to achieve branch coverage. Therefore, d is a measure of the number of test cases needed for branch coverage (actually, the number needed in practice is closer to $d/4$ than to d). The primary result is expressed in terms of the mean number of test cases required per decision, as shown in the table below (after WEYU88A):

Strategy	t/d	$t = a + bd$
ACU all-c	.43	1.87 + 0.52d
APU all-p	.70	1.01 + 0.76d
APU all-p*	.39	104.28 + 0.02d
AU all-uses	.72	1.42 + 0.81d
ADUP all-du-paths	.81	1.40 + 0.92d

The all-p* entry refers to a study by Shimeall and Levenson reported by Weyuker in a revised version of WEYU88A. The study covered eight numerical Pascal programs used in combat simulation. The programs ranged in size from 1186 to 2489 statements and had from 173 to 434 decisions, with a mean of 277 decisions. The regression line is not as meaningful a predictor of the number of test cases needed to achieve APU because of the relatively small range of number of decisions in the sample: t/d is probably a more reliable indicator of testing complexity for these programs. Note that this value is almost half of the value obtained for APU for the small Kernighan and Plauger programs. There are no data to reliably determine how t/d for APU changes with program size.

The surprising result is that ADUP doesn't even take twice as many test cases as ACU or APU; furthermore, the modest number of test cases is not much greater than required for P_2. The experiments further showed that although theoretically AC and AP are incomparable, achieving AP generally satisfied AC also. The results are comparable to those of Ntafos (NTAF84A, NTAF84B).

Data-flow testing concepts have been around a long time. Data flow testing practice predates the formal analysis of these strategies. Although data flow testing came under theoretical scrutiny after statement and branch testing the use of data flow testing strategies coincides with the use of branch testing in the late 1960s (BEND70C, SCHL70). Just as statement and branch coverage were found to be cost-effective testing strategies, even when unsupported by automation, data-flow testing has been found effective. Finding data-flow-covering test sets, especially for the all-uses strategy, is not more nor less difficult than finding branch-covering test sets—merely more tedious if you want to avoid redundant tests. There's more bookkeeping because you have to keep track of which variables are covered and where, in addition to branch coverage. Bender and Associates (BEND85) markets a proprietary design and test methodology in which AU (in addition to P_1 and P_2) testing plays a prominent role.* Experience with AU on critical software and a long history of experience at IBM (BEND70C) is convincing evidence of the practicality and effectiveness of data flow testing strategies.

Data-flow testing does entail additional record keeping, for which a computer is most effective. Even relatively simple tools that just keep track of which variables are defined and where and in which (if any) subsequent statement the definition is used can significantly reduce the effort of data-flow testing. Because one entry/exit path test case typically passes through a bunch of definitions and uses for many different vari-

---

* Because, as for statement versus branch coverage, for unstructured code such as assembly language, FORTRAN, or COBOL, AU does not necessarily guarantee APU, which in turn need not guarantee P_2, etc.

ables, test design is not very different than for P_1 or P_2. In Weyuker's experiments (WEYU88A), subjects did not specifically try to use the selected strategy—they tested in accordance to a strategy of their choice, and the tool, ASSET, told them the extent to which the test set had satisfied the criteria. The following sources also deal with data-flow testing tools: BEND70C, FOSD76A, FRAN88, HARR89, HERM76, KORE85, KORE88A, KORE88B, KORE89, LASK90A, LYLE87, OSTR88B, POLL87B, SNEE86, WILS82, WEYU88A, and WEYU90.

While most users of data-flow testing strategies have found it expedient and cost-effective to create supporting tools, as of the time of writing, commercial data-flow testing tools have yet to come on the market. The ease with which data-flow testing tools can be incorporated into compilers, and the general increase in awareness of the efficacy of data-flow testing combine to foreshadow intense commercial tools development in the future.

5. TESTABILITY TIPS

1. No data-flow anomalies, even if "harmless."
2. Try to do all data-flow operations on one variable at the same program level. That is, avoid defining an object in a subroutine and using it in the calling program, or vice versa. When all data-flow operations on a variable are all done at the same program level, you avoid an integration testing problem for that variable. The closer your design meets this objective, the likelier you are to find a data-flow anomaly in unit tests rather than in integration or higher-level component tests.
3. If you can't achieve item 2 for a variable, then at least try to have complementary operations such as open/close or define/kill done at the same program level.
4. Try especially hard to keep the *p*-uses of a variable at the same level as they are defined. This helps you to avoid data-flow anomalies and control-flow problems that can only be detected in the integrated components; that is, more of the control flow can be verified in unit testing.
5. No data object aliases, "bit sharing," and the utilization of unassigned bits within bytes. "Waste" a little space if that makes data structures cleaner and references more consistent.
6. Use strong typing and user-defined types if and as supported by the source language. Use a preprocessor to enforce strong typing if not supported by the language.

7. Use explicit, rather than implicit (as in FORTRAN), declaration of all data objects even if not required by the language. Use explicit initialization of all data objects if it is not done automatically by the language processor.

8. Bias the design to a regular pattern of object creation, use, and release, in that order: i.e., create/assign/fetch, use, return/clear/kill. Put data declarations at the top of the routine even if the language permits declarations anyplace. Return and clear objects at a central point, as close as possible to the exit. In other words, waste a little space and hold it a little longer in the interest of data-flow regularity.

6. SUMMARY

1. Data are as important as code and will become more important.

2. Data integrity is as important as code integrity. Just as common sense dictates that all statements and branches be exercised on under test, all data definitions and subsequent uses must similarly be tested.

3. What constitutes a data flow anomaly is peculiar to the application. Be sure to have a clear concept of data flow anomalies in your situation.

4. Use all available tools to detect those anomalies that can be detected statically. Let the extent and excellence of static data-flow anomaly detection be as important a criterion in selecting a language processor as produced object code efficiency and compilation speed. Use the slower compiler that gives you slower object code if it can detect more anomalies. You can always recompile the unit after it has been debugged.

5. The data-flow testing strategies span the gap between all paths and branch testing. Of the various available strategies, AU probably has the best payoff for the money. It seems to be no worse than twice the number of test cases required for branch testing, but the resulting code is much more reliable. AU is not too difficult to do without supporting tools, but use the tools as they become available.

6. Don't restrict your notion of data-flow anomaly to the obvious. The symbols d, k, u, and the associated anomalies, can be interpreted (with profit) in terms of file opening and closing, resource management, and other applications.

6
DOMAIN TESTING

1. SYNOPSIS

Programs as input data classifiers: domain testing attempts to determine whether the classification is or is not correct. Application of domain testing to interfaces and integration, domain design, software design for testability, and limitations.

2. DOMAINS AND PATHS

2.1. The Model

Domain testing can be based on specifications and/or equivalent implementation information. If domain testing is based on specifications, it is a functional test technique; if based on implementations, it is a structural technique. Domain testing, as practiced, is usually applied to one input variable or to simple combinations of two variables, based on specifications. For example, you're doing domain testing when you check extreme values of an input variable. Domain testing as a theory, however, has been primarily structural.

All inputs to a program can be considered as if they are numbers. For example, a character string can be treated as a number by concatenating bits and looking at them as if they were a binary integer. This is the view in domain testing, which is why this strategy has a mathematical flavor.

Before doing whatever it does, a routine must classify the input and set it moving on the right path. Figure 6.1 is a schematic representation of this notion. Processing begins with a classifier section that partitions the input vector into cases. An invalid input (e.g., value too big) is just a special processing case called "reject," say. The input then passes to a hypothetical subroutine or path that does the processing. In domain testing we focus on the classification aspect of the routine rather than on the calculations.

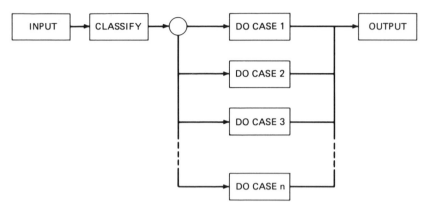

Figure 6.1. Schematic Representation of Domain Testing.

Structural knowledge is not needed for this model—only a consistent, complete specification of input values for each case. Even though we might not use structural information, we can infer that for each case there must be at least one path to process that case. That path need not be obvious and at the level of the tested routine. For example, case classification and/or case processing could be buried in a low-level subroutine. Because domain testing can be a functional test technique, not only do we need not know anything about the hypothetical path, but usually we don't care. When we talk about "paths through the routine" in this chapter, it is understood that we mean actual paths in the routine, paths in subroutines, table entries, or whatever else is needed to process each case. If we base domain testing on structure rather than on specifications, the hypothetical paths will be actual paths.

2.2. A Domain Is a Set

An input domain is a set. If the source language supports set definitions (e.g., Pascal set types, C enumerated types) less testing is needed because the compiler (compile-time and run-time) does much of it for us. Domain testing doesn't work well with arbitrary discrete sets of data objects because there are no simple, general strategies. In Section 3 below we discuss domain problems (ugly domains): arbitrary, discrete sets suffer from many of those problems. Our discussion will focus on domains that either are numerical or can be thought of as numerical.

The language of set theory is natural for domain testing. We speak of connected and disconnected domains, closure properties, boundaries, intersections and unions, and so on. Readers who were victimized by the "new math" may remember these concepts from elementary school and may have wondered what use they were; they will be useful now. Readers unfamiliar with set theory should read an introduction such as a high school text. Computer science graduates and software engineers usually know some set theory but probably never used it for anything practical. We won't be using deep concepts, but a terminology review might be in order.

2.3. Domains, Paths, and Predicates

In domain testing, predicates are assumed to be interpreted in terms of input vector variables. If domain testing is applied to structure, then predicate interpretation must be based on actual paths through the routine—that is, based on the implementation control flowgraph. Conversely, if domain testing is applied to specifications, interpretation is based on a specified data flowgraph for the routine; but usually, as is the nature of specifications, no interpretation is needed because the domains are specified directly. I will be deliberately vague about whether we're dealing with implementations or specifications when the discussion applies equally well to either. For the most part, though, there will be a specification bias because that's where I believe domain testing has the best payoff.

For every domain there is at least one path through the routine. There may be more than one path if the domain consists of disconnected parts or if the domain is defined by the union of two or more domains. Unless stated otherwise, we'll assume that domains consist of a single, connected part. We'll also assume (for now) that the routine has no loops. Domains are defined by their boundaries. Domain boundaries are also where most domain bugs occur. For every boundary there is at least one predicate that specifies what numbers belong to the domain and what numbers don't. For example, in the statement IF x>0 THEN ALPHA ELSE BETA we know that numbers greater than zero belong to ALPHA processing domain(s) while zero and smaller numbers belong to BETA domain(s). A domain may have one or more boundaries—no matter how many variables define it. For example, if the predicate is $x^2 + y^2 < 16$, the domain is the inside of a circle of radius 4 about the origin. Similarly, we could define a spherical domain with one boundary but in three variables. Domains are usually defined by many boundary segments and therefore by many predicates.

In typical programs, domain boundary predicates alternate with processing. A domain might be defined by a sequence of predicates—say A,

B, and C. First evaluate A and process the A cases, then evaluate B and do B processing, and then evaluate C and finish up. With three binary predicates, there are up to eight (2^3) domains, corresponding to eight possible combinations of TRUE/FALSE outcomes of the three predicates. It could be as few as two domains if, for example, the ABC (boolean) case is processed one way and the rest of the cases ($\overline{A} + \overline{B} + \overline{C}$) another way.

To review:

1. A domain for a loop-free program corresponds to a set of numbers defined over the input vector.
2. For every domain there is at least one path through the routine, along which that domain's processing is done.
3. The set of interpreted predicates traversed on that path (i.e., the path's predicate expression) defines the domain's boundaries.

2.4. Domain Closure

Figure 6.2 shows three situations for a one-dimensional domain—i.e., a domain defined over one input variable; call it x. As in set theory, a domain boundary is **closed** with respect to a domain if the points on the boundary belong to the domain. If the boundary points belong to some other domain, the boundary is said to be **open.** Figure 6.2 shows three domains called D1, D2, and D3. In Figure 6.2a, D2's boundaries are closed both at the minimum and maximum values; that is, both points belong to D2. If D2 is closed with respect to x, then the adjacent domains (D1 and D3) must both be open with respect to x. Similarly, in Figure

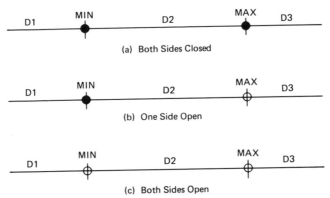

Figure 6.2. Open and Closed Domains.

6.2b, D2 is closed on the minimum side and open on the maximum side, meaning that D1 is open at the minimum (of D2) and D3 is closed at D2's maximum. Figure 6.2c shows D2 open on both sides, which means that those boundaries are closed for D1 and D2. The importance of domain closure is that incorrect closure bugs are frequent domain bugs. For example, $x >= 0$ when $x > 0$ was intended.

2.5. Domain Dimensionality

Every input variable adds one dimension to the domain. One variable defines domains on a number line, two variables define planar domains, three variables define solid domains, and so on. Don't confuse the domain's dimensionality with the number of boundary predicates. There must be at least one boundary predicate or there's nothing to test from the point of view of domain testing; however, there's no limit to the number of boundary predicates. Every new predicate slices through previously defined domains and cuts (at least one of) them in half. A piece of salami (the input vector space) is a three-dimensional object (three variables), but a food processor can create far more than three slices or chunks—but no less than two or else it isn't slicing.

Every boundary slices through the input vector space with a dimensionality which is less than the dimensionality of the space. Thus, planes are cut by lines and points, volumes by planes, lines and points, and *n*-spaces by **hyperplanes.** Because a domain could consist of only points along a line, or for that matter a single point, the dimensionality of the predicate can be any value less than the dimensionality of the space. Spaces of more than three dimensions are called *n*-spaces. Things that cut through *n*-spaces are called **hyperplanes** (not starships). An input array with dimension 100 is not unusual, but it is a 100-dimensional space. Input spaces of dozens of dimensions are common for even modest routines. It's obvious that pictures, intuition, and visualization rapidly become useless. Domain testing can be done manually for one or two dimensions, but it is tool-intensive in general.

2.6. The Bug Assumptions

The bug assumption for domain testing is that processing is okay but the domain definition is wrong. An incorrectly implemented domain means that boundaries are wrong, which may in turn mean that control-flow predicates are wrong. Although we can infer that an incorrect boundary results in a control-flow bug, we can't assume that the bug is at the level of the routine we're testing. The faulty boundary could be decided by a lower-level subroutine, by a faulty call to an otherwise correct subroutine, or by a faulty table entry. We also assume that once the input vector is set on the right path, it will be correctly processed. This last assumption implies that domain testing should be augmented by other testing to verify that processing is correct: for example, at least one case within the domain. Many different bugs can result in domain errors. Here is a sample of more common ones:

1. *Double-Zero Representation*—In computers or languages that (unfortunately) have a distinct positive and negative zero, boundary errors for negative zero are common.

2. *Floating-Point Zero Check*—A floating-point number can equal zero only if the previous definition of that number set it to zero or if it is subtracted from itself, multiplied by zero, or created by some operation that forces a zero value. Floating-point zero checks should always be done about a small interval, typically called "epsilon," which for that application has been defined as "close enough to zero for all practical purposes."

3. *Contradictory Domains*—An implemented domain can never be ambiguous or contradictory, but a specified domain can. A contradictory domain specification means that at least two supposedly distinct domains overlap. Programmers resolve contradictions by assigning overlapped regions to one or the other domain for a 50-50 chance of error.

4. *Ambiguous Domains*—Ambiguous domains means that the union of the specified domains is incomplete; that is, there are either missing domains or holes in the specified domains. Not specifying what happens to points on the domain boundary is a common ambiguity.

5. *Overspecified Domains*—The domain can be overloaded with so many conditions that the result is a null domain. Another way to put it is to say that the domain's path is unachievable.

6. *Boundary Errors*—Domain boundary bugs are discussed in further detail in Section 4, below, but here's a few: boundary closure bug, shifted, tilted, missing, extra boundary.

7. *Closure Reversal*—A common bug. The predicate is defined in terms of $>=$. The programmer chooses to implement the logical complement and incorrectly uses $<=$ for the new predicate; i.e., $x >= 0$ is incorrectly negated as $x <= 0$, thereby shifting boundary values to adjacent domains.

8. *Faulty Logic*—Compound predicates (especially) are subject to faulty logic transformations and improper simplification. If the pred-

icates define domain boundaries, all kinds of domain bugs can result from faulty logic manipulations.

2.7. Restrictions

2.7.1. General

Domain testing has restrictions, as do other testing techniques. They aren't restrictions in the sense that you can't use domain testing if they're violated—but in the sense that if you apply domain testing to such cases, tests are unlikely to be productive because they may not reveal bugs or because the number of tests required to satisfy the criterion is greater than practicality warrants. In testing (other than faulty outcome prediction, improper execution, or other test design and execution bugs), there are no invalid tests—only unproductive tests.

2.7.2. Coincidental Correctness

Coincidental correctness is assumed not to occur. Domain testing isn't good at finding bugs for which the outcome is correct for the wrong reasons. Although we're not focusing on outcome in domain testing, we still have to look at outcomes to confirm that we're in the domain we think we're in. If we're plagued by coincidental correctness we may misjudge an incorrect boundary. Note that this implies weakness for domain testing when dealing with routines that have binary outcomes (i.e., TRUE/ FALSE). If the binary outcome is INSIDE/OUTSIDE (the domain), as in data-validation routines, domain testing will probably be effective. But if the domain is a disconnected mess of small subdomains, each of which has a binary outcome or if outcomes are restricted to a few discrete values, then coincidental correctness is likely and domain testing may not be revealing.

2.7.3. Representative Outcome

Domain testing is an example of **partition testing. Partition-testing** strategies divide the program's input space into domains such that all inputs within a domain are equivalent (not equal, but equivalent) in the sense that any input represents all inputs in that domain. If the selected input is shown to be correct by a test, then processing is presumed correct, and therefore all inputs within that domain are expected (perhaps unjustifiably) to be correct. Most test techniques, functional or structural, fall under partition testing and therefore make this **representative outcome** assumption. Another way to say it is that only one function is calculated in a domain and that adjacent domains calculate different functions. This is not equivalent to barring coincidental correctness—coincidental correctness concerns the value of functions, whereas a representative outcome concerns the functions themselves. For example, x^2 and 2^x are equal for $x = 2$, but the functions are different. The functional differences between adjacent domains are usually simple, such as $x + 7$ versus $x + 9$, rather than x^2 versus 2^x.

2.7.4. Simple Domain Boundaries and Compound Predicates

Each boundary is defined by a simple predicate rather than by a compound predicate. We want to avoid, among other things, inconsistent boundary closures. Compound predicates in which each part of the predicate specifies a different boundary are not a problem: for example, x >= 0 .AND. x < 17, just specifies two domain boundaries by one compound predicate. As an example of a compound predicate that specifies one boundary, consider: x = 0 .AND. y >= 7 .AND. y <= 14. This predicate specifies one boundary equation ($x = 0$) but alternates closure, putting it in one or the other domain depending on whether $y < 7$ or $y > 14$.

Compound predicates that include ORs can create concave domains (see Section 3.3.7), domains that are not simply connected (see Section 3.3.8) and violate the requirement that adjacent domains compute different functions. A domain defined by a predicate such as ABC + DEF defines two subdomains (by three boundaries corresponding to ABC or three boundaries corresponding to DEF). These subdomains can be separated, adjacent but not overlapped, partially overlapped, or one can be contained within the other; all of these are problematic.

Eliminating compound predicates is usually enough to guarantee simple boundary closures and connected, convex domains, but it is probably too strong a requirement. The predicates usually employ numerical relational operators: >, >=, =, <=, <>, and <. Although elaborate boundary closures can be constructed using these operators and compound predicates, it's not likely, except in mathematical software. In real situations, exotic boundaries don't come up often, but multiply connected and/or overlapped domains can and do occur with compound predicates. Note also that if one leg of a binary predicate is compound with only ANDs, then the other leg, because it is a boolean negation, *must* contain ORs and therefore can create disconnected, overlapped, or concave domains. Treat compound predicates with respect because they're more complicated than they seem.

2.7.5. Functional Homogeneity of Bugs

Whatever the bug is, it will not change the functional form of the boundary predicate. For **linear predicates** (i.e., boundary predicates that are linear functions) the bug is such that the resulting predicate will still be linear. For example, if the predicate is $ax >= b$, the bug will be in the value of a or b but it will not change the predicate to $a^x >= b$, say.

2.7.6. Linear Vector Space

A **linear (boundary) predicate** is defined by a linear inequality (*after interpretation in terms of input variables*),* using only the simple relational operators $>$, $>=$, $=$, $<=$, $<>$, and $<$. Most papers on domain testing, such as WHIT81, assume linear boundaries—not a bad assumption because in practice most boundary predicates *are* linear. A more general assumption is that boundaries can be embedded in a linear vector space. For example, the predicate $x^2 + y^2 > a^2$ is not linear in rectangular coordinates, but by transforming to polar coordinates we obtain the equivalent linear predicate $r > a$. Similarly, a polynomial boundary can be transformed into a linear vector space by $y_1 = x$, $y_2 = x^2$, $y_3 = x^3$, ... Polynomial and other nonlinear boundaries have been examined by Zeil and White (ZEIL81, ZEIL84). The difficulties with nonlinear boundaries are practical and theoretical. The practical problems are twofold: significant increase in the number of tests needed to confirm boundaries and major escalation in calculations to determine test points. In real testing, asking for a linear vector space boils down to simple linear predicates.

2.7.7. Loop-free Software

Loops are problematic for domain testing. The trouble with loops is that each iteration can result in a different predicate expression (after interpretation), which means a possible domain boundary change. If a loop is an overall control loop on transactions, say, there's no problem. We "break" the loop and use domain testing for the transaction process. If the loop is **definite** (that is, if we know on entry exactly how many times it will loop), then domain testing may be useful for the processing within the loop, and loop testing discussed in Chapter 3 can be applied to the looping

---

* Emphasize linearity "after interpretation in terms of input variables." A predicate could *appear* to be linear, say $x + y > 0$, but not be linear after interpretation because there had been, say, a previous assignment such as $x := y^2$. Similarly, a nonlinear predicate could become linear after interpretation. To make matters worse, the interpretation could depend on the path—linear for some paths and nonlinear for others. Despite these potential (but rare) difficulties, it's a useful technique.

values. The really troublesome loops for domain testing are indefinite loops, such as in iterative procedures.

Despite the theoretical difficulties of applying domain testing to software with loops, White and Wiszniewski (WHIT88, WISZ85, WISZ87) have investigated the problem, especially testing complexity. Early research indications are that domain-testing tools for programs with loops may emerge, but it will take time to determine whether the loop methodology is cost-effective in practice.

3.   NICE DOMAINS AND UGLY DOMAINS

3.1.   Where Do Domains Come From?

Domains are often created by salesmen or politicians. I shouldn't knock salesmen and politicians, but we know that they aren't as careful about "minor" issues of consistency as we'd like them to be—especially if by ignoring such problems they befriend the customer and make the sale. There's always a salesman at the top of the design process—a person who negotiates functionality with a buyer in the loosest possible way while providing the greatest possible appearance of consistency and completeness. It's an emotional appeal rather than a rational process that submits to logic. There's always a salesman in the act—be it a retailer who sells software to a user or a manager who "sells" the project up the line (or up the creek). Don't fault salesmen for their (typical) shortsighted view and desire for instant gratification—it's an essential aspect of a personality needed to get a job done. And if they didn't sell the "impossible" once in a while, where would progress be? I don't fault them—I don't even want to change them—but as a designer and tester I've learned to be cynical about their domain "definitions." As for politicians? The difficulties you have with your income tax returns were caused by politically defined domains.

Domains are and will be defined by an imperfect iterative process aimed at achieving (user, buyer, voter) satisfaction. We saw in Chapter 2 that requirement bugs are among the most troublesome of all. Many requirement bugs can be viewed as ill-defined domains—meaning ill-defined domain boundaries. The first step in applying domain testing should be to analyze domain definitions in order to get (at least) consistent and complete domain specifications. As designers and testers, we have been far too timid about challenging specified domains. Most domain problems discussed below (Section 3.4) can be avoided.

3.2. Specified Versus Implemented Domains

Implemented domains can't be incomplete or inconsistent. Every input will be processed (rejection is a process), possibly forever. Inconsistent domains will be made consistent. Conversely, specified domains can be incomplete and/or inconsistent. **Incomplete** in this context means that there are input vectors for which no path is specified, and **inconsistent** means that there are at least two contradictory specifications over the same segment of the input space. If a program is based on such specified domains, because the program can't be either incomplete or inconsistent (in the above sense), there must be a bug.

3.3. Nice Domains

3.3.1. General

Figure 6.3 shows some nice, typical, two-dimensional domains. The boundaries have several important properties discussed below: they are linear, complete, systematic, orthogonal, consistently closed, simply connected, and convex. To the extent that domains have these properties, domain testing is as easy as testing gets. To the extent that these properties don't apply, testing is as tough as it gets. What's more important is that bug frequencies are much lower for nice domains than for ugly domains.

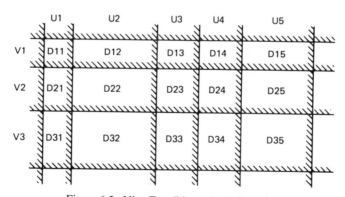

Figure 6.3. Nice Two-Dimensional Domains.

3.3.2. Linear and Nonlinear Boundaries

Nice domain boundaries are defined by linear inequalities or equations—*after interpretation in terms of input variables*. The impact on testing stems from the fact that it takes only two (test) points to determine a straight line, three points to determine a plane, and in general $n + 1$ points to determine an n-dimensional hyperplane. Add one point to test boundary closure correctness and you have it all.

The restriction to linear boundaries might seem to severely restrict the applicability of domain testing, but that's not so. Cohen (COHE78) studied 50 COBOL programs and found only one nonlinear predicate out of 1070. Studies by Knuth (FORTRAN) and Elshoff (PL/1) reported in WHIT80A support the observation that almost all boundary predicates met in practice are linear. There are no published data on how many nonlinear predicates could be linearized by simple transformations (see Section 6.2 below). My guess is that, in practice, more than 99.99% of all boundary predicates are either directly linear or can be linearized by simple variable transformations.

3.3.3. Complete Boundaries

Nice domain boundaries are complete in that they span the number space from plus to minus infinity in all dimensions. Figure 6.4 shows some incomplete boundaries. Boundaries A and E have gaps. Such boundaries can come about because the path that hypothetically corresponds to them is unachievable, because inputs are constrained in such a way that such values can't exist, because of compound predicates that define a single

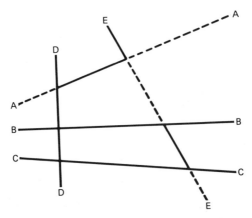

Figure 6.4. Incomplete Domain Boundaries.

boundary, or because redundant predicates convert such boundary values into a null set. The advantage of complete boundaries is that one set of tests is needed to confirm the boundary no matter how many domains it bounds. If the boundary is chopped up and has holes in it, then every segment of that boundary must be tested for every domain it bounds.

3.3.4. Systematic Boundaries

By **systematic boundaries** I mean boundary inequalities related by a simple function such as a constant. In Figure 6.3 for example, the domain boundaries for u and v differ only by a constant. We want relations such as

$$f_1(X) >= k_1 \quad \text{or} \quad f_1(X) >= g(1,c)$$
$$f_2(X) >= k_2 \qquad f_2(X) >= g(2,c)$$
$$\dots\dots\dots\dots \qquad \dots\dots\dots\dots\dots$$
$$f_i(X) >= k_i \qquad f_i(X) >= g(i,c)$$

where f_i is an arbitrary linear function, X is the input vector, k_i and c are constants, and $g(i,c)$ is a decent function over i and c that yields a constant, such as $k + ic$. The first example is a set of parallel lines, and the second example is a set of systematically (e.g., equally) spaced parallel lines. I would also call a set of lines through a point, such as the spokes of a wheel, if equally spaced in angles, systematic. If the boundaries are systematic and if you have one tied down and generate tests for it, the tests for the rest of the boundaries in that set can be automatically generated.

3.3.5. Orthogonal Boundaries

The U and V boundary sets in Figure 6.3 are **orthogonal;** that is, every inequality in V is perpendicular to every inequality in U. The importance of this property cannot be minimized. If two boundary sets are orthogonal, then they can be tested independently. It's the difference between linear and nonlinear test growth. In Figure 6.3 we have six boundaries in U and four in V. We can confirm the boundary properties in a number of tests proportional to $6 + 4 = 10$ ($O(n)$). If we tilt the boundaries to get Figure 6.5, we must now test the intersections. We've gone from a linear number of cases to a quadratic: from $O(n)$ to $O(n^2)$.*

---

* The notation $O(n)$ means of the order of. For example, $O(n)$ is a linear growth, $O(n^2)$ is a quadratic growth, and $O(2^n)$ is an exponential growth.

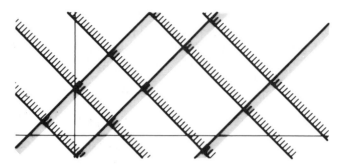

Figure 6.5. Tilted Boundaries.

Actually, there are two different but related orthogonality conditions. Sets of boundaries can be orthogonal to one another but not orthogonal to the coordinate axes (condition 1), or boundaries can be orthogonal to the coordinate axes (condition 2). The first case allows us to simplify intersection testing. The second case means that boundaries are functions of only one variable. Both are desirable properties. Figure 6.6 shows the difference. The boundaries defined by x ($x = A_1$, . . .) are orthogonal to the x axis and are therefore functions only of x. The other set of boundaries, though systematic, is not orthogonal to either coordinate axis and therefore not to the other set of boundaries. Orthogonality can depend on the coordinate system chosen. For example, concentric circles intersected by equally spaced spokes aren't orthogonal in rectangular coordinates but if you express the variables in polar coordinates, testing is no worse than for Figure 6.3.

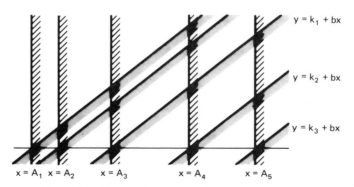

Figure 6.6. Linear, Nonorthogonal Domain Boundaries.

3.3.6.   Closure Consistency

Figure 6.6 shows another desirable domain property: boundary closures are consistent and systematic. The shaded areas on the boundary denote that the boundary belongs to the domain in which the shading lies—e.g., the boundary lines belong to the domains on the right. Consistent closure means that there is a simple pattern to the closures—for example, using the same relational operator for all boundaries of a set of parallel boundaries.

Inconsistent closures are often not fundamental; they're often arbitrary and result from hasty solutions rather than analysis. The programmer has to know how to treat the points on every domain boundary. As a programmer you know all about domains and especially adjacent domains, even if you haven't talked about them in these terms before. You spot a boundary ambiguity and you ask "What do I do when . . . *equals* . . .?" If you don't know that there's a pattern to the boundaries, or that boundaries enclose a case in a certain way, then the answer is likely to be arbitrary. Another source of inconsistent closures is a misguided attempt to "simplify" the problem. The salesman doesn't want to burden you with "complexities" such as dealing with $>=$ rather than $>$. She doesn't realize that programming one relational operator is the same as another so he says, "Use .GT. rather than .GE.", because he thinks that software will be simpler as a result. I've wasted more time than I can reckon trying to program an arbitrary requirement intended to "simplify" my work. Pay special attention to domain boundary closures during requirements reviews. Look for closure patterns and deviations from patterns. Confirm that specified closures are actual rather than arbitrary requirements. You'll simplify not only programming but also testing.

3.3.7.   Convex

A geometric figure (in any number of dimensions) is **convex** if you can take two arbitrary points on any two different boundaries, join them by a line and all points on that line lie within the figure. Nice domains are convex; dirty domains aren't. Linear convex domains look like polished, n-dimensional diamonds. Linear domains with concavities are like diamonds with chips gouged out of them. The reliability of domain testing breaks down for domains with concavities—specifically, the n-on, one-off strategy discussed in Section 4.2 of this chapter may not work. We should start by looking at the specification for signs of concavity. You can smell a suspected concavity when you see phrases such as: ". . . except if

. . . ," "However . . . ," ". . . but not. . . ." In programming, it's often the buts in the specification that kill you.

3.3.8. Simply Connected

Nice domains are **simply connected;** that is, they are in one piece rather than pieces all over the place interspersed with other domains (more "buts," "excepts," etc.). Nice domains are solid rather than laced through with exceptions like termite-infested beams. Simple connectivity is a weaker requirement than convexity; if a domain is convex it is simply connected, but not vice versa.

Consider domain boundaries defined by a compound predicate of the (boolean) form ABC. Say that the input space is divided into two domains, one defined by ABC and, therefore, the other defined by its negation $\overline{A} + \overline{B} + \overline{C}$. The inverse predicate is the union of three predicates, which can define up to three overlapped domains. If the first domain is convex, its complement can't be convex or simply connected—it must have a hollow created by the first domain. If one domain slices out a hunk of number space, the complementary domain must have holes or be in pieces. For example, suppose we define valid numbers as those lying between 10 and 17 inclusive. The invalid numbers are the disconnected domain consisting of numbers less than 10 and greater than 17.

Simple connectivity, especially for default cases, may be impossible. It would be a poor idea to implement default cases as the primary driver of the domain logic if the default domain was concave or multiply connected. The smart strategy would be to do case logic first and let defaults fall through. Conversely, if the default domain is simply connected, the union of the working cases may not be simply connected but is surely concave, so the smart design (and test) strategy would be to do default case analysis first and to fall through to working cases.

3.4. Ugly Domains and How Programmers and Testers Treat Them

3.4.1. General

Some domains are born ugly and some are uglified by bad specifications. Programmers in search of nice solutions will "simplify" essential complexity out of existence. Testers in search of brilliant insights will be blind to essential complexity and therefore miss important cases. Every simplification of ugly domains by programmers, as discussed below, can be either good or bad. If the ugliness results from bad specifications and the programmer's simplification is harmless, then the programmer has made ugly good. But if the domain's complexity is essential (e.g., the income tax code), such "simplifications" constitute bugs. We'll assume (in this section) that domain complexities are essential and can't be removed—but remember, that's still the goal driving designers and testers.

3.4.2. Nonlinear Boundaries

Nonlinear boundaries are so rare in ordinary programming that there's no information on how programmers might "correct" such boundaries if they're essential. I just don't see that as a statistically significant source of bugs. If a domain boundary is essentially nonlinear, it's unlikely that programmers will make it linear by accident or by erroneous thinking.

3.4.3. Ambiguities and Contradictions

Figure 6.7 shows several domain ambiguities and contradictions. Remember that although specifications can be ambiguous and/or contradictory, programs can't.

Domain ambiguities are holes in the input space. The holes may lie within domains or in cracks between domains. A hole in a one-variable input space is easy to see. An ambiguity for two variables can be difficult to spot, especially if boundaries are lines going every which way. Ambiguities in three or more variables are almost impossible to spot without formal analysis—which means tools. Because programs can't be ambiguous, programmers must (whether or not they realize it) associate every ambiguity with some domain. Therefore, valid ambiguous cases may be rejected or assigned to the wrong domain and invalid ambiguous cases

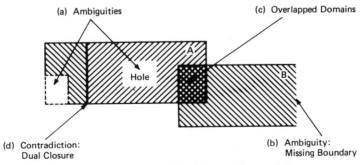

Figure 6.7. Domain Ambiguities and Contradictions.

may be accepted. Because the ambiguity is not consciously realized, we can assume that the result is as likely to be a bug as not. Formal ambiguity detection is provided by specification languages and tools designed for this purpose.

Two kinds of contradictions are possible: overlapped domain specifications and overlapped closure specifications. Figure 6.7c shows overlapped domains. The programmer's reaction will be to treat the overlap as belonging either to domain A or to domain B. Let's grant that situation a 50-50 bug chance. The tester faced with an unrecognized domain contradiction similarly assigns the overlapped area to one or the other domains. The result is an almost certain argument between designer and tester, when in fact both are wrong, as is the specification.

Figure 6.7d shows a dual closure assignment. This is actually a special kind of overlap. It looks different because we're conscious of the difference between one and two dimensions. The general case, of n-dimensional domains means boundaries of $n - 1$ or fewer dimensions—that is, boundary hyperplanes. The two cases (Figures 6.7c and 6.7d) are just overlapped (contradictory) domains with a two-dimensional overlap and a one-dimensional overlap, respectively.

3.4.4. Simplifying the Topology

The programmer's and tester's reaction to complex domains is the same—simplify. There are three generic cases: concavities, holes, and disconnected pieces. Programmers introduce bugs and testers misdesign test cases by: smoothing out concavities (Figure 6.8a), filling in holes (Figure 6.8b), and joining disconnected pieces (Figure 6.8c). Connecting disconnected boundary segments and extending boundaries out to infinity are other ways to simplify the domain's topology. Overlooking special cases or merging supposedly equivalent cases (as a result of a "great" but faulty insight) does one or more of these things.

The negation of a compound predicate with ANDs is always a compound predicate with ORs—and these predicates can create complex domain topologies. If you have a compound predicate, there's nothing simple about inverting the decision. If you "simplify" the program by inverting decisions, are you sure that you haven't inadvertently simplified essential domain complexity?

3.4.5. Rectifying Boundary Closures

If domain boundaries are parallel but have closures that go every which way (left, right, left, . . .) the natural reaction is to make closures go the

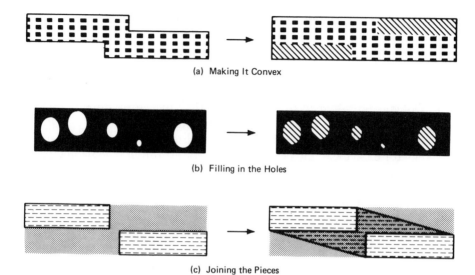

(a) Making It Convex

(b) Filling in the Holes

(c) Joining the Pieces

Figure 6.8. Simplifying the Topology.

same way (see Figure 6.9). If the main processing concerns one or two domains and the spaces between them are to be rejected, the likely treatment of closures is to make all boundaries point the same way. For example, every bounding hyperplane is forced to belong to the domain or every bounding hyperplane is forced outside of the domain. Again, it's the programmers' and testers' search for simple rules to cover all cases that results in consistent but incorrect closures.

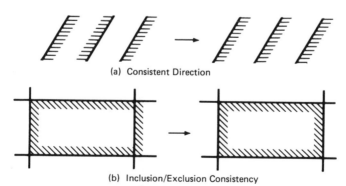

(a) Consistent Direction

(b) Inclusion/Exclusion Consistency

Figure 6.9. Forcing Closure Consistency.

4. DOMAIN TESTING (WHIT78A, WHIT80A, WHIT85B, WHIT87)

4.1. Overview

The domain-testing strategy is simple, albeit possibly tedious.

1. Domains are defined by their boundaries; therefore, domain testing concentrates test points on or near boundaries.
2. Classify what can go wrong with boundaries, then define a test strategy for each case. Pick enough points to test for all recognized kinds of boundary errors.
3. Because every boundary serves at least two different domains, test points used to check one domain can also be used to check adjacent domains. Remove redundant test points.
4. Run the tests and by posttest analysis (the tedious part) determine if any boundaries are faulty and if so, how.
5. Run enough tests to verify every boundary of every domain.

4.2. Domain Bugs and How to Test for Them

4.2.1. General

An **interior point** (Figure 6.10) is a point in the domain such that all points within an arbitrarily small distance (called an **epsilon neighborhood**) are also in the domain. A **boundary point** is one such that within an epsilon neighborhood there are points both in the domain and not in the domain. An **extreme point** is a point that does not lie between any two other arbitrary but distinct points of a (convex) domain.

An **on point** is a point on the boundary. If the domain boundary is closed, an **off point** is a point near the boundary but in the adjacent

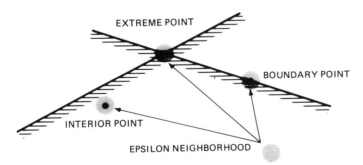

Figure 6.10. Interior, Boundary, and Extreme Points.

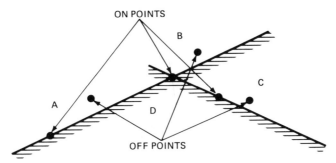

Figure 6.11. On Points and Off Points.

domain. If the boundary is open, an off point is a point near the boundary but in the domain being tested; see Figure 6.11. You can remember this by the acronym COOOOI: **C**losed **Off O**utside, **O**pen **Off I**nside.

Figure 6.12 shows generic domain bugs: closure bug, shifted boundaries, tilted boundaries, extra boundary, missing boundary.

4.2.2. *Testing One-Dimensional Domains*

Figure 6.13 shows possible domain bugs for a one-dimensional open domain boundary. The closure can be wrong (i.e., assigned to the wrong

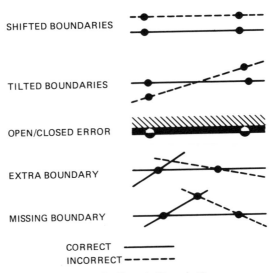

Figure 6.12. Generic Domain Bugs.

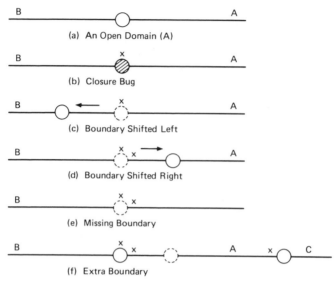

Figure 6.13. One-Dimensional Domain Bugs, Open Boundaries.

domain) or the boundary (a point in this case) can be shifted one way or the other, we can be missing a boundary, or we can have an extra boundary. In Figure 6.13a we assumed that the boundary was to be open for A. The bug we're looking for is a closure error, which converts > to >= or < to <= (Figure 6.13b). One test (marked x) on the boundary point detects this bug because processing for that point will go to domain A rather than B.

In Figure 6.13c we've suffered a boundary shift to the left. The test point we used for closure detects this bug because the bug forces the point from the B domain, where it should be, to A processing. Note that we can't distinguish between a shift and a closure error, but we do know that we have a bug.

Figure 6.13d shows a shift the other way. The on point doesn't tell us anything because the boundary shift doesn't change the fact that the test point will be processed in B. To detect this shift we need a point close to the boundary but within A. The boundary is open, therefore by definition, the off point is in A (**Open Off Inside**). This point also suffices to detect a missing boundary because what should have been processed in A is now processed in B. To detect an extra boundary we have to look at two domain boundaries. In this context an extra boundary means that A has been split in two. The two off points that we selected before (one for each

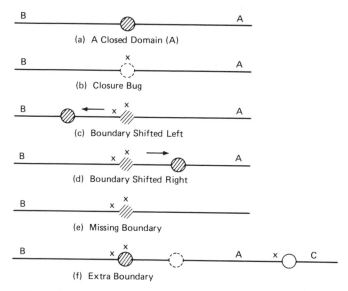

Figure 6.14. One-Dimensional Domain Bugs, Closed Boundaries.

boundary) does the job. If point C had been a closed boundary, the on test point at C would do it.

For closed domains look at Figure 6.14. As for the open boundary, a test point on the boundary detects the closure bug. The rest of the cases are similar to the open boundary, except now the strategy requires off points just outside the domain.

4.2.3. Testing Two-Dimensional Domains

Figure 6.15 shows domain boundary bugs for two-dimensional domains. A and B are adjacent domains and the boundary is closed with respect to A, which means that it is open with respect to B. We'll first discuss cases for closed boundaries; turn the figure upside down to see open boundary cases.

1. *Closure Bug*—Figure 6.15a shows a faulty closure, such as might be caused by using a wrong operator (for example, $x >= k$ when $x > k$ was intended, or vice versa). The two on points detect this bug because those values will get B rather than A processing.
2. *Shifted Boundary*—In Figure 6.15b the bug is a shift up, which converts part of domain B into A processing, denoted by A'. This

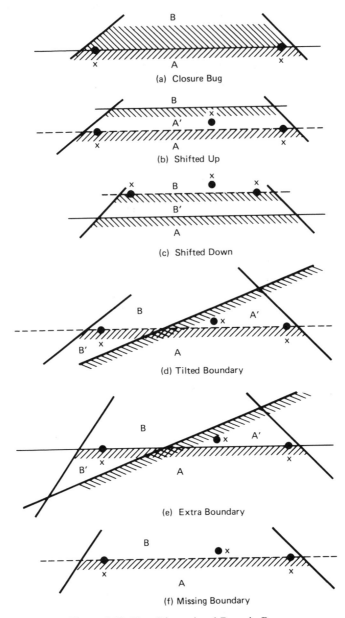

(a) Closure Bug

(b) Shifted Up

(c) Shifted Down

(d) Tilted Boundary

(e) Extra Boundary

(f) Missing Boundary

Figure 6.15. Two-Dimensional Domain Bugs.

result is caused by an incorrect constant in a predicate, such as $x + y >= 17$ when $x + y >= 7$ was intended. The off point (closed off outside) catches this bug. Figure 6.15c shows a shift down that is caught by the two on points.

3. *Tilted Boundary*—A tilted boundary occurs when coefficients in the boundary inequality are wrong. For example, $3x + 7y > 17$ when $7x + 3y > 17$ was intended. Figure 6.15d has a tilted boundary, which creates erroneous domain segments A' and B'. In this example the bug is caught by the left on point. Try tilting your pencil along the boundary in various ways and you'll see that every tilt can be caught by the fact that some point or points go to the wrong domain.

4. *Extra Boundary*—An extra boundary is created by an extra predicate. An extra boundary will slice through many different domains and will therefore cause many test failures for the same bug. The extra boundary in Figure 6.15e is caught by two on points, and depending on which way the extra boundary goes, possibly by the off point also. Note that this extra boundary must result in different functions for A' versus A and B' versus B. If it doesn't—i.e., $f(A) = f(A')$ and/or $f(B) = f(B')$—there is a redundant and useless predicate but no actual bug insofar as functional testing is concerned.

5. *Missing Boundary*—A missing boundary is created by leaving a boundary predicate out. A missing boundary will merge different domains and, as the extra boundary can, will cause many test failures although there is only one bug. A missing boundary, shown in Figure 6.15f, is caught by the two on points because the processing for A and B is the same—either A or B processing. You can't detect a missing boundary if your domain testing is based on the implementation because no structural test technique can detect a missing path. In detecting a missing boundary you are comparing a specified domain, for which you select test points, with the implemented domains.

Turn the figure upside down and consider the B domain, which is open. The off point is correct, by the definition of on and off points, and the discussion is essentially the same as before.

Figure 6.16 summarizes domain testing for two-dimensional domains; it shows a domain all but one of whose boundaries are closed. There are two on points (closed circles) for each segment and one off point (open circles). That's all the testing needed to do domain testing in two dimensions. Note that the selected test points are shared with adjacent domains, so the number of cases needed is reduced. To test a two-dimensional domain whose boundaries may be incomplete, with s boundary segments,

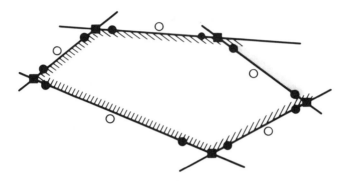

Figure 6.16. Domain-Testing Strategy Summary.

we need at least $2s$ test points if we can share them with other domains and at most $3s$ points if we can't.

The on points for two adjacent boundary segments can also be shared if both those segments are open or if both are closed (see Figure 6.17). A single extreme point replaces the two on points near the boundary intersection. If two adjacent boundary segments aren't both open or both closed, then two different on points are needed. Try different bug cases to see this.

Although the above domain-testing strategy doesn't require us to test the intersections of the boundaries (the **extreme points**), it's a good idea to do so because bugs tend to congregate in corners. If the basic strategy (for two dimensions) of two on points and one off point per boundary segment shows the boundaries to be correct, what can we expect to learn from intersection testing? Look for a blowup, crash, or endless loop. Testing extreme points doesn't require much extra work because you had to find them in order to know where to put the on points.

Domain testing is blind to small domain errors. Whatever off points we pick, they are within an epsilon neighborhood of the boundary. A shift of less than this value or a small enough tilt will not be caught. Other refinements of domain testing, especially for small errors and discrete spaces,

Figure 6.17. Shared on Points.

are discussed in WHIT78A: read that paper if you're building a domain-testing tool.

4.2.4. Equality and Inequality Predicates

Equality predicates such as $x + y = 17$ define lower-dimensional domains. For example, if there are two input variables, a two-dimensional space, an equality predicate defines a line—a one-dimensional domain. Similarly, an equality predicate in three dimensions defines a planar domain. We get test points for equality predicates by considering adjacent domains (Figure 6.18). There are three domains. A and B are planar while C, defined by the equality boundary predicate between A and B, is a line. Applying the two-on, one-off rule to domains A and B and remembering **Open Off Inside**, we need test point b for B and point a for A and two other points on C (c and c') for the on points. This is equivalent to testing C with two on and two off points. There is a pathological situation in which the bug causes the boundary to go through the two selected off points: it can be detected by another on point at the intersection between the correct domain line and the two off points (marked d). Because such bugs require careful design and because our failure to catch them depends on an unfortunate choice of the two off points, they can be ignored.

4.2.5. Random Testing?

Look at Figure 6.16. Let's add one typical test case someplace in the middle of the domain to verify the computation (not really needed). Domain testing, especially when it incorporates extreme points, has two virtues: it verifies domain boundaries efficiently, and many selected test

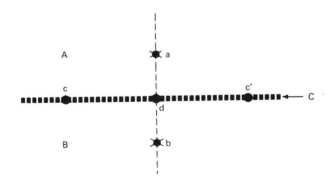

Figure 6.18. Equality Predicates.

cases (on points and extreme points) correspond to cases where experience shows programmers have trouble. Consider Figure 6.16. What is the probability that a set of randomly chosen test points will meet the above criteria? End of argument against random testing.*

4.2.6. Testing n-Dimensional Domains

For domains defined over an n-dimensional input space with p boundary segments, the domain testing strategy generalizes to require at most $(n + 1)p$ test points per domain, consisting of n on points and one off point (see WHIT78A). When extreme point sharing is possible, the number of points required per domain can be as little as $2p$ per domain. Domain boundaries which are orthogonal to the coordinate axes, have consistent closures, and extend over the entire number space can be tested independently of other boundaries. Equality predicates defined over m dimensions ($m < n$) create a subspace of $n - m$ dimensions, which is then treated the same way as general n-dimensional domains.

4.3. Procedure

The procedure is conceptually straightforward. It can be done by hand for two dimensions and a few domains. Without tools the strategy is practically impossible for more than two variables.

1. Identify input variables.
2. Identify variables which appear in domain-defining predicates, such as control-flow predicates.
3. Interpret all domain predicates in terms of input variables. We'll assume that the interpreted predicates are linear or can be easily transformed to linear (see Section 6.2 below). Note that interpretation need not be based on actual paths. For example, if all variable assignments that lead to an uninterpreted predicates are specified, then interpretation can be based on a "path" through this set of specifications. This path may or may not correspond to implemented paths. In other words, the paths we want are not paths in the control flowgraph but paths in the specified data flowgraph.

---

* Not really—random test points have value when used to determine statistically valid notions of confidence: e.g., what is the probability that this routine will fail in use? See DURA84 and HAML88. Random test data though, as a means for breaking software or catching bugs, is not effective, and even its proponents suggest augmenting it with domain boundary and extreme points: but see JENG89 for conditions under which random testing is either better or worse.

4. For p binary predicates, there are at most 2^p combinations of TRUE-FALSE values and therefore, at most 2^p domains. Find the set of all non-null domains (see Chapter 10). The result is a boolean expression in the predicates consisting of a set of AND terms joined by ORs—for example, ABC + DEF + GH + IJKL, where the capital letters denote predicates. Each **product term** (that is, term consisting of predicates joined by ANDs) is a set of linear inequalities that defines a domain or a part of a multiply connected domain.

5. Solve these inequalities (see a book on linear algebra or linear programming) to find all the extreme points of each domain. White (WHIT86) discusses a method called "the scattering method" based on linear programming that yields a usable set of test points.

6. Use the extreme points to solve for nearby on points and to locate midspan off points for every domain.

More details on how to (build tools that) determine test points can be found in PERE85 and WHIT86. If it seems to you that you are rapidly becoming involved in linear algebra, simultaneous-equation solving, linear programming, and a lot of supporting software, you're right. I said at the outset that this was a tool-intensive strategy, but don't feel cheated. What you should ask yourself is: "Did the person who specified these domains, their closures, their extreme points, and all the rest—did that person go through the above analysis in order to verify the validity of the specified domains? Did she have the foggiest notion of the complexity she specified?"

4.4. Variations, Tools, Effectiveness

Domain testing, although it's been around for over a decade, has not progressed as far toward day-to-day application as other strategies. Variations have been explored that vary the number of on and off points and/or the extreme points. The basic domain testing strategy discussed here is called the $N \times 1$ strategy because it uses N on points and one off point. Clarke et al. (CLAR82, RICH85) discuss strategies that use N on and N off points per boundary segment ($N \times N$ strategy) and strategies based on extreme points and off points near extreme points ($V \times V$ strategy, V for "vertex"). As with all testing techniques, many variations are possible if you consider the way to pick on points, off points, and extreme points. Also, as we'll see in Section 6, it's possible to weaken the basic strategy and to consider boundary hyperplanes as the basic thing to test rather than domain boundary segments caused by intersections of those hyperplanes. As with all test techniques, more research will lead to sharper strategies that find more bugs with fewer tests and a better understanding of how the variations relate to one another.

We don't have many statistics on the cost-effectiveness of domain testing. Richardson and Clarke (RICH85) discuss a generalization that they call "partition analysis," which includes domain testing, computation verification, and both structural and functional information. Their methodology applied to the Kernighan and Plauger and other test sets shows promise in that almost all bugs were caught.

The present tool situation is par for the course. Some specification-based tools such as T (PROG88), use heuristic domain-testing principles based on the observation that bugs are likelier at the extreme points of domains. Most researchers in domain testing have built experimental tools to assist them, as with other test techniques, but to date there are no commercial tools that incorporate strict domain testing.

The fact that domain testing is tool-intensive should not be a barrier to its effective exploitation. An appropriate perspective can be gained by looking at the related field of hardware logic testing, which is also tool-intensive. Logic testers are ahead of software testers because they've been at it longer and because their problem is simpler. The operative mode of hardware testing is extremely tool-intensive. Why should we expect, why should we restrict, software testing methods to what can be done by hand? After all, what *are* computers for?

5. DOMAINS AND INTERFACE TESTING

5.1. General

Don't be disappointed by domain testing because it's difficult to apply to two dimensions and humanly impossible for more than two. Don't reject it because it seems that all a person can do is handle one dimension at a time and you can't (yet) buy tools to handle more than one dimension. The conceptual vocabulary of domain testing, even one variable at a time, has a lot to offer us in integration testing. Recall that we defined integration testing as testing the correctness of the interface between two otherwise correct components. Components A and B have been demonstrated to satisfy their component tests, and as part of the act of integrating them we want to investigate possible inconsistencies across their interface. Although the interface between two components can be a subroutine call, shared data objects, values left in registers or global variables, or some combination thereof, it's convenient to talk about the interface as if it is a subroutine call. We're looking for bugs in that "call" when we do interface testing. Another way to put this is to say that we're looking for incompatible notions of what constitutes "good" values in the call. Let's assume that the call sequence is correct and that there are no type incompatibilities. What's left is a possible disagreement about domains—the variables' domain as seen by the caller and the called routine. For a single variable, the **domain span** is the set of numbers between (and including) the smallest value and the largest value. For every input variable we want (at least): compatible domain spans and compatible closures. Note that I said "compatible" and not "equal." As we'll see, domains need not be equal to be compatible.

5.2. Domains and Range

The set of output values produced by a function is called the **range** of the function, in contrast with the **domain,** which is the set of input values over which the function is defined. In most of testing we are only minimally concerned with output values. We have to examine them to confirm that the correct function has been implemented, but other than that, we place no restrictions on output values. Thus, for most testing, our aim has been to specify input values and to predict and/or confirm output values that result from those inputs. Interface testing requires that we select the output values of the calling routine. A more precise statement of the kind of compatibility needed between caller and called is to say that the caller's range must be compatible with the called routine's domain. An interface test consists of exploring the correctness of the following mappings:

caller domain → caller range   (caller unit test)
caller range   → called domain   (integration test)
called domain → called range   (called unit test)

Another way to put this is to say that the caller's range is the caller's notion of the called routine's domain. We'll usually be looking at things from the point of view of the called routine and therefore be talking in terms of domains.

5.3. Closure Compatibility

Assume that the caller's range and the called domain spans the same numbers—say, 0 to 17. Figure 6.19 shows the four ways in which the caller's range closure and the called's domain closure can agree. I've turned the number line on its side. The thick line means closed and the thin line means open. Figure 6.19 shows the four cases consisting of

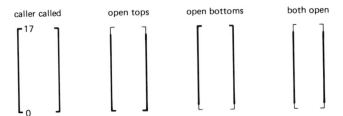

Figure 6.19. Range/Domain Closure Compatibility.

domains that are closed both on top (17) and bottom (0), open top and closed bottom, closed top and open bottom, and open top and bottom. Figure 6.20 shows the twelve different ways the caller and the called can disagree about closure. Not all of them are necessarily bugs. The four cases in which a caller boundary is open and the called is closed (marked with a "?") are probably not buggy. It means that the caller will not supply such values but the called can accept them. Note that inconsistencies even if harmless in one domain may be erroneous in adjacent domains. If there are only two domains (valid, not valid) and we're looking at the valid domain, then the inconsistency is harmless; otherwise it's a bug.

5.4. Span Compatibility

Figure 6.21 shows three possibly harmless span incompatibilities. I've eliminated closure incompatibilities to simplify things. In all cases, the caller's range is a subset of the called's domain. That's not necessarily a bug. Consider, for example, a square-root routine that accepts negative numbers and provides an imaginary square root for them. The routine is used by many callers; some require complex number answers and some don't. This kind of span incompatibility is a bug only if the caller expects

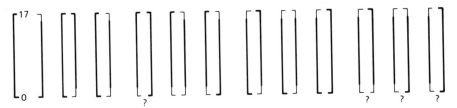

Figure 6.20. Equal-Span Range/Domain Compatibility Bugs.

Figure 6.21. Harmless Range/Domain Span Incompatibility Bug.
(Caller Span Is Smaller Than Called.)

the called routine to validate the called number for the caller. If that's so, there are values that can be included in the call, which from the caller's point of view are invalid, but for which the called routine will not provide an error response.

Figure 6.22a shows the opposite situation, in which the called routine's domain has a smaller span than the caller expects. All of these examples are buggy. In Figure 6.22b the ranges and domains don't line up; hence good values are rejected, bad values are accepted, and if the called routine isn't robust enough, we have crashes. Figure 6.22c combines these notions to show various ways we can have holes in the domain: these are all probably buggy.

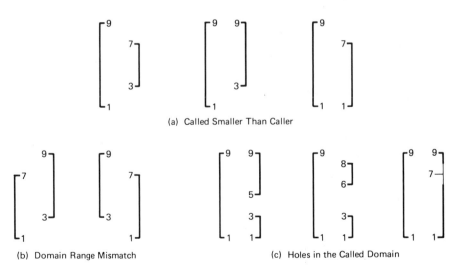

(a) Called Smaller Than Caller

(b) Domain Range Mismatch   (c) Holes in the Called Domain

Figure 6.22. Buggy Range/Domain Mismatches.

5.5. Interface Range/Domain Compatibility Testing

I tried to generalize caller/called range/domain incompatibilities by first considering combinations of closure and span errors for one variable. That led to a vast combination of cases that were no more revealing than those shown above. I curbed my ambition and tried to picture all possible range/domain disagreements for two variables simultaneously. The result would have been called (had I persisted) *Beizer's Picture Book of Two-Dimensional Range/Domain Incompatibilities*. It was a fruitless and pointless exercise because for interface testing, bugs are more likely to concern single variables rather than peculiar combinations of two or more variables. Without automation, it's impractical to even consider double-error cases, never mind higher dimensions. That's why we test one variable at a time.

Test every input variable independently of other input variables to confirm compatibility of the caller's range and the called routine's domain span and closure of every domain defined for that variable. For subroutines that classify inputs as "valid/invalid" the called routine's domain span and closure (for valid cases) is usually broader than the caller's span and closure. The reason is that common subroutines serve more than one mistress and must accept a span of values equal to the union of all caller's ranges for that variable. Therefore, the burden of providing valid inputs is always on the caller, not the called. There are two boundaries to test and it's a one-dimensional domain; therefore, it requires one on and one off point per boundary or a total of two on points and two off points for the domain—pick the off points appropriate to the closure (COOOOI).

If domains divide processing into several cases, you must use normal domain-testing ideas and look for exact range/domain boundary matches (span and closure). You should be able to lump all valid cases into a contiguous "superdomain" so that this set can be tested for compatibility with the called routine's valid set. Then it might be possible that mere compatibility, rather than an exact match, will suffice for the top and bottom domains. The caller range's lower bound must be compatible only with the called domain's lower bound—similarly for the caller's and called's range/domain upper bounds.

5.6. Finding the Values

Start with the called routine's domains and generate test points in accordance to the domain-testing strategy used for that routine in component testing. A good component test should have included all the interesting domain-testing cases, and as a consequence there's no need to repeat the work. Those test cases are the values for which you must find the input values of the caller. If the caller's domains are linear, then this is another exercise in solving inequalities. Some things to consider:

1. The solution may not be unique. That doesn't matter because you need *any* caller input that will produce the required output.
2. There may be no solution for the specific points you need. In that case you'll probably have to make do with the maximum and minimum values that can be produced as outputs by the caller. Note that if the caller's domains are ugly (nonlinear, incomplete boundaries, unsystematic, not orthogonal, and so on), the problem can be very difficult. For nice domains, you do it one variable at a time and that's no big deal.
3. In general, you must find and evaluate *an* inverse function for the caller. Note "*an* inverse" rather than "*the* inverse."
4. Unless you're a mathematical whiz you won't be able to do this without tools for more than one variable at a time. We have very little data on the frequency of interface range/domain incompatibility bugs for single variables on no data on the frequencies of such bugs for several variables simultaneously. Consequently, there's no point in heavy investment in complicated multivariable tests whose effectiveness is unknown.

6. DOMAINS AND TESTABILITY

6.1. General

The best way to do domain testing is to avoid it by making things so simple that it isn't needed. The conceptual vocabulary of domain testing is a rich source of insights into design. We know what makes domain testing trivial: orthogonal domain boundaries, consistent closure, independent boundaries, linear boundaries, and the other characteristics discussed in Section 3.3. We know what makes domain testing difficult. What can we, as designers, do? Most of what we can do consists of applying algebra to the problem.

6.2. Linearizing Transformations

In the unlikely event that we're faced with essential nonlinearity we can often convert nonlinear boundaries to equivalent linear boundaries. This is done by applying **linearizing transformations.** The methods are centuries old. Here is a sample.

1. *Polynomials*—A boundary is specified by a polynomial or multinomial in several variables. For a polynomial, each term (for example, $x, x^2, x^3, \ldots$) can be replaced by a new variable: $y_1 = x$, $y_2 = x^2$, $y_3 = x^3, \ldots$. For multinomials you add more new variables for terms such as $xy, x^2y, xy^2, \ldots$. You're trading the nonlinearity of the polynomial for more dimensions. The advantage is that you transform the problem from one we can't solve to one for which there are many available methods (e.g., linear programming for finding the set of on and off points.)

2. *Logarithmic Transforms*—Products such as xyz can be linearized by substituting $u = \log(x)$, $v = \log(y)$, $w = \log(z)$. The original predicate ($xyz > 17$, say) now becomes $u + v + w > 2.83$.

3. *More General Transforms*—Other linearizable forms include $x/(ax + b)$ and ax^b. You can also linearize (approximately) by using the Taylor series expansion of nonlinear functions, which yields an infinite polynomial. Lop off the low-order terms to get an approximate polynomial and then linearize as for polynomials. There's a rich literature on even better methods for finding approximating polynomials for functions.

6.3. Coordinate Transformations

Nice boundaries come in parallel sets. Parallel boundary sets are sets of linearly related boundaries: that is, they differ only by the value of a constant. Finding such sets is straightforward. Its an $O(n^2)$ procedure for n boundary equations. Pick a variable, say x. It has a coefficient a_i in inequality i. Divide each inequality by it's x coefficient so that the coefficients of the transformed set of inequalities is unity for variable x. If two inequalities are parallel, then all the coefficients will be the same and they will differ only by a constant. A systematic comparison will find the parallel sets, if any. There are more efficient algorithms, and any serious tool builder would do well to research the issue. We now have parallel sets of inequalities. For each such set, pick one representative, any one, and put the rest aside for now; but keep track of how many different boundaries each represents. We now have a bunch of linear inequalities that are not parallel to one another.

The next objective is to extract, from the set of nonparallel inequalities determined above, a subset that can, by suitable coordinate transformations, be converted into a set of orthogonal boundary inequalities. If you'll recall, the reason for doing this is to obtain a new set of variables in terms of which the inequalities can be tested one at a time, independently of the other inequalities. Generally, we have more inequalities (n, say) than we have variables (m, say) so we'll not be able to pack them all into an m-dimensional space such that they are all independent. But we can pick m of them. I don't claim the following to be the best possible way—only a reasonable heuristic. Convert the inequalities to equalities—we're interested in the boundaries only, and they're specified by equalities. Start with the equation that represents the most boundaries, then pick the equation that represents the next most boundaries, etc. Continue adding equations until they're all used up or until you have m of them. After you select the equations, you apply a procedure called Gram-Schmidt orthogonalization (see KOLM88), which transforms your original set of variables X into a new, orthogonal set of variables U. For these new variables the inequalities are of the form $u_i >= k_i$, which you'll agree is easy to test. One test per hyperplane confirms the on point, another test confirms the inequality's direction. If the hyperplane represents several parallel hyperplanes, then you'll need two tests each to confirm them. There's no need to test intersections with the other nonparallel hyperplanes if funny things aren't happening to the boundary segments—that is, if the inequality's direction applies to the entire boundary hyperplane and the hyperplane extends to plus and minus infinity with the same closure all the way. But your choice of the m hyperplanes was arbitrary. Furthermore, parallel hyperplanes had been eliminated, so that any m could have been transformed to an orthogonal coordinate set. Therefore, as my mathematician friend Tom Seidman pointed out, you didn't have to test the boundary segments in the first place and you didn't have to do the transformation. In other words, given a (nice) k-dimensional hyperplane, its correctness can be confirmed by $k + 1$ tests, no matter how many domains it splits the world into. We need another test for the off point, for a total of $k + 2$ tests per hyperplane.

The $N \times 1$ domain-testing strategy is a worst-case strategy that allows arbitrary things to be done to the closure of each and every domain boundary segment. If we postulate reasonable bugs (as contrasted to carefully designed bugs) testing requirements are considerably reduced. As with all strategies, reducing the strength of the strategy by leaving out test cases increases your vulnerability to certain kinds of bugs. If those bugs cannot be reasonably expected, then nothing of value has been sacrificed.

6.4. A Canonical Program Form

Go back to Figure 6.1 and consider it now as a design objective. I'll make a few changes to it, though, starting with a variable transformation that linearizes and orthogonalizes as many inequalities as possible in order to simplify testing. The routine's structure then looks something like this:

1. Input the data.
2. Apply linearizing transforms to as many predicates as possible.
3. Transform to an orthogonal coordinate system.
4. For each set of parallel hyperplanes in the orthogonal space, determine the case by a table lookup or by an efficient search procedure (e.g., binary halving) to put the value of that variable into the right bin.
5. Test the remaining inequalities (those that couldn't be brought into the orthogonal space) to determine the required subcase.
6. You can now direct the program to the correct case processing routine by a table lookup or by a tree of control-flow predicates based on the case numbers for each dimension.

Testing is clearly divided into the following: testing the predicate and coordinate transformations; testing the individual case selections (independently of one another); testing the control flow (now over very simple predicates—or table-driven); and then testing the case processing. The resulting routine is probably very big, but also fast. You can compact it by merging various steps, alternating case determination with processing, and so on, but you're starting from a base of a canonical form that, though big, is clear. The bugs don't go away, however, because now you have added the possibility of an erroneously programmed predicate or coordinate transformation. If that's more complicated than using the original variables in control-flow predicates scattered throughout, you might have made things worse. I'm not suggesting that the above canonical form is *the* way programs should be written but that it is a starting point for a rational examination of more design options than you're probably seeing now—to convert a purely intuitive procedure into a more mechanical one. Think about it.

6.5. Great Insights?

Sometimes programmers have great insights into programming problems that result in much simpler programs than one might have expected. My favorite example is the calendar routine. It's easier to start the year on March 1 rather than January 1 because leap year corrections are then applied to the "last" day of the year. Isn't that just a coordinate change? In retrospect, when we look at some of our productive insights, insights that made a tough programming problem easy, many of them can be explained in terms of a judicious change to a new coordinate system in which the problem becomes easy. There's ample precedence for such things in other engineering disciplines—a good coordinate systems can break the back of many tough problems. Designers! Instead of waiting for inspiration to grant you the favor of a great insight, go out and look for them. Make the domains explicit. Separate domain definition from processing. Look for transformations to new, orthogonal, coordinate sets that are therefore easy to test. Examine your transformed variables and see whether you can find a clean functionally meaningful interpretation for them—you usually can. Testers! Look for ways to organize tests based on specifications into a minimal set of domain-verifying tests.

7. SUMMARY

1. Programs can be viewed as doing two different things: (a) classifying input vectors into domains, and (b) doing the processing appropriate to the domain. Domain testing focuses on the classification aspect and explores domain correctness.
2. Domains are specified by the intersections of inequalities obtained by interpreting predicates in terms of input variables. If domain testing is based on structure, the interpretation is specific to the control-flow path through the set of predicates that define the domain. If domain testing is based on specifications, the interpretation is specific to the path through a specification data flowgraph.
3. Every domain boundary has a closure that specifies whether boundary points are or are not in the domain. Closure verification is a big part of domain testing.
4. Almost all domain boundaries found in practice are based on linear inequalities. Those that aren't can often be converted to linear inequalities by a suitable linearization transformation.
5. Nice domains have the following properties: linear boundaries, boundaries that extend from plus to minus infinity in all variables, have systematic inequality sets, form orthogonal sets, have consistent closures, are convex, and create domains that are all in one piece. Nice domains are easy to test because the boundaries can be tested one at a time, independently of the other boundaries. If domains aren't nice, examine the specifications to see whether they can be changed to make the boundaries nice; often what's difficult about a boundary or domain is arbitrary rather than based on real requirements.
6. As designers, guard against incorrect simplifications and transformations that make essentially ugly domains nice. As testers, look for such transformations.
7. The general domain strategy for arbitrary convex, simply connected, linear domains is based on testing at most $(n + 1)p$ test

points per domain, where n is the dimension of the interpreted input space and p is the number of boundaries in the domain. Of these, n points are on points and one is an off point. Remember the definition of off point—COOOOI.

8. Real domains, especially if they have nice boundaries, can be tested in far less than $(n + 1)p$ points: as little as $O(n)$.

9. Domain testing is easy for one dimension, difficult for two, and tool-intensive for more than two. Beg, borrow, or build the tools before you attempt to apply domain testing to the general situation. Finding the test points is a linear programming problem for the general case and trivial for the nicest domains.

10. Domain testing is only one of many related partition testing methods which includes more points, such as n-on + n-off, or extreme points and off-extreme points. Extreme points are good because bugs tend to congregate there.

11. The domain-testing outlook is a productive tactic for integration interface testing. Test range/domain compatibility between caller and called routines and all other forms of intercomponent communications.

12. Instead of waiting for the programming muse to strike you with a brilliant intuition that will simplify your implementation, use the canonical model as a mental tool that you can exploit to systematically look for brilliant insights. As a tester, use the canonical program model as a framework around which to organize your test plan.

7

METRICS AND COMPLEXITY

1. SYNOPSIS

Measuring software complexity. Halstead's metrics, token counts, Mc-Cabe's metric, hybrid metrics. Application and implementation.

2. METRICS, WHAT AND WHY

2.1. Philosophy

One of the characteristics of a maturing discipline is the replacement of art by science. Science is epitomized by quantitative methods. In classical Greece, for example, early physics was dominated by discussions of the "essence" of physical objects, with almost no attempts to quantify such "essences." They were struggling with what questions should be asked. Quantification was impossible until the right questions were asked. By the sixteenth century, physics began to be quantified—first by Galileo and then by others. In the eighteenth century, we called physical scientists "natural philosophers" recognizing that the right questions hadn't been asked, and that all was not yet, even in principle, amenable to quantification. Today, physics is as quantified as science can get and far removed from its speculative roots in philosophy.*

Computer science (I think that the term is presumptuous—we're still more of a craft than a science) is following the same quantification path. Ultimately, we hope to get precise estimates of labor, resources, and reliability from formal specifications by mechanical means—ultimately, that is. If there's a note of scepticism it's because so much of what we want to quantify is tied to erratic human behavior. Should we expect greater success over a shorter period of time than economists and sociolo-

---

* But modern particle physics borders on mysticism and seems poised for a return to speculative philosophy.

213

gists have had? Our objective then is not necessarily the ultimate truth, the "real" model of how programs and systems behave, but a partial, practical, truth that is adequate for the practitioner. Does it matter whether our models of software complexity are right if, right or wrong in some abstract sense, they correlate well with reality? We have programs to write and systems to debug. We can leave the search for truth to the theorists and be content with pragmatism. What works is what counts. For metrics in general, see CURR86, DAVI88C, GILB77, GRAD87, HARR82, LEVI86, LIHF87 (especially), LIND89, PERL81, POLL87A, RAMA85 and WEYU88B.

2.2. Historical Perspective

There's no record of programming labor estimates on ENIAC, but I'm sure they fell far short of reality. The first programmer, Lady Lovelace, who coded for Charles Babbage's wonderful but unfinished computer in the nineteenth century, I'm sure often said "Just one more week, Mr. Babbage, and it'll be done." Lucky for her the hardware was never finished, so she didn't have to go beyond desk checking. By the mid-1950s individual programmers had coalesced into programming groups, which meant there was now a new profession—programmer manager. The managers, who were responsible for productivity and quality, began to measure software effort in terms of "number of lines of code." That was used to predict programming costs, testing costs, running time, number of bugs, salaries, the gross national product, the inflation rate of the peso, and who knows what else. It is today still the primary quantitative measure in use: "Count the number of lines of code, and you know all there is to know."

A landmark study by Weinwurm, Zagorski, and Nelson debunked any such simplistic measure (NELS67, WEIN65). They showed that cost was heavily influenced by such things as the number of meetings attended, the number of items in the database, the relative state of hardware development (if new hardware), documentation requirements, and other factors that didn't relate directly to simple measures such as lines of code. The study also debunked popular programmer's myths, such as "real-time software is much more difficult than batch processing." The study is important because it's one of the earliest serious large-scale efforts to quantify the issues in programming. Furthermore, the base for this study was not a bunch of small homework exercises, but a big group of system programs, spanning the range from subroutines to systems. As a basis for cost estimating, these studies have yet to be surpassed by anything that's been published. Despite the fact that the study thoroughly debunked the myths, despite the fact that contemporary estimation programs such as COCOMO (BOEH81) use many factors to predict cost, resources, and schedules—despite these facts, the lines-of-code metric stubbornly remains the most popular (and inaccurate) one in use, much as it was (ab)used a quarter of a century ago.

2.3. Objectives

2.3.1. How Big Is It?

Science begins with quantification: you can't do physics without a notion of length and time; you can't do thermodynamics until you measure temperature. The most fundamental question you can ask is "How big is it?" Without defining what "big" means, it's obvious that it makes no sense to say "This program will need more testing than that program" unless we know how big they are relative to one another. Comparing two strategies also needs a notion of size. The number of tests required by a strategy should be normalized to size. For example, "Strategy A needs 1.4 tests per unit of size, while strategy B needs 4.3 tests per unit of size."

What is meant by "size" is not obvious in the early phases of science development. Newton's use of mass instead of weight was a breakthrough for physics, and early researchers in thermodynamics had heat, temperature, and entropy hopelessly confused. We seem to be doing about as well (or as badly) as the sixteenth- and seventeenth-century physicists did at a comparable phase of development. "Size" isn't obvious for software. Levitin, in his critique of metrics (LEVI86) discusses fundamental problems in our most popular metric, the seemingly obvious "lines of code." You can't measure "size" if it's based on a subjective ruler—try doing physics or engineering with rubber rulers and spasmodic clocks. Metrics must be objective in the sense that the measurement process is algorithmic and will yield the same result no matter who applies it.

2.3.2. The Questions

Our objective in this book is not to quantify all of computer science, but only to explore those **metrics** of complexity that have proved their worth in practice. To see what kinds of metrics we need, let's ask some questions:

1. When can we stop testing?
2. How many bugs can we expect?
3. Which test technique is more effective?

4. Are we testing hard or are we testing smart?
5. Do we have a strong program or a weak test suite?

I won't answer any of these questions in this book because we don't know enough about software and testing to provide answers—at least not with the strength of a physical law. What we can do is take another lesson from physics: measurement leads to empirical "laws," which in turn lead to physical laws. Thus, Kepler's precise measurements* of planetary motion provided the foundations on which Newton could build physics; Mendel's experiments* provided the foundations on which the laws of genetics are based. Quantitative, empirical laws were used by engineers and artisans long before there was a satisfactory theory to explain such laws. Roman aqueducts, for example, can be shown to be structurally and hydraulically almost optimum, based on theory that's less than 100 years old.

If you want answers to the above questions, then you'll have to do your own measuring and fit your own empirical laws to the measured data. How that's done is discussed in Section 6, below. For now, keep in mind that all the metrics discussed below are aimed at getting empirical laws that relate program size (however it be measured) to expected number of bugs, expected number of tests required to find bugs, test technique effectiveness, etc.

2.3.3. Desirable Metric Properties

A useful metric should satisfy several requirements:**

1. It can be calculated, uniquely, for all programs to which we apply it.
2. It need not be calculated for programs that change size dynamically or programs that in principle cannot be debugged.
3. Adding something to a program (e.g., instructions, storage, processing time) can never decrease the measured complexity.

The first requirement ensures a usable, objective, measure; the second says that we won't try to apply it to unreasonable programs; and the third is formalized common sense. It's another way of saying that the program is at least as complicated as any of its parts.

---

* But recent evidence shows that Kepler cooked the data to fit his theory. Ditto for Mendel.
** A formal examination of metrics requirements by Weyuker (WEYU88B) formally extends these concepts and evaluates the extent to which several popular metrics, including statement count, cyclomatic number, Halstead's effort metric, and data-flow complexity do or do not meet them.

2.3.4. Metrics Taxonomy

There's no agreement in the literature on how to classify metrics—and there are so many metrics to classify. Here are some broad categories: **linguistic** metrics, **structural** metrics, and **hybrid** metrics. Each can be applied to either programs or specifications; to date, however, application to programs has dominated. The taxonomy is not rigid because a narrowly defined linguistic metric can define a structural property. For example, cyclomatic complexity can be defined in terms of links and nodes in the control flowgraph or alternatively by the number of equivalent branches in the program.

Linguistic Metrics—Metrics based on measuring properties of program or specification text without interpreting what that text means or the ordering of components of the text. For example: lines of code, number of statements, number of unique operators, number of unique operands, total number of operators, total number of operands, total number of keyword appearances, total number of tokens.

Structural Metrics—Metrics based on structural relations between objects in the program—usually metrics on properties of control flowgraphs or data flowgraphs; for example, number of links, number of nodes, nesting depth.

Hybrid Metrics—Metrics based on some combination of structural and linguistic properties of a program or based on a function of both structural and linguistic properties.

3. LINGUISTIC METRICS

3.1. General

Linguistic metrics measure some property of text without interpreting what is measured. A metric is (mainly) linguistic if its value doesn't change when you rearrange the text. Linguistic metrics, to date, have been applied mostly to program text. They can be just as easily applied to formal specifications, but because formal, processable specifications are rare, there is almost no experience with such usage; but see RAMA85.

3.2. Lines of Code, Statement Count, and Related Metrics

3.2.1. What Is It?

Count the number of lines of code in a program and use that number as a measure of complexity. If then, bugs appear to occur at 1% per line, a

1000-line program should have 10 bugs and a 10,000 line program should have 100. Going further, if we find that it takes an average of twenty tests to find a bug, we might infer (empirically) the expected number of tests needed per line of code.

I have an easier metric: weigh the listing—or if you don't have a scale, measure its thickness with a ruler. In today's electronic programming world, you could just count the number of k of storage used to store the program text. Why not use listing weight? Why is it that when I propose measuring programs by listing weight people think I'm pulling their leg but they take me seriously and consider it "scientific" when I suggest lines of code? Is listing weight really less scientific? Think about it. There's a high correlation between the weight of the listing or its thickness and the number of statements in it. On a big project, it probably correlates to better than 95%. Within a project with all paper supplied by the same vendor and all listings done under the same printing utility, the formats are regular. I think that if you were to gather statistics over one big project or many small projects (that used the same paper), then the weight of the listings would correlate as well to the bug rate and test efforts as do lines of code. Yet, "lines of code" sounds reasonable and scientific, and "listing weight" seems to be an outrageous put-on. Who's putting whom on? The fact is that it makes *exactly* as much sense (or nonsense) to say "This is a 230-gram* program" as it does to say "This is a 500-line program."

3.2.2. What to Count and Not Count

Early users of lines of code did not include data declarations, comments, or any other lines that did not result in object code. Later users decided to include declarations and other unexecutable statements but still excluded comments and blank lines. The reason for this shift is the recognition that contemporary code can have 50% or more data statements and that bugs occur as often in such statements as in "real" code. There is a rationale for including comments. The quality of comments materially affects maintenance costs because the maintenance programmer will depend on the comments more than anything else to do her job. Conversely, too many blank lines and wordy but information-poor comments will increase maintenance effort. The problem with including comments is that we must be able to distinguish between useful and useless comments, and there's no rigorous way to do that. The same can be said of blank lines and format-

---

* Note my use of "gram" rather than carat, drachm, gera, mina, nsp, ounce, pennyweight, pound, shekel, or talent in order to make my weight metric more "scientific."

ting text: a little helps us read the code but too much forces us into excessive page turning.

The lines-of-code metric has obvious difficulties. The count depends on the printing format. For example, it depends on the print-line length. Are we using line lengths of 50, 60, 72, 80, or 128 characters? Programming standards and individual style change lines of code, especially for data declarations. As an example, my data declarations in BASIC usually take more lines of code than needed so that they can look neat, can be ordered by object type (string, real, integer), by semantic type (counter, pointer), and so on. By making the program more legible, I've increased the line count, thereby making my version of the program seem more complex when in fact I've made it easier to understand. Similarly, for languages that permit multiple statements on each line: putting an entire loop on a line reduces apparent complexity, but overcrowding a line by arbitrarily packing statements makes the program text more obscure. The final weakness of this metric is that if we apply a "pretty printer" format program to source code, inevitably increasing the line count, we get an apparent complexity increase despite the fact that intelligibility has been improved. A rubbery ruler, lines of code.

Lines of code makes more sense for source languages in which there's a high correlation between statement count and lines of code. For example: assembly languages, old Basic, and FORTRAN.

3.2.3. Statement Counts

Some of the difficulties with lines of code can be overcome by using statements instead—but this evokes new problems that are as bad as those of lines of code. The problem, aptly stated by Levitin (LEVI86) is that there's no unique way to count statements in some languages (e.g., Pascal), and there's no simple rule for defining "statement" across different languages. Just as subjectivity is involved in applying lines of code, there's subjectivity in deciding what is and what is not to be called a statement (for some languages).

3.2.4. How Good (Bad) Are They?

Thayer, Lipow and Nelson, in their monumental software reliability study (THAY76) showed error rates ranging from 0.04% to 7% when measured against statement counts, with the most reliable routine being one of the largest. The same lack of useful correlation is shown in Rubey (RUBE75). Curtis, Sheppard, and Milliman (CURT79A) show that lines of code is as good as other metrics for small programs, but is optimistic for big programs. Moderate performance is also reported for lines of code by Schneidewind (SCHN79A). The definitive report on the relation between program size and bug rate is Lipow's (LIPO82). In his study of 115,000 JOVIAL statements, he found a nonlinear relation between bugs per line of code and statements; but also included other factors related to language type and modularization. Small programs had an error rate of 1.3% to 1.8%, with big programs increasing from 2.7% to 3.2%. Lipow's study, however, and most of the others, only included executable lines and not data declarations. The bottom line is that lines of code is reasonably linear for small programs (under 100 lines) but increases nonlinearly with program size. It seems to correlate with maintenance costs. Statement count shows the same correlation. These metrics are certainly better than guesses or nothing at all.

3.3. Halstead's Metrics

3.3.1. What Are They?

Halstead's metrics are based on a combination of arguments derived from common sense, information theory, and psychology. The clearest exposition is still to be found in Halstead's *Elements of Software Science* (HALS77). It's an easy-to-read little book that should be read before applying these metrics. The following exposition is intended only as an introductory overview. The set of metrics are based on two, easily measured, parameters of programs:

n_1 = the number of distinct operators in the program (e.g., keywords)
n_2 = the number of distinct operands in the program (e.g., data objects)

From these he defines **program length,** which is not to be confused with the number of statements in a program, by the following relation:

$$H = n_1 \log_2 n_1 + n_2 \log_2 n_2 \qquad (1)*$$

---

* The late Maurice Halstead used N for this metric, as has the rest of the literature. I have several reasons for departing from that practice. The use of H for "Halstead length" is a fitting tribute to Halstead's contribution to computer science. The term usually used for this metric is "program length," which is easily confused with statement count or lines-of-code. "Halstead's metric" or "Halstead length" cannot be so confused. Finally, the form of the definition is reminiscent of information theory's "information content," to which it is related. In information theory, the information content is denoted by h and is calculated by a similar expression.

In calculating the Halstead length, paired operators such as "BEGIN...END," "DO...UNTIL," "FOR...NEXT," "(...)" are usually treated as a single operator, which is what they actually are. For any given program it's possible to count the actual operator and operand appearances.

$$N_1 = \text{program operator count}$$
$$N_2 = \text{program operand count}$$

The actual Halstead length is evidently

$$N = N_1 + N_2 \tag{2}$$

The actual length is effectively a static count of the number of tokens in the program (see Section 3.4 below).

Halstead also defines a program's **vocabulary** as the sum of the number of distinct operators and operands. That is:

$$n = \text{vocabulary} = n_1 + n_2 \tag{3}$$

The central claim to Halstead's conjecture (equation 1) is that the program's actual Halstead length (N) can be calculated from the program's vocabulary even though the program hasn't been written. It does not tell us how long the program will be in terms of statements, but it is an amazing claim nevertheless. Its immediate importance is that it's often possible to get an operand count and to estimate operator counts before a program is written. This is especially true when the program is written after a data dictionary already exists. If a program is written using 20 keywords out of a total of 200 in the language, and it references 30 data objects, its Halstead length should be $20 \log_2 20 + 30 \log_2 30 = 233.6$. How well does H (the predicted Halstead length) compare with N, (the actual Halstead length measured on the program)? The answer is: closely. The validity of the relation has been experimentally confirmed, many times, independently over a wide range of programs and languages. Furthermore, the relation appears to hold when a program is subdivided into modules.

The bug prediction formula is based on the four values: n_1, n_2, N_1 and N_2:

$$B = \frac{(N_1 + N_2)\log_2(n_1 + n_2)}{3000} \tag{4}$$

All of which are easily measured parameters of a program. A program then that accesses 75 data objects a total of 1300 times and uses 150 operators a total of 1200 times, should be expected to have $(1300 + 1200)\log_2(75 + 150)/3000 = 6.5$ bugs.

In addition to the above equations, Halstead also derived relations that predict programming effort and time, and they also seem to correlate with experience. The time prediction is expectably nonlinear, showing 2.4 hours for a 120-statement program, 230 hours for a 1000-statement program, and 1023 hours for a 2000-statement program. Although the correlation is not perfect, it is at least of the right order of magnitude. Over a set of 24,000 statements, the predicted 31,600 work hours agreed with the actual 36,000 within 12%. Though not perfect, it is better than most simple metrics, but is not better than multifactor models such as COCOMO.

3.3.2. How Good?

Confirmation of these metrics has been extensively published by Halstead and others. The most solid confirmation of the bug prediction equation is by Lipow (LIPO82), who compared actual to predicted bug counts to within 8% over a range of programs sizes from 300 to 12,000 executable statements. The analysis was of postcompilation bugs, so that syntax errors caught by the compiler are properly excluded. However, of the 115,000 statements in the experiment, only the 75,000 executable statements were examined. It would be interesting to see whether better accuracy would have been obtained had all declarations been included in the analysis. Ottenstein, in an earlier report (OTTE79), showed similar good correlation. Curtis (CURT79A) shows that Halstead's metrics are at least twice as good as lines of code and are not improved by augmenting them with lines of code or with McCabe's metric.

There has been extensive experimental confirmation of the utility of Halstead's metrics, to the point that they have been firmly established as the principal linguistic metric. It is likely that if ever a true software science emerges, it will be based in part on Halstead's work. Other confirming studies include FEUE79A, FEUE79B, FITS80, FUNA76, GAFF84, LIPO86, and OTTE79. Critiques are to be found in CURT79A, DEYO79, DUNN82, LEVI86, LEVI87, LASS79, SHEP79C, and ZWEB79.

3.3.3. The Hidden Assumptions and Weaknesses

Because Halstead's metric is the best established (serious) linguistic metric we have, it's fitting that it be subjected to the harshest criticism. There are fewer hidden assumptions in Halstead's work than in other comparable efforts, but some assumptions and weaknesses still remain. Some of the following weaknesses apply to all linguistic metrics.

1. *Modularity*—Modularity is not ignored because each call, together with the parameters of the call sequence, will contribute to the values of n_1, n_2, N_1, and N_2, and therefore to the predicted bug count. Note that Halstead treats each distinct subroutine call as a unique operator and not just as the one keyword "CALL." In this respect, the impact of hypermodularity on bug rate is not ignored. The criticism is that Halstead does not distinguish between a programmer's "own" subfunctions and a subfunction provided by another programmer. Each is given equal weight. The metric might be improved by fudging the weight given to external calls by multiplying it with a constant k_f, greater than 1, which is a measure of the thickness of the semantic fog that exists whenever two programmers attempt to communicate. For own subroutines and modules, the index is equal to 1, and Halstead's criterion relating to optimum module size (see HALS77) holds. For external calls, the fog index might be as high as 5 (depending on the documentation clarity) and would result in bigger components produced by a single programmer. Common subroutines and macros in a library are treated as language extensions and have unity fog index as for built-in language features. If this isn't valid, then documentation must be improved to the point where such calls are no more difficult than built-in keywords.

2. *Database Impact and Declarations*—Halstead isn't to be faulted on this one. It's just that most evaluators and confirmers have continued the erroneous practice of ignoring unexecutable statements such as declarations and data statements—which is to say that most initialization and data structure bugs are ignored. They can't be faulted for this entirely, because in many cases errors in data declarations and initializing data statements are not even counted as bugs. If a true bug count is used, one that includes declaration errors and data statement bugs, then declarations and data statements, equates, constant declarations, and any other statements that affect not just what code is produced, but what data are loaded, should also be counted in determining Halstead's metrics. If such bugs are ignored, the corresponding declarations should not be counted.

3. *Operator/Operand Ambiguity*—There is a hidden assumption that code is code and data are data, and never the twain should meet. If Halstead's metrics are rigidly applied to an assembly language program that does extensive modification of its own code (ugh!) it will

predict the same bug count as a routine that performs the same operations on a fixed data area. Trying to expand the bug prediction or program length equations to such dynamically varying calls would make it impossible to do a static calculation of the metrics. Only a dynamic count would do. In principle, the method still works. Each modified instruction, after each modification, would increase the operator count. Say that a programmer implemented a flag by changing a NOOP instruction to an unconditional branch (a common practice at one time), that instruction, in addition to its appearance as a unique operand, would also contribute two unique operators. The bug prediction would be clearly raised. Whether it would be increased to the point where it would correctly predict the catastrophic impact of instruction modification remains to be seen.

The issue in code-data ambiguity is not with instruction modification, but with code masquerading as data. That is, with data whose actual function is control—as in jump tables, finite-state machines, undeclared internal languages and their interpreters, and similar, effective and useful programming tactics. There is nothing inherently weak in Halstead's approach if we count such things correctly. Control and instructions in the guise of data are operators and not operands. State tables are tables of operators and operands. In the same vein, in languages that permit subroutine names in a call, each value of a subroutine name parameter should be treated as if it were different operator. Similarly for calls that permit a variable number of operands—each value constitutes a different operator. Both of these are instances of dynamically bound objects, which no static metric can handle. See Section 3.4 below.

4. *Data-Type Distinctions*—In strongly typed languages that force the explicit declaration of all types and prohibit mixed-type operations unless a type conversion statement has been inserted, the weakness does not exist if we count all type conversation statements, whether or not they result in object code. If we count all declarations, including user-defined type declarations, there is no weakness in Halstead's metrics. The problem arises in the more common languages that permit mixed operations (e.g., integer floating-point addition) and that have no user-defined types. In principle, each use of an operator must be linked with type of data over which it operates. For example, if a language has integers and short and long operands, and mixed-mode operations are allowed for any combination, then each of the basic arithmetic operators (add, subtract, multiply, divide) actually represents six operators each, one for each combination of operand types. If a language has four types of arithmetic operands,

then each of the basic operators correspond to ten operators, and so on for all combinations of data types and all arithmetic operators.

5. *Call Depth*—No notice is made of call depth. A routine that calls ten different subroutines as a sequence of successive calls would actually be considered more complex than a routine that had ten nested calls. If the totality of the routines and all that it calls were considered, the bug prediction would be the same for both because the total operator and operand counts would be the same. A nonunity fog index associated with each call, which would be multiplicative with depth would raise the predicted bug rate for deeply nested calls. This would be more realistic. Call depth is a structural property and therefore this criticism applies to all linguistic metrics.

6. *Operator Types*—An IF-THEN-ELSE statement is given the same weight as a FOR-UNTIL, even though it's known that loops are more troublesome. This is an example of a broader criticism—that operators and operands are treated equally, with no correlation to the bug incidence associated with specific operators or with operand types.

7. *General Structure Issues*—Of these, the fact that nesting is ignored (nested loops, nested IF-THEN-ELSE, and so on) is probably the most serious critique. A Basic statement such as

$$100 \quad A = B + C @ D = SIN(A) \quad N = 9$$

is less bug-prone than

$$100 \quad D = SIN(B + C) \qquad\qquad N = 6$$

but is claimed to have a higher bug potential. This claim is true if it is assumed that bugs are dominated by typographical errors, but untrue in reality. The first structure is more prone to typographical errors, but is clearer. The second structure is less prone to typographical errors, but is more prone to nesting errors. If we counted $SIN(B + C)$ as a different operator than $SIN(A)$, this problem is taken care of, but this may be an overly harsh use of operator counts. In general, then, a nested sequence of operators, be they loops or logic, is more complicated than an unnested sequence with the same operator and operand count. The possible solution might be a nesting fog index that increases by multiplication with increasing depth. Again, the weakness is generic to all linguistic metrics that ignore structure.

The gist of the above criticism is not so much with Halstead's metrics, but with the way we should apply them. They have proved their worth, but that doesn't mean we should accept and apply them blindly and in a doctrinaire, orthodox, immutable, and rigid manner. It's too early for that. The above critique implies methods of improvement; although some of those suggestions may in practice prove effective, most will probably prove to make little difference or to be outright wrong. It is only by trying, by making variations, by meticulous and honest recording of data, that we will find what components and what interpretations are really useful and the context to which those interpretations apply. The main value of Halstead's work is not in the "theorems"—because they're not really theorems in the sense that they can be proved deductively from axioms—but that he provided strong, cogent, albeit intuitive, arguments for the general functional form that our empirical "laws" should take and what the significant parameters of such "laws" should be.

3.4. Token Count

Levitin, in his incisive critique of linguistic metrics (LEVI86), makes a strong argument for the use of program **token** count rather than lines of code, statement count, or Halstead's length. A **token** in a programming language is the basic syntactic unit from which programs are constructed. Tokens include keywords, labels, constants, strings, and variable names. Token counting is easy because the first stage of compilation is to translate the source code into equivalent numerical tokens. The number of tokens is easily obtained as a by-product of compilation. Token count gets around the subjectivity problems we have with statement counts and lines of code.

There are two possible ambiguities: paired delimiters and dynamically bound objects. Paired delimiters are usually converted by the compiler into two tokens and then eliminated by the (typical) subsequent translation to parenthesis-free form (i.e., polish prefix or suffix form). Although syntactically, paired delimiters function as a single object, there is a strong case for treating them as two objects, in that a paired delimiter *is* more complex than a single operator, and bugs can occur with mismatched paired delimiters if both a begin and end delimiter are dropped or added. In some languages it is possible to add or drop a single half of the pair and still have a syntactically correct program because the second half is optional—for example, if a single END is used to service a bunch of BEGINs or a single ENDIF concludes a nesting of IF. . .THENs. The pragmatic approach is not to agonize over the point but to simply use the compiler's token count as the metric, however it treats paired delimiters. The issue is not important because at worst it introduces a statistically small error.

Levitin's argument (LEVI89) with respect to dynamically bound objects such as a variable number of objects in a call or a variable subroutine name in a call is that you cannot define a static metric over such objects— the size is dynamic and only a metric defined over the program at run-time will do. Dynamic binding violates our second desirable metric property. The observation is important because it clarifies the issue—the fact that the use of dynamically bound objects is much more complex than statically bound objects. A static count can still be used, but the metric should be augmented with a count of the instances of dynamically bound objects as determined at compile time, which could result in additional tokens when bound. That is, the metric consists of two parts: the static token count and unbound token count. This approach gets around the problems of how to count dynamic subroutine names in calls, pointer variables, variable number of objects in a call, etc. We would expect the unbound variable count to have a much higher coefficient in a bug prediction formula, say.

Why this simple, obvious, linguistic metric has been all but ignored in the literature is as mysterious to me as it is to Levitin. Its only significant weaknesses are those that apply to all purely linguistic metrics: e.g., ignoring nesting depth and treating all operators as equivalent. We should progress from simpler to more complicated metrics only to the extent that we have to in order to get good empirical laws. Most metrics, as actually used, are applied to source code, so that some of the utility of Halstead's conjecture is eroded—why estimate N (effectively the token count) from n_1 and n_2 using Halstead's conjecture when the compiler can give you the actual value directly?

4.   STRUCTURAL METRICS

4.1.   General

Structural metrics take the opposite viewpoint of linguistic metrics. Linguistic complexity is ignored while attention is focused on control-flow or data-flow complexity—metrics based on the properties of flowgraph models of programs. Graph theory is more than a half-century old but the study of graph-theoretic problems and metrics goes back three centuries: see MAYE72. If it's a graph (i.e., it consists of links and nodes) then there are hundreds of interesting metrics that can be applied to it: metrics whose mathematical properties have been studied in minute detail. The thrust of structural metrics research has not been so much the invention of new graph-theoretic metrics but the investigation of the utility of known graph-theoretic metrics. McCabe's use of the cyclomatic number (MCCA76) is an archetypal example.

4.2. Cyclomatic Complexity (McCabe's Metric)

4.2.1. Definition

McCabe's cyclomatic complexity metric (MCCA76) is defined as:

$$M = L - N + 2P$$

where

L = the number of links in the graph
N = the number of nodes in the graph
P = the number of disconnected parts of the graph (e.g., a calling program and a subroutine)

The number M that appeared alongside the flowgraphs in Chapter 3 was McCabe's metric for that flowgraph. In all the examples, except for the one on page 73, there was only one connected part, and consequently the value of P was 1. Figure 7.1 shows some more examples and their associated M values.

This metric has the intuitively satisfying property that the complexity of several graphs considered as a set is equal to the sum of the individual graphs' complexities. You can see this by analyzing Figure 7.2. Two disconnected graphs having N_1, L_1 and N_2, L_2 nodes and links respectively, are combined and treated as a single entity with $N_1 + N_2$ nodes and $L_1 + L_2$ links. The arithmetic shows directly that the complexity of the sum is equal to the sum of the complexities.

This metric can also be calculated by adding one to the number of binary decisions in a structured flowgraph with only one entry and one exit. If all decisions are not binary, count a three-way decision as two binary decisions and N-way case statements as $N - 1$ binary decisions. Similarly, the iteration test in a DO or other looping statement is counted as a binary decision. The rationale behind this counting of N-way decisions is that it would take a string of $N - 1$ binary decisions to implement an N-way case statement.

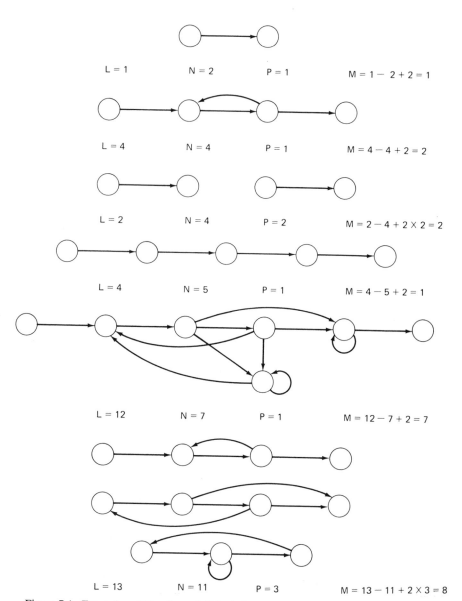

Figure 7.1. Examples of Graphs and Calculation of McCabe's Complexity Metric.

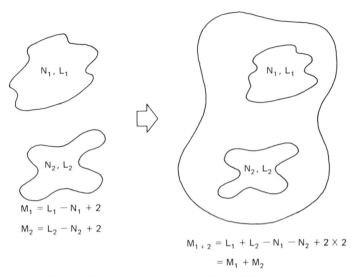

$$M_1 = L_1 - N_1 + 2$$

$$M_2 = L_2 - N_2 + 2$$

$$M_{1+2} = L_1 + L_2 - N_1 - N_2 + 2 \times 2$$

$$= M_1 + M_2$$

Figure 7.2. Complexity Sum and Sum of Complexities.

4.2.2.   Applications to Test Plan Completeness and Inspections

Evaluate the cyclomatic complexity of the program's design (e.g., from the design control flowgraph). As part of self-inspection, reevaluate the complexity by counting decisions in the code. Any significant difference should be explained, because it's more likely that the difference is due to a missing path, an extra path, or an unplanned deviation from the design than to something else. Having verified the code's cyclomatic complexity, compare the number of planned test cases to the code's complexity. In particular, count how many test cases are intended to provide coverage. If the number of covering test cases is less than the cyclomatic complexity, there is reason for caution, because one of the following may be true:

1. You haven't calculated the complexity correctly. Did you miss a decision?
2. Coverage is not really complete; there's a link that hasn't been covered.
3. Coverage is complete, but it can be done with a few more but simpler paths.
4. It might be possible to simplify the routine.

Warning: Don't be rigid in applying the above because the relation between cyclomatic complexity and the number of tests needed to achieve branch coverage is circumstantial. Use it as a guideline, not as an immutable fact.

4.2.3. When to Subroutine

McCabe's metric can be used to help decide whether it pays to make a piece of code which is common to two or more links into a subroutine. Consider the graph of Figure 7.3. The program has a common part that consists of N_c nodes and L_c links. This is the part being considered for conversion to a subroutine. This common part recurs k times in the body of the main program. The main program has N_m nodes and L_m links over and above the common part. The total number of links and nodes for the main program, therefore, is $L_m + kL_c$ and $N_m + kN_c$. When the common parts are removed, an additional link must be added to the main program to replace the code by a subroutine call. The subroutine's code must be augmented with an additional entry node and exit node. The following table summarizes the transformation:

	EMBEDDED COMMON PART	SUBROUTINE FOR COMMON PART
Main nodes	$N_m + kN_c$	N_m
Main links	$L_m + kL_c$	$L_m + k$
Subnodes	0	$N_c + 2$
Sublinks	0	L_c
Main complexity	$L_m + kL_c - N_m + kN_c + 2$	$L_m + k$
Subcomplexity	0	$L_c - N_c - 2 + 2 = L_c - N_c = M$
Total complexity + 2	$L_m + kL_c - N_m + kN_c + 2$	$L_m + L_c - N_m - N_c + k + 2$

The break-even point occurs when the total complexities are equal. A little algebra shows that this is independent of the main routine's complexity and is equal to: $M_c = k/(k - 1)$. For one call ($k = 1$), the total complexity must increase no matter how complex the subroutine itself is. For two calls, the crossover occurs at a complexity of 2 for the subroutine. For more calls, the crossover complexity decreases and is asymptotic to 1. In general, then, creating subroutines out of straight-line code (complexity of 1) tends to increase net complexity rather than reduce it, if one takes into account the complexity of the calls and the fact that there are separate routines. Of course, you would not use this analysis as the sole criterion for deciding whether or not to make a subroutine out of common code.

One of the popular fads of the 1970s was blind modularization. Rules such as "No subroutine shall contain more than a hundred statements"

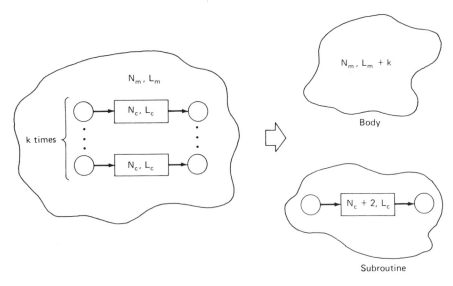

Figure 7.3. Subroutine Complexity.

were used in the hope of reducing bug frequency. Presumably, if programmers followed such rules, the programs would be simpler, easier to debug, more reliable, and so on. This rule was, unfortunately, put into several government specifications. The statistics (discussed below) show that McCabe's metric is a better measure of complexity than lines of code. It's intuitively better because it takes into account the increase in complexity resulting from subdividing a routine—something which lines of code does not do. If anything, McCabe's metric underestimates the impact of subdividing code, because it says that the complexity of the whole is equal to the sum of the complexities of its parts—which is neat, but it is an underestimate because complexity increases nonlinearly with more parts. The above analysis warns us that complexity can increase, rather than decrease, with modularization—as the following experience with my favorite bad project shows:*

The system was a multicomputer, distributed-processing, distributed-database kind of thing—a tough proposition at best. Of all the silly rules

---

* It was a really bad project, but it had its good sides. I will never again witness so many bad design practices and such a lack of testing discipline (which supplied ample material for this book) under one roof. It was a real project, and it was rotten from keelson to hounds. Obviously, I can't identify it without risking a libel suit. As for discussing bad projects and what appears to be an uncommon frequency of them in my experience—it's not that I've had bad luck, but that consultants aren't usually called in for good projects. As for discussing bad projects at all, there's more to be learned from our mistakes than from our triumphs.

that this benighted project adopted in the interest of improving programmer productivity and software reliability, the silliest was an absolute, unappealable restriction of all modules to less than fifty *object-code* instructions.

Because the program was written in a higher-order language, and because the call/return sequence took up about half of the object code, what resulted were thousands of tiny subroutines and modules hardly more than ten source statements long. The typical number of calls per module was 1.1 ($k = 1.1$), which meant that the subroutines would have had to have a complexity of 10 or greater, if net complexity was to be reduced. But the fifty-object-statement rule kept the average complexity down to about 1.01. This hypermodularity increased the predicted test and debug effort to several times as much as had been estimated for unit design, test, and debugging. Because the hyperfine modularity and the other rules adopted were supposed to eliminate *all* bugs, the labor estimated for system integration and test was an order of magnitude less than it should have been. My estimates of the labor needed to integrate this vast horde of tiny, gnat-like subroutines was about 30 or 40 times higher than the project's management expected. My predictions were not politely received, to say the least, and my association with the project ended soon after. They quietly dropped that rule (so I heard) when they redesigned the system for the version that did (after a fashion) work.

I don't advocate great complicated unwashed masses of overly verbose code that rambles on and on and on and on, page after page after page, beyond the scope of human ken. Programs like that are also untestable. But consider this when setting modularity rules: in addition to the net increase in complexity due to breaking a function up, there is a further increase attributable to additional code in a calling sequence and possibly additional declarations. All of these increases add to the bug rate and testing labor. Furthermore, each subdivision creates a new interface between the calling routine and called routine, and all interfaces breed bugs. Partition cannot be dictated by an arbitrary rule but must result from a trade analysis whose resulting optimum value is unlikely to exist at either extreme of the range.

4.2.4.   A Refinement

Myers (MYER77) points out a weakness of McCabe's metric and suggests the use of a refinement thereto. A decision statement in languages such as FORTRAN can contain a compound predicate of the form: IF A & B & C THEN . . . . A statement such as this could be implemented as a string of IFs, resulting in a different complexity measure. Figure 7.4 shows three

IF (A.AND.B.AND.C) THEN . . . ELSE

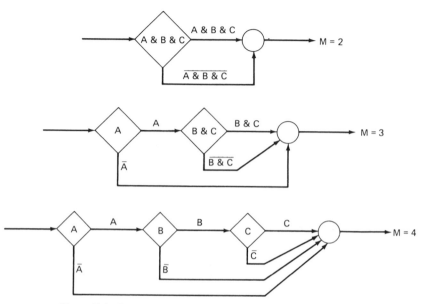

Figure 7.4. Cyclomatic Complexity and Compound Predicates.

alternate, equivalent, representations of the same IF-THEN-ELSE statement. If the compound predicate is used in a single statement as in the first case, the complexity of the construct is only two, but if it is broken down into its constituent parts, the complexity increases to four. However, intuitively, all three constructs should have the same complexity. The refinement consists of accounting for each term of the predicate expression separately. For a predicate expression of the form A&B&C . . . , each predicate should be counted as if it was a decision. In more complicated expressions, such as A&B&C OR D&E . . . , again count each predicate. If a predicate appears more than once in an expression, you can take a pessimistic point of view and count each appearance or a slightly optimistic point of view and count only the first appearance.

4.2.5. How Good a Measure; A Critique

Statistics on how well McCabe's metric correlates with design, test, and debugging difficulty are encouraging (BELF79, CHEN78A, CURT79A, ENDR75, FEUE79A, FEUE79B, LIPO77, SCHN79A, SCHN79B,

SCHN79D, SHEP79C, THAY76, WALS79, ZOLN77).* The reported results confirm the utility of McCabe's metric as a convenient rule of thumb that is significantly superior to statement count.

McCabe advises partitioning routines whose metric exceeds 10. Walsh confirms this advice (WALS79) by citing a military software project to which the metric was applied. They found that 23% of the routines with a metric value greater than 10 accounted for 53% of the bugs. Walsh further states that in the same study of 276 procedures, the routines with M greater than 10 had 21% more errors per line of code than those with metric values below 10. Feuer (FEUE79A, FEUE79B) cites mixed results but provides strong correlation between the metric (actually, decision counts) and error rates for big programs. Curtis (CURT79A) also shows fair predictability. For other references related to structural complexity, McCabe's metric, and related subjects see BAKE79A, BAKE80, PAIG75A, PAIG77, PAIG78, SCHN79B, and WOOD78.

It's too early to tell whether this metric will eventually serve as a true bug predictor. It's not likely. The main appeal of M is its simplicity. People have long used program length as the main criterion for judging software complexity. Simple measures are inherently inaccurate but they can provide useful rules of thumb. McCabe's metric should be used in combination with token count to get a quick measure of complexity.

McCabe's metric has some additional weaknesses. It makes no real distinction as to the direction of flow. For example, an IF-THEN-ELSE statement has the same complexity as a single loop. This situation is not intuitively satisfying because we know that loops are more troublesome than simple decision sequences. Case statements, which provide a nice, regular structure, are given a high complexity value, which is also coun-terintuitive. It also tends to judge highly regular, repetitive control structures unfairly. Conversely, if these weaknesses were to be rectified, it could only be done by increasing the complexity of the metric itself and taking it out of the realm of an easy-to-use measure of complexity.

The strongest criticism of this metric is its shaky theoretical foundation (EVAN84). McCabe wanted to relate the cyclomatic complexity to the number of test cases needed—that is, to use cyclomatic complexity as a coverage metric. His testing strategy ("structured testing," MCCA82) is based on selecting control-flow paths that satisfy graph-theoretic properties on which this metric is based. The cyclomatic number of a graph is the number of paths in the base set of paths for strongly connected,

---

* Not all of these references provide direct information for McCabe's metric. Some (ENDR75, THAY76) provide correlations to decision counts and similar metrics that can be converted to McCabe's metric. Note also that if we forget the structural basis of cyclomatic complexity and merely use equivalent binary decision count or simple predicate count, then this metric can be obtained by purely linguistic means.

undirected, graphs. That is, for graphs whose exit is connected to the entry **(strongly connected)** and for which all links are bidirectional **(undirected),** all paths can be built out of a combination of paths in the base set. McCabe's conjecture was that adequate coverage could be achieved by using a base set of test paths. Evangelist (EVAN84) says no and provides counterexamples. Furthermore, research has failed to provide either a theoretical basis for this conjecture or to relate McCabe's heuristic testing strategies to any other structural testing strategy even though the strategy appears to be pragmatically effective. Despite these criticisms, whether McCabe's reasoning is valid or invalid, cyclomatic complexity (or more often, equivalent binary decision count) is a firmly established, handy rule of thumb for structural complexity.

4.2.6. Utility Summary

Cyclomatic complexity provides some useful rules of thumb:

1. Bugs per line of code increase discontinuously for M greater than 10.
2. Arbitrary modularity rules based on length, when applied to straight-line code that has few calls or only one call, increase rather than reduce complexity.
3. The amount of design, code, test design, and test effort is better judged by cyclomatic complexity than by lines of code.
4. Routines with high complexity, say 40 or more, should be given close scrutiny, especially if that complexity is not due to the use of case statements or other regular control structures. If the complexity is due to loops and raw logic, consideration should be given to subdividing the routine into smaller, less complex segments in order to avoid the nonlinear increase in effort associated with high complexity.
5. Cyclomatic complexity establishes a useful lower-bound rule of thumb for the number of cases required to achieve branch coverage—especially when based on simple predicate counts rather than raw decision counts (i.e., use the number of simple predicates plus 1). If fewer test cases than M are proposed, look for missing cases or the possibility of simplifying the logic or using tests that are less complicated.

4.3. Other Structural Metrics

Many other structural metrics have been proposed and investigated. Chen (CHEN78A) combines structural properties with information theoretic concepts. Gong (GONG85) combines decisions and nesting depth. Rodriguez and Tsai (RODR86) apply structural concepts to data flowgraphs, as do Tai (TAIK84) and Tsai et al. (TSAI86). Van Verth (VANV87) proposes using a combination of control flow and data flow, as does Whitworth (WHIT80B). This list is incomplete as the number of papers on alternate complexity metrics is as great as those on alternate testing strategies. The problem with these metrics is that confirming statistics on their usefulness is lacking. It is intuitively clear that cyclomatic complexity over data flowgraphs should be as useful a metric as cyclomatic complexity over control flowgraphs but corroboration is still lacking (OVIE80).

5. HYBRID METRICS

The appearance of McCabe's and Halstead's metrics spurred the proposal, development, refinement, and validation of a host of similar and related metrics, or totally different alternatives based on different assumptions. Some of those cited below preceded McCabe's and Halstead's work and some followed. It's too early to tell which will be experimentally confirmed independently over a range of projects and applications, no matter how rational and sensible their basis might be. Some of the more interesting and promising alternatives are presented in BAKE79A, BAKE80, BELF79, CHAP79, CHEN78A, DEYO79, EVAN84, FEUE79B, GILB77, LIPO77, MCCL78B, PAIG80, RAMA88, SCHN79B, VANV87, WHIT80B, and ZONL77. Most of these metrics and their variations recognize one or more weaknesses in the popular metrics and seek to measure reliability and/or predict bug counts through refinement or alternative formulation of the problem. It is inevitable that increased predictability and fidelity can only be achieved at a cost of increased sophistication, complexity of evaluation, and difficulty of use.

6. METRICS IMPLEMENTATION

6.1. The Pattern of Metrics Research

You may well ask why you, who may be concerned with getting next week's release working, should care about how metrics research is done. There are several reasons:

1. Like it nor not, sooner or later, what you do will be measured by metrics. As a programmer or tester, the quality of your work and your personal productivity will be tied (rightly or wrongly) to metrics whose validity ranges from statistically sound, to theoretically

sound but not germane, to downright stupid. Understanding the research issues may help you to tell them apart.

2. Metrics *are* useful—to programmers, testers, and managers, and almost any complexity metric (even listing weight) is better than no metric at all.

3. If you're using any complexity metric at all, you're either doing metrics research yourself or you're a subject in a metrics research experiment. Some experiments are better (worse) than others. I don't really mind being run like a rat through a maze but I'd like to know about it.

Let's go back to how a (good) metrics research project is done:

1. A new metric is proposed, based on previous metrics, a functional combination of previous metrics, wholly new principles, intuition, valid or invalid reasoning, or whatever. The metric's definition is refined to the point where a tool that measures it can be written.

2. The metric is compared by correlation analysis to previous metrics: lines of code, Halstead's length, Halstead's volume, and cyclomatic complexity are favorites. The correlation analysis is done over a set of known programs such as a set of programs for which metric values were previously published. The new metric shows a high correlation to the old metrics. Metrics that don't correlate well usually die a quiet death. Correlation with previous metrics is important because we know how well (or how poorly) such metrics correlate with things we're interested in, such as number of tests required, expected number of remaining bugs, programming effort, and so on.

3. The metric is used to predict interesting characteristics of programming and software for new code or for maintenance. Statistics are gathered and the predictions are compared with actual results. Good predictors are retained, bad predictors remain unpublished.

4. The metric is "tweaked" (i.e., refined) to provide better predictions and step 3 above is repeated. This process continues until the predictor stabilizes.

5. A more sophisticated alternative is to throw a whole bunch of possible metrics into a pot and do the above steps with the additional refinement of using regression analysis (DRAP81) to obtain a weighted multifactor metric.

Most published metrics research doesn't get beyond step 2, and little has been published that gets past the iteration between steps 3 and 4. We seem to have more papers that critique old metrics and that propose new metrics (to be subsequently critiqued by others) than papers that show how useful a specific metric is. Useful comparisons and criticisms of various metrics can be found in BAKE79A, CURR86, CURT79A, DAVI88C, EVAN84, FEUE79A, FEUE79B, GRAD87, HARR82, LEVI86, LIHF87, LIND89, NEJM88, PAIG80, RODR86, RODR87, VANV87, and WEYU88B. The most useful information on metrics research, though, is never published because the sponsors of that research consider the information too valuable and too proprietary to divulge it to their competitors.

6.2. A Pattern for Successful Applications

Successful applications of metrics abound but aren't much talked about in the public literature (but see GRAD87). Mature metrics (emphasis on mature—see below) can help us predict expected number of latent bugs, help us decide how much testing is enough and how much design effort, cost, elapsed time, and all the rest we expect from metrics. Here's what it takes to have a success.

1. *Any Metric Is Better Than None*—A satnav system or loran is better than a compass, but even a compass beats navigating with your head stuck in the bilges. Correlate what you're interested in with listing weight if that's the best you can do. Implement token counting and cyclomatic complexity as the next step. Worry about the fancy metrics later.

2. *Automation Is Essential*—Any metrics project that relies on having the programmers fill out long questionnaires or manually calculate metric values is doomed. They never work. If they work once, they won't the second time. If we've learned anything, it's that a metric whose calculation isn't fully automated isn't worth doing: it probably harms productivity and quality more than any benefit we can expect from metrics.

3. *Empiricism Is Better Than Theory*—Theory is at best a guide to what makes sense to include in a metrics project—there's no theory sufficiently sound today to warrant the use of a single, specific metric above others. Theory tells you what to put into the empirical pot. It's the empirical, statistical data that you must use for guidance.

4. *Use Multifactor Rather Than Single Metrics*—All successful metrics programs use a combination (typically linear) of several different metrics with weights calculated by regression analysis. Some organizations measure more than 200 factors but only a few of these end up with significant coefficients in prediction formulas.

5. *Avoid Naive Statistics*—Getting empirical laws from measured data is old hat to statisticians and they know how to avoid the statistical gaffes that trap the unwary amateur. I saw one big project go down the tubes because of naive statistics. They predicted the safe release point with exquisite precision but no accuracy—"We can ship the release on June 25 at 2:04:22.71 P.M. (plus or minus three centuries)." Bring a professional statistician in to assure yourself that the metrics are significant when compared to random events. Use a statistician to tell you how much confidence is or isn't warranted in the predictions.

6. *Don't Confuse Productivity Metrics with Complexity Metrics*—Productivity is a characteristic of programmers and testers. Complexity is a characteristic of programs. It's not always easy to tell them apart. Examples of productivity metrics incorrectly used in lieu of complexity metrics are: number of shots it takes to get a clean compilation, percentage of modules that passed testing on the first attempt, number of test cases required to find the first bug. There's nothing wrong with using productivity metrics as an aid to project management, but that's a whole different story. Automated or not, a successful metrics program needs programmer cooperation. If complexity and productivity are mixed up, be prepared for either or both to be sabotaged to uselessness.

7. *Let Them Mature*—It takes a lot of projects and a long time for metrics to mature to the point where they're trustworthy. If the typical project takes 12 months, then it takes ten to fifteen projects over a 2- to 3-year period before the metrics are any use at all.

8. *Maintain Them*—As design methods change, as testing gets better, and as QA functions to remove the old kind of bugs, the metrics based on that past history loses its utility as a predictor of anything. The weights given to metrics in predictor equations have to be revised and continually reevaluated to ensure that they continue to predict what they are intended to predict.

9. *Let Them Die*—Metrics wear out just like test suites do, for the same reason—the pesticide paradox. Actually, it's not that the metric itself wears out but that the importance we assign to the metric changes with time. I've seen projects go down the tubes because of worn-out metrics and the predictions based on them.

7. TESTABILITY TIPS

We don't have testability metrics yet—but we have complexity metrics and we know that more complexity means more bugs and more testing to find those bugs. It's not that you shouldn't design complicated software, but that you should know your design's complexity.

1. Use Halstead's conjecture, Eq. (1), to estimate the token count before coding. You can estimate the number of operands (n_2) from the data dictionary and the number of operators (n_1) from your experience with the language and the number of subroutine and function calls you expect to make.

2. Use the number of equivalent binary decisions in your PDL or design control–flowgraph as an estimator of control-flow complexity. Remember that there's a jump in the bug potential for cyclomatic complexity at around 10 to 15. Remember that cyclomatic complexities of more than 40 (excluding neat case statements) are probably over your (and anyone's) head. Learn your own limits and your own ability to handle control-flow complexity.

3. If you use a design methodology or data-structuring tools that allow you to find the total data-flow complexity, use that as a guide to how much data complexity you can tolerate.

4. Once you have compiled code, use token counts, and if you have the tools for it, also control-flow and data-flow cyclomatic complexity. Compare these metrics to the precoding estimates to be sure that you haven't inadvertently buried yourself in complexity. Break it up before testing and debugging if you're in over your head.

5. As testers and designers, support your QA group and agitate for corporate, project, and personal statistics that relate the expected number of bugs and the expected number of tests needed to shake out those bugs to the primary complexity metrics (tokens, control flow, data flow). Agitate for tools that will pull this stuff out for you directly as a by-product of compilation. Don't stop using your intuition and common sense—use the statistics to sharpen them.

We all have personal complexity barriers. The barriers we can safely hurdle get bigger with experience, stabilize to some maximum personal level, and then get smaller as we age and lose vitality. A by-product of experience is that we have a better understanding of our personal barriers and are less likely to get in over our heads—that's called wisdom. Because there's less wasted effort banging our heads against barriers we can't conquer, net productivity (that is, the production of fully tested, reliable software as distinct from raw code) generally increases with experience. Exploit the complexity metrics and their relation (however fuzzy that relation may be) to testing requirements and bug potentials to learn about yourself, in weeks and months, what others have taken years and decades to learn.

8. SUMMARY

1. Computer science is still far from a quantitative science. Because of the high human content, the model is more likely to be that of economics than of physics.
2. Three complexity metrics appear to be basic: token count, control-flow cyclomatic complexity, and data-flow cyclomatic complexity. Learn to use these instead of lines of code.
3. Don't bother with metrics that aren't automated: the payoff is probably less than the effort, and the accuracy is dubious.
4. As testers and designers we want to relate the metric value to a prediction of the expected number of bugs in a piece of code and the expected number of tests needed to find those bugs. That relation, today, is best obtained empirically from data gathered over a long period of time and many different pieces of software. The specific values are personal; that is, they differ widely between applications, organizations, projects, and individuals. Until we understand the underlying cause of bugs we'll have to make do with such personal, empirical "rules."
5. All metrics today, and the relations derived from them, are at best quantified rules of thumb dressed up in statistical finery—they provide guidance. Don't use them as rigid rules.
6. Metrics are based on statistics. It's as important to know how much statistical confidence is warranted in a metric as it is to know the results that the metric claims to predict. Don't get trapped by naive statistics.

8

PATHS, PATH PRODUCTS, AND REGULAR EXPRESSIONS

1. SYNOPSIS

Path expressions are introduced as an algebraic representations of sets of paths in a graph. With suitable arithmetic laws (BRZO62A, BRZO62B, BRZO63, MCNA60, PRAT83) and weights, path expressions are converted into algebraic functions or **regular expressions** that can be used to examine structural properties of flowgraphs, such as the number of paths, processing time, or whether a data-flow anomaly can occur. These expressions are then applied to problems in test design and debugging.

2. MOTIVATION

This chapter and its continuation, Chapter 12, are the two most abstract chapters in this book; but that doesn't mean that they're difficult. Considering the generally pragmatic orientation of this book, some motivation for this abstraction is warranted. I could be high-handed and patronizing and say: "Trust me, it's good for you," but you're too intelligent to let me get away with that. This stuff *is* good for you and I do want you to trust me about it; but I would rather you take the effort needed to master the subject and then to see all the nice ways it can be applied. So here's some motivation for you.

1. I introduced flowgraphs as an abstract representation of programs. I assume that by now you appreciate their utility and want to know how playing with flowgraphs is really done.
2. Almost any question you have about programs can be cast into an equivalent question about an appropriate flowgraph. This chapter tells you how to do that.

3. The concepts discussed in this chapter will help you better understand and exploit syntax testing (Chapter 9) and state testing (Chapter 11), both of which yield applicable test methods.
4. EE's have been using flowgraphs to design and analyze circuits for more than 50 years (MAYE72) and logic designers for more than 30 years. Get on the bandwagon.
5. Most software development, testing, and debugging tools use flowgraph analysis techniques (or should). You can better exploit your tools if you understand them.
6. If you're a test tool builder, I don't know how you can get along without these concepts.

3.   PATH PRODUCTS AND PATH EXPRESSIONS

3.1.   Overview

Our flowgraphs (Chapter 3) denoted only control-flow connectivity; that is, links had no property other than the fact that they connected nodes. In Chapter 5, on data-flow testing, we expanded the notation to add **link weights;** that is, every link was annotated with a letter or sequence of letters that denoted the sequence of data-flow actions on that link. We'll now generalize the idea of link weights so that they can denote almost anything of interest that can be derived from the program's structure.

The simplest weight we can give to a link is a name. Using link names as weights, we then convert the graphical flowgraph into an equivalent algebraic-like expression which denotes the set of all possible paths (finite or infinite) from entry to exit for that flowgraph. The same basic algorithm is then used in subsequent sections with different kinds of weights to do data-flow anomaly detection, timing analyses, and to solve various debugging and testing problems.

3.2.   Basic Concepts

Every link of a graph can be given a name; the link name will be denoted by lowercase italic letters. In tracing a path or path segment through a flowgraph, you traverse a succession of link names. The name of the path or path segment that corresponds to those links is expressed naturally by concatenating those link names. If you traverse links a, b, c, and d along some path, the name for that path segment is $abcd$. This path name is also called a **path product.** Figure 8.1 shows some examples.

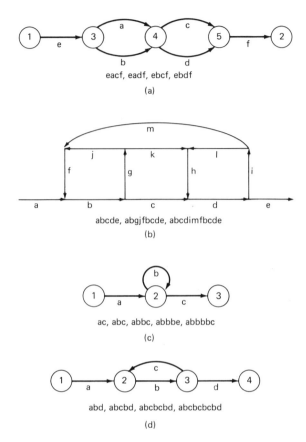

Figure 8.1. Examples of Paths.

Consider a pair of nodes in a graph and the set of paths between those nodes. Denote that set of paths by uppercase letters such as X or Y. The members of that set can be listed as follows for Figure 8.1c:

ac, abc, abbc, abbbc, . . .

Alternatively, that same set of paths can be denoted by:

ac + abc + abbc + abbbc + · · ·

The "+" sign is understood to mean "or." That is, between the two nodes of interest, paths *ac*, or *abc*, or *abbc*, and so on can be taken. Any expression that consists of path names and "ORs" and which denotes a set of paths (not necessarily the set of all paths) between two nodes is called a **path expression.**

3.3. Path Products

The name of a path that consists of two successive path segments is conveniently expressed by the concatenation or **path product** of the segment names. For example, if X and Y are defined as

$$X = abcde$$
$$Y = fghij$$

then the path corresponding to X followed by Y is denoted by

$$XY = abcdefghij$$

Similarly,

$$YX = fghijabcde$$
$$aX = aabcde$$
$$Xa = abcdea$$
$$XaX = abcdeaabcde$$

If X and Y represent sets of paths or path expressions, their product represents the set of paths that can be obtained by following every element of X by any element of Y in all possible ways. For example,

$$X = abc + def + ghi$$
$$Y = uvw + z$$

Then

$$XY = abcuvw + defuvw + ghiuvw + abcz + defz + ghiz$$

If a link or segment name is repeated, that fact is denoted by an exponent. The exponent's value denotes the number of repetitions:

$$a^1 = a; a^2 = aa; a^3 = aaa; a^n = aaaa \ . \ . \ . \ n \text{ times.}$$

Similarly, if

$$X = abcde$$

then

$$X^1 = abcde$$
$$X^2 = abcdeabcde \qquad = (abcde)^2$$
$$X^3 = abcdeabcdeabcde = (abcde)^2abcde$$
$$\quad = abcde(abcde)^2 \qquad = (abcde)^3$$

The path product is not commutative (that is, XY does not necessarily equal YX), but expressions derived from it may be commutative. The path product is associative, but expressions derived from it may not be; that is,

Rule 1:   A(BC) = (AB)C = ABC

where A, B, and C are path names, sets of path names, or path expressions.

The zeroth power of a link name, path product, or path expression is also needed for completeness. It is denoted by the numeral "1" and denotes the "path" whose length is zero—that is, the path that doesn't have any links.* 1 is a multiplicative identity element; that is, it has the same properties as the number 1 in ordinary arithmetic.

$$a^0 = 1$$
$$X^0 = 1$$

3.4. Path Sums

The "+" sign was used to denote the fact that path names were part of the same set of paths. Consider the set of paths that can lie between two arbitrary nodes of a graph. Even though these paths can traverse intermediate nodes, they can be thought of as "parallel" paths between the two nodes. The **path sum** denotes paths in parallel between two nodes. Links a and b in Figure 8.1a are parallel paths and are denoted by $a + b$. Similarly, links c and d are parallel paths between the next two nodes and are denoted by $c + d$. The set of all paths between nodes 1 and 2 of Figure 8.1a can be thought of as a set of parallel paths between nodes 1 and 2 and can be denoted by $eacf + eadf + ebcf + ebdf$. If X and Y are sets of paths that lie between the same pair of nodes, then X + Y denotes the union of

---

* The first edition and the literature on regular expressions use the Greek letter lambda (λ) for this. I've switched to an ordinary "1" to simplify the notation and to make it more familiar.

those sets of paths. As an example,

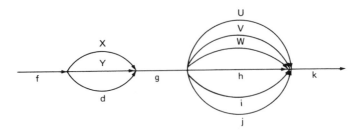

The first set of parallel paths is denoted by $X + Y + d$ and the second set by $U + V + W + h + i + j$. The set of all paths in this flowgraph is

$$f(X + Y + d)g(U + V + W + h + i + j)k$$

Keep in mind in the above example that the uppercase letters can represent individual segment names (*pqrst,* say) or sets of segment names, such as *pqrst + pqrsst + pqrssst +* $\cdot$ $\cdot$ $\cdot$. Because the path sum is a set union operation, it is clearly commutative and associative; that is,

Rule 2: $X + Y = Y + X$
Rule 3: $(X + Y) + Z = X + (Y + Z) = X + Y + Z$

3.5 Distributive Laws

The product and sum operations are distributive, and the ordinary rules of multiplication apply; that is,

Rule 4: $A(B + C) = AB + AC$ and $(B + C)D = BC + BD$

Applying these rules to Figure 8.1a yields

$$e(a + b)(c + d)f = e(ac + ad + bc + bd)f$$
$$= eacf + eadf + ebcf + ebdf$$

for the set of all paths from node 1 to node 2 .

3.6. Absorption Rule

If X and Y denote the same set of paths, then the union of these sets is unchanged; consequently,

Rule 5: $X + X = X$ (absorption rule)

Similarly, if a set consists of path names and a member of that set is added to it, the "new" name, which is already in that set of names, contributes nothing and can be ignored. For example, if

$$X = a + aa + abc + abcd + def$$

then

$$X + a = X + aa = X + abc = X + abcd = X + def = X$$

It follows that any arbitrary sum of identical path expressions reduces to the same path expression.

3.7. Loops

Loops can be understood as an infinite set of parallel paths. Say that the loop consists of a single link b. Then the set of all paths through that loop point is

$$b^0 + b^1 + b^2 + b^3 + b^4 + b^5 + \cdots$$

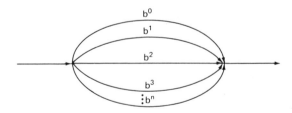

This potentially infinite sum is denoted by b^* for an individual link and by X^* when X is a path expression. If the loop must be taken at least once, then it is denoted by a^+ or X^+. The path expressions for Figure 8.1c and 8.1d, respectively, as expressed by this notation, are

$$ab^*c = ac + abc + abbc + abbbc + \cdots$$

and

$$a(bc)^*bd = abd + abcbd + abcbcbd + a(bc)^3bd + \cdots$$

Evidently

$$aa^* = a^*a = a^+$$

and

$$XX^* = X^*X = X^+$$

It is sometimes convenient to denote the fact that a loop cannot be taken more than a certain, say n, number of times. A bar is used under the exponent to denote that fact as follows:

$$X^{\underline{n}} = X^0 + X^1 + X^2 + X^3 + \cdots + X^{n-1} + X^n$$

The following rules can be derived from the previous rules:

Rule 6: $X^{\underline{n}} + X^{\underline{m}} = X^{\underline{n}}$ if n is bigger than m
$\qquad\qquad\qquad\quad = X^{\underline{m}}$ if m is bigger than n
Rule 7: $X^{\underline{n}}X^{\underline{m}} \quad = X^{\underline{n+m}}$
Rule 8: $X^{\underline{n}}X^* \quad\; = X^*X^{\underline{n}} = X^*$
Rule 9: $X^{\underline{n}}X^+ \quad\; = X^+X^{\underline{n}} = X^+$
Rule 10: $X^*X^+ \quad\; = X^+X^* = X^+$

3.8. Identity Elements

Returning to the meaning of terms such as a^0 or X^0, which denote the path whose length is zero, the following rules, previously used without explanation, apply:

Rule 11: $1 + 1 = 1$
Rule 12: $1X = X1 = X$ Following or preceding a set of paths by a path of zero length doesn't change the set.
Rule 13: $1^n = 1^{\underline{n}} = 1^* = 1^+ = 1$ No matter how often you traverse a path of zero length, it is still a path of zero length.
Rule 14: $1^+ + 1 = 1^* = 1$

The final notation needed is the empty set or the set that contains no paths, not even the zero-length path 1. The null set of paths is denoted by the numeral 0.* Zero, in this algebra, plays the same role as zero does in

---

* As with the unit element λ, the first edition and regular expression literature use the Greek letter phi (Φ) for the null set.

ordinary arithmetic. That is, it obeys the following rules:

Rule 15: $X + 0 = 0 + X = X$
Rule 16: $X0 = 0X = 0$ If you block the paths of a graph fore or aft by
a graph that has no paths, there won't be any paths.
Rule 17: $0^* = 1 + 0 + 0^2 + \cdots = 1$

The meaning and behavior of zero and one (the identity elements) given above apply only to path names. Other applications have different identity elements with different properties.

4. A REDUCTION PROCEDURE

4.1. Overview

This section presents a reduction procedure for converting a flowgraph whose links are labeled with names into a path expression that denotes the set of all entry/exit paths in that flowgraph. The procedure is a node-by-node removal algorithm. You follow these steps, which initialize the process:

1. Combine all serial links by multiplying their path expressions.
2. Combine all parallel links by adding their path expressions.
3. Remove all self-loops (from any node to itself) by replacing them with a link of the form X^*, where X is the path expression of the link in that loop.

The remaining steps are in the algorithm's loop:

4. Select any node for removal other than the initial or final node. Replace it with a set of equivalent links whose path expressions correspond to all the ways you can form a product of the set of inlinks with the set of outlinks of that node.
5. Combine any remaining serial links by multiplying their path expressions.
6. Combine all parallel links by adding their path expressions.
7. Remove all self-loops as in step 3.
8. Does the graph consist of a single link between the entry node and the exit node? If yes, then the path expression for that link is a path expression for the original flowgraph; otherwise, return to step 4.

Each step will be illustrated and explained in further detail in the next sections. Note the use of the phrase "*a* path expression," rather than "*the* path expression." A flowgraph can have many equivalent path expressions between a given pair of nodes; that is, there are many different ways to generate the set of all paths between two nodes without affecting the content of that set. The appearance of the path expression depends, in general, on the order in which nodes are removed.

4.2. Cross-Term Step (Step 4)

The cross-term step* is the fundamental step of the reduction algorithm. It removes a node, thereby reducing the number of nodes by one. Successive applications of this step eventually get you down to one entry and one exit node. The following diagram shows the situation at an arbitrary node that has been selected for removal:

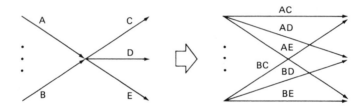

The rationale for this step is intuitively obvious. Whatever the set of paths represented by, say, A and C, there can be no other paths for the combination other than those represented by AC. Similarly, the removal of the node results in the AD, AE, BC, BD, and BE path expressions or path sets. If the path expressions are path names, it is clear that the resulting path names will be the names obtained by traversing the pair of links. If the path expressions denote sets of paths or path sums, using the definition of multiplication and the distributive rule produces every combination of incoming and outgoing path segments, as in

$$(a + b)(c + d) = ac + ad + bc + bd$$

---

* Also known as the star-mesh transformation in signal flowgraph literature. See BRZO63, MAYE72.

Applying this step to the graph of Figure 8.1b, we remove several nodes in order; that is,

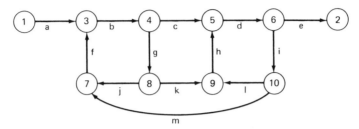

Remove node 10 by applying step 4 and combine by step 5 to yield

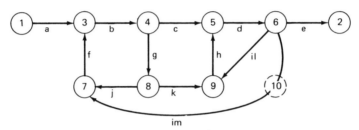

Remove node 9 by applying steps 4 and 5 to yield

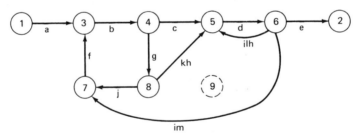

Remove node 7 by steps 4 and 5, as follows:

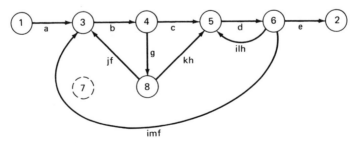

Remove node 8 by steps 4 and 5, to obtain

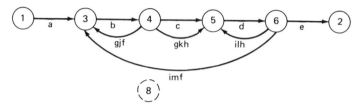

4.3. Parallel Term (Step 6)

Removal of node 8 above led to a pair of parallel links between nodes 4 and 5. Combine them to create a path expression for an equivalent link whose path expression is $c + gkh$; that is,

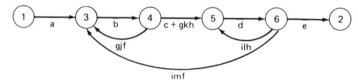

4.4. Loop Term (Step 7)

Removing node 4 leads to a loop term. The graph has now been replaced with the following equivalent, simpler graph:

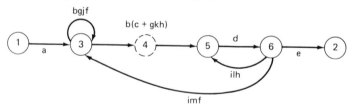

There are two ways of looking at the loop-removal operation:

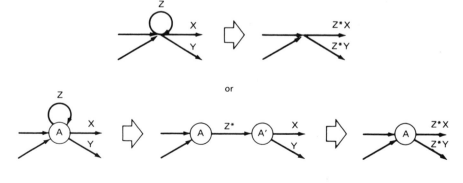

In the first way, we remove the self-loop and then multiply all outgoing links by Z*. The second way shows things in more detail. We split the node into two equivalent nodes, call them A and A′ and put in a link between them whose path expression is Z*. Then we remove node A′ using steps 4 and 5 to yield outgoing links whose path expressions are Z*X and Z*Y.

Continue the process by applying the loop-removal step, as follows:

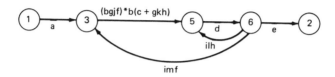

Removing node 5 produces

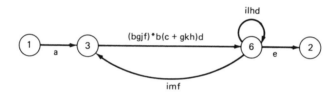

Remove the loop at node 6 to yield

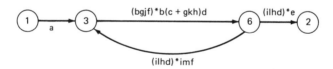

Remove node 3 to yield

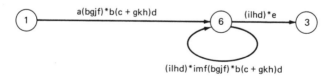

Removing the loop and then node 6 results in the following ugly expression:

$$a(bgjf)^*b(c + gkh)d((ilhd)^*imf(bgjf)^*b(c + gkh)d)^*(ilhd)^*e$$

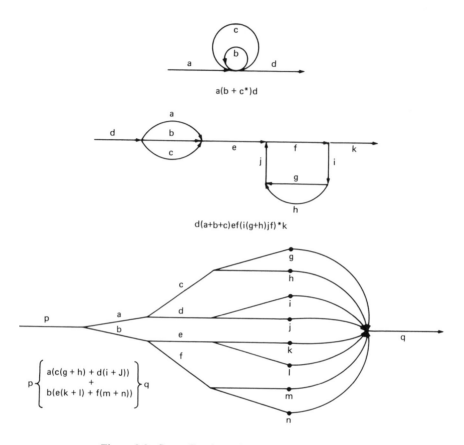

Figure 8.2. Some Graphs and Their Path Expressions.

We shouldn't blame the expression for being ugly because it was, after all, derived from an ugly, unstructured monster of a graph. With structured code, the path expressions are tamer. Figure 8.2 shows examples.

4.5. Comments, Identities, and Node-Removal Order

I said earlier that the order in which the operations are done affects the appearance of the path expressions. Such appearances of differences also result in identities that can sometimes be used to simplify path expressions.

I1: $(A + B)*$ $\qquad = (A* + B*)*$
I2: $\qquad\qquad\qquad\qquad = (A*B*)*$

I3: $= (A^*B)^*A^*$
I4: $= (B^*A)^*B^*$
I5: $= (A^*B + A)^*$
I6: $= (B^*A + B)^*$
I7: $(A + B + C + \cdot \cdot \cdot)^* = (A^* + B^* + C^* + \cdot \cdot \cdot)^*$
I8: $= (A^*B^*C^* \cdot \cdot \cdot)^*$

These can be derived by considering different orders of node removals and then applying the series-parallel-loop rules. Each change in order can produce a different appearance for the path expression and therefore a path expression identity. Don't make the mistake of applying these identities to finite exponents or $+$. These identities hold only because they denote infinite sets of paths. These identities are not very important anyhow, because we will rarely deal with path expressions as such but rather with other kinds of expressions derived from the path expressions by using link weights and link arithmetics. As an example of misapplying the identities, consider:

$$(A + B)^2 \neq (A^2 + B^2)^2 \neq (A^2B^2)^2$$

If A consists of the single link a and B is link b, the three expressions correspond to the following sets of paths:

$$(A + B)^2 = aa + ab + bb + ba$$
$$(A^2 + B^2)^2 = (a^4 + a^2b^2 + b^2a^2 + b^4)$$
$$(A^2B^2)^2 = a^2b^2a^2b^2 = (a^2b^2)^2$$

This algorithm can be used to find the path expression between any two nodes in a graph, including a node and itself. It is not restricted to finding the path expression between the entry and the exit of a flowgraph, although that might be the most common and most useful application. The method is tedious and cumbersome, what with having to constantly redraw the graph. In Chapter 12 I'll present a more powerful version of the same algorithm that can find the path expression between every pair of nodes with less work than this graphical method requires.

5. APPLICATIONS

5.1. General

The previous sections of this chapter are more abstract than I and most readers are apt to like. They are, I admit, remote from the substantive problems of testing and test design. The purpose of all that abstraction was to present one very generalized concept—the path expression and one very generalized way of getting it, the node-removal algorithm, so that the same concepts would not have to be discussed over and over again as one variation on a theme after another. Every application follows this common pattern:

1. Convert the program or graph into a path expression.
2. Identify a property of interest and derive an appropriate set of "arithmetic" rules that characterizes the property.
3. Replace the link names by the link weights (remember them?) for the property of interest. The path expression has now been converted to an expression in some algebra, such as ordinary algebra, regular expressions, or boolean algebra. This algebraic expression summarizes the property of interest over the set of all paths.
4. Simplify or evaluate the resulting "algebraic" expression to answer the question you asked.

If it seems that the above algorithm requires you to invent a new form of arithmetic for each application, that's true, but it's far less formidable than it seems. In practice you don't do it as outlined above. You substitute the weights (the properties associated with the links) first and simplify as you develop the path expression, using the right kind of arithmetic as you remove the nodes. This is apt to be hazy in the abstract, so let's get to the first application.

5.2. How Many Paths in a Flowgraph?

5.2.1. The Question

The question is not simple. Here are some ways you could ask it:

1. What is the maximum number of different paths possible?
2. What is the fewest number of paths possible?
3. How many different paths are there really?
4. What is the average number of paths?

In all that follows, by "path" I mean paths from the entrance to the exit of a single-entry/single-exit routine.* The first question has a straightforward answer and constitutes the first application. The second question

---

* Not a fundamental requirement. See Chapter 12 for paths from any node to any other node, including multi-entry and multi-exit routines.

concerns the fewest number of paths and is inherently difficult. No satisfactory algorithm exists; but I'll present an approximate solution for
nicely structured flowgraphs. If we know both of these numbers (maximum and minimum number of possible paths) we have a good idea of how
complete our testing is. Suppose that the minimum number of possible
paths is 15 and the maximum is 144 and that we had planned only 12 test
cases. The discrepancy should warn us to look for incomplete coverage.
Consider two routines with comparable structure and comparable testing
requirements—one with a maximum path count of 1000 and the other
with a maximum path count of 100. In both cases, say that coverage was
achievable with 10 paths. We should have more confidence in the routine
with a lower maximum path count, because the 10 paths is closer to
satisfying the all-paths testing strategy for the 100-path routine than it is
for the 1000-path routine.

Determining the actual number of different paths is an inherently difficult problem because there could be unachievable paths resulting from
correlated and dependent predicates. In fact, it is generally unsolvable by
static analysis. If all the predicates are uncorrelated and independent, not
only does the flowgraph have no loops, but the actual, minimum, and
maximum numbers of paths are the same.

Asking for "the average number of paths" is meaningless. The questions one should ask are questions such as: What is the mean path length
over all paths? What is the mean processing time considering all paths?
What is the most likely path? Such questions involve a notion of probability. A model for that is also provided as an application in the next section.
It should not require deep analysis to find the "typical" or normal path. It
should be obvious: the one that runs straight through the program. That
should be tested, of course, and tested first, even though it will probably
be the least revealing path of all.

5.2.2. *Maximum Path Count Arithmetic*

Label each link with a link weight that corresponds to the number of paths
that that link represents. Typically, that's one to begin with; but if the link
represented a subroutine call, say, and you wanted to consider the paths
through the subroutine in the path count, then you would put that number
on the link. Also mark each loop with the maximum number of times that
the loop can be taken. If the answer is infinite, you might as well stop the
analysis because it's clear that the maximum number of paths will be
infinite. There are three cases of interest: parallel links, serial links, and
loops. In what follows, A and B are path expressions and W_A and W_B are
algebraic expressions in the weights.

CASE	PATH EXPRESSION	WEIGHT EXPRESSION
PARALLELS*	$A + B$	$W_A + W_B$
SERIES	AB	$W_A W_B$
LOOP	A^n	$\displaystyle\sum_{j=0}^{n} W_A^j$

The arithmetic is ordinary algebra. This is an upper bound for the number of paths because the model can include unachievable paths. The rationale behind the parallel rule is simple. The path expressions denote the paths in a set of paths corresponding to that expression. The weight is the number of paths in each set. Assuming that the path expressions were derived in the usual way, they would have no paths in common, and consequently the sum of the paths for the union of the sets is at most the sum of the number of paths in each set. The series rule is explained by noting that each term of the path expression (say the first one A) will be combined with each term of the second expression B, in all possible ways. If there are W_A paths in A and W_B paths in B, then there can be at most $W_A W_B$ paths in the combination. The loop rule follows from the combination of the series and parallel rules, taking into account going through zero, once, twice, and so on. If you know for a fact that the minimum number of times through the loop is not zero but some other number, say j, then you do the summation from j to n rather than from 0 to n.

5.2.3. A Concrete Example

Here is a reasonably well-structured program. Its path expression, with a little work, is:

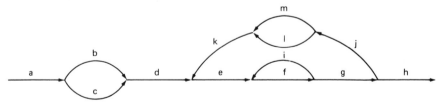

$$a(b + c)d\{e(fi)^*fgj(m + l)k\}^*e(fi)^*fgh$$

Each link represents a single link and consequently is given a weight of "1" to start. Let's say that the outer loop will be taken exactly four times

---

* Adjustments may be needed to avoid overcounting if both sets contain the zero-length path "1." If X and Y have W_X and W_Y paths, respectively, then $W_{X+Y} = W_X + W_Y - 1$. Otherwise the zero-length path would be counted twice.

and the inner loop can be taken zero to three times. The steps in the reduction are as follows:

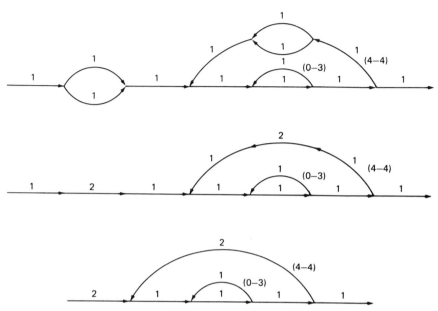

For the inner loop,

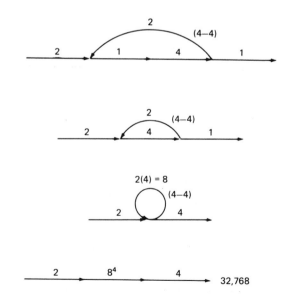

Alternatively, you could have substituted a "1" for each link in the path expression and then simplified, as follows:

$$1(1 + 1)1(1(1 \times 1)^3 1 \times 1 \times 1(1 + 1)1)^4 1(1 \times 1)^3 1 \times 1 \times 1$$
$$= 2(1^3 1 \times (2))^4 1^3$$

but
$$1^3 = 1 + 1^1 + 1^2 + 1^3 = 4$$
$$= 2(4 \times 2)^4 \times 4 \qquad = 2 \times 8^4 \times 4$$
$$= 32,768$$

This is the same result we got graphically. Reviewing the steps in the reduction, we:

1. Annotated the flowgraph by replacing each link name with the maximum number of paths through that link (1) and also noted the number of possibilities for looping. The inner loop was indicated by the range (0–3) as specified, and the outer loop by the range (4–4).
2. Combined the first pair of parallels outside of the loop and also the pair corresponding to the IF-THEN-ELSE construct in the outer loop. Both yielded two possibilities.
3. Multiplied things out and removed nodes to clear the clutter.
4. Took care of the inner loop: there were four possibilities, leading to the four values. Then we multiplied by the link weight following (originally link *g*) whose weight was also 1.
5. Got rid of link *e*.
6. Used the cross-term to create the self-loop with a weight of $8 = 2 \times 4$ and passed the other 4 through.

We have a test designer's bug. I've contradicted myself. I said that the outer loop would be taken exactly four times. That doesn't mean it will be taken *zero* or four times. Consequently, there is a superfluous "4" on the outlink in Step 6. Therefore the maximum number of different paths is 8192 rather than 32,768.

5.3. Approximate Minimum Number of Paths

5.3.1. Structured Code

The node-by-node reduction procedure can also be used as a test for structured code. Structured code can be defined in several different ways

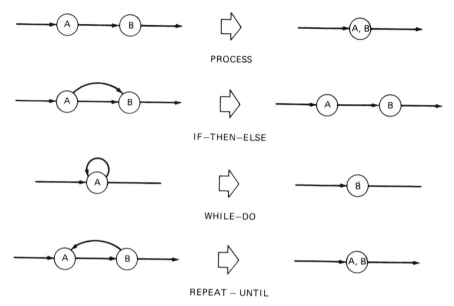

Figure 8.3. Structured-Flowgraph Transformations.

that do not involve ad hoc rules such as not using GOTOs. A graph-based definition by Hecht (HECH77B) is as follows:

A **structured flowgraph** is one that can be reduced to a single link by successive application of the transformations of Figure 8.3.

Note that the cross-term transformation is missing. An alternate characterization by McCabe (MCCA76) states that

Flowgraphs that do not contain one or more of the graphs shown in Figure 8.4 as subgraphs are **structured.**

5.3.2.   *Lower Path Count Arithmetic*

A lower bound on the number of paths in a routine can be approximated for structured flowgraphs. It is not a true lower bound because, again, unachievable paths could reduce the actual number of paths to a lower number yet. The appropriate arithmetic is as follows:

CASE	PATH EXPRESSION	WEIGHT EXPRESSION
PARALLEL	A + B	$W_A + W_B$
SERIES	AB	$MAX(W_A, W_B)$
LOOP	A^n	$1, W_1$

The parallel case is the same as before. The values of the weights are the number of members in a set of paths. There could be an error here because both sets could contain the zero-length path, but because of the way the loop expression is defined, this cannot happen. The series case is explained by noting that each term in the first set will combine with at least one term in the second set. The minimum number of combinations

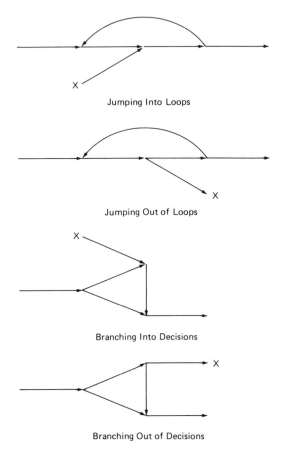

Jumping Into Loops

Jumping Out of Loops

Branching Into Decisions

Branching Out of Decisions

Figure 8.4. Unstructured Subgraphs.

must be the greater of the number of possibilities in the first set and the second set. The loop case requires that you use the minimum number of loops—possibly zero. Loops are always problematic. If the loop can be bypassed, then you can ignore the term in the loop. I don't think that this is a meaningful lower bound, because why is there a loop if it's not to be taken? By using a value of 1, we are asserting that we'll count the number of paths under the assumption that the loop will be taken once. Because in creating the self-loop we used the cross-term expression, there will be a contribution to the links following the loop, which will take things into account.

Alternatively, you could get a higher lower bound by arguing that if the loop were to be taken once, then the path count should be multiplied by the loop weight. This however, would be equivalent to saying that the loop was assumed to be taken both zero and once because, again, the cross-term that created the self-loop was multiplied by the series term. Generally, if you ask for a minimum number of paths, it's more likely that the minimum is to be taken under the assumption that the routine will loop once—because it is consistent with coverage.

Applying this arithmetic to the earlier example gives us the identical steps until step 3, where we pick it up:

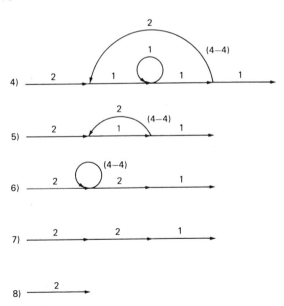

If you go back to the original graph on page 260 you'll see that it takes at least two paths to cover and that it can be done in two paths. The reason for restricting the algorithm to structured graphs is that for unstructured graphs the result can depend on the order in which nodes are removed. Structured or not, it's worth calculating this value to see if you have at least as many paths as the minimum number of paths calculated this way. If you have fewer paths in your test plan than this minimum you probably haven't covered. It's another check.

5.4. The Probability of Getting There

5.4.1. The Problem

I suggested in Chapter 3 that, if anything, path selection should be biased toward the low- rather than the high-probability paths. This raises an interesting question: What is the probability of being at a certain point in a routine? This question can be answered under suitable assumptions, primarily that all probabilities involved are independent, which is to say that all decisions are independent and uncorrelated. This restriction can be removed, but the method is beyond the scope of this book. We use the same algorithm as before—node-by-node removal of uninteresting nodes.

5.4.2. Weights, Notation, Arithmetic

Probabilities can come into the act only at decisions (including decisions associated with loops). Annotate each outlink with a weight equal to the probability of going in that direction. Evidently, the sum of the outlink probabilities must equal 1. For a simple loop, if the loop will be taken a mean of N times, the looping probability is $N/(N + 1)$ and the probability of not looping is $1/(N + 1)$. A link that is not part of a decision node has a probability of 1. The arithmetic rules are those of ordinary arithmetic.

CASE	PATH EXPRESSION	WEIGHT EXPRESSION
PARALLEL	A + B	$P_A + P_B$
SERIES	AB	$P_A P_B$
LOOP	A*	$P_A/(1 - P_L)$

In this table, P_A is the probability of the link leaving the loop and P_L is the probability of looping. The rules are those of ordinary probability theory. If you can do something either from column A with a probability of P_A or from column B with a probability P_B, then the probability that you do either is $P_A + P_B$. For the series case, if you must do both things, and their probabilities are independent (as assumed), then the probability that you do both is the product of their probabilities.

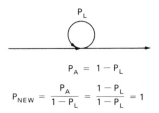

$$P_A = 1 - P_L$$

$$P_{NEW} = \frac{P_A}{1 - P_L} = \frac{1 - P_L}{1 - P_L} = 1$$

A loop node has a looping probability of P_L and a probability of not looping of P_A, which is obviously equal to $1 - P_L$. Following the rule, all we've done is replace the outgoing probability with 1—so why the complicated rule? After a few steps in which you've removed nodes, combined parallel terms, removed loops and the like, you might find something like this:

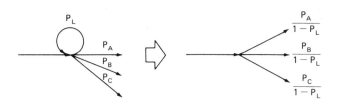

because $P_L + P_A + P_B + P_C = 1$, $1 - P_L = P_A + P_B + P_C$, and

$$\frac{P_A}{1 - P_L} + \frac{P_B}{1 - P_L} + \frac{P_C}{1 - P_L} = \frac{P_A + P_B + P_C}{1 - P_L} = 1$$

which is what we've postulated for any decision. In other words, division by $1 - P_L$ renormalizes the outlink probabilities so that their sum equals unity after the loop is removed.

5.4.3. *Example*

Here is a complicated bit of logic. We want to know the probability associated with cases A, B, and C.

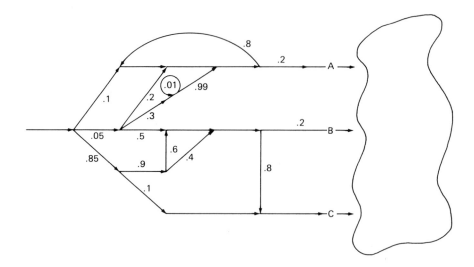

I'll do this in three parts, starting with case A. Note that the sum of the probabilities at each decision node is equal to 1. Start by throwing away anything that isn't on the way to case A, and then apply the reduction procedure. To avoid clutter, we usually leave out probabilities equal to 1—they're understood.

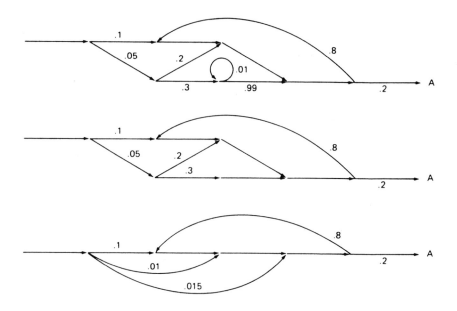

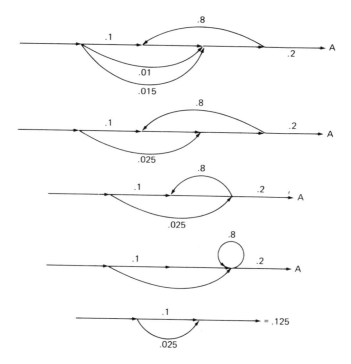

Case B is simpler:

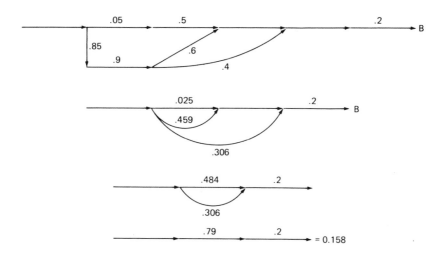

Case C is similar and should yield a probability of $1 - 0.125 - 0.158 = 0.717$:

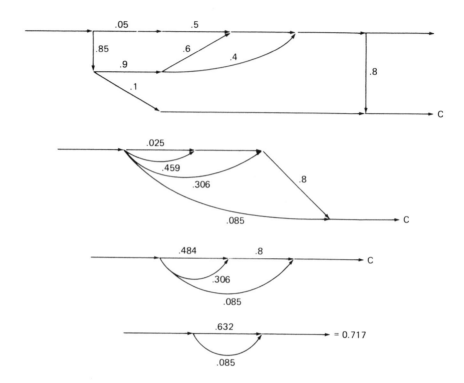

This checks. It's a good idea when doing this sort of thing to calculate all the probabilities and to verify that the sum of the routine's exit probabilities does equal 1. If it doesn't, then you've made calculation error or, more likely, you've left out some branching probability. Calculating the probability of reaching a point in a routine is not completely trivial, as you can see. If the logic is convoluted, simplistic methods of estimating can be very far off. It's better to analyze it.

How about path probabilities? That's easy. Just trace the path of interest and multiply the probabilities as you go. Alternatively, write down the path name and do the indicated arithmetic operation. Say that a path consisted of links a, b, c, d, e, and the associated probabilities were .2, .5, 1., .01, and 1 respectively. Path $abcbcbcdeabddea$ would have a probability of 5×10^{-10}. Long paths are usually improbable. Covering with short, simple paths is usually covering with high-probability paths. If you're going to make an argument related to testing based on probabilities, be prepared to evaluate those probabilities. If someone refutes a test based on probabilities, be prepared to demand an evaluation thereof rather than a haphazard guess.

Another good practice is to calculate the sum of the probabilities of the paths in the test set. A routine could have millions of paths but can be covered by ten or twenty. Calculate the sum of the probabilities for those paths and compare the sum with unity. Given two proposed sets of tests, the set whose path probability sum is greater provides a statistically more complete test than the set whose path probability sum is smaller. Be careful how you apply this because:

1. Getting the probabilities can be very difficult.
2. Correlated and dependent predicates do not follow the simple rules of multiplication and addition. A comparison made in such cases could be misleading.
3. The probabilities of the covering path set tend to be small. Don't expect to compare test plan A with a probability sum of 0.9 to test plan B with a sum of 0.8—it's more likely to be a comparison of 10^{-3} to 10^{-5}.

5.5. The Mean Processing Time of a Routine

5.5.1. The Problem

Given the execution time of all statements or instructions for every link in a flowgraph and the probability for each direction for all decisions, find the mean processing time for the routine as a whole. Under suitable assumptions, specifically that the decisions are uncorrelated and independent, the following algorithm gives you the results. In practice, getting the probabilities is half the work. Data dependencies and correlated decisions can be handled with modifications of the algorithm. Furthermore, the standard deviation and higher moments can also be calculated. For more information, see BEIZ78.

5.5.2. The Arithmetic

The model has *two* weights associated with every link: the processing time for that link, denoted by T, and the probability of that link. The rules for the probabilities are identical to those discussed in Section 5.4. The rules for the mean processing times are:

CASE	PATH EXPRESSION	WEIGHT EXPRESSION
PARALLEL	A + B	$T_{A+B} = (P_A T_A + P_B T_B)/(P_A + P_B)$
		$P_{A+B} = P_A + P_B$
SERIES	AB	$T_{AB} = T_A + T_B$
		$P_{AB} = P_A P_B$
LOOP	A*	$T_A = T_A + T_L P_L/(1 - P_L)$
		$P_A = P_A/(1 - P_L)$

The parallel term is the mean of the processing time over all the parallel .inks. Because the first node could have links that do not terminate on the second node of the parallels, we must divide by the sum of the parallel probabilities to get the proper mean. The serial term is intuitively obvious as the sum of the two processing times. The probability portion of the loop term is the same as before. The processing-time component consists of two parts. The part that was on the link leaving the loop (T_A) and the contribution of the loop. The loop contribution is most easily understood by substituting the value $N/(N + 1)$ for the probability of looping, under the assumption that the routine was expected to loop N times. The $P_L/(1 - P_L)$ term then reduces to just N. If the routine is expected to loop N times, and each time takes T_L seconds, and thereafter it does T_A seconds' worth of work, then the mean time through the entire process is $T_A + NT_L$.

5.5.3.   An Example

As an example, we'll use our old standby now annotated with branch probabilities, loop probabilities, and processing times for each link. The probabilities are given in parentheses. The node-removal order will be as in the previous use of this graph. It helps to remove nodes from the inside of loops to the outside.

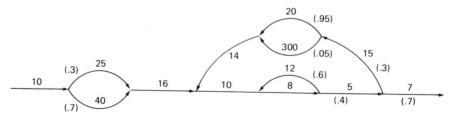

1. Start with the original flowgraph annotated with probabilities and processing time in microseconds or in instructions or whatever else is convenient.

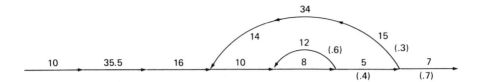

2. Combine the parallel links of the outer loop. The result is just the mean of the processing times for the links because there aren't any other links leaving the first node. Also combine the pair of links at the beginning of the flowgraph.

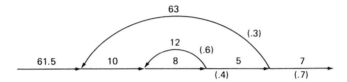

3. Combine as many serial links as you can.

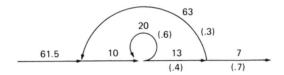

4. Use the cross-term step to eliminate a node and to create the inner self-loop.

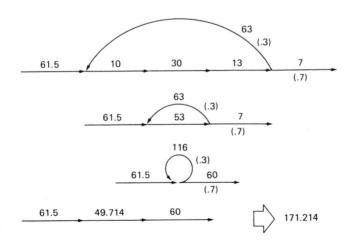

5.6. Push/Pop, Get/Return

5.6.1. The Problem

This model can be used to answer several different questions that can turn up in debugging. It can also help decide which test cases to design. The question is: given a pair of complementary operations such as PUSH (the stack) and POP (the stack), considering the set of all possible paths through the routine, what is the net effect of the routine? PUSH or POP? How many times? Under what conditions? Here are some other examples of complementary operations to which this model applies:

GET/RETURN a resource block.

OPEN/CLOSE a file.

START/STOP a device or process.

5.6.2. Push/Pop Arithmetic

CASE	PATH EXPRESSION	WEIGHT EXPRESSION
PARALLEL	A + B	$W_A + W_B$
SERIES	AB	$W_A W_B$
LOOPS	A*	W_A^*

An arithmetic table is needed to interpret the weight addition and multiplication operations. Typically, the exponent for loops will be the normal exponent. As before, we must be careful with loops: if a specific number of loops will be taken, the nonlooping term is not multiplied for the links following the loop. The numeral 1 is used to indicate that nothing of interest (neither PUSH nor POP) occurs on a given link. "H" denotes PUSH and "P" denotes POP. The operations are commutative, associative, and distributive.

PUSH/POP MULTIPLICATION TABLE

X	H PUSH	P POP	1 NONE
H	H^2	1	H
P	1	P^2	P
1	H	P	1

PUSH/POP ADDITION TABLE

+	H PUSH	P POP	1 NONE
H	H	P + H	H + 1
P	P + H	P	P + 1
1	H + 1	P + 1	1

Example:

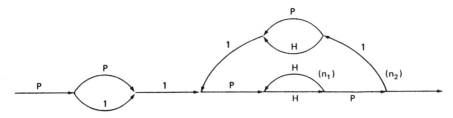

$$P(P + 1)1\{P(HH)^{n_1}HP1(P + H)1\}^{n_2}P(HH)^{n_1}HPH$$

Simplifying by using the arithmetic tables,

$$(P^2 + P)\{P(HH)^{n_1}(P + H)\}^{n_1}(HH)^{n_1}$$
$$(P^2 + P)\{H^{2n_1}(P^2 + 1)\}^{n_2}H^{2n_1}$$

The circumstances under which the stack will be pushed, popped, or left alone by the routine can now be determined. Table 8.1 shows several combinations of values for the two looping terms—n_1 is the number of times the inner loop will be taken and n_2 the number of times the outer loop will be taken.

These expressions state that the stack will be popped only if the inner loop is not taken. The stack will be left alone only if the inner loop is iterated once, but it may also be pushed. For all other values of the inner loop, the stack will only be pushed.

Exactly the same arithmetic tables are used for GET/RETURN a buffer block or resource, or, in fact, for any pair of complementary operations in which the total number of operations in either direction is cumulative. As another example, consider INCREMENT/DECREMENT of a counter. The question of interest would be: For various loop counts, considering the set of all possible paths, is the net result a positive or negative count and what are the values? The arithmetic tables for GET/RETURN are:

X	G	R	1
G	G^2	1	G
R	1	R^2	R
1	G	R	1

+	G	R	1
G	G	G + R	G + 1
R	G + R	R	R + 1
1	G + 1	R + 1	1

M_1	M_2	PUSH/POP
0	0	$P + P^2$
0	1	$P + P^2 + P^3 + P^4$
0	2	$\sum_{1}^{6} P^i$
0	3	$\sum_{1}^{8} P^i$
1	0	$1 + H$
1	1	$\sum_{0}^{3} H^i$
1	2	$\sum_{0}^{5} H^i$
1	3	$\sum_{0}^{7} H^i$
2	0	$H^2 + H^3$
2	1	$\sum_{4}^{7} H^i$
2	2	$\sum_{6}^{11} H^i$
2	3	$\sum_{8}^{15} H^i$

Table 8.1. Result of the PUSH/POP Graph Analysis

Example:

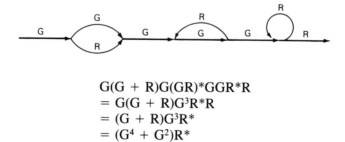

$$G(G + R)G(GR)^*GGR^*R$$
$$= G(G + R)G^3R^*R$$
$$= (G + R)G^3R^*$$
$$= (G^4 + G^2)R^*$$

This expression specifies the conditions under which the resources will be balanced on leaving the routine. If the upper branch is taken at the first decision, the second loop must be taken four times. If the lower branch is taken at the first decision, the second loop must be taken twice. For any other values, the routine will not balance. Therefore, the first loop does not have to be instrumented to verify this behavior because its impact should be nil. The first decision and the second loop should be instrumented.

5.7. Limitations and Solutions

The main limitation to these applications is the problem of unachievable paths. The node-by-node reduction procedure, and most graph-theory-based algorithms work well when all paths are possible, but may provide misleading results when some paths are unachievable. The approach to handling unachievable paths (for any application) is to partition the graph into subgraphs so that all paths in each of the subgraphs are achievable. The resulting subgraphs may overlap, because one path may be common to several different subgraphs. Each predicate's truth-functional value potentially splits the graph into two subgraphs. For n predicates, there could be as many as 2^n subgraphs. Here's the algorithm for one predicate:

1. Set the value of the predicate to TRUE and strike out all FALSE links for that predicate.
2. Discard any node, other than an entry or exit node, that has no incoming links. Discard all links that leave such nodes. If there is no exit node, the routine probably has a bug because there is a predicate value that forces an endless loop or the equivalent.
3. Repeat step 2 until there are no more links or nodes to discard. The resulting graph is the subgraph corresponding to a TRUE predicate value.
4. Change "TRUE" to "FALSE" in the above steps and repeat. The resulting graph is the subgraph that corresponds to a FALSE predicate value.

Only correlated predicates whose values exclude paths should be included in this analysis—not all predicates that may control the program flow. You can usually pick out the subgraphs by inspection because only one or two predicates, each of which appears in only a few places, cause the unachievable paths. If it isn't that simple, the routine is probably more complicated than it should be. A side benefit of the partitioning is that it may suggest a simpler, cleaner, and easier-to-test routine. The cost of this simplicity is probably a modest increase in the number of statements, which is partially paid for by an improvement in running time. Ask yourself why the routine is hard to analyze and why a formal analysis was required to see how various sets of paths were mutually exclusive. More often it's because the routine's a murky pit than because it's deep and elegant.

6. REGULAR EXPRESSIONS AND FLOW-ANOMALY DETECTION

6.1. The Problem

The generic flow-anomaly detection problem (note: not just data-flow anomalies, but *any* flow anomaly) is that of looking for a specific sequence of operations considering all possible paths through a routine. Let's say the operations are SET and RESET, denoted by *s* and *r* respectively, and we want to know if there is a SET followed immediately by a SET or a RESET followed immediately by a RESET (i.e., an *ss* or an *rr* sequence). Unlike the previous examples, we will not take advantage of a possible arithmetic over the various operations because we are interested in knowing whether a specific sequence occurred, not what the net effect of the routine is. Here are some more application examples:

1. A file can be opened (*o*), closed (*c*), read (*r*), or written (*w*). If the file is read or written to after it's been closed, the sequence is nonsensical. Therefore, *cr* and *cw* are anomalous. Similarly, if the file is read before it's been written, just after opening, we may have a bug. Therefore, *or* is also anomalous. Furthermore, *oo* and *cc*, though not actual bugs, are a waste of time and therefore should also be examined.

2. A tape transport can do a rewind (*d*), fast-forward (*f*), read (*r*), write (*w*), stop (*p*), and skip (*k*). There are rules concerning the use of the transport; for example, you cannot go from rewind to fast-forward without an intervening stop or from rewind or fast-forward to read or write without an intervening stop. The following sequences are anomalous: *df*, *dr*, *dw*, *fd*, and *fr*. Does the flowgraph lead to anomalous sequences on any path? If so, what sequences and under what circumstances?

3. The data-flow anomalies discussed in Chapter 5 requires us to detect the *dd*, *dk*, *kk*, and *ku* sequences. Are there paths with anomalous data flows?

4. You suspect a bug that could occur only if two operations, *a* and *b*, occurred in the order *aba* or *bab*. Is there a path along which this is possible?

6.2. The Method

Annotate each link in the graph with the appropriate operator or the null operator 1. Simplify things to the extent possible, using the fact that $a + a = a$ and $1^2 = 1$. Other combinations must be handled with care, because it may not be the case that a null operation can be combined with another operation. For example, $1a$ may not be the same thing as a alone. You now have a **regular expression** that denotes all the possible sequences of operators in that graph. You can now examine that regular expression for the sequences of interest. A useful theorem by Huang (HUAN79) helps simplify things:

Let A, B, C, be nonempty sets of character sequences whose smallest string is at least one character long. Let T be a two-character string of characters. Then if T is a substring of (i.e., if T appears within) AB^nC, then T will appear in AB^2C.

  As an example, let

$$A = pp$$
$$B = srr$$
$$C = rp$$
$$T = ss$$

The theorem states that ss will appear in $pp(srr)^nrp$ if it appears in $pp(srr)^2rp$. We don't need the theorem to see that ss does not appear in the given string. However, let

$$A = p + pp + ps$$
$$B = psr + ps(r + ps)$$
$$C = rp$$
$$T = p^4$$

Is it obvious that there is a p^4 sequence in AB^nC? The theorem states that we have only to look at

$$(p + pp + ps)[psr + ps(r + ps)]^2rp$$

Multiplying out the expression and simplifying shows that there is no p^4 sequence.

  A further point of Huang's theorem is directly useful in test design. He shows that if you substitute $1 + X^2$ for every expression of the form X^*, the paths that result from this substitution are sufficient to determine whether a given two-character sequence exists or not. Incidentally, the above observation is an informal proof of the wisdom of looping twice discussed in Chapter 3. Because data-flow anomalies are represented by two-character sequences, it follows from Huang's theorem that looping twice is what you need to do to find such anomalies.

6.3. A Data-Flow Testing Example (HUAN79)

Here is a flowgraph annotated with the operators at the links that correspond to the variables of interest:

The *ku* bug is clear from the regular expression. It will occur whenever the first loop is not taken. The second part of Huang's theorem states that the following expression is sufficient to detect any two-character sequence:

$$d(r + 1)r[1 + (udr)^2]ur(1 + d^2)ru$$

This makes the *dd* bug obvious. A *kk* bug cannot occur because there is no left-hand term that ends in *k*. Similarly, a *dk* bug cannot occur, because the only left-hand term ending in *d* is the last parenthesis, which is followed by *uk*.

$$(drr + dr)(1 + udrudr)(urru + urd^2ru)$$

There's no point in following through, because the bugs have been found. Generally, you would have to do this for every variable of interest. Also, the weights used with any link will change from variable to variable because different things are being done with each variable. For this reason, it's best to write down the path expression and to substitute the operators later. That way, you don't have to constantly redraw the graph and redo the path expression.

A better way to do this is to subscript the operator with the link name. Doing it this way, you don't lose the valuable path information. When two or more links or operators are combined, combine the link names. Here's the problem done over again with this feature added:

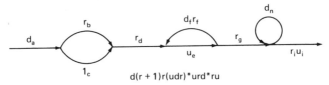

The path expression is

$$a(b + c)d(ef)^*egh^*i$$

The regular expression is

$$d_a(r_b + 1_c)r_d(u_e d_f r_f)^* u_e r_g d_h^* r_i u_i$$

Applying Huang's theorem:

$$d_a(r_b + 1_c)r_d(1 + (u_e d_f r_f)^2)u_e r_g(1 + d_h^2)r_i u_i$$
$$(d_a r_b r_d + d_{ac} r_d)(u_e r_g + u_e d_f r_f u_e d_f r_f u_e r_g)(r_i u_i d_h^2 r_i u_i)$$

The resulting expression tells us the same thing and preserves the path names so that we can work back to see what paths are potentially responsible for the bug or, alternatively, what paths must be tested to assure detection of the problem.

Although it's a good idea to learn how to do this analysis by hand as a step in understanding the algorithms, actual application should be based on data-flow analysis tools. Unless you do a lot of practicing, you probably won't achieve enough facility with these methods to use them without tools.

6.4. Generalizations, Limitations, and Comments

Huang's theorem can be easily generalized to cover sequences of greater length than two characters. Beyond three characters, though, things get complex and this method has probably reached its utilitarian limit for manual application.

If A, B, and C are nonempty sets of strings of one or more characters, and if T is a string of k characters, and if T is a substring of AB^nC, where n is greater than or equal to k, then T is a substring of AB^kC. A sufficient test for strings of length k can be obtained by substituting $P^{\underline{k}}$ for every appearance of P^* (or $P^{\underline{n}}$, where n is greater than or equal to k). Recall that

$$P^{\underline{k}} = 1 + P + P^2 + P^3 + \cdot \cdot \cdot + P^k$$

A warning concerning the use of regular expressions: there are almost no other useful identities beyond those shown earlier for the path expressions. There are some nice theorems for finding sequences that occur at the beginnings and ends of strings (BRZO62B) but no nice algorithms for finding strings buried in an expression. The mathematics for finding initial and terminal substrings is analogous to taking derivatives of algebraic expressions, and things get abstract fast. Because you can usually see whether a sequence starts or ends a regular expression by inspection, the additional mathematics hardly seem worthwhile. The main use of regular expressions is as a convenient notation and method of keeping track of paths and sets of paths. Once you learn it, doing the algebra and manipulating the expression is easier than tracing (and perhaps missing) paths on a flowgraph.

A final caution concerns unachievable paths. Static flow analysis methods can't determine whether a path is or is not achievable. Unless the flow analysis includes symbolic execution or similar techniques, the impact of unachievable paths will not be included in the analysis. That could lead to either optimistic or pessimistic values depending on the model and application. The flow-anomaly application, for example, doesn't tell us that there *will* be a flow anomaly—it tells us that if the path is achievable, then there will be a flow anomaly. Such analytical problems go away, of course, if you take the trouble to design routines for which all paths are achievable.

7. SUMMARY

1. A flowgraph annotated with link names for every link can be converted into a path expression that represents the set of all paths in that flowgraph. A node-by-node reduction procedure is used.
2. By substituting link weights for all links, and using the appropriate arithmetic rules, the path expression is converted into an algebraic expression that can be used to determine the minimum and maximum number of possible paths in a flowgraph, the probability that a given node will be reached, the mean processing time of a routine, and other models.
3. With different, suitable arithmetic rules, and by using complementary operators as weights for the links, the path expression can be converted into an expression that denotes, over the set of all possible paths, what the net effect of the routine is.
4. With links annotated with the appropriate weights, the path expression is converted into a regular expression that denotes the set of all operator sequences over the set of all paths in a routine. Rules for determining whether a given sequence of operations are possible are given. In other words, we have a generalized flow-anomaly detec-

tion method that'll work for data-flow anomalies or any other flow anomaly.

5. All flow analysis methods lose accuracy and utility if there are unachievable paths. Expand the accuracy and utility of your analytical tools by designs for which all paths are achievable. Such designs are *always* possible.

9

SYNTAX TESTING

1. SYNOPSIS

System inputs must be validated. Internal and external inputs conform to formats, which can usually be expressed in **Backus-Naur form**—a specification form that can be mechanically converted into more input-data validation tests than anyone could want to execute.

2. WHY, WHAT, AND HOW

2.1. Garbage

"Garbage-in equals garbage-out" is one of the worst cop-outs ever invented by the computer industry. We know when to use that one! When our program screws up and people are hurt. An investigation is launched and it's discovered that an operator made a mistake, the wrong tape was mounted, or the source data were inconsistent, or something like that. That's the time to put on the guru's mantle, shake your head, disclaim guilt, and mutter, "What do you expect? Garbage-in equals garbage-out."

Can we say that to the families of the airliner crash victims? Will you offer that excuse for the failure of the intensive care unit's monitoring system? How about a nuclear reactor meltdown, a supertanker run aground, or a war? GIGO is no explanation for anything except our failure to install good data-validation checks, or worse, our failure to test the system's tolerance for bad data. Garbage shouldn't get in—not in the first place or in the last place. Every system must contend with a bewildering array of internal and external garbage, and if you don't think the world is hostile, how do you plan to cope with alpha particles?

2.2. Casual and Malicious Users

Systems that interface with the public must be especially robust and consequently must have prolific input-validation checks. It's not that the users of automatic teller machines, say, are willfully hostile, but that there are so many of them—so many of them and so few of us. It's the million-monkey phenomenon: a million monkeys sit at a million typewriters for a million years and eventually one of them will type *Hamlet*. The more users, the less they know, the likelier that eventually, on pure chance, someone will hit every spot at which the system's vulnerable to bad inputs.

There are malicious users in every population—infuriating people who delight in doing strange things to our systems. Years ago they'd pound the sides of vending machines for free sodas. Their sons and daughters invented the "blue box" for getting free telephone calls. Now they're tired of probing the nuances of their video games and they're out to attack computers. They're out to get *you*. Some of them are programmers. They're persistent and systematic. A few hours of attack by one of *them* is worse than years of ordinary use and bugs found by chance. And there are so many of them; so many of them and so few of us.

Then there's crime. It's estimated that computer criminals (using mostly hokey inputs) are raking in hundreds of millions of dollars annually. A criminal can do it with a laptop computer from a telephone booth in Arkansas. Every piece of bad data accepted by a system—every crash-causing input sequence—is a chink in the system's armor that smart criminals can use to penetrate, corrupt, and eventually suborn the system for their own purposes. And don't think the system's too complicated for them. They have your listings, and your documentation, and the data dictionary, and whatever else they need.* There aren't many of them, but they're smart, motivated, and possibly organized.

2.3. Operators

Roger and I were talking about operators and the nasty things they can do, and the scenarios were getting farfetched. Who'd think of mounting a tape with a write-ring installed, writing a few blocks, stopping, opening the transport's door, dismounting the tape reel without unloading the buffers, removing the ring, remounting the tape without telling the system, and then attempting to write a new block? The malice we ascribed to the operators was embarrassing. I said to Roger, the designer most con-

---

* Accountants are the most successful embezzlers—why wouldn't the "best" computer criminal be a programmer?

cerned with the impact of operator shenanigans, "What the operators have done to these systems in the past is bad enough—just imagine how they'd act if they knew how we talked about them."

To which he snapped, "If they knew how we talked about them, they'd probably act the way we expect them to!"

I'm not against operators and I don't intend to put them down. They're our final defense against our latent bugs. Too often they manage, by intuition, common sense, and brilliance, to snatch a mere catastrophe from the jaws of annihilation. Operators make mistakes—and when they do, it can be serious. It's right that they probe the system's defenses, catalog its weaknesses and prepare themselves for the eventualities we didn't think of.

2.4.   The Internal World

Big systems have to contend not only with a hostile external environment but also a hostile internal environment. Malice doesn't play a role here, but oversight, miscommunication, and chance can be just as deadly. Any big system is subdivided into loosely coupled subsystems and consequently, there are many internal interfaces. Each interface presents another opportunity for data corruption and may require explicit internal-data validation. Furthermore, hardware can fail in bizarre ways that will cause it to pump streams of bad data into memory, across channels, and so on. Another piece of software may fail and do the same. And then there're always alpha particles.

2.5.   What to Do

Input validation is the first line of defense against a hostile world. Good designers design their system so that it just doesn't accept garbage—good testers subject systems to the most creative garbage possible. Input-tolerance testing is usually done as part of system testing, such as in a formal feature test or in a final acceptance test, so it's usually done by independent testers.

This kind of testing and test design is more fun than any other kind I know of: it's great therapy and they pay you for it. My family and pets loved it when I was doing these tests; after I was through kicking and stomping the programmers around, there wasn't a mean bone left in my body.

But to be really diabolical takes organization, structure, discipline, and method. Taking random potshots and waiting for inspirations with which to victimize the programmer won't do the job. Syntax testing is a primary tool of dirty testing, and method beats sadism every time.

2.6. Applications and Hidden Languages

Opportunities for applying syntax testing abound in most systems because most systems have **hidden languages.** A **hidden language** is a programming language that hasn't been recognized as such. Remember the Third Law (Chapter 2, Section 3.4.1.): *Code Migrates to Data.* One of the ways this happens is by taking control information and storing it as data (in lists or tables, say) and then interpreting that data as statements in an unrecognized and undeclared, internal, high-level language. Syntax testing is used to validate and break the explicit or (usually) implicit parser of that language. The troubles with these hidden languages are: there's no formal definition of syntax; the syntax itself is often buggy; and parsing is inexorably intertwined with processing. The key to exploiting syntax testing is to learn how to recognize hidden languages. Here are some examples:

1. User and operator commands are obvious examples of languages. Don't think that it doesn't pay to use syntax-testing methods because you only have a few commands. I've found it useful for only one or two dozen commands. For mainframe systems there are system operator commands and also a big set of user OS commands. For PC or any other application that can be used interactively, there are application-specific command sets.
2. The counterpart to operator and user command languages for batch processing are job control languages: either at the operating system level (e.g., JCL) or application-specific.
3. In Chapter 4, Section 5.2, I wrote about transaction-control languages. Reread that section for this application.
4. A system-wide interprocess-communication convention has been established. Isn't that a minilanguage? A precompilation preprocessor has been implemented to verify that the convention is followed: use syntax-testing thinking to test it.
5. An offline database generator package is used to create the database. It has a lot of fields to look at and many rules to follow—and more syntax to check.
6. Any internal format used for interprocess communications that does not consist of simple, fixed fields should be treated to a syntax test—for example, project or application calling sequence conventions, or a macro library.

7. Almost any communication protocol has, in part, a command language and/or formats that deserve syntax testing. Even something as simple as using a telephone can be tested by syntax testing methods.
8. A complicated application may have several hidden languages: an external language for user commands and an internal language, not apparent to the user, out of which the applications are built. The internal languages could be subtle and difficult to recognize. For example, a language could consist of a pattern of calls to worker subroutines. A deep call tree with a big common subroutine library can be viewed as a **syntax graph** (see below). A tip-off for syntax testing is that there are a few high-level routines with subroutine or function names in the call and a big common subroutine library. When you see that kind of a call tree, think of syntax testing.

I wouldn't use syntax-testing methods against a modern compiler. The way modern compiler construction is automated almost guarantees that syntax testing won't be effective. By extension, if the hidden language is out in the open and implemented as a real language, then syntax testing will probably fail—not because the tests won't be valid but because they won't reveal enough bugs to warrant the effort. Syntax testing is a shotgun method that depends on creating many test cases. Although any one case is unlikely to reveal a bug, the fact that many cases are used and that they are very easy to design makes the method effective. It's almost impossible for the kinds of bugs that syntax testing exposes to remain by the time (typically, in system testing) that syntax testing is used if it is used against a modern compiler. Also, for most programming languages there's no need to design these tests because you can buy a test oracle for the compiler at a far lower cost than you can design the tests.

2.7. The Graph We Cover

Look at the back of almost any Pascal reference manual, and you'll see several pages of graphs such as the one shown in Figure 9.1. It is a graph because it has nodes joined by links. The nodes shown here are either circles or boxes. The links are arrows as usual. The circles enclose actual characters. The boxes refer to other parts of the syntax graph, which you can think of as subroutine calls. The meanings attached to this graph are slightly different than those we've used before:

1. An arrow or link means "is followed by."
2. A branch point at a node with two or more outlinks means "or."

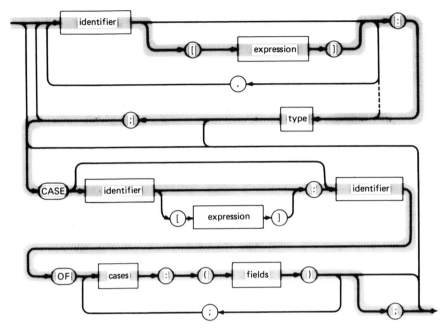

Figure 9.1. Pascal Fields Definition Graph. (Courtesy of Microsoft.)

We can interpret one path through this graph to get an example of *"fields."* The marked path is equivalent to:

"A *fields* (can) consist of an *identifier* followed by "[" followed by an *expression* followed by "]:" followed by a *type* ";CASE", another *identifier*, ":", yet another *identifier*, "OF", *cases*, ":(", *fields*, and ending with ");".

What do you do when you see a graph? COVER IT! Do you know how to do syntax testing? Of course you do! Look at Figure 9.1. You can test the normal cases of this syntax by using a covering set of paths through the graph. For each path, generate a *fields* that corresponds to that path. There are two explicit loops in the graph, one at the top that loops around *identifier* and another at the bottom following the "OF." There is an implicit loop that you must also test: note that *fields* calls itself recursively. I would start with a set of covering paths that didn't hit the recursion loop and only after that was satisfactory, hit the recursive cases.

In syntax testing, we must test the syntax graph with (at least) a covering set of test cases, but we usually go much further and also test with a set of cases that cannot be on the graph—the dirty cases. We generate these by methodically screwing up one circle, box, or link at a time. Look at the comma in the top loop: we can remove it or put something else in its place for two dirty test cases. We can also test a link that doesn't exist, such as following the comma with a *type* as indicated by the dotted arrow.

You also know the strategy for loops. The obvious cases are: not looping, looping once, looping twice, one less than the maximum, the maximum, and one more than the maximum. The not-looping case is often productive, especially if it is a syntactically valid but semantically obscure case. The cases near the maximum are especially productive. You know that there must be a maximum value to any loop and if you can't find what that value is, then you're likely to draw blood by attempting big values.

2.8. Overview

Syntax testing consists of the following steps:

1. Identify the target language or format (hidden or explicit).
2. Define the syntax (format) of the language, formally, in a convenient notation such as **Backus-Naur form (BNF).**
3. Test and debug the syntax to assure that it is complete and consistent and that it satisfies the intended semantics.
4. Normal condition testing consists of a covering set of input strings including critical loop values. The difficult part about normal case testing is predicting the outcome and verifying that the processing was correct. That's ordinary functional testing—i.e., semantics. Covering the syntax graph assures that all options have been tested. This is a minimum mandatory requirement with the analogous strengths and weaknesses of branch testing for control flowgraphs. It isn't "complete" syntax testing by any measure.
5. Syntax testing methods pay off best for dirty testing. Test design is a top-down process that consists of methodically identifying which component is to be cruddied-up and how.
6. Much of syntax test design can and should be automated by relatively simple means.
7. Test execution automation is essential for syntax testing because this method produces so many tests.

3. A GRAMMAR FOR FORMATS

3.1. Objectives

Every input has a syntax. That syntax may be formally specified or undocumented and "just understood," but it does exist. Data validation consists (in part) of checking the input for correct syntax. It's best when the syntax is defined in a formal language—best for the designer and the tester. Whether the designer creates the data-validation software from a formal specification or not is not important to the tester, but the tester needs a formal specification to create useful garbage. That specification is conveniently expressed in Backus-Naur form, which is very similar to regular expressions.

Regular expressions were introduced in Chapter 8 as an algebraic representation of all the paths in a graph. It's usually more convenient to deal with the algebraic version of graphs than with the pictorial version. Get comfortable with going back and forth between algebraic forms and pictorial forms for graphs and with talk about "covering a graph" even if there's no pictorial graph around. This isn't new to you because you worked with paths through an algebraic representation of a graph long before you heard about flowgraphs: what did you mean by "paths through code"?

3.2. BNF Notation (BACK59)

3.2.1. The Elements

Every input can be considered as if it were a string of characters. The software accepts valid strings and rejects invalid ones. If the software fails on a string, we've really got it. If it accepts an invalid string, then it's guilty of GIGO. There's nothing we can do about syntactically valid strings whose values are valid but wrong—that kind of garbage we have to accept. The syntax definition must be formal, starting with the most elementary parts, the characters themselves. Here's a sample definition:

alpha_characters ::= A/B/C/D/E/F/G/H/I/J/K/L/M/N/O/P/Q/
R/S/T/U/V/W/X/Y/Z
numerals ::= 1/2/3/4/5/6/7/8/9
zero ::= 0
signs ::= !/#/$/%/&/*/(/)/−/+/=/;/:/''/'/,/.?
space ::= sp

The left-hand side of the definitions is the name given to the collection of objects on the right-hand side. The string "::=" is interpreted as a single symbol that means "is defined as." The slash "/" means "or." We could have used the plus sign for that purpose as with regular expressions but that wouldn't be in keeping with the established conventions for BNF. We are using BNF to define a miniature language. The "::=" is part of the language in which we talk about the minilanguage, called the **metalanguage.** Spaces are always confusing because we can't display them on paper. We use *sp* to mean a space. The actual spaces on this page have no meaning. Similarly, an italicized (or underlined) symbol is used for any other single character that can't conveniently be printed, such as *null* (*nl*), *end-of-text* (*eot*), *clear-screen, carriage-return* (*cr*), *line-feed* (*lf*), *tab, shift-up* (*su*), *shift-down* (*sd*), *index, backspace* (*bs*), and so on. The underlined space, as in *alpha_characters,* is used as usual in programming languages to connect words that comprise a single object.

3.2.2. BNF Operators

The operators are the same as those used in path expressions and regular expressions: "or," concatenate, (which doesn't need a special symbol), "*", and "+". Exponents, such as A^n, have the same meaning as before—*n* repetitions of the strings denoted by the letter A. Syntax is defined in BNF as a set of definitions. Each definition may in turn refer to other definitions or to itself in such a way that eventually it gets down to the characters that form the input string. Here's an example:

word ::= *alpha_character alpha_character* / *numeral sp numeral*

I've defined an input string called *word* as a pair of *alpha_characters* or a pair of *numerals* separated by a space. Here are examples of *word*s and non*word*s, by this definition:

*word*s   : AB, DE, XY, 3 *sp* 4, 6 *sp* 7, 9 *sp* 9, 1 *sp* 2
non*word*s : AAA, A *sp* A1, A), 11, 111, WORD, NOT *sp* WORD, +

There are 722 possible *word*s in this format and an infinite number of non*word*s. If the strings are restricted to four characters, there are more than a million non*word*s. The designer wants to detect and accept *word*s and reject non*word*s; the tester wants to generate non*word*s and force the program to deal with them.

3.2.3. Repetitions

As before, *object*$^{1-3}$ means one to three *object*s, *object** means zero or more repetitions of *object* without limit, and *object*$^+$ means one or more repetitions of *object*. Neither the star (*) nor the plus (+) can legitimately appear in any syntax because both symbols mean a possibly infinite number of repetitions. That can't be done in finite memory or in the real world. The software must have some means to limit repetitions. It can be done by an explicit test associated with every + or * operator, in which case you should replace the operator with a number. Another way to limit the repetitions is by placing a global limit on the length of any string. The limit then applies to all commands and it may be difficult to predict what the actual limit is for any specific command. You test this kind of limit by maximum-length strings. Yet another way to implement limits is to limit a common resource such as stack or array size. Again, the limits for a specific command may be unpredictable because it is a global limit rather than a format-specific limit. The way to test this situation is with many repetitions of short strings. For example, using as many as possible minimum-length *identifiers* and not including *expression* in the first loop of Figure 9.1: "ID1,ID2,ID3,ID4,....ID999:*type*" will do the job.

One of the signs of weak software is the ease with which you can destroy it by overloading its repetition-limiting mechanisms. If the mechanism doesn't exist, you can probably scribble all over the stack or code— crash-crash, tinkle-tinkle, goody-goody.

3.2.4. Examples

This is an example and not a real definition of a telephone number:

special_digit	::=	1/2/5
zero	::=	0
other_digit	::=	3/4/6/7/8/9
ordinary_digit	::=	*special_digit* / *zero* / *other_digit*
exchange_part	::=	*other_digit*^{2} *ordinary_digit*
number_part	::=	*ordinary_digit*^{4}
phone_number	::=	*exchange_part number_part*

According to this definition, the following are *phone_number*s,

3469900, 9904567, 3300000

and these are not:

> 5551212, 5510000, 123, 8, ABCDEFG, 572-5580, 886-0144.

Another example:

operator_command ::= *mnemonic field_unit*$^{1-8}$ +

An *operator_command* consists of a *mnemonic* followed by one to eight *field_units* and a plus sign.

field_unit	::= *field delimiter*
mnemonic	::= *first_part second_part*
delimiter	::= *sp* / , / . / $ / *sp*$^{1-42}$
field	::= *numeral / alpha / mixed / control*
first_part	::= *a_vowel a_consonant*
second_part	::= *b_consonant alpha*
a_vowel	::= A/E/I/O/U
a_consonant	::= B/D/F/G/H/J/K/L/M/N/P/Q/R/S/T/V/X/Z
b_consonant	::= B/G/X/Y/Z/W/M/R/C
alpha	::= *a_vowel / a_consonant / b_consonant*
numeral	::= 1/2/3/4/5/6/7/8/9/0
control	::= $/*/%/*sp*/@
mixed	::= *control alpha control* / *control numeral control* / *control control control*

Here are some valid *operator_commands:*

ABXW A. B. C. 7. +

UTMA W *sp sp sp sp* +

While the following are not *operator_commands:*

ABC *sp* +

A *sp* BCDEFGHIJKLMNOPQR *sp*^{47} +

The telephone number example and the operator command example are different. The telephone number started with recognizable symbols and constructed the more complicated components from them—a bottom-up definition. The command example started at the top and worked down to the real characters—a top-down definition. These two ways of defining things are equivalent—it's only a matter of the order in which the definition lines are printed. The top-down order is generally more useful and it's the usual form for language design. Looking at the definition from the top down leads you to some tests and looking from the bottom up can lead to different tests.

As a final notational convenience, it's sometimes useful to enclose an expression in parentheses to reduce the number of steps in the definition. For example, the definition step for *field_unit* could have been simplified as follows:

$$\textit{operator\_command} \ ::= \ \textit{mnemonic (field delimiter)}^{1-8} \ +$$

This is fine if the syntax doesn't use parentheses that can confuse you in the definitions; otherwise use some other bracket symbols such as < and >. BNF notation can also be expanded to define optional fields, conditional fields, and the like. In most realistic formats of any complexity, you won't be able to get everything expressed in this notation—nor is it essential that you do so; additional narrative descriptions may be needed.

4.   TEST CASE GENERATION

4.1.   Generators, Recognizers, and Approach

A data-validation routine is designed to recognize strings that have been explicitly or implicitly defined in accordance with an input syntax. It either accepts the string, because it is recognized as valid, or rejects it and takes appropriate action. The routine is said to be a **string recognizer.** Conversely, the tester attempts to generate strings and is said to be a **string generator.** There are three possible kinds of incorrect actions:

1. The recognizer does not recognize a good string.
2. It accepts a bad string.
3. It may accept or reject a good string or a bad string, but in so doing, it fails.

Even small specifications lead to many good strings and far more bad strings. There is neither time nor need to test them all. String errors can be categorized as follows:

1. *High-Level Syntax Errors*—The strings have violations at the topmost level in a top-down BNF syntax specification.

2. *Intermediate-Level Syntax Errors*—Syntax errors at any level other than the top or bottom.
3. *Field-Syntax Errors*—Syntax errors associated with an individual field, where a **field** is defined as a string of characters that has no subsidiary syntax specification other than the identification of characters that compose it. A field is the lowest level at which it is productive to think in terms of syntax testing.
4. *Delimiter Errors*—Violation of the rules governing the placement and the type of characters that must appear as separators between fields.
5. *Syntax-Value Errors*—When the syntax of one field depends on values of other fields, there is a possibility of an interaction between a field-value error and a syntax error—for example, when the contents of a control field dictate the syntax of subsequent fields. This is a messy business that permits no reasonable approach. It needs syntax testing combined with domain testing, but it's better to redesign the syntax.
6. *State-Dependency Errors*—The permissible syntax and/or field values is conditional on the state of the system or the routine. A command used for start-up, say, may not be allowed when the system is running. If state behavior is extensive, consider state testing (Chapter 11).

Errors in the values of the fields or the relation between field values are domain errors and should be tested accordingly.

4.2. Test Case Design

4.2.1. Strategy

The strategy is to create one error at a time, while keeping all other components of the input string correct; that is, in the absence of the single error, the string would have been accepted. Once a complete set of tests has been specified for single errors, do the same for double errors and then triple errors. However, if there are of the order of N single-error cases, there will be of the order of N^2 double-error and N^3 triple-error cases. Once past the single errors, it takes a lot of judicious pruning to keep the number of tests reasonable. This is almost impossible to do without looking at the implementation details.

4.2.2. Top, Intermediate, and Field-Level Syntax Errors

Say that the topmost syntax level is defined as:

item ::= *atype* / *btype* / *ctype* / *dtype etype*

Here are some obvious test cases:

1. *Do It Wrong*—Use an element that is correct at some other lower syntax level, but not at this level.
2. *Use a Wrong Combination.* The last element is a combination of two other elements in a specified order. Mess up the order and combine the wrong things:

   dtype atype / *btype etype* / *etype dtype* / *etype etype* / *dtype dtype*

3. *Don't Do Enough*—For example,

   dtype / *etype*

4. *Don't Do Nothing.* No input, just the end-of-command signal or carriage return. Amazing how many bugs you catch this way.
5. *Do Too Much*—For example:

   atype btype ctype dtype etype / *atype atype atype* /
   dtype etype atype / *dtype etype etype* / *dtype etype*[128]

Focus on one level at a time and keep the level above and below as correct as you can. It may help to draw a definition graph; we'll use the telephone number example (see Figure 9.2).

TOP LEVEL
1. Do nothing.
2. An *exchange_part* by itself.
3. A *number_part* by itself.
4. Two *exchange_parts*.
5. Two *number_parts*.
6. An *exchange_part* and two *number_parts*.
7. Two *exchange_parts* and one *number_part*.

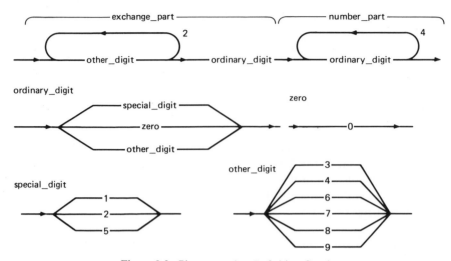

Figure 9.2. Phone_number Definition Graph.

NEXT LEVEL

  8. Bad *exchange_part*.

      8.1—do nothing—covered by test 3 above.

      8.2—no *other_digit*.

      8.3—two *special_digit*s.

      8.3—three *special_digit*s.

      8.4—et cetera.

  9. Bad *number_part*.

      9.1—not enough *digit*s.

      9.2—too many *digit*s.

      9.3—et cetera.

THIRD LEVEL

10. Bad *ordinary_digit*.

      10.1—not a digit—use an alphabetic.

      10.2—not a digit—use a control character.

      10.3—not a digit—use a delimiter.

      10.4—not a digit—leave it out.

      10.5—et cetera.

FOURTH LEVEL

11. Bad *other_digit*—as with bad *ordinary_digit*.

12. Bad *special_digit*—as with bad *ordinary_digit*.

13. Et cetera.

Check the levels above and below as you generate cases. Not everything generated by this procedure produces bad cases, and the procedure may lead to the same test case by two different paths. The corruption of one element could lead to a correct but different string. Such tests are useful because logic errors in the string recognizer might miscategorize the string. Similarly, if a test case (either good or bad) can be generated via two different paths, it is an especially good case because there is a potential for confusion in the routine. I like test cases that are difficult to design and difficult to recognize as either good or bad because if I'm confused, it's likely that the designer will also be confused. It's not that designers are dumb and testers smart, but designers have much more to do than testers. To design and execute syntax-validation tests takes 5% to 10% of the effort needed to design, code, test, validate, and integrate a syntax-validation routine. The designer has 10 to 20 times as much work to do as does the tester. Given equal competence, if the tester gets confused with comparatively little to do, it's likely that the overloaded designer will be more confused by the same case.

Now look at Figure 9.3. I generated this syntax graph from Figure 9.2 by inserting the subsidiary definitions and simplifying by using regular expression rules. The result is much simpler. It can obviously be covered by one test for the normal path and there are far fewer dirty tests:

1. Start with a *special_digit.*
2. Start with a *zero.*
3. Only one *other_digit* before a *zero.*
4. Only one *other_digit* before a *special_digit.*
5. Not enough digits.
6. Too many digits.
7. Selected nondigits.

You could get lavish and try starting with two *zero*s, two *special_digit*s, *zero* followed by *special_digit,* and *special_digit* followed by *zero,* thereby hitting all the double-error cases of interest; but there's not much more you can do to mess up this simplified graph. Should you do it? No! The implementation will tend to follow the definition and so will the bugs.

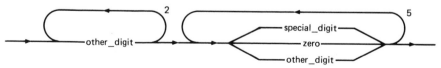

Figure 9.3. Phone_number Graph Simplified.

Therefore, there's a richer possibility for variations of bad strings to which the simplified version is not vulnerable. Don't expect to find opportunities for such simplifications in the syntax of mature programming languages—the language designers usually do as much simplification as makes sense before the syntax is released. For formats, operator commands, and hidden languages, there are many such opportunities. The lesson to be learned from this is that you should always simplify the syntax graph if you can. The implementation will be simpler, it will take fewer tests to cover the normal cases, and there will be fewer meaningful dirty tests.

4.2.3. Delimiter Errors

Delimiters are characters or strings placed between two fields to denote where one ends and the other begins. Delimiter problems are an excellent source of test cases. Therefore, it pays to identify the delimiters and the rules governing their syntax.

1. *Missing Delimiter*—This kind of error causes adjacent fields to merge. This may result in a different, but valid, field or may be covered by another kind of syntax error.
2. *Wrong Delimiter*—It's nice when several different delimiters are used and there are rules that specify which can be used where. Mix them up and use them in the wrong places.
3. *Not a Delimiter*—There are some characters or strings that are not delimiters but could be put into that position. Note the possibility of changing adjacent field types as a result.
4. *Too Many Delimiters*—The number of delimiters appearing at a field boundary may be variable. This is typical for spaces, which can serve as delimiters. If the number of delimiters is specified as 1 to N, it pays to try 0, 1, 2, $N - 1$, N, $N + 1$, and also an absurd number of delimiters, such as 127, 128, 255, 256, 1024, and so on.
5. *Paired Delimiters*—These delimiters represent another juicy source of test cases. Parentheses are the archetypal paired delimiters. There could be several kinds of paired delimiters within a syntax. If paired delimiters can nest, as in "(()( )", there are a whole set of new evils to perpetrate. For example, "BEGIN...BEGIN...END", "BEGIN...END...END". Nested paired delimiters provide opportunities for matching ambiguities. For example, "((()(()))" has a matching ambiguity and it's not clear where the missing parenthesis belongs.

6. *Tolerant Delimiters*—The delimiter may be optional or several alternate formats may be acceptable. In communications systems, for example, the start of message is defined as ZCZC, but many systems allow any one of the four characters to be corrupted. Therefore, #CZC, Z#ZC, ZC#C, and ZCZ# (where "#" denotes any character) are all acceptable; there are many nice confusing ways to put in a bad character here:
   a. A blank.
   b. Z or C in the wrong place—CCZC, ZZZC, ZCCC, ZCZZ (catches them every time!).
   c. Something off-the-wall—especially important control characters in some other context.

Tolerance is most often provided for delimiters but can also be provided for individual fields and higher levels of syntax. It's a sword of many edges—more than two for sure—all of them dangerous. Syntax tolerance is provided for user and operator convenience and in the interest of making the system humane and robust. But it also makes the format-validation design job and testing format-validation designs more complicated. Format tolerance is sophisticated and takes sophisticated designs to implement and, consequently, many more and more complicated tests to validate. If you can't do the whole job from design to thorough validation, there's no point in providing the tolerance. Most users and operators prefer a solid system with rigid syntax rules to a system with tolerant rules that don't always work.

4.2.4. Field-Value Errors

Field-value errors are clearly a domain-testing issue, and domain testing is where it's at. Whether you choose to implement field-value errors in the context of syntax testing or the other way around (i.e., syntax testing under domain testing) or whether you choose to implement the two methods as separate test suites depends on which aspect dominates. Syntax-testing methods will usually wear out more quickly than will domain testing. For that reason, it pays to separate domain and syntax tests into different suites. You may not be able to separate the two test types because of (unfortunately) context-dependent syntax—either field values whose domain depends on syntax or syntax that depends on field values (ugh!). Here's a reminder of what to look for: boundary values and near-boundary values, excluded values, binary values for integers, and values vulnerable to semantic type changes and representation changes.

4.2.5. Context-Dependent Syntax Errors

Components of the syntax may be interrelated and may be related by field values of other fields. The first field could be a code that specifies the syntax of subsequent fields. As an example:

> *command*   ::= *pilot_field syntax_option*
> *pilot_field*   ::= 1/2/3/4/5/6/7/8/9
> *syntax_option* ::= *option1 / option2 / option3 / . . .*

The specification further states that *option1* must be preceded by "1" as the value of the *pilot_field*. Actually, it would have been better had the specification be written as:

> *command* ::= 1 *option1 / 2 option2 / 3 option3 / . . .*

but that's not always easy to do. The test cases to use are clearly invalid combinations of syntactically valid field values and syntactically valid options. If you can rewrite the specification, as in the above example, to avoid such field-value dependencies, then it's better you do so; but if so doing means vast increases in formality, which could be handled more clearly with a side-bar notation that specifies the relation, then it's better to stick to the original form of the specification. The objective is to make things as clear as possible to the designer and to yourself, and excessive formality can destroy clarity just as easily as modest formality can enhance it.

4.2.6. State-Dependency Errors

The string or field value that may be acceptable at one instant may not be acceptable at the next because validity depends on the transaction's or the system's state. As an example, say that the operator's command-input protocol requires confirmation of all commands. After every command the system expects either an acknowledgment or a cancellation, but not another command. A valid command at that point should be rejected, even though it is completely correct in all other respects. As another example, the system may permit, as part of a start-up procedure, commands that are forbidden after the system has been started, or it may forbid otherwise normal commands during a start-up procedure. A classical example occurs in communications systems. The start of message sequence ZCZC is allowed tolerance (see page 301) when it occurs at the beginning of a message. However, because the system has to handle

Polish language words such as: "zczalny", "jeszcze", "deszcz", and "zczotka" (BEIZ79), the rules state that any subsequent start-of-message sequence that occurs prior to a correct end-of-message sequence (NNNN) must be intolerant; the format is changed at that point and only an exact "ZCZC" will be accepted.

I divide state-dependency errors into "simple" and "complicated." The simple ones are those that can be described by at most two states. All the rest are complicated and are best handled by the methods of Chapter 11. The simple ones take two format or two field-value specifications—and require at worst double the work.

4.3. Sources of Syntax

4.3.1. General

Where do you get the syntax? Here's another paradox for you. If the syntax is served up in a nice, neat, package, then syntax-testing methods probably won't be effective and if syntax testing is effective, you'll have to dig out and formally define the syntax yourself. Where do you get the syntax?

Ideally, it comes to you previously defined, formally defined, in BNF or an equivalent, equally convenient notation.* That's the case for common programming languages, command languages written by and for programmers, and languages and formats defined by a formal standard.

4.3.2. Designer-Tester Cooperation and Design Specifications

If there is no BNF specification, I try to get the designers to create one—at least the first version of one. Realistically, though, if a BNF specification does not exist, the designers will have to create a document that can be easily converted into one or what is she designing to? If you get the designer to create the first version of the BNF specification, you may find that it is neither consistent nor complete. Test design begins with requests for clarification of that preliminary specification. Many serious bugs can be avoided this way. Do it yourself if you can't get the designers to create the first version of the BNF specification. It doesn't really matter whether it's complete or correct, as long as it's down on paper and formal. Present your specification version to the designers and say that tests will be de-

---

* I'll use the term "BNF specification" in the sequel to mean actual BNF or specifications in any other metalanguage that can be used for the same purpose. Many other metalanguages have been developed, but BNF is the most popular and it has the advantage of being almost the same as regular expressions.

fined accordingly. There may be objections, but the result should be a reasonably correct version in short order.

Using a BNF specification is the easiest way to design format-validation test cases. It's also the easiest way for designers to organize their work, but sadly they don't always realize that. You can't begin to design tests unless you agree on what is right or wrong. If you try to design tests without a formal specification, you'll find that you're throwing cases out, both good and bad, as the designers change the rules in response to the cases you show them. If you can't get agreement on syntax early in the project, put off syntax test design and concentrate on some other area. Alternatively, and more productively, participate in the design under the guise of getting a specification tied down. You'll prevent lots of bugs that way.

It can boomerang, though. I pushed for a BNF specification of operator commands on one project. The commands had been adapted from a previous system in the same family whose formats were clearly specified but not in BNF. This designer fell in love with BNF and created a monster that was more complicated than a combination of Ada and COBOL—and mostly wrong. To make matters worse, his first version of the operator's manual was written in top-down BNF, so operators had to plow through several levels of abstract syntax to determine which keys to hit. Good human engineering will dictate simple, clean, easy-to-understand syntax for user and operator interfaces. Similarly, internal formats for interprocess communications should also be simple. There's usually a topmost syntax level, several field options, and a few subfields. Recursive definitions are rare (or should be). We do find useful recursive definitions in operating system command languages or data query languages for things such as sorting, data object specifications, and searching; but in general, recursive definitions are rare and more likely to be a syntax-specification error than a real requirement. Be suspicious if the syntax is so complicated that it looks like a new programming language. That's not a reasonable thing to expect users or operator to employ.

4.3.3. Manuals as Sources

Manuals, such as instruction manuals, reference manuals, and operator manuals are the obvious place to start for command languages if there isn't a formal syntax document and you can't get designers to do the job for you. The syntax in manuals may be fairly close to a formal syntax definition. Manuals are good sources because more often than not, we're dealing with a maintenance situation, rehosting, or a rewrite of an old application. But manuals can be mushy because the manual writer tries to convey complicated syntactic issues in a language that is "easy for those dumb users and operators."*

4.3.4. Help Screens and Systems

Putting user information such as command syntax into HELP systems and on-line tutorial is becoming more commonplace, especially for PC software because it's cheaper to install a few hundred K of HELP material on a floppy than it is to print a few hundred pages of instruction manual. You may find the undocumented syntax on these screens. If you have both manuals and help systems, compare them and find out which one is correct.

4.3.5. Data Dictionary and Other Design Documents

For internal hidden languages, your most likely source of syntax is the data dictionary and other design documents. Also look at internal interface standards, style manuals, and design practice memos. Common subroutine and macro library documents are also good sources. Obviously you can't expect designers to hand you the syntax of a language whose existence they don't even recognize.

4.3.6. Prototypes

If there's a prototype, then it's likely to embody much of the user interface and command language syntax you need. This source will become more useful in the future as prototyping gains popularity. But remember that a prototype doesn't really have to work, so what you get could be incomplete or wrong.

---

* Another war story about my favorite bad software vendor, Coddler Incorporated—a pseudonym invented to protect me from lawsuits. They had a word processing programming language that was putatively designed for use by word processing operators. The language's syntax description in the manual was sketchy and wrong. It's the only programming language that ever defeated me because after weeks of trying I still couldn't write more than 20 statements without a syntax error. When I asked them for complete documentation of the language's syntax, I was told that, as a mere user, I wasn't entitled to such "proprietary" information. We dragged the syntax out of that evil box experimentally and discovered so many context and state dependencies that it was clear to us that they had broken new grounds in language misdesign. What was even worse, when they confronted you with a syntax error, it was presented by reference to the tokenized version of the source after compilation rather than to the source—you guessed it, the token table was also "proprietary." We dragged that out experimentally also and discovered even more state dependencies. Syntax testing that garbage dump was like using hydrogen bombs against a house of cards. The ironic thing about this experience was that we were trying to use this "language" and its "processor" to automate the design of syntax tests for the system we were testing.

4.3.7. *Programmer Interviews*

The second most expensive way to get user and operator command syntax is to drag the information out of the implementing programmer's head by interviews. I would do it only after I had exhausted all other sources. If you're forced to do this as your only source, then syntax testing may be pointless because a low-level programmer is making user interface or system architecture decisions and the project's probably aground on the reef—it just hasn't sunk yet. Syntax testing is then just a cruel way to demonstrate that fact—pitiful.

4.3.8. *Experimental*

The most expensive possible way to get the syntax is by experimenting with the running program. Think back to the times you've had to use a new system without an instruction manual and of how difficult it was to work out even a few simple commands—now think of how much work that can be for an entire set of commands; but for dirty old code, it's sometimes the only way. You got it. Take what you know of the syntax and express it in BNF. Apply syntax testing to that trial syntax and see what gets accepted, what gets rejected, and what causes crashes and data loss. You'll have a few surprises that will cause you to change your syntax graph. Change it and start over again until either the money runs out or the program's been scrapped. Looking at the code may help, but it often doesn't because, as often as not, parsing, format validation, domain validation, and processing are hopelessly intertwined and splattered across many components and many levels. It's usually pretty tender software. If you have to live with it, think in terms of putting a proper format validation front end on such junk (see Section 6 below) and avoid the testing altogether.

4.4. Ambiguities and Contradictions

Unless it's the syntax of a programming language or a communication format or it's derived from a previous system or from some other source that's been in use for a long time, it's unlikely that the syntax of the formats you're testing will be correct the first time you test it. There will be valid cases that are rejected and other cases, valid or otherwise, for which the action is unpredictable. I mean fundamental errors in the syntax itself and not in the routines that analyze the format. If you have to create the formal syntax in order to design tests, you are in danger of creating the format you want rather than the one that's being implemented. That's not necessarily bad if what you want is a simpler, more reliable, and easier format to use, implement, and test.

Ambiguities are easy to spot—there's a dangling branch on the definition tree. That is, something appears on the right-hand side of a definition, but there's no definition with that term on the left-hand side. An obvious contradiction occurs when there are two or more definitions for the same term. As soon as you permit recursive definitions, state dependencies, and context-dependent syntax, the game's over for easy ambiguity and contradiction spotting—in fact, the problem's known to be unsolvable. Approaches to detecting ambiguities and contradictions in the general case is a language-validation problem and beyond the scope of this book by a wide margin. I'm assuming that we're dealing only with the simpler and more obvious ambiguities and contradictions that become apparent when the format is set down formally (e.g., written in BNF) for the first time.

The point about syntactic ambiguities and contradictions (as I've said several times before) is that although a specification can have them, a program, because it is deterministic, is always unambiguous and consistent. Therefore, without looking at the code, even before the code's been designed, you know that there *must* be bugs in the implementation. Take advantage of every ambiguity and contradiction you detect in the format to push the format's design into something that has fewer exception conditions, fewer state dependencies, fewer field correlations, and fewer variations. Keep in close contact with the format's designer, who is often also the designer of the format-analysis routine. Maintain a constant pressure of weird cases, interactions, and combinations. Whenever you see an opportunity to simplify the format, communicate that observation to the format's designer: he'll have less to design and code, you'll have less to test, and the user will thank you both for a better system. It's true that flaws in the syntax may require a more elaborate syntax and a more complicated implementation. However, my experience has been that the number of instances in which the syntax can be simplified outnumber by about 10 to 1 the instances in which it's necessary to complicate it.

4.5.   Where Did the Good Guys Go?

Syntax test design is like a lot of other things that are hard to stop once you've started. A little practice with this technique and you find that the most innocuous format leads to hundreds of tests; but there are dangers to this kind of test design.

1. *It's Easy to Forget the Normal Cases*—I've done it often. You get so entangled in creative garbage that you forget that the system must also be subjected to good inputs. I've made it a practice to check every test area explicitly for the normal case. Covering the syntax definition graph does it.

2. *Don't Go Overboard with Combinations*—It takes iron nerves to do this. You've done all the single-error cases, and in your mind you know exactly how to create the double- and higher-error cases. And there are so many of them that you can create an impressive mound of test cases in short order. "How can the test miss anything if I've tried 1000 input format errors?," you think. Remind yourself that any one strategy is inherently limited to discovering certain types of bugs. Remind yourself that those N^2 double-error cases and N^3 triple-error cases may be no more effective than trying every value from 1 to 1023 in testing a loop. Don't let the test become top-heavy with syntax tests at the expense of everything else just because syntax tests are so easy to design.

3. *Don't Ignore Structure*—Just because you can design thousands of test cases without looking at the code that handles those cases doesn't mean you should do it that way. Knowing the program's design may help you eliminate cases wholesale without sacrificing the integrity and thoroughness of the test. As an example, say that operator-command keywords are validated by a general-purpose preprocessor routine. The rest of the input character string is passed to the appropriate handler for that operator command only after the keyword has been validated. There would be no point to designing test cases that deal with the interaction of keyword errors, the delimiter between the keyword and the first field, and format errors in the first field. You don't have to know a whole lot about the implementation. Often, just knowing what parts of the format are handled by which routines is enough to avoid designing a lot of impressive but useless error combinations that won't prove a thing. The bug that could creep across that kind of interface would be so exotic that you would have to design it. If it takes several hours of work to postulate and "design" a bug that a test case is supposed to catch, you can safely consider that test case as too improbable to worry about—certainly in the context of syntax testing.

4. *There's More than One Kind of Test*—Did you forget that you designed path tests and domain tests—that there are state tests to design (Chapter 11), data-flow tests (Chapter 5), or logic-based tests (Chapter 10)? Each model of the system's behavior leads to tests

designed from a different point of view, but many of these tests overlap. Although redundant tests are harmless, they cost money and little is learned from them.

5. *Don't Make More of the Syntax Than There Is*—You can increase or decrease the scope of the syntax by falsely making it more or less tolerant than it really is. This may lead to the false classification of some good input strings as bad and vice versa—not a terrible problem, because if there is confusion in your mind, there may be confusion in the designer's mind. At worst, you'll have to reclassify the outcome of some cases from "accept" to "reject," or vice versa.

6. *Don't Forget the Pesticide Paradox*—Syntax tests wear out fast. Programmers who don't change their design style after being mauled by syntax testing can probably be thrashed by any testing technique, now and forever. However they do it, by elegant methods or by brute force, good programmers will eventually become immune to syntax testing.

5. IMPLEMENTATION AND APPLICATION

5.1. Execution Automation

5.1.1. General

Syntax testing, more than any other technique I know, forces us into test execution automation because it's so easy to design so many tests (even by hand) and because design automation is also easy. Syntax testing is a shotgun method which—like all shotgun methods—is effective only if there are a lot of pellets in your cartridge. How many ducks will you bring down if you have to throw the pellets up one at a time?

An automation platform is a prerequisite to execution automation. The typical dedicated (dumb) terminal is next to useless. Today, the box of choice is a PC with a hard disc and general-purpose terminal emulator software such as CROSSTALK MK-4 (CROS89). If you've still got 37xx or VTxxx terminals, or teleprinters, or even cardwallopers around and someone wants to foist them off on you as test platforms, resist—violently. Dumb terminals are hardly better than paper tape and teleprinters.

5.1.2. Manual Execution

Manual execution? Don't! Even primitive automation methods such as putting test cases on paper tape (see the first edition) was better than doing it manually. I found that the only way it could be done by hand was to use three persons, as in the following scenario. If that doesn't convince you to automate, then you're into compulsive masochism.

Use three persons to do it. The one at the terminal should be the most fumble-fingered person in the test group. The one with the test sheet should be almost illiterate. The illiterate calls out one character at a time, using her fingers to point to it, and moving her lips as she reads. The fumble-fingered typist scans the keyboard (it helps if he's very myopic) and finally finds it.

"A" the illiterate calls out.

"A" the typist responds when he's got his finger on the key. He presses it and snatches it away in fear that it will bite him.

"Plus" the reader shouts.

"No, dammit!" the third person, the referee, interrupts (the only one in the group who acts as if she had brains).

The idiot typist looks for the "DAMMIT" key.* . . .

So I'm exaggerating: but it's very hard to get intelligent humans to do stupid things with consistency. Syntax testing is dominated by stupid input errors that you've carefully designed.

5.1.3. Capture/Replay

See Chapter 13 for a more detailed discussion of capture/replay systems. A **capture/replay** system captures your keystrokes and stuff sent to the screen and stores them for later execution. However you've designed your syntax tests, execute them the first time through a capture/replay system if that's the only kind of execution automation you can manage. These systems (at least the acceptable ones) have a built-in editor or can pass the test data to a word processor for editing. That way, even if your first execution is faulty, you'll be able to correct it.

5.1.4. Drivers

Build or buy a **driver**—a program that automatically sequences through a set of test cases usually stored as data. Don't build the bad strings (especially) as code in an ordinary programming language because you'll be going down a diverging infinite sequence of test testing.

---

* Don't snicker. Ask your friends who work in PC software customer service how many times they've had inquiries from panicked novices who couldn't find the "ANYKEY" key—as in ". . . then hit any key."

5.1.5. *Scripting Languages*

A **scripting language** is a language used to write test scripts. CASL (CROS89, FURG89) is nice scripting language because it can be used to emulate any interface, work from strings stored as data, provide smart comparisons for test outcome validation, editing, and capture/replay.

5.2. Design Automation

5.2.1. *General*

Syntax testing is a good place to begin a test design automation effort because it's so easy and has such a high, immediate payoff. It's about the only test design automation area in which you can count on a payback the first time out.

5.2.2. *Primitive Methods*

You can do design automation with a word processor. If you don't have that, will you settle for a copying machine and a bottle of white-out? Design a covering set of correct input strings. If you want to, because you have to produce paper documentation for every test case, bracket your test strings with control sequences such as "$$$XXX" so that you'll be able to extract them later on. Let's say you're doing operator commands. Pick any command and reproduce the test sheet as often as you need to cover all the bad cases for that command. Then, using the word processor's search-and-replace feature, replace the correct substring with the chosen bad substring. If you use the syntax definition graph as a guide, you'll see how to generate all the single-error cases by judicious uses of search-and-replace commands. Once you have the single-error cases done, go on to the double errors if you don't already have more cases than you can handle. With double errors you have to examine each case to be sure that it is still an error case rather than a correct case—similarly for triple and higher errors. If you're starting with a capture/replay system, then you can do the editing either in the system's own editor or with a word processor. It's really more difficult to describe than to do. Think about how you might automate syntax test design with just a copying machine and a hardy typist: then graduate to a word processor. If you understand these primitive methods, then you'll understand how to automate much of syntax test design.

5.2.3. Scripting Languages

A scripting language and processor such as CASL has the features needed to automate the replacement of good substrings by bad ones on the fly. You can use random number generators to select which incorrect, single, character will be used in any spot. Similarly for replacing incorrect keywords by correct ones and for deciding whether or not to delete mandatory fields. You can play all kinds of game with this, but remember that you'll not be able to predict which produced strings are right or wrong. This is a good approach to use if your main purpose is to stress the software rather than to validate the format validation software. If you want to do it right, whatever language you do it in, you have to get more sophisticated.

5.2.4. Random String Generators

Why not just use a random number generator to generate completely random strings? Two reasons: random strings get recognized as invalid too soon, and even a weak front end will catch most bad strings. The probability of hitting vulnerable points is too low, just as it was for random inputs in domain testing—there are too many bad strings in the world. A random string generator is very easy to build. You only have to be careful about where you put string terminators such as carriage returns. Throw the dice for the string length and then pack random characters (except string terminators) in *front* of the terminator until you've reached the required length. Easy but useless. Even with full automation and running at night, this technique caught almost nothing of value.

5.2.5. Getting Sophisticated

Getting sophisticated means building an anti-parser. It's about as complicated as a simple compiler. The language it compiles is BNF, and instead of producing output code it produces structured garbage. I'll assume that you know the rudiments of how a compiler works—if not, this section is beyond you.

As with a compiler, you begin with the lexical scan and build a symbol table. The symbols are single characters, keywords, and left-hand sides of definitions. Keep the three lists separate and replace the source symbols with numerical tokens. Note that each definition string points to one or more other definition strings, characters, or keywords—i.e., to other tokens in the symbol table. There are two ways to screw up—bad tokens and bad pointers.

Start with a covering set of correct test cases. This can be done by hand or by trial and error with random number generators or by using flow-analyzer techniques such as are used in path test generators. Given a good string, you now scan the definition tree by using a tree search procedure. At every node in the subtree corresponding to your good test case you can decide whether you're going to use an incorrect token or an incorrect branch to a subsidiary definition. Use random numbers to replace individual characters, keywords, or pointers to other definitions. Double errors work the same way except that they use the single-error strings as a seed. Similarly, triple-error cases are built on using the double-error cases as a seed. They grow fast.

Another way to look at automated syntax test generation is to view the normal cases as path test generation over BNF as the source language. The errored cases are equivalent to creating **mutations** (BUDD81, WHIT87) of the source ''code.'' There is no sensitization problem because all paths are achievable.

If you've read this far, then you know that you can't guarantee bad strings, even for single-error cases because that's a known unsolvable problem. Double errors increase the probability of correct strings because of error cancellations. The only (imperfect) way to sort the good from the bad is to use the BNF specification as data to a parser generator and then use the generated parser to sort for you—it can't be perfect but it should do for simple operator commands. What's the point of generating test strings and using an automatically created parser to sort the good from the bad? If you've got such a parser, use *it* instead of the code you're testing? If we were dealing with entirely new code and a new command language, it would be better to generate the parser and avoid the testing. Using the generated parser as above is useful if it's an older system under maintenance and your objective is to build a big syntax-testing suite where one didn't exist before.

5.3. Productivity, Training, and Effectiveness

I used syntax test design as basic training for persons new to a test group. With very little effort they can churn out hundreds of good tests. It's a great confidence builder for people who have never done formal test design before and who may be intimidated by the prospect of subjecting a senior designer's masterpiece to a barrage of calculated heartburn. With nothing more sophisticated for automation than a word processor and a copying machine, a testing trainee can usually produce twenty to thirty fully documented test cases *per hour* after a few days of training.

Syntax testing is also an excellent way of convincing a novice tester that testing is infinite and that the tester's problem is not generating tests but knowing which ones to cull. When my trainees told me that they had run out of ideas, it was time to teach them syntax testing. I would always ask them to produce *all* single-, double-, and triple-error cases for a few well-chosen operator commands. Think about it.

5.4. Ad-Lib Tests

Whenever you run a formal system test there's always someone in the crowd who wants to try ad-lib tests. And almost always, the kind of test they want to ad-lib is an input-syntax error test. I used to object to ad-libbing, because it didn't prove anything—I thought. It doesn't prove anything substantive about the system, assuming you've done a good job of testing—which is why I used to object to it. It may save time to object to ad-lib tests, but it's not politic. Allowing the ad-lib tests demonstrates that you have confidence in the system and your test. Because a system-wide functional demonstration should have been through a dry run in advance, the actual test execution is largely ceremonial (or should be) and the ad-libbers are part of the ceremony, just as hecklers are part of the ball game—it adds color to the scene.

You should never object if the system's final recipient has cooked up a set of tests of his own. If they're carefully constructed, and well documented, and all the rest, you should welcome yet another independent assault on the system's integrity. Ad-lib tests aren't like that. The customer has a hotshot operator who's earned a reputation for crashing any system in under 2 minutes, and she's itching to get her mitts on yours. There's no prepared set of tests, so you know it's going to be ad-libbed. Agree to the ad-libbing, but only after all other tests have been done. Here's what happens:

1. Most of the ad-lib tests will be input strings with format violations, and the system will reject them—as it should.
2. Most of the rest are good strings that look bad. The system accepts the strings and does as it was told to do, but the ad-lib tester doesn't recognize it. It will take a lot of explanation to satisfy the customer that it was a cockpit error.
3. A few seemingly good strings will be correctly rejected because of a correlation problem between two field values or a state dependency. These situations will also take a lot of explanation.
4. At least once, the ad-lib tester will shout "Aha!" and claim that the system was wrong. It will take days to dig out the documentation

that shows that the way the system behaves for that case is precisely the way the customer insisted that it behave—over the designer's objections.

5. Another time the ad-lib tester will shout ''Aha!'' but, because the inputs weren't documented and because nonprinting characters were used, it won't be possible to reproduce the effect. The ad-lib tester will be forever convinced that the system has a flaw.

6. There may be one problem, typically related to an interpretation of a specification ambiguity, whose resolution will probably be trivial.

This may be harsh to the ad-lib testers of the world, but such testing proves little or nothing if the system is good, if it's been properly tested from unit on up, and if there has been good quality control. If ad-lib tests do prove something, then the system's so shaky and buggy that it deserves the worst that can be thrown at it.

6. TESTABILITY TIPS

6.1. The Tip

Here's the whole testability tip:

1. Bring the hidden languages out of the closet.
2. Define the syntax, formally, in BNF.
3. Simplify the syntax definition graph.
4. Build a parser.

I'll quell the objections to the last step by pointing out that building a minicompiler is a typical senior-year computer science project these days. I find that interesting because although most computer science majors build a compiler once in their lifetime, they'll never have a chance to build a real compiler once they're out in the world—we just don't need that many programming language compilers. So drag out the old notebooks to remember how it was done and if you learned your programming before compiler building was an undergraduate exercise, get one of the kids to do it for you.

6.2. Compiler Overview

This overview is superficial and intended only to illustrate testability issues. Compilation consists of three main steps: **lexical analysis, parsing,** and **code production.** In our context, we deal most often not with a compiler as such, but with an **interpreter;** but if we're testing hidden languages, then indeed we may be interested in a compiler. The main difference between an interpreter and compiler is that an interpreter works one statement at a time and does the equivalent of code production on the fly.

1. *Lexical Analysis*—The lexical analysis phase accomplishes the following:
   a. The analyzer knows enough about parsing to identify individual fields, where we define a **field** as a linguistic element that uses no lower-level definitions. That is, a field is defined solely in terms of primitive elements such as characters.
   b. Identifies interfield separators or delimiters.
   c. Classifies the field (e.g., integer, string, operator, keyword, variable names, program labels). Some fields, such as numbers or strings, may be translated at this point.
   d. New variable names and program labels are put into a **symbol table** and replaced by a pointer to that table. If a variable name or program label is already in the table, its appearance in the code is replaced by the pointer. The pointer is an example of a **token.**
   e. **Keywords** (e.g., STOP, IF, ELSE) are also replaced by tokens as are single-character operators. Numbers and strings are also put in a table and replaced by pointers.
   f. Delimiters are eliminated where possible, such as interfield delimiters. If the language permits multiple statements per line and there are statement delimiters, statements will be separated so that subsequent processing will be done one statement at a time. Similarly, multiline statements are combined and thereafter treated as a single string.
   g. The output of the lexical analysis phase is the partially translated version of the source in which all linguistic components have been replaced by tokens. The act of replacing these components by tokens is called **tokenizing.**
2. *Parsing*—Parsing is done on tokenized strings. There are many different strategies used for parsing, and they depend on the kind of statement, the language, and the compiler's objectives. There is also a vast literature on the subject. For general information you can start with LEER84 or MAGI84. From our point of view, the validation aspect of parsing consists of showing that the string to be parsed corresponds to a path in the syntax graph. The output of the parser is a tree with the statement identifier at the top, primitive elements (e.g., characters and keywords) at the bottom, and with intermediate

nodes corresponding to definitions that were traversed along the path through the syntax graph.

3. *Code Production*—Code production consists of scanning the above tree (bottom-up, say) in such a way as to assure that all objects needed are available when they are needed and then replacing the tokens with sequences of instructions that accomplish what the tokens signify. From our point of view and our typical use of syntax testing, the equivalent to code production is a call to a worker subroutine or transfer of control to the appropriate program point.

6.3. Typical Software

Unlike the above operation with its clear separation of lexical analysis, parsing, and production, the typical software for (operator command, say) syntax validation and command processing follows what I like to call:

$$(lex\_a\_little + parse\_a\_little + process\_a\_little)*$$

Because the three aspects of command interpretation are hopelessly intermixed, a single bug can involve all three aspects. In other words, the ground for bugs is much more fertile.

6.4. Separation of Phases

Separation of the three phases means that it is virtually impossible for a bug to involve, say, the interaction between processing, say, and parsing. We can handle the lexical testing by low-level syntax testing based on one field at a time and be confident that we can ignore lexical-level field interactions, except where field delimiters are involved. Similarly, because most delimiters are eliminated during lexical analysis, we don't have to bother with combinations of syntax errors and long delimiter strings. Lexical-parsing separation means that test strings with combined lexical and syntax errors will not be productive. Parsing-processing separation means that we can separate domain testing from syntax testing. Domain analysis is the first stage of processing and follows parsing, and it is therefore independent of syntax. The bottom line of phase separation is the wholesale elimination of possible double-error and higher-order vulnerabilities and therefore the need to even consider such cases.

In addition to more robust software that's easier to test, there's a payoff in maintenance. The lexical definitions, the syntax, and the equivalent of code that points to working subroutines that do the actual processing can all be stored in tables rather than as code. Separation means separate maintenance. If a processing routine is wrong, there's no need to change the lexical analyzer or parser. If a new command is to be added, chances are that only the parser and keyword table will be affected. Similarly for enhancing existing commands.

What's the price? Possibly more memory, possibly more processing time, but probably neither. The ad hoc *lex_a_little, parse_a_little* code is a jumbled mess that often contains a lot of code redundancy and wasted reprocessing. My own experience has been that in every instance where we replaced an old-style format analyzer and processor with an explicit lex analyzer and parser, even though we had planned on more time and more space, to our surprise the new software was tighter and faster.

6.5. Prerequisites

The language must be decent enough so that it is possible to do lexical analysis before parsing and parsing before processing. That means that it is possible to pull out the tokens in a single left-to-right pass over the string and to do it independently of any other string or statement in the language. The kind of thing that can't be handled for example, are formats such as: "If the first character of the string is an alpha, then every fourth character following it is a token delimiter and the last token is a symbol; but if the first character is numeric, only spaces and parentheses are delimiters and any contiguous string of alphas unbroken by a delimiter is a symbol."—hopeless.

The above is an example of a **context-dependent language.** Languages with more virtuous properties are called **context-free.** We're not dealing with general purpose programming languages here but with simpler mini-languages such as human-interface languages and internal hidden languages. The only excuse for context dependencies is that they were inherited. If it's an internal language then it can, and should, be changed to remove such dependencies. If it's a human-interface language, then the context dependencies must be ripped out because humans can't really deal with such command structures.

7. SUMMARY

1. Syntax testing begins with a validated format specification. That may be half the work of designing syntax tests.
2. Express the syntax in a formal language such as BNF.

3. Simplify the syntax definition graph before you design.
4. Design syntax tests level by level from top to bottom making only one error at a time, one level at a time, leaving everything else as correct as possible.
5. Test the valid cases by (at least) covering the definition graph.
6. Concentrate on delimiters, especially paired delimiters, and delimiter errors that could cause syntactic ambiguities.
7. Stress all BNF exponent (loop) values as for loop testing.
8. Test field-value errors and state dependencies by domain testing and state testing, as appropriate.
9. Cut multiple-error tests sharply at two and three simultaneous errors. Look for the bugs along the baseboards and in the corners.
10. Take advantage of the design to simplify the test and vice versa.
11. Don't forget the valid cases.
12. Document copiously and automate, automate, automate—use capture/replay systems and editors to create the tests and build or buy drivers to run them (Chapter 13).
13. Give the ad-lib testers the attention they crave and deserve but remember that they can probably be replaced by a random string generator and aren't much more useful.

AND

14. Don't forget to cover the valid cases.

10

LOGIC-BASED TESTING

1. SYNOPSIS

The functional requirements of many programs can be specified by **decision tables,** which provide a useful basis for program and test design. Consistency and completeness can be analyzed by using boolean algebra, which can also be used as a basis for test design. Boolean algebra is trivialized by using **Karnaugh-Veitch charts.**

2. MOTIVATIONAL OVERVIEW

2.1. Programmers and Logic

"Logic" is one of the most often used words in programmers' vocabularies but one of their least used techniques. This chapter concerns logic in its simplest form, **boolean algebra,** and its application to program and specification test and design. Boolean algebra is to logic as arithmetic is to mathematics. Without it, the tester or programmer is cut off from many test and design techniques and tools that incorporate those techniques.

2.2. Hardware Logic Testing

Logic has been, for several decades, the primary tool of hardware logic designers. Today, hardware logic design and more important in the context of this book, hardware logic *test* design, are intensely automated. Many test methods developed for hardware logic can be adapted to software logic testing. Because hardware testing automation is 10 to 15 years ahead of software testing automation, hardware testing methods and its associated theory is a fertile ground for software testing methods.*

---

* Hardware testing is ahead of software testing not because hardware testers are smarter than software testers but because hardware testing is easier. I say this from the perspective of a former hardware logic designer and tester who has worked in both camps and therefore has a basis for comparison.

Hardware testing methods will eventually filter into the software testers' toolkits, but there's another ongoing trend that provides an even stronger motivation. The distinction between hardware and software is blurring. Hardware designers talk about **silicon compilers**—compilers that start with a specification in a high-order language and automatically produce integrated circuit layouts. Similarly, the decision to implement a feature as hardware or software may one day be left to a silicon/software compiler. The hardware designers look more like programmers each day and we can expect them to meet at a middle ground where boolean algebra will be basic to their common language of discourse.

2.3. Specification Systems and Languages
(BERZ85, CHIU85, HAYE85, KEMM85, VESS86)

As programming and test techniques have improved, the bugs have shifted closer to the process front end, to requirements and their specifications. These bugs range from 8% to 30% of the total and because they're first-in and last-out, they're the costliest of all. The impact of specification systems and languages was discussed in Chapter 2, Section 3.2.4.

The trouble with specifications is that they're hard to express. Logicians have struggled with this problem since Aristotle's time. Boolean algebra (also known as the **sentential calculus**) is the most basic of all logic systems. Higher-order logic systems are needed and used for formal specifications. That does not necessarily mean that future programmers will have to live with upside-down A's and backward E's because much of logical analysis can be and is embedded in tools. But these tools incorporate methods to simplify, transform, and check specifications, and the methods are to a large extent based on boolean algebra. So even if you have a relatively painless specification system, to understand why your specification was rejected or how it was transformed, you'll have to understand boolean algebra.

2.4. Knowledge-Based Systems

The **knowledge-based system** (also **expert system,** or **"artificial intelligence" system**) has become the programming construct of choice for many applications that were once considered very difficult (WATE86). Knowledge-based systems incorporate knowledge from a knowledge domain such as medicine, law, or civil engineering into a database. The data can then be queried and interacted with to provide solutions to problems in that domain. One implementation of knowledge-based systems is to incorporate the expert's knowledge into a set of rules. The user can then provide data and ask questions based on that data. The user's data is processed through the rule base to yield conclusions (tentative or definite) and requests for more data. The processing is done by a program called the **inference engine.** From the point of view of testing, there's nothing special about the inference engine—it's just another piece of software to be tested, and the methods discussed in this book apply. When we talk about testing knowledge-based systems, it's not the inference engine that concerns us, but testing the validity of the expert's knowledge and the correctness of the transcription (i.e., coding) of that knowledge into a rule base. Both of these testing areas are beyond the scope of this book; but understanding knowledge-based systems and their validation problems requires an understanding of formal logic (BELL87) to which the content of this chapter is basic.

2.5. Overview

We start with **decision tables** because: they are extensively used in business data processing; decision-table preprocessors as extensions to CO-BOL are in common use; boolean algebra is embedded in the implementation of these processors. The next step is a review of boolean algebra (included to make this book self-contained). I included decision tables because the engineering/mathematically trained programmer may not be familiar with them, and boolean algebra because the business data processing programmer may have had only cursory exposure to it. That gets both kinds of readers to a common base, which is the use of decision tables and/or boolean algebra in test and software design.

Although *programmed tools* are nice to have, most of the benefits of boolean algebra can be reaped by wholly manual means if you have the right *conceptual tool:* the **Karnaugh-Veitch** diagram is that conceptual tool. Few programmers, unless they're retreaded logic designers like me, or unless they had a fling with hardware design, learn about this method of doing boolean algebra. Without it, boolean algebra is tedious and error-prone and I don't wonder that people won't use it. With it, with practice, boolean algebra is no worse than arithmetic.

3. DECISION TABLES (HURL83, VESS86)

3.1. Definitions and Notation

Table 10.1 is a **limited-entry decision table.** It consists of four areas called the **condition stub,** the **condition entry,** the **action stub,** and the **action**

CONDITION ENTRY

	RULE 1	RULE 2	RULE 3	RULE 4
CONDITION 1	YES	YES	NO	NO
CONDITION 2	YES	I	NO	I
CONDITION 3	NO	YES	NO	I
CONDITION 4	NO	YES	NO	YES
ACTION 1	YES	YES	NO	NO
ACTION 2	NO	NO	YES	NO
ACTION 3	NO	NO	NO	YES

CONDITION STUB (CONDITION 1–4), ACTION STUB (ACTION 1–3)

ACTION ENTRY

Table 10.1. An Example of a Decision Table.

entry. Each column of the table is a rule that specifies the conditions under which the actions named in the action stub will take place. The **condition stub** is a list of names of conditions. A rule specifies whether a condition should or should not be met for the rule to be satisfied. "YES" means that the condition must be met, "NO" means that the condition must not be met, and "I" means that the condition plays no part in the rule, or it is **immaterial** to that rule. The **action stub** names the actions the routine will take or initiate if the rule is satisfied. If the action entry is "YES," the action will take place; if "NO," the action will not take place. Table 10.1 can be translated as follows:

1a. Action 1 will take place if conditions 1 and 2 are met and if conditions 3 and 4 are not met (rule 1), or if conditions 1, 3, and 4 are met (rule 2).

"Condition" is another word for predicate: either a predicate in a specification or a control-flow predicate in a program. To say that a "condition is satisfied or met" is to say that the predicate is true. Similarly for "not met" and "false." Decision-table literature uses "condition" and "satisfied" or "met." In this book we prefer to use "predicate" and TRUE/ FALSE.

Restating the conditions for action 1 to take place:

1b. Action 1 will be taken if predicates 1 and 2 are true and if predicates 3 and 4 are false (rule 1), or if predicates 1, 3, and 4 are true (rule 2).

2. Action 2 will be taken if the predicates are all false, (rule 3).

3. Action 3 will take place if predicate 1 is false and predicate 4 is true (rule 4).

	RULE 5	RULE 6	RULE 7	RULE 8
CONDITION 1	I	NO	YES	YES
CONDITION 2	I	YES	I	NO
CONDITION 3	YES	I	NO	NO
CONDITION 4	NO	NO	YES	I
DEFAULT ACTION	YES	YES	YES	YES

Table 10.2. The Default Rules for Table 10.1.

It is not obvious from looking at this specification whether or not all sixteen possible combinations of the four predicates have been covered. In fact, they have not; a combination of YES, NO, NO, NO, for predicates 1 through 4 respectively, is not covered by these rules. In addition to the stated rules, therefore, we also need a **default rule** that specifies the default action to be taken when all other rules fail. The default rules for Table 10.1 is shown in Table 10.2. Decision tables can be specified in specialized languages that will automatically create the default rules.* Consequently, when programming in such languages, it is not necessary to make an explicit default specification; but when decision tables are used as a tool for test case design and specification analysis, the default rules and their associated predicates must be explicitly specified or determined. If the set of rules covers all the combinations of TRUE/FALSE (YES/NO) for the predicates, a default specification is not needed.

3.2. Decision-Table Processors

Decision tables can be automatically translated into code and, as such, are a higher-order language. The decision table's translator checks the source decision table for consistency and completeness and fills in any required default rules. The usual processing order in the resulting object code is, first, to examine rule 1. If the rule is satisfied, the corresponding action takes place. Otherwise, rule 2 is tried. This process continues until either a satisfied rule results in an action or no rule is satisfied and the default action is taken. Decision tables as a source language have the virtue of clarity, direct correspondence to specifications, and maintain-

---

* Exactly the same situation occurs for languages with an IF P_1 THEN . . . ELSE IF P_2 . . . ELSE . . . construct. The last ELSE is the default case executed when none of the previous predicates is satisfied.

ability. The principal deficiency is possible object-code inefficiency. There was a time when it was thought by some that decision tables would herald a new era in programming. Their use, it was claimed, would eliminate most bugs and poor programming practices and would reduce testing to trivia. Such claims are rarely made now, but despite such unrealistically high hopes, decision tables have become entrenched as a useful tool in the programmer's kit, especially in business data processing.

3.3. Decision Tables as a Basis for Test Case Design

If a specification is given as a decision table, it follows that decision tables should be used for test case design. Similarly, if a program's logic is to be implemented as decision tables, decision tables should also be used as a basis for test design. But if that's so, the consistency and completeness of the decision table is checked by the decision-table processor; therefore, it would seem that there would be no need to design those test cases. True, testing is not needed to expose contradictions and inconsistencies, but testing is still needed to determine whether the rules themselves are correct and to expose possible bugs in processing on which the rules' predicates depend.

Even if you can specify the program's logic as a decision table, it is not always possible or desirable to implement the program as a decision table because the program's logical behavior is only part of its behavior. The program interfaces with other programs, there are restrictions, or the decision-table language may not have needed features. Any of these reasons could be sufficient to reject a decision-table implementation. The use of a decision-table *model* to design tests is warranted when:

1. The specification is given as a decision table or can be easily converted into one.
2. The order in which the predicates are evaluated does not affect interpretation of the rules or the resulting action—i.e., an arbitrary permutation of the predicate order will not, or should not, affect which action takes place.
3. The order in which the rules are evaluated does not affect the resulting action—i.e., an arbitrary permutation of rules will not, or should not, affect which action takes place.
4. Once a rule is satisfied and an action selected, no other rule need be examined.
5. If several actions can result from satisfying a rule, the order in which the actions are executed doesn't matter.

These restrictions mean that the action selected is based on the combination of predicate truth values and nothing else. It might seem that these restrictions eliminate many potential applications but, despite external appearances, the rule evaluation order often doesn't matter. For example, if you use an automatic teller machine, the card must be valid, you must enter the right password, and there must be enough money in your account. It really doesn't matter in which order these predicates are evaluated. The specific order chosen may be sensible in that it might be more efficient, but the order is not inherent in the program's logic: the ordering is a by-product of the way we mapped parallel data flows into a sequential, Von Neumann language.

The above restrictions have further implications: (1) the rules are complete in the sense that every combination of predicate truth values, including the default cases, are inherent in the decision table, and (2) the rules are consistent if and only if every combination of predicate truth values results in only one action or set of actions. If the rules were inconsistent, that is if at least one combination of predicate truth values was implicit in two or more rules, then the action taken could depend on the order in which the rules were examined in contradiction to requirement 3 above. If the set of rules were incomplete, there could be a combination of inputs for which no action, normal or default, were specified and the routine's action would be unpredictable.

3.4. Expansion of Immaterial Cases

Improperly specified **immaterial entries** (I) cause most decision-table contradictions. If a condition's truth value is immaterial in a rule, satisfying the rule does not depend on the condition. It doesn't mean that the case is impossible. For example,

Rule 1: "If the persons are male and over 30, then they shall receive a 15% raise."

Rule 2: "But if the persons are female, then they shall receive a 10% raise."

The above rules state that age is material for a male's raise, but immaterial for determining a female's raise. No one would suggest that females either under or over 30 are impossible. If there are n predicates there are 2^n cases to consider. You find the cases by expanding the immaterial cases. This is done by converting each I entry into a pair of entries, one with a YES and the other with a NO. Each I entry in a rule doubles the number of cases in the expansion of that rule. Rule 2 in Table 10.1 con-

		RULE 2			RULE 4		
	RULE 2.1	RULE 2.2	RULE 4.1	RULE 4.2	RULE 4.3	RULE 4.4
CONDITION 1	YES	YES	NO	NO	NO	NO
CONDITION 2	YES	NO	YES	YES	NO	NO
CONDITION 3	YES	YES	YES	NO	NO	YES
CONDITION 4	YES	YES	YES	YES	YES	YES

Table 10.3. Expansion of Immaterial Cases for Rules 2 and 4.

tains one I entry and therefore expands into two equivalent subrules. Rule 4 contains two I entries and therefore expands into four subrules. The expansion of rules 2 and 4 are shown in Table 10.3.

Rule 2 has been expanded by converting the I entry for condition 2 into a separate rule 2.1 for YES and 2.2 for NO. Similarly, condition 2 was expanded in rule 4 to yield intermediate rules 4.1/4.2 and 4.3/4.4, which were then expanded via condition 3 to yield the four subrules shown.

The key to test case design based on decision tables is to expand the immaterial entries and to generate tests that correspond to all the subrules that result. If some conditions are three-way, an immaterial entry expands into three subrules. Similarly, an immaterial n-way case statement expands into n subrules.

If no default rules are given, then all cases not covered by explicit rules are perforce default rules (or are intended to be). If default rules are given, then you must test the specification for consistency. The specification is complete if and only if n (binary) conditions expand into exactly 2^n unique subrules. It is consistent if and only if all rules expand into subrules whose condition combinations do not match those of any other rules. Table 10.4

	RULE 1	RULE 2		RULE 1.1	RULE 1.2	RULE 2.1	RULE 2.2
CONDITION 1	YES	YES		YES	YES	YES	YES
CONDITION 2	I	NO		YES	NO	NO	NO
CONDITION 3	YES	I		YES	YES	YES	NO
CONDITION 4	NO	NO		NO	NO	NO	NO
ACTION 1	YES	NO		YES	YES	NO	NO
ACTION 2	NO	YES		NO	NO	YES	YES

Table 10.4. The Expansion of an Inconsistent Specification.

is an example of an inconsistent specification in which the expansion of two rules yields a contradiction.

Rules 1 and 2 are contradictory because the expansion of rule 1 via condition 2 leads to the same set of predicate truth values as the expansion of rule 2 via condition 3. Therefore action 1 or action 2 is taken depending on which rule is evaluated first.

3.5. Test Case Design (GOOD75, LEWA76, TAIA87)

Test case design by decision tables begins with examining the specification's consistency and completeness. This is done by expanding all immaterial cases and checking the expanded tables. Also, make the default case explicit and treat it as just another set of rules for the default action. Efficient methods are given in later sections. Once the specifications have been verified, the objective of the test cases is to show that the implementation provides the correct action for all combinations of predicate values.

1. If there are k rules over n binary predicates, there are at least k cases to consider and at most 2^n cases. You can design test cases based on the unexpanded rules, with one case per rule, or based on the expanded rules with 2^n tests. Find input values to force each case.

2. It is not usually possible to change the order in which the *predicates* are evaluated because that order is built into the program,* but if the implementation allows the order to be changed by input values, augment the test cases by using different predicate evaluation orders. Try all pairs of interchanges for a representative set of values. For example, if the normal order is predicate A followed by B, try a test in which B is followed by A. For N predicates, there will be $N(N - 1)/2$ interchanges for each combination of predicate truth values.

3. It is not usually possible to change the order in which the *rules* are evaluated because that order is built into the program, but if the implementation allows the rule evaluation order to be modified, test

---

* Predicate and rule evaluation order could be variable in a system in which operators use explicit identifiers for every input field in a command. For example, the input specification might be of the form

$$A = 1, B = 3, C = 17, D = ABCDE. \ . \ . \ , \text{ and so on.}$$

A tolerant implementation would allow these fields in any order. Similarly, an input packet could consist of several dozen or possibly a variable number of input blocks, each of which was self-identifying and could therefore be tolerated in any order. Finally, complicated forms can have conditional subforms, which can result in the same data being input in different orders, depending on the path taken through the form and on the values of previous data. All such examples can result in variable orders of predicate evaluation and/or variable orders of rule evaluation.

different orders for the rules by pairwise interchanges. One set of predicate values per rule should suffice.

4. Identify the places in the routine where rules are invoked or where the processors that evaluate the rules are called. Identify the places where actions are initiated. Instrument the paths from the rule processors to the actions so that you can show that the correct action was invoked for each rule.

3.6. Decision Tables and Structure

Decision tables can also be used to examine a program's structure (GOOD75). Figure 10.1 shows a program segment that consists of a decision tree. These decisions, in various combinations, can lead to actions 1, 2, or 3. Does this flowgraph correspond to a complete and consistent set of conditions?

The corresponding decision table is shown in Table 10.5. You can almost read it from the flowgraph. If the decision appears on a path, put in a YES or NO as appropriate. If the decision does not appear on the path, put in an I. Rule 1 does not contain decision C, therefore its entries are: YES, YES, I, YES. Expanding the immaterial cases for Table 10.5 leads to Table 10.6.

Sixteen cases are represented in Table 10.5, and no case appears twice. Consequently, the flowgraph appears to be complete and consistent. As a

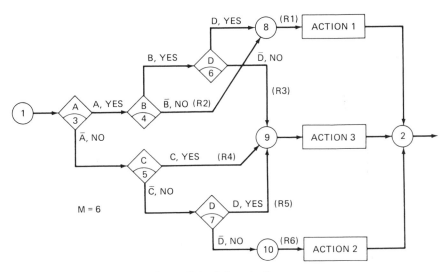

Figure 10.1. A Sample Program.

	RULE 1	RULE 2	RULE 3	RULE 4	RULE 5	RULE 6
CONDITION A	YES	YES	YES	NO	NO	NO
CONDITION B	YES	NO	YES	I	I	I
CONDITION C	I	I	I	YES	NO	NO
CONDITION D	YES	I	NO	I	YES	NO
ACTION 1	YES	YES	NO	NO	NO	NO
ACTION 2	NO	NO	YES	YES	YES	NO
ACTION 3	NO	NO	NO	NO	NO	YES

Table 10.5. The Decision Table Corresponding to Figure 10.1.

	R1	RULE 2	R3	RULE 4	R5	R6
CONDITION A	Y Y	Y Y Y Y	Y Y	N N N N	N N	N N
CONDITION B	Y Y	N N N N	Y Y	Y Y N N	N Y	Y N
CONDITION C	Y N	N N Y Y	Y N	Y Y Y Y	N N	N N
CONDITION D	Y Y	Y N N Y	N N	N Y Y N	Y Y	N N

Table 10.6. The Expansion of Table 10.5.

first check, before you look for all sixteen combinations, count the number of Y's and N's in each row. They should be equal. I found my bug that way.

Consider the following specification whose putative flowgraph is shown in Figure 10.2:

1. If condition A is met, do process A1 no matter what other actions are taken or what other conditions are met.
2. If condition B is met, do process A2 no matter what other actions are taken or what other conditions are met.
3. If condition C is met, do process A3 no matter what other actions are taken or what other conditions are met.
4. If none of the conditions is met, then do processes A1, A2, and A3.
5. When more than one process is done, process A1 must be done first, then A2, and then A3. The only permissible cases are: (A1), (A2), (A3), (A1,A3), (A2,A3) and (A1,A2,A3).

Table 10.7 shows the conversion of this flowgraph into a decision table after expansion. There are eight cases, and all paths lead to the evaluation

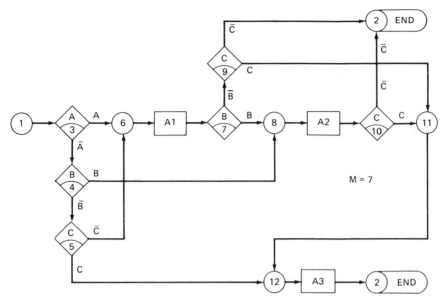

Figure 10.2. A Troublesome Program.

of all three predicates even though some predicates on some paths may be evaluated more than once. We can use the predicate notation introduced in Chapter 3 and name the rules by their corresponding combination of predicate truth values to make things clearer.

As clever as this design may seem, perhaps because it is clever, it has a bug. The programmer tried to force all three processes to be executed for the $\overline{A}\,\overline{B}\,\overline{C}$ cases but forgot that the B and C predicates would be done again, thereby bypassing processes A2 and A3. This would have been

RULES

	$\overline{A}\,\overline{B}\,\overline{C}$	$\overline{A}\,\overline{B}\,C$	$\overline{A}\,B\,C$	$\overline{A}\,B\,\overline{C}$	$A\,B\,\overline{C}$	$A\,B\,C$	$A\,\overline{B}\,C$	$A\,\overline{B}\,\overline{C}$
CONDITION A	NO	NO	NO	NO	YES	YES	YES	YES
CONDITION B	NO	NO	YES	YES	YES	YES	NO	NO
CONDITION C	NO	YES	YES	NO	NO	YES	YES	NO
ACTION 1	YES	NO	NO	NO	YES	YES	YES	YES
ACTION 2	YES	NO	YES	YES	YES	YES	NO	NO
ACTION 3	YES	YES	YES	NO	NO	YES	YES	NO

Table 10.7. Decision Table for Figure 10.2.

easily found by the techniques of the next section, but for the moment, if the processes had been instrumented and if all eight cases were used to test, the bug would have been revealed. Note that testing based on structure alone would reveal nothing because the design was at fault—it did something, but what it did didn't match the specification.

4. PATH EXPRESSIONS AGAIN

4.1. General

4.1.1. The Model

Logic-based testing is structural testing when it's applied to structure (e.g., control flowgraph of an implementation); it's functional testing when it's applied to a specification. As with all test techniques, we start with a model: we focus on one program characteristic and ignore the others. In logic-based testing we focus on the truth values of control flow predicates.

4.1.2. Predicates and Relational Operators

A **predicate** is implemented as a process whose outcome is a truth-functional value. Don't restrict your notion of predicate to arithmetic relations such as $>$, $>=$, $=$, $<=$, $<$, $\neq$. Predicates are based on **relational operators,** of which the arithmetic relational operators are merely the most common. Here's a sample of some other relational operators: ... is a member of ..., ... is a subset of ..., ... is a substring of ..., ... is a subgraph of ..., ... dominates ..., ... is dominated by ..., ... is the greatest lower bound of ..., ... hides ..., ... is in the shadow of ..., ... is above ..., ... is below .... The point about thinking of predicates as processes that yield truth values is that it usually pays to look at predicates top-down—typically from the point of view of predicates as specified in requirements rather than from the point of view of predicates as implemented. Almost all programming languages have arithmetic relational operators and few others. Therefore, in most languages you construct the predicates you need by using the more primitive arithmetic relations. For example, you need a set membership predicate for numbers (e.g., . . . is a member of . . .) but it's implemented as an equality predicate in a loop that scans the whole set.

4.1.3. Case Statements and Multivalued Logics

Predicates need not be restricted to binary truth values (TRUE/FALSE). There are multiway predicates, of which the FORTRAN three-way IF is the most notorious and the case statement the most useful. There are multivalued logics such as Post-algebras that can be used to analyze such predicate structures, but their use is technically difficult and semantically tricky. Three-valued logics are used routinely at the hardware interfaces between chips to reduce the number signal lines needed. For our purpose, logic-based testing is restricted to binary predicates. If you have case statements, you have to analyze things one case at a time if you're to use these methods. If you have many case statements, there will be a lot of bookkeeping and you're probably pushing the applicability of logic-based testing.

4.1.4. What Goes Wrong with Predicates

Several things can go wrong with predicates, especially if the predicate has to be interpreted in order to express it as a predicate over input values.

1. The wrong relational operator is used: e.g., $>$ instead of $<=$.
2. The predicate expression of a compound predicate is incorrect: e.g., $A + B$ instead of AB.
3. The wrong operands are used: e.g., $A > X$ instead of $A > Z$.
4. The processing leading to the predicate (along the predicate's interpretation path) is faulty.

Logic-based testing is useful against the first two bug types, whereas data flow testing is more useful against the latter two.

4.1.5. Overview

We start by generating path expressions by path tracing as in Chapter 8, but this time, our purpose is to convert the path expressions into boolean algebra, using the predicates' truth values (e.g., A and $\overline{A}$) as weights. Once we have predicate expressions that cover all paths, we can examine the logical sum of those expressions for consistency and ambiguity. We then consider a hierarchy of logic-based testing strategies and associated coverage concepts starting with simple branch testing and going on to explore strategies up to complete path testing.

4.2. Boolean Algebra

4.2.1. Notation

Let's take a structural viewpoint for the moment and review the steps taken to get the predicate expression of a path.

1. Label each decision with an uppercase letter that represents the truth value of the predicate. The YES or TRUE branch is labeled with a letter and the NO or FALSE branch with the same letter overscored.
2. The truth value of a path is the product of the individual labels. Concatenation or products mean "AND." For example, the straight-through path of Figure 10.2, which goes via nodes 3, 6, 7, 8, 10, 11, 12, and 2, has a truth value of ABC. The path via nodes 3, 6, 7, 9 and 2 has a value of $AB\overline{C}$.
3. If two or more paths merge at a node, the fact is expressed by use of a plus sign (+) which means "OR."

Using this convention, the truth-functional values for several of the nodes can be expressed in terms of segments from previous nodes. Use the node name to identify the point.

$$N6 = A + \overline{A}\,\overline{B}\,\overline{C}$$
$$N8 = (N6)B + \overline{A}B = AB + \overline{A}\,\overline{B}\,\overline{C}B + \overline{A}B$$
$$N11 = (N8)C + (N6)\overline{B}C$$
$$N12 = N11 + \overline{A}\,\overline{B}C$$
$$N2 = N12 + (N8)\overline{C} + (N6)\overline{B}\,\overline{C}$$

The expression for node 6 can be rewritten as:

"Either it is true that decision A is satisfied (YES) *OR* it is true that decision A is not satisfied (NO) *AND* decision B is not satisfied *AND* decision C is not satisfied, OR both."

The "OR" in boolean algebra is always an **inclusive OR,** which means "A or B or both." The **exclusive OR,** which means "A or B, but *not* both" is $A\overline{B} + \overline{A}B$. Each letter in a boolean expression represents the truth or falsity of a statement such as:

"It is snowing outside."
"Decision A is satisfied."
"A mouse is green when it is spinning."

There are only two numbers in boolean algebra: zero (0) and one (1). One means "always true" and zero means "always false." "Truth" and "falsity" should not be taken in the ordinary sense but in a more technical sense—such as meaning that a specific bit is set. Actually, it doesn't matter whether it is or is not snowing outside. If a program's decision is evaluated as corresponding to "it is snowing," then we say that the statement is true or that the value of the variable that represents it is 1.

4.2.2. The Rules of Boolean Algebra

Boolean algebra has three operators:

× meaning *AND*. Also called multiplication. A statement such as AB means "A and B are both true." This symbol is usually left out as in ordinary algebra.

+ meaning *OR*. "A + B" means "either A is true or B is true or both."

$\overline{A}$ meaning *NOT*. Also **negation** or **complementation.** This is read as either "not A" or "A bar." The entire expression under the bar is negated. For example, $\overline{A}$ is a statement that is true only when statement A is false. The statement $(A + \overline{B})$ is translated as, "It is not true that either A is true or B is not true or both."

We usually dispense with the clumsy phraseology of "it is true" or "it is false" and say "equals 1" or "equals 0" respectively. With these preambles, we can set down the laws of boolean algebra:

1.	$A + A$	$= A$	If something is true, saying it
	$\overline{A} + \overline{A}$	$= \overline{A}$	twice doesn't make it truer, ditto for falsehoods.
2.	$A + 1$	$= 1$	If something is always true, then "either A or true or both" must also be universally true.
3.	$A + 0$	$= A$	
4.	$A + B$	$= B + A$	Commutative law.
5.	$A + \overline{A}$	$= 1$	If either A is true or not-A is true, then the statement is always true.
6.	AA	$= A$	
	$\overline{A}\overline{A}$	$= \overline{A}$	
7.	$A \times 1$	$= A$	
8.	$A \times 0$	$= 0$	

9. $A B = B A$

10. $A \overline{A} = 0$ A statement can't be simultaneously true and false.

11. $\overline{\overline{A}} = A$ "You ain't not going" means you are. How about, "I ain't not never going to get this nohow."?

12. $\overline{0} = 1$

13. $\overline{1} = 0$

14. $\overline{A + B} = \overline{A}\,\overline{B}$ Called "De Morgan's theorem or law."

15. $\overline{AB} = \overline{A} + \overline{B}$

16. $A(B + C) = AB + AC$ Distributive law.

17. $(AB)C = A(BC)$ Multiplication is associative.

18. $(A + B) + C = A + (B + C)$ So is addition.

19. $A + \overline{A}B = A + \overline{B}$ Absorptive law.

20. $A + AB = A$

In all of the above, a letter can represent a single sentence or an entire boolean algebra expression. Individual letters in a boolean algebra expression are called **literals.** The product of several literals is called a **product term** (e.g., ABC, DE). Usually, product terms are simplified by removing duplicate appearances of the same literal barred or unbarred. For example, AAB and $A\overline{B}C\overline{B}$ are replaced by AB and $A\overline{B}C$ respectively. Also, any product term that has both a barred and unbarred appearance of the same literal (e.g., $\overline{A}BAC$) is removed because it equals zero by rule 10. An arbitrary boolean expression that has been multiplied out so that it consists of the sum of products (e.g., ABC + DEF + GH) is said to be in **sum-of-products form.** Boolean expressions can be simplified by successive applications of rules 19 and 20. We'll discuss much easier ways to do this in Section 5 below. The result of such simplifications is again in the sum of product form and each product term in such a simplified version is called a **prime implicant.** For example, ABC + AB + DEF reduces by rule 20 to AB + DEF; that is, AB and DEF are prime implicants.

4.2.3. *Examples*

The path expressions of Section 4.2 can now be simplified by applying the rules. The steps are shown in detail to illustrate the use of the rules. Usually, it's done with far less work. It pays to practice.

$$N6 = A + \overline{A}\,\overline{B}\,\overline{C}$$
$$= A + \overline{B}\,\overline{C}$$
    : Use rule 19, with "B" $= \overline{B}\,\overline{C}$.

$$N8 = (N6)B + \overline{A}B$$
$$= (A + \overline{B}\,\overline{C})B + \overline{A}B \qquad \text{: Substitution.}$$
$$= AB + \overline{B}\,\overline{C}B + \overline{A}B \qquad \text{: Rule 16 (distributive law).}$$
$$= AB + B\overline{B}C + \overline{A}B \qquad \text{: Rule 9 (commutative multiplication).}$$
$$= AB + 0C + \overline{A}B \qquad \text{: Rule 10.}$$
$$= AB + 0 + \overline{A}B \qquad \text{: Rule 8.}$$
$$= AB + \overline{A}B \qquad \text{: Rule 3.}$$
$$= (A + \overline{A})B \qquad \text{: Rule 16 (distributive law).}$$
$$= 1 \times B \qquad \text{: Rule 5.}$$
$$= B \qquad \text{: Rules 7, 9.}$$

Similarly,

$$N11 = (N8)C + (N6)\overline{B}C$$
$$= BC + (A + \overline{B}\,\overline{C})\overline{B}C \qquad \text{: Substitution.}$$
$$= BC + A\overline{B}C \qquad \text{: Rules 16, 9, 10, 8, 3.}$$
$$= C(B + \overline{B}A) \qquad \text{: Rules 9, 16.}$$
$$= C(B + A) \qquad \text{: Rule 19.}$$
$$= AC + BC \qquad \text{: Rules 16, 9, 9, 4.}$$
$$N12 = N11 + \overline{A}\,\overline{B}C$$
$$= AC + BC + \overline{A}\,\overline{B}C$$
$$= C(B + \overline{A}\,\overline{B}) + AC$$
$$= C(\overline{A} + B) + AC$$
$$= C\overline{A} + AC + BC$$
$$= C + BC$$
$$= C$$
$$N2 = N12 + (N8)\overline{C} + (N6)\overline{B}\,\overline{C}$$
$$= C + B\overline{C} + (A + \overline{B}\,\overline{C})\overline{B}\,\overline{C}$$
$$= C + B\overline{C} + \overline{B}\,\overline{C}$$
$$= C + \overline{C}(B + \overline{B})$$
$$= C + \overline{C}$$
$$= 1$$

The deviation from the specification is now clear. The functions should have been:

$$N6 = A + \overline{A}\,\overline{B}\,\overline{C} = A + \overline{B}\,\overline{C} \qquad \text{: correct.}$$
$$N8 = B + \overline{A}\,\overline{B}\,\overline{C} = B + \overline{A}\,\overline{C} \qquad \text{: wrong, was just B.}$$
$$N12 = C + \overline{A}\,\overline{B}\,\overline{C} = C + \overline{A}\,\overline{B} \qquad \text{: wrong, was just C.}$$

4.2.4. *Paths and Domains*

Consider a loop-free entry/exit path and assume for the moment that all predicates are simple. Each predicate on the path is denoted by a capital letter (either overscored or not). The result is a term that consists of the product of several literals. For example, $\overline{A}BC$. If a literal appears twice in a product term then not only can one appearance be removed but it also means that the decision is redundant. If a literal appears both barred and unbarred in a product term, then by rule 10 the term is equal to zero, which is to say that the path is unachievable.

A product term on an entry/exit path specifies a domain because each of the underlying predicate expressions specifies a domain boundary over the input space. Now let's allow the predicates to be compound and again trace a path from entry to exit. Because the predicates are compound, the boolean expression corresponding to the path will be (after simplification) a sum of product terms such as ABC + DEF + GH. Because this expression was derived from one path, the expression also specifies a domain. However, the domain now need not be simply connected. For example, each of the product terms ABC, DEF, and GH could correspond to three separate, disconnected subdomains. If any one of the product terms is included in another, as in ABC + AB, then it means that the domain corresponding to ABC is wholly contained within the domain corresponding to AB and it is always possible to eliminate the included subdomain (ABC in this case) by boolean algebra simplification. Moreover, if the product of any two terms is not zero, then the two domains overlap even though one may not be contained in the other.

An alternative design could have eliminated the compound predicates by providing a separate path for each product term. For example, we can implement ABC + DEF + GH as one path using a compound predicate or as three separate paths (ABC, DEF, and GH) that specify three separate domains that happen to call the same processing subroutine to calculate the outcomes.

Let's say that we've rewritten our program, design, or specification such that there is one and only one product term for each domain: call these $D_1, D_2, \ldots D_i, \ldots D_m$. Consider any two of these product terms, D_i and D_j. For every i not equal to j, D_iD_j must equal zero. If the product doesn't equal zero, then there's an overlap of the domains, which is to say a contradictory domain specification. Furthermore, the sum of all the D_i must equal 1 or else there is an ambiguity. Actually, the same will hold even if the D_i are not simple product terms but arbitrary boolean expressions that could result from compound predicates—i.e., domains that are not simply connected.

4.2.5. Test Case Design

It is, in principle, necessary to design a test case for each possible TRUE/FALSE combination of the predicates. In general, as in the example, the predicates are correlated, so not all paths are achievable. If the predicates were all uncorrelated, then each of the 2^n combinations would correspond to a different path, a different domain, and their sum would correspond to a minimum-covering set.

Although it is possible to have ambiguities and contradictions in a specification (given, say, as a list of conditions), it is *not* possible for a program to have contradictions or ambiguities if:

1. The routine has a single entry and a single exit.
2. No combination of predicate values leads to nonterminating loops.
3. There are no pieces of dangling code that lead nowhere.

Under these circumstances, the boolean algebra expression corresponding to the set of all entry/exit paths must equal 1 exactly. If it doesn't, either you've made a mistake in evaluating it or there are pieces of unreachable code or nonterminating code for some predicate-value combination.

Let's consider a hierarchy of test cases for an arbitrary loop-free routine that has compound predicates. The routine has one entry and exit and has no dead-end code. Because the predicates may be compound, the boolean algebra expression of a domain will generally be a sum of products after simplification. We can build a hierarchy of test strategies by considering how we test for each domain and the whole routine.

The most complete test case set you can use is one where the paths correspond to all 2^n combinations of predicate values, which we know is equivalent to all paths. There can be no more cases than this (from the point of view of logic-based testing), but testing can usually be achieved with fewer test cases. For example, branch coverage of Figure 10.2 can be achieved by using all the cases except ABC and $\overline{AB}\overline{C}$: and there are several other combinations that do not include all 2^n cases but still provide branch coverage. To find a set of covering paths, write out all 2^n combinations. Each combination specifies a path. Add combinations until branch coverage has been achieved.

Typically, we're interested in the boolean algebra expression corresponding to paths from one node to another. For example, from the entry to the point at which processing specific to a domain is done. We had three other points of interest in this routine, corresponding to the three processes. Those nodes were N6, N8, and N12. The simplified product-form boolean algebra expression for those nodes specifies the test cases needed for each. Any one prime implicant in the boolean expression covering all the paths from the entry to the node is sufficient to reach the node. The expansion of the expression for that node specifies all possible ways of reaching that node, although all terms may not be needed to provide coverage to that point. For example:

$$N6 = A + \overline{B}\,\overline{C}$$
$$= A\overline{B}\,\overline{C} + A\overline{B}C + AB\overline{C} + ABC + \overline{A}\,\overline{B}\,\overline{C}$$

Any term starting with A will get us to node 6, and it doesn't matter what happens subsequently. The only other way to get to node 6 is via $\overline{A}\,\overline{B}\,\overline{C}$. This is exactly what the simplified version of the expression for N6 said. A gets you there and the other predicates are immaterial. Consequently, the $A\overline{B}\,\overline{C}$ obtained from the expansion of $\overline{B}\,\overline{C}$ is also immaterial, and only the $\overline{A}\,\overline{B}\,\overline{C}$ term remains. N8 is reached by B, no matter what values the other predicates may have. In particular, $\overline{A}\,B$ and AB provide all the ways to get to node 8. Node 12 can be reached by C, but all four terms in C's expansion are needed to get there in all possible ways.

Note that it does not matter whether the predicates at a decision are simple or compound. Say that a predicate at a node is X + YZ. We can replace it by a new variable, say U = X + YZ. The analysis is the same as before, and when we're through, we can replace every instance of U with the equivalent expression in X, Y, and Z. Why bother when we can work directly with the compound predicate? So although we started with structure-based path predicate expressions and notions of branch coverage, we end up with notions of predicate coverage. The set of paths used to reach any point of interest in the flowgraph (such as the exit) can be characterized by an increasingly more thorough set of test cases:

1. *Simplest*—Use any prime implicant in the expression to the point of interest as a basis for a path. The only values that must be taken are those that appear in the prime implicant. All predicates not appearing in the prime implicant chosen can be set arbitrarily. If we chose the $\overline{B}\,\overline{C}$ prime implicant for node 6, we could still get to node 6, whether we chose A or $\overline{A}$. If we picked the A prime implicant, it doesn't matter what we do about B or C. Note that this still leaves us exposed to problems of compound predicates discussed in Chapter 3, Section 3.4.
2. *Prime Implicant Cover*—Pick input values so that there is at least one path for each prime implicant at the node of interest.
3. *All Terms*—Test all expanded terms for that node—for example,

five terms for node 6, four for node 8, and four for node 12. That is, at least one path for each term.

4. *Path Dependence*—Because in general, the truth value of a predicate is obtained by interpreting the predicate, its value may depend on the path taken to get there. Do every term by every path to that term.

The exit is treated as any other point of interest except that it should have a value of 1 for its boolean expression, which when expanded yields all 2^n combinations of predicate values. A set of covering paths could be achieved with fewer than 2^n test cases. K. C. Tai (TAIK87, TAIK89) has investigated strategies that can, with some restrictions, test for both relational operator errors and boolean expression errors using of the order of n tests for n predicates rather than 2^n. The pragmatic utility of these strategies and other logic-based test strategies is currently unknown because we do not know how frequently the kinds of bugs these strategies expose occur in actual software.

4.3. Boolean Equations

Loops complicate things because we may have to solve a boolean equation to determine what predicate-value combinations lead to where. Furthermore, the boolean expression for the end point does not necessarily equal 1. Consider the flowgraph of Figure 10.3.

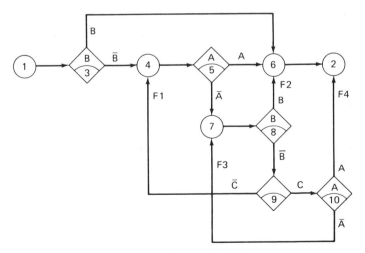

Figure 10.3. A Flowgraph with Loops.

Assign a name to any node whose value you don't know yet and write the expressions down, one at a time, working backward to something you do know, simplifying as you go. It's usually convenient to give names to links. The names represent the boolean expression corresponding to that link. I've named the links F1, F2, F3, and F4.

$$N4 = \overline{B} + F1$$
$$F1 = \overline{B}\,\overline{C}N7$$
$$N4 = \overline{B} + \overline{B}\,\overline{C}N7$$
$$\quad = \overline{B}$$
$$N6 = B + AN4$$
$$\quad = B + A\overline{B}$$
$$\quad = A + B$$
$$N7 = \overline{A}N4 + F3$$
$$\quad = \overline{A}\,\overline{B} + F3$$
$$F3 = N7\overline{B}C\overline{A}$$
$$N7 = \overline{A}\,\overline{B} + \overline{A}\,\overline{B}CN7$$
$$\quad = \overline{A}\,\overline{B}$$
$$N2 = N6 + F4$$
$$\quad = A + B + F4$$
$$F4 = A\overline{B}CN7$$
$$N2 = A + B + A\overline{B}CN7$$
$$\quad = A + B$$

You might argue that this is a silly flowgraph, but it illustrates some interesting points. The fact that the expression for the end point does not reduce to 1 means that there are predicate-value combinations for which the routine will loop indefinitely. Because the flowgraph's exit expression is A + B, the condition under which it does not exit is the negation of this or $\overline{(A + B)}$, which by De Morgan's theorem (rule 14) equals $\overline{A}\,\overline{B}$. This term when expanded yields $\overline{A}\,\overline{B}C + \overline{A}\,\overline{B}\,\overline{C}$, which identifies the two ways of looping, via nodes 7,8,9,10 and 4,5,7,8,9, respectively. It is conceivable that this unstructured horror could have been deliberately constructed (other than as a tutorial example, that is), but it's not likely. If the predicate values are independent of the processing, this routine must loop indefinitely for $\overline{A}\,\overline{B}$. A test consisting of all eight predicate-value combinations would have revealed the loops. Alternatively, the fact that the exit expression did not equal 1 implied that there had to be a loop. Feeding the logic back into itself this way, usually in the interest of saving some code or some work, leads to simultaneous boolean equations, which are rarely as easy to solve as the given example; it may also lead to dead paths and infinite loops.

5. KV CHARTS

5.1. The Problem

It's okay to slug through boolean algebra expressions to determine which cases are interesting and which combination of predicate values should be used to reach which node; it's okay, but not necessary. If you had to deal with expressions in four, five, or six variables, you could get bogged down in the algebra and make as many errors in designing test cases as there are bugs in the routine you're testing. The **Karnaugh-Veitch chart** (this is known by every combination of "Karnaugh" and/or "Veitch" with any one of "map," "chart," or "diagram") reduces boolean algebraic manipulations to graphical trivia (KARN53, VEIT52). Beyond six variables these diagrams get cumbersome, and other techniques such as the Quine-McCluskey (MCCL56, QUIN55) method (which are beyond the scope of this book) should be used.

5.2. Simple Forms

Figure 10.4 shows all the boolean functions of a single variable and their equivalent representation as a KV chart. The charts show all possible truth values that the variable A can have. The heading above each box in the chart denotes this fact. A "1" means the variable's value is "1" or

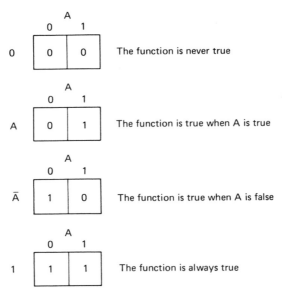

Figure 10.4. KV Charts for Functions of a Single Variable.

TRUE. A "0" means that the variable's value is 0 or FALSE. The entry
in the box (0 or 1) specifies whether the function that the chart represents
is true or false for that value of the variable. We usually do not explicitly
put in 0 entries but specify only the conditions under which the function is
true.

Figure 10.5 shows eight of the sixteen possible functions of two variables. Each box corresponds to the combination of values of the variables
for the row and column of that box. The single entry for $\overline{A}\,\overline{B}$ in the first
chart is interpreted that way because both the A and B variables' value for
the box is 0. Similarly, $A\overline{B}$ corresponds to A = 1 and B = 0, $\overline{A}B$ to A = 0
and B = 1, and AB to A = 1 and B = 1. The next four functions all have

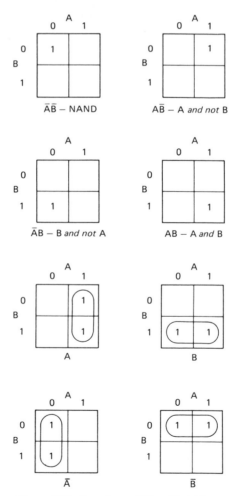

Figure 10.5. Functions of Two Variables.

two nonzero entries, and each entry forms an adjacent pair. A pair may be **adjacent** either horizontally or vertically but not diagonally. Any variable that changes in either the horizontal or vertical direction does not appear in the expression. In the fifth chart, the B variable changes from 0 to 1 going down the column, and because the A variable's value for the column is 1, the chart is equivalent to a simple A. Similarly, in the sixth chart it is the A variable that changes in the B = 1 row, and consequently the chart is equivalent to B. Similarly for $\overline{A}$ and $\overline{B}$.

Figure 10.6 shows the remaining eight functions of two variables. The interpretation of these charts is a combination of the interpretations of the

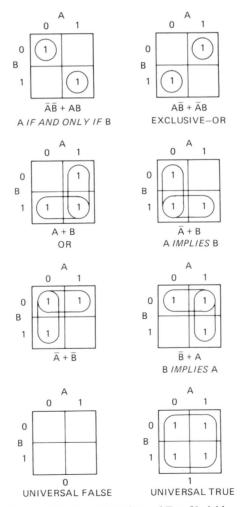

Figure 10.6. More Functions of Two Variables.

previous charts in Figure 10.5. The first chart has two 1's in it, but be-cause they are not adjacent, each must be taken separately. They are written using a plus sign. Because the first is $\overline{A}\,\overline{B}$ and the second AB, the entire chart is equivalent to $\overline{A}\,\overline{B}$ + AB. Similarly, the second chart is equivalent to $\overline{A}B$ + $A\overline{B}$. The next four charts have three 1's in them, and each can be grouped into adjacent groups of two (remember, adjacency is either horizontal or vertical).* Each adjacent group is a prime implicant and is therefore written down connected to the others by a "+." The first example consists of two adjacent groups of two boxes, corresponding to $\overline{A}$ (vertical group) and B (horizontal group), to yield $\overline{A}$ + B. The last case has all boxes filled with 1's and consequently, whatever the value of the variables might be, the function equals 1. The four entries in this case form an adjacent grouping of four boxes. It is clear now why there are sixteen functions of two variables. Each box in the KV chart corresponds to a combination of the variables' values. That combination might or might not be in the function (i.e., the box corresponding to that combina-tion might have a 1 or 0 entry).

Since n variables lead to 2^n combinations of 0 and 1 for the variables, and each such combination (box) can be filled or not filled, leading to 2^{2^n} ways of doing this. Consequently for one variable there are $2^{2^1} = 4$ func-tions, 16 functions of 2 variables, 256 functions of 3 variables, 16,384 functions of 4 variables, and so on. The third example of Figure 10.6 explains rule 19 on page 336. In fact, it's trivially obvious:

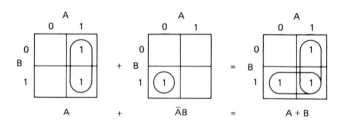

I've used the fact that KV charts are boolean functions. Given two charts over the same variables, arranged the same way, their product is the term by term product, their sum is the term by term sum, and the negation of a chart is gotten by reversing all the 0 and 1 entries in the chart. The procedure for simplifying expressions using KV charts is to fill in each term one at a time, and then to look for adjacencies and to rewrite

---

* Overlapping and multiple use is allowed because A + AB = A.

the expression in terms of the largest groupings you can find that cover all the 1's in the chart. Say the expression is $\overline{A}\overline{B} + A\overline{B} + AB$, then

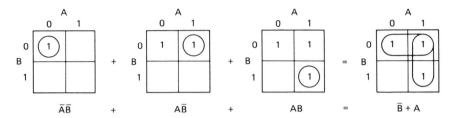

5.3. Three Variables

KV charts for three variables are shown below. As before, each box represents an elementary term of three variables with a bar appearing or not appearing according to whether the row-column heading for that box is 0 or 1. Note that I've labeled the column headings in an unusual way "00, 01, 11, 10" rather than with the expected "00, 01, 10, 11." Recall that the variable whose value did not change is the one we ended with. This labeling preserves the adjacency properties of the chart. However, note that adjacencies can go around corners, because 00 is adjacent to 10. The meaning of "adjacency" can now be specified more precisely: two boxes are **adjacent** if they change in only one bit, and two groupings are adjacent if they change in only one bit. A three-variable chart can have groupings of 1, 2, 4, and 8 boxes. A few examples will illustrate the principles:

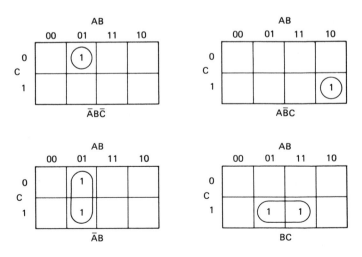

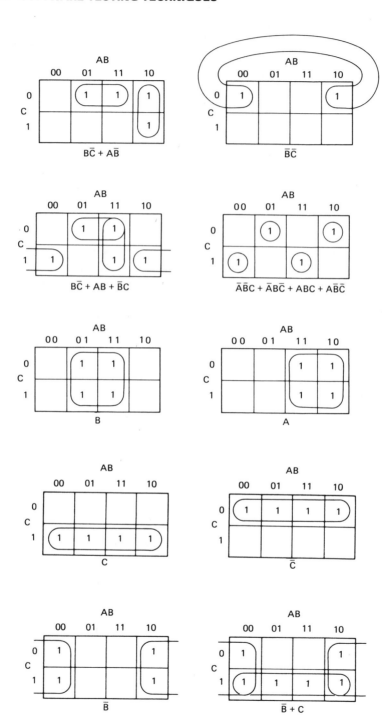

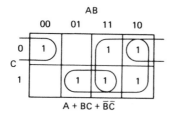

$A + BC + \overline{B}\overline{C}$

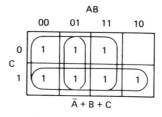

$\overline{A} + B + C$

You'll notice that there are several ways to circle the boxes into maximum-sized covering groups. All such covering sets are equivalent, no matter how different they might appear to be. As an example, consider

$$BC + \overline{A}\,\overline{B}C + A\overline{B}C$$

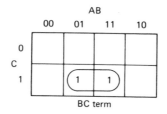

BC term

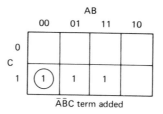

$\overline{A}\overline{B}C$ term added

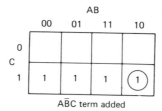

$A\overline{B}C$ term added

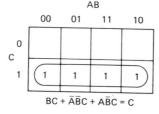

$BC + \overline{A}\overline{B}C + A\overline{B}C = C$

5.4. Four Variables and More

The same principles hold for four and more variables. A four-variable chart and several possible adjacencies are shown below. Adjacencies can now consist of 1, 2, 4, 8, and 16 boxes, and the terms resulting will have 4, 3, 2, 1, and 0 literals in them respectively:

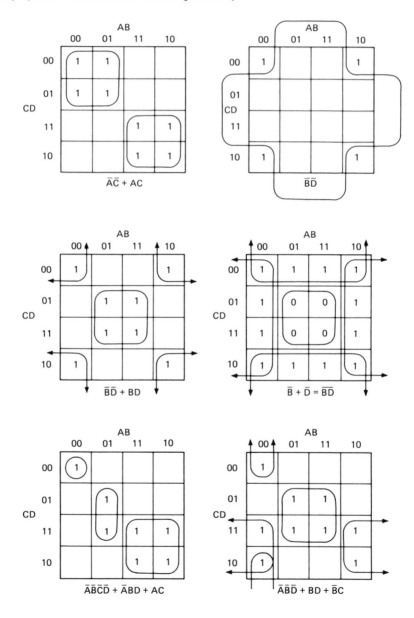

As with three-variable charts, the way you can group adjacent entries to cover all the 1s in the chart is not unique, but all such ways are equivalent, even though the resulting boolean expressions may not look the same.

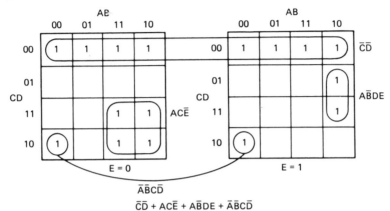

$$\overline{C}\overline{D} + AC\overline{E} + A\overline{B}DE + \overline{A}\overline{B}C\overline{D}$$

This is a five-variable chart with some of the adjacencies shown: things start to get cumbersome. For the hardy, there is a six-variable chart.

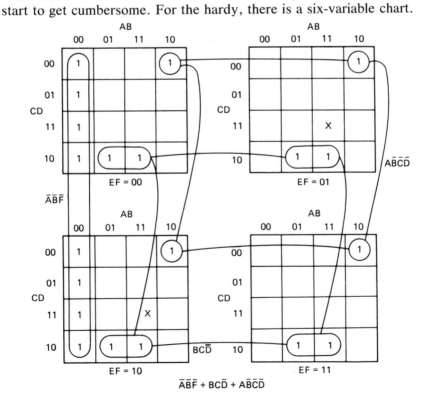

$$\overline{A}\overline{B}\overline{F} + BC\overline{D} + A\overline{B}\overline{C}\overline{D}$$

The two points labeled "X" are not adjacent because the subcharts on which they appear are diagonal to one another. If you really have to do a lot of work with six variables, you can build a three-dimensional tic-tac-toe game (4 × 4 × 4) out of transparent plastic. I once used eight transparent chessboards to do nine-variable problems—it was impressive but it didn't work very well.

5.5.   Even More Testing Strategies?

The KV map leads to yet another family of testing strategies to play with whose pragmatic utility is unknown. You developed a boolean algebra expression for every interesting action (e.g., domain). Consider any one of these and how you might go from the weakest to the strongest set of logic-based test cases:

1. Use one prime implicant per domain. You'll obviously miss parts of the domain not covered by the prime implicant you chose—e.g., for disconnected domains. Within this strategy there's a hierarchy also.
2. Use the prime implicant with the fewest variables (i.e., largest adjacency set or, equivalently, fewest domain boundaries) and work down to the prime implicant with the greatest number of variables (smallest adjacency set or most domain boundaries). For the five variable map above, the cases are: $\overline{C}D$, $AC\overline{E}$, $A\overline{B}DE$ and $\overline{A}\,\overline{B}C\overline{D}$.
3. Overcome the obvious weaknesses of the above strategy (not all subdomains are covered) by using one test per prime implicant.
4. Every term in the product form for n variables has at most n literals but, because of simplifications made possible by adjacencies, terms may have fewer than n literals, say k. Any term with k literals can be expanded into two terms with $k + 1$ literals. For example, $A = AB + A\overline{B}$. This is equivalent to considering maximum-size adjacency groups, and working down to smaller groups. Ultimately all terms contain n literals, which for the routine as a whole is equivalent to testing 2^n cases.

6.   SPECIFICATIONS

6.1.   General

There's no point in getting into design and coding until you're sure that the specification is logically consistent and complete. This section shows you how much of specification analysis can be done using the KV chart, pencil, and paper. You'll need to use such methods until your automated specification system and language comes on stream—which could be a long wait. Alternatively, if you have a specification system, this section gives you an insight into some of the processing done by it. The procedure for specification validation is straightforward:

1. Rewrite the specification using consistent terminology.
2. Identify the predicates on which the cases are based. Name them with suitable letters, such as A, B, C.
3. Rewrite the specification in English that uses only the logical connectives AND, OR, and NOT, however stilted it might seem.
4. Convert the rewritten specification into an equivalent set of boolean expressions.
5. Identify the default action and cases, if any are specified.
6. Enter the boolean expressions in a KV chart and check for consistency. If the specifications are consistent, there will be no overlaps, except for cases that result in multiple actions.
7. Enter the default cases and check for consistency.
8. If all boxes are covered, the specification is complete.
9. If the specification is incomplete or inconsistent, translate the corresponding boxes of the KV chart back into English and get a clarification, explanation, or revision.
10. If the default cases were not specified explicitly, translate the default cases back into English and get a confirmation.

6.2.   Finding and Translating the Logic

This is the most difficult part of the job, because it takes intelligence to disentangle intentions that are hidden by ambiguities inherent in English and by poor English usage. We cast the specifications into sentences of the following form:

"IF predicate THEN action."

The predicates are written using the AND, OR, and NOT boolean connectives. Therefore, the problem should be one of finding the keywords: IF, THEN, AND, OR, and NOT. Unfortunately we have to deal with the real world of specifications and specification writers, where clarity ranges from elusive, through esoteric, into incomprehensible. Here is a sample of phrases that have been or can be used (and abused) for the words we need:

IF—based on, based upon, because, but, if, if and when, only if, only when, provided that, when, when or if, whenever.

THEN—applies to, assign, consequently, do, implies that, infers that, initiate, means that, shall, should, then, will, would.

AND—all, and, as well as, both, but, in conjunction with, coincidental with, consisting of, comprising, either . . . or, furthermore, in addition to, including, jointly, moreover, mutually, plus, together with, total, with.

OR—and, and if . . . then, and/or, alternatively, any of, anyone of, as well as, but, case, contrast, depending upon, each, either, either . . . or, except if, conversely, failing that, furthermore, in addition to, nor, not only . . . but, although, other than, otherwise, or, or else, on the other hand, plus.

NOT—but, but not, by contrast, besides, contrary, conversely, contrast, except if, excluding, excepting, fail, failing, less, neither, never, no, not, other than.

EXCLUSIVE OR—but, by contrast, conversely, nor, on the other hand, other than, or.

IMMATERIAL—independent of, irregardless, irrespective, irrelevant, regardless, but not if, whether or not.

The above is *not* a list of recommended synonyms for specification writers because I've included many examples of bad usage. Several entries appear in more than one list—a source of danger. There are other dangerous phrases, such as "respectively," "similarly," "conversely," "and so forth," and "etc." More than one project's been sunk by an "etc." The main point, maybe the only point, of translating the specification into unambiguous English that uses IF, THEN, AND, OR, and NOT, is that this form is less likely to be misinterpreted.

Start rewriting the specification by getting rid of ambiguous terms, words, and phrases and expressing it all as a long list of IF. . .THEN statements. Then identify the actions and give them names such as A1, A2, A3, etc. Break the actions down into small units at first. All actions at this point should be mutually exclusive in the sense that no one action is part of another. If some actions always occur in conjunction with other actions and vice versa, then lump them into one action and give it a new name. Now substitute the action names in the sentences. Identify the

"OR" components of all sentences and rewrite them so that each "OR" is on a separate line. You now have a specification of the form

> IF A AND B AND C, THEN A1,
> IF C AND D AND F, THEN A1,
> IF A AND B AND D, THEN A2,
>
> . . .

Now identify all the NOTs, which can be knotty because some sentences may have the form $\overline{(A + B + C)}$ or $\overline{A}\,\overline{B}\,\overline{C}$. Put phrases in parentheses if that helps to clarify things. The only English now remaining are the A's, B's and C's, which should resemble predicates of the form, "A is true" or "NOT A . . .". Identify all the predicates in both negated and unnegated form and group them. Select a single representative for each, preferably the clearest one, or rewrite the predicates if that helps. Give each predicate a letter. You now have a set of boolean expressions that can be retranslated back into English preparatory to confirmation. An alternative is a table. List the predicates on one side and the actions on the other—a decision table is a handy format—and use that instead of English sentences. It's helpful to expand the immaterial cases and show the 2^n combinations of predicate values explicitly. Immaterial cases are always confusing.

This process should be done as early as possible because the translation of the specification into boolean algebra may require discussion among the specifiers, especially if contradictions and ambiguities emerge. If the specification has been given as a decision table or in another equally unambiguous tabular form, then most of the above work has been avoided and so has much of the potential confusion and the bugs that inevitably result therefrom.

6.3. Ambiguities and Contradictions

Here is a specification:

$$
\begin{aligned}
A1 &= B\overline{C}\,\overline{D} + A\overline{B}\,\overline{C}D \\
A2 &= A\overline{C}\,\overline{D} + A\overline{C}D + A\overline{B}\,\overline{C} + AB\overline{C} \\
A3 &= BD + BC\overline{D} \\
ELSE &= B\overline{C} + \overline{A}\,\overline{B}\,\overline{C}\,\overline{D}
\end{aligned}
$$

Here is the KV chart for this specification (I've used the numerals 1, 2, 3, and 4 to represent the actions and the default case):

	AB			
CD	00	01	11	10
00	4	1	1, 2	2
01		3	2, 3	1, 2
11	4	3	3	4
10	4	3	3	4

There is an ambiguity, probably related to the default case: $\overline{A}\,\overline{B}\,\overline{C}D$ is missing. The specification layout seems to suggest that this term also belongs to the default action. I would ask the question twice:

1. Is $\overline{A}\,\overline{B}\,\overline{C}D$ also to be considered a default action?
2. May the default action be rephrased as $\overline{B}C + \overline{A}\,\overline{B}$?

You might get contradictory answers, in which case, you may have to rephrase your question or, better yet, lay out all the combinations in a table and ask for a resolution of the ambiguities. There are several boxes that call for more than one action. If the specification did not explicitly call out both actions in a sentence, such as, "IF $AB\overline{C}D$ then *both* action 1 and action 2 shall be taken," I would treat each box that contained more than one action as a potential conflict. Similarly, if the specification did say, ". . . both A1 and A2 . . ." but did not mention A3, as in the $AB\overline{C}D$ entry, I would also question that entry.

If no explicit default action is specified, then fill out the KV chart with explicit entries for the explicitly specified actions, negate the entire chart, and present the equivalent expression as a statement of the default. In the above example, had no default action been given, all the blank spaces would have been replaced with 1's and the $\overline{B}C + \overline{A}\,\overline{B}$ expression would have resulted.

Be suspicious of almost complete groups of adjacencies. For example, if a term contains seven adjacent boxes and lacks only one to make a full eight adjacency, question the missing box. I would question 3 out of 4, 6 or 7 out of 8, 13 through 15 out of 16, and so on, especially if the missing boxes are not themselves adjacent.

It's also useful to present the new version of the specification as a table that shows all cases explicitly and also as a compact version in which you've taken advantage of the possibility of simplifying the expression by using a KV chart. You present the table and say that, "This table can also be expressed as . . . ." There may be disagreement. The specifier might insist that the table does not correspond to the specification and that the table also does not correspond to your compact statement, which you know was derived from the table by using boolean algebra. Don't be smug if that happens. Just as often as the seeming contradiction will be due to not understanding the equivalence, it will be due to a predicate that has not been explicitly stated.

6.4. Don't-Care and Impossible Terms

There are only three things in this universe that I'm certain are impossible:

1. Solving a provably unsolvable problem, such as creating a universal program verifier.
2. Knowing both the exact position and the exact momentum of a fundamental particle.
3. Knowing what happened before the "big bang" that started the universe.

Everything else is improbable, but not impossible. So-called "impossible" cases can be used to advantage to simplify logic and, consequently, to simplify the programs that implement that logic. There are two kinds of so-called impossible conditions: (1) the condition cannot be created or is seemingly contradictory or improbable; and (2) the condition results from our insistence on forcing a complex, continuous world into a binary, logical mold. Most program illogical conditions are of the latter kind. There are twelve cases for something, say, and we represent those cases by 4 bits. Our conversion from the continuous world to the binary world has "created" four impossible cases. The external world can also contain "impossible" and "mutually exclusive" cases, such as female fighter pilots, consistent specifications, honest mechanics and politicians, insincere used-car salesmen and funeral directors, and blind editors. The seemingly impossible cases of semantic origin can appear to occur within a program because of malfunctions or alpha particles. The supposed impossibilities of the real world can come into being because the world changes. Consequently, you can take advantage of an "impossible" case only when you are sure that there is data validation or protection in a preceding module or when appropriate illogical condition checks are made elsewhere in the program. Taking advantage of "impossible" and "illogical" cases is a dangerous practice and should be avoided, but if you insist on doing that sort of thing, you might as well do it right:

1. Identify all "impossible" and "illogical" cases and confirm them.
2. Document the fact that you intend to take advantage of them.
3. Fill out the KV chart with the possible cases and then fill in the impossible cases. Use the combined symbol ∅, which is to be interpreted as a 0 or 1, depending on which value provides the greatest simplification of the logic. These terms are called **don't-care terms,** because the case is presumed impossible, and we don't care which value (0 or 1) is used.

Here is an example:

		AB		
	00	01	11	10
00	∅	1		
01	1	∅	∅	
11	∅	1	1	1
10	1	1	1	1

(CD labels the rows)

By not taking advantage of the impossible conditions, we get the resulting boolean expression

$$C\overline{D} + CB + CA + \overline{A}B\overline{D} + \overline{A}\,\overline{B}CD$$

By taking advantage of the impossible conditions, we get:

$$C + \overline{A}$$

The corresponding flowgraphs are shown in Figure 10.7. The B and D decisions have disappeared for the second case. This a two-edged sword.

By reducing the logic's complexity we reduced instructions, data references for B and D, and the routine's complexity, and thereby reduced the probability of bugs. However, the routine now depends on nature's good graces, how thoroughly preceding routines have done data validation, and how thoroughly data validation will be done after this design has been modified in maintenance. It is not obvious whether long-term quality has been improved or degraded.

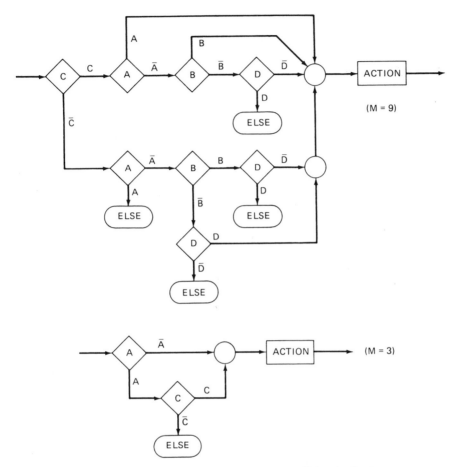

Figure 10.7. Reducing Complexity by Simplifying the Logic.

7. TESTABILITY TIPS

Logic-intensive software designed by the seat of the pants is almost never right. We learned this lesson decades ago in the simpler hardware logic design arena. It is in our interest as software engineers to use the simplest possible predicate expressions in our design. The objective is not to simplify the code in order to save a few bytes of memory but to reduce the opportunities for bugs. Hardware logic designers learned that there were many advantages to designing their logic in a **canonical form**—that is, a form that followed certain rules. The testability considerations of this chapter apply to loop-free software, or to the portion of the software that is loop-free; for example, a logic-intensive program segment within a loop can be examined by these means. You can start either from specifications or, if you're doing a redesign, from code. I'll speak to the latter case because it's more general. Think in terms of redesign if you have sensitization difficulties.

1. Identify your predicates (simple or compound).
2. If starting from code, get a branch covering set of path predicates.
3. Interpret the predicates so that they are expressed in terms of the input vector for the chosen path.
4. Simplify the path predicate expression for each selected path. If any expression is logically zero, the path is unachievable. Pick another path or paths to achieve branch coverage.
5. If any path predicate expression equals logical 1 then all other paths must be unachievable—find and fix the design bug.
6. The logical sum of the path predicate expressions must equal 1 or else there is an unsuspected loop, dangling code, or branch coverage is an inadequate test criterion.

The canonical processor has three successive stages:

1. Predicate calculator.
2. Logic analyzer.
3. Domain processor.

The **predicate calculator** transforms (e.g., processes) the input vector to get the values of the variables that are actually used in the predicates. Every predicate is evaluated exactly once, so that it's truth value is known. The **logic analyzer** forms the predicate expression appropriate to the case and directs the control flow to the appropriate domain processor. Because each predicate defines a domain boundary and each predicate expression defines a domain, there is a one-to-one correspondence between the various outcomes of the logic analyzer and the domains. The **domain processor** does the processing appropriate to each domain, for example, with a separate hunk of code for each domain. Only one control-flow statement (a case statement) is needed—one case, one predicate expression, one domain. The canonical form, if it is achieved, has the following obvious advantages:

1. Branch coverage and all-paths coverage are identical.
2. All paths are achievable and easy to sensitize.
3. Separation simplifies maintenance.

The above canonical form is an ideal that you cannot expect to achieve. Achieving it could mean redundant software, excessive nesting depth (if you encapsulate the redundancies in subroutines), or slow execution on some paths; conversely, however, the canonical form can be faster and tighter. You may be able to achieve it locally, or globally but not both; but you don't know unless you try. And why try? Because it works. The proof comes from hardware design, where we learned, three decades ago, that seat-of-the-pants logic was buggy, slow, dangerous, and hard to build, test, and maintain.

8. SUMMARY

1. Use decision tables as a convenient way to organize statements in a specification—possibly as an intermediate step toward a more compact and more revealing equivalent boolean algebra expression.
2. Label the links following binary decisions with a weight that corresponds to the predicate's logical value, and evaluate the boolean expressions to the nodes of interest.
3. Simplify the resulting expressions or solve equations and then simplify if you cannot directly express the boolean function for the node in terms of the path predicate values.
4. The boolean expression for the exit node should equal 1. If it does not, or if attempting to solve for it leads to a loop of equations, then there are conditions under which the routine will loop indefinitely. The negation of the exit expression specifies all the combinations of predicate values that will lead to the loop or loops.
5. Any node of interest can be reached by a test case derived from the expansion of any prime implicant in the boolean expression for that node.
6. The set of all paths from the entry to a node can be obtained by expanding all the prime implicants of the boolean expression that corresponds to that node. A branch-covering set of paths, however, may not require all the terms of the expansion.
7. You don't do boolean algebra by algebra. You use KV charts for up to six variables. Keep quadrille-ruled paper pads handy.
8. For logic-intensive routines, examine specification completeness and consistency by using boolean algebra via KV charts. Use the canonical form as a model of clean logic.
9. Be careful in translating English into boolean algebra. Retranslate and discuss the retranslation of the algebra with the specifier. Be

tricky and use alternate, logically equivalent forms to see whether they (specifiers) are consistent and whether they really want what they say they want.

10. Question all missing entries, question overlapped entries if there was no explicit statement of multiple actions, question all almost-complete groups.

11. Don't take advantage of don't-care cases or impossible cases unless you're willing to pay the maintenance penalties; but if you must, get the maximum payoff by making the resulting logic as simple as you can and document all instances in which you take advantage of don't-care cases.

11

STATES, STATE GRAPHS, AND TRANSITION TESTING

1. SYNOPSIS

The **state graph** and its associated **state table** are useful models for describing software behavior. The **finite-state machine** is a functional testing tool and testable design programming tool. Methods analogous to path testing are described and discussed.

2. MOTIVATIONAL OVERVIEW

The **finite-state machine** is as fundamental to software engineering as boolean algebra. State testing strategies are based on the use of finite-state machine models for software structure, software behavior, or specifications of software behavior. Finite-state machines can also be implemented as table-driven software, in which case they are a powerful design option. Independent testers are likeliest to use a finite-state machine model as a guide to the design of functional tests—especially system tests. Software designers are likelier to want to exploit and test finite-state machine software implementations. Finally, finite-state machine models of software abound in the testing literature, much of which will be meaningless to readers who don't know this subject. Among the affected testing topics are protocols, concurrent systems, system failure and recovery, system configuration, and distributed data bases (BARN72, DAVI88A, HOLZ87, PETE76).

3.   STATE GRAPHS

3.1.   States

The word **"state"** is used in much the same way it's used in ordinary English, as in "state of the union," or "state of health." The Oxford English Dictionary defines "state" as: "A combination of circumstances or attributes belonging for the time being to a person or thing."

A program that detects the character sequence "ZCZC" can be in the following states:

1. Neither ZCZC nor any part of it has been detected.
2. Z has been detected.
3. ZC has been detected.
4. ZCZ has been detected.
5. ZCZC has been detected.

A moving automobile whose engine is running can have the following states with respect to its transmission:

1. Reverse gear
2. Neutral gear
3. First gear
4. Second gear
5. Third gear
6. Fourth gear

A person's checkbook can have the following states with respect to the bank balance:

1. Equal
2. Less than
3. Greater than

A word processing program menu can be in the following states with respect to file manipulation:

1. Copy document
2. Delete document
3. Rename document
4. Create document
5. Compress document
6. Copy disc
7. Format disc
8. Backup disc
9. Recover from backup

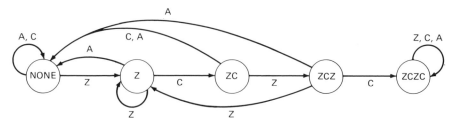

Figure 11.1. One-Time ZCZC Sequence-Detector State Graph.

States are represented by **nodes.** States are numbered or may be identified by words or whatever else is convenient. Figure 11.1 shows a typical **state graph.** The automobile example is really more complicated because: (1) the engine might or might not be running, (2) the car itself might be moving forward or backward or be stopped, and (3) the clutch might or might not be depressed. These factors multiply the above six states by $2 \times 3 \times 2 = 12$, for a total of 72 rather than 6 states. Each additional factor that has alternatives multiplies the number of states in a model by the number of alternatives. The number of states of a computer is 2 raised to the power of the number of bits in the computer; that is, all the bits in main memory, registers, discs, tapes, and so on. Because most interesting factors are binary, and because each factor doubles the number of states, state graphs are most useful for relatively simple functional models involving at most a few dozen states and only a few factors.

3.2. Inputs and Transitions

Whatever is being modeled is subjected to inputs. As a result of those inputs, the state changes, or is said to have made a **transition.** Transitions are denoted by links that join the states. The input that causes the transition are marked on the link; that is, the inputs are link weights. There is one outlink from every state for every input. If several inputs in a state cause a transition to the same subsequent state, instead of drawing a bunch of parallel links we can abbreviate the notation by listing the several inputs as in: "input1, input2, input3. . .". A **finite-state machine** is an abstract device that can be represented by a state graph having a finite number of states and a finite number of transitions between states.

The ZCZC detection example can have the following kinds of inputs:

1. Z
2. C
3. Any character other than Z or C, which we'll denote by A

The state graph of Figure 11.1 is interpreted as follows:

1. If the system is in the "NONE" state, any input other than a Z will keep it in that state.
2. If a Z is received, the system transitions to the "Z" state.
3. If the system is in the "Z" state and a Z is received, it will remain in the "Z" state. If a C is received, it will go to the "ZC" state; if any other character is received, it will go back to the "NONE" state because the sequence has been broken.
4. A Z received in the "ZC" state progresses to the "ZCZ" state, but any other character breaks the sequence and causes a return to the "NONE" state.
5. A C received in the "ZCZ" state completes the sequence and the system enters the "ZCZC" state. A Z breaks the sequence and causes a transition back to the "Z" state; any other character causes a return to the "NONE" state.
6. The system stays in the "ZCZC" state no matter what is received.

As you can see, the state graph is a compact representation of all this verbiage.

3.3. Outputs

An output* can be associated with any link. Outputs are denoted by letters or words and are separated from inputs by a slash as follows: "input/output." As always, "output" denotes anything of interest that's observable and is not restricted to explicit outputs by devices. Outputs are also link weights. If every input associated with a transition causes the same output, then denote it as: "input 1, input 2, . . . input 3/output." If there are many different combinations of inputs and outputs, it's best to draw a separate parallel link for each output.

Consider now, as an example, a simplified specification for a tape transport write-error recovery procedure, such as might be found in a tape driver routine:**

"If no write errors are detected, (input = OK), no special action is taken (output = NONE). If a write error is detected (input = ERROR), backspace the tape one block and rewrite the block (output = RE-

---

* "Output" rather than "outcome" because the outcome consists of the output *and* a transition to the new state. "Output" used in this context can mean almost anything observable and is not restricted to tangible outputs by devices, say.

** Our objective here is not to design a tape driver but to illustrate how a specification, good or bad, sensible or not, can be modeled by a state graph.

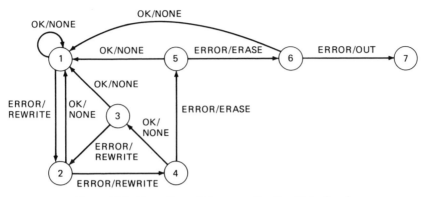

Figure 11.2. Tape Control Recovery Routine State Graph.

WRITE). If the rewrite is successful (input = OK), ignore the fact that there has been a rewrite. If the rewrite is not successful, try another backspace and rewrite. Return to the original state if and only if there have been two successive successful writes. If there have been two successive rewrites and a third error occurs, backspace ten centimeters and erase forward from that point (output = ERASE). If the erasure works (input = OK), return to the initial state. If it does not work, backspace another ten centimeters, erase and treat the next write attempt as for the first erasure. If the second erasure does not clear the problem, put the tape transport out of service.''

The state graph is shown in Figure 11.2. As in the previous example, the inputs and actions have been simplified. There are only two kinds of inputs (OK, ERROR) and four kinds of outputs (REWRITE, ERASE, NONE, OUT-OF-SERVICE). Don't confuse outputs with transitions or states. This can be confusing because sometimes the name of the output is the same as the name of a state.* Similarly, don't confuse the input with the state, as in the first transition and the second state of the ZCZC detection example.

3.4. State Tables

Big state graphs are cluttered and hard to follow. It's more convenient to represent the state graph as a table (the **state table** or **state-transition table**)

---

* An alternate, but equivalent, representation of behavior, called a "Moore model" (MOOR56), associates outputs with states rather than with transitions. The model used in this book is called a "Mealy model" (MEAL55), in which outputs are associated with transitions. Mealy models are more useful because of the way software of this kind is usually implemented. Also, the Mealy model makes both inputs and outputs link weights, which makes it easier to use the methods of Chapter 12 for analysis.

INPUT

STATE	OKAY	ERROR
1	1/NONE	2/REWRITE
2	1/NONE	4/REWRITE
3	1/NONE	2/REWRITE
4	3/NONE	5/ERASE
5	1/NONE	6/ERASE
6	1/NONE	7/OUT
7	. . .	. . .

Table 11.1. State Table for Figure 11.2.

that specifies the states, the inputs, the transitions, and the outputs. The following conventions are used:

1. Each row of the table corresponds to a state.
2. Each column corresponds to an input condition.
3. The box at the intersection of a row and column specifies the next state (the transition) and the output, if any.

The state table for the tape control is shown in Table 11.1.

I didn't specify what happens in state 7 because it's not germane to the discussion. You would have to complete the state graph for that state and for all the other states (not shown) that would be needed to get the tape back into operation. Compare the tabular representation with the graphical representation so that you can follow the action in either notation.

3.5. Time Versus Sequence

State graphs don't represent time—they represent sequence. A transition might take microseconds or centuries; a system could be in one state for milliseconds and another for eons, or the other way around; the state graph would be the same because it has no notion of time. Although the finite-state machine model can be elaborated to include notions of time in addition to sequence, such as timed Petri nets (DAVI88A, MURA89, PETE81), the subject is beyond the scope of this book.

3.6. Software Implementation

3.6.1. Implementation and Operation

There is rarely a direct correspondence between programs and the behavior of a process described as a state graph. In the tape driver example, for instance, the inputs would occur over a period of time. The routine is probably activated by an executive, and the inputs might be status-return interrupts from the tape control hardware. Alternatively, the inputs might appear as status bits in a word in memory reserved for that transport. The tape control routine itself is probably reentrant, so it can be used simultaneously by all transports.

The state graph represents the total behavior consisting of the transport, the software, the executive, the status returns, interrupts, and so on. There is no simple correspondence between lines of code and states. The state table, however, forms the basis for a widely used implementation shown in the PDL program below. There are four tables involved:

1. A table or process that encodes the input values into a compact list (INPUT_CODE_TABLE).
2. A table that specifies the next state for every combination of state and input code (TRANSITION_TABLE).
3. A table or case statement that specifies the output or output code, if any, associated with every state-input combination (OUTPUT_TABLE).
4. A table that stores the present state of every device or process that uses the same state table—e.g., one entry per tape transport (DEVICE_TABLE).

The routine operates as follows, where # means concatenation:

```
BEGIN
PRESENT_STATE := DEVICE_TABLE(DEVICE_NAME)
ACCEPT INPUT_VALUE
INPUT_CODE := INPUT_CODE_TABLE(INPUT_VALUE)
POINTER := INPUT_CODE#PRESENT_STATE
NEW_STATE := TRANSITION_TABLE(POINTER)
OUTPUT_CODE := OUTPUT_TABLE(POINTER)
CALL OUTPUT_HANDLER(OUTPUT_CODE)
DEVICE_TABLE(DEVICE_NAME) := NEW_STATE
END
```

1. The present state is fetched from memory.
2. The present input value is fetched. If it is already numerical, it can be used directly; otherwise, it may have to be encoded into a numerical value, say by use of a case statement, a table, or some other process.
3. The present state and the input code are combined (e.g., concatenated) to yield a pointer (row and column) of the transition table and its logical image (the output table).
4. The output table, either directly or via a case statement, contains a pointer to the routine to be executed (the output) for that state-input combination. The routine is invoked (possibly a trivial routine if no output is required).
5. The same pointer is used to fetch the new state value, which is then stored.

There could be a lot of code between the end of this flow and the start of a new pass. Typically, there would be a return to the executive, and the state-control routine would only be invoked upon an interrupt. Many variations are possible. Sometimes, no input encoding is required. In other situations, the invoked routine is itself a state-table-driven routine that uses a different table.

3.6.2. Input Encoding and Input Alphabet

Only the simplest finite-state machines, such as a character sequence detector in a compiler's lexical analyzer, can use the inputs directly. Typically, we're not interested in the actual input characters but in some attribute represented by the characters. For example, in the ZCZC detector, although there are 256 possible ASCII characters (including the inverse parity characters), we're only interested in three different types: "Z," "C," and "OTHER." The input encoding could be implemented as a table lookup in a table that contained the following codes: "OTHER" = 0, "Z" = 1 and "C" = 2. Alternatively, we could implement it as a process: IF INPUT = "Z" THEN CODE := 1 ELSE IF INPUT = "C" THEN CODE := 2 ELSE CODE := 0 ENDIF.

The alternative to input encoding is a huge state graph and table because there must be one outlink in every state for every possible different input. Input encoding compresses the cases and therefore the state graph. Another advantage of input encoding is that we can run the machine from a mixture of otherwise incompatible input events, such as characters, device response codes, thermostat settings, or gearshift lever positions. The set of different encoded input values is called the **input alphabet.** The word "input" as used in the context of finite-state machines always means a "character" from the input alphabet.

3.6.3. Output Encoding and Output Alphabet

There can be many different, incompatible, kinds of outputs for transitions of a finite-state machine: a single character output for a link is rare in actual applications. We might want to output a string of characters, call a subroutine, transfer control to a lower-level finite-state machine, or do nothing. Whatever we might want to do, there are only a finite number of such distinct actions, which we can encode into a convenient **output alphabet.** We then have a hypothetical (or real) output processor that invokes the action appropriate to the output code. Doing nothing is also considered an action and therefore requires its own code in the output alphabet. The word "output" as used in the context of finite-state machines means a "character" from the output alphabet.

3.6.4. State Codes and State-Symbol Products

We speak about finite-state machines as if the states are numbered by an integer. If there are n states and k different inputs, both numbered from zero, and the state code and input code are S and I respectively, then the pointer value is $Sk + I$ or $In + S$ depending on how you want to organize the tables. If the state machine processor is coded in an HOL then you can use a two-dimensional array and use two pointers (state code and input code); the multiplication will be done by object code. Finite-state machines are often used in time-critical applications because they have such fast response times. If a multiplication has to be done, the speed is seriously affected. A faster implementation is to use a binary number of states and a binary number of input codes, and to form the pointer by concatenating the state and input code. The speed advantage is obvious, but there are also some disadvantages. The table is no longer compact; that is, because the number of states and the number of input codes are unlikely to be both binary numbers, the resulting table must have holes in it. Like it or not, those holes correspond to state-input combinations and you have to fill them, if only with a call to an error recovery routine. The second disadvantage is size. Even in these days of cheap memory, excessive table size can be a problem, especially, for example, if the finite-state machine is part of embedded software in a ROM. For the above reasons, there may be another encoding of the combination of the state number and the input code into the pointer. The term **state-symbol product** is used to mean the value obtained by any scheme used to convert the combined state and input code into a pointer to a compact table without holes. This conversion could be done by multiplication and addition, by concatenation, or even by a hash-coding scheme for very big tables. When we talk about "states" and "state codes" in the context of finite-state machines, we mean the (possibly) hypothetical integer used to denote the state and not the actual form of the state code that could result from an encoding process. Similarly, "state-symbol product" means the hypothetical (or actual) concatenation used to combine the state and input codes.

3.6.5.   Application Comments for Designers

An explicit state-table implementation is advantageous when either the control function is likely to change in the future or when the system has many similar, but slightly different, control functions. Their use in telecommunications, especially telephony, is common. This technique can provide fast response time—one pass through the above program can be done in ten to fifteen machine instruction execution times. It is not an effective technique for very small (four states or less) or big (256 states or more) state graphs. In the small case, the overhead required to implement the state-table software would exceed any time or space savings that one might hope to gain. In big state tables, the product of input values and states is big—in the thousands—and the memory required to store the tables becomes significant. The usual approach for big state graphs is to partition the problem into a hierarchy of finite-state machines. The output of the top level machine is a call to a subsidiary machine that processes the details. In telephony, for example, two-level tables are common and three- and four-level tables are not unusual.

3.6.6.   Application Comments for Testers

Independent testers are not usually concerned with either implementation details or the economics of this approach but with how a state-table or state-graph representation of the behavior of a program or system can help us to design effective tests. If the programmers have implemented an explicit finite-state machine then much of our work has been done for us and we have to be concerned with the kinds of bugs that are inherent in the implementation—which is good reason for understanding such implementations. There is an interesting correlation, though: when a finite-state machine *model* is appropriate, so is a finite-state machine *implementation*. Sometimes, showing the programmers the kinds of tests developed from a state-graph description can lead them to consider it as an implementation technique.

4. GOOD STATE GRAPHS AND BAD

4.1. General

This is a book on testing so we deal not just with good state graphs, but also with bad ones. What constitutes a good or a bad state graph is to some extent biased by the kinds of state graphs that are likely to be used in a software test design context. Here are some principles for judging:

1. The total number of states is equal to the product of the possibilities of factors that make up the state.
2. For every state and input there is exactly one transition specified to exactly one, possibly the same, state.
3. For every transition there is one output action specified. That output could be trivial, but at least one output does something sensible.*
4. For every state there is a sequence of inputs that will drive the system back to the same state.**

Figure 11.3 shows examples of improper state graphs.

A state graph must have at least two different input codes. With only one input code, there are only a few kinds of state graphs you can build: a bunch of disconnected individual states; disconnected strings of states that end in loops and variations thereof; or a strongly connected state graph in which all states are arranged in one grand loop. The latter can be implemented by a simple counter that resets at some fixed maximum value, so this elaborate modeling apparatus is not needed.

If I seem to have violated my own rules regarding outputs—I have. The ZCZC detector example didn't have output codes. There are two aspects of state graphs: (1) the states with their transitions and the inputs that cause them, and (2) the outputs associated with transitions. Just as in the flowgraph model we concentrated on control structure and tended to ignore processing that did not directly affect control flow, in state testing we may ignore outputs because it is the states and transitions that are of primary interest. Two state graphs with identical states, inputs, and transitions could have vastly different outputs, yet from a state-testing point of view, they could be identical. Consequently, we reduce the clutter

---

* State graphs without outputs can't do anything in the pragmatic world and can consequently be ignored. For output, include anything that could cause a subsequent action—perhaps setting only one bit.
** In other words, we've restricted the state graphs to be strongly connected. This may seem overly narrow, because many state graphs are not strongly connected; but in a software context, the only nonstrongly connected state graphs are those used to set off bombs and other infernal machines or those that deal with bootstraps, initialization, loading, failure, recovery, and illogical, unrecoverable conditions. A state graph that is not strongly connected usually has bugs.

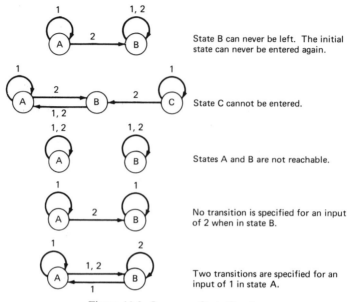

Figure 11.3. Improper State Graphs.

caused by explicit output specifications if outputs are not interesting at the moment.

4.2. State Bugs

4.2.1. Number of States

The number of states in a state graph is the number of states we choose to recognize or model. In practice, the state is directly or indirectly recorded as a combination of values of variables that appear in the data base. As an example, the state could be composed of the value of a counter whose possible values ranged from 0 to 9, combined with the setting of two bit flags, leading to a total of $2 \times 2 \times 10 = 40$ states. When the state graph represents an explicit state-table implementation, this value is encoded so bugs in the number of states are less likely; but the encoding can be wrong. Failing to account for all the states is one of the more common bugs in software that can be modeled by state graphs. Because an explicit state-table mechanization is not typical, the opportunities for missing states abound. Find the number of states as follows:

1. Identify all the component factors of the state.
2. Identify all the allowable values for each factor.
3. The number of states is the product of the number of allowable values of all the factors.

Before you do anything else, before you consider one test case, discuss the number of states you think there are with the number of states the programmer (or you, if you're wearing a programmer's hat) thinks there are. Differences of opinion are common. There's no point in designing tests intended to check the system's behavior in various states if there's no agreement on how many states there are. And if there's no agreement on how many states there are, there must be disagreement on what the system does in which states and on the transitions and the outputs. If it seems that I'm giving undue emphasis to the seemingly trivial act of counting states, it's because that act often exhumes fundamental design deficiencies. You don't need to wait until the design is done. A functional specification is usually enough, inasmuch as state testing is primarily a functional test tool. I read the functional specification and identify the factors and then the number of possible values for each factor. Then I question the designer. I want to get an identification or recognition for each state—with one state corresponding to each combination of condition values. It's gratifying work. It's gratifying to hear, "Oh yeah, I forgot about that one." Make up a table, with a column for every factor, such that all combinations of factors are represented. Before you get concurrence on outputs or transitions or the inputs that cause the transitions, get concurrence from the designer (or confirm for yourself) that every combination listed makes sense.

4.2.2. Impossible States

Some combinations of factors may appear to be impossible. Say that the factors are:

GEAR	R, N, 1, 2, 3, 4	= 6 factors
DIRECTION	Forward, reverse, stopped	= 3 factors
ENGINE	Running, stopped	= 2 factors
TRANSMISSION	Okay, broken	= 2 factors
ENGINE	Okay, broken	= 2 factors
TOTAL		= 144 states

But broken engines can't run, so the combination of factors for engine condition and engine operation yields only 3 rather than 4 states. Therefore, the total number of states is at most 108. A car with a broken transmission won't move for long, thereby further decreasing the number of feasible states. The discrepancy between the programmer's state count and the tester's state count is often due to a difference of opinion concerning "impossible states."

We should say "supposedly impossible" rather than "impossible." There are always alpha particles and bugs in other routines. The implicit or explicit record of the values of the factors in the computer is not always the same as the values of those factors in the world—as was learned at Three Mile Island. One of the contributing factors to that fiasco was a discrepancy between the actual position of an actuator and its reported position. The designers had falsely assumed that it was "impossible" for the actuator's actual position to be at variance with its reported position. Two states, "Actuator-UP/Actuator Position-DOWN" and "Actuator-DOWN/Actuator-Position-UP," were incorrectly assumed to be impossible.

Because the states we deal with inside computers are not the states of the real world but rather a numerical representation of real-world states, the "impossible" states can occur. Wrack your brains for a devious scenario that gets the program into the impossible states, even if the world can't produce such states. If you can't come by such states honestly, invoke alpha particles or lighting storms. A robust piece of software will not ignore impossible states but will recognize them and invoke an illogical-condition handler when they appear to have occurred. That handler will do whatever is necessary to reestablish the system's correspondence to the world.*

---

* The most bizarre case I have ever seen of correspondence loss between the computer's notion of the state and the world's notion of the state occurred at a major international air freight depot more than two decades ago. The computer controlled a vast automated warehouse used to transship and rearrange air cargo loads. Pallets were taken off aircraft and loaded into the automatic warehouse. Automated forklift trucks trundled up and down the aisles and lofted the pallets into push-through bins that were stacked six stories high. Other forklift trucks pulled the pallets out and automatically put them onto conveyors bound for the aircraft on which the pallets belonged. Unfortunately, the designers had made several errors: (1) the power-transient protection was inadequate for the environment, (2) the hardware was not duplicated, (3) there appeared to be no automatic recovery software, (4) the data-validation checks that should have continually verified the correspondence between the computer's notion of what the bins contained (stored as disc sectors) and the actual contents of the bins were either missing or faulty, but surely inadequate, and (5) test sophistication matched design sophistication. It worked fine for a few days; then came the lightning storm. Correspondence between the computer's version of the bins and the actual bins was lost, but the system kept doing it's thing—a thing out of Walt Disney's *Fantasia* (The Sorcerer's Apprentice). The warehouse was glutted and gutted in hours as automatic forklift trucks tried to stuff more pallets into full bins and remove nonexistent pallets from empty bins. They shut down. The old warehouse, of course, had been decommissioned by then. They then hired hundreds of university students to clamber about the six-story warehouse to identify just what was where. The tons of frozen liver that had not been placed in a refrigerated section were found in a few days. It took much longer to find the corpses in their coffins.

4.2.3. *Equivalent States*

Two states are **equivalent** if every sequence of inputs starting from one state produces exactly the same sequence of outputs when started from the other state. This notion can also be extended to sets of states. Figure 11.4 shows the situation.

Say that the system is in state S and that an input of *a* causes a transition to state A while an input of *b* causes a transition to state B. The blobs indicate portions of the state graph whose details are unimportant. If, starting from state A, *every* possible sequence of inputs produces *exactly* the same sequence of outputs that would occur when starting from state B, then there is no way that an outside observer can determine which of the two sets of states the system is in without looking at the record of the state. The state graph can be reduced to that of Figure 11.5 without harm.

The fact that there is a notion of state equivalency means that there is an opportunity for bugs to arise from a difference of opinion concerning which states are equivalent. If you insist that there is another factor, not recognized by the programmer, such that the resulting output sequence for a given input sequence is different depending on the value of that factor, then you are asserting that two inequivalent sets of states have been inadvertently merged. Conversely, if you cannot find a sequence of inputs that results in at least one different output when starting from either of two supposedly inequivalent states, then the states *are* equivalent and should be merged if only to simplify the software and thereby reduce the probability of bugs. Be careful, though, because equivalent states could come about as a result of good planning for future enhancements. The two states are presently indistinguishable but could in the future become distinguished as a result of an enhancement that brings with it the distinguishing factor.

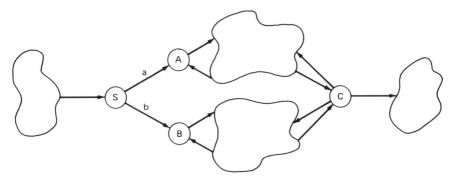

Figure 11.4. Equivalent States.

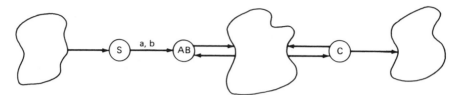

Figure 11.5. Equivalent States of Figure 11.4 Merged.

Equivalent states can be recognized by the following procedures:

1. The rows corresponding to the two states are identical with respect to input/output/next state but the name of the next state could differ. The two states are differentiated only by the input that distinguishes between them. This situation is shown in Figure 11.6. Except for the *a,b* inputs, which distinguish between states A and B, the system's behavior in the two states is identical for every input sequence; they can be merged.
2. There are two sets of rows which, except for the state names, have identical state graphs with respect to transitions and outputs. The two sets can be merged (see Figure 11.7).

The rows are not identical, but except for the state names (A1 = B2, A2 = B2, A3 = B3), the system's action, when judged by the relation between the output sequence produced by a given input sequence, is identical for either the A or the B set of states. Consequently, this state graph can be replaced by the simpler version shown in Figure 11.7c.

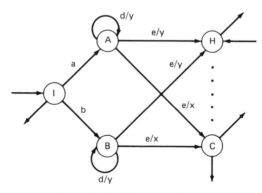

Figure 11.6. Equivalent States.

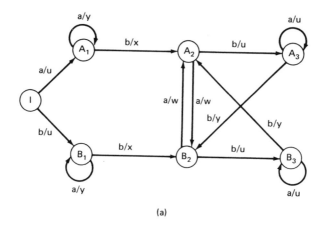

(a)

INPUT

STATE	a	b
I	A_1/Y	B_1/U
A_1	A_1/Y	A_2/X
B_1	B_1/Y	B_2/X
A_2	B_2/W	A_3/U
B_2	A_2/W	B_3/U
A_3	A_3/U	B_2/Y
B_3	B_3/U	A_2/Y

(b)

(c)

Figure 11.7. Merged Equivalent States.

Don't expect to have corresponding states or sets of states so neatly labeled in terms of equivalences. There are more formal methods (beyond the scope of this book—see MILL66) for identifying and spotting such equivalences. The process can also be automated. Because we are using state graphs as a test design tool rather than as a program design tool and because the state graphs we deal with are usually small, a sketch of the state graphs of the two versions (the tester's and the designer's) is usually

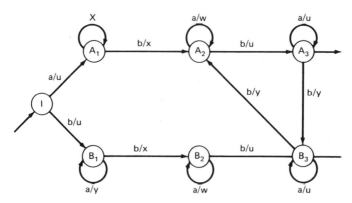

Figure 11.8. Unmergeable States.

enough to expose the similarities and the possibility of merging equivalent states.

Bugs are often the result of the unjustifiable merger of seemingly equivalent states. Two states or two sets of states appear to be equivalent because the programmer has failed to carry through to a proof of equivalence for *every* input sequence. The first few sequences looked good. Figure 11.8 is an example.

The input sequence *abbbb* produces the output sequence *uxuyy*, while the input sequence *bbbbb* produces the output sequence *uxuyu*. The two sets of states are not equivalent, although an incomplete analysis might lead you to believe that they are.

4.3. Transition Bugs

4.3.1. Unspecified and Contradictory Transitions

Every input-state combination must have a specified transition. If the transition is impossible, then there must be a mechanism that prevents that input from occurring in that state—look for it. If there is no such mechanism, what will the program do if, through a malfunction or an alpha particle, the impossible input occurs in that state? The transition for a given state-input combination may not be specified because of an oversight. *Exactly one transition must be specified for every combination of input and state.* However you model it or test it, the system will do *something* for every combination of input and state. It's better that it does what you want it to do, which you assure by specifying a transition rather than what some bugs want it to do.

A program can't have contradictions or ambiguities. Ambiguities are impossible because the program will do *something* (right or wrong) for every input. Even if the state does not change, by definition this is a transition to the same state. Similarly, software can't have contradictory transitions because computers can only do one thing at a time. A seeming contradiction could come about in a model if you don't account for *all* the factors that constitute the state and all the inputs. A single bit may have escaped your notice; if that bit is part of the definition of the state it can double the number of states, but if you're not monitoring that factor of the state, it would appear that the program had performed contradictory transitions or had different outputs for what appeared to be the same input from the same state. If you, as a designer, say while debugging "sometimes it works and sometimes it doesn't," you've admitted to a state factor of which you're not aware—a factor probably caused by a bug. Exploring the real state graph and recording the transitions and outputs for each combination of input and state may lead you to discover the bug.

4.3.2. An Example

Specifications are one of the most common source of ambiguities and contradictions. Specifications, unlike programs, can be full of ambiguities and contradictions. The following example illustrates how to convert a specification into a state graph and how contradictions can come about. The tape control routine will be used. Start with the first statement in the specification and add to the state graph one statement at a time. Here is the first statement of the specification:

Rule 1:   The program will maintain an error counter, which will be incremented whenever there's an error.

I don't yet know how many states there will be, but I might as well start by naming them with the values of the error counter. The initial state graph might look like this:

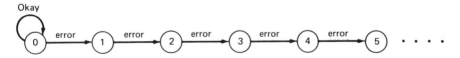

There are only two input values, "okay" and "error." A state table will be easier to work with, and it's much easier to spot ambiguities and contradictions. Here's the first state table:

INPUT

STATE	OKAY	ERROR
0	0/none	1/
1		2/
2		3/
3		4/
4		5/
5		6/
6		7/
7		8/

There are no contradictions yet, but lots of ambiguities. It's easy to see how ambiguities come about—just stop the specification before it's finished. Let's add the rules one at a time and fill in the state graph as we go. Here are the rest of the rules; study them to see if you can find the problems, if any:

Rule 2: If there is an error, rewrite the block.

Rule 3: If there have been three successive errors, erase 10 centimeters of tape and then rewrite the block.

Rule 4: If there have been three successive erasures and another error occurs, put the unit out of service.

Rule 5: If the erasure was successful, return to the normal state and clear the error counter.

Rule 6: If the rewrite was unsuccessful, increment the error counter, advance the state, and try another rewrite.

Rule 7: If the rewrite was successful, decrement the error counter and return to the previous state.

Adding rule 2, we get

INPUT

STATE	OKAY	ERROR
0	0/NONE	1/REWRITE
1		2/REWRITE
2		3/REWRITE
3		4/REWRITE
4		5/REWRITE
5		6/REWRITE
6		7/REWRITE
7		8/REWRITE

Rule 3: If there have been three successive errors, erase 10 centimeters of tape and then rewrite the block.

INPUT

STATE	OKAY	ERROR
0	0/NONE	1/REWRITE
1		2/REWRITE
2		3/REWRITE, ERASE, REWRITE
3		4/REWRITE, ERASE, REWRITE
4		5/REWRITE, ERASE, REWRITE
5		6/REWRITE, ERASE, REWRITE
6		7/REWRITE, ERASE, REWRITE
7		8/REWRITE, ERASE, REWRITE

Rule 3, if followed blindly, causes an unnecessary rewrite. It's a minor bug, so let it go for now, but it pays to check such things. There might be an arcane security reason for rewriting, erasing, and then rewriting again.

Rule 4: If there have been three successive erasures and another error occurs, put the unit out of service.

INPUT

STATE	OKAY	ERROR
0	0/NONE	1/RW
1		2/RW
2		3/ER, RW
3		4/ER, RW
4		5/ER, RW
5		6/OUT
6		
7		

Rule 4 terminates our interest in this state graph so we can dispose of states beyond 6. The details of state 6 will not be covered by this specification; presumably there is a way to get back to state 0. Also, we can credit the specifier with enough intelligence not to have expected a useless rewrite and erase prior to going out of service.

Rule 5: If the erasure was successful, return to the normal state and clear the counter.

INPUT

STATE	OKAY	ERROR
0	0/NONE	1/RW
1		2/RW
2		3/ER, RW
3	0/NONE	4/ER, RW
4	0/NONE	5/ER, RW
5	0/NONE	6/OUT
6		

Rule 6: If the rewrite was unsuccessful, increment the error counter, advance the state, and try another rewrite.

Because the value of the error counter is the state, and because rules 1 and 2 specified the same action, there seems to be no point to rule 6 unless yet another rewrite was wanted. Furthermore, the order of the actions is wrong. If the state is advanced before the rewrite, we could end up in the wrong state. The proper order should have been: output = attempt-rewrite and then increment the error counter.

Rule 7: If the rewrite was successful, decrement the error counter and return to the previous state.

INPUT

STATE	OKAY	ERROR
0	0/NONE	1/RW
1	0/NONE	2/RW
2	1/NONE	3/ER, RW
3	0/NONE 2/NONE	4/ER, RW
4	0/NONE 3/NONE	5/ER, RW
5	0/NONE 4/NONE	6/OUT
6		

Rule 7 got rid of the ambiguities but created contradictions. The specifier's intention was probably:

Rule 7A: If there have been no erasures and the rewrite is successful, return to the previous state.

We're guessing, of course, and we could be wrong, especially if the issue is obscure and the technical details unfamiliar. The only thing you can assume is that it's unlikely that a satisfactory implementation will result from a contradictory specification. If the state graph came from a design specification, be especially stupid. Be literal in your interpretation and smile when the designer accuses you of semantic nit-picking. It's tragic how such "purely semantic" issues turn out to cause tough bugs.

4.3.3. Unreachable States

An **unreachable state** is like unreachable code—a state that no input sequence can reach. An unreachable state is not impossible, just as unreachable code is not impossible. Furthermore, there may be transitions from the unreachable state to other states; there usually are because the state became unreachable as a result of incorrect transitions.

Unreachable states can come about from previously "impossible" states. You listed all the factors and laid out a state table. Some of these states corresponded to previously "impossible" states. The designer, perhaps after some rough persuasion, agrees that something should be done about the unreachable states. "Easy," he thinks, "provide no transitions into them." Yet there should still be a transition *out* of all such states. At least there should be a transition to an error-recovery procedure or an exception handler.

An isolated, unreachable state here and there, which clearly relates to impossible combinations of real-world state-determining conditions, is acceptable, but if you find groups of connected states that are isolated from others, there's cause for concern. There are two possibilities: (1) There is a bug; that is, some transitions are missing. (2) The transitions are there, but you don't know about it; in other words, there are other inputs and associated transitions to reckon with. Typically, such hidden transitions are caused by software operating at a higher priority level or by interrupt processing.

4.3.4. Dead States

A **dead state,** (or set of dead states) is a state that once entered cannot be left. This is not necessarily a bug, but it is suspicious. If the software was designed to be the fuse for a bomb, we would expect at least one such state. A set of states may appear to be dead because the program has two modes of operation. In the first mode it goes through an initialization process that consists of several states. Once initialized, it goes to a strongly connected set of working states, which, within the context of the routine, cannot be exited. The initialization states are unreachable to the working states, and the working states are dead to the initialization states. The only way to get back might be after a system crash and restart. Legitimate dead states are rare. They occur mainly with system-level issues and device handlers. In normal software, if it's not possible to get from any state to any other, there's reason for concern.

4.4. Output Errors

The states, the transitions, and the inputs could be correct, there could be no dead or unreachable states, but the output for the transition could be incorrect. Output actions must be verified independently of states and transitions. That is, you should distinguish between a program whose state graph is correct but has the wrong output for a transition and one whose state graph is incorrect. The likeliest reason for an incorrect output is an incorrect call to the routine that executes the output. This is usually a localized and minor bug. Bugs in the state graph are more serious because they tend to be related to fundamental control-structure problems. If the routine is implemented as a state table, both types of bugs are comparably severe.

4.5. Encoding Bugs

It would seem that encoding bugs for input coding, output coding, state codes, and state-symbol product formation could exist as such only in an explicit finite-state machine implementation. The possibility of such bugs is obvious for a finite-state machine implementation, but the bugs can also occur when the finite-state machine is implicit. If the programmer has a notion of state and has built an implicit finite-state machine, say by using a bunch of program flags, switches, and "condition" or "status" words, there may be an encoding process in place.

Make it a point *not* to use the programmer's state numbers and/or input codes. As a tester, you're dealing with an abstract machine that you're going to use to develop tests. *The behavior of a finite-state machine is invariant under all encodings.* That is, say that the states are numbered 1 to *n*. If you renumber the states by an arbitrary permutation, the finite-state machine is unchanged—similarly for input and output codes. Therefore, if you present your version of the finite-state machine with a different encoding, and if the programmer objects to the renaming or claims that behavior is changed as a result, then use that as a signal to look for encoding bugs. You may have to look at the implementation for these, especially the data dictionary. Look for "status" codes and read the list carefully. The key words are "unassigned," "reserved," "impossible," "error," or just gaps.

The implementation of the fields as a bunch of bits or bytes tells you the potential size of the code. If the number of code values is less than this potential, there is an encoding process going on, even if it's only to catch values that are out of range. In strongly typed languages with user-defined semantic types, the encoding process is probably a type conversion from a set membership, say, to a pointer type or integer. Again, you may have to look at the program to spot potential bugs of this kind.

5. STATE TESTING

5.1. Impact of Bugs

Let's say that a routine is specified as a state graph that has been verified as correct in all details. Program code or tables or a combination of both must still be implemented. A bug can manifest itself as one or more of the following symptoms:

1. Wrong number of states.
2. Wrong transition for a given state-input combination.
3. Wrong output for a given transition.
4. Pairs of states or sets of states that are inadvertently made equivalent (factor lost).
5. States or sets of states that are split to create inequivalent duplicates.
6. States or sets of states that have become dead.
7. States or sets of states that have become unreachable.

5.2. Principles

The strategy for state testing is analogous to that used for path-testing flowgraphs. Just as it's impractical to go through every possible path in a flowgraph, it's impractical to go through every path in a state graph. A path in a state graph, of course, is a succession of transitions caused by a sequence of inputs. The notion of coverage is identical to that used for flowgraphs—pass through each link (i.e., each transition must be exercised). Assume that some state is especially interesting—call it the initial state. Because most realistic state graphs are strongly connected, it should be possible to go through all states and back to the initial state, when starting from there. But don't do it. Even though most state testing can be done as a single case in a grand tour, it's impractical to do it that way for several reasons:

1. In the early phases of testing, you'll never complete the grand tour because of bugs.
2. Later, in maintenance, testing objectives are understood, and only a few of the states and transitions have to be retested. A grand tour is a waste of time.

3. There's so much history in a long test sequence and so much has happened that verification is difficult.

The starting point of state testing is:

1. Define a set of covering input sequences that get back to the initial state when starting from the initial state.
2. For each step in each input sequence, define the expected next state, the expected transition, and the expected output code.

A set of tests, then, consists of three sets of sequences:

1. Input sequences.
2. Corresponding transitions or next-state names.
3. Output sequences.

5.3.   Limitations and Extensions

Just as link coverage in a flowgraph model of program behavior did not guarantee "complete testing," state-transition coverage in a state-graph model does not guarantee complete testing. Things are slightly better because it's not necessary to consider any sequence longer than the total number of states. *Note:* Everything discussed in this section applies equally well to control flowgraphs with suitable translation.

Chow (CHOW78) defines a hierarchy of paths and methods for combining paths to produce covers of a state graph. The simplest is called a "0 switch," which corresponds to testing each transition individually. The next level consists of testing transition sequences consisting of two transitions, called "1 switches." The maximum-length switch is an $n - 1$ switch, where n is the number of states. Chow's primary result shows that in general, a 0 switch cover (which we recognize as branch cover for control flowgraphs) can catch output errors but may not catch some transition errors. In general, one must use longer and longer covering sequences to catch transition errors, missing states, extra states, and the like. The theory of what constitutes a sufficient number of tests (i.e., input sequences) to catch specified kinds of state-graph errors is still in its infancy and is beyond the scope of this book. Furthermore, practical experience with the application of such theory to software as exists is limited, and the efficacy of such methods as bug catchers has yet to be demonstrated sufficiently well to earn these methods a solid place in the software tester's tool repertoire. Work continues and progress in the form of semiautomatic test tools and effective methods are sure to come. Meanwhile, we have the following experience:

1. Simply identifying the factors that contribute to the state, calculating the total number of states, and comparing this number to the designer's notion catches some bugs.
2. Insisting on a justification for all supposedly dead, unreachable, and impossible states and transitions catches a few more bugs.
3. Insisting on an explicit specification of the transition and output for every combination of input and state catches many more bugs.
4. A set of input sequences that provide coverage of all nodes and links is a mandatory minimum requirement.
5. In executing state tests, it is essential that means be provided (e.g., instrumentation software) to record the sequence of states (e.g., transitions) resulting from the input sequence and not just the outputs that result from the input sequence.

5.4. What to Model

Because every combination of hardware and software can in principle be modeled by a sufficiently complicated state graph, this representation of software behavior is applicable to every program. The utility of such tests, however, is more limited. The state graph is a behavioral model—it is functional rather than structural and is thereby far removed from the code. As a testing method, it is a bottom-line method that ignores structural detail to focus on behavior. It is advantageous to look into the database to see how the factors that create the states are represented in order to get a state count. More than most test methods, state testing yield the biggest payoffs during the design of the tests rather than during the running thereof. Because the tests can be constructed from a design specification long before coding, they help catch deep bugs early in the game when correction is inexpensive. Here are some situations in which state testing may prove useful:

1. Any processing where the output is based on the occurrence of one or more sequences of events, such as detection of specified input sequences, sequential format validation, parsing, and other situations in which the order of inputs is important.
2. Most protocols between systems, between humans and machines, between components of a system (CHOI84, CHUN78, SARI88).
3. Device drivers such as for tapes and discs that have complicated retry and recovery procedures if the action depends on the state.
4. Transaction flows where the transactions are such that they can stay in the system indefinitely—for example, online users, tasks in a multitasking system.

5. High-level control functions within an operating system. Transitions between user states, supervisor's states, and so on. Security handling of records, permission for read/write/modify privileges, priority interrupts and transitions between interrupt states and levels, recovery issues and the safety state of records and/or processes with respect to recording recovery data.

6. The behavior of the system with respect to resource management and what it will do when various levels of resource utilization are reached. Any control function that involves responses to thresholds where the system's action depends not just on the threshold value, but also on the direction in which the threshold is crossed. This is a normal approach to control functions. A threshold passage in one direction stimulates a recovery function, but that recovery function is not suspended until a second, lower threshold is passed going the other way.

7. A set of menus and ways that one can go from one to the other. The currently active menus are the states, the input alphabet is the choices one can make, and the transitions are invocations of the next menu in a menu tree. Many menu-driven software packages suffer from dead states—menus from which the only way out is to reboot.

8. Whenever a feature is directly and explicitly implemented as one or more state-transition tables.

5.5. Getting the Data

As is so often the case in the independent tester's life, getting the data on which the model is to be based is half the job or more. There's no magic for doing that: reading documents, interviews, and all the rest. State testing, more than most functional test strategies, tends to have a labor-intensive data-gathering phase and tends to need many more meetings to resolve issues. This is the case because most of the participants don't realize that there's an essential state-machine behavior. For nonprogrammers, especially, the very concept of finite-state machine behavior may be missing. Be prepared to spend more time on getting data than you think is reasonable and be prepared to do a lot of educating along the way.

5.6. Tools

Good news and bad news: The telecommunications industry, especially in telephony, has been using finite-state machine implementations of control functions for decades (BAUE79). They also use several languages/systems to code state tables directly. Similarly, there are tools to do the same for hardware logic designs. That's the good news. The bad news is that these systems and languages are proprietary, of the home-brew variety, internal, and/or not applicable to the general use of software implementations of finite-state machines. The most successful tools are not published and are unlikely to be published because of the competitive advantage they give to the users of those tools.

6. TESTABILITY TIPS

6.1. A Balm for Programmers

Most of this chapter has taken the independent tester's viewpoint and has been a prescription for making programmers squirm. What is testability but means by which programmers can protect themselves from the ravages of sinister independent testers? What is testability but a guide to cheating—how to design software so that the pesticide paradox works and the tester's strongest technique is made ineffectual? The key to testability design is easy: build explicit finite-state machines.

6.2. How Big, How Small?

I understand every two-state finite-state machine because, including the good and bad ones, there are only eight of them. There are about eighty possible good and bad three-state machines, 2700 four-state machines, 275,000 five-state machines, and close to 100 million six-state machines, most of which are bad. We learned long ago, as hardware logic designers, that it paid to build explicit finite-state machines for even very small machines. I think you can safely get away with two states, it's getting difficult for three states, a heroic act for four, and beyond human comprehension for five states. That doesn't mean that you have to build your finite-state machine as in the explicit PDL example given above, but that you must do a finite-state machine model and identify how you're implementing every part of that model for anything with four or more states.

6.3. Switches, Flags, and Unachievable Paths

Something may look like a finite-state machine but not be one. Figure 11.9a shows a program with a switch or flag. Someplace early in the routine we set a flag, A, then later we test the flag and go one way or the other depending on its value. In Figure 11.9b we've rewritten the routine

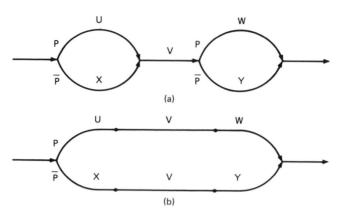

Figure 11.9. Program with One Switch Variable.

to eliminate the flag. As soon as the flag value is calculated, we branch. The cost is the cost of converting segment V into a subroutine and calling it twice. But note that we went from four paths, two of which are unachievable to two paths, both of which are achievable and both of which are needed to achieve branch coverage.

In Figure 11.10, the situation is more complicated. There are three switches this time. Again, where we go depends on the switch settings calculated earlier in the program. We can put the decision up front and branch directly, and again use subroutines to make each path explicit and do without the switches. The advantages of this implementation is that if any of the combinations are not needed, we merely clip out that part of the decision tree, as in Figure 11.10c. Again, all paths are achievable and all paths are needed for branch cover.

Figure 11.11 is similar to the previous two except that we've put the switched parts in a loop. It's even worse if the loop includes the switch value calculations (dotted link). We now have a very difficult situation. We don't know which of these paths are achievable and which are or are not required. What is or is not achievable depends on the switch settings. Branch coverage won't do it: we must do or attempt branch coverage in every possible state.

6.4. Essential and Inessential Finite-State Behavior

Program flags and switches are predicates deferred. There is a significant, qualitative difference between finite-state machines and combinational machines. A combinational machine selects paths based on the values of

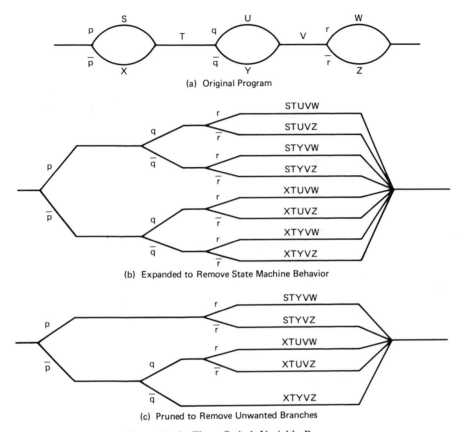

(a) Original Program

(b) Expanded to Remove State Machine Behavior

(c) Pruned to Remove Unwanted Branches

Figure 11.10. Three-Switch-Variable Program.

predicates, the predicates depend only on prior processing and the predicates' truth values will not change once they have been determined. Any path corresponds to a boolean algebra expression over the predicates. Furthermore, it does not matter in which order the decisions are made. The fact that there is an ordering is a consequence of a sequential, Von Neumann computer architecture. In a parallel-data-flow machine, for ex-

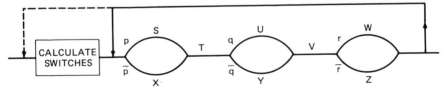

Figure 11.11. Switches in a Loop.

ample, the decisions and path selections could be made simultaneously. Sequence and finite-state behavior are in this case implementation consequences and not essential. The combinational machine has exactly one state and one transition back to itself for all possible inputs. The control logic of a combinational program can be described by a decision table or a decision tree.

The simplest essential finite-state machine is a flip-flop. There is no logic that can implement it without some kind of feedback. You cannot describe this behavior by a decision table or decision tree unless you provide feedback into the table or call it recursively. It must have a loop or the equivalent.

The problem with nontrivial finite-state machine behavior is that to do the equivalent of branch testing, say, you must do it over for every state. Why take on that extra burden if the finite-state machine behavior isn't essential?

Most programmers' implementation of finite-state behavior is not essential—it appears to be convenient. Most programmers, having implemented finite-state behavior, will not test it properly. I've yet to see a programmer who implemented a routine with 10 flags rerun the tests for all 1024 possible flag settings.

Learn to distinguish between essential and inessential finite-state behavior. It's not essential if you can do it by a parallel program in a hypothetical data-flow machine. It's not essential if a decision-table model will do it for you or if you can program it as a big decision tree. It's not essential if the program's exit expression (Chapter 10), even with explicit loops, equals unity. It's not essential if there's a nonunity exit expression but it turns out that you don't really want to loop under the looping conditions. I'm not telling you to throw away your "harmless" little flags and switches and not to implement inessential finite-state machine behavior. All I ask is that you be prepared to repeat your tests in every state.

6.5. Design Guidelines

I'll assume that you've checked the design and the specification and that you're not about to implement inessential finite-state machine behavior. What should you do if you must build finite-state machines into your code?

1. Learn how it's done in hardware. I know of no books on finite-state machine design for programmers. There are only books on hardware

logic design and switching theory, with a distinct hardware flavor and you'll have to adapt their methods to software.

2. Start by designing the abstract machine. Verify that it is what you want to do. Do an explicit analysis, in the form of a state graph or table, for anything with three states or more.

3. Start with an explicit design—that is, input encoding, output encoding, state code assignment, transition table, output table, state storage, and how you intend to form the state-symbol product. Do this at the PDL level. But be sure to document that explicit design.

4. Before you start taking shortcuts, see if it really matters. Neither the time nor the memory for the explicit implementation usually matters. Do a prototype based on the explicit design and analyze that or measure it to see what the processing time actually is and if that's significant. Remember that explicit finite-state machines are usually very fast and that the penalty is likelier to be a memory cost than a time cost. Test the prototype thoroughly, as discussed above. The prototype test suite should be kept for later use.

5. Take shortcuts by making things implicit only as you must to make significant reductions in time or space and only if you can show that such savings matter in the context of the whole system. After all, doubling the speed of your implementation may mean nothing if all you've done is shaved 100 microseconds from a 500-millisecond process. The order in which you should make things implicit are: output encoding, input encoding, state code, state-symbol product, output table, transition table, state storage. That's the order from least to most dangerous.

6. Consider a hierarchical design if you have more than a few dozen states.

7. Build, buy, or implement tools and languages that implement finite-state machines as software if you're doing more than a dozen states routinely.

8. Build in the means to initialize to any arbitrary state. Build in the transition verification instrumentation (the coverage analyzer). These are much easier to do with an explicit machine.

7. SUMMARY

1. State testing is primarily a functional testing tool whose payoff is best in the early phases of design.

2. A program can't have contradictory or ambiguous transitions or outputs, but a specification can and does. Use a state table to verify the specification's validity.

3. Count the states.
4. Insist on a specification of transition and output for every combination of input and states.
5. Apply a minimum set of covering tests.
6. Instrument the transitions to capture the sequence of states and not just the sequence of outputs.
7. Count the states.

12

GRAPH MATRICES
AND APPLICATIONS

1. SYNOPSIS

Graph matrices are introduced as another representation for graphs; some useful tools resulting therefrom are examined. Matrix operations, relations, node-reduction algorithm revisited, equivalence class partitions.

2. MOTIVATIONAL OVERVIEW

2.1. The Problem with Pictorial Graphs

Graphs were introduced as an abstraction of software structure early in this book and used throughout. Yet another graph that modeled software behavior was introduced in Chapter 11. There are many other kinds of graphs, not discussed in this book, that are useful in software testing. Whenever a graph is used as a model, sooner or later we trace paths through it—to find a set of covering paths, a set of values that will sensitize paths, the logic function that controls the flow, the processing time of the routine, the equations that define a domain, whether the routine pushes or pops, or whether a state is reachable or not. Even algebraic representations such as BNF and regular expressions can be converted to equivalent graphs. Much of test design consists of tracing paths through a graph and most testing strategies define some kind of cover over some kind of graph.

Path tracing is not easy, and it's subject to error. You can miss a link here and there or cover some links twice—even if you do use a marking pen to note which paths have been taken. You're tracing a long complicated path through a routine when the telephone rings—you've lost your place before you've had a chance to mark it. I get confused tracing paths, so naturally I assume that other people also get confused.

One solution to this problem is to represent the graph as a matrix and to use matrix operations equivalent to path tracing. These methods aren't necessarily easier than path tracing, but because they're more methodical and mechanical and don't depend on your ability to "see" a path, they're more reliable.

Even if you use powerful tools that do everything that can be done with graphs, and furthermore, enable you to do it graphically, it's still a good idea to know how to do it by hand; just as having a calculator should not mean that you don't need to know how to do arithmetic. Besides, with a little practice, you might find these methods easier and faster than doing it on the screen; moreover, you can use them on the plane or anywhere.

2.2. Tool Building

If you build test tools or want to know how they work, sooner or later you'll be implementing or investigating analysis routines based on these methods—or you should be. Think about how a naive tool builder would go about finding a property of all paths (a possibly infinite number) versus how one might do it based on the methods of Chapter 8. But Chapter 8 was graphical and it's hard to build algorithms over visual graphs. The properties of graph matrices are fundamental to test tool building.

2.3. Doing and Understanding Testing Theory

We talk about graphs in testing theory, but we prove theorems about graphs by proving theorems about their matrix representations. Without the conceptual apparatus of graph matrices, you'll be blind to much of testing theory, especially those parts that lead to useful algorithms.

2.4. The Basic Algorithms

This is not intended to be a survey of graph-theoretic algorithms based on the matrix representation of graphs. It's intended only to be a basic toolkit. For more on this subject, see EVEN79, MAYE72, PHIL81. The basic toolkit consists of:

1. Matrix multiplication, which is used to get the path expression from every node to every other node.
2. A partitioning algorithm for converting graphs with loops into loop-free graphs of equivalence classes.
3. A collapsing process (analogous to the determinant of a matrix), which gets the path expression from any node to any other node.

3. THE MATRIX OF A GRAPH

3.1. Basic Principles

A **graph matrix** is a square array with one row and one column for every
node in the graph. Each row-column combination corresponds to a relation between the node corresponding to the row and the node corresponding to the column. The relation, for example, could be as simple as the
link name, if there is a link between the nodes. Some examples of graphs
and their associated matrices are shown in Figure 12.1a through g. Observe the following:

1. The size of the matrix (i.e., the number of rows and columns) equals
    the number of nodes.
2. There is a place to put every possible direct connection or link
    between any node and any other node.
3. The entry at a row and column intersection is the link weight of the
    link (if any) that connects the two nodes in that direction.
4. A connection from node i to node j does not imply a connection from
    node j to node i. Note that in Figure 12.1h the (5,6) entry is m, but
    the (6,5) entry is c.
5. If there are several links between two nodes, then the entry is a sum;
    the "+" sign denotes parallel links as usual.

In general, an entry is not just a simple link name but a path expression
corresponding to the paths between the pair of nodes. Furthermore, as
with the graphs, an entry can be a link weight or an expression in link
weights (see Chapter 8 for a refresher). Finally, "arithmetic operations"
are the operations appropriate to the weights the links represent.

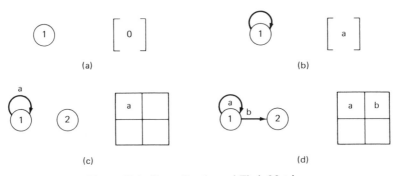

Figure 12.1. Some Graphs and Their Matrices.

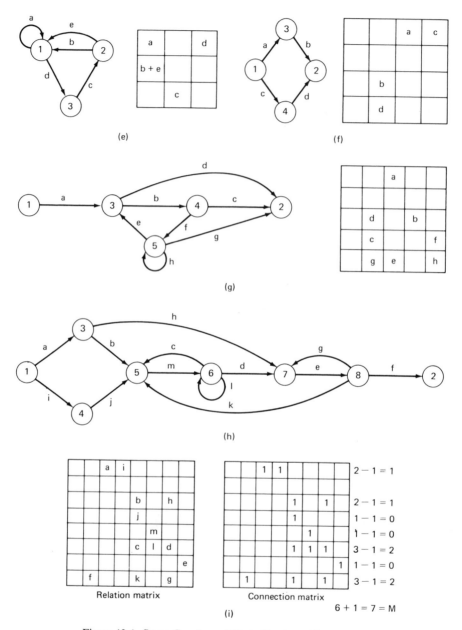

Figure 12.1. Some Graphs and Their Matrices. (Continued)

3.2. A Simple Weight

The simplest weight we can use is to note that there is or isn't a connection. Let "1" mean that there is a connection and "0" that there isn't. The arithmetic rules are:

$$1 + 1 = 1, \quad 1 + 0 = 1, \quad 0 + 0 = 0,$$
$$1 \times 1 = 1, \quad 1 \times 0 = 0, \quad 0 \times 0 = 0.$$

A matrix with weights defined like this is called a **connection matrix.** The connection matrix for Figure 12.1h is obtained by replacing each entry with 1 if there is a link and 0 if there isn't. As usual, to reduce clutter we don't write down 0 entries. Each row of a matrix (whatever the weights) denotes the outlinks of the node corresponding to that row, and each column denotes the inlinks corresponding to that node. A branch node is a node with more than one nonzero entry in its row. A junction node is a node with more than one nonzero entry in its column. A self-loop is an entry along the diagonal. Because rows 1, 3, 6, and 8 of Figure 12.1h all have more than one entry, those nodes are branch nodes. Using the principle that a case statement is equivalent to $n - 1$ binary decisions, by subtracting 1 from the total number of entries in each row and ignoring rows with no entries (such as node 2), we obtain the equivalent number of decisions for each row. Adding these values and then adding 1 to the sum yields the graph's cyclomatic complexity.

3.3. Further Notation

Talking about the "entry at row 6, column 7" is wordy. To compact things, the entry corresponding to node i and column j, which is to say the link weights between nodes i and j, is denoted by a_{ij}. A self-loop about node i is denoted by a_{ii}, while the link weight for the link between nodes j and i is denoted by a_{ji}. The path segments expressed in terms of link names and, in this notation, for several paths in the graph of Figure 12.1h are:

$$
\begin{aligned}
abmd \quad &= a_{13}a_{35}a_{56}a_{67}; \\
degef \quad &= a_{67}a_{78}a_{87}a_{78}a_{82}; \\
ahekmlld &= a_{13}a_{37}a_{78}a_{85}a_{56}a_{66}a_{66}a_{67};
\end{aligned}
$$

because

$$a_{13} = a, \quad a_{35} = b, \quad a_{56} = m, \quad a_{66} = l, \quad a_{67} = d, \text{ etc.}$$

The expression "$a_{ij}a_{jj}a_{jm}$" denotes a path from node i to j, with a self-loop at j and then a link from node j to node m. The expression "$a_{ij}a_{jk}a_{km}a_{mi}$" denotes a path from node i back to node i via nodes j, k, and m. An expression such as "$a_{ik}a_{km}a_{mj} + a_{in}a_{np}a_{pj}$" denotes a pair of paths between nodes i and j, one going via nodes k and m and the other via nodes n and p.

This notation may seem cumbersome, but it's not intended for working with the matrix of a graph but for expressing operations on the matrix. It's a very compact notation. For example,

$$\sum_{k=1}^{n} a_{ik}a_{kk}a_{kj}$$

denotes the set of all possible paths between nodes i and j via one intermediate node. But because "i" and "j" denote any node, this expression is the set of all possible paths between any two nodes via one intermediate node.

The **transpose** of a matrix is the matrix with rows and columns interchanged. It is denoted by a superscript letter "T," as in A^T. If $C = A^T$ then $c_{ij} = a_{ji}$. The **intersection** of two matrices of the same size, denoted by A#B is a matrix obtained by an element-by-element multiplication operation on the entries. For example, $C = A\#B$ means $c_{ij} = a_{ij}\#b_{ij}$. The multiplication operation is usually boolean AND or set intersection. Similarly, the **union** of two matrices is defined as the element-by-element addition operation such as a boolean OR or set union.

4. RELATIONS

4.1. General

This isn't a section on aunts and uncles but on abstract relations that can exist between abstract objects, although family and personal relations can also be modeled by abstract relations, if you want to. A **relation** is a property that exists between two (usually) objects of interest. We've had many examples of relations in this book. Here's a sample, where a and b denote objects and R is used to denote that a has the relation R to b:

1. "Node a *is connected* to node b" or aRb where "R" means "is connected to."
2. "$a >= b$" or aRb where "R" means "greater than or equal."
3. "a *is a subset* of b" where the relation is "is a subset of."

4. "It takes 20 microseconds of processing time to get from node a to node b." The relation is expressed by the number 20.
5. "Data object X is defined at program node a and used at program node b." The relation between nodes a and b is that there is a *du* chain between them.

Let's now redefine what we mean by a graph.

A **graph** consists of a set of abstract objects called **nodes** and a relation R between the nodes. If aRb, which is to say that a has the relation R to b, it is denoted by a **link** from a to b. In addition to the fact that the relation exists, for some relations we can associate one or more properties. These are called **link weights.** A link weight can be numerical, logical, illogical, objective, subjective, or whatever. Furthermore, there is no limit to the number and type of link weights that one may associate with a relation.

"Is connected to" is just about the simplest relation there is: it is denoted by an unweighted link. Graphs defined over "is connected to" are called, as we said before, **connection matrices.*** For more general relations, the matrix is called a **relation matrix.**

4.2. Properties of Relations

4.2.1. General

The least that we can ask of relations is that there be an algorithm by which we can determine whether or not the relation exists between two nodes. If that's all we ask, then our relation arithmetic is too weak to be useful. The following sections concern some properties of relations that have been found to be useful. Any given relation may or may not have these properties, in almost any combination.

4.2.2. Transitive Relations

A relation R is **transitive** if aRb and bRc implies aRc. Most relations used in testing are transitive. Examples of transitive relations include: is connected to, is greater than or equal to, is less than or equal to, is a relative of, is faster than, is slower than, takes more time than, is a subset of, includes, shadows, is the boss of. Examples of **intransitive** relations in-

---

* Also "adjacency matrix"; see EVEN79.

clude: is acquainted with, is a friend of, is a neighbor of, is lied to, has a *du* chain between.

4.2.3. Reflexive Relations

A relation R is **reflexive** if, for every *a*, *a*R*a*. A reflexive relation is equivalent to a self-loop at every node. Examples of reflexive relations include: equals, is acquainted with (except, perhaps, for amnesiacs), is a relative of. Examples of **irreflexive relations** include: not equals, is a friend of (unfortunately), is on top of, is under.

4.2.4. Symmetric Relations

A relation R is **symmetric** if for every *a* and *b*, *a*R*b* implies *b*R*a*. A symmetric relation means that if there is a link from *a* to *b* then there is also a link from *b* to *a*; which furthermore means that we can do away with arrows and replace the pair of links with a single **undirected** link. A graph whose relations are not symmetric is called a **directed graph** because we must use arrows to denote the relation's direction. A graph over a symmetric relation is called an **undirected graph.**[*] The matrix of an undirected graph is symmetric ($a_{ij} = a_{ji}$ for all i, j).

Examples of symmetric relations: is a relative of, equals, is alongside of, shares a room with, is married (usually), is brother of, is similar (in most uses of the word), OR, AND, EXOR. Examples of **asymmetric** relations: is the boss of, is the husband of, is greater than, controls, dominates, can be reached from.

4.2.5. Antisymmetric Relations

A relation R is **antisymmetric** if for every *a* and *b*, if *a*R*b* and *b*R*a*, then *a* = *b*, or they are the same elements.

Examples of antisymmetric relations: is greater than or equal to, is a subset of, time. Examples of **nonantisymmetric** relations: is connected to, can be reached from, is greater than, is a relative of, is a friend of.

4.3. Equivalence Relations

An **equivalence relation** is a relation that satisfies the reflexive, transitive, and symmetric properties. Numerical equality is the most familiar exam-

---

[*] Strictly speaking, we should distinguish between undirected graphs (no arrows) and bidirected graphs (arrow in both directions); but in the context of testing applications, it doesn't matter.

ple of an equivalence relation. If a set of objects satisfy an equivalence relation, we say that they form an **equivalence class** over that relation. The importance of equivalence classes and relations is that any member of the equivalence class is, with respect to the relation, equivalent to any other member of that class. The idea behind **partition-testing strategies** such as domain testing and path testing, is that we can partition the input space into equivalence classes. If we can do that, then testing any member of the equivalence class is as effective as testing them all. When we say in path testing that it is sufficient to test one set of input values for each member of a branch-covering set of paths, we are asserting that the set of all input values for each path (e.g., the path's domain) is an equivalence class with respect to the relation that defines branch-testing paths. If we furthermore (incorrectly) assert that a strategy such as branch testing is sufficient, we are asserting that satisfying the branch-testing relation implies that all other possible equivalence relations will also be satisfied— that, of course, is nonsense.

4.4. Partial Ordering Relations

A **partial ordering relation** satisfies the reflexive, transitive, and antisymmetric properties. Partial ordered graphs have several important properties: they are loop-free, there is at least one maximum element, there is at least one minimum element, and if you reverse all the arrows, the resulting graph is also partly ordered. A **maximum element** a is one for which the relation xRa does not hold for any other element x. Similarly, a **minimum element** a, is one for which the relation aRx does not hold for any other element x. Trees are good examples of partial ordering. The importance of partial ordering is that while strict ordering (as for numbers) is rare with graphs, partial ordering is common. Loop-free graphs are partly ordered. We have many examples of useful partly ordered graphs: call trees, most data structures, an integration plan. Also, whereas the general control-flow or data-flow graph is not always partly ordered, we've seen that by restricting our attention to partly ordered graphs we can sometimes get new, useful strategies. Also, it is often possible to remove the loops from a graph that isn't partly ordered to obtain another graph that is.

5. THE POWERS OF A MATRIX

5.1. Principles

Each entry in the graph's matrix (that is, each link) expresses a relation between the pair of nodes that corresponds to that entry. It is a direct relation, but we are usually interested in indirect relations that exist by virtue of intervening nodes between the two nodes of interest. Squaring the matrix (using suitable arithmetic for the weights) yields a new matrix that expresses the relation between each pair of nodes via one intermediate node under the assumption that the relation is transitive. The square of the matrix represents all path segments two links long. Similarly, the third power represents all path segments three links long. And the kth power of the matrix represents all path segments k links long. Because a matrix has at most n nodes, and no path can be more than $n - 1$ links long without incorporating some path segment already accounted for, it is generally not necessary to go beyond the $n - 1$ power of the matrix. As usual, concatenation of links or the weights of links is represented by multiplication, and parallel links or path expressions by addition.

Let A be a matrix whose entries are a_{ij}. The set of all paths between any node i and any other node j (possibly i itself), via all possible intermediate nodes, is given by

$$a_{ij} + \sum_{k=1}^{n} a_{ik}a_{kj} + \sum_{k=1}^{n}\sum_{m=1}^{n} a_{ik}a_{km}a_{mj} + \sum_{k}^{n}\sum_{m}^{n}\sum_{l}^{n} a_{ik}a_{km}a_{ml}a_{lj}$$

$$+ \cdots \sum_{k=1}^{n}\sum_{m=1}^{n}\sum_{l=1}^{n} \cdots \sum_{p=1}^{n} a_{ik}a_{km}a_{ml} \cdots a_{qp}a_{pj}$$

As formidable as this expression might appear, it states nothing more than the following:

1. Consider the relation between every node and its neighbor.
2. Extend that relation by considering each neighbor as an intermediate node.
3. Extend further by considering each neighbor's neighbor as an intermediate node.
4. Continue until the longest possible nonrepeating path has been established.
5. Do this for every pair of nodes in the graph.

5.2.   Matrix Powers and Products

Given a matrix whose entries are a_{ij}, the square of that matrix is obtained by replacing every entry with

$$a_{ij} = \sum_{k=1}^{n} a_{ik}a_{kj}$$

More generally, given two matrices A and B, with entries a_{ik} and b_{kj}, respectively, their product is a new matrix C, whose entries are c_{ij}, where:

$$c_{ij} = \sum_{k=1}^{n} a_{ik}b_{kj}$$

$$\begin{bmatrix} a_{11}a_{12}a_{13}a_{14} \\ a_{21}a_{22}a_{23}a_{24} \\ a_{31}a_{32}a_{33}a_{34} \\ a_{41}a_{42}a_{43}a_{44} \end{bmatrix} \times \begin{bmatrix} b_{11}b_{12}b_{13}b_{14} \\ b_{21}b_{22}b_{23}b_{24} \\ b_{31}b_{32}b_{33}b_{34} \\ b_{41}b_{42}b_{43}b_{44} \end{bmatrix} = \begin{bmatrix} c_{11}c_{12}c_{13}c_{14} \\ c_{21}c_{22}c_{23}c_{24} \\ c_{31}c_{32}c_{33}c_{34} \\ c_{41}c_{42}c_{43}c_{44} \end{bmatrix}$$

$$c_{11} = a_{11}b_{11} + a_{12}b_{21} + a_{13}b_{31} + a_{14}b_{41}$$
$$c_{12} = a_{11}b_{12} + a_{12}b_{22} + a_{13}b_{32} + a_{14}b_{42}$$
$$c_{13} = a_{11}b_{13} + a_{12}b_{23} + a_{13}b_{33} + a_{14}b_{43}$$
$$\cdot \cdot \cdot$$
$$\cdot \cdot \cdot$$
$$\cdot \cdot \cdot$$
$$c_{32} = a_{31}b_{12} + a_{32}b_{22} + a_{33}b_{32} + a_{34}b_{42}$$
$$\cdot \cdot \cdot$$
$$\cdot \cdot \cdot$$
$$\cdot \cdot \cdot$$
$$c_{44} = a_{41}b_{14} + a_{42}b_{24} + a_{43}b_{34} + a_{44}b_{44}$$

The indexes of the product [e.g., (3,2) in c_{32}] identify, respectively, the row of the first matrix and the column of the second matrix that will be combined to yield the entry for that product in the product matrix. The c_{32} entry is obtained by combining, element by element, the entries in the third row of the A matrix with the corresponding elements in the second column of the B matrix. I use two hands. My left hand points and traces across the row while the right points down the column of B. It's like patting your head with one hand and rubbing your stomach with the other at the same time: it takes practice to get the hang of it. Applying this to the matrix of Figure 12.1g yields

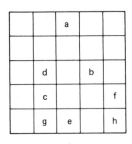

	a					ad		ab			abc			abf
d	b					bc		bf			bfg	bfe		bfh
c		f				fg	fe	fh			fed + fhg	fhe	feb	fh²
g	e	h				ed + hg	he	eb	h²		ebc + hed + h²g	h²e	heb	ebf + h³

A   A²   A³

$A^2A = AA^2$; that is, matrix multiplication is associative (for most interesting relations) if the underlying relation arithmetic is associative. Therefore, you can get A^4 in any of the following ways: A^2A^2, $(A^2)^2$, A^3A, AA^3. However, because multiplication is not necessarily commutative, you must remember to put the contribution of the left-hand matrix in front of the contribution of the right-hand matrix and not inadvertently reverse the order. The loop terms are important. These are the terms that appear along the **principal diagonal** (the one that slants down to the right). The initial matrix had a self-loop about node 5, link *h*. No new loop is revealed with paths of length 2, but the cube of the matrix shows additional loops about nodes 3 (*bfe*), 4 (*feb*), and 5 (*ebf*). It's clear that these are the same loop around the three nodes.

If instead of link names you use some other relation and associated weight, as in Chapter 8, and use the appropriate arithmetic rules, the matrix displays the property corresponding to that relation. Successive powers of the matrix display the property when considering paths of length exactly 2, exactly 3, and so on. The methods of Chapter 8 and the applications discussed there carry over almost unchanged into equivalent matrix methods.

5.3. The Set of All Paths

Our main objective is to use matrix operations to obtain the set of all paths between all nodes or, equivalently, a property (described by link weights) over the set of all paths from every node to every other node, using the appropriate arithmetic rules for such weights. The set of all paths between all nodes is easily expressed in terms of matrix operations. It's given by the following infinite series of matrix powers:

$$\sum_{i=1}^{\infty} A^i = A + A^2 + A^3 \cdots A^{\infty}$$

This is an eloquent, but practically useless, expression. Let I be an *n* by *n* matrix, where *n* is the number of nodes. Let I's entries consist of multiplicative identity elements along the principal diagonal. For link names, this can be the number "1." For other kinds of weights, it is the multiplicative identity for those weights. The above product can be rephrased as:

$$A(I + A + A^2 + A^3 + A^4 \cdots A^{\infty})$$

But often for relations, $A + A = A$, $(A + I)^2 = A^2 + A + A + I = A^2 + A + I$. Furthermore, for any finite n,

$$(A + I)^n = I + A + A^2 + A^3 \ldots A^n$$

Therefore, the original infinite sum can be replaced by

$$\sum_{i=1}^{\infty} A^i = A(A + I)^{\infty}$$

This is an improvement, because in the original expression we had both infinite products and infinite sums, and now we have only one infinite product to contend with. The above is valid whether or not there are loops. If we restrict our interest for the moment to paths of length $n - 1$, where n is the number of nodes, the set of all such paths is given by

$$\sum_{i=1}^{n-1} A^i = A(A + I)^{n-2}$$

This is an interesting set of paths because, with n nodes, no path can exceed $n - 1$ nodes without incorporating some path segment that is already incorporated in some other path or path segment. Finding the set of all such paths is somewhat easier because it is not necessary to do all the intermediate products explicitly. The following algorithm is effective:

1. Express $n - 2$ as a binary number.
2. Take successive squares of $(A + I)$, leading to $(A + I)^2$, $(A + I)^4$, $(A + I)^8$, and so on.
3. Keep only those binary powers of $(A + I)$ that correspond to a 1 value in the binary representation of $n - 2$.
4. The set of all paths of length $n - 1$ or less is obtained as the product of the matrices you got in step 3 with the original matrix.

As an example, let the graph have 16 nodes. We want the set of all paths of length less than or equal to 15. The binary representation of $n - 2$ (14) is $2^3 + 2^2 + 2$. Consequently, the set of paths is given by

$$\sum_{i=1}^{15} A^i = A(A + I)^8(A + I)^4(A + I)^2$$

This required one multiplication to get the square, squaring that to get the fourth power, and squaring again to get the eighth power, then three more multiplications to get the sum, for a total of six matrix multiplications without additions, compared to fourteen multiplications and additions if gotten directly.

A matrix for which $A^2 = A$ is said to be **idempotent.** A matrix whose successive powers eventually yields an idempotent matrix is called an **idempotent generator**—that is, a matrix for which there is a k such that $A^{k+1} = A^k$. The point about idempotent generator matrices is that we can get properties over all paths by successive squaring. A graph matrix of the form $(A + I)$ over a transitive relation is an idempotent generator; therefore, anything of interest can be obtained by even simpler means than the binary method discussed above. For example, the relation "connected" does not change once we reach A^{n-1} because no connection can take more than $n - 1$ links and, once connected, nodes cannot be disconnected. Thus, if we wanted to know which nodes of an n-node graph were connected to which, by whatever paths, we have only to calculate: A^2, $A^2A^2 = A^4 \cdot \cdot \cdot A^p$, where p is the next power of 2 greater than or equal to n. We can do this because the relation "is connected to" is reflexive and transitive. The fact that it is reflexive means that every node has the equivalent of a self-loop, and the matrix is therefore an idempotent generator. If a relation is transitive but not reflexive, we can augment it as we did above, by adding the unit matrix to it, thereby making it reflexive. That is, although the relation defined over A is not reflexive, A + I is. A + I is an idempotent generator, and therefore there's nothing new to learn for powers greater than $n - 1$, the length of the longest nonrepeating path through the graph. The nth power of a matrix A + I over a transitive relation is called the **transitive closure** of the matrix.

5.4. Loops

Every loop forces us into a potentially infinite sum of matrix powers. The way to handle loops is similar to what we did for regular expressions. Every loop shows up as a term in the diagonal of some power of the matrix—the power at which the loop finally closes—or, equivalently, the length of the loop. The impact of the loop can be obtained by preceding every element in the row of the node at which the loop occurs by the path expression of the loop term starred and then deleting the loop term. For example, using the matrix for the graph of Figure 12.1e, we obtain the following succession of powers for A + I:

1		a		
	1			
d	1	b		
c		1	f	
h*g	h*e		1	

$(A + I)*$

1	ad	a	ab	
	1			
d+ bc	1	b	bf	
c + fh*g	fh*e	1	f	
h*g+ h*ed	h*e	h*eb	1	

$(A + I)^2 *$

1	ad + abc	a	ab	abf
	1			
d + bc + bfh*g	1 + bfh*e	bf	bf	
c + fh*g + fh*ed	fh*e	1 + fh*eb	f	
h*e(d + bc) + h*g + h*ed	h*e	h*eb	1 + h*ebf	

$(A + I)^3 *$

The first matrix $(A + I)$ had a self-loop about node 5 link h. Moving link h out to the other entries in the row, leaving the "1" entry at the $(5,5)$ position, yielded the $h*g$ and the $h*e$ entries at $(5,2)$ and $(5,3)$ respectively. No new loops were closed for the second power. The third-power matrix has a loop about node 3, whose expression is $bfh*e$. Consequently, all other entries in that row are premultiplied by $(bfh*e)*$, to yield $(bfh*e)*(d + bc + bfh*g)$ for $(3,2)$, $(bfh*e)*b$ for $(3,4)$, and $(bfh*e)*bf$ for $(3,5)$. Similarly, the $fh*eb$ term in the $(4,4)$ entry is removed by multiplying every other nonzero term in the fourth row by $(fh*eb)*$, and the elements in the fifth row is multiplied by $(h*ebf)*$ to get rid of the loop.

Applying this method of characterizing all possible paths is straightforward. The above operations are interpreted in terms of the arithmetic appropriate to the weights used. Note, however, that if you are working with predicates and you want the logical function (predicate function, truth-value function) between every node and every other node, this may lead to loops in the logical functions. The specific "arithmetic" for handling predicate loops has not been discussed in this book. The information can be found in any good text on switching and automata theory, such as MILL66. Code that leads to predicate loops is not very nice, not well structured, hard to understand, and harder to test—and anyone who codes that way deserves the analytical difficulties arising therefrom. Predicate loops come about from declared or undeclared program switches and/or unstructured loop constructs. This means that the routine's code remembers. If you didn't realize that you put such a loop in, you probably didn't intend to. If you did intend it, you should have expected the loop.

5.5. Partitioning Algorithm (BEIZ71, SOHO84)

Consider any graph over a transitive relation. The graph may have loops. We would like to partition the graph by grouping nodes in such a way that every loop is contained within one group or another. Such a graph is partly ordered. There are many used for an algorithm that does that:

1. We might want to embed the loops within a subroutine so as to have a resulting graph which is loop-free at the top level.
2. Many graphs with loops are easy to analyze if you know where to break the loops.
3. While you and I can recognize loops, it's much harder to program a tool to do it unless you have a solid algorithm on which to base the tool.

The way to do this is straightforward. Calculate the following matrix: $(A + I)^n \# (A + I)^{nT}$. This groups the nodes into strongly connected sets of nodes such that the sets are partly ordered. Furthermore, every such set is an equivalence class so that any one node in it represents the set. Now consider all the places in this book where we said "except for graphs with loops" or "assume a loop-free graph" or words to that effect. If you can bury the loop in a real subroutine, you can as easily bury it in a conceptual subroutine. Do the analysis over the partly ordered graph obtained by the partitioning algorithm and treat each loop-connected node set as if it is a subroutine to be examined in detail later. For each such component, break the loop and repeat the process. You now have a divide-and-conquer approach for handling loops. Here's an example, worked with an arbitrary graph:

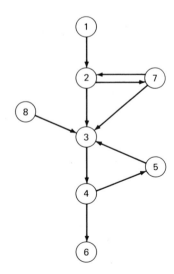

The relation matrix is

1	1						
	1	1					1
		1	1				
			1	1	1		
		1		1			
					1		
	1	1				1	
		1					1

The transitive closure matrix is

1	1	1	1	1	1	1	
	1	1	1	1	1	1	
		1	1	1	1		
		1	1	1	1		
		1	1	1	1		
					1		
	1	1	1	1	1	1	
		1	1	1	1		1

Intersection with its transpose yields

1							
	1					1	
		1	1	1			
		1	1	1			
		1	1	1			
					1		
	1					1	
							1

You can recognize equivalent nodes by simply picking a row (or column) and searching the matrix for identical rows. Mark the nodes that match the pattern as you go and eliminate that row. Then start again from the top with another row and another pattern. Eventually, all rows have been grouped. The algorithm leads to the following equivalent node sets:

$$A = [1]$$
$$B = [2,7]$$
$$C = [3,4,5]$$
$$D = [6]$$
$$E = [8]$$

whose graph is

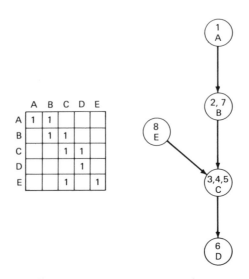

	A	B	C	D	E
A	1	1			
B		1	1		
C			1	1	
D				1	
E			1		1

5.6. Breaking Loops And Applications

And how do you find the point at which to break the loops, you ask? Easy. Consider the matrix of a strongly connected subgraph. If there are entries on the principal diagonal, then start by breaking the loop for those links. Now consider successive powers of the matrix. At some power or another, a loop is manifested as an entry on the principal diagonal. Furthermore, the regular expression over the link names that appears in the diagonal entry tells you all the places you can or must break the loop. Another way is to apply the node-reduction algorithm (see below), which will also display the loops and therefore the desired break points.

The divide-and-conquer, or rather partition-and-conquer, properties of the equivalence partitioning algorithm is a basis for implementing tools. The problem with most algorithms is that they are computationally intensive and require of the order of n^2 or n^3 arithmetic operations, where n is the number of nodes. Even with fast, cheap computers it's hard to keep up with such growth laws. The key to solving big problems (hundreds of nodes) is to partition them into a hierarchy of smaller problems. If you can go far enough, you can achieve processing of the order of n, which is fine. The partition algorithm makes graphs into trees, which are relatively easy to handle.

6.   NODE-REDUCTION ALGORITHM

6.1.   General

The matrix powers usually tell us more than we want to know about most graphs. In the context of testing, we're usually interested in establishing a relation between two nodes—typically the entry and exit nodes—rather than between every node and every other node. In a debugging context it is unlikely that we would want to know the path expression between every node and every other node; there also, it is the path expression or some other related expression between a specific pair of nodes that is sought: for example, "How did I get *here* from *there*?" The method of this section is a matrix equivalence to the node-by-node reduction procedure of Chapter 8. The advantage of the matrix-reduction method is that it is more methodical than the graphical method of Chapter 8 and does not entail continually redrawing the graph. It's done as follows:

1. Select a node for removal; replace the node by equivalent links that bypass that node and add those links to the links they parallel.
2. Combine the parallel terms and simplify as you can.
3. Observe loop terms and adjust the outlinks of every node that had a self-loop to account for the effect of the loop.
4. The result is a matrix whose size has been reduced by 1. Continue until only the two nodes of interest exist.

6.2.   Some Matrix Properties

If you numbered the nodes of a graph from 1 to n, you would not expect that the behavior of the graph or the program that it represents would change if you happened to number the nodes differently. Node numbering is arbitrary and cannot affect anything. The equivalent to renumbering the nodes of a graph is to interchange the rows and columns of the corresponding matrix. Say that you wanted to change the names of nodes i and j to j and i, respectively. You would do this on the graph by erasing the names and rewriting them. To interchange node names in the matrix, you must interchange both the corresponding rows and the corresponding columns. Interchanging the names of nodes 3 and 4 in the graph of Figure 12.1g results in the following:

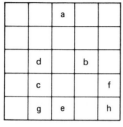
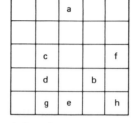
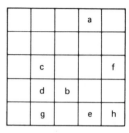

a) Original   b) Rows 3 and 4 interchanged   c) Interchange complete

If you redraw the graph based on c, you will see that it is identical to the original except that node 3's name has been changed to 4, and node 4's name to 3.

6.3. The Algorithm

The first step is the most complicated one: eliminating a node and replacing it with a set of equivalent links. Using the example of Figure 12.1g, we must first remove the self-loop at node 5. This produces the following matrix:

		a		
	d		b	
	c			f
	h*g	h*e		

The reduction is done one node at a time by combining the elements in the last column with the elements in the last row and putting the result into the entry at the corresponding intersection. In the above case, the f in column 5 is first combined with $h*g$ in column 2, and the result $(fh*g)$ is added to the c term just above it. Similarly, the f is combined with $h*e$ in column 3 and put into the 4,3 entry just above it. The justification for this operation is that the column entry specifies the links entering the node, whereas the row specifies the links leaving the node. Combining every column entry with the corresponding row entries for that node produces exactly the same result as the node-elimination step in the graphical-reduction procedure. What we did was: $a_{45}a_{52} = a_{42}$ or $f \times h*g = a_{52}$, but because there was already a c term there, we have effectively created a parallel link in the (5,2) position leading to the complete term of $c + fh*g$. The matrix resulting from this step is

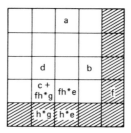

If any loop terms had occurred at this point, they would have been taken care of by eliminating the loop term and premultiplying every term in that row by the loop term starred. There are no loop terms at this point. The next node to be removed is node 4. The b term in the (3,4) position will combine with the (4,2) and (4,3) terms to yield a (3,2) and a (3,3) term, respectively. Carrying this out and discarding the unnecessary rows and columns yields

		a
	d + bc + bfh*g	bfh*e

Removing the loop term yields

		a
	(bfh*e)* × (d + bc + bfh*g)	

There is only one node to remove now, node 3. This will result in a term in the (1,2) entry whose value is

$$a(bfh*e)*(d + bc + bfh*g)$$

This is the path expression from node 1 to node 2. Stare at this one for awhile before you object to the $(bfh*e)*$ term that multiplies the d; any fool can see the direct path via d from node 1 to the exit, but you could miss the fact that the routine could circulate around nodes 3, 4, and 5 before it finally took the d link to node 2.

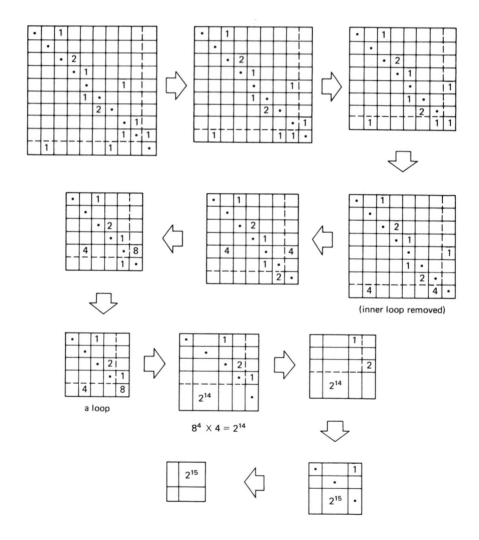

(inner loop removed)

a loop

$8^4 \times 4 = 2^{14}$

6.4. Applications

6.4.1. General

The path expression is usually the most difficult and complicated to get. The arithmetic rules for most applications are simpler. In this section we'll redo applications from Chapter 8, using the appropriate arithmetic rules, but this time using matrices rather than graphs. Refer back to the corresponding examples in Chapter 8 to follow the successive stages of the analysis.

6.4.2. Maximum Number of Paths

The matrix corresponding to the graph on page 261 is on the opposite page. The successive steps are shown. Recall that the inner loop about nodes 8 and 9 was to be taken from zero to three times, while the outer loop about nodes 5 and 10 was to be taken exactly four times. This will affect the way the diagonal loop terms are handled.

6.4.3. The Probability of Getting There

A matrix representation for the probability problem on page 268 is

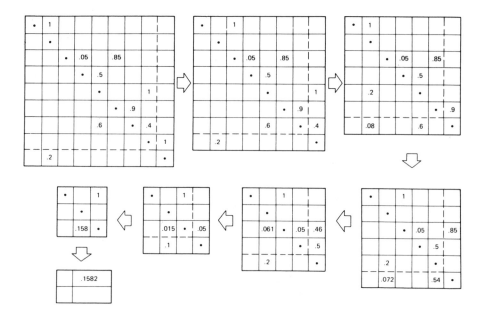

6.4.4. Get/Return Problem

The GET/RETURN problem on page 276 has the following matrix reduction:

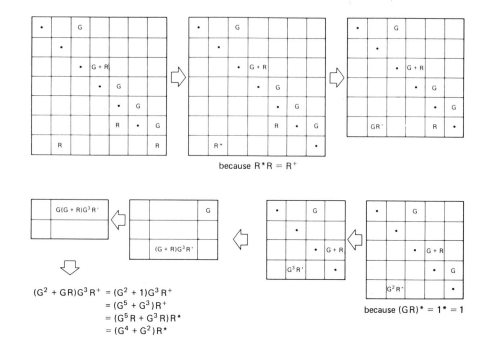

because $R*R = R^+$

because $(GR)* = 1* = 1$

$$(G^2 + GR)G^3 R^+ = (G^2 + 1)G^3 R^+$$
$$= (G^5 + G^3)R^+$$
$$= (G^5 R + G^3 R)R*$$
$$= (G^4 + G^2)R*$$

6.5. Some Hints

Redrawing the matrix over and over again is as bad as redrawing the graph to which it corresponds. You actually do the work in place. Things get more complicated, and expressions get bigger as you progress, so you make the low-numbered boxes larger than the boxes corresponding to higher-numbered nodes, because those are the ones that are going to be removed first. Mark the diagonal lightly so that you can easily see the loops. With these points in mind, the work sheet for the timing analysis graph on page 272 looks like this:

	171.2143 (1)	61.5 (1)			
	60 109.71 (.7) (1.0)	116 (.3)	10 (1)		
	50 (.7)	106 (.3)	20 (.6)	13 43 (.4) (1)	8 (1)
	7 (.7)	63 (.3)			
			12 (.6)	5 (.4)	

This may appear difficult to follow, but it becomes obvious when you try it out for yourself. A lot of tedium can be saved by judicious node numbering. Leave complicated, knotty areas until last so that you won't have to carry a whole lot of nasty terms all through the analysis. And because the last node to be removed is node 2 in the matrix, I've made it a practice to label the first node in the graph "node 1" and the last node in the graph "node 2," as I've usually done throughout this book.

7. BUILDING TOOLS

7.1. Matrix Representation in Software

7.1.1. Overview

We draw graphs or display them on screens as visual objects; we prove theorems and develop graph algorithms by using matrices; and when we want to process graphs in a computer, because we're building tools, we represent them as linked lists. We use linked lists because graph matrices are usually very sparse; that is, the rows and columns are mostly empty.

7.1.2. Node Degree and Graph Density

The **out-degree** of a node is the number of outlinks it has. The **in-degree** of a node is the number of inlinks it has. The **degree** of a node is the sum of the out-degree and in-degree. The average degree of a node (the mean over all nodes) for a typical graph defined over software is between 3 and 4. The degree of a simple branch is 3, as is the degree of a simple junction. The degree of a loop, if wholly contained in one statement, is only 4. A mean node degree of 5 or 6 say, would be a very busy flowgraph indeed.

7.1.3. What's Wrong with Arrays?

We can represent the matrix as a two-dimensional array for small graphs with simple weights, but this is not convenient for larger graphs because:

1. *Space*—Space grows as n^2 for the matrix representation, but for a linked list only as kn, where k is a small number such as 3 or 4.
2. *Weights*—Most weights are complicated and can have several components. That would require an additional weight matrix for each such weight.
3. *Variable-Length Weights*—If the weights are regular expressions, say, or algebraic expressions (which is what we need for a timing analyzer), then we need a two-dimensional string array, most of whose entries would be null.
4. *Processing Time*—Even though operations over null entries are fast, it still takes time to access such entries and discard them. The matrix representation forces us to spend a lot of time processing combinations of entries that we know will yield null results.

The matrix representation *is* useful in building prototype tools based on untried algorithms. It's a lot easier to implement algorithms by using direct matrix representations, especially if you have matrix manipulation subroutines or library functions. Matrices are reasonable to about 20–30 nodes, which is good enough for testing most prototype tools.

7.1.4. Linked-List Representation

Give every node a unique name or number. A link is a pair of node names. The linked list for Figure 12.1g on page 400 is:

1,3;*a*

2,

3,2;*d*

3,4;*b*

4,2;*c*

4,5;*f*

5,2;*g*

5,3;*e*

5,5;*h*

Note that I've put the list entries in lexicographic order. The link names will usually be pointers to entries in a string array where the actual link weight expressions are stored. If the weights are fixed length then they can be associated directly with the links in a parallel, fixed entry–length array. Let's clarify the notation a bit by using node names and pointers.

List Entry	Content
1	node1,3;*a*
2	node2,exit
3	node3,2;*d*
	,4;*b*
4	node4,2;*c*
	,5;*f*
5	node5,2;*g*
	,3;*e*
	,5;*h*

The node names appear only once, at the first link entry. Also, instead of naming the other end of the link, we have just the pointer to the list position in which that node starts. Finally, it is also very useful to have back pointers for the inlinks. Doing this we get

List Entry	Content	List Entry	Content
1	node1,3;*a*	4	node4,2;*c*
2	node2,exit		,5;*f*
	3,	5	3,
	4,		node5,2;*g*
	5,		,3;*e*
3	node3,2;*d*		,5;*h*
	,4;*b*		4,
	1,		5,
	5,		

It's important to keep the lists sorted in lexicographic ordering with the following priorities: node names or pointers, outlink names or pointers, inlink names or pointers. Because the various operations will result in nearly sorted lists, a sort algorithm, such as stringsort, that's optimum for such lists is an essential subroutine.

7.2. Matrix Operations

7.2.1. Parallel Reduction

This is the easiest operation. Parallel links after sorting are adjacent entries with the same pair of node names. For example:

$$\text{node}17,21;x$$
$$,44;y$$
$$,44;z$$
$$,44;w$$

We have three parallel links from node 17 to node 44. We fetch the weight expressions using the y, z, and w pointers and we obtain a new link that is their sum:

$$\text{node}17,21;x$$
$$,44;y \quad \text{(where } y = y + z + w).$$

7.2.2. Loop Reduction

Loop reduction is almost as easy. A loop term is spotted as a self-link. The effect of the loop must be applied to all the outlinks of the node. Scan the link list for the node to find the loop(s). Apply the loop calculation to every outlink, except another loop. Remove that loop. Repeat for all loops about that node. Repeat for all nodes. For example removing node 5's loop:

List Entry	Content		Content After
5	node5,2;g	$\rightarrow$	node5,2;$h*g$
	,3;e	$\rightarrow$	,3;$h*e$
	,5;h	$\rightarrow$	
	4,		4,
	5,		

7.2.3. Cross-Term Reduction

Select a node for reduction (see Section 7.3 below for strategies). The cross-term step requires that you combine every inlink to the node with every outlink from that node. The outlinks are associated with the node you've selected. The inlinks are obtained by using the back pointers. The new links created by removing the node will be associated with the nodes of the inlinks. Say that the node to be removed was node 4.

List Entry	Content Before	
2	node2,exit	node2,exit
	3,	3,
	4,	4,
	5,	5,
3	node3,2;*d*	node3,2;*d*
	,4;*b*	,2;*bc*
		,5;*bf*
	1,	1,
	5,	5,
4	node4,2;*c*	
	,5;*f*	
	3,	
5	node5,2;*h*g*	node5,2;*h*g*
	,3;*h*e*	,3;*h*e*
	4,	

As implemented, you can remove several nodes in one pass if you do careful bookkeeping and keep your pointers straight. The links created by node removal are stored in a separate list which is then sorted and thereafter merged into the master list.

7.2.4. *Addition, Multiplication, and Other Operations*

Addition of two matrices is straightforward. If you keep the lists sorted, then simply merge the lists and combine parallel entries.

Multiplication is more complicated but also straightforward. You have to beat the node's outlinks against the list's inlinks. It can be done in place, but it's easier to create a new list. Again, the list will be in sorted order and you use parallel combination to do the addition and to compact the list.

Transposition is done by reversing the pointer directions, resulting in a list that is not correctly sorted. Sorting that list provides the transpose. All other matrix operations can be easily implemented by sorting, merging, and combining parallels.

7.3. Node-Reduction Optimization

The optimum order for node reduction is to do lowest-degree nodes first. The idea is to get the lists as short as possible as quickly as possible. Nodes of degree 3 (one in and two out or two in and one out) reduce the total link count by one link when removed. A degree-4 node keeps the link count the same, and all higher-degree nodes increase the link count. Although this is not guaranteed, by picking the lowest-degree node available for reduction you can almost prevent unlimited list growth. Because processing is dominated by list length rather than by the number of nodes on the list, this strategy is effective. For large graphs with 500 or more nodes and an average degree of 6 or 7, the difference between not optimizing the node-reduction order and optimizing it was about 50:1 in processing time.

8. Summary

1. Working with pictorial graphs is tedious and a waste of time. Graph matrices are used to organize the work.
2. The graph matrix is the tool of choice for proving things about graphs and for developing algorithms.
3. As implemented in tools, graph matrices are usually represented as linked lists.
4. Most testing problems can be recast into an equivalent problem about some graph whose links have one or more weights and for which there is a problem-specific arithmetic over the link weights. The link-weighted graph is represented by a relation matrix.
5. Relations as abstract operators are well understood and have interesting properties which can be exploited to create efficient algorithms. Properties of interest include transitivity, reflexivity, symmetry, asymmetry, and antisymmetry. These properties in various combinations define ordering, partial ordering, and equivalence relations.
6. The powers of a relation matrix define relations spanning one, two, three, and up to the maximum number of links that can be included in a path. The powers of the matrix are the primary tool for finding properties that relate any node to any other node.
7. The transitive closure of the matrix is used to define equivalence classes and to convert an arbitrary graph into a partly ordered graph.

8. The node reduction algorithm first presented in Chapter 8 is redefined in terms of matrix operations.
9. There is an old and copious literature on graph matrices and associated algorithms. Serious tool builders should learn that literature lest they waste time reinventing ancient algorithms or on marginally useful heuristics.

13

IMPLEMENTATION

1. SYNOPSIS

Testing within the software development process. Programmers versus independent testers. Self-test strategies for programmers. Data sources and strategies for testers. Tests as products. Test execution automation and test design automation tools.

2. OVERVIEW

2.1. General

This chapter concerns the testing process and how to apply the techniques discussed in the previous chapters. It is not intended to be a comprehensive discussion of how test techniques are used in the real world—that is a process question and the subject of another book. This chapter puts test techniques into perspective with testing as it is, and should be, done.

2.2. Who Does What Kind of Tests

2.2.1. The Testing Spectrum

Testing is divided into three main phases: (1) unit and component testing, (2) integration testing, and (3) system testing. The phases are not distinct; rather, they represent points along a continuous spectrum of test activities that start with unit testing and end with field testing. Both structural and functional test techniques can and should be applied in all three phases; however, there is a higher concentration of structural techniques for units and components and, conversely, system testing is mostly functional.

428

2.2.2. Component Testing

Component testing is firmly in the programmers' hands. In an attempt to improve the software development process, there have been experiments aimed at determining whether component testing should be done by programmers and, if so, to what extent. These experiments have ranged from no programmer component testing at all to total control of all testing by the designer. The consensus, as measured by successful projects (rather than by toy projects in benign environments) puts component testing and responsibility for software quality firmly in the programmer's hands.

2.2.3. System Testing

System testing is less firmly in the independent testers' hands. There are three stages of organizational development with respect to system testing and who does it.

1. *Stage 1: Preconscious*—The preconscious phase is marked by total ignorance of independent testing. It's business as usual, as it's been done for decades. It works for small projects (four to five programmers) and rapidly becomes catastrophic as project size and program complexity increases. Today, most software development is still dominated by this state of happy ignorance.
2. *Stage 2: Independent Testing*—Independent testing marks most successful project of more than 50K lines of new code. Independent system testing is a feature of many government software development specifications. This testing typically includes detailed requirements testing, most dirty testing, stress testing, and system testing areas such as performance, recovery, security, and configuration.
3. *Stage 3: Enlightened Self-Testing*—Some software development groups that have implemented a successful stage 2 process have returned system testing responsibility to the designers and done away with independent testing. This is not a reactionary move but an enlightened move. It has worked in organizations where the ideas and techniques of testing and software quality assurance have become so thoroughly embedded in the culture that they have become unquestioned software development paradigms. The typical prerequisites for enlightened self-testing are 5–10 years of effective independent testing with a continual circulation of personnel between design and test responsibility. Enlightened self-testing may superficially appear to be the same as the preconscious state, but it is not. Component testing is as good as it can be, a metrics-driven process,

and real quality assurance (as distinct from mere words) is integral to the culture. Attempts, such as they are, to leapfrog stage 2 and go directly from stage 1 to stage 3 have usually been disastrous: the result is a stage 1 process embedded in stage 2 buzzwords. It seems that stage 2 is an essential step to achieve the quality acculturation prerequisite to a stage 3 process.

4. *Beyond Stage 3*—As you might guess, some successful stage 3 groups are looking beyond it and a return to independent testing. Are we doomed to a cyclic process treadmill? Probably not. What we're seeing is a reaction to an imperfectly understood process. Eventually, we will learn how to relate the characteristics of a software product and the developing culture to the most effective balance between enlightened self-testing and independent testing.

2.2.4. Integration Testing

Integration is a no-man's land. Part of the problem is that in many groups it is hopelessly confused with system testing—where "integration testing" is used synonymously with "testing the integrated system." With such semantic confusion, there can be no integration testing worthy of the name.

Assuming that "integration testing" is used as I've defined it, as testing the interfaces and interactions between otherwise functionally and structurally correct components, where on the self-test/independent-test axis should integration testing be placed? I don't know.

It's clear that programmers should integrate their own work—is it possible for them to do otherwise? But how about integrating the work of several programmers? Low-level integration up to aggregates of about 20,000 lines of code is usually done by developers. Integration of big components and subsystems from 50,000 lines up is usually done by independent test and integration groups. And for very big software (10 million-plus lines of code) there may be several levels of independent integration groups. But there are no rules or hard facts to tell us where to put this activity. Take your choice: all integration by the developers; separate developers, integration testers, and system testers; all integration of the work of different programmers by an independent integration group.

I've seen all of these strategies and their variations succeed brilliantly or fail miserably. It seems to depend more on culture and history than anything substantive we can measure about software. Similar groups working on similar products (say, minicomputer operating systems) will adopt totally different placements of integration testing, and quality doesn't seem to be affected (for the good or for the bad) by the placement.

We don't understand. Consequently, we should be very cautious in making changes and even more cautious in jumping to conclusions about the effect (good or bad) of the changes we do implement.

2.3. Adversarial Roles

Independent testing, as it has evolved, has taken on adversarial overtones—to put it politely. At the extremes, independent testing is viewed as the programmers' nemesis. This is a sad state of affairs, is counterproductive, and may lead to expensive but bad software. It isn't a testing problem, but a management problem. The warfare mentality results from imposing independent testing on software developers before they're ready for it, or imposing the trappings of independent test and QA with no real intention of changing anything in the process. Consequently, testers are paid less than programmers, viewed as unproductive leeches, overruled by programmers, subordinated to schedule pressures, and otherwise abused. Given that background, is it any wonder that they'll take the opportunities they get to make programmers miserable beyond the needs of software quality?

The independent tester's role *is* adversarial, but that doesn't mean obnoxious. The tester *must* question, *must* be critical, *must* try to break the software, and that will make some (immature) programmers uncomfortable. When independent testing works well, it works in a spirit of cooperation. A delicate balance is achieved in which developers rely on testers to find the problems that they, the developers, despite their best testing efforts, could not find. The developers welcome the independent assault on their product's integrity (but not the developers' integrity) and everyone cheers when a bug is found. The developers welcome the testers' suggestions for design approaches that will lead to more robust, more reliable products. Conversely, the testers don't allow the programmers to abrogate their primary responsibility for quality; they don't permit a "Don't worry about it, the testers will find it" mentality to develop.

3.   STRATEGIES FOR PROGRAMMERS

3.1. Who's Responsible?

Programmers are responsible for software quality—quality in their own work, quality in the products that incorporate their work, and quality at the interfaces between components. Quality has never been and will never be, tested in. The responsibility is both moral and professional.

3.2. Programming in Perspective

3.2.1. Realities

The effectiveness, application, and the specific techniques used are meaningful only in the context of programming as it is done. Here are some realities of contemporary programming that provide a cultural infrastructure over which testing is done.

3.2.2. Cooperative Programming

Contemporary programming is cooperative because the products we build are beyond the ability of individual programmers or even small programming groups. Cooperative programming means that attention must be paid to human interfaces and to processes and procedures that facilitate accurate interpersonal communications. That in turn means that much of a programmer's time is spent doing things that seem to have nothing to do with programming—such as documentation, test planning and execution, inspections, and so on. The day of the lone programmer struggling to build an elegant algorithm is long gone—it's about as germane to programming today as two young bicycle builders (the Wright brothers) are to building a 747. Forget that lone-hacker image if you still cherish it. And if contemporary software engineering with its procedural structure bothers you, if you're blind to the opportunities for expressing your personal creativity within its necessary constraints, if the fast-tight algorithm is still the driving force in your designs—then get out! Find another domain, such as an R&D sandbox or an unreconstructed software shop, in which to play at programming.

3.2.3. Maintenance

Programming is dominated by maintenance rather than new-code production. That's another reality with which many programmers are unhappy. Maintenance is often viewed as the lowest form of work—only jerks, novices, dweebs, and women do it. Reality is that most programmers will spend most of their time modifying and adapting existing software: the new-software development based on a "clean slate" will increasingly become rarer. If that's another fact of programming life that discomfits you, then that's another reason to review your professional aspirations.

   In maintenance, most of your time is spent trying to understand someone else's code; testing to explore behavioral quirks; trying to understand without getting bogged down in structural details; trying to impose behavioral changes without disrupting the design—in other words, adopting an attitude closer to that of an independent tester than a new-code programmer. Maintenance usually means maintenance of someone else's code. And if that isn't independent testing, then I don't know what is.

Unfortunately, our testing theory and techniques are theory and techniques for new-code production rather than for maintenance. Maintenance testing theory is in its infancy (KORE89, LEUN88, LEUN89, POLL87B). In addition to obvious pragmatic differences between maintenance testing and new-code testing, there are also theoretical differences: differences that will lead to new testing techniques and to modifications of existing techniques. Meanwhile, what do we do about maintenance testing? The most important thing you can do is not to throw your tests away. The second thing you can do is not to reject techniques because they seem to be overkill for the maintenance situation, but to adapt the technique and perhaps to overtest while waiting for sharper guidelines to emerge.

3.2.4. Reusability

The ideal of a software equivalent of an integrated-circuit chip has been around as long as software. The barrier to reusable software has never been technical—it's been financial and managerial. Reusable software doesn't get built if no one's willing to pay the price. New languages and programming techniques won't do it—they never have. It takes bucks and guts. Bucks to pay the fivefold extra cost of developing and testing the more generalized, more robust, reusable component; bucks to pay for a protracted development; guts to take the entrepreneurial plunge and assert that there is a market for the component if it is developed.

But reusability seems to be around the corner because bucks and guts are replacing short-term thinking. What will this mean to programming? The most obvious impact is that software developers will spend more of their time integrating reusable components than developing new components. It means that developers will look a lot more like independent testers and integrators.

3.2.5. A New Software Morality

Good software works, meets requirements, is robust, and is easy to understand, easy to integrate, and easy to test. Furthermore, it keeps these qualities over a long period of time because it is a permanent product rather than a transitory one. Software quality has almost nothing to do with algorithmic elegance, compactness, or speed—in fact, *those* attributes do more harm to quality than good. Good algorithms, compactness, and speed *do* matter for a small part of software—such a small part of software that I can safely discount these attributes as having anything to do with quality. Most programmers will never find themselves in a situation where they matter. Unfortunately, most programmers have been led to believe, because of their early training, hacker folklore, and hero myths that led them into programming, their early experiences with toy programs, that "good" means elegant, compact, and fast. Here's a software morality update.

1. *Test*—If you can't test it, don't build it. If you don't test it, rip it out.
2. *Put Testing Up Front*—You can't achieve testability if it's an afterthought that follows design and coding. Tests are as important as code because code is garbage unless it is tested.
3. *Don't Be a Functional Overachiever*—If it isn't called for, don't build it. There's no requirement, therefore no specification, therefore no test criteria, therefore you can't test it. And if you do "test" it, who'll understand?
4. *Don't Put in Private Hooks*—Hooks for future enhancements and functionality are architectural issues. Your hooks won't be consistent with someone else's hooks so they won't be used in the future unless you happen to be the project leader. You can't test the private hooks because there's no supporting data structures or corequisite components. See rule 1.
5. *Decouple*—Don't take advantage of hardware peculiarities, operating system quirks, the compiler, residues left by other components, physical anything, data structure details, environment, processing done by other components. Do what you can to reduce the dependency of your component's proper behavior on the proper behavior or the invariant behavior of other components. Always ask yourself what will happen if the other component is changed. And if coupling is essential, document the potential vulnerability of your component to the continued good graces of the other component.
6. *Don't Squeeze*—Don't squeeze space, time, or schedule. Don't allow shortsighted bosses concerned with next week's progress report or the quarterly stockholders' report to squeeze them for you. If you can't fight them, document your objections and the expected consequences and/or vote with your feet.

3.3. Self-Inspection

3.3.1. General

Inspections (FAGA76) are one of the most cost-effective quality processes. Another truism of programming is that what can be done in public is better if done first in private. That holds for testing and also for inspections. How should programmers inspect their own software and how can a knowledge of testing techniques fit into that inspection process?

3.3.2. Self-Inspection Versus Classical Desk Checking

Classical desk checking was an essential step in the early days of software when programmers might have to wait several months to get enough computer time to even begin testing. The only alternative in those days was extensive manual simulation of the computer—the programmer was expected to "play" computer and to do as good a job as was humanly possible at that gruesome task. People are lousy computers, and the attempted simulation was far from perfect. It was possible only because the scope of most programs in those days would be reckoned as toys by today's standards. There are still today, sadly, many programmers, managers, and organizational cultures that cling to the idea of manual computer simulation as the main test and inspection method.

3.3.3. Objectives of Self-Inspection

If you have a formal inspection methodology in place, then the first objective of self-inspection should be to do, yourself, whatever the inspection process calls for. You will not get the full benefits of an inspection because an essential part of all inspection and review methods is the interactions of other humans and the diversity of viewpoints.

The ground rules of self-inspection should be to do things that humans can do, preferably well, and computers can't, and not to do things that computers can do exquisitely and humans poorly, if at all. Here are some examples:

1. *Syntax Checking*—If humans could do syntax checking, we wouldn't have so many syntax errors. If you do syntax checking well, you probably don't have many syntax errors, and it's not likely that inspecting for syntax errors will reveal anything. If you do have syntax errors, it proves that you're no good at syntax checking, so what do you expect to catch by manual syntax checking?

2. *Cross-Reference Checks*—Check the program for undeclared variables, unreferenced labels, uninitialized values, and so on. This should be done by the source language processor. Unfortunately, some assemblers are notoriously poor in this respect. Humans aren't terrible at this job, but it's a terrible job. Other alternatives: build your own cross-reference generator (not that big a deal); change languages or development environment; vote with your feet.

3. *Convention Violations*—Good projects have conventions for naming variables, labels, subroutines, and so on. The conventions may specify the first few letters of mnemonics and leave the last three to the programmer. Similarly, there may be conventions for the length of the mnemonic, use of numerics, and so on. Stylistic conventions may prohibit certain constructs. Checking for style violations is a form of syntax checking and should be automated, but often it isn't. Agitate for language features and preprocessors that support formal stylistic conventions and the automatic checking thereof. If you don't have such facilities, protect yourself by reducing stylistic freedom within your own routine. Use systematic label naming conventions. Name things so that it will be possible to tell at a glance that something is awry. If automatic facilities are not available, you will have to check it yourself (or better yet, get someone else to check it for you—while you check that person's code) as part of self-inspection. Go through the program one convention at a time, rather than trying to check all conventions simultaneously. It's actually faster and more thorough to methodically read the program ten times for ten different conventions than to attempt to read it once for all ten conventions simultaneously.

4. *Detailed Comparison*—This step went the way of the dinosaur along with keypunching. It was essential that the coding sheet be compared, character by character, to the code on keypunched cards. The main economic justification for doing away with keypunching was the difficulty of this odious, mind-boggling task. Programs should be entered directly at terminals with no humans between the programmer and the compiler. If you have to program in an archaic environment and can't vote with your feet, get a copy of the first edition to see how to do it.

5. *Read Your Code*—Even if you entered the program directly at the terminal or into a PC, there are typing errors that don't violate style or syntax. The persistence of tygopraphical errors is amazing. This book was proofread many times by proofreaders and editors, who are really excellent at it, and yet, tygophraphical errors remain. How many did you find so far? Do this check with a ruler. Expose only

one line at a time. Do it a word at a time, a character at a time, and say the letters, and move your lips as you read. This is no place for glancing or speed-reading. Try it on this paragraph,

Read the code at least four times: for typographical errors, for data structures, for control flow, and for processing. It's easier, faster, and more reliable to read it four times than to try to do it all in one pass.

6. *The Control Flowgraph*—Create the flowgraph from the compiled code and compare it to the design flowgraph or PDL—it's best to use a flowgraph generator. You can't automate the comparison because comparing design intentions as expressed in the original PDL to what was coded and to the flowgraph produced from the code entails notions of equivalence presently beyond the ken of computers.

7. *Path Sensitizing*—The final step in self-inspection should be path sensitizing. Design the paths from the design PDL but attempt to sensitize them from the code. If you can force all the paths you intended, it may prove nothing, but if there are paths or segments in the coded version that appeared to be reasonable in the design but that you cannot force from the code, then you've probably found a bug. Simulate only the part of the processing that you must to sensitize the paths. Once you have successfully found sensitizing values for a branch-covering set of the test paths, you have perforce checked every line of code involved in the control flow and every decision. That is, your self-inspection has achieved branch coverage and you're not likely to learn anything more from self-inspection; get to work running your test cases.

As usual, I've prescribed a procedure that entails a lot of work. It's a trade. Either you do the work now, in a systematic, unpressured way, or you or someone else will have to do it later on the test floor. Or worse, you may have to get up in the middle of the night, when the snow is piled a foot high, and battle your way to the airport so that you can catch the last plane to Frittersville. Remember, "There's never enough time to do it right, but there's always enough time to do it over."

3.4. Test Case Design

Test case design starts when you understand enough of the requirements to design tests. It progresses concurrently with the other two pillars of programming—data structures and code. All three should progress at about the same rate although at times one or the other may be ahead.

Because you start with functionality, your earliest test cases will be based on functional techniques. As design progresses and more structure is revealed, new test cases will take on a structural flavor. Just as you go back and revise data structures to accommodate code and code to match data structures, you should revise tests to reflect changes in data structures and code *and code and data structures to reflect changes in test approaches*. Testing starts when all three areas have been brought to a final level of detail.

3.5. Test Type Priority

Although there is a heavier reliance on structural methods, most of your initial tests will have a functional outlook—tests against specified requirements. Design and run these first and worry about coverage later. If your software is clean and testable, then covering the requirements will also achieve high structural coverage for any coverage metric or technique you use. A coverage monitor tool is essential. The order in which you design tests should be roughly as follows:

1. Clean tests against requirements.
2. Additional structural tests for branch coverage, as needed.
3. Additional tests for data-flow coverage as needed.
4. Domain tests not covered by the above.
5. Special techniques as appropriate—syntax, loop, state, etc.
6. Any dirty tests not covered by the above.

A coverage monitor appropriate to the techniques you use is essential if you're to avoid a lot of unrevealing, redundant tests. Tools such as reported by Weyuker (WEYU88A) let you test in whatever order you wish from whatever point of view you like, but provide you with continual information of what has and hasn't been covered under which criteria.

3.6. Learn to "Cheat"

The objective of an independent test suite is to break the program and the objective of the program is to break the test suite. How does a programmer "break" a test suite, you ask? You break the test suite if it fails to reveal bugs. You break the test suite when it's built on test techniques that don't work against your design. The same holds for inspections and reviews. You break those when they don't reveal bugs. As a programmer you have the right to know what new tests will be thrown against your software by independent testers—just as they have a right to know your source code so that they can pick at the vulnerable spots. Every test technique carries within it the seeds of its own futility. You cheat by exploiting such weaknesses. You want to make branch testing ridiculous? Don't have unachievable paths. You want domain testing to fail? Do explicit domain analysis. You want to make mincemeat out of syntax testing? Build a table-driven parser. There isn't a sneaky trick in the tester's repertoire that you can't outmaneuver. But remember that with automated regression testing and permanent test products, you won't be able to cheat by going back to design practices that were caught by earlier testing strategies. You should assume that all previous tests will be run.

4. STRATEGIES FOR INDEPENDENT TESTERS

4.1. General

Independent testing is 50% digging, 25% test design and execution, and 25% for the rest. "Digging" means digging into the data structure, the code, the requirements, and the programmer's mind. The purpose of digging is to learn where your limited test resources will be best spent—to find the points at which the software's most likely to be most vulnerable.

4.2. Database Gold

4.2.1. General

Data structure documents, especially the data dictionary, are the richest source of test ideas. They are also the resource most often underutilized by independent testers. If there is no centrally administered, configuration-controlled data dictionary or the equivalent, then the data structure is where you should concentrate, and you might think that you have to create the data structure document yourself. Don't fall into that trap. If there's no data dictionary, the project is down the tubes. Do only as much data analysis as you need to prove the point.

The principles of database-driven testing are simple:

1. Examine every functionally significant data object for conformance to the system's functional objectives.
2. Find all contradictions in the database and get them resolved by the designers.
3. Design tests to confirm that the knottier contradictions have been properly resolved.

If you had to do the above completely, it would be an endless task. Be comfortable with the thought that the method will pay off statistically and that the greatest value is bug prevention rather than bugs caught. You can work in a functional area for weeks, catch dozens of problems, earn your pay several times over in prevented bugs, and yet not design a single test.

4.2.2.   Simple Fields and Parameters

Simple fields don't depend on other fields, they have individual meanings, and they can be easily related back to functional requirements. All the checks that applied to data in individual-routine testing, such as in path sensitizing, or in domain testing apply here. Because these fields relate to the functional requirements in a direct way, given a field value, it should be straightforward to design a transaction that will force that value to occur and to design domain boundary tests.

1. *Numerical Fields*—Domain boundary values: minimum, less than minimum, one more than minimum, typical, one less than maximum, maximum, one more than maximum, excluded values, and boundaries near excluded values. Use off-points for floating-point variables.
2. *Bit Fields*—All 2^n combinations are not needed: one bit set at a time, one bit reset at a time, none set, and all set.
3. *Case Control Fields*—All cases.
4. *Structural Boundary Checks*—What you test depends on how the computer accesses data. Say it's a 32-bit machine with word, half-word, and character addressing. Any field that doesn't fit on one of these natural boundaries should be given additional checks for values that come close, especially for values that could cause overflow into an adjacent word. Variable-length fields should be tested with values that force the minimum and maximum length and try to exceed the maximum length. If field-access macros are used or if the source language is strongly typed, this kind of check will prove little or nothing.

4.2.3.   Semantic Shifts

A **semantic shift** occurs when the same object means different things to different people—a common source of bugs. You find this in the database check when a field has two different names and has been equated by an equate statement in the declarations. For example, say that you have a security field and a priority field, and that they have been equated. Because they refer to what appears to be different functional requirements, it is apparent that there is a difference of opinion over the field's meaning.*

Excavating semantic shifts is not a machine job because we have no computers that can say that "security" and "priority" are or are not the same. They might be in some systems or even in some parts of one system and not in another part of the same system. When you spot what appears to be a semantic shift, try to find a counterexample from the users' point of view: a low-priority high-security input, for example. Any combination that does not match the equated values must be explained by the designers. If the boundary values and excluded values do not match exactly, you can be sure that it's a real bug. Barring obvious inconsistencies, the history of the semantic shift can give you insight into what kinds of tests to design. Here are some possible histories for semantic shifts:

1. There was a time, earlier in the project, when the semantic shift did not exist; the separation of the two functions occurred later. There should be two different fields, which the counterexamples should spot.

2. There were two fields originally and the designers knew it. They examined all combinations and came to the conclusion that they could equate the values, even though it didn't make functional sense. They could do it, but a routine here and there had to be "adjusted," to make the match work. It's a bad idea. It'll be a hellish maintenance task in the future. Furthermore, there will be at least one programmer who's working under the assumption that the two fields are different. Test with counterexamples and combinations that "just can't happen."

3. The confusion is caused by bad specifications. For example, the specification discusses both input and output formats under the heading of "format" and assumes that you know that they are not identical. Or else, the difference is referred to in a subsection under "Operator Training." Because neither the input- nor output-processing designer reads the section on operator training, it's no wonder the semantic shift gets in.

---

* The most dramatic semantic shift I ever saw caused a multimillion-dollar rocket and satellite to destroy themselves on the launch pad. A hardware designer saw two switches, the first labeled "initiate final-stage separation sequence," the other labeled "initiate *test* of final-stage separation sequence." He wired them in parallel in an attempt to improve reliability. During the countdown, when they started the final-stage checkout: the final-stage rockets ignited, the protective covers flew off the satellite, and it sprouted antennae and tried to go into orbit—a hundred feet off the ground. Semantic shifts are like that.

4. People don't talk the same language. What do "vector," "index," "queue," "pointer," "benchmark," "overlay," "executive," "direct," "indirect," and "random" mean to you? I've run into at least two different meanings for each of these terms—sometimes on the same project. One person uses the phrase "indirect input vector pointer," another uses "indirect vector input pointer," a third person uses "indirect pointer input vector," or "input vector indirect pointer"—see what I mean? Then the database coordinator equates them all—glorious bug.

The worst semantic shifts occur between specifications and designers—so the design is consistent, but wrong. Treat the specification as if it were written in a foreign language and translated into English by a person who understood neither the foreign language nor English, nor the application. Distrust jargon—it's likelier to be local than universal. Translate technicalities into English (or your native language). Ask all parties to the equate what "indirect pointer vector input" really means in functional terms. Be *very* stupid and dense when you ask such questions. People may be impatient at first, but after a while they'll realize that you're not so stupid after all.

Semantic shifts are uncommon, but they deserve attention because they are very expensive. They tend to have ugly diffused implications, and correcting them may mean modifying many routines, the database, or fundamental design assumptions. If you don't catch them now, they'll probably remain in the system until the customer's acceptance test is run.

4.2.4. Type Changes

When a field is accessed in different ways, under different structural assumptions, there has been a type change (e.g., when a field is treated as a bit field, character field, or integer in several different parts of a program). Any type change is suspect, although it may not be a bug. The only nice thing about type changes is that usually you're able to spot them because two fields, which are described as different (e.g., bit versus character) but occupy the same space, are equated. Given these elementary kinds of type changes, you should look for a more basic semantic shift behind it.

4.2.5. Representation Changes

A functional object is represented in several different ways in the database. For example, you could have a case variable that specified priority as high, medium, low, and routine. Elsewhere in the database there is a numerical priority field and priorities are listed as 1 to 12. In a third place, it is a binary field with four priority bits. They all appear to refer to "priority," but they appear to be incompatible. Ask:

1. Are the total number of cases the same? If not, why not?
2. Are the excluded values the same?
3. Can you arrange them in a consistent manner, one for one, with the excluded values corresponding?
4. Do all the values correspond to functionally meaningful cases?

If you have three fields, check this three ways: A against B, B against C, and A against C. For four fields make six sets of comparisons. In general, do all pairwise comparisons.

Representation changes are not necessarily bugs. The fourth question is the key. You might find six external priorities, but sixteen internal priorities, some of which match the external ones and some of which don't. Furthermore, the internal priority of a transaction type might not be consistent with the external priority, but this does not mean there is a bug. For example, external priorities could be deliberately reversed for some phases of internal processing in the interest of processing efficiency or some other technical consideration. Although there may be no bug, representation changes are confusing, so programmers could make mistakes with respect to one representation or another. Use test cases that force apparent reversals, inconsistent boundary values, and inconsistent excluded values.

4.2.6. Splatters, Mergers, and Overlaps

Several fields are defined that cover the same physical space. There is a semantic shift and also a structure change. Field A is the lower 3 bits of one word. Field B is the upper 4 bits of the adjacent word, and C is some field that includes all or part of both of them, and all of them appear to relate to things that have functional significance. Ask:

1. Are the domains of the fields consistent?
2. Can you force cases that correspond to the inconsistencies?
3. Find functional cases that do not fit the overlap. What prevents these impossible transactions?

4.2.7. Access Method Differences

Access method differences apply to tables that have multiple entries and multiple fields per entry. You can access such tables in one of two ways:

use an offset that corresponds to the field location within the entry and increment by entry size, or go to the entry and then access the specific field. A routine that accesses a single field of all entries uses the first method, whereas a routine that accesses several fields in the same entry uses the second method. Access method differences are not usually bugs. Furthermore, that kind of simple access method change may be very difficult to spot in the database documentation. You can spot this sort of change when the entries and fields are accessed by an index or by a combination of direct access and indexes. The key is to find all the indexes or pointers by which the field is accessed. This is documented explicitly in a proper database dictionary or is supplied automatically through the use of field-access macros. In a higher-order language, the method of documentation, if any, may be more difficult to spot. You play the same game with the pointers that you play with individual fields: minimum and maximum boundaries, excluded values, and so on. Boundary mismatches are not necessarily bugs, but they should be investigated.

4.2.8. Dynamic Resources

Dynamically allocated resources have many uses. Each usage has an associated set of field definitions. But some fields, such as link fields, status fields, image disc addresses, and other administrative fields are common to all uses. Typically, for any one resource, it is possible to describe a tree of nested data structures. The top of the tree has only those fields that are common to all uses. The next level down has the first kind of split, and so on, as shown in Figure 13.1.

Most of the fields will correspond to internal things and are therefore not good sources of questions. You can't tell which routines will use a given format without looking at the code, but it's a safe bet that formats that are close to one another on the tree will be used for similar, and possibly interactive, purposes. Look for the same functional objects stored in different ways or in different places in nearby objects. For example, a priority field is always represented as a two-character field in a half-dozen different objects that are on the same tree branches, but in several places it appears in a different part of the object. It would be better if they were in the same location throughout, but if they're not, there's a likelihood of confusion over which version to use where. Explore the use of the resource for each such field with the designers and see whether you can create a transaction that will use more than one of these objects. Use this as a starting point and continue to investigate conflicting locations farther and farther away on the tree. If you find a conflicting location for a

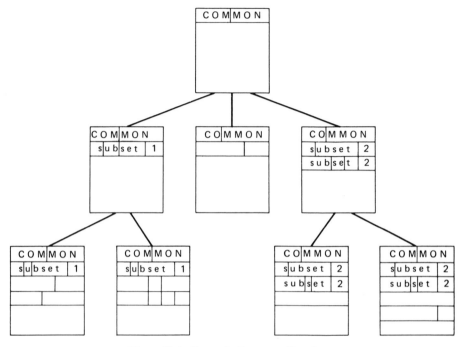

Figure 13.1. Dynamic Resource Structure.

functional field and you can create a transaction that uses both of the conflicting locations, include that transaction in your test.

4.2.9.   Version Changes

All changes in the data dictionary should be flagged from version to version. You cannot just look at the data dictionary once; like the programmers, you must check to see whether any fields have changed in a way that is likely to cause trouble. Don't do this for all fields—only for those that have direct functional meaning. You should be tracking them anyhow to see if there have been any functional changes that would necessitate new test cases or obviate old ones. Read the database and look for the changes. Compare the old version to the new. Pay special attention to reserved fields that are no longer reserved; to fields that were "to be determined" and have now been determined; to cases and values that are newly defined; and especially to cases, fields, and values that were defined and are no longer defined.

4.3. Reading Code and Other Design Documents

There's a common but misguided point of view among programmers and testers that independent testers should not have access to source code because that's "unfair" or might inadvertently subvert their objectivity. What's supposed to be "fair" about dirty testing? We're not playing kid games—we're out to bust software and we're not going to do that if we have to be "fair" (read "ignorant"). As for bias, any tester who's so weak-willed as to be swayed by a little judicious code reading doesn't belong in independent testing. An independent tester's main job is bug prevention. In that capacity, she *must* be a critic. It is only by looking at the code that the tester can spot the bad designs. Testing is aimed at those places in the design where you feel that the designers have not been responsive to quality issues.

Looking at code and other design documents is also a source of quality assurance over the quality of the tests themselves. If you're a good tester and critic and the designers respond to your criticism by design changes, then your critical ability is confirmed. If they don't change the design and your tests based on that fact breaks the software, again your critical ability is confirmed. But if they don't change and the software ignores your tests, then you have been given essential feedback that will guide to the future production of more revealing tests—you can't lose.

4.4. Requirements

I've left requirements as a data source until last because that the obvious place to start functional test design. Specification systems and tools or some other means of automating the entire requirements list (or cross-reference matrix) is essential. No magic here. No avoiding it either. The whole list must be tested in detail, or the requirement doesn't work. But if you had a choice between cutting dirty tests and an equal number of clean tests, the rational place to cut is the clean tests because you can be reasonably sure that the designers have tried the easy cases many times. Some tests are marginal in the sense that they're not dirty, but they correspond to weird or anomalous conditions which could theoretically happen. Again, cut the normal cases before the anomalous cases.*

---

* Poston's law (Bob Poston of Programming Environments Inc.) is: "The percentage of test cases classified as anomalous by designers increases as the shipping date approaches."

4.5. Tests and the Threat of Tests

A good threat is worth a thousand tests. Another common myth of independent testing is that the designers shouldn't be allowed to see the test cases because they might ''cheat.'' Children's games again. You *want* them to cheat and invalidate your tests! That's the point of it all! You have limited resources, though, and you know that you can think of many more test cases than you have time or resources to implement. Develop and publish your cases in a series of increasingly more detailed documents. An early test plan might have only a one-line description of a test case that could take several days to detail and test. You can go into a lot of detail without executing the actual test and spending the time or resources. That's what I mean by a good threat. It's like the professor who gives you a list of 1000 questions and say's that 20 of them will be on the final exam—and that's about the ratio you should strive to achieve—fifty to one, fifty threatened tests for each actual test run. It's testing leverage.

Good techniques for producing massive threats are syntax testing, domain boundary crossings, feature interactions, state testing, and predicate truth value combinations.

5. TESTS AS SOFTWARE PRODUCTS

5.1. Throwaway Tests?

Here's a proposal for programmers: when you've got the software installed and running to the users' satisfaction, throw away the documentation and especially the source because the computer only needs object to run. Insane? If it's an insane proposal for code, why is it a common practice for half of the labor content—tests? Why do programmers throw away their test cases and test databases once the tests are run? Why are independent tests only documented on paper? Why is half of the product thrown away? Who's insane?

5.2. Tests, Subtests, Scripts, and Suites

If you're going to be rational and treat tests as permanent objects then you'll need as formal a method of keeping track of them as you use for code. The lowest level is a **subtest,** which is the testing equivalent of a line of code. Subtests are grouped into **tests,** which must be run as a set, typically because the outcome of one subtest is the input or the initial condition for the next subtest in the test. Tests can be run independently of one another but are typically defined over the same database. A **test suite** is a set of related tests, usually pertaining to a group of features or software component and usually defined over the same database. Suites are combined into **groups.** I've found that the four-level hierarchy was essential for most testing. Other testers have used five- or six-level groupings.

Just as you establish programming conventions you must have test conventions that define documentation standards, mnemonics, versions, and all the rest. Tests must be treated as if they are code in a real or hypothetical scripting language.

5.3. Test Configuration Control

Test configuration control is more complicated than software configuration control because there are more factors to consider and more variations. I'll assume that the suite is the basic configuration-controlled test object.

1. *Software Configuration Control History*—Test suites target configuration-controlled software products, but for functional tests they may be used against several different products. The suite must point to the products it tested and the product must point to the suite(s) that tested it.
2. *Suite Configuration Data*—The suite is a product in its own right and therefore needs a version number, release number, dates, authorization, and so on, exactly as for software.
3. *Test Database Configuration Data*—The supporting test database often entails as much labor as test suite design. Furthermore, a given test database may be used for different suite versions and a given suite version may be used with several different test databases. Typically, it pays to control the test databases as objects separate from the suites. Suites and databases must point to each other.
4. *Test Bed Configuration*—This includes many things: hardware physical configuration, platform software configuration, operating system version, sysgen details, test terminals, test tools, etc. It must be possible to precisely recreate the entire test situation or else it may be impossible to resolve some of the nastiest configuration-dependent bugs that show up in the field. That means that *everything* that impinges on testing must be configuration-controlled.

6. TOOLS

6.1. General

Testing is tool-intensive and will become more so as time goes on. Almost all current research in test techniques leads to methods that cannot be implemented by hand except by the most dedicated or desperate testers. Therefore, testing requires an investment in testing tools. One can question whether or not the return on that investment (especially the investment in tool usage training) is worth the cost. The only survey we know of was done in Japan by Nomura (NOMU87). This survey of 200 Japanese software development groups rated test tools as having the highest productivity return: ahead of a standard process, ahead of CASE, ahead of programming and design tools, and ahead of reviews.

The decade or so that elapsed between the writing of the first edition of this book and the current edition has been marked by a rapid and radical change in the way testing is done. Previously, testing was manual. Such tools that existed were mostly in the research phase. Few commercial products existed and it was difficult to predict which research products would come into general use. The situation has now stabilized to the point where many of the past uncertainties have been resolved.

As of this writing there is a sharp trichotomy between private, commercial, and research tools. Advanced testing techniques are all tool-intensive, and consequently most testing researchers build tools that embody their strategies. Some of these tools are very sophisticated and powerful, but they have yet to be implemented on a commercial platform. Private noncommercial tool development dominates the scene. The testing leaders have tool development groups that incorporate research results, internal developments, and past experience into tools that suit their specific testing environments. Most of these tools are too application-, environment-, or culture-specific to warrant export to a wider domain. Nor do the leaders want to make these tools available because they correctly see the tool and the software testing techniques embodied in the tool as a significant contribution to their competitive edge. Some of the best tools are unpublished and likely to remain so. For general surveys of tools and their use see FAIR81, FREN88, MILL86, NOMU87, and OSTE81.

The commercial situation for tools is still dynamic, especially in the case of unit test tools based on path testing. It is not possible to survey tools in depth in this book because of potentially rapid obsolescence. For such information, consult a periodical commercial tools guide such as DATA90 or SQET90. Test tools have evolved with generic features, which are discussed below. Recognize, though, that any specific commercial tool may implement some, all, or none of the features discussed below. Every service provided by the tools can be had without them and our earlier, manual testing experience showed that despite the labor, these were things worth doing—with or without the tools.

6.2. Fundamental Tools

6.2.1. Coverage Certifiers

A **coverage certifier** or **coverage monitor** records the amount (and type) of coverage achieved by a set of test cases over the same component. Coverage certifiers are also the oldest known test tools (HIRS67, WARN64): they have been in routine use at IBM, among others, for more than two decades. Coverage certifiers are usually integrated with a test driver or within a comprehensive test environment. Branch coverage is generally done under an interpreter and is therefore difficult, or even meaningless, if used at the system level. Instruction coverage can be monitored by less disruptive, hardware-based tools and is typically the only kind of coverage monitoring available for higher-level component testing. Modern hardware architectures, especially cache memories, can provide misleading coverage data because although the monitor detects that the instruction was fetched, there is no way to determine whether in fact it was or was not executed. Ultimately, instruction, statement, and branch coverage should be a built-in hardware function. Computer designers have recognized this fact and we should expect hardware support to increase in the future.

Note: The kind of coverage measured by a coverage certifier is often not specified. That is, unless you ask, you don't know whether you're monitoring statement coverage, branch coverage, or both—for source code, for object, or for memory words. Some of the research and private monitors are very elaborate and provide many different kinds of sophisticated coverage recording, but other tools have hardly been worth the using. Unless I knew otherwise, I would assume that a coverage certifier provided only object level instruction word use monitoring, and appearances and claims to the contrary, I would further assume that the reported coverage was unreliable if the computer had a cache memory. I'd want to verify more sophisticated coverage certification claims by testing.

Coverage certification, especially statement and branch, are recognized as important, basic tools to measure the effectiveness of a test suite or proposed strategy. Consequently, they are often implemented as an adjunct to some other test tool. Typically, modern tools have coverage certifiers built in, and the independent stand-alone coverage monitor has become the exception. For more information on coverage certifiers see: BEND70C, BUYA82, COLL82, COLL84, FUJI80, GANN80, HIRS67, KORE88A, SCHI69, SNEE86, STON88, WARN64, and WEYU88A.

6.2.2. Flowgraph Generators and Analyzers

I include in this category tools that produce control and data-flow graphs, call graphs, static analyzers of various kinds, and symbolic execution packages. Such tools, as stand-alone tools, are rapidly disappearing because their functions are integrated into a broader testing or debugging tool. For example, structural test generators usually produce flowgraphs as a by-product and also do symbolic execution in support of path sensitization. For more information on these tools see CLAR76, CLAR81, GANN80, JACE84, KEMM85, OSTE76, OSTE77, OSTE81, PLOE79, RYDE79, SARR84, and WILS82.

6.2.3. Metrics Support

Metrics must be automated if they're to be useful and, as a consequence, metrics support is incorporated in almost all new tools. The metrics include the usual, expected, coverage metrics, various complexity metrics such as Halstead's, McCabe's, tokens, etc. Metrics support figures heavily in most research tools because they are needed to evaluate the effectiveness of test strategies. As stand-alone tools, though, metrics packages are becoming the exception. For metrics tools see CURR86, GRAD87, POLL87A, RAMA85, and SCHN79B.

6.2.4. Instrumentation Support

Instrumentation has long been recognized as a fundamental part of all structural testing strategies. As such, stand-alone path instrumentation has all but been absorbed into more comprehensive tools. Earlier papers on instrumentation facilities include ANDR81, CHEN78B, HUAN79, RAMA75B, and STUK77.

6.3. Test Execution Automation

6.3.1. General

Test execution automation automates the setup and running of tests that have been either automatically or manually generated. Test execution automation is a mandatory prerequisite to test design automation because most design automation schemes produce vast numbers of tests that cannot be executed without automation. It is also a fundamental prerequisite to any kind of regression testing. Most commercial test tools support execution automation and most test generators include execution automation support.

6.3.2. Capture/Replay

The **capture/replay** (also capture/playback) tool is the most popular commercial tool of all—so much so that when some people speak of test automation they mean capture/replay. The tool is simple: conceptually and to use. It is typically hosted on a PC. The tester executes the test manually from the PC keyboard and the capture/replay software captures the keystrokes and the responses that are sent to the screen. Later, the tester can specify which tests are to be replayed. The system then compares the new outcomes to the stored outcomes and reports discrepancies. To be useful, capture/replay systems must have the following features:

1. *Test Editor*—This feature may be provided either by porting the captured data to a word processor or by a test editor. Without some kind of editing facility, a capture/replay system is useless. The editor is obviously used to correct executed tests, but more important, to create variations on tests without having to rerun the tests.

2. *Smart Comparator*—Direct, character-by-character comparators are almost useless because in most realistic testing situations, there are many fields that can be ignored or whose values cannot be predicted (e.g., time of day), but whose outcomes do not affect test validity. Smart comparison means the ability to specify the verification criteria including such things as ignoring fields, tolerances on fields, and different timings and sequences.

3. *Internal/External*—Capture/replay systems may be limited to only working on object code within the same PC or may serve as a terminal to be used over a communication link with another computer whose software is under test; both kinds are available, and both are useful. The internal tool is useful only as a unit test tool, whereas the external variant is useful for higher-level testing, such as system testing.

4. *Single/Multi-thread*—The simplest tool can run only one line at a time, which makes it a limited tool for many system testing applica-

tions. More elaborate capture/replay systems can capture and replay entire scenarios along several lines and do the fancy kinds of timing and sequence comparisons that may be needed.

5. *Exception Reports*—Another useful property. Typically, once regression suites have been built using these tools, test runs may be very long (hours or days) and it is essential that the tool reports comparison failures by exception. Tools that do not do this are useful only in the capture phase but seriously limited as a driver.

It is interesting to note that the single most popular test automation tool is conspicuously absent in the research domain—perhaps because it is so simple and because it tells us almost nothing about testing. This tool, though useful, is dangerous. In a sense, it is not even a test tool because it captures everything—good or bad behavior—but tells us nothing about whether the software is or is not working correctly. The outcomes must be examined for correctness just as for manual testing. The payback for capture/replay is never in the first execution, but in regression testing.

Capture/replay is the tool of choice for transition to an automated test environment from a manual environment. It is an excellent tool for converting manual test suites to automated test suites and as such is a fundamental test tool. It is also a useful aid to reverse engineering of software and rehosting. Today, capture/playback facilities are becoming integrated into more comprehensive test drivers and total testing environments. The stand-alone capture/playback tool is becoming the exception. For more information on capture/playback tools consult SQET90.

6.3.3. Stubs and Drivers

A **stub** is a simulator of a called subroutine. You're doing unit testing on component X, which calls subcomponent Y. Y is either not available for testing at the moment or you don't want to be confused by Y's actions; so you replace Y with a dummy subroutine that uses the same calling sequence but provides "canned" outcomes for its processing. A stub can provide outcomes for only a small subset of the possible outcomes of the routine it simulates—for example, only for narrowly selected paths. If the stub is realistic in every way, it is no longer a stub but the actual routine. There are commercial tools (DATA90, SQET90) that help to generate stubs and to test with them.

A **driver** is the opposite of a stub, and more. Instead of simulating the called subroutine, it simulates the calling component and perhaps the entire environment under which the component is to be tested. A complete test driver, in addition to simulating the caller, provides the following services:

1. *Test Case Initialization*—Initializes the environment to the state specified for each test and starts the test going. Typically, a test or subtest consists of a single entry/exit path.
2. *Input Simulation*—Provides simulated inputs to the tested unit, including simulation of operator keystrokes and I/O responses, as required.
3. *Outcome Comparison*—Compares the actual outcome to the expected outcome specified by the test designer. Typically, it is a "smart" comparator to which you can specify which fields matter, which should be ignored, tolerances, etc.
4. *Path Instrumentation and Verification*—Verifies that the specified path was achieved.
5. *Reporting*—Typically, report by exception for failed test cases, but has controls to allow complete documentation of all cases run, pass or fail.
6. *Passage to Next Test*—Provides automatic resetting of initial conditions and execution of the next test case in the series.
7. *Debugging Support*—Captures the environment (e.g., dumps) for crashes and/or passes control directly to debug package.

Where commercial drivers do not exist—or where the peculiarities of the language, computer, environment, etc., prevent the effective use of packaged drivers—most organizations implement special-purpose test drivers by writing programs for the purpose. This approach automates the test execution process and ensures repeatability. Most test groups have found that even such labor-intensive drivers are worth the investment. The simplest drivers are less than a capture/replay system, whereas elaborate drivers approach a complete testing environment. In addition to commercial test drivers, see CONK89, GANN80, HOLT87, LEMP89, PANZ76, PANZ78A, PANZ78B, RAMA79, STAK89, STON88, and TSAL86.

6.3.4. Test Environments

The complexity of large-scale functional testing has led to the development of supporting test environments. These are conceptually similar to CASE systems but are typically restricted to testing objectives. Environments may range from support of a single tester at a PC to elaborate systems that control hundreds of testers and a test bed measured in acres. I've grouped environments under execution automation because most environments support it rather than test design automation. There are no commercial test environments today, although some elaborate drivers come close. The features of complete environments include: tie to configuration control systems, capture/replay, metrics support, extensive reporting and authorization features, test data base management, test-bed management, scheduling and resource allocation, test driving, incident tracking, reliability modeling, software development support, to name a few. Test environments are described and discussed in: BASI87, BURK88, BUTL89, CHOW88, CONK89, DEGA81, ELLI89, FRAN88, FREE88, FREN88, FURG89, GANN80, GERH88, GOMA82, HEND89, LASK90A, MATT88, MILL81B, PATR88, PERE86, RAMA75A, RAPP88, STON88, TSAL86, WEYU88A, YINB80, and YOSH87.

6.4.   Test Design Automation

6.4.1.   General

Much of test tools research has focused on test design automation or partial automation. Automation is essential because many of the most effective strategies, such as data-flow testing and domain testing, are too tedious without automation support. It has become the norm for testing researchers to build automation and support tools that embody various strategies.

6.4.2.   Structural Generators

Structural test generators attempt to generate a covering set of test cases based on source code. That is, at best, it does the whole job of path selection, sensitization, and outcome prediction. These generators are almost always coupled to a driver and coverage certifier so that, together, they become a complete test tool. Most structural test generators center on path testing as the primary strategy, although other strategies may be incorporated.

Structural test generators don't live up to their promise—nor can they—because the entire "job," as defined above, is unsolvable. The biggest difficulty is with sensitizing arbitrarily specified paths. As for outcome prediction, the generator simply records the actual outcome once the path has been achieved. Some generators (KORE89) use a search procedure to find a covering path set while others use various combinations of static analysis, symbolic execution, and heuristics to find a covering path set. The objective for most tools is statement and branch coverage.

In a fundamental sense, all structural test generators are silly—but that doesn't mean they're useless. They're silly because the best they can do is to provide a set of test cases that demonstrates that the program works the way the program works—bugs and all. In other words, structural test generators are kiddie testing at its worst. In the hands of lazy programmers and venal test designers, they are the devil's own invention because they create the illusion of thorough testing when in fact nothing at all has been tested. More than one software project has gone down the tubes relying on structural test generators in the naive belief that good unit testing was being done.

In the hands of a disciplined designer or tester who understands their fundamental fallacy, they are a great shortcut to unit test design. The point is that most of the software is correct and it's a lot easier to confirm that the covering set of tests is a valid set of tests than it is to create such a set from scratch. In other words, you examine a test path created by the generator and confirm that it makes sense. Then you use the sensitization values provided and confirm that indeed that is the way you expect the routine to go. Finally, you confirm that the produced outcome is what it should be. If you don't get lazy or trapped, the test design and execution labor will have been cut to a fraction of what it would be for manually designed tests.

Structural test generators are discussed in CICU75, CLAR76, CLAR78, HARR89, KORE89, LIND88, MILL75, MILL77C, RAMA75A, RAMA76, STON88, and VOGE80.

6.4.3. Data-Flow Test Generators

Data-flow generators produce test cases or support test case production based on data-flow criteria. As such, they also include most path-testing strategies. Data-flow testing support tools abut debugging tools on one side and environments on the other. Coverage certification for multiple criteria is a common feature. Weyuker's description (WEYU88A) is interesting because it shows how a tool that embodies sophisticated testing strategies can be used without the user being an expert in the strategy. Structural generators centered on data-flow concepts are discussed in BEND70C, FOSD76A, FRAN88, HARR89, HERM76, KORE85, KORE88A, KORE88B, KORE89, LASK90A, LYLE87, POLL87B, SNEE86, SOLO86, WEIS86, WEYU88A, and WILS82.

6.4.4.   Functional Generators

Functional test generator development has been slower than structural test generators because of the difficulty of providing a formal framework for specifications. Although there has been much work on specification and test-scripting languages (BERZ85, BLUM87, HALL78, PANZ76, and WILK77), many of the language efforts have relied on constructs that are closer to the predicate calculus than to natural languages—this too has hindered the development of functional test generators. Papers on functional test generators include GERH88, HALL78, JALO83, OSTR86, OSTR88A, and STAK89.

6.4.5.   Other Generators

Every structural or functional test technique can be supported by an appropriate test generator but progress in such generators (aside from that discussed above) and publication of results have been sparse. Although finite-state machine testing and implementation is common in telephony, little has been openly published (BAUE79, CHOW88, WILK77) probably because of the competitive advantage such methods provide. In domain testing, we have only WHIT85B, although some commercial tools employ heuristic domain test generation strategies. Most domain testing, as done, is based on one variable at a time, under the assumption that the domain boundaries are orthogonal. Many researchers in domain testing have incorporated domain test generators, usually based on structure rather than on functionally defined domains.

6.4.6.   Random Test Data Generators

There is an easy way to generate test cases that does not rely on a deep analysis of the program's structure, either automated or manual: by using random test data. There are several difficulties and weaknesses in random test data, especially if that is the only kind of test that's done.

1. Random data produce a statistically insignificant sample of the possible paths through most routines (HUAN75, MORA78). Because it may be difficult to determine how many achievable paths there are, even copious tests based on random data may not allow you to produce a statistically valid prediction of the routine's reliability.
2. There is no assurance of coverage. Running the generator to the point of 100% coverage could take centuries.
3. If the data are generated in accordance with statistics that reflect

expected data characteristics, the test cases will be biased to the normal paths—the very paths that are least likely to have bugs.

4. There may be no rational basis for predicting the statistical characteristics of the users. In such cases it isn't even random testing, it's arbitrary testing.

5. It may be difficult or impossible to predict the desired outputs and therefore to verify that the routine is working properly; all you might learn is that it did not blow up, but not whether or not what it did made sense. In many cases, the only way to produce the output against which to make a comparison is to run the equivalent of the routine—and the equivalent is as likely to have bugs as the routine being tested.

The main justification for random testing has always been that it is perceived as an essential prerequisite to doing software reliability modeling and predictions. The software test and QA world is deeply divided on this point and I'm a firm fence sitter until the dust settles one way or the other. Because automatic random test generation is so easy, and because so much has been written about it in the context of software reliability, many groups looking for an easy alternative to rigorous testing have adopted random testing as the main or sole testing strategy. As we have seen, random testing is hardly better than unsystematic domain and syntax testing. Because of its appeal and danger, most writers on random testing, who understand its limitations, make a point of noting that it should never be used as a sole technique—but that's a warning too often ignored.

If random testing is to be used, instead of generating test cases in accordance with the probability of traversals at decisions, the test cases should be generated in accordance with the complementary probability. That is, if the probability of branching in a given direction is P, test paths should be generated so that the probability of branching for the test cases is $1 - P$ at that decision. This would, at least, bias the paths away from the normal cases and toward the weird cases that are more likely to have bugs. In other words, force the cases to the domain boundaries and, especially, the boundary crossing points.

As a supplementary method of generating test cases, particularly when applied at a system level, using random test data is not a bad idea—assuming that it is possible to run the system on a test bed with a test data generator and then to force the system through thousands and millions of cases. If done as part of system-level stress testing (BEIZ84), random testing is more effective yet—until it wears out, that is.

6.5. Tool Usage and Training

One of the sad experiences with tools has been that even in organizations where testing was mature and backed by management and a reasonable budget was provided for tools, actual usage of the tool, measured a year after the purchase, was very low—about 5% (GRUM88, SQES88). Typically, that meant that each tool was used by one person—the person who sponsored the tool. Why actual tool usage has been far lower than tool purchase is probably a result of shortsighted thinking and expectations of miracles. Most important, though, is inadequate training budgets. Software testing tools can be based on sophisticated principles that even superintelligent testers and programmers can't be expected to grasp at one sitting or even in a 3-day seminar. In addition to formal training in tool usage, the user must be given ample time to acquire facility with the tool's use. By "ample" I mean weeks and months, not hours and days. Furthermore, instead of expecting miraculous increases in productivity, one should expect the first or first few products to show lower productivity and possibly lower quality for the same effort—and the schedule will surely be extended. The payoff comes on the second or third project and continues thereafter. If management expectations are that the tool will be introduced and used without disrupting the schedule, if it is expected that the tester and programmer will both learn the new techniques *and* retain the old schedule, if the ground rule is that there shall be no investment allowed to learn the tool, then is it any wonder that the potential user doesn't even try. A reasonable budget is to assume about ten times the tool's cost for training, at least 3 or 4 weeks to reach the productivity break-even point per user of a simple tool, and no break-even expectations until the third project. On any given project or task, it is probably cheaper and faster to continue to do things by hand than it is to invest in automation. That was true for widget production at the start of the industrial revolution and is true for software today: the payoff for testing and software quality, as for manufactured products, has been and will always be in the long run.

Appendix

BUG STATISTICS AND TAXONOMY

NOTICE—The author and publisher give the reader the right to copy and use this appendix (and only this appendix) subject to use of one of the following credit lines to be used on all print or electronic copies.

EXPLANATION AND NOTATION—This document is a taxonomy for bugs. I had intended at first to adopt the IEEE draft standard on bug classification (ANSI87E), but decided not to because it doesn't cover the territory.

Bugs are categorized by a 4-digit number, perhaps with subnumbers using the point system; e.g., "1234.1.6." The "x" that appears is a place holder for possible future filling in of numbers as the taxonomy is (inevitably) expanded. For example:

3xxx—structural bugs in the implemented software
   32xx—processing bugs
      322x—expression evaluation
         3222—arithmetic expressions
            3222.1—wrong operator

The last digit in a set is always a 9: e.g., 9xxx, 39xx, 329x, 3229, 3226.9. This is the category to use when a finer breakdown is not available: e.g., an unclassified bug is a 9xxx bug, an unclassified structural bug is desig-

460

nated as 39xx, an unclassified processing bug is 329x, an unclassified expression evaluation bug is 3229, unclassified arithmetic bug is a 3222.9 bug.

I've adopted this numbering plan and convention so that I can combine data from various sources, which are based on different taxonomies, to different levels of detail.

BUG STATISTICS

This is a spreadsheet dump for combined bug statistics gathered from many different sources: AKIY71, BELF79, BOEH75A, BOIE72, BONN88, DNIE78, DRAB88, ELSH76B, ENDR75, EVAN88, GANN76, GILB77, GOEL78B, HAUG64, HOFF77, ITOH73, LITE76, NASA88, RADA81, REIF79A, RUBE75, SCHI78, SCHN75, SCHN79A, SCHW71, SHOO75, THAY76, and WAGO73. The columns denote:

 1. *Category Number*—1xxx, 11xx, 119x. . . .
 2. *Bug Category Name*—e.g., requirements incorrect.
 3. *Bug Type or Subtype Count*—e.g., 111x has a count of 222.
 4–6. *Subgroup Count*—e.g., 11xx = 649, 13xx = 224, 15xx = 13.
 5–7. *Group Count*—e.g., 1xxx = 1317, 2xxx = 2624. Note that type, subgroup, and group counts progress from left to right. How many columns are used depends on how fine the group breakdown is.
 8. *Total Percentage*—The column shows the percentage of this bug category compared to the total number of bugs; e.g., 1xxx = 8.12% of the whole, 11xx = 4.00%, and 111x = 1.37%.
 9. *Group Percentages*—The column percentages relative to the group. You can determine the group by going up to the nearest 100% entry; e.g., 11xx (incorrect requirements) is 49.28% of all requirements bugs, whereas ambiguous requirements are 0.15% of all requirements bugs.
 10. *Subgroup Percentages*—As for group percentages, except for subgroups; e.g., case completeness (23xx) can be subdivided into missing (75.13%), duplicated or overlapped (5.18%), extraneous output (18.65%), and miscellaneous (1.04%).

		TOTAL	SUM1	SUM2	SUM3	SUM4	SUM5	Percent of Total	Percent Group	Percent Subgroup
	KLOC (WITH COMMENTS)	6877.26								
	TOTAL NUMBER OF BUGS	16209	16209	16209	16209	16209	16209			
	BUGS/KLOC	2.36								
1xxx	FUNCTIONAL REQUIREMENTS				1317	1317	1317	8.12%	100.00%	
11xx	REQUIREMENTS INCORRECT		649	649				4.00%	49.28%	100.00%
111x	Incorrect	222						1.37%	16.86%	34.21%
114x	Ambiguous	2						0.01%	0.15%	0.31%
119x	Other requirements	425						2.62%	32.27%	65.49%
12xx	REQUIREMENTS LOGIC			153				0.94%	11.62%	100.00%
124x	Inconsistent, incompatible		62					0.38%	4.71%	40.52%
1249	Other inconsistencies	62						0.38%	4.71%	40.52%
129x	Other requirements logic problems	91	91					0.56%	6.91%	59.48%
13xx	REQUIREMENTS COMPLETENESS		224	224				1.38%	17.01%	100.00%
131x	Incomplete	138						0.85%	10.48%	61.61%
132x	Missing, not specified	84						0.52%	6.38%	37.50%
139x	Other completeness problems	2						0.01%	0.15%	0.89%
15xx	PRESENTATION, DOCUMENTATION		13	13				0.08%	0.99%	100.00%
152x	Presentation, documentation	1						0.01%	0.08%	7.69%
159x	Other presentation problems	12						0.07%	0.91%	92.31%
16xx	REQUIREMENTS CHANGES			278				1.72%	21.11%	100.00%
162x	Features		175					1.08%	13.29%	62.95%
1621	Feature added	37						0.23%	2.81%	13.31%
1622	Feature deleted	3						0.02%	0.23%	1.08%
1623	Feature changed	110						0.68%	8.35%	39.57%
1629	Other feature changes	25						0.15%	1.90%	8.99%
164x	Domain changes	5	5					0.03%	0.38%	1.80%
165x	User messages and diagnostics	8	8					0.05%	0.61%	2.88%
167x	External interfaces	22	22					0.14%	1.67%	7.91%
169x	Other requirements changes	68	68					0.42%	5.16%	24.46%
2xxx	FUNCTIONALITY AS IMPLEMENTED			2624	2624	2624	2624	16.19%	100.00%	
21xx	CORRECTNESS		456					2.81%	17.38%	100.00%
211x	Feature not understood	70						0.43%	2.67%	15.35%
218x	Feature interaction	32						0.20%	1.22%	7.02%
219x	Other feature bugs	354						2.18%	13.49%	77.63%
22xx	COMPLETENESS, FEATURES		231					1.43%	8.80%	100.00%
221x	Missing feature	56						0.35%	2.13%	24.24%
223x	Duplicated, overlapped feature	155						0.96%	5.91%	67.10%
229x	Other feature completeness	20						0.12%	0.76%	8.66%

		TOTAL	SUM1	SUM2	SUM3	SUM4	SUM5	Percent of Total	Percent Group	Percent Subgroup
23xx	COMPLETENESS, CASES		193					1.19%	7.36%	100.00%
231x	Missing case	145						0.89%	5.53%	75.13%
233x	Duplicated, overlapped case	10						0.06%	0.38%	5.18%
234x	Extraneous output data	36						0.22%	1.37%	18.65%
239x	Other case completeness bugs	2						0.01%	0.08%	1.04%
24xx	DOMAIN BUGS		778					4.80%	29.65%	100.00%
241x	Domain misunderstood, wrong	306						1.89%	11.66%	39.33%
242x	Boundary location error	457						2.82%	17.42%	58.74%
243x	Boundary closure	11						0.07%	0.42%	1.41%
249x	Other domain bugs	4						0.02%	0.15%	0.51%
25xx	USER MESSAGES AND DIAGNOSTICS	857	857					5.29%	32.66%	100.00%
26xx	EXCEPTION CONDITION MISHANDLED	79	79					0.49%	3.01%	100.00%
29xx	OTHER FUNCTIONAL BUGS	30	30					0.19%	1.14%	100.00%
3xxx	STRUCTURAL BUGS						4082	25.18%	100.00%	
31xx	CONTROL FLOW AND SEQUENCING			2078	2078	2078		12.82%	50.91%	100.00%
311x	General structure		155					0.96%	3.80%	7.47%
3119	Other general structure	155						0.96%	3.80%	7.47%
312x	Control logic and predicates		561					3.46%	13.74%	26.99%
3128	Other control-flow predicate bug	268						1.65%	6.56%	12.90%
3129	Other control-flow logic bugs	293						1.81%	7.18%	14.10%
314x	Loops and iterations		120					0.74%	2.94%	5.77%
3142	Terminal value or condition	54						0.33%	1.32%	2.60%
3144	Iteration variable processing	1						0.01%	0.02%	0.05%
3149	Other loop and iteration	65						0.40%	1.59%	3.13%
315x	Control initialization and/or stop		10					0.06%	0.24%	0.48%
3159	Other control state bugs	10						0.06%	0.24%	0.48%
319x	Other control flow, sequencing	1232	1232					7.60%	30.18%	59.28%
32xx	PROCESSING					2004		12.36%	49.09%	100.00%
321x	Algorithmic, fundamental	121	121	121	121			0.75%	2.96%	6.04%
322x	Expression evaluation	0	0		445			2.75%	10.90%	22.21%
3222	Arithmetic expressions		278	278				1.72%	6.81%	13.87%
3222.3	Sign	30						0.19%	0.73%	1.50%
3222.9	Other arithmetic	248						1.53%	6.08%	12.38%
3224	Logic, boolean, not control predicate	167	167	167				1.03%	4.09%	8.33%
323x	Initialization	303	303	303	303			1.87%	7.42%	15.12%
324x	Cleanup	10	10	10	10			0.06%	0.24%	0.50%
325x	Precision, accuracy	88	88	88	88			0.54%	2.16%	4.39%
326x	Execution time	47	47	47	47			0.29%	1.15%	2.35%
329x	Other processing	990	990	990	990			6.11%	24.25%	49.40%

		TOTAL	SUM1	SUM2	SUM3	SUM4	SUM5	Percent of Total	Percent Group	Percent Subgroup
4xxx	DATA				3638	3638	3638	22.44%	100.00%	
41xx	DATA DEFINITION, STRUCTURE, DECLARATION			1805				11.14%	49.62%	100.00%
413x	Static initial or default value		157					0.97%	4.32%	8.70%
414x	Duplication and aliases		11					0.07%	0.30%	0.61%
4149	Other duplication and aliases	11						0.07%	0.30%	0.61%
419x	Other data structure definition	1637	1637					10.10%	45.00%	90.69%
42xx	DATA ACCESS AND HANDLING			1831				11.30%	50.33%	100.00%
421x	Type		359					2.21%	9.87%	19.61%
4212	Wrong type	10						0.06%	0.27%	0.55%
4214	Type transformation	84						0.52%	2.31%	4.59%
4216	Scaling, units	237						1.46%	6.51%	12.94%
4219	Other type bugs	28						0.17%	0.77%	1.53%
423x	Value		236					1.46%	6.49%	12.89%
4232	Initialization	236						1.46%	6.49%	12.89%
424x	Duplication and aliases		10					0.06%	0.27%	0.55%
4249	Other duplication and aliases	10						0.06%	0.27%	0.55%
426x	Resources		11					0.07%	0.30%	0.60%
4269	Other dynamic resource	11						0.07%	0.30%	0.60%
428x	Access		677					4.18%	18.61%	36.97%
4281	Wrong object accessed	244						1.51%	6.71%	13.33%
4282	Access rights violation	8						0.05%	0.22%	0.44%
4283	Data-flow anomaly	115						0.71%	3.16%	6.28%
4285	Saving or protecting bug	10						0.06%	0.27%	0.55%
4287	Access mode, direct/indirect	113						0.70%	3.11%	6.17%
4288	Object boundary, structure	115						0.71%	3.16%	6.28%
4289	Other access bug	72						0.44%	1.98%	3.93%
429x	Other data access and handling	538	538					3.32%	14.79%	29.38%
49xx	OTHER DATA PROBLEMS	2	2	2				0.01%	0.05%	100.00%
5xxx	IMPLEMENTATION				1601	1601	1601	9.88%	100.00%	
51xx	CODING AND TYPOGRAPHICAL		322	322				1.99%	20.11%	100.00%
511x	Coding wild card, typographical	26						0.16%	1.62%	8.07%
519x	Other, general coding bugs	296						1.83%	18.49%	91.93%
52xx	STANDARDS VIOLATION			318				1.96%	19.86%	100.00%
527x	Format	15	15					0.09%	0.94%	4.72%
528x	Comments	68	68					0.42%	4.25%	21.38%
529x	Other standards, style violation	235	235					1.45%	14.68%	73.90%
53xx	DOCUMENTATION		960	960				5.92%	59.96%	100.00%
531x	Incorrect	550						3.39%	34.35%	57.29%
532x	Inconsistent	9						0.06%	0.56%	0.94%
534x	Incomplete	146						0.90%	9.12%	15.21%
539x	Other documentation, general	255						1.57%	15.93%	26.56%
59xx	OTHER IMPLEMENTATION	1	1	1				0.01%	0.06%	100.00%

		TOTAL	SUM1	SUM2	SUM3	SUM4	SUM5	Percent of Total	Percent Group	Percent Subgroup
6xxx	INTEGRATION				1455	1455	1455	8.98%	100.00%	
61xx	INTERNAL INTERFACES			859				5.30%	59.04%	100.00%
611x	Component invocation		27					0.17%	1.86%	3.14%
6119	Other component invocation	27						0.17%	1.86%	3.14%
612x	Interface parameter, invocation		128					0.79%	8.80%	14.90%
6121	Wrong parameter	75						0.46%	5.15%	8.73%
6126	Parameter sequence	2						0.01%	0.14%	0.23%
6129	Other invocation parameter bugs	51						0.31%	3.51%	5.94%
613x	Component return		70					0.43%	4.81%	8.15%
6131	Parameter identity wrong	37						0.23%	2.54%	4.31%
6139	Other parameter bugs on return	33						0.20%	2.27%	3.84%
614x	Initialization, state	221	221					1.36%	15.19%	25.73%
619x	Other, internal interfaces	413	413					2.55%	28.38%	48.08%
62xx	EXTERNAL INTERFACES AND TIMING			518				3.20%	35.60%	100.00%
621x	Interrupts	94	94					0.58%	6.46%	18.15%
622x	Devices, drivers		137					0.85%	9.42%	26.45%
6222	Device, driver, init and/or state	3						0.02%	0.21%	0.58%
6224	Device, driver, command bug	28						0.17%	1.92%	5.41%
6226	Return data, status, misinterpreted	24						0.15%	1.65%	4.63%
6229	Other device, driver	82						0.51%	5.64%	15.83%
623x	I/O timing and throughput	23	23					0.14%	1.58%	4.44%
629x	Other, external interface, timing	264	264					1.63%	18.14%	50.97%
69xx	OTHER INTEGRATION	78	78	78				0.48%	5.36%	100.00%
7xxx	SYSTEM, SOFTWARE ARCHITECTURE			282	282	282	282	1.74%	100.00%	
71xx	O/S CALL, USE BUG		47					0.29%	16.67%	100.00%
711x	Invocation, command	5						0.03%	1.77%	10.64%
714x	Space	3						0.02%	1.06%	6.38%
719x	Other OS call, use bugs	39						0.24%	13.83%	82.98%
72xx	SOFTWARE ARCHITECTURE		139					0.86%	49.29%	100.00%
721x	Interlocks and semaphores	56						0.35%	19.86%	40.29%
724x	Resource management and control	8						0.05%	2.84%	5.76%
729x	General software architecture	75						0.46%	26.60%	53.96%
73xx	RECOVERY AND ACCOUNTABILITY	4	4					0.02%	1.42%	100.00%
74xx	PERFORMANCE		64					0.39%	22.70%	100.00%
742x	Response time, delay	44						0.27%	15.60%	68.75%
749x	Other performance, unspecified	20						0.12%	7.09%	31.25%

		TOTAL	SUM1	SUM2	SUM3	SUM4	SUM5	Percent of Total	Percent Group	Percent Subgroup
75xx	INCORRECT DIAGNOSTIC, EXCEPTIONS	16	16					0.10%	5.67%	100.00%
76xx	PARTITIONS, OVERLAYS	3	3					0.02%	1.06%	100.00%
77xx	SYSGEN/ENVIRONMENT	9	9					0.06%	3.19%	100.00%
8xxx	TEST DEFINITION OR EXECUTION			447	447	447	447	2.76%	100.00%	
81xx	TEST DESIGN BUGS		11					0.07%	2.46%	100.00%
811x	Requirements misunderstood	3						0.02%	0.67%	27.27%
819x	Other test design bugs	8						0.05%	1.79%	72.73%
82xx	TEST EXECUTION BUGS		355					2.19%	79.42%	100.00%
823x	Database	6						0.04%	1.34%	1.69%
824x	Configuration	66						0.41%	14.77%	18.59%
828x	Verification act	28						0.17%	6.26%	7.89%
829x	Other test execution bugs	255						1.57%	57.05%	71.83%
83xx	TEST DOCUMENTATION	11	11					0.07%	2.46%	100.00%
84xx	TEST CASE COMPLETENESS	64	64					0.39%	14.32%	100.00%
89xx	OTHER TEST DESIGN/ EXECUTION BUGS	6	6					0.04%	1.34%	100.00%
9xxx	OTHER BUGS, UNSPECIFIED	763	763	763	763	763	763	4.71%	100.00%	100.00%

BUG TAXONOMY

1xxx: FUNCTIONAL BUGS: REQUIREMENTS AND FEATURES: bugs having to do with requirements as specified or as implemented.

11xx: REQUIREMENTS INCORRECT: the requirement or a part of it is incorrect.

111x: Incorrect: requirement is wrong.

112x: Undesirable: requirement is correct as stated but it is not desirable.

113x: Not needed: requirement is not needed.

12xx: LOGIC: the requirement is illogical or unreasonable.

121x: Illogical: illogical, usually because of a self-contradiction which can be exposed by a logical analysis of cases.

122x: Unreasonable: logical and consistent but unreasonable with respect to the environment and/or budgetary and time constraints.

123x: Unachievable: requirement fundamentally impossible or cannot be achieved under existing constraints.

124x: Inconsistent, incompatible: requirement is inconsistent with other requirements or with the environment.

1242: Internal: the inconsistency is evident within the specified component.

1244: External: the inconsistency is with external (to the component) components or the environment.

1248: Configuration sensitivity: the incompatibility is with one or more configurations (hardware, software, operating system) in which the component is expected to work.

13xx: COMPLETENESS: the requirement as specified is either ambiguous, incomplete, or overly specified.

131x: Incomplete: the specification is incomplete; cases, features, variations or attributes are not specified and therefore not implemented.

132x: Missing, unspecified: the entire requirement is missing.

133x: Duplicated, overlapped: specified requirement totally or partially overlaps another requirement either already implemented or specified elsewhere.

134x: Overly generalized: requirement as specified is correct and consistent but is overly generalized (e.g., too powerful) for the application.

137x: Not downward compatible: requirement as specified will mean that objects created or manipulated by prior versions can either not be processed by this version or will be incorrectly processed.

138x: Insufficiently extendable: requirement as specified cannot be expanded in ways that are likely to be needed—important hooks are left out of specification.

14xx: VERIFIABILITY: specification bugs having to do with verifying that the requirement was correctly or incorrectly implemented.

141x: Unverifiable: the requirement, if implemented, cannot be verified by any means or within available time and budget. For example, it is possible to design a test, but the outcome of the test cannot be verified as correct or incorrect.

142x: Untestable: it is not possible to design and/or execute tests that will verify the requirement. Untestable is stronger than unverifiable.

15xx: PRESENTATION: bugs in the presentation or documentation of requirements. The requirements are presumed to be correct, but the form in which they are presented is not. This can be important for test design automation systems, which demand specific formats.

152x: Presentation, documentation: general presentation, documentation, format, media, etc.

153x: Standards: presentation violates standards for requirements.

16xx: REQUIREMENT CHANGES: requirements, whether or not correct, have been changed between the time programming started and testing ended.

162x: Features: requirement changes concerned with features.

1621: Feature added: a new feature has been added.

1622: Feature deleted: previously required feature deleted.

1623: Feature changed: significant changes to feature, other than changes in cases.

163x: Cases: cases within a feature have been changed. Feature itself is not significantly modified except for cases.

1631: Cases added.

1632: Cases deleted.

1633: Cases changed: processing or treatment of specific case(s) changed.

164x: Domain changes: input data domain modified: e.g., boundary changes, closure, treatment.

165x: User messages and diagnostics: changes in text, content, or conditions under which user prompts, warning, error messages, etc. are produced.

166x: Internal interfaces: direct internal interfaces such as call sequences, or indirect interfaces (e.g., via data structures) have been changed.

167x: External interfaces: external interfaces, such as device drivers, protocols, etc. have been changed.

168x: Performance and timing: changes to performance requirements (e.g., throughput) and/or timings.

2xxx: FUNCTIONALITY AS IMPLEMENTED: requirement known or assumed to be correct, implementable, and testable, but implementation is wrong.

21xx: CORRECTNESS: having to do with the correctness of the implementation.

211x: Feature misunderstood, wrong: feature as implemented is not correct—not as specified.

218x: Feature interactions: feature is correctly implemented by itself, but has incorrect interactions with other features, or specified or implied interaction is incorrectly handled.

22xx: COMPLETENESS, FEATURES: having to do with the completeness with which features are implemented.

221x: Missing feature: An entire feature is missing.

222x: Unspecified feature: a feature not specified has been implemented.

223x: Duplicated, overlapped feature: feature as implemented duplicates or overlaps features implemented by other parts of the software.

23xx: COMPLETENESS, CASES: having to do with the completeness of cases within features.

231x: Missing case.

232x: Extra case: cases that should not have been handled are handled.

233x: Duplicated, overlapped case: duplicated handling of cases or partial overlap with other cases.

234x: Extraneous output data: data not required are output.

24xx: DOMAINS: processing case or feature depends on a combination of input values. A domain bug exists if the wrong processing is executed for the selected input-value combination.

241x: Domain misunderstood, wrong: misunderstanding of the size, shape, boundaries, or other characteristics of the specified input domain for the feature or case. Most bugs related to handling extreme cases are domain bugs.

242x: Boundary locations: the values or expressions that define a domain boundary are wrong: e.g., "X>=6" instead of "X>=3".

243x: Boundary closures: end points and boundaries of the domain are incorrectly associated with an adjacent domain: e.g., "X>=0" instead of "X>0".

244x: Boundary intersections: domain boundaries are defined by a relation between domain control variables. That relation, as implemented, is incorrect: e.g., "IF X>0 AND Y>0 ..." instead of "IF X>0 OR Y>0 ...".

25xx: USER MESSAGES AND DIAGNOSTICS: user prompt or printout or other form of communication is incorrect. Processing is assumed to be correct: e.g., a false warning, failure to warn, wrong message, spelling, formats.

26xx: EXCEPTION CONDITIONS MISHANDLED: exception conditions such as illogicals, resource problems, failure modes, which require special handling, are not correctly handled or the wrong exception-handling mechanisms are used.

3xxx: STRUCTURAL BUGS: bugs related to the component's structure: i.e., the code.

31xx: CONTROL FLOW AND SEQUENCING: bugs specifically related to the control flow of the program or the order and extent to which things are done, as distinct from what is done.

311x: General structure: general bugs related to component structure.

3112: Unachievable path: a functionally meaningful processing path in the code for which there is no combination of input values that will force that path to be executed. Do not confuse with unreachable code. The code in question might be reached by some other path.

3114: Unreachable code: code for which there is no combination of input values that will cause that code to be executed.

3116: Dead-end code: code segments that once entered cannot be exited, even though it was intended that an exit be possible.

312x: Control logic and predicates: the path taken through a program is directed by control flow predicates (e.g., boolean expressions). This category addresses the implementation of such predicates.

3122: Duplicated logic: control logic that should appear only once is inadvertently duplicated in whole or in part.

3124: Don't care: improper handling of cases for which what is to be done does not matter either because the case is impossible or because it really doesn't matter: e.g., incorrectly assuming that the case is a don't-care case, failure to do case validation, not invoking the correct exception handler, improper logic simplification to take advantage of such cases.

3126: Illogicals: improper identification of, or processing of, illogical or impossible conditions. An illogical is stronger than a don't care. Illogicals usually mean that something bad has happened and that recovery is needed. Examples of bugs include: illogical not really so, failure to recognize illogical, invoking wrong handler, improper simplification of control logic to take advantage of the case.

3128: Other control-flow predicate bugs: control-flow problems that can be directly attributed to the incorrect formulation of a control flow predicate: e.g., "IF A>B THEN ..." instead of "IF A<B THEN ...".

313x: Case selection bug: simple bugs in case selections, such as improperly formulated case selection expression, GOTO list, or bug in assigned GOTO.

314x: Loops and iteration: bugs having to do with the control of loops.

3141: Initial value: initial iteration value wrong: e.g., "FOR I 3 TO 17 ..." instead of "FOR I = 8 TO 17."

3142: Terminal value or condition: value, variable, or expression used to control loop termination is incorrect: e.g., "FOR I = 1 TO 7 ..." instead of "FOR I = 1 TO 8."

3143: Increment value: value, variable, or expression used to control loop increment value is incorrect: e.g., "FOR I = 1 TO 7 STEP 2 ..." instead of "FOR I = 1 TO 7 STEP 5 ...".

3144: Iteration variable processing: where end points and/or increments are controlled by values calculated within the loop's scope, a bug in such calculations.

3148: Exception exit condition: where specified values or conditions or relations between variables force an abnormal exit to the loop, either incorrect processing of such conditions or incorrect exit mechanism invoked.

315x: Control initialization and/or state: bugs having to do with how the program's control flow is initialized and changes of state that affect the control flow: e.g., switches.

3152: Control initialization: initializing to the wrong state or failing to initialize.

3154: Control state: for state-determined control flows, incorrect transition to a new state from the current state: e.g., input condition X requires a transition to state B, given that the program is in state A, instead, the transition is to state C. Most incorrect GOTOs are included in this category.

316x: Incorrect exception handling: any incorrect invocation of a control-flow exception handler not previously categorized.

32xx: PROCESSING: bugs related to processing under the assumption that the control flow is correct.

321x: Algorithmic, fundamental: inappropriate or incorrect algorithm selected, but implemented correctly: e.g., using an incorrect approximation, using a shortcut string search algorithm that assumes string characteristics that may not apply.

322x: Expression evaluation: bugs having to do with the way arithmetic, boolean, string, and other expressions are evaluated.

3222: Arithmetic: bugs related to evaluation of arithmetic expressions.

3222.1: Operator: wrong arithmetic operator or function used.

3222.2: Parentheses: syntactically correct bug in placement of parentheses or other arithmetic delimiters.

3222.3: Sign: bug in use of sign.

3224: Logical or boolean, not control: bug in the manipulation or evaluation of boolean expressions that are not (directly) part of control-flow predicates: e.g., using wrong mask, AND instead of OR, incorrect simplification of boolean function.

3226: String manipulation: bug in string manipulation.

3226.1: Beheading: the beginning of a string is cut off when it should not have been or not cut off when it should have been.

3226.2: Curtailing: as for beheading but for string end.

3226.3: Concatenation order: strings are concatenated in wrong order or concatenated when they should not be.

3226.3.1: Append instead of precede.

3226.3.2: Precede instead of append.

3226.4: Inserting: having to do with the insertion of one string into another.

3226.5: Converting case: case conversion (upper to lower, say) is incorrect.

3226.6: Code conversion: string is converted to another code incorrectly or not converted when it should be.

3226.7: Packing, unpacking: strings are incorrectly packed or unpacked.

3228: Symbolic, algebraic: bugs in symbolic processing of algebraic expressions.

323x: Initialization: bugs in initialization of variables, expressions, functions, etc. used in processing, excluding initialization bugs associated with declarations and data statements and loop initialization.

324x: Cleanup: incorrect handling of cleanup of temporary data areas, registers, states, etc. associated with processing.

325x: Precision, accuracy: insufficient or excessive precision, insufficient accuracy and other bugs related to number representation system used.

326x: Execution time: excessive (usually) execution time for processing component.

4xxx: DATA: bugs in the definition, structure, or use of data.

41xx: DATA DEFINITION, STRUCTURE, DECLARATION: bugs in the definition, structure, and initialization of data: e.g., in DATA statements. This category applies whether the object is declared statically in source code or created dynamically.

411x: Type: the data object type, as declared, is incorrect: e.g., integer instead of floating, short instead of long, pointer instead of integer, array instead of scalar, incorrect user-defined type.

412x: Dimension: for arrays and other objects that have a dimension (e.g., arrays, records, files) by which component objects can be indexed, a bug in the dimension, in the minimum or maximum dimensions, or in redimensioning statements.

413x: Initial, default values: bugs in the assigned initial values of the object (e.g., in DATA statements), selection of incorrect default values, or failure to supply a default value if needed.

414x: Duplication and aliases: bugs related to the incorrect duplication or failure to create a duplicated object.

4142: Duplicated: duplicated definition of an object where allowed by the syntax.

4144: Aliases: object is known by one or more aliases but specified alias is incorrect; object not aliased when it should have been.

415x: Scope: the scope, partition, or components to which the object applies is incorrectly specified.

4152: Local should be global: a locally defined object (e.g., within the scope of a specific component) should have been specified more globally (e.g., in COMMON).

4154: Global should be local: the scope of an object is too global; it should have been declared more locally.

4156: Global/local inconsistency or conflict: a syntactically acceptable conflict between a local and/or global declaration of an object (e.g., incorrect COMMON).

416x: Static/dynamic resources: related to the declaration of static and dynamically allocated resources.

4162: Should be static resource: resource is defined as a dynamically allocated object but should have been static (e.g., permanent).

4164: Should be dynamic resource: resource is defined as static but should have been declared as dynamic.

4166: Insufficient resources, space: number of specified resources is insufficient or there is insufficient space (e.g., main memory, cache, registers, disc) to hold the declared resources.

4168: Data overlay bug: data objects are to be overlaid but there is a bug in the specification of the overlay areas.

42xx: DATA ACCESS AND HANDLING: having to do with access and manipulation of data objects that are presumed to be correctly defined.

421x: Type: bugs having to do with the object type.

4212: Wrong type: object type is incorrect for required processing: e.g., multiplying two strings.

4214: Type transformation: object undergoes incorrect type transformation: e.g., integer to floating, pointer to integer, specified type transformation is not allowed, required type transformation not done. Note: type transformation bugs can exist in any language, whether or not it is strongly typed, whether or not there are user-defined types.

4216: Scaling, units: scaling or units (semantic) associated with object is incorrect, incorrectly transformed, or not transformed: e.g., FOOT-POUNDS to STONE-FURLONGS.

422x: Dimension: for dynamically variable dimensions of a dimensioned object, a bug in the dimension: e.g., dynamic redimension of arrays, exceeding maximum file length, removing one more than the minimum number of records.

423x: Value: having to do with the value of data objects or parts thereof.

4232: Initialization: initialization or default value of object is incorrect. Not to be confused with initialization and default bugs in declarations. This is a dynamic initialization bug.

4234: Constant value: incorrect constant value for an object: e.g., a constant in an expression.

424x: Duplication and aliases: bugs in dynamic (run time) duplication and aliasing of objects.

4242: Object already exists: attempt to create an object that already exists.

4244: No such object: attempted reference to an object that does not exist.

426x: Resources: having to do with dynamically allocated resources and resource pools, in whatever memory media they exist: main, cache, disc, bulk RAM. Included are queue blocks, control blocks, buffer blocks, heaps, files.

4262: No such resource: referenced resource does not exist.

4264: Wrong resource type: wrong resource type referenced.

428x: Access: having to do with the access of objects as distinct from the manipulation of objects. In this context, accesses include read, write, modify, and (in some instances) create and destroy.

4281: Wrong object accessed: incorrect object accessed: e.g., "X := ABC33" instead of "X := ABD33".

4282: Access rights violation: access rights are controlled by attributes associated with the caller and the object. For example, some callers can only read the object, others can read and modify. Violations of object access rights are included in this category whether or not a formal access rights mechanism exists; that is, access rights could be specified by programming conventions rather than by software.

4283: Data-flow anomaly: data-flow anomalies involve the sequence of accesses to an object: e.g., reading or initializing an object before it has been created, or creating and then not using.

4284: Interlock bug: where objects are in simultaneous use by more than one caller, interlocks and synchronization mechanisms may be used to ensure that all data are current and changed by only one caller at a time. These are not bugs in the interlock or synchronization mechanism but in the use of that mechanism.

4285: Saving or protecting bug: application requires that the object be saved or otherwise protected in different program states or, alternatively, not protected. These bugs are related to the incorrect usage of such protection mechanisms or procedures.

4286: Restoration bug: application requires that a previously saved object be restored prior to processing: e.g., POP the stack, restore registers after interrupt. This category includes bugs in the incorrect restoration of data objects and not bugs in the implementation of the restoration mechanism.

4287: Access mode, direct/indirect: object is accessed by wrong means: e.g., direct access of an object for which indirect access is required; call by value instead of name, or vice versa; indexed instead of sequential, or vice versa.

4288: Object boundary or structure: access to object is partly correct, but the object structure and its boundaries are handled incorrectly: e.g., fetching 8 characters of a string instead of 7, mishandling word boundaries, getting too much or too little of an object.

5xxx: IMPLEMENTATION: bugs having to do with the implementation of the software. Some of these, such as standards and documentation, may not affect the actual workings of the software. They are included in the bug taxonomy because of their impact on maintenance.

51xx: CODING AND TYPOGRAPHICAL: bugs that can be clearly attributed to simple coding, as well as typographical bugs. Classification of a bug into this category is subjective. If a programmer believed that the correct variable, say, was "ABCD" instead of "ABCE", then it would be classified as a 4281 bug (wrong object accessed). Conversely, if E was changed to D because of a typewriting bug, then it belongs here.

511x: Coding wild card, typographical: all bugs that can be reasonably attributed to typing and other typographical bugs.

512x: Instruction, construct misunderstood: all bugs that can be reasonably attributed to a misunderstanding of an instruction's operation or HOL statement's action.

52xx: STANDARDS VIOLATION: bugs having to do with violating or misunderstanding the applicable programming standards and conventions. The software is assumed to work properly.

521x: Structure violations: violations concerning control-flow structure, organization of the software, etc.

5212: Control flow: violations of control-flow structure conventions: e.g., excessive IF-THEN-ELSE nesting, not using CASE statements where required, not following dictated processing order, jumping into or out of loops, jumping into or out of decisions.

5214: Complexity: violation of maximum (usually) or minimum (rare) complexity guidelines as measured by some specified complexity metric: e.g., too many lines of code in module, cyclomatic complexity greater than 200, excessive Halstead length, too many tokens.

5215: Loop nesting depth: excessive loop nesting depth.

5216: Modularity and partition: modularity and partition rules not followed: e.g., minimum and maximum size, object scope, functionally dictated partitions.

5217: Call nesting depth: violations of component (e.g., subroutine, subprogram, function) maximum nesting depth, or insufficient depth where dictated.

522x: Data definition, declarations: the form and/or location of data object declaration is not according to standards.

523x: Data access: violations of conventions governing how data objects of different kinds are to be accessed, wrong kind of object used: e.g., not using field-access macros, direct access instead of indirect, absolute reference instead of symbolic, access via register, etc.

524x: Calling and invoking: bugs in the manner in which other processing components are called, invoked, or communicated with: e.g., a direct subroutine call that should be indirect, violation of call and return sequence conventions.

526x: Mnemonics, label conventions: violations of the rules by which names are assigned to objects: e.g., program labels, subroutine and program names, data object names, file names.

527x: Format: violations of conventions governing the overall format and appearance of the source code: indentation rules, pagination, headers, ID block, special markers.

528x: Comments: violations of conventions governing the use, placement, density, and format of comments. The content of comments is covered by 53xx, documentation.

53xx: DOCUMENTATION: bugs in the documentation associated with the code or the content of comments contained in the code.

531x: Incorrect: documentation statement is wrong.

532x: Inconsistent: documentation statement is inconsistent with itself or with other statements.

533x: Incomprehensible: documentation cannot be understood by a qualified reader.

534x: Incomplete: documentation is correct but important facts are missing.

535x: Missing: major parts of documentation are missing.

6xxx: INTEGRATION: bugs having to do with the integration of, and interfaces between, components. The components themselves are assumed to be correct.

61xx: INTERNAL INTERFACES: bugs related to the interfaces between communicating components with the program under test. The components are assumed to have passed their component level tests. In this context, direct or indirect transfer of data or control information via a memory object such as tables, dynamically allocated resources, or files, constitute an internal interface.

611x: Component invocation: bugs having to do with how software components are invoked. In this sense, a "component" can be a subroutine, function, macro, program, program segment, or any other sensible processing component. Note the use of "invoke" rather than "call," because there may be no actual call as such: e.g., a task order placed on a processing queue is an invocation in our sense, though (typically) not a call.

6111: No such component: invoked component does not exist.

6112: Wrong component: incorrect component invoked.

612x: Interface parameter, invocation: having to do with the parameters of the invocation, their number, order, type, location, values, etc.

6121: Wrong parameter: parameters of the invocation are incorrectly specified.

6122: Parameter type: incorrect invocation parameter type used.

6124: Parameter structure: structural details of parameter used are incorrect: e.g., size, number of fields, subtypes.

6125: Parameter value: value (numerical, boolean, string) of the parameter is wrong.

6126: Parameter sequence: parameters of the invocation sequence in the wrong order, too many parameters, too few parameters.

613x: Component invocation return: having to do with the interpretation of parameters provided by the invoked component on return to the invoking component or on release of control to some other component. In this context, a record, a subroutine return sequence, or a file can qualify for this category of bug. Note that the bugs included here are *not* bugs in the component that created the return data but in the receiving component's subsequent manipulation and interpretation of that data.

6131: Parameter identity: wrong return parameter accessed.

6132: Parameter type: wrong return parameter type used; that is, the component using the return data interprets a return parameter incorrectly as to type.

6134: Parameter structure: return parameter structure misinterpreted.

6136: Return Sequence: sequence assumed for return parameters is incorrect.

614x: Initialization, state: invoked component not initialized or initialized to the wrong state or with incorrect data.

615x: Invocation in wrong place: the place or state in the invoking component at which the invoked component was invoked is wrong.

616x: Duplicate or spurious invocation: component should not have been invoked or has been invoked more often than necessary.

62xx: EXTERNAL INTERFACES AND TIMING: having to do with external interfaces, such as I/O devices and/or drivers, or other software not operating under the same control structure. Data passage by files or messages qualify for this bug category.

621x: Interrupts: bugs related to incorrect interrupt handling or setting up for interrupts: e.g., wrong handler invoked, failure to block or unblock interrupts.

622x: Devices and drivers: incorrect interface with devices or device drivers or incorrect interpretation of return status data.

6222: Device, driver, initialization or state: incorrect initialization of device or driver, failure to initialize, setting device to the wrong state.

6224: Device, driver, command bug: bug in the command issued to a device or driver.

6226: Device, driver, return/status misinterpretation: return status data from device or driver misinterpreted or ignored.

623x: I/O timing or throughput: bugs having to do with timings and data rates for external devices such as: not meeting specified timing requirements (too long or too short), forcing too much throughput, not accepting incoming data rates.

7xxx: SYSTEM AND SOFTWARE ARCHITECTURE: bugs that are not attributable to a component or to the interface between components but affect the entire software system or stem from architectural errors in the system.

71xx: OS bug: bugs related to the use of operating system facilities. Not to be confused with bugs in the operating system itself.

711x: Invocation, command: erroneous command given to operating system or OS facility incorrectly invoked.

712x: Return data, status misinterpretation: data returned from operating system or status information ignored or misinterpreted.

714x: Space: required memory (cache, disc, RAM) resource not available or requested in the wrong way.

72xx: Software architecture: architectural problems not elsewhere defined.

721x: Interlocks and semaphores: bugs in the use of interlock mechanisms and interprocess communications facilities. Not to be confused with bugs in these mechanisms themselves: e.g., failure to lock, failure to unlock, failure to set or reset semaphore, duplicate locking.

722x: Priority: bugs related to task priority: e.g., priority too low or too high, priority selected not allowed, priority conflicts.

723x: Transaction-flow control: where the path taken by a transaction through the system is controlled by an implicit or explicit transaction flow-control mechanism, these are bugs related to the definition of such flows. Note that all components and their interfaces could be correct but this kind of bug could still exist.

724x: Resource management and control: bugs related to the management of dynamically allocated shared resource objects: e.g., not returning a buffer block after use, not getting an object, failure to clean up an object after use, getting wrong kind of object, returning object to wrong pool.

725x: Recursive calls: bugs in the use of recursive invocation of software components or incorrect recursive invocation.

726x: Reentrance: bugs related to reentrance of program components: e.g., a reentrant component that should not be reentrant, a nonreentrant component that should be, a reentrant call that should be nonreentrant.

73xx: RECOVERY, ACCOUNTABILITY: bugs related to the recovery of objects after failure and to the accountability for objects despite failures.

74xx: PERFORMANCE: bugs related to the throughput-delay behavior of software under the assumption that all other aspects are correct.

741x: Throughput inadequate.

742x: Response time, delay: response time to incoming events too long at specified load or too short (rare), delay between outgoing events too long or too short.

743x: Insufficient users: maximum specified number of simultaneous users or task cannot be accommodated at specified transaction delays.

748x: Performance parasites: any bug whose primary or only symptom is a performance degradation: e.g., the harmless but needless repetition of operations, fetching and returning more dynamic resources than needed.

75xx: INCORRECT DIAGNOSTIC, EXCEPTION: diagnostic or error message incorrect or misleading. Exception handler invoked is wrong.

76xx: PARTITIONS AND OVERLAYS: memory or virtual memory is incorrectly partitioned, overlay to wrong area, overlay or partition conflicts.

77xx: SYSGEN OR ENVIRONMENT: wrong operating system version, incorrect system generation, or other host environment problem.

8xxx: TEST DEFINITION OR EXECUTION BUGS: bugs in the definition, design, execution of tests or the data used in tests. These are as important as "real" bugs.

81xx: DESIGN BUGS: bugs in the design of tests.

811x: Requirements misunderstood: test and component are mismatched because test designer did not understand requirements.

812x: Incorrect outcome predicted: predicted outcome of test does not match required or actual outcome.

813x: Incorrect path predicted: outcome is correct but was achieved by the wrong predicted path. The test is only coincidentally correct.

814x: Test initialization: specified initial conditions for test are wrong.

815x: Test data structure or value: data objects used in tests or their values are wrong.

816x: Sequencing bug: the sequence in which tests are to be executed, relative to other tests or to test initialization, is wrong.

817x: Configuration: the hardware and/or software configuration and/or environment specified for the test is wrong.

818x: Verification method, criteria: the method by which the outcome will be verified is incorrect or impossible.

82xx: EXECUTION BUGS: bugs in the execution of tests as contrasted with bugs in their design.

821x: Initialization: tested component not initialized to the right state or values.

822x: Keystroke or command: simple keystroke or button hit error.

823x: Database: database used to support the test was wrong.

824x: Configuration: configuration and/or environment specified for the test was not used during the run.

828x: Verification act: the act of verifying the outcome was incorrectly executed.

83xx: TEST DOCUMENTATION: documentation of test case or verification criteria is incorrect or misleading.

84xx: TEST CASE COMPLETENESS: cases required to achieve specified coverage criteria are missing.

CITED REFERENCES
AND BIBLIOGRAPHY

Note: Numbers in italics following an entry denote the text page(s) on which the entry is cited.

ABEJ79   Abe, J., Sakamura, K., and Aiso, H. An analysis of software project failures. Fourth International Conference on Software Engineering, Munich, Germany, September 17–19, 1979. *2, 56, 461*
           Example of the use of metrics to predict the end of system feature testing based on test passage history.

AKIY71   Akiyama, K. An example of software system debugging. *Proceedings of the 1971 IFIP Congress.* Amsterdam, The Netherlands: North-Holland, 1971. *461, 488*
           Bug statistics on routines ranging in size from 700 to 5500 instructions with correlation to the number of decisions and subroutine calls. Proportion of bugs found in unit testing, integration testing, and system testing.

ALBE76   Alberts, D. S. The economics of software quality assurance. *Proceedings of the 1976 National Computer Conference.* Montvale, N.J.: AFIPS Press, 1976. *2*

ALLE72   Allen, F. E., and Cocke, J. Graph theoretic constructs for program control flow analysis. IBM Research Report RC3923, T. J. Watson Research Center, Yorktown Heights, N.Y., 1972.

ANDE79   Anderson, R. B. *Proving Programs Correct.* New York: John Wiley & Sons, 1979.

ANDR81   Andrews, D. M., and Benson, J. P. An automated program testing method and its implementation. Fifth International Conference on Software Engineering, San Diego, Calif., March 9–12, 1981. *451*

ANSI83A   ANSI/IEEE Standard 729-1983. Glossary of Software Engineering Terminology.

ANSI83B   ANSI/IEEE Standard 828-1983. Software Configuration Management Plans.

ANSI83C   ANSI/IEEE Standard 829-1983. Software Test Documentation.

ANSI84A   ANSI/IEEE Standard 730-1984. Software Quality Assurance Plans.

ANSI84B   ANSI/IEEE Standard 830-1984. Software Requirements Specifications.

ANSI86A   ANSI/IEEE Standard 983-1986. Software Quality Assurance Planning.

ANSI87A   ANSI/IEEE Standard 1002-1987. Taxonomy for Software Engineering Standards.
           Includes bibliography of many important DOD, FIPS/NBS standards on software engineering. Listing of IEEE standards activities under way including: reliability measurement, review and audits, configuration management, error classification, productivity metrics, project management, verification and validation, maintenance, software quality metrics, third-party software acquisition, user documentation, life-cycle process.

ANSI87B   ANSI/IEEE Standard 1008-1987. Software Unit Testing. *75*

ANSI87C   ANSI/IEEE Standard 1012-1987. Software Verification and Validation Plans.

ANSI87D   ANSI/IEEE Standard 1016-1987. Software Design Descriptions.

ANSI87E   ANSI/IEEE Standard P1044/D3. Draft Standard of: A Standard Classification for Software Errors, Faults, and Failures.

BACK59   Backus, J. The syntax and the semantics of the proposed international algebraic language. *Proceedings of the ACM-GAMM Conference*. Paris, France: Information Processing, 1959. *291*

BAKE79A   Baker, A. L., and Zweben, S. H. A comparison of measures of control flow complexity. Third Computer Software and Applications Conference, Chicago, Ill., November 1979. *235, 237, 239*

BAKE80   Baker, A. L. A comparison of measures of control flow complexity. *IEEE Transactions on Software Engineering* **6:**506–511 (1980). *235, 237*

BARN72   Barnes, B. H. A programmer's view of automata. *Computing Surveys* **4:**222–239 (1972). *363*
           Introduction to state graphs and related automata theory topics from a software application perspective.

BASI87   Basili, V. R., and Selby, R. W. Comparing the effectiveness of software testing strategies. *IEEE Transactions on Software Engineering* **13:**1278–1296 (1987). *7, 90, 455*
           A (rare) controlled experiment designed to explore the relative effectiveness of functional versus structural testing, coverage metrics, professional versus student programmers.

BAUE79   Bauer, J. A., and Finger, A. B. Test plan generation using formal grammars. Fourth International Conference on Software Engineering, Munich, Germany, September 17–19, 1979. *390, 457*

Use of state graph model for processes and automated test case generation. Examples of application to telephony.

BEIZ71   Beizer, B. *The Architecture and Engineering of Digital Computer Complexes.* New York: Plenum Press, 1971. *411*

BEIZ78   Beizer, B. *Micro-Analysis of Computer System Performance.* New York: Van Nostrand Reinhold, 1978.
Analytical models of software processing time, memory utilization, queueing theory, system models, mass memory latency models, model validation, and system tuning.

BEIZ79   Beizer, B. *Organizacja Systemow Komputerowyc.* Warsaw, Poland: Panstwowe Wydawnictwo Naukowe, 1979. *303*
Polish edition of BEIZ71.

BEIZ84   Beizer, B. *Software System Testing and Quality Assurance.* New York: Van Nostrand Reinhold, 1984.
Companion to this book. Test and QA management, integration testing, system testing. Organization of testing, functional testing, formal acceptance testing, stress testing, software reliability, bug prediction methods, software metrics, test teams, adversary teams, design reviews, walkthroughs, etc.

BELA80   Belady, B. L. A. Software geometry. International Computer Symposium, Taipei, China, December 1980.
Definition of structural metric as mean nesting level.

BELF76   Belford, P. C., and Taylor, D. S. Specification verification—a key to improving software reliability. *Proceedings of the PIB Symposium on Computer Software Engineering.* New York: Polytechnic Institute of New York, 1976. *35, 461*
Verification of specifications, use of specification languages, and related subjects.

BELF79   Belford, P. C., Berg, R. A., and Hannan, T. L. Central flow control software development: A case study of the effectiveness of software engineering techniques. Fourth International Conference on Software Engineering, Munich, Germany, September 17-19, 1979. *59, 234, 237, 461*
Decision-to-decision paths as a measure of complexity. Statistics on bugs caught during design review, unit testing, and system testing based on 24,000 lines of executable code. Statistics show that limiting the module size is not effective and that module sizes of 100 to 200 lines would be better than 50 lines of executable code.

BELL87   Bellman, K. L., and Walter, D. O. Testing rule-based expert systems. Computer Science Laboratory Report, The Aerospace Corporation, November 1, 1987. *322*

BEND70C   Bender, R. A., and Pottorff, E. L. Basic testing: a data flow analysis

technique. IBM System Development Division, Poughkeepsie Laboratory, TR-00.2108, October 9, 1970. *170, 171, 451, 456*
Early description of effectiveness of data flow testing.

BEND85   Bender, R. A., and Becker, P. Code analysis. Bender and Associates, P.O. Box 849, Larkspur, CA 94939. *170*
Proprietary software development and test methodology that features use of data-flow testing techniques.

BERZ85   Berzins, V., and Gray, M. Analysis and design in MSG.84: formalizing functional specifications. *IEEE Transactions on Software Engineering* **11:**657–670 (1985). *35, 321, 457*

BLUM87   Blum, R., and Klandrud, T. A communication systems simulation language translator. Proceedings of the Summer Computer Simulation Conference, Montreal, Canada, July 1987. *457*

BOEH73   Boehm, B. W. Software and its impact: a quantitative assessment. *Datamation* **19:**48–59 (May 1973).

BOEH75A   Boehm, B. W., McClean, R. K., and Urfrig, D. B. Some experience with automated aids to the design of large-scale reliable software. *IEEE Transactions on Software Engineering* **1:**125–133 (1975). *56, 461*
Software error statistics.

BOEH75B   Boehm, B. W. Software design and structuring. In *Practical Strategies for Developing Large Software Systems* (Ellis Horowitz, editor). Reading, Mass.: Addison-Wesley, 1975. *2, 90*

BOEH75C   Boehm, B. W. The high cost of software. In *Practical Strategies for Developing Large Software Systems* (Ellis Horowitz, editor). Reading, Mass.: Addison-Wesley, 1975. *1*

BOEH79   Boehm, B. W. Software engineering—as it is. Fourth International Conference on Software Engineering, Munich, Germany, September 17–19, 1979.
Survey of the state of the art in testing and software engineering. Good aphorisms.

BOEH81   Boehm, B. W. *Software Engineering Economics*. Englewood Cliffs, N.J.: Prentice-Hall, 1981. *215*
Source book for all aspects of software economics.

BOHM66   Bohm, C., and Jacopini, G. Flow diagrams, Turing machines, and languages with only two formation rules. *Communications of the ACM* **9:**366–371 (1966). *62*
Proof that single-entry/single-exit programs can be constructed without GOTOs using only the IF-THEN-ELSE and DO-WHILE constructs.

BOIE72   Boies, S. J., and Gould, J. D. A behavioral analysis of programming—on the frequency of syntactical errors. IBM Research Report

RC-3907, T. J. Watson Research Center, Yorktown Heights, N.Y., June 1972. *56, 461*

BONN88 Bonnstetter, B. Unisys Corporation, Clear Lake, Iowa. Private communication of bug statistics. *461*

BOWD77 Bowditch, N. *American Practical Navigator,* 70th edition, Washington, D.C.: Defense Mapping Agency Hydrographic Center (1977). *148*
Kotlaric's sight reduction method. What *our* discipline should strive to be when it grows up.

BRIT85 Britcher, R. H., and Gaffney, J. E. Reliable size estimates for software systems decomposed as state machines. Ninth International Computer Software and Applications Conference, Chicago, Ill., October 9–11, 1985.
Representation of program as finite-state machine relates state machine size, Halstead length, and program size.

BROW73 Brown, J. R., and Lipow, M. The quantitative measurement of software safety and reliability. TRW Report SDP-1176, 1973. *1*

BRZO62A Brzozowski, J. A. A survey of regular expressions and their application. *IRE Transactions on Electronic Computers* **11:**324–335 (1962). *243*
Survey of regular expression theory and its application to logic design and finite automata.

BRZO62B Brzozowski, J. A. Canonical regular expressions and minimal state graphs for definite events. *Proceedings of the PIB Symposium on the Mathematical Theory of Automata.* New York: Polytechnic Press (John Wiley), 1963. *243, 282*

BRZO63 Brzozowski, J. A., and McCluskey, E. J., Jr. Signal flow graph techniques for sequential circuit state diagrams. *IEEE Transactions on Electronic Computers* **12:**67–76 (1963). *243, 252*
Basic paper that applies Mason's flowgraphs to regular expressions and state graphs of finite-state machines.

BUDD81 Budd, T. A. Mutation analysis: ideas, examples, problems, and prospects. In *Computer Program Testing* (B. Chandrasekaran and S. Radicchi, editors). New York: Elsevier North-Holland, 1981. *313*

BURK88 Burke, R. Black-box regression testing—an automated approach. Fifth International Conference on Testing Computer Software, Washington D.C., June 13–16, 1988. *455*

BUTL89 Butler, R. W., Mejia, J. D., Brooks, P. A., and Hewson, J. E. Automated testing for real-time systems. Sixth International Conference on Testing Computer Software, Washington D.C., May 22–25, 1989. *455*

BUYA82 Buyansky, D. V., and Schatz, J. W. No. 1A ESS laboratory support

system—erasable flag facility. Sixth International Conference on Software Engineering, Tokyo, Japan, September 13–16, 1982. *451*
Hardware/software coverage analyzer.

CARD86   Card, D. N., Church, V. E., and Agresti, W. W. An empirical study of software design practices. *IEEE Transactions on Software Engineering* **12:**264–271 (1986).
Bug frequency statistics from large FORTRAN sample.

CERI81   Ceriani, M., Cicu, A., and Maiocchi, M. A methodology for accurate software test specification and auditing. In *Computer Program Testing* (B. Chandrasekaran and S. Radicchi, editors). New York: Elsevier North-Holland, 1981.
Experience with test development methods, controls, practices.

CHAN81   Chandrasekaran, B., and Radicchi, S. (editors). *Computer Program Testing.* Summer School on Computer Program Testing held at SOGESTA, Urbino, Italy, June 29–July 3, 1981. New York: Elsevier North-Holland, 1981.
Collection of previously published and original papers concerned with testing theory and practice.

CHAP79   Chapin, N. A measure of software complexity. *Proceedings of the 1979 National Computer Conference.* Montvale, N.J.: AFIPS Press, 1979. *237*

CHEL87   Chellappa, M. Nontraversable paths in a program. *IEEE Transactions on Software Engineering* **13:**751–755 (1987).
Finite-state machine representation of the program flowgraph and analysis of unachievable paths.

CHEN78A   Chen, E. T. Program complexity and programmer productivity. *IEEE Transactions on Software Engineering* **4:**187-194 (1978). *234, 236, 237*
Defines a complexity metric based on structure and information theory. Shows discontinuous productivity change with increased complexity.

CHEN78B   Chen, W. T., Ho, J. P., and Wen, C. H. Dynamic validation of programs using assertion checking facilities. Second Computer Software and Applications Conference, Chicago, Ill., November 1978. *451*

CHIU85   Chi, U. H. Formal specification of user interfaces: a comparison and evaluation of four axiomatic approaches. *IEEE Transactions on Software Engineering* **11:**671–685 (1985). *321*

CHOI84   Choi, T. Y. On the recoverability of finite state protocols. Eighth International Computer Software and Applications Conference, Chicago, Ill., November 7–9, 1984. *389*

CHOW78   Chow, T. S. Testing software design modeled by finite state machines. *IEEE Transactions on Software Engineering* **4:**78–186 (1978). *388*

Testing software modeled by state graphs with examples from telephony. Definition of n-switch coverage as a generalization of statement coverage. Categorizes types of state graph errors and shows relation between type of coverage and the kind of errors that can and can't be caught.

CHOW88   Chow, C. H., and Lam, S. S. PROSPEC: an interactive programming environment for designing and verifying communication protocols. *IEEE Transactions on Software Engineering* **14:**327–338 (1988). *455, 457*

CHUN78   Chung, P., and Gaiman, B. Use of state diagrams to engineer communications software. Third International Conference on Software Engineering, Atlanta, Ga., May 10–12, 1978. *389*

CHUS87   Chusho, T. Test data selection and quality estimation based on the concepts of essential branches for path testing. *IEEE Transactions on Software Engineering* **13:**509–517 (1987).
Another path coverage metric and path selection algorithms for producing more efficient covering test sets. For tool builders.

CICU75   Cicu, A., Maiocchi, M., Polillo, R., and Sardoni, A. Organizing tests during software evolution. International Conference on Reliable Software, Los Angeles, Calif., April 1975. *456*

CLAR76   Clarke, L. A. A system to generate test data and symbolically execute programs. *IEEE Transactions on Software Engineering* **2:**215–222 (1976). *451, 456*

CLAR78   Clarke, L. A. Testing: achievements and frustrations. Second Computer Software and Applications Conference, Chicago, Ill., November 1978. *456*

CLAR81   Clarke, L. A., and Richardson, D. J. Symbolic evaluation methods—implementation and applications. In *Computer Program Testing* (B. Chandrasekaran and S. Radicchi, editors). New York: Elsevier North-Holland, 1981. *451*
Use of static and dynamic symbolic evaluation as a test method. Methods and tools for symbolic evaluation.

CLAR82   Clarke, L. A., Hassel, J., and Richardson, D. J. A close look at domain testing. *IEEE Transactions on Software Engineering* **8:**380–390 (1982). *201*

CLAR85   Clarke, L. A., Podgurski, A., Richardson, D. J., and Zeil, S. J. A comparison of data flow path selection criteria. *IEEE Transactions on Software Engineering* **11:**244–251 (1985).

CLAR86   Clarke, L. A., Podgurski, A., Richardson, D. J., and Zeil, S. J. An investigation of data flow path selection criteria. Workshop on Software Testing, Banff, Canada, July 15–17, 1986. *166*
Formal analysis, comparison, and ordering of various coverage criteria.

COHE78   Cohen, E. I. *A Finite Domain-Testing Strategy for Computer Program Testing.* Ph.D. dissertation, The Ohio State University, June 1978. *184*

COLL82   Collofello, J. S., and Klinkel, G. D. An automated Pascal test coverage assessment tool. Sixth International Computer Software and Applications Conference, Chicago, Ill., November 8–12, 1982. *451*

COLL84   Collofello, J. S., and Ferrara, A. F. An automated Pascal multiple condition test coverage tool. Eighth International Computer Software and Applications Conference, Chicago, Ill., November 7–9, 1984. *451*

CONK89   Conklin, J. Automated repetitive testing. Sixth International Conference on Testing Computer Software, Washington D.C., May 22–25, 1989. *454, 455*

CROS89   Crosstalk Communications. *Crosstalk Mk.4 User's Guide, Reference Manual.* Rosswell, Ga.: Digital Communications Associates, Inc., 1989. *309, 311*

CURR86   Currans, N. A comparison of counting methods for software science and cyclomatic complexity. Pacific Northwest Software Quality Conference, Portland, Oregon, 1986. *214, 239, 451*

       Halstead's metrics, McCabe's metric, lines of code, bugs, correlated and compared. Based on study of 30 "C" modules. No module size given. Correlation between alternative ways of counting McCabe's complexity.

CURT79A   Curtis, B., Sheppard, S. B., and Milliman, P. Third time charm: stronger predictions of programmer performance by software complexity metrics. Fourth International Conference on Software Engineering, Munich, Germany, September 17–19, 1979. *219, 222, 234, 235, 239, 498*

       Continuation of related experiments (see SHEP79C). Correlation between McCabe, Halstead, and program length metrics. Halstead's metric appears to be a better predictor than either length or McCabe's metric. Study dealt with small FORTRAN routines.

CURT80B   Curtis, B. Measurement and experimentation in software engineering. *Proceedings of the IEEE* **68:**1144–1157 (1980).

       Survey of complexity metrics including McCabe's and Halstead's.

DATA90   Daybreak Technologies Inc. *Data Sources Software Products Guide.* Cherry Hill, N.J.: Data Sources Inc., 1990. *449, 453*

       Periodical guide to software products.

DAVI88A   Davis, A. M. A comparison of techniques for the specification of external system behavior. *Communications of the ACM* **31:**1098–1115 (1988). *35, 363, 368*

       Survey of state graphs, state tables, decision tables, decision trees, program design languages, Petri nets, requirement languages, and specification languages in developing requirements and tests from them.

DAVI88B   Davis, A. M. *Software Requirements: Analysis and Specification.* Englewood Cliffs, N.J.: Prentice-Hall, 1988. *35*

DAVI88C   Davis, J. S, and LeBlanc, R. J. A study of the applicability of complexity measures. *IEEE Transactions on Software Engineering* **14:**1366–1372 (1988). *214, 239*

DEGA81   Degano, P., and Levi, G. Software development and testing in an integrated programming environment. In *Computer Program Testing* (B. Chandrasekaran and S. Radicchi, editors). New York: Elsevier North-Holland, 1981. *455*

DEMI78   DeMillo, R. A., Lipton, R. J., and Sayward, F. G. Hints on test data selection: help for the practicing programmer. *IEEE Computer* **11(4):**34–43 (1978).

DEON74   Deo, N. *Graph Theory with Applications to Engineering and Computer Science.* Englewood Cliffs, N.J.: Prentice-Hall, 1974.

DERE76   DeRemer, F., and Kron, H. K. Programming-in-the-large versus programming-in-the-small. *IEEE Transactions on Software Engineering* **2:**80–86 (1976). *14*
           Discussion of linguistic features that abet the construction and testing of large programs.

DEYO79   DeYoung, G. E., and Kampen, G. R. Program factors as predictors of program readability. Third Conference on Computer Software and Applications, Chicago, Ill., November 6–8, 1979. *222, 237*

DNIE78   Dniesirowski, A., Guillaume, J. M., and Mortier, R. Software engineering in avionics applications. Third International Conference on Software Engineering, Atlanta, Ga., May 10–12, 1978. *56, 461*
           Good bug categories. Statistics on bugs caught during specification, design, and coding and the kind of testing used to catch them. Also effort required to catch bugs.

DRAB88   Drabick, R. Eastman Kodak Company, Software Systems Division, Rochester, N.Y. *461*
           Private communication of bug statistics.

DRAP81   Draper, N., and Smith, H. *Applied Regression Analysis* (second edition). New York: John Wiley & Sons, 1981. *238*
           Primary reference for regression analysis.

DUNN82   Dunn, R., and Ullman, R. *Quality Assurance for Computer Software.* New York: McGraw-Hill, 1982. *222*

DURA84   Duran, J. W, and Ntafos, S. C. An evaluation of random testing. *IEEE Transactions on Software Engineering* **10:**438–443 (1984). *200*
           Experiment on five mathematical routines with random test data and coverage (several metrics) achieved. Points out that uncovered

branches tend to be for exception conditions and suggests combination with other techniques.

ELLI89   Ellis, R. A. Testing of embedded software in real-time controllers using emulation. Sixth International Conference on Testing Computer Software, Washington D.C., May 22–25, 1989. *455*

ELSH76B   Elshoff, J. L. An analysis of some commercial PL/I programs. *IEEE Transactions on Software Engineering* **2:**113–120 (1976). *56, 461*

ELSH78B   Elshoff, J. L., and Marcotty, M. On the use of the cyclomatic number to measure program complexity. *ACM SIGPLAN Notices* **13:**33–40 (1978).

ELSH84   Elshoff, J. L. Characteristic program complexity measures. Seventh International Conference on Software Engineering, Orlando, Fla., March 26–29, 1984.
          Twenty metrics, including Halstead's, applied to 585 PL/I procedures and correlated.

ENDR75   Endres, A. An analysis of errors and their causes in system programs. *IEEE Transactions on Software Engineering* **1:**140–149 (1975). *2, 56, 90, 234, 235, 461*
          Detailed error categories and bug statistics.

EVAN84   Evangelist, M. An analysis of control flow complexity. Eighth International Computer Software and Applications Conference, Chicago, Ill., November 7–9, 1984. *235, 236, 237, 239*
          Critiques of Halstead's and McCabe's metrics and suggested fixes.

EVAN88   Evans, G. K., NCR Corporation, West Columbia, SC.
          Private communication of bug statistics. *461*

EVEN79   Even, S. *Graph Algorithms*. Potomac, Md.: Computer Science Press, 1979. *398, 403*
          Resource material.

FAGA76   Fagan, M. E. Design and code inspections to reduce errors in program development. *IBM Systems Journal* **3:**182–211 (1976). *7, 8, 435*
          Kill the bugs before they hatch. Required reading because of inspection's effectiveness. Bug statistics, inspection checklists, inspections versus walkthroughs.

FAIR81   Fairley, R. E. Software testing tools. In *Computer Program Testing* (B. Chandrasekaran and S. Radicchi, editors). New York: Elsevier North-Holland, 1981. *449*

FEUE79A   Feuer, A. R., and Fowlkes, E. G. Some results from an empirical study of computer software. Fourth International Conference on Software Engineering, Munich, Germany, September 17–19, 1979. *222, 234, 235, 239*
          Study of 197 PL/I routines averaging 54 statements. Focus on

maintainability. Shows that program size is a good guide to maintainability and that decision density is better suited to big programs.

FEUE79B   Feuer, A. R., and Fowlkes, E. B. Relating computer program maintainability to software measures. Proceedings of the 1979 National Computer Conference. Montvale, N.J.: AFIPS Press, 1979. *222, 234, 235, 237, 239*
Study of 123 PL/I modules in business data processing applications. Relates complexity measure to maintainability. Applies Halstead's metric to maintainability question.

FISC79   Fischer, K. F., and Walker, M. J. Improved software reliability through requirements verification. *IEEE Transactions on Reliability* **28:**233–240 (1979). *35*

FITS80   Fitsos, G. P. Vocabulary effects in software science. Fourth International Conference on Computer Software And Applications, Chicago, Ill., October 27–31, 1980. *222*

FORM84   Forman, I. R. An algebra for data flow anomaly detection. Seventh International Conference on Software Engineering, Orlando, Fl., March 26–29, 1984.
Use of regular expressions generated from program flowgraphs for data-flow anomalies.

FOSD76A   Fosdick, L. D., and Osterweil, L. J. Data flow analysis in software reliability. *ACM Computing Surveys* **8:**305–330 (1979). *171, 456*
Use of graphs, survey of symbolic execution methods, path expressions derived from flowgraphs, detection of data-flow anomalies.

FOST80   Foster, K. A. Error sensitive test case analysis (ESTCA). *IEEE Transactions on Software Engineering* **6:**258–264 (1980).
Three rules for structural testing based on input-data domains: useful rules for arithmetic processing.

FRAN86   Frankl, P. G., and Weyuker, E. J., Data flow testing in the presence of unexecutable paths. Workshop on Software Testing, Banff, Canada, July 15–17, 1986. *166*
Formal analysis, comparison, ordering, of data-flow test criteria for programs with unachievable paths.

FRAN88   Frankl, P. G., and Weyuker, E. J. An applicable family of data flow testing criteria. *IEEE Transactions on Software Engineering* **14:**1483–1498 (1988). *159, 162, 163, 166, 169, 171, 455, 456*
Continuation and expansion of FRAN86.

FREE88   Freeman, P. A., and Hunt, H. S. Software quality improvement through automated testing. Fifth International Conference on Testing Computer Software, Washington D.C., June 13–16, 1988. *455*

FREN88   French, I. G. Independent verification and validation (IV&V) in Ada software environments. National Institute for Software and Productivity Conference, Washington D.C., April 20–22, 1988.

FSTC83   Federal Software Testing Center. *Software Tools Survey*. Office of Software Development Report OSD/FSTC-83/015, 1983. *449, 455*
     Survey of 100 software development tools, language, source.

FUJI80   Fujimura, N., and Ushijima, K. Experience with a COBOL analyzer. Fourth Computer Software and Applications Conference, Chicago, Ill., October 27–31, 1980. *451*
     COBOL statement coverage analyzer, execution counter, and (almost) branch coverage analyzer.

FUNA76   Funami, Y., and Halstead, M. A software physics analysis of Akiyama's debugging data. *Proceedings of the PIB Symposium on Computer Software Engineering*. New York: Polytechnic Institute of New York, 1976. *222*
     Oft-cited paper showing correlation of Halstead's metrics to bug counts and cost based on nine modules totaling 25,000 executable assembly language instructions (see AKIY71).

FURG89   Furgerson, D. F., Coutu, J. P., Reinemann, J. K., and Novakovich, M. R. Automated testing of a real-time microprocessor operating system. Sixth International Conference on Testing Computer Software, Washington D.C., May 23–25, 1989. *311, 455*
     Description of application of Crosstalk CASL scripting language to test script design and to construction of a testing environment.

GABO76   Gabow, H. N., Maheshwari, S. N., and Osterweil, L. J. On two problems in the generation of program test paths. *IEEE Transactions on Software Engineering* **2:**227–231 (1976).
     Construction of constrained paths.

GAFF84   Gaffney, J. E., Jr. Estimating the number of faults in code. *IEEE Transactions on Software Engineering* **10:**459–464 (1984). *222, 497*
     Shows that bug density is relatively insensitive to source language, but see LIPO86 and TRAC86 for rebuttal.

GANN76   Gannon, J. D. Data types and programming reliability—some preliminary evidence. *Proceedings of the PIB Symposium on Computer Software Engineering*. New York: Polytechnic Institute of New York, 1976. *46, 56, 461*
     Discussion of data types and data type operands. Summary of errors related to data types.

GANN79   Gannon, C. Error detection using path testing and static analysis. *IEEE Computer* **12:**26–31 (1979). *90*

GANN80   Gannon, C. A debugging, testing, and documentation tool for JOVIAL J73. Fourth International Conference on Computer Software and Applications, Chicago, Ill., October 27–31, 1980. *451, 454, 455*

Description of multifunction tool for JOVIAL source, including static and data-flow analysis, coverage, timing, and test driver.

GEIG79 Geiger, W., Gmeiner, L., Trangoth, H., and Voges, U. Program testing techniques for nuclear reactor protection systems. *IEEE Computer* **12**:10–17 (1979).
Structural component testing, tools, static analysis tool (SADAT), instrumentation.

GELP87 Gelperin, D., and Hetzel, W. Software Quality Engineering, Jacksonville, Fla. *3*
Motto on lapel pin and bumper stickers, Fourth International Conference on Software Testing, Washington D.C., June 15–18, 1987.

GERH88 Gerhart, S. L. A broad spectrum toolset for upstream testing, verification, and analysis. Second Workshop on Software Testing, Verification, and Analysis, Banff, Canada, July 19–21, 1988. *455, 457*

GHEZ81 Ghezzi, C. Levels of static program testing. In *Computer Program Testing* (B. Chandrasekaran and S. Radicchi, editors). New York: Elsevier North-Holland, 1981. *155*
Survey of static analysis methods and tools. Application to data-flow anomaly detection.

GILB77 Gilb, T. *Software Metrics*. Cambridge, Mass.: Winthrop, 1977. *56, 214, 237, 461*
Source book for almost all possible metrics.

GIRG86 Girgis, M. R., Woodward, M. R. An experimental comparison of the error exposing ability of program testing criteria. Workshop on Software Testing, Banff, Canada, July 15–17, 1986. *90*
Error-seeding experiment compares effectiveness of four control-flow test criteria, four data-flow test criteria, and mutation testing for computational and domain bugs.

GLIG87 Gligor, V. D., Chandersekaran, C. S., Jiang, W. D., Johri, A., Luckenbaugh, G. K., and Reich, L. E. A new security testing method and its application to the secure xenix kernel. *IEEE Transactions on Software Engineering* **13**:169–183 (1987).
Hybrid functional/structural testing applied to security kernel testing.

GOEL78B Goel, A. L., and Okumoto, K. Analysis of recurrent software errors in a real-time control system. ACM Annual Conference, 1978. *56, 461*

GOMA82 Gomaa, H., and Martello, S. J. A partially automated method for testing interactive systems. Sixth Computer Software and Applications Conference, Chicago, Ill., November 8–12, 1982. *455*

GONG85 Gong, H. S., and Schmidt, M. A complexity metric based on selection and nesting. *ACM Sigmetrics—Performance Evaluation Review* **13**(1):14–19 (1985). *237*

Proposed structural metric augments cyclomatic complexity to include nesting depth.

GOOD75   Goodenough, J. B., and Gerhart, S. L. Toward a theory of test data selection. *IEEE Transactions on Software Engineering* **1:**156–173 (1975). *26, 93, 328, 329*

Seminal paper. Limitations of structural testing and formal methods of proof. Formal definitions for reliable tests, valid tests, complete tests, and successful tests. Use of decision tables as an aid to test case design.

GOOD79   Goodenough, J. B. A survey of program testing issues. In *Research Directions in Software Technology* (Peter Wegner, editor). Cambridge, Mass.: MIT Press, 1979. *1*

GOOD80   Goodenough, J. B., and McGowan, C. L. Software quality assurance: testing and validation. *Proceedings of the IEEE* **68:**1093–1098, (1980).

Comparison of hardware and software life cycles, testing, research. Proposed methodology to improve software quality.

GOUR83   Gourlay, J. S. A mathematical framework for the investigation of testing. *IEEE Transactions on Software Engineering* **9:**686–709 (1983).

Fundamental paper for serious theorists. Formal definitions. Compares theoretical relative "power" of alternate test strategies. Excellent exposition for the mathematically mature.

GRAD87   Grady, R. B, and Caswell, D. L. *Software Metrics: Establishing a Company-Wide Program.* Englewood Cliffs, N.J.: Prentice-Hall, 1987. *214, 239, 451*

A practical guide to implementing metrics in an industrial setting.

GREE76   Green, T. F., Schneidewind, N. F., Howard, G. T., and Parisequ, R. Program structures, complexity, and error characteristics. *Proceedings of the PIB Symposium on Computer Software Engineering.* New York: Polytechnic Institute of New York, 1976.

GRUM88   Gruman, G. Management cited in bleak SQA survey. *IEEE Software* **5:**102–103 (May 1988). *459*

HALE81   Haley, A., and Zweben, S. Module integration testing. In *Computer Program Testing* (B. Chandrasekaran and S. Radicchi, editors). New York: Elsevier North-Holland, 1981.

Formal investigation of integration testing with a domain-testing flavor. Paths within tested called subcomponents. Integration strategy.

HALL78   Hallin, T. G., and Hansen, R. C. Toward a better method of software testing. Second Computer Software and Applications Conference, Chicago, Ill., November 1978. *457*

HALS75   Halstead, M. H. Software physics: basic principles. IBM Technical

Report RJ-1582, T. J. Watson Research Center, Yorktown Heights, N.Y., 1975. *220, 223*

HALS77   Halstead, M. H. *Elements of Software Science.* New York: Elsevier North-Holland, 1977.

HAML88   Hamlet, R., and Taylor, R. Partition testing does not inspire confidence. Second Workshop on Software Testing, Verification, and Analysis, Banff, Canada, July 19–21, 1988. *200*

HANF70   Hanford, K. V. Automatic generation of test cases. *IBM System Journal* **9**:242–257 (1979).
         Use of BNF and syntax-directed software to generate syntactically valid test cases of PL/I code for testing a PL/I compiler.

HANS78   Hanson, W. J. Measurement of program complexity by the pair cyclomatic number, operator count. *ACM SIGPLAN Notices* **13**:29–32 (1978).

HANT76   Hantler, S. L., and King, J. C. An introduction to proving the correctness of programs. *ACM Computing Surveys* **8**(3):331–353 (1976).

HARR82   Harrison, W., Magel, K., Kluczny, R., and DeKock, A. Applying software complexity metrics to program maintenance. *IEEE Computer* **15**:65–79 (1982). *214, 239*
         Excellent survey of a baker's dozen of metrics.

HARR88   Harrold, M. J. *An Approach to Incremental Testing.* Ph.D. dissertation, University of Pittsburgh, 1988 (Technical report 89-1).

HARR89   Harrold, M. J., and Soffa, M. L. An incremental data flow testing tool. Sixth International Conference on Testing Computer Software, Washington D.C., May 22–25, 1989. *171, 456*

HAUG64   Haugk, G., Tsiang, S. H., and Zimmerman, L. System testing of the number 1 electronic switching system. *Bell System Technical Journal* **43**:2575–2592 (1964). *56, 461*

HAYE85   Hayes, I. J. Applying formal specifications to software development in industry. *IEEE Transactions on Software Engineering* **11**:169–178 (1985). *35, 321*

HECH72   Hecht, M. S., and Ullman, J. D. Flow graph reducibility. *SIAM Journal on Computing* **1**:188–202 (1972).

HECH77B Hecht, M. S. *Flow Analysis of Computer Programs.* New York: Elsevier North-Holland, 1977. *263*
         A clear exposition of graph theory applied to the analysis of programs. Primarily aimed at questions related to compiler design and code optimization. Large bibliography. For the mathematically mature.

HEND75   Henderson, P. Finite state modeling in program development. IEEE 1975 International Conference on Reliable Software, Los Angeles, Calif., April 1975.

HEND89   Henderson, B. M. Big brother—automated test controller. Sixth International Conference on Testing Computer Software, Washington D.C., May 22–25, 1989. *455*

HENN84   Hennel, M. A., Hedley, D., and Riddell, I. J. Assessing a class of software tools. Seventh International Conference on Software Engineering, Orlando, Fla., March 26–29, 1984. *90*
          Branch, statement, and jump-to-jump path segment coverage metrics. COBOL and PL/I. Error detection effectiveness and bug types versus percent for each coverage type.

HENR81   Henry, S., Kafura, D., and Harris, K. On the relationships among three software metrics. *Performance Evaluation Review* **10**:3–10 (1981).
          McCabe's, Halstead's, and Thayer's metrics compared and correlated with each other and with bug rates.

HERA88   Herath, J., Yamaguchi, Y., Saito, N., and Yuba, T. Data flow computing models, languages, and machines for intelligence computations. *IEEE Transactions on Software Engineering:* **14**:1805–1828 (1988).
          Although the paper is aimed at intelligence processing, the overview and tutorial is one of the best around.

HERM76   Herman, P. M. A data flow analysis approach to program testing. *The Australian Computer Journal:* 92–96 (November 1976). *171, 456*
          Early published discussion of data-flow testing methods and tools.

HETZ73   Hetzel, W. C. (editor). *Program Test Methods.* Englewood Cliffs, N.J.: Prentice-Hall, 1972. *12*
          Basic book on testing. Comprehensive pre-1972 bibliography on testing and related subjects.

HETZ84   Hetzel, W. C. *The Complete Guide to Software Testing.* Wellesley, Mass.: QED Information Sciences, 1984.
          A pragmatic introduction to the organization and execution of testing with a commercial data processing flavor.

HIRS67   Hirsch, I. N. MEMMAP/360. Report TR P-1168, IBM Systems Development Division, Product Test Laboratories. Poughkeepsie, N.Y., February 3, 1967. *59, 75, 450, 451*
          Earliest known description of a software statement and branch coverage analyzer.

HOFF77   Hoffmann, H. M. *An Experiment in Software Error Occurrence and Detection.* M.S. thesis, Naval Postgraduate School, Monterey, Calif., June 1977. *56, 461*

HOLT87   Holt, D. A general purpose driver for UNIX. Fourth International Conference on Testing Computer Software, Washington, D.C., June 15–18, 1987. *454*

HOLZ87   Holzman, G. J. Automated protocol validation in *Argos:* assertion

proving and scatter searching. *IEEE Transactions on Software Engineering* **13:**683–696 (1987). *363*
  Experience in automatically generated state-machine-based testing cases as applied to protocol verification. Application and strategies for systems having up to 10^{24} states.

HORE79   Horejs, J. Finite semantics: a technique for program testing. Fourth International Conference on Software Engineering, Munich, Germany, September 17–19, 1979.

HOSO83   Hosoya, R., and Hotta, H. Static detection of ADA programming errors through joint analysis of data flow and value range. Seventh International Computer Software and Applications Conference, Chicago, Illinois, November 9–11, 1983.
  Static analysis combines data-flow anomaly analysis and input domain checks.

HOUG81   Houghton, R. C., Jr. *Features of Software Development Tools*. National Bureau of Standards Special Publication 500-74, 1981.
  Survey of software development tools and features.

HOUG82   Houghton, R. C., Jr. *Software Development Tools*. National Bureau of Standards Special Publication 500-88, 1982.
  Description of NBS database on software development tools, abstracts.

HOUG83   Houghton, R. C., Jr. Software development tools: a profile. *IEEE Computer* **16**(5):63 (1983).
  Survey article describing NBS's software development tools database.

HOWD76   Howden, W. E. Reliability of the path analysis testing strategy. *IEEE Transactions on Software Engineering* **2:**208–215 (1976). *90*
  Proof that the automatic generation of a finite test set that is sufficient to test a routine is not a computable problem. Formal definition of computation error, path error, and other kinds of errors.

HOWD78A Howden, W. E. A survey of static analysis methods. In *Software Testing and Validation Techniques* (second edition) (E. Miller and W. E. Howden, editors). New York: IEEE Computer Society Press, 1981.

HOWD78B Howden, W. E. A survey of dynamic analysis methods. In *Software Testing and Validation Techniques* (second edition) (E. Miller and W. E. Howden, editors). New York: IEEE Computer Society Press, 1981. *23*

HOWD78C Howden, W. E. Empirical studies of software validation. In *Software Testing and Validation Techniques* (second edition) (E. Miller and W. E. Howden, editors). New York: IEEE Computer Society Press, 1981.

HOWD78D Howden, W. E. Theoretical and empirical studies of program testing. *IEEE Transactions on Software Engineering* **4:**293–298 (1978). *90*
    Symbolic trace, algebraic value trace, reliability of various methods.

HOWD78E Howden, W. E. An evaluation of the effectiveness of symbolic testing. *Software Practice and Experience* **8:**381–397 (1978).
    Shows that path testing is 64% effective.

HOWD80 Howden, W. E. Functional program testing. *IEEE Transactions on Software Engineering* **6:**162–169 (1980).
    Use of testing applied mostly to testing mathematical software—combined functional/structural testing.

HOWD81 Howden, W. E. Completeness criteria for testing elementary program functions. Fifth International Conference on Software Engineering, San Diego, Calif., March 9–12, 1981.

HOWD86 Howden, W. E. A functional approach to program testing and analysis. *IEEE Transactions on Software Engineering* **12:**997–1005 (1986).

HUAN75 Huang, J. C. An approach to program testing. *ACM Computing Surveys* **7:**113–128 (1975). *93, 457*
    Structural testing, graph models, path coverage, path count, path predicates; discusses use of inserted counters in links to measure test thoroughness.

HUAN79 Huang, J. C. Detection of data flow anomaly through program instrumentation. *IEEE Transactions on Software Engineering* **5:**226–236 (1979). *82, 154, 279, 280, 451*

HURL83 Hurley, R. B. *Decision Tables in Software Engineering.* New York: Van Nostrand Reinhold, 1983. *322*
    Introductory text to decision tables.

IEEEST IEEE Standards: see also, ANSI/IEEE.

IEEE87A IEEE Standard 1016-1987. Software Design Descriptions.

IEEE87B IEEE Standard P1044. Draft Standard for Classification of Software Errors, Faults, and Failures. *34*
    Draft standard provides comprehensive taxonomy/classification of bugs, their symptoms, and causes. Good basis for setting metrics and bug categories.

IEEE87C *Software Engineering Standards.* New York: IEEE/Wiley, 1987.
    Collection of ANSI/IEEE standards on software engineering, including (1987): 729-1983, 730-1984, 828-1983, 829-1983, 830-1984, 983-1986, 990-1986, 1002-1987, 1008-1987, 1012-1986, 1016-1987.

ITOH73 Itoh, D., and Izutani, T. Fadebug-1, a new tool for program debugging. IEEE Symposium on Computer Software Reliability, 1973. *56, 461*

Summary of findings on the utility of path-tracing test tool. Statistics on bug types.

JACE84   Jachner, J., and Agarwal, V. K. Data flow anomaly detection. *IEEE Transactions on Software Engineering* **10**:432–437 (1984). *451*
Algorithms for static analysis of data-flow anomalies.

JALO83   Jalote, P. Specification and testing of abstract data types. Seventh International Computer Software and Applications Conference, Chicago, Ill., November 7–11, 1983. *457*

JENG89   Jeng, B., and Weyuker, E. J. Some observations on partition testing. *Proceedings of the ACM SIGSOFT 89, Third Symposium on Testing, Analysis, and Verification (TAV3)*, Key West Fla., December 13–15, 1989. *200*

JENS85   Jensen, H. A., and Vairavan, K. An experimental study of software metrics for real-time software. *IEEE Transactions on Software Engineering* **11**:231–234 (1985).
Correlation analysis of Halstead's length, volume, programming effort, McCabe's complexity, and Belady's band metric for 202 Pascal modules.

KARN53   Karnaugh, M. The map method for synthesis of combinational logic circuits. *Transactions of the AIEE (Part I)* **72**:593–598 (1953). *343*

KAVI87   Kavi, K. M., Buckles, B. P., and Bhat, N. U. Isomorphism between Petri nets and dataflow graphs. *IEEE Transactions on Software Engineering* **13**:1127–1134 (1987). *128, 130*

KEMM85   Kemmerer, R. A. Testing formal specifications to detect design errors. *IEEE Transactions on Software Engineering* **11**:32–43 (1985). *321, 451*

KERN76   Kernighan, B. W., and Plauger, P. J. *Software Tools*. Reading, Mass.: Addison-Wesley, 1976. *90, 168*

KODR77   Kodres, U. R. Analysis of real time systems by data flowgraphs. (First) Computer Software and Applications Conference, Chicago, Ill., November 1977. *128*

KOLM88   Kolman, B. *Introductory Linear Algebra With Applications* (fourth edition). New York: Macmillan and Company, 1988. *209*
Introductory text used in computer sciences curricula.

KORE85   Korel, B., and Laski, J. A tool for data flow oriented program testing. Second Conference on Software Development Tools, Techniques, and Alternatives, San Francisco, Calif., December 2–5, 1985. *166, 167, 171, 456*

KORE88A   Korel, B., and Laski, J. STAD—a system for testing and debugging: user perspective. Second Workshop on Software Testing, Verification, and Analysis. Banff, Canada, July 19–21, 1988. *171, 451, 456*

KORE88B   Korel, B. PELAS—Program error-locating assistant system. *IEEE*

Transactions on Software Engineering **14:**1253–1260 (1988). *171, 456*

KORE88C Korel, B., and Laski, J. Dynamic program slicing. *Information Processing Letters* **29:**155–163 (1988). *168*

KORE89 Korel, B. TESTGEN—a software test data generation system. Sixth International Conference on Testing Computer Software, Washington D.C., May 22–25, 1989. *171, 433, 455, 456*

KRAU73 Krause, K. W., Smith, R. W., and Goodwin, M. A. Optimal software test planning through automated network analysis. IEEE Symposium on Computer Software Reliability, 1973.
Early example of path testing, graph models, coverage, and automated generation of paths.

LASK83 Laski, J. W., and Korel, B. A data flow oriented program testing strategy. *IEEE Transactions on Software Engineering* **SE-9:**347–354 (1983). *166, 167*

LASK90A Laski, J. Data flow testing in STAD. *Journal for Systems and Software 1990* (preprint). *171, 455, 456*

LASS79 Lassez, J. L., and Van Den Knijff, D. Evaluation of length and level for simple program schemes. Third International Conference on Computer Software and Applications, Chicago, Ill., November 6–8, 1979. *222*

LEER84 Lee, R. C. T, Shen, C. W., and Chang, S. C. Compilers. In *Handbook of Software Engineering*, C. R. Vick and C. V. Ramamoorthy, (editors). New York: Van Nostrand Reinhold, 1984. *316*

LEMP89 Lemppenau, W. W. Hybrid load and functional testing of SPC-PABX software for analog or digital subscribers and trunk lines. Sixth International Conference on Testing Computer Software, Washington D.C., May 22–25, 1989. *454*

LEUN88 Leung, H. K. N., and White, L. J. A Study of Regression Testing. Technical Report TR-88-15. Department of Computer Science, University of Alberta, Edmonton, Canada, September 1988. *92, 433*
Formal investigation of regression testing. Definition of reusable, testable, obsolete, changed, and new test cases. Formal study of test plan selection and test plan update under regression. Algorithm, tools.

LEUN89 Leung, H. K. N., and White, L. J. A study of regression testing. *Proceedings Sixth International Conference on Software Testing.* Washington, D.C., May 22–25, 1989. *433*

LEVI86 Levitin, A. V. How to measure software size, and how not to. Tenth International Computer Software and Applications Conference, Chicago, Ill., October 8–10, 1986. *214, 215, 219, 222, 226, 239*
Incisive critique of metrics: lines of code, statement, Halstead's. Suggests use of token count.

LEVI87   Levitin, A. V. Investigating predictability of program size. Eleventh International Computer Software and Applications Conference, Tokyo, Japan, October 7–9, 1987. *222*

LEVI89   Levitin, A. V. Private communications. *227*

LEWA76   Lew, A., and Tamanaha, D. Decision table programming and reliability. Second International Conference on Software Engineering, Long Beach, Calif., 1976. *328*

LIHF87   Li, H. F., and Chung, W. K. An empirical study of software metrics. *IEEE Transactions on Software Engineering* **13:**697–708 (1987). *214, 239*

           Comparison and correlation of 31 different software metrics applied to 250 small programs by students.

LIND88   Lindquist, T. E., and Jenkins, J. R. Test case generation with IOgen. *IEEE Software* **5**(1):72–79 (1988). *456*

LIND89   Lind, R. K., and Vairavan, K. An experimental investigation of software metrics and their relation to software development effort. *IEEE Transactions on Software Engineering* **15:**649–653 (1989). *214, 239*

LINJ89   Lin, J. C., Lo, S. C., Wang, H. S., and Chung, C. G. Local coverage criteria for structural program testing. Sixth International Conference on Software Testing, Washington D.C., May 22–25, 1989. *92*

           Examination and ranking of partial branch and statement coverage as in maintenance or regression testing.

LIPO77   Lipow, M., and Thayer, T. A. Prediction of software failures. Annual Symposium on Reliability and Maintainability, January 18–20, 1977. *234, 237*

LIPO82   Lipow, M. Number of faults per line of code. *IEEE Transactions on Software Engineering* **8:**437–439 (1982). *220, 222*

LIPO86   Lipow, M. Comments on "Estimating the number of faults in code" and two corrections to published data. *IEEE Transactions on Software Engineering* **12:**584–585 (1986). *222, 488*

           Rebuttal to GAFF84's comments on LIPO82.

LITE76   Litecky, C. R., and Davis, G. B. A study of errors, error proneness, and error diagnosis in COBOL. *Communications of the ACM* **19:**33–37 (1976). *56, 461*

LYLE87   Lyle, J. R., and Weiser, M. Automatic program bug location by program slicing. Second International Conference on Computers and Applications, Beijing, People's Republic of China, June 23–27, 1987. *168, 171, 456*

LYLE88   Lyle, J. R. Using program decomposition to guide modifications. *Proceeding of the Conference on Software Maintenance*. Phoenix, Ariz., October 24–27, 1988. pp 265–269. *167*

MAGI84   Maginnis, J. B. Compiler construction. In *The Handbook of Computers and Computing* (A. H. Seidman and I. Flores, editors). New York: Van Nostrand Reinhold, 1984. *316*

MANN78   Manna, Z., and Waldinger, R. The logic of computer programming. *IEEE Transactions on Software Engineering* **4**:199–229 (1978). *24, 26*
     Survey of methodology and limitation of proofs of program correctness. Numerical programming examples.

MARI60   Marimont, R. B. Application of graphs and boolean matrices to computer programming. *SIAM Review* **2**:259–268 (1960).

MATT88   Matthews, R. S., Muralidhar, K. H., and Sparks, S. MAP 2.1 conformance testing tool. *IEEE Transactions on Software Engineering* **14**:363–374 (1988). *455*

MAYE72   Mayeda, W. *Graph Theory*. New York: John Wiley & Sons, 1972. *227, 244, 252, 398*
     Still one of the best introductions to graph theory and related subjects. Many applications.

MCCA76   McCabe, T. J. A complexity measure. *IEEE Transactions on Software Engineering* **2**:308–320 (1976). *228, 363*
     Definition of cyclomatic complexity, subgraphs that lead to structured code, putative relation of number of branch-covering paths to cyclomatic complexity.

MCCA82   McCabe, T. J. (editor). *Structured Testing*. Silver Spring, MD: IEEE Computer Society Press, 1982. *235*
     A tutorial on testing and collection of important previously published papers including CURT79A, MYER77, SCHN79A, and WALS79.

MCCL56   McCluskey, E. J., Jr. Minimization of boolean functions. *Bell System Technical Journal* **35**:1417–1444 (1956). *343*
     A "must" method for more than six boolean variables and for boolean function minimization software design.

MCCL78B   McClure, C. A model for program complexity. Third International Conference on Software Engineering, Atlanta, Ga., May 10–12, 1978. *237*

MCNA60   McNaughton, R., and Yamada, H. Regular expressions and state graphs for automata. *IRE Transactions on Electronic Computers* **9**:39–47 (1960). *243*
     Survey of the theory of regular expressions as applied to finite-state machines. Proof of fundamental theorems.

MEAL55   Mealy, G. H. A method for synthesizing sequential circuits. *Bell System Technical Journal* **34**:1045–1079 (1955). *367*

MILL66   Miller, R. E., *Switching Theory*. New York: John Wiley & Sons, 1966. *379*
     Basic reference on switching and automata theory.

MILL74   Miller, E. F., et al. Structurally based automatic program testing. *Proceedings IEEE EASCON*. New York: IEEE, 1974.

MILL75   Miller, E. F., and Melton, R. A. Automated generation of test case data sets. International Conference on Reliable Software, Los Angeles, Calif., April 1975. *456*

MILL77C   Miller, E. F. Program testing: art meets theory. *IEEE Computer* **10**:42–51 (1977). *90, 456*
           Survey of testing theory and practice.

MILL78A   Miller, E. F., and Howden, W. E. (editors). *Tutorial: Software Testing and Validation Techniques* (second edition). New York: IEEE Computer Society Press, 1981.
           A bargain resource for pre-1981 literature; huge bibliography up to and including 1981.

MILL78B   Miller, E. F. Program testing—an overview for managers. (First) Computer Software and Applications Conference, Chicago, Ill., November 1978. *1*

MILL81   Miller, E. F. Experience with industrial software quality testing. In *Computer Program Testing* (B. Chandrasekaran and S. Radicchi, editors). New York: Elsevier North-Holland, 1981.
           Summary of testing experiences in commercial/industrial setting. Relative effectiveness of inspections, ad hoc testing, different coverage criteria, unit, component, system testing.

MILL81B   Miller, E. F., Henderson, J. G., and Mapp, T. E. A software test bed: philosophy, implementation, and application. In *Computer Program Testing* (B. Chandrasekaran and S. Radicchi, editors). New York: Elsevier North-Holland, 1981. *455*

MILL86   Miller, E. F. Mechanizing software testing. TOCG Meeting, Westlake Village, Calif., April 15, 1986. *449*

MOOR56   Moore, E. F. Gedanken experiments on sequential machine. In *Automata Studies. Annals of Mathematical Studies, No. 34*. Princeton, N.J.: Princeton University Press, 1956. *367*

MORA78   Moranda, P. B. Limits to program testing with random number inputs. Second Computer Software and Applications Conference, Chicago, Ill., November 1978. *457*

MURA89   Murata, T. Petri nets: properties, analysis and applications. *Proceedings of the IEEE* **77**:541–580 (1989). *130, 133, 368*
           In-depth tutorial, huge bibliography.

MYER77   Myers, G. J. An extension to the cyclomatic measure of program complexity. *ACM SIGPLAN Notices* **12**:62–64 (1977). *67, 233, 498*

MYER78   Myers, G. J. A controlled experiment in program testing and code walkthroughs/inspections. *Communications of the ACM* **21**(9):760–768 (1978). *1*

Relative effectiveness of testing, inspections and walkthrough investigated under controlled experiments.

MYER79   Myers, G. J. *The Art of Software Testing.* New York: John Wiley & Sons, 1979. *1, 5, 120*

NAFT72   Naftaly, S. M., and Cohen, M. C. Test data generators and debugging systems . . . workable quality control. *Data Processing Digest* **18:**(1972).
Survey of automatic test data generation tools.

NASA88   The Software Engineering Laboratory. NASA/GSFC, Code 552, Greenbelt, MD., 20771. Jon Valett and Frank McGarry. *461*
Private communication of large database bug statistics, consisting of 1.7 millions lines of code, 25 projects, 10–12 years, and 5500 bugs.

NEJM88   Nejmeh, B. A. NPATH: a measure of execution path complexity and its application. *Communications of the ACM* **31**(2):188–200 (1988). *239*

NELS67   Nelson, E. A. *A Management Handbook for the Estimation of Computer Programming Costs.* System Development Corporation, TM-3225/000/01, Santa Monica, Calif., March 1967. *214*

NOMU87   Nomura, T. Use of software engineering tools in Japan. Ninth International Conference on Software Engineering, Monterey, Calif., March 30–April 2, 1987. *449*
Survey of 200 Japanese software development groups rates test tools as having the highest productivity return; more important than a standard process, programming and design tools, and reviews.

NTAF78   Ntafos, S. C. *A Graph Theoretic Approach to Program Testing.* Ph.D. dissertation, Northwestern University, 1978.
Path-covering problems and other subjects applicable to automatic test data generation.

NTAF79   Ntafos, S. C., and Hakimi, S. L. On path cover problems in digraphs and applications to program testing. *IEEE Transactions on Software Engineering* **5:**520–529 (1979).
Theorems and algorithms on generating a minimal structural path-covering test; for tool builders.

NTAF84A   Ntafos, S. C. An evaluation of required element testing strategies. Seventh International Conference on Software Engineering, Orlando, Fla., March 26–29, 1984. *169, 170*
Hybrid technique based on data-flow analysis and path testing applied to fourteen mathematical routines and test effectiveness compared to random and branch testing, measured by mutation analysis.

NTAF84B   Ntafos, S. C. On required element testing. *IEEE Transactions on Software Engineering* **10:**795–803 (1984). *161, 166, 168, 170*
More detailed discussion of NTAF84A.

NTAF88   Ntafos, S. C. A comparison of some structural testing strategies. *IEEE Transactions on Software Engineering* **14:**868–874 (1988). *92, 166*
          Survey, comparison, ranking structural testing strategies.

OSTE76   Osterweil, L. J., and Fosdick, L. DAVE—a validation error detection and documentation system for Fortran programs. *Software Practices and Experience* **6:**473–486 (1976). *451*

OSTE77   Osterweil, L. J. The detection of unexecutable program paths through static data flow analysis. (First) Computer Software and Applications Conference, Chicago, Ill., November 1977. *451*

OSTE81   Osterweil, L. J., Fosdick, L. D., and Taylor, R. N. Error and anomaly diagnosis through data flow analysis. In *Computer Program Testing* (B. Chandrasekaran and S. Radicchi, editors). New York: Elsevier North-Holland, 1981. *449, 451*
          Discussion of static data-flow analysis and relation to program optimization by compilers. Synchronization and scheduling anomalies.

OSTR86   Ostrand, T. J., Sigal, R., and Weyuker, E. Design for a tool to manage specification-based testing. Workshop on Software Testing, Banff, Canada, July 15–17, 1986. *457*

OSTR88A   Ostrand, T. J., and Balcer, M. J. The category-partition method for specifying and generating functional tests. *Communications of the ACM* **31**(6):676–686 (1988). *457*

OSTR88B   Ostrand, T. J., and Weyuker, E. J. Using data flow analysis for regression testing. *Proceedings Sixth Annual Pacific Northwest Software Quality Conference,* Portland, Ore., September 19–20, 1988. *167, 171*

OTTE79   Ottenstein, L. M. Quantitative estimates of debugging requirements. *IEEE Transactions on Software Engineering* **5:**504–514 (1979). *222*
          Use of Halstead's metrics to estimate remaining bugs. Data on bugs, use and validation of metrics on several projects.

OVIE80   Oviedo, E. I. Control flow, data flow and program complexity. Fourth Computer Software and Applications Conference, Chicago, Ill., October 27–31, 1980. *237*

OXLE84   Oxley, D., Sauber, W., and Cornish, M. Software development for data-flow machines. In *Handbook of Software Engineering* (C. R. Vick and C. V. Ramamoorthy, editors). New York: Van Nostrand Reinhold, 1984. *147*

PAGE84   Page, G., McGarry, F. E., and Card, D. N. A practical experience with independent verification and validation. Eighth International Computer Software and Applications Conference, Chicago, Ill., November 7–9, 1984.
          A negative view on the value of independent testing.

PAIG73   Paige, M. R., and Balkovich, E. E. On testing programs. IEEE Symposium on Computer Software Reliability, New York, N.Y., May 1973.
Structural testing based on graph model; coverage.

PAIG75A   Paige, M. R. Program graphs, an algebra, and their implication for programming. *IEEE Transactions on Software Engineering* **1**:286–291 (1975). *235*

PAIG77   Paige, M. R., and Holthouse, M. A. On sizing software testing for structured programs. IEEE International Symposium on Fault Tolerant Computing, Los Angeles, Calif. June 28–30, 1977. *235*

PAIG78   Paige, M. R. An analytical approach to software testing. Second Computer Software and Applications Conference, Chicago, Ill., November 1978. *235*

PAIG80   Paige, M. R. A metric for software test planning. Fourth International Conference on Computer Software and Applications, Chicago, Ill., October 27–31, 1980. *237, 239*

PANZ76   Panzl, D. J. Test procedures: a new approach to software verification. Second International Conference on Software Engineering, Long Beach, Calif., 1976. *454, 457*

PANZ78A   Panzl, D. J. Automatic software test drivers. *IEEE Computer* **11**:44–50 (1978). *454*

PANZ78B   Panzl, D. J. Automatic revision of formal test procedures. Third International Conference on Software Engineering, Atlanta, Ga., May 10–12, 1978. *454*

PATR88   Patrick, D. P. Certification of automated test suites with embedded software. National Institute for Software and Productivity Conference, Washington D.C., April 20–22, 1988. *455*

PERE85   Perera, I. A., and White, L. J. Selecting Test Data For The Domain Testing Strategy. Technical Report TR-85-5, Department of Computer Science, University of Alberta, Edmonton, Alberta, Canada, 1985. *201*

PERE86   Perelmuter, I. M. Directions of automation in software testing. Third Conference on Testing Computer Software, Washington, D.C., September 29–October 1, 1986. *455*

PERL81   Perlis, A., Sayward, F., and Shaw, M. *Software Metrics: An Analysis and Evaluation*. Cambridge, Mass.: MIT Press, 1981. *214*
Survey of metrics, literature, research; large bibliography (pre-1981).

PETE76   Peters, L. J., and Tripp, L. L. Software design representation schemes. *Proceedings of the PIB Symposium on Computer Software Reliability*. New York: Polytechnic Institute of New York (1976). *121, 130, 133, 363*

Survey of software models, including HIPO charts, activity charts, structure charts, control graphs, decision tables, flowcharts, transaction diagrams, and others. Critiques and suggestions for new models.

PETE80   Peters, L. J. Software representation and composition techniques. *IEEE Proceedings* **68:**1085–1093 (1980). *133*

Survey of software models and associated design methods, including Leighton diagrams, design trees, structure charts, SADT diagrams, flowcharts, Hamilton-Zeldin diagrams, decision tables, Nassi-Shneiderman model, data-flow diagrams.

PETE81   Petersen, J. L. *Petri Net Theory and the Modeling of Systems.* Englewood Cliffs, N.J.: Prentice-Hall, 1981. *130, 368*

Basic text on Petri nets.

PHIL81   Phillips, D. T., and Garcia-Diaz, A. *Fundamentals of Network Analysis.* Englewood Cliffs, N.J.: Prentice-Hall, 1981. *398*

PLOE79   Ploedereder, E. Pragmatic techniques for program analysis and verification. Fourth International Conference on Software Engineering, Munich, Germany, September 17–19, 1979. *451*

POLL87A   Pollock, G. M., and Sheppard, S. A design methodology for the utilization of metrics within various phases of the software lifecycle model. Eleventh International Computer Software and Applications Conference, Tokyo, Japan, October 7–9, 1987. *214, 451*

Survey of metrics and description of a general-purpose metrics tool.

POLL87B   Pollock, L. L., and Soffa, M. L. An incremental version of iterative data flow analysis. Report COMP TR87-58, Rice University, Department of Computer Science, Houston, Tex., August 1987. *171, 433, 456*

POWE82   Powell, P. B. (editor) *Software Validation, Verification, and Testing Techniques and Tool Reference Guide.* National Bureau of Standards Special Publication 500-93, 1982.

Survey of testing, verification, validation, tools and techniques with comments on effectiveness and supporting and resources needed for each.

PRAT83   Prather, R. E., Theory of program testing—an overview. *Bell System Technical Journal* **62:**3073–3105 (1983). *243*

Tutorial overview.

PRAT87   Prather, R. E., and Myers, J. P. Jr. The path prefix software testing strategy. *IEEE Transactions on Software Engineering* **13:**761–765 (1987). *79*

Path selection tactics. Theoretical justification for intuitively appealing methods.

PROG88 $T^{(tm)}$ *User Guide*. Tinton Falls, N.J.: Programming Environments Inc., 1988. *35, 202*

QUIN55   Quine, W. V. A way to simplify truth functions. *The American Math Monthly* **52:**627–631 (1955). *343*
Like the McCluskey method (MCCL56), but cumbersome.

RADA81   Radatz, J. W. Analysis of IV&V data. Rome Air Development Center Report RADC-TR-81-145, June 1981. *1, 2, 461*
Study of five big DOD projects (averaging 120K lines of code). Bug statistics, categories, economics of independent testing.

RAMA66   Ramamoorthy, C. V. Analysis of graphs by connectivity considerations. *Journal of the ACM* **13:**211–222 (1966).
Early paper on graph models of programs.

RAMA75A   Ramamoorthy, C. V., and Ho, S. F. Testing large software with automated evaluation systems. *IEEE Transactions on Software Engineering* **1:**46–58 (1975). *455, 456*

RAMA75B   Ramamoorthy, C. V., and Kim, K. H. Optimal placement of software monitors aiding systematic testing. *IEEE Transactions on Software Engineering* **1:**403–410 (1975). *111, 451*
Use of monitor software inserted in code to measure path traversals and to detect errors. Algorithm for optimum placement of a minimum number of probes.

RAMA76   Ramamoorthy, C. V., Ho, S. F., and Chen, W. T. On the automated generation of program test data. *IEEE Transactions on Software Engineering* **2:**293–300 (1976). *456*
Structural testing; path generation, problems of arrays, difficulty of solving constraint equations, random generation of test cases that satisfy constraints. FORTRAN CASEGEN and automated test case generator.

RAMA79   Ramamoorthy, C. V., Bastani, F. B., Favaro, J. M., Mok, Y. R., Nam, C. W., and Suzuki, K. A systematic approach to the development and validation of critical software for nuclear power plants. Fourth International Conference on Software Engineering, Munich, Germany, September 17–19, 1979. *454*

RAMA85   Ramamoorthy, C. V., Tsai, W. T., Yamaura, T., and Bhide, A. Metrics guided methodology. Ninth International Computer Software and Applications Conference, Chicago, Ill., October 9–11, 1985. *130, 214, 217, 451*
Metric taxonomy and properties; various program models and associated metrics; role in design and test.

RAMA88   Ramamurthy, B., and Melton, A. A synthesis of software science measures and the cyclomatic number. *IEEE Transactions on Software Engineering* **14:**1116–1121 (1988). *237*
Proposed hybrid metric based on Halstead's and cyclomatic complexity; comparisons.

RAPP82   Rapps, S., and Weyuker, E. J. Data flow analysis techniques for test data selection. Sixth International Conference on Software Engineering, Tokyo, Japan, September 13–16, 1982. *159, 162, 163, 166*

RAPP85   Rapps, S., and Weyuker, E. J. Selecting software test data using data flow information. *IEEE Transactions on Software Engineering* **11:**367–375 (1985). *455*

RAPP88   Rapps, J. C compilation system testing. Fifth International Conference on Testing Computer Software, Washington D.C., June 13-16, 1988.

REDW83   Redwine, S. T., Jr. An engineering approach to software test data design. *IEEE Transactions on Software Engineering* **9:**191–200 (1983).
       Pragmatic approach to test design.

REIF77   Reifer, D. J., and Trattner, S. A glossary of software tools and techniques. *IEEE Computer* **10:**52–62 (1977).
       Seventy tools and their application to testing.

REIF79A   Reifer, D. J. Software failure modes and effects analysis. *IEEE Transactions on Reliability* **28:**247–249 (1979). *56, 461*

REIF79B   Reifer, D. J. Software quality assurance tools and techniques. In *Software Quality Management* (J. D. Cooper and M. J. Fisher, editors). New York: Petrocelli Books, 1979.
       Survey of tools, their use, and taxonomy.

RICH81   Richardson, D. J., and Clarke, L. A. A partition analysis method to increase program reliability. Fifth International Conference on Software Engineering, San Diego, Calif., March 9–12, 1981.
       Partition analysis testing; functional/structural hybrid based on domain testing.

RICH85   Richardson, D. J., and Clarke, L. A. Partition analysis: a method combining testing and verification. *IEEE Transactions on Software Engineering* **11:**1477–1490 (1985). *201, 202*

RODR86   Rodriguez, V., and Tsai, W. T. Software metrics interpretation through experimentation. Tenth International Computer Software and Applications Conference, Chicago, Ill., 1986. *239*
       Statistical comparison of Halstead's, cyclomatic complexity, lines-of-code, data-flow, and other metrics for bug prediction and maintenance effort.

RODR87   Rodriguez, V., and Tsai, W. T. Evaluation of software metrics using discriminant analysis. Eleventh International Computer Software and Applications Conference, Tokyo, Japan, October 7–9, 1987. *239*
       Statistical investigation of the ability of seven metrics to distinguish between simple and complicated software.

RUBE75   Rubey, R. J., Dana, J. A., and Biche, P. W. Quantitative aspects of software validation. *IEEE Transactions on Software Engineering* **1:**150–155 (1975). *56, 219, 461*

RUGG79   Ruggiero, W., Estrin, G., Fenchel, R., Razouk, R., Schwabe, D., and Vernon, M. Analysis of data-flow models using the SARA graph model of behavior. *Proceedings of the 1979 National Computer Conference.* Montvale, N.J.: AFIPS Press, 1979. *128, 130*

RYDE79   Ryder, B. G. Constructing the call graph of a program. *IEEE Transactions on Software Engineering* **5:**216–226 (1979). *451*
          Algorithm for automatic construction of call tree or program graph.

SARI88   Sarikaya, B. Protocol test generation, trace analysis and verification technique. Second Workshop on Software Testing, Verification, and Analysis, Banff, Canada, July 19–21, 1988. *389*

SARR84   Sarraga, R. F. Static data flow analysis of PL/I programs with the PROBE system. *IEEE Transactions on Software Engineering* **10:**451–459 (1984). *451*

SCHE65   Scheff, B. Decision-table structure as input format for programming automatic test equipment systems. *IEEE Transactions on Electronic Computers* **14:**248–250 (1965).
          Decision tables used in automatic test generation.

SCHI69   Schiller, H. Using MEMMAP to measure the extent of program testing. Report TR 00.1836, IBM Systems Development Division, Poughkeepsie, N.Y., February 10, 1969. *59, 75, 451*
          Description of the use of an early software statement/branch coverage analyzer.

SCHI78   Schick, G. J., and Wolverton, R. W. An analysis of competing software reliability models. *IEEE Transactions on Software Engineering* **4:**104–120 (1978). *56, 461*
          Survey of the history, development, and experience with software reliability models.

SCHL70   Schlender, P. J. Path analysis techniques. Memo, IBM System Development Division, Poughkeepsie, N.Y., April 27, 1970. *170*
          Early discussion of data-flow testing (all definitions); notes (without proof) that branch coverage is usually assured by all definitions.

SCHN75   Schneidewind, N. F. Analysis of error processes in computer software. Conference on Reliable Software, Los Angeles, Calif., April 1975. *56, 461*

SCHN79A   Schneidewind, N. F., and Hoffman, H. M. An experiment in software error data collection and analysis. *IEEE Transactions on Software Engineering* **5:**276–286 (1979). *56, 220, 234, 461, 498*
          Study of 500 modules averaging 480 statements, each with a total sample of 250K statements. Breakdown by bug type and project phase during which bug was discovered. Shows that McCabe's metric correlates well with the number of bugs and time to correct them, but not with time to find them. Shows qualitative change in bug density and labor near $M = 5$.

SCHN79B   Schneidewind, N. F. Software metrics for aiding program develop-
           ment debugging. *Proceedings of the 1979 National Computer Con-
           ference*. Montvale, N.J.: AFIPS Press, 1979. *234, 235, 237, 451*
           Comparison of measures of complexity and their relation to dis-
           covered bugs. Reachability matrix and uses thereof.

SCHN79C   Schneidewind, N. F. Application of program graphs and complexity
           analysis to software development and testing. *IEEE Transactions on
           Reliability* **28:**192–198 (1979).
           Tutorial on graphs. Fundamental circuit matrix and relation to
           McCabe's metric. Experiments on ALGOL code; 173 bugs found in
           2000 statements.

SCHN79D   Schneidewind, N. F. Case study of software complexity and error
           detection simulation. Third International Software and Applications
           Conference, Chicago, Ill., November 1979. *234*

SCHU87   Schultz, R. D., and Cardenas, A. F. An approach and mechanism
           for auditable and testable advanced transaction processing systems.
           IEEE Transactions on Software Engineering **13:**666–676 (1987).
           Proposed design and facilities based on transaction flows intended
           to improve transaction processing system testability and auditabil-
           ity.

SCHW71   Schwarts, J. T. An overview of bugs. In *Debugging Techniques in
           Large Systems* (R. Rustin, editor). Englewood Cliffs, N.J.: Prentice-
           Hall, 1971. *56, 461*
           Nature of bugs and their sources. Difference between debugging
           and testing.

SHED80   Shedley, E. I., *The Medusa Conspiracy*. New York: Viking, 1980.
           Espionage thriller dealing with bugs that lead to potential nuclear
           holocaust and Middle East war. Shedley, a notorious liar, claims to
           be a professional software type.

SHEN85   Shen, V. Y., Yu, T. J., Thebaut, S. M., and Paulsen, L. R. Identify-
           ing error-prone software—an empirical study. *IEEE Transactions
           on Software Engineering* **11:**317–324 (1985).
           Empirical study of 1423 modules averaging 420 lines of code relat-
           ing Halstead's and McCabe's metrics to bug density.

SHEP79C   Sheppard, S. B., Curtis, W., Milliman, P., Borst, M. A., and Love,
           T. First-year results from a research program on human factors in
           software engineering. *Proceedings of the 1979 National Computer
           Conference*. Montvale, N.J.: AFIPS Press, 1979. *222, 234*
           Experiment using thirty-six programmers working on small pro-
           grams. Study shows good correlation between McCabe's and Hal-
           stead's metrics, but neither metric is especially effective for small
           routines.

SHEP80   Sheppard, S. B., Milliman, P., and Curtis, W. Experimental evalua-
           tion of on-line program construction. Fourth International Computer

Software and Applications Conference, Chicago, Ill., October 27–31, 1980.

Correlation of McCabe's and Halstead's metrics with productivity.

SHIY87   Shi, Y., Prywes, N., Szymanski, B., and Pnueli, A. Very high level concurrent programming. *IEEE Transactions on Software Engineering* **13**:1038–1046 (1987). *147*

SHOO75   Shooman, M. L., and Bolsky, M. I. Types, distributions and test and correction times for programming errors. Conference on Reliable Software, Los Angeles, Calif., April 1975. *2, 56, 461*

SNEE86   Sneed, H. M. Data coverage measurement in program testing. Workshop on Software Testing, Banff, Canada, July 15–17, 1986. *169, 171, 451, 456*

Reports experience with use of data coverage metrics; tools, comparison of effectiveness with control flow coverage.

SOFT88   Software Research Inc. *SPECTEST® Description, METATEST® Description*. San Francisco: Software Research Inc., 1988. *35*

SOHO84   So, H. H. Graph theoretic modeling and analysis in software engineering. In *Handbook of Software Engineering* (C. R. Vick and C. V. Ramamoorthy, editors). New York: Van Nostrand Reinhold, 1984. *411*

SQES88   Software Quality Engineering. *Survey of Software Test Practices*. Jacksonville, Fla.: Software Quality Engineering, 1988. *459*

Periodical survey of software testing practices based on attendees at the International Conference on Software Testing.

SQET90   Software Quality Engineering. *Tools Guide*. Jacksonville, Fla.: Software Quality Engineering, 1990. *449, 453*

Periodical tools guide specific to software testing.

STAK89   Staknis, M. E. The use of software prototypes in software testing. Sixth International Conference on Testing Computer Software, Washington, D.C., May 22–25, 1989. *454, 457*

STET86   Stetter, F. Comments on "Number of faults per line of code." *IEEE Transactions on Software Engineering* **12**:1145 (1986).

Bug estimation formula based on Halstead's metrics.

STON88   Stone, A., Ritchie, R. Hoey, J., and Best, K. Automated testing and quality metrics for Ada. National Institute for Software and Productivity Conference, Washington, D.C., April 20–22, 1988. *451, 454, 455, 456*

STUK77   Stucki, L. G. New directions in automated tools for improving software quality. In *Current Trends in Programming Methodology, Volume II: Program Validation* (Raymond T. Yeh, editor). Englewood Cliffs, N.J.: Prentice-Hall, 1977. *451*

SUNO81   Sunohara, T., Takano, A., Uehara, K. and Ohkawa, R. Program complexity measure for software development management. Fifth

International Conference on Software Engineering, San Diego, Calif., March 9–12, 1981.

McCabe's, Halstead's, lines of code, and other metrics compared and correlated to productivity and bug rate for 137 modules.

SYMO88 Symons, C. R. Function point analysis: difficulties and improvements. *IEEE Transactions on Software Engineering* **14:**2–11 (1988).

Critique and proposed enhancement of popular function point metric used for COBOL software.

TAIA87 Tai, A., Hecht, M., and Hecht, H. Enhanced condition table method for verification of critical software. Eleventh Conference on Computer Software and Applications, Tokyo, Japan, October 7–9, 1987. *328*

TAIK84 Tai, K. C. A program complexity metric based on data flow information in control graphs. Seventh International Conference on Software Engineering, Orlando, Fla., March 26–28, 1984. *237*

Topological complexity metric for data flows.

TAIK87 Tai, K. C., and Su, H. K. Test generation for boolean expressions. Eleventh Conference on Computer Software and Applications, Tokyo, Japan, October 7–9, 1987. *341*

TAIK89 Tai, K. C. What to do beyond branch testing? Sixth International Conference on Testing Computer Software, Washington, D.C., May 23–25, 1989. *341*

THAY76 Thayer, T. A. Software reliability study. Report RADC-TR77-216, Rome Air Development Center. (Also: Thayer, T. A., Lipow, A. M., and Nelson, E. C. Software reliability study. Final Technical Report, TRW Defense and Space Systems Group, February 1976. *2, 90, 219, 234, 235, 461*

The watershed study on software reliability. More than 300 pages of software-related statistics.

TRAC86 Trachtenberg, M. Validating Halstead's theory with system 3 data. *IEEE Transactions on Software Engineering* **12:**584 (1986). *488*

TSAI86 Tsai, W. T., Lopez, M. A., Rodriguez, V., and Volovik, D. An approach to measuring data structure complexity. Tenth International Computer Software And Applications Conference, Chicago, Ill., October 8–10, 1986. *237*

Proposed topological complexity metric for data structure.

TSAL86 Tsalaikhin, L. Dialog with a tester (architecture and functions of one unit test facility. Workshop on Software Testing, Banff, Canada, July 15–17, 1986. *454, 455*

VANV87 Van Verth, P. B. A program complexity model that includes procedures. Eleventh International Computer Software and Applications Conference, Tokyo, Japan, October 7–9, 1987. *237, 239*

Proposed hybrid data-flow/control-flow structural metric; comparisons.

VEIT52   Veitch, E. E. A chart method for simplifying truth functions. ACM Annual Conference, 1952. *343*

VESS86   Vessey, I., and Weber, R. Structured tools and conditional logic: an empirical investigation. *Communications of the ACM* **29**(1):48–57 (1986). *321, 322*
    Comparison of structured English, decision tables, and decision trees as tools for representing conditional logic.

VOGE80   Voges, U., Gmeiner, L., and von Mayrhauser, A. A. SADAT—an automated test tool. *IEEE Transactions on Software Engineering* **6**:286–290 (1980). *456*

WAGO73   Wagoner, W. L. The final report on a software reliability measurement study. The Aerospace Corporation, El Segundo, Calif., August 1973. *56, 461*

WALS79   Walsh, T. J. A software reliability study using a complexity measure. *Proceedings of the 1979 National Computer Conference.* Montvale, N.J.: AFIPS Press, 1979. *235, 498*
    McCabe's metric applied to 276 routines in the Aegis system. Discusses break at $M = 10$.

WARN64   Warner, C. D., Jr. Evaluation of program testing. TR 00.1173, IBM Data Systems Division Development Laboratories, Poughkeepsie, N.Y., July 28, 1964. *59, 75, 450, 451*
    Earliest known use of a hardware instruction coverage monitor: COBOL and FORTRAN source.

WATE86   Waterman, D. A. *A Guide to Expert Systems.* Reading, Mass.: Addison-Wesley, 1986. *321*
    Introductory text to knowledge-based systems.

WEIN65   Weinwurm, F. G., and Zagorski, H. J. Research into the management of computer programming: a transitional analysis of cost estimation techniques. TM-27 1/100/00m, System Development Corporation, Santa Monica, Calif., November 1965. *7, 214*
    Statistics on cost, labor factors, and development time.

WEIS81   Weiser, M. Program slicing. *Proceedings of the Fifth International Conference on Software Engineering,* March 1981, pp. 439–449.

WEIS82   Weiser, M. Programmers use slices when debugging. *Communications of the ACM* **25**:446–452 (1982). *167, 168*

WEIS84   Weiser, M. Program slicing. *IEEE Transactions on Software Engineering* **SE-10**:352–357 (1984).

WEIS85A   Weiser, M. D., Gannon, J. D., and McMullin, P. R. Comparison of structural test coverage metrics. *IEEE Software* **2**:80–85 (March 1985).
    Comparison of data definition-use (*du*-path), statement, branch coverage metrics and variations.

WEIS85B   Weiss, D. M., and Basili, V. R. Evaluating software development by analysis of changes: some data from the software engineering laboratory. *IEEE Transactions on Software Engineering* **11:**157–168 (1985). *2*

Bug statistics by type, effort to correct, emphasis on software modification, large medium-sized FORTRAN programs.

WEIS86   Weiser, M., and Lyle, J. R. Experiments on slicing-based debugging aids. *Proceedings of the First Workshop on Empirical Studies of Programmers,* Washington, D.C. June 5–6, 1986, Norwood, N.J.: Ablex Publishing, pp. 187–197. *456*

WEYU80   Weyuker, E. J., and Ostrand, T. J. Theories of program testing and the application of revealing subdomains. *IEEE Transactions on Software Engineering* **6:**236–246 (1980).

WEYU86   Weyuker, E. J. Axiomatizing software test data adequacy. *IEEE Transactions on Software Engineering* **12:**1128–1138 (1986).

Clarifications, definitions, axioms, and theorems formalizing the concept of useful test sets toward a more rational testing theory.

WEYU88A   Weyuker, E. J. An empirical study of the complexity of data flow testing. Second Workshop on Software Testing, Verification, and Analysis. Banff, Canada, July 19–21, 1988. *92, 169, 171, 438, 451, 455, 456*

WEYU88B   Weyuker, E. J. Evaluating software complexity measures. *IEEE Transactions on Software Engineering* **14:**1357–1365 (1988). *214, 216, 239*

Formal analysis of axioms for complexity metrics. Evaluation of several popular metrics and their problems.

WEYU90   Weyuker, E. J. The cost of data flow testing—an empirical study. *IEEE Transactions on Software Engineering* **16:** February (1990). *169, 171*

WHIT78A   White, L. J., Cohen, E. I., and Chandrasekaran, B. A domain strategy for computer program testing. Technical Report OSU-CISRC-TR-78-4, Computer and Information Science Research Center, Ohio State University, Columbus, Ohio, August 1978. *192, 199*

WHIT78B   White, L. J., Teng, F. C., Kuo, H., and Coleman, D. An error analysis of the domain testing strategy. Technical Report OSU-CISRC-TR-78-2, Computer and Information Science Research Center, Ohio State University, Columbus, Ohio, December 1978.

WHIT80A   White, L. J., and Cohen, E. I. A domain strategy for computer program testing. *IEEE Transactions on Software Engineering* **6:**247–257 (1980). *184, 192*

Use of linear predicates and associated inequalities to establish test cases, boundary choices, etc. Generalization to *n*-dimensional problems.

WHIT80B   Whitworth, M. H., and Szulewski, P. A. The measurement of control and data flow complexity in software designs. Fourth Computer Software and Applications Conference, Chicago, Ill., October 27–31, 1980. *237*

WHIT81   White, L. J. Basic mathematical definitions and results in testing. In *Computer Program Testing* (B. Chandrasekaran and S. Radicchi, editors). New York: Elsevier North-Holland, 1981.
Survey and synthesis of prior work in testing theory. Goodenough-Gerhart theorem of testing, computability issues, reliable test sets, Howden's error types.

WHIT85B   White, L. J., and Sahay, P. N. A computer system for generating test data using the domain strategy. IEEE SOFTFAIR Conference II, San Francisco, Calif., December 2–5, 1985. *192, 457*

WHIT86   White, L. J., and Perera, I. A. An alternative measure for error analysis of the domain testing strategy. Workshop on Software Testing, Banff, Canada, July 15–17, 1986. *201*

WHIT87   White, L. J. Software testing and verification. In *Advances in Computers,* volume 26, 335–391. Orlando, Fla.: Academic Press, 1987. *7, 100, 192, 313*
Superior tutorial and overview of theory status. Functional versus structural testing, mathematical models of testing, data-flow analysis, coverage, mutation analysis, path testing, domain testing, theoretical results, decidability results.

WHIT88   White, L. J., and Wiszniewski, B. W. Complexity of testing iterated borders for structured programs. Second Workshop on Software Testing, Verification, and Analysis, Banff, Canada, July 19–21, 1988. *182*

WILK77   Wilkens, E. J. Finite state techniques in software engineering. (First) Computer Software and Applications Conference, Chicago, Ill., November 1977. *457*
Application of finite-state machine models to software design.

WILS82   Wilson, C., and Osterweill, L. J. A data flow analysis tool for the C programming language. Sixth Computer Software and Applications Conference, Chicago, Ill., November 8–12, 1982. *171, 451, 456*

WISZ85   Wiszniewski, B. W. Can domain testing overcome loop analysis? Ninth International Computer Software and Applications Conference, Chicago, Ill., October 9–11, 1985. *182*

WISZ87   Wiszniewski, B. W., and White, L. J. Testing of paths of computer programs with loops by induction. Private communication. *182*

WOLV75   Wolverton, R. W. The cost of developing large scale software. In Practical Strategies for Developing Large Software Systems. (E. Horowitz, editor). Reading, Mass.: Addison-Wesley, 1975. *1*

WOOD78   Woods, J. L. Path Selection for Symbolic Execution Systems. Ph.D. dissertation, University of Massachusetts, 1978. *235*

WOOD80   Woodward, M. R., Hedley, D., and Hennell, M. A. Experience with
          path analysis and testing of programs. *IEEE Transactions on Soft-
          ware Engineering* **2:**278–286 (1976).
              Using link count as a metric; path testing; and two measures of
          coverage.

YEHR80   Yeh, R. T., and Zave, P. Specifying software requirements. *IEEE
          Proceedings* **68:**1077–1085 (1980). *35*
              Examines specifications as a source of program bugs and suggests
          methodology for specification design.

YINB80   Yin, B. H. Software design testability analysis. Fourth Computer
          Software and Applications Conference, Chicago, Ill., October 27–
          31, 1980. *455*

YOSH87   Yoshizawa, Y., Kubo T., Satoh, T., Totsuka, K., Haraguchi, M.,
          and Moriyama, H. Test and debugging environment for large scale
          operating systems. Eleventh International Computer Software and
          Applications Conference, Tokyo, Japan, October 7–9, 1987. *455*

ZEIL81   Zeil, S. J., and White, L. J. Sufficient test sets for path analysis
          testing strategies. Fifth International Conference on Software Engi-
          neering, San Diego, Calif., March 9–12, 1981. *100*
              Linearly domained program results. Minimal test sets, criteria for
          revealing tests, how many cases, theorems for tool builders.

ZEIL84   Zeil, S. J. Perturbation testing for computation errors. Seventh In-
          ternational Conference on Software Engineering, Orlando, Fla.,
          March 26–29, 1984.

ZEIL88   Zeil, S. J. Selectivity of data-flow and control-flow path criteria.
          *Proceedings of Second Workshop on Software Testing, Verification,
          and Analysis.* July 19–21, Banff, Canada, 1988. pp. 216–222. *166*

ZELK78   Zelkowitz, M. V. Perspective on software engineering. *ACM Com-
          puting Surveys* **10:**197–214 (1978).
              Survey of the state of the art and the issues in software engineer-
          ing.

ZOLN77   Zolnowski, J. C., and Simmons, R. B. Measuring program complex-
          ity. *Proceedings COMPCON Fall 1977.* New York: IEEE, 1977.
          235, 237

ZWEB79   Zweben, S. H., and Fung, K. C. Exploring software science rela-
          tions in COBOL and APL. Third International Conference on Com-
          puter Software and Application, Chicago, Ill., November 6–8, 1979.
          222

ZWEB81   Zweben, S. H. Computer program testing: an introduction. In *Com-
          puter Program Testing* (B. Chandrasekaran and S. Radicchi, edi-
          tors). New York: Elsevier North-Holland, 1981.
              Tutorial overview, basic definitions.

GLOSSARY/INDEX

NOTE: Numbers printed in boldface refer to definitions in the text.

bug *continued*

, **functional,** a bug whose symptoms are incorrect, missing, or superfluous functionality, most often caused by an incorrect or incomplete specification of function, rather than by an implementation error. 12, 34–36, 57, **466–468**

, functional homogeneity of, **181**

, **hardware,** a programmer's cry of joy when she's deluded herself into believing that the hardware is at fault instead of her program. The counter-cry (actually a low mutter) of hardware designers and service technicians is "dumb programmer!" About as rare as unicorns and the prerequisite condition that enables their captors. 18

importance, 27–**28**, 31, 58

, illegitimate birth, 131, 135

, **initialization,** bugs related to the incorrect initialization of data. *See also: data–flow anomaly.* 38, 40, 47, 49, 51, 82, 83, 90, 223, **469, 470, 474**

, instrumentation, 114

, integration, **21,** 44, 48, 53, 57, 154, **473–474**

, **interactive,** bugs arising from the interaction of routines wherein the routines are individually correct but collectively erroneous. 50–51

, **interface,** bugs manifested at the interface between routines, such as an improper calling sequence. 13, 48–50, 90, 233, **467, 473–474**

, interlock, 51, 136, **472, 475**

, **intermittent,** bugs whose symptoms occur with no apparent pattern. 381

, **language,** bugs in the syntax of a language or implementation of a language processor. Rare for standard programming languages, common for hidden or ad hoc languages. 142

, latent, 286

, load-dependent, 51

locality hypothesis, **19**

, **location-dependent,** bug whose manifestation depends on where in absolute or virtual space the routine or its data are loaded. 87, 113

, logic, 37–38, 76, 178–179, **466, 469, 470**

, loop, 36, 80

, lost daughter, 131, 135

, operating system, 18, 50, **475**

, output, 386

, parameter conflict, 40, 42

, **peek-a-boo,** a bug whose symptoms disappear when the suspected routine is instrumented in order to catch it. Often location dependent. **113**

, predicate, 333, 469

prediction, 221–222, 235

preprocessor, 42

prevention, 3, 4, 8, 46, 52, 55–56, 106, 440, 446

private versus public, 4

, process(ing), 38, **469–470**

, protocol, 48

, race condition, 49, 113

rate, 8, 20

COCOMO, 215, 222
code
  , comparison, 436
  /data ambiguity, 223–224
  /data separation, 19
  , dead, 342
  importance, 76
  masquerading as data, 41
  , new, 59, 76, 116–117
  production (by compiler), **316,** 317
  reading, 8, 436, 437, 446
  redundant, 106
  , table-driven, 40
  , "tight," 8
coding conventions, 46, 436
coincidental correctness, any condition in which the outcome of a test is as expected but the fact that the outcome is correct is a coincidence and a consequence of the unrevealing nature of the test (e.g., $2 + 2 = 4$ and so does 2×2 and 2^2). **109**–110, 111, 119, 179, 180
comment, 48, 218
communication system, 24, 127, 138, 302, 306, 372, 390
commutative operator, 247
compile(r) (*see also: translator*), 8, 24, 37, 39, 42, 47, 98, 147, 315–317
  phases, 317–318
  , run-time resident portion, 156
  , silicon, **321**
  testing, 288
  -time processing, the interpretive execution of source code by compiler during compilation. **43**
compilation, conditional, a feature of a compiler which permits control over the statements to be compiled conditional on control statements or commands to the compiler. For example, marked statements are (not) to be compiled this time. **114**
complementary operations, a pair of operations that negate each other, such as push/pop, do/undo, start/stop. 151, 171, 172, 274–277
complementation, **335**
complete
  specification, 325, 352–353
  path, **71**
  testing, erroneously used to mean 100% branch coverage. The notion is specific to a test selection criterion: i.e., testing is "complete" when the tests specified by the criterion have been passed. Absolutely complete testing is impossible. 24–26, 72, 77, 230, 339
complexity, 18, 235, 358–359
  barrier, software is always enhanced (over time) to the maximum complexity that software builders can manage. **9,** 32, 36, 241

data, flow, test(ing) *continued*
    effectiveness, 168–171
    history, 170
    motivation, 145–146
    overview, 163
    terminology, 162–163
    tools, 155, 169, 171, 281, 456
  , global, 46, 51
  initialization, 82
  , local, 46, 51
  object state, the state of an object with reference to its availability for use as in: defined, undefined, open, closed, etc. 154
  representation change, 38, 442–443
  residue, 19, 41
  specification, 44–45, 218
  , static, 41–43
  structure, **45**–47, 405, 437, 439, 444
  type (*see also: semantic, type*), 8, **45**, 224, 442
  use, 150–154
    , computational, **151**–152
    , defined, **151**
    , killed, **151**
    , predicate, **151**–152
    , undefined, **151**
  validation, 43–44, 284, 285, 286, 291, 295
  , vulnerability to bad, 284
dead
  code, 342
  state, **385**
  variable, 156
debugger, one who engages in the intuitive art of correctly determining the cause (e.g., bug) of a set of symptoms. 1, 168
  , symbolic, 110, 113
debugging, the act of attempting to determine the cause of the symptoms of malfunctions detected by testing or by frenzied user complaints. Contrast with *testing.* 6, 7, **10,** 139, 140, 167–168, 244, 454
  cost, 71, 92, 233, 235
  (vs.) testing, 4–5, 9–10
  theory, 10, 167
  tools, 110, 114, 168, 244
decision (*see also: predicate, branch*), a node in a program's control flow with two or more outlinks. **60, 62**
  , binary, **62,** 92, 228, 328
  count metric, 230, 235, 241
  , jumping into or out of, 264
  node, **65**

graph, matrix *continued*
    , sparse, 422
    transitive closure, **410**
    transpose, **402**, 425
    union, **402**
  , maximum element, **405**
  , minimum element, **405**
  , partitioning, 398
  , partly ordered, **405**
  , pictorial, 397
  , strongly-connected, 235–**236**, 412
  theory, 227, 477, 485, 498
  , **undirected,** a graph whose links have no arrowheads. **236, 404**
guilt, 1, 2, 44

Halstead
  bug frequency predictor, 221–222, 508
  conjecture (i.e., "theorem"), 221, 227, 241
  length, **220,** 221, 481
  metric, 220–226
  vocabulary, **221**
hardware, 18, 49–50, 286
  logic design, 394–395
  testing, 50, 130, 202, 320–321
hard testing, the massive use of dumb (i.e., unrevealing) tests.
harness, test. *See: test driver*
help screens, 305
higher order language (HOL), 19, 35–36, 116, 444
hook, any data structure or part thereof or program or statement therein intended
      for the future retrofit of new features. 34, 119, 377, 434
horrible loops, **80–81,** 83–84, 119, 264, 411
Huang's theorem, 82, 84, 279–282
Hulk, The Incredible, from the early 80's television series of the same name. The
      hero, David Banner, when stressed or hurt is transmogrified into The
      Incredible Hulk, a benevolent green giant of vast strength and minuscule
      intellect. 12
human interface, 15, 28, 46, 285–286, 301, 304
hypermodularity, 223, 233
hyperplane, the n-dimensional analog of a plane surface. **177**

Ill-formed program, 89
illogical condition, 71, 357, 358, 469
immaterial case (decision table), **323, 326**–328, 355
impossible case, 37, 326, 357–358, 361
impossible state, 375–376
incidence matrix, 158
incident, when the execution of a test produces an unexpected outcome or the
      validation criteria are not satisfied, there has been an incident. Further

high probability of detecting specified classes of bugs; tests aimed at specific bug types.

spaghetti code, a program whose control structure is so entangled by a surfeit of GOTOs that its flowgraph resembles a bowl of spaghetti. Typical of bad, old software. The only thing worse is *Pachinko code*. 36, 63